A Companion to American Fiction 1865–1914

Blackwell Companions to Literature and Culture

This series offers comprehensive, newly written surveys of key periods and movements, and certain major authors, in English literary culture and history. Extensive volumes provide new perspectives and positions on contexts and on canonical and postcanonical texts, orientating the beginning student in new fields of study and providing the experienced undergraduate and new graduate with current and new directions, as pioneered and developed by leading scholars in the field.

A COMPANION TO

AMERICAN FICTION

1865–1914

EDITED BY **ROBERT PAUL LAMB AND G. R. THOMPSON**

Blackwell
Publishing

BLACKWELL PUBLISHING
350 Main Street, Malden, MA 02148–5020, USA
9600 Garsington Road, Oxford OX4 2DQ, UK
550 Swanston Street, Carlton, Victoria 3053, Australia

First published 2005 by Blackwell Publishing Ltd

1 2005

Library of Congress Cataloging-in-Publication Data

A companion to American fiction, 1865–1914 / edited by Robert Paul Lamb and G.R. Thompson.
p. cm.—(Blackwell companions to literature and culture ; 35)
Includes bibliographical references and index.
ISBN-13: 978-1-4051-0064-9 (hard cover : alk. paper)
ISBN-10: 1-4051-0064-8 (hard cover : alk. paper)
1. American fiction—19th century—History and criticism—Handbooks, manuals, etc.
2. American fiction—20th century—History and criticism—Handbooks, manuals, etc. I. Lamb,
Robert Paul, 1951–II. Thompson, Gary Richard, 1937–III. Series.

PS377.C665 2005
813′.409—dc22
2004029758

A catalogue record for this title is available from the British Library.

Set in 11/13 pt Garamond 3
by SPI Publisher Services, Pondicherry, India
Printed and bound in India by
Replika Press Pvt. Ltd

Picture research by Helen Nash

For further information on
Blackwell Publishing, visit our website:
www.blackwellpublishing.com

Contents

Illustrations

All captions and accompanying text are by the editors.

Notes on Contributors

Michael Anesko teaches English and American literature at Pennsylvania State University. His books include *"Friction with the Market": Henry James and the Profession of Authorship* (1986) and *Letters, Fictions, Lives: Henry James and William Dean Howells* (1997).

Bert Bender is Professor of English at Arizona State University. His books include *Evolution and the "Sex Problem": American Narratives during the Eclipse of Darwin* (2004), *The Descent of Love: Darwin and the Theory of Sexual Selection in American Fiction, 1871–1926* (1996), and *Sea-Brothers: The Tradition of American Sea Fiction from Moby-Dick to the Present* (1988).

Christine Bold is Professor of English at the University of Guelph, Canada. She is the author of *Selling the Wild West: Popular Western Fiction, 1860–1960* (1987) and *Writers, Plumbers, and Anarchists: The WPA Writers' Project in Massachusetts* (2005), and co-author of *Remembering Women Murdered by Men: Memorials across Canada* by the Cultural Memory Group (2006). Currently, she is editing the *Dictionary of Literary Biography* volume on American dime novelists and writing a revisionist history of popular Westerns, 1860–1920.

Sidney H. Bremer is Campus Dean and Executive Officer at the University of Wisconsin at Marinette. A Professor of English in the University of Wisconsin Colleges, she earned her Ph.D. from Stanford University. She has published on women's, ethnic, and urban studies and US literature in *PMLA*, *Soundings*, and other journals, and is the author of *Urban Intersections: Meetings of Life and Literature in United States Cities* (1992) and the co-editor of *Revolution in Art and Ideas at the Turn of the Twentieth Century* (1993).

Dickson D. Bruce, Jr., is Professor of History at the University of California at Irvine, specializing in nineteenth-century America with emphases on African American thought and on the antebellum South. His books include *And They All Sang Hallelujah: Plain-Folk Camp-Meeting Religion, 1800–1845* (1974), *Violence and Culture in the Antebellum South* (1979), *Black American Writing from the Nadir: The Evolution of a Literary Tradition, 1877–1915* (1989), *Archibald Grimké: Portrait of a Black Independent* (1993), and *The Origins of African American Literature, 1680–1865* (2001).

William E. Cain is Mary Jewett Gaiser Professor of English and American Studies at Wellesley College. He is the author of *The Crisis in Criticism: Theory, Literature, and Reform in English Studies* (1984) and *F. O. Matthiessen and the Politics of Criticism* (1988), and his many edited books include *William Lloyd Garrison and the Fight Against Slavery: Selections from The Liberator* (1995), *The Blithedale Romance: A Cultural and Critical Edition* (1996), and *A Historical Guide to Henry David Thoreau* (2000). He has also written a study of American literary and cultural criticism, 1900–45, included in *The Cambridge History of American Literature*, vol. 5 (2003), and has co-authored with Sylvan Barnet several books on literature and composition.

Gregg Camfield is Professor of English at the University of the Pacific. He is the author of *The Oxford Companion to Mark Twain* (2003), *Sentimental Twain: Samuel Clemens in the Maze of Moral Philosophy* (1994), and *Necessary Madness: The Humor of Domesticity in Nineteenth-Century American Literature* (1997), in addition to numerous articles and reviews on American literature and culture. He serves on the editorial board of the University of California–Iowa Mark Twain Project, and is co-editing a volume on Twain's early journalism for the project.

Clare Colquitt is Associate Professor of English at San Diego State University, where she currently serves as Graduate Director. She is co-editor, with Susan Goodman and Candace Waid, of *A Forward Glance: New Essays on Edith Wharton* (1999). She has been a Fulbright Senior Professor of American literature at the Ernst-Moritz-Arndt Universität, Greifswald and the Friedrich-Schiller-Universität, Jena.

Christophe Den Tandt teaches American and English literature as well as literary theory at the Free University of Brussels (Université Libre de Bruxelles). A recipient of the American Studies Association's Gabriel Prize, he is the author of *The Urban Sublime in American Literary Naturalism* (1998) and of many articles on popular culture.

Kathleen Diffley is Associate Professor of English at the University of Iowa and Executive Director of the Midwest Modern Language Association. She is the author of *Where My Heart Is Turning Ever: Civil War Stories and Constitutional Reform, 1861–1876* (1992) and editor of *To Live and Die: Civil War Stories in the Popular Press, 1861–1876*

(2002). She is currently at work on a book-length study about telling the war in a magazine culture shaped by market concerns.

Robert M. Dowling is Assistant Professor of English at Central Connecticut State University and holds a Ph.D. in English and American studies from the Graduate Center of the City University of New York. His areas of specialization are late nineteenth- and early twentieth-century American literature, ethnic studies, urban studies, and American cultural history. He has published numerous essays on these subjects and a book, entitled *Slumming in New York: From the Waterfront to Mythic Harlem*, is forthcoming.

Clare Virginia Eby is Professor of English at the University of Connecticut and the author of *Dreiser and Veblen, Saboteurs of the Status Quo* (1998), editor of the Dreiser Edition of *The Genius* and the Norton Critical Edition of Upton Sinclair's *The Jungle* (2003), and co-editor, with Leonard Cassuto, of *The Cambridge Companion to Theodore Dreiser* (2004). She is currently researching a book on Progressive era marriages.

Grace Farrell is Rebecca Clifton Reade Professor of English at Butler University. Her books include *Lillie Devereux Blake: Retracing a Life Erased* (2002), an edition of Lillie Devereux Blake's *Fettered for Life, or, Lord and Master: A Story of To-Day* (1996), *Critical Essays on Isaac Bashevis Singer* (1996), *Isaac Bashevis Singer: Conversations* (1992), and *From Exile to Redemption: The Fiction of Isaac Bashevis Singer* (1987).

Winfried Fluck is Professor of English at the Free University of Berlin (Freie Universität Berlin). His most recent books include *Theories of American Culture: Theories of American Studies* (2003), *Wie viel Ungleichheit verträgt die Demokratie? Armut und Reichtum in den USA* (with Welf Werner, 2003), *German? American? Literature? New Directions in German-American Studies* (with Werner Sollors, 2002), *Pragmatism and Literary Studies* (1999), *Das kulturelle Imaginäre: eine Funkionsgeschichte des amerikanischen Romans, 1790–1900* (1997), *The Historical and Political Turn in Literary Studies* (1995), and *Inszenierte Wirklichkeit: der amerikanische Realismus, 1865– 1900* (1992).

Nancy Glazener is Associate Professor of English at the University of Pittsburgh, where she teaches a range of courses in US literature and women's studies. She is the author of *Reading for Realism: The History of a U.S. Literary Institution, 1850–1910* (1997). Her current book project is provisionally entitled "Modern Hypocrisy: The Public, the Private, and the Secular in US Literature."

June Howard is Professor of English, American Culture, and Women's Studies at the University of Michigan at Ann Arbor. In addition to articles on late nineteenth-century American literature, she is the author of *Publishing the Family* (2001) and *Form and History in American Literary Naturalism* (1985), and the editor of *New Essays on The*

Country of the Pointed Firs (1994) in the Cambridge University Press series on "The American Novel."

J. Gerald Kennedy is William A. Reade Professor of English at Louisiana State University. He is the author of *The Narrative of Arthur Gordon Pym and the Abyss of Interpretation* (1995), *Imagining Paris: Exile, Writing, and American Identity* (1993), *Poe, Death, and the Life of Writing* (1987), and *The Astonished Traveler: William Darby, Frontier Geographer and Man of Letters* (1981); and the editor of *Romancing the Shadow: Poe and Race* (with Liliane Weissberg, 2001), *The Narrative of Arthur Gordon Pym of Nantucket and Related Tales* (1994), *A Historical Guide to Edgar Allan Poe* (2001), *French Connections: Hemingway and Fitzgerald Abroad* (with Jackson R. Bryer, 1999), *Modern American Short Story Sequences: Composite Fictions and Fictive Communities* (1995), and *American Letters and the Historical Consciousness: Essays in Honor of Lewis P. Simpson* (with Daniel Mark Fogel, 1987). He is currently writing a book entitled "Inventing America: Literary Nation-Building and Cultural Conflict, 1820–1850."

Robert Paul Lamb is Associate Professor of English and American Studies at Purdue University, West Lafayette. The recipient of Harvard University's Bowdoin Prize and over two dozen department and university teaching awards from Purdue and Harvard, he has published a monograph entitled *James G. Birney and the Road to Abolitionism* (1994) and many articles on authors and topics including Melville, Whitman, Hemingway, Frank Norris, pedagogy, and literary theory. He recently completed a book entitled "Hemingway and the Modern Short Story: A Study in Craft" and is currently writing a book on Mark Twain and nineteenth-century political thought provisionally entitled "Citizen Twain: A Political Biography of Samuel Langhorne Clemens."

John Matteson is Assistant Professor of English at John Jay College of Criminal Justice, City University of New York, where he teaches literature and legal writing. His work has appeared in such journals as *Harvard Theological Review, New England Quarterly, CrossCurrents*, and *Melville Society Extracts*. His forthcoming book on Bronson and Louisa May Alcott will be published by W. W. Norton and Company.

William E. Moddelmog is the author of *Reconstituting Authority: American Fiction in the Province of the Law, 1880–1920* (2000) and of essays on law and literature. He was formerly an Assistant Professor at The Ohio State University, Newark, and is currently an attorney with the Office of Legislative Counsel in Sacramento, California.

Thomas Peyser is Associate Professor of English at Randolph–Macon College. He is the author of *Utopia and Cosmopolis: Globalization in the Era of American Literary Realism* (1998) and a novel, *W.W.* (2000).

S. K. Robisch is Assistant Professor of English at Purdue University, West Lafayette. His principal interests are American and ecological literatures. He is writing a book entitled "Big Holy Dog: Wolves and the Wolf Myth in North American Literature."

John Carlos Rowe is University of Southern California Associates' Professor of the Humanities. His most recent authored books include *The New American Studies* (2002), *Literary Culture and U.S. Imperialism: From the Revolution to World War II* (2000), *The Other Henry James* (1998), and *At Emerson's Tomb: The Politics of Classic American Literature* (1997). His new projects are *A Rediscovery of America: Multicultural Literature and the New Democracy* and Blackwell's *A Companion to American Studies*.

William J. Scheick is the J. R. Millikan Centennial Professor at the University of Texas at Austin. He has published many books, including *The Splintering Frame: The Later Fiction of H. G. Wells* (1984), *Contemporary American Women Writers: Narrative Strategies* (1985), *Fictional Structure and Ethics: The Turn-of-the-Century English Novel* (1990), and *The Ethos of Romance at the Turn of the Century* (1994).

Sarah Way Sherman is Associate Professor of English and American Studies at the University of New Hampshire. Her publications include *Sarah Orne Jewett, an American Persephone* (1989) and the Centennial Edition of Jewett's *The Country of the Pointed Firs and Other Stories* (1997). She is also general series editor for the University Press of New England's "Becoming Modern: New Nineteenth-Century Studies." Her current project is a book entitled "Sacramental Shopping: US Fictions and Modern Consumerism, 1868–1925."

Gwen Athene Tarbox, an Associate Professor of English at Western Michigan University, specializes in literary history, youth culture, and women's studies. She is author of *The Clubwomen's Daughters: Collectivist Impulses in Progressive-era Girls' Fiction* (2000). Her current scholarly project, *Angry Young Women: Essays on Girls' Culture in Contemporary America*, explores the ways in which female adolescents have reacted to the media-created phenomenon of "girl power."

G. R. Thompson is Professor of English and Comparative Literature at Purdue University, West Lafayette. The former editor of *ESQ: A Journal of the American Renaissance* (1972–8) and *Poe Studies* (1968–80), he is the author of *Neutral Ground: New Traditionalism and the American Romance Controversy* (with Eric Carl Link, 1999), *The Art of Authorial Presence: Hawthorne's Provincial Tales* (1993), *Romantic Arabesque, Contemporary Theory, and Postmodernism: The Example of Poe's Narrative* (*ESQ* prize monograph, 1989), and *Poe's Fiction: Romantic Irony in the Gothic Tales* (1973). His edited books include the Norton Critical Edition of *The Selected Writings of Edgar Allan Poe* (2004), *Edgar Allan Poe: Essays and Reviews* (1984), *Ruined Eden of the Present: Hawthorne, Melville, and Poe* (with Virgil L. Lokke, 1981), *Romantic Gothic Tales,*

1790–1840 (1979), *The Gothic Imagination: Essays in Dark Romanticism* (1974), and *Ritual, Realism, and Revolt: Major Traditions in the Drama* (with J. C. Taylor, 1972).

Gerald Vizenor is Professor of American Studies at the University of New Mexico and Professor Emeritus at the University of California, Berkeley. He is the author of many books and essays on Native histories, critical studies, and literature, including *The People Named the Chippewa: Narrative Histories* (1984) and *Manifest Manners: Narratives on Postindian Survivance* (1994). He won the American Book Award for *Griever: An American Monkey King in China* (1987, 1990), and received a Distinguished Achievement Award from the Western Literature Association (2005). His most recent books include *Fugitive Poses: Native American Indian Scenes of Absence and Presence* (1998), *The Trickster of Liberty: Native Heirs to a Wild Baronage* (1988, 2005), and two novels, *Chancers* (2000) and *Hiroshima Bugi: Atomu 57* (2003). Vizenor is series editor of "American Indian Literature and Critical Studies" for the University of Oklahoma Press, and, with Diane Glancy, series editor of "Native Storiers: A Series of American Narratives" for the University of Nebraska Press.

Linda Wagner-Martin is Frank Borden Hanes Professor of English at the University of North Carolina at Chapel Hill. She has written biographies of Sylvia Plath, Gertrude Stein, Barbara Kingsolver, and Zelda Fitzgerald, and has authored and edited a number of books on modernist writers including, among others, William Carlos Williams, Denise Levertov, John Dos Passos, Ernest Hemingway, William Faulkner, and Gertrude Stein. She is the president of the Ernest Hemingway Foundation and Society, and she has received grants from the Guggenheim Foundation, the Rockefeller Foundation, the National Endowment for the Humanities, the American Council of Learned Societies, and the Bunting Institute.

Candace Waid is the author of *Edith Wharton's Letters from the Underworld: Fictions of Women and Writing* (1991), the editor of the Norton Critical Edition of Wharton's *The Age of Innocence* (2002), and co-editor, with Susan Goodman and Clare Colquitt, of *A Forward Glance: New Essays on Edith Wharton* (1999). In addition to teaching for a decade on the faculty of Yale University, where she worked extensively on the Wharton Collection, she has been a visiting professor at the Institut du Monde Anglophone at the Sorbonne and at the École Normale Superieure. Currently Associate Professor at the University of California at Santa Barbara, she teaches American literature with a focus on race and regional culture.

Christopher P. Wilson is Professor of English at Boston College, and the author of *The Labor of Words: Literary Professionalism in the Progressive Era* (1985), *White Collar Fictions: Class and Social Representation in American Literature, 1885–1925* (1992), and *Cop Knowledge: Police Power and Cultural Representation in Twentieth Century America* (2000). He is currently at work on a study of crime, social memory, and political authority in the contemporary era.

Acknowledgments

We wish to thank our friends at Blackwell, whose consummate professionalism and warm support made this project possible: Andrew McNeillie, who initiated the process and shepherded it through its early stages; Emma Bennett, Jenny Hunt, and Helen Nash; and most especially our superb copy-editor, Gillian Somerscales, whose talents and hard work run throughout this volume, and Karen Wilson, whose kindness, encouragement, and infinite patience with her tardy editors were those of a saint. We couldn't have asked for more.

Editors' Introduction
Robert Paul Lamb and G. R. Thompson

I

In 1865, after four years of bloody civil conflict, the federation of states begun three-quarters of a century earlier was at last indisputably a nation. The triumph of the American experiment, far from inevitable at the start of the war, came at a cost of 620,000 dead and 375,200 wounded, which was over one-third of all combatants and 3.2 percent of the nation's entire population. Slavery was abolished, westward expansion intensified, and stability brought capital investment, rapid industrialization, the growth of railroads linking the nation, the rise of great cities, and an influx of immigrants from southern and eastern Europe and Asia that led to a hitherto unimaginable cultural diversity. Between 1860 and 1920 the national population more than tripled, from 31,443,000 to 105,710,000. From 1860 to 1900, the urban population of the entire nation increased fourfold, from six million to twenty-four million, as displaced rural populations from both home and abroad settled in urban areas. During those four decades the population of New York City rose from 1,080,330 to 3,437,202, and Chicago, with 109,000 residents on the eve of the war, became the nation's second largest city with a population of 1,698,575. By the start of the Great War in 1914, the United States had evolved from a loosely knit union of local economies, cultures, and peoples into a modern nation-state and global power, and "the American Century" had begun.

This national narrative of progress contained within it other, very different narratives. The Native population of the continental United States, which estimates place as high as five million people in 1492, and which had dwindled to 600,000 by 1800, would reach a low point of 250,000 in the 1890s. The history of Natives between 1864 and 1890 was marked by broken treaties, forced relocation, the near-extermination of their primary source of sustenance (the bison population was reduced from roughly ten million to about one thousand in a mere two and a half decades), and unprovoked assaults – euphemistically called "Indian Wars" – on peaceful civilians by federal troops, from the barbaric Sand Creek Massacre of 1864 to the slaughter of three hundred men, women, and children at Wounded Knee in 1890. The four million African Americans freed from a life of hereditary chattel slavery in 1865, after a glimpse of freedom and citizenship during twelve years of Reconstruction, were condemned to a new kind of bondage in the era of Jim Crow: a period of segregation, political and legal disenfranchisement, sharecropping, economic privation, vagrancy laws, convict labor, and such terrorist tactics as mutilations, immolations, and lynchings. In the 1890s alone, an average of eighty African Americans were lynched every year, many of them in public spectacles attended by white families.

To say that the 14 million immigrants who came to America between 1860 and 1900 fared better is not to say much. Unlike the midcentury immigration from Ireland, these "New Immigrants" were peoples who hailed from non-Anglophone cultures: Italians, Jews, Poles, Russians, Greeks, Bohemians, Turks, Austro-Hungarians, Chinese, Japanese, and others. For the most part herded into squalid urban ghettoes in a land whose language and culture they did not understand, they endured overcrowding, poverty, disease, crime, lack of economic opportunity, and hostility from nativist groups (i.e. "native-born" whites). The anti-Catholicism of the antebellum period shifted to anti-radicalism, with the already established white citizens viewing the new immigrants as infected with unwelcome European ideologies such as socialism and communism, and blaming them for urban problems and labor unrest.

America's glowing cities, so well showcased by such public events as the Phila-delphia Centennial Exposition of 1876 and Chicago's Columbian Exposition of 1893, were an indication of the nation's newfound self-confidence and expansive attitude, an attitude nicely captured in the opening chapters of Theodore Dreiser's 1900 novel *Sister Carrie*. The overall quality of life, in terms of life expectancy, education, and consumption of consumer items, rose remarkably during this period. For example, illiteracy was halved, from 11 percent to 6 percent in the white population and from 80 percent to 45 percent among African Americans. And in the first 14 years of the twentieth century, deaths caused by diseases dropped by almost a half. But never before had there been such huge disparities of wealth, nor had the nation ever seemed so sharply divided into haves and have-nots. These contrasts were particularly evident in the big cities. By 1890, 9 percent of the population owned 71 percent of the nation's wealth, and roughly 40 percent of all Americans lived below the poverty line. Thus progress and poverty went hand in hand, as reflected in the radically different fictional worlds of, say, Henry James and Edith Wharton, on the one hand, and Theodore Dreiser and Upton Sinclair on the other. It was perhaps symbolically apt that the 1893 Exposition, with its acclaimed model "White City," took place during the worst depression the nation had hitherto seen, with over 150,000 businesses becoming insolvent and nearly one-fifth of the nation's workforce unable to find employment.

America's great industries – steel production, petroleum, the railroads, electricity, textiles, meatpacking, the automobile, and toolmaking, to name but a few – grew to such an extent between 1865 and 1914 that they changed almost every facet of national life. As industrialization made all sectors of the American economy less labor-intensive, the value of production per agricultural worker rose by 43 percent between 1870 and 1900, while the value per worker in manufacturing and mining increased by a remarkable 76 percent. The revolution in agricultural production meant that the nation could feed itself, and sell its produce throughout the world as well, with fewer people engaged in farming. In 1870, 52 percent of American workers were farmers, but by 1890 they were outnumbered for the first time by workers in manufacturing and mining, and by 1900 agricultural workers made up only 40 percent of the labor force. During that same period from 1870 to 1900, farm products, despite their increase, dropped from 53 to 33 percent of the nation's commodity output, while manufacturing and mining rose from 35 to 58 percent. As agriculture itself became big business with larger economies of scale, Jefferson's dream of a nation of yeoman farmers faded and, with the country's ten largest cities producing nearly 40 percent of the manufactures, the excess rural population went off to the cities in search of jobs.

The nation's industries quickly consolidated into larger and larger entities, monopolies and consortia run by interlocking directorates. Headed by powerful men dubbed the "Robber Barons," abetted by friendly courts and an even friendlier Congress, and supported by federal troops, state militias, and private armies of hired thugs, these conglomerates came close to taking over the nation, presenting the sort of threat of concentrated power that Americans had feared since the years preceding the American Revolution. But as big business became dominant, labor began to organize itself to fight against the abuses of lock-outs, "yellow dog" contracts (forbidding employees to join a union), scabs, blacklists, court injunctions, company towns and stores, wages in the form of scrip rather than money, arbitrary wage cuts, child labor, 12- to 14-hour work days, dangerous working conditions, and physical coercion. From the mid-1870s to 1914, there was a major strike every year in America, and the strife was so intense and extensive that one social historian has referred to it as "the other civil war." The Great Railroad Strike of 1877 was the first nationwide strike in American history: protesting drastic cuts in barely subsistence wages and a rise of serious injuries and deaths in the workplace, not only the railroad workers themselves, but also farmers, craftsmen, coal miners, and the unemployed brought the nation's railroads to a standstill. By the conclusion of the strike, which involved some hundred thousand workers, one hundred people were dead and a thousand had been imprisoned. In 1886 alone there were roughly fifteen hundred strikes, affecting half a million workers. Between one and two thousand strikes took place every year during the 1890s, together involving nearly three-quarters of a million workers. Labor strikes were usually accompanied by violence, with workers carrying personal weapons on one side, and well-armed state militia, National Guards, federal troops, local police, and hired Pinkerton guards on the other. In many cases the violence amounted to authorized murder, as in the "Ludlow Massacre" in Colorado in 1914. When coal miners employed by John D. Rockefeller's Colorado Fuel and Coal Company struck because they were forbidden to join the United Mine

Workers of America, they were evicted from their company-owned shacks and moved their families into tents for shelter. On the morning of April 20, in a premeditated attack, company guards and state militia doused the tents with kerosene, set them ablaze, and sprayed the area with machine-gun fire, killing 20 people, including two women and 11 children. The perpetrators were never punished, and the miners who survived were subsequently arrested and blacklisted. The emergence of mass society during this half century of American history was indeed a period of striking achievement — there is no gainsaying that fact; but it was also a time of tragedy.

As one might expect, literary productions in this period of upheaval and transformation were rich in cultural representations and far more diverse than they had been during the relatively culturally homogeneous antebellum years. A partial list of authors who wrote important fictional narratives during these years is impressive: Harriet Beecher Stowe (born 1811), Frances Ellen Watkins Harper (b. 1825), John William De Forest (b. 1826), Rose Terry Cooke (b. 1827), Lew Wallace (b. 1827), Helen Hunt Jackson (b. 1830), John Esten Cooke (b. 1830), Rebecca Harding Davis (b. 1831), Louisa May Alcott (b. 1832), Horatio Alger (b. 1832), Lillie Devereux Blake (b. 1833), Artemus Ward (b. 1834), Frank Stockton (b. 1834), Mark Twain (b. 1835), Augusta Jane Evans (b. 1835), Bret Harte (b. 1836), Thomas Bailey Aldrich (b. 1836), William Dean Howells (b. 1837), John Burroughs (b. 1837), Edward Eggleston (b. 1837), Henry Adams (b. 1838), John Muir (b. 1838), Albion Tourgée (b. 1838), Constance Fenimore Woolson (b. 1840), Ambrose Bierce (b. 1842), Sidney Lanier (b. 1842), Henry James (b. 1843), Elizabeth Stuart Phelps (b. 1844), George Washington Cable (b. 1844), Hjalmar Hjorth Boyesen (b. 1848), Joel Chandler Harris (b. 1848), Sarah Orne Jewett (b. 1849), James Lane Allen (b. 1849), Mary Noailles Murfree (b. 1850), Edward Bellamy (b. 1850), Lafcadio Hearn (b. 1850), Kate Chopin (b. 1851), Mary E. Wilkins Freeman (b. 1852), Grace King (b. 1852), Thomas Nelson Page (b. 1853), Harold Frederic (b. 1856), L. Frank Baum (b. 1856), Alice Brown (b. 1857), Henry Blake Fuller (b. 1857), Gertrude Atherton (b. 1857), Charles Waddell Chesnutt (b. 1858), Pauline Elizabeth Hopkins (b. 1859), Hamlin Garland (b. 1860), Owen Wister (b. 1860), Abraham Cahan (b. 1860), Charlotte Perkins Gilman (b. 1860), Henry Harland (b. 1861), Edith Wharton (b. 1862), O. Henry (b. 1862), Geneva Stratton-Porter (b. 1863), Richard Harding Davis (b. 1864), Sui Sin Far (b. 1865), George Ade (b. 1866), David Graham Phillips (b. 1867), Finley Peter Dunne (b. 1867), W. E. B. Du Bois (b. 1868), Mary Austin (b. 1868), Charles Alexander Eastman (b. 1868), Robert Herrick (b. 1868), Booth Tarkington (b. 1869), Frank Norris (b. 1870), Stephen Crane (b. 1871), Theodore Dreiser (b. 1871), James Weldon Johnson (b. 1871), Winston Churchill (b. 1871), Paul Laurence Dunbar (b. 1872), Sutton Elbert Griggs (b. 1872), Zane Grey (b. 1872), Willa Cather (b. 1873), Gertrude Stein (b. 1874), Ellen Glasgow (b. 1874), Zona Gale (b. 1874), Alice Dunbar-Nelson (b. 1875), Zitkala Ša (b. 1876), Jack London (b. 1876), Upton Sinclair (b. 1878), James Branch Cabell (b. 1879), and Ernest Poole (b. 1880). These authors documented the myriad ongoing changes in American society; they preserved in their works the vanishing worlds of their childhoods; they offered penetrating critiques of race, racism, gender, class, nativism, imperialism, capitalism, war, poverty, local societies, and national politics; and they introduced into American literature peoples and regions previously unrepresented. They did so in texts that mixed literary modes – sentimentalism, the romance, realism, naturalism, regionalism, and modernism. If America's population, culture, society, economy, and political life were forever transformed during the half century between 1865 and 1914, so too was its literature.

Nearly all of the abovementioned authors, and many others, are discussed in this volume, and this list serves as a reminder of how few of the important authors and texts of a given period find their way into undergraduate, or even graduate curricula, crowded out as they are by hypercanonized texts in the ideologically constructed canon. A list of the authors by their dates of birth also shows how a classification by generation, which organizes these writers by their formative periods, is at odds with the usual methods by which they are classified in literary histories. Thus Stephen Crane and Frank Norris, commonly viewed as "nineteenth-century naturalists," are actually nearly a decade younger than Edith Wharton, a "twentieth-century realist/ naturalist/modernist." Crane and Norris are also from the same generation as Willa Cather and Gertrude Stein, two leading twentieth-century modernists. All literary histories and generic classifications are critical constructions. They are vital to understanding the literature of a period, but should never be mistaken for the primary reality: literary and cultural histories are never as rich as what they purport to represent.

II

Anonymously reviewing the first edition of his own *Leaves of Grass* in 1855, Walt Whitman proclaimed, "An American bard at last!" and further intoned, "You have come in good time, Walt Whitman!" Neither possessing Whitman's justifiable *chutzpah* nor able to avail ourselves of his anonymity, we nevertheless confess to a good deal of pride in the present volume, which is unprecedented in scope among collections devoted to this crucial period in American literary history. Previous such companions have taken the form of smaller sections in volumes covering the breadth of American literature, like the *Columbia Literary History of the United States*, or else have been collections of essays on the period that consist of a couple of overviews with each of the remaining pieces focusing on one or two specific novels apiece. But *A Companion to American Fiction 1865–1914* is comprehensive, providing overviews of a wealth of topics central to the period. Thus the reader will find essays not only on realism, naturalism, and regionalism – the three historical genres most closely iden- tified with these years – but also on the romance and on sentimental and domestic fiction, which are mainly associated with the previous period, and on modernism, which would come to full fruition later. These kinds of writing existed, in some cases flourished, during this period, and also found their way into realist, naturalist, and regionalist texts; as Nancy Glazener reminds us in her essay, "all fictional works cross genres." Similarly, the volume contains essays not only on such expected topics as race, gender, class, and ethnicity, but also on other important issues like Darwinism, law, the city, consumer culture, the frontier, and even children's literature and ecocriticism. There is no other such comprehensive and multifaceted collection of essays on the period.

From its conception, this volume has been intended to serve several purposes: to provide an introduction to the historical and aesthetic genres, thematic concerns, historical and cultural contexts, and major authors of this period; to serve as a reference tool, offering distillations of the most recent and up-to-date scholarship in the fields covered; and to present in one volume original essays on these topics. Consequently, the book is aimed at a large and diverse audience: advanced undergraduates contemplating the pursuit of a graduate education; graduate students in English departments, History departments, American Studies programs, and Comparative Literature programs; young faculty members preparing courses in nineteenth- and early twentieth-century literature; established faculty members seeking the latest perspectives on the period; and even non-specialists and general intellectuals who are interested in these areas of inquiry. To that end, our contributors, although they come from strong theoretical backgrounds, have attempted – we think successfully – to present their ideas in accessible, jargon-free prose, writing in such a way as to reach the largest possible audience while, at the same time, maintaining an intellectual rigor that will appeal to specialists in these fields. The individual essays are autonomous and the editors have refrained from any effort – other than in their initial choices of topics – to fashion a monolithic perspective running throughout the book. Sometimes the contributors will take different views of the same author, text, or thematic material. Far from worrying about the expression of such differences, we welcome and indeed expected it. We feel that such a process is in the best interests of honest academic inquiry, that it serves to demonstrate the richness of the period and its literary productions, and that, most of all, it is from a multiplicity of viewpoints, ideological frameworks, and contexts that the fullest picture of literary history emerges.

The book is organized into three parts, the first of which is devoted to historical traditions and genres. The historical genre most closely associated with these years is realism, and in the opening essay Nancy Glazener locates American realism in its larger Anglophone contexts and its relations with other contemporary genres such as the romance and sentimental fiction. She also delineates the nature of realist fictional practices and examines the challenges to realism and the traditional realist canon presented by women and minority authors hitherto excluded from consideration. The romance is a genre traditionally confined to the antebellum period, but William J. Scheick shows how it continued to flourish in the late nineteenth century. Providing a critical taxonomy for examining the wealth of postbellum romances, he introduces popular texts neglected by criticism, recontextualizes canonical texts as romances, and links the postbellum romance genre to utopian fiction, sentimentalism, satire, gender, race, class, and the transformation of American culture. Like the romance, sentimentalism is a vibrant element in postbellum narrative that most critics focus on only as it appears in the earlier part of the nineteenth century. Gregg Camfield offers a historical overview of the seventeenth-century origins and development of sentimentalism, and then proceeds to explore its importance in post-Civil War American literature and culture – especially its relationship to politics, religion, social class, childhood, domesticity, and nostalgia, and its entwinement with realism. Realist narrative appeared on the European scene roughly three decades before it began in America. Although early American realism coincided with the peak of French, British, and Russian realism, its indebtedness to European realists has only rarely been examined. Winfried Fluck examines the relations between American realists and their European counterparts – in terms of influence, and also of the significant departures that made American realism in the works of such authors as Howells, James, Chopin, and Dreiser both different and particularly "modern."

Contrary to the traditional view, realism, as these first essays show, should not be classified as a mode or historical genre in opposition to the already established literary genres of sentimentalism and the romance. Nor is it easily distinguished from the other significant historical genres that emerged in late nineteenth-century America. Naturalism, which reached its height in the 1890s, is usually viewed as the offspring of realism. But whether it is entirely other, merely a late form of realism, a transgeneric blend of realism and the romance, or a return to the romance per se – on this question, critics differ. Christophe Den Tandt provides a historiography of the scholarship on naturalism – from orthodox to the most recent revisionist – and, drawing upon the perspectives of these critics and of the naturalists themselves, maps out a new way of viewing naturalism and its relation to other late nineteenth-century literary discourses. Regionalism is another historical genre associated with the period and with realism, but it already existed in the antebellum period and simply intensified after the war. Like sentimentalism, regionalism can be found in texts of other genres, and can be seen as an element of most narrative. June Howard examines the postwar vogue for local color and regional fiction, as Americans began viewing themselves in national and even global contexts; she also ties this phenomenon to changes in the print marketplace, showing that this literature played an important role in the process of national integration.

Although modernism did not fully emerge in American narrative until after World War I, its foundations were already present in the first decades of the twentieth century, years in which it was well underway in American poetry and Anglo-European fiction. Linda Wagner-Martin examines the pre-1914 roots of American modernist fiction, focusing on how the expectations of the reading public and the gendered situations of women authors led those authors, many of whom would become full-blown modernists after 1914, to adopt narrative strategies that would later exert a great influence on American modernism in its heyday. The final essay in part I is devoted to a literary, rather than a historical genre: the short story and what critics refer to as the short story "cycle" or "sequence." The bulk of scholarship on the

American short story has focused on earlier romance writers and later modernists and contemporary authors, with only a handful of authors who wrote stories between 1865 and 1914 attracting attention. But J. Gerald Kennedy shows how the form was affected by postwar developments in publishing and by the emergence of regionalism, realism, and naturalism. He presents a rich canvas of short story writers in the period and explores, as well, the re-emergence of the short story sequence, or linked story collection, that would come to full fruition in the modern period.

The second part of this book, which is devoted to "contexts and themes," is its most diverse. It contains essays on the narratives of people who share historical experiences and traditions (e.g. Native Americans, ethnic groups, African Americans, women); essays on narratives that foreground particular kinds of place and space (e.g. nature, the frontier, the city); essays on what might be called sub-genres of narrative (e.g. the literature of the Civil War and Reconstruction, utopian fiction, children's fiction); and essays that treat themes that run throughout the period (e.g. class, law, the influence of Darwin, consumer culture). S. K. Robisch introduces us to the relatively recent but burgeoning field of ecocriticism and ecological literary study, demonstrating how nature writing and ecological narratives reorient our conceptions of literary history and literary classification. He delineates the major tenets of industrial-era nature writing and shows how ecocritical readings of an ecological narrative by Sarah Orne Jewett and the nature writing of John Muir deepen our understanding of both the texts and their cultural contexts. Christine Bold turns our attention to the mono-logical myth of the American West as it was constructed by such figures as Theodore Roosevelt, Frederick Remington, Owen Wister, William "Buffalo Bill" Cody, and Frederick Jackson Turner, and was later canonized by scholars. She then vastly complicates this male Anglo-American myth – which is still prevalent in American culture – by bringing in the long-erased voices, texts, and presences of Native American, Hispanic American, African American, and women authors, turning the larger traditional narrative into a multicultural and historically accurate one. Most collections of this sort do not include an essay on Native American narratives, which are, instead, classified as a subset of ethnic narratives and recast into discourses amenable to Euro-American sensibilities. But Gerald Vizenor takes us into the world of peoples caught between coerced cultural assimilation and physical extermin-ation, in what is, along with chattel slavery, one of the two most appalling chapters in American history. Juxtaposing Native voices with the ways in which their narratives have been misconstrued by white culture, he demonstrates how these stories represent a spirit of survivance – of diplomatic, strategic resistance, and aesthetic irony – that has been the hallmark of Native narratives ever since.

The West was not the only contested site of national identity. Kathleen Diffley shows how the coming of the Civil War and the conflict itself were differently represented in the narratives of women and men, Northerners and Southerners, African Americans and whites, and by combatants and non-combatants. She then illustrates how these different perspectives continued on into the literature of Recon-struction, which presented competing visions about the future of African Americans, relations between women and men, and the nation itself. The two essays that follow focus exclusively on the respective narrative traditions of women and African Americans in this period. Grace Farrell shows the ways in which women authors represented the struggles of middle-class, professional, and African American women in late nineteenth-century patriarchal culture, in these years between the apogee of the domestic novelists and the emergence of women modernists. She resurrects important but long-forgotten texts and offers reinterpretations of others that are still being read, revealing the faulty assumptions upon which the canon has rested. Dickson D. Bruce, Jr. examines African American narratives in the period. He delineates the rhetorical strategies authors employed in their efforts to combat racism and the pernicious racist stereotypes prevalent in white culture, as well as the internalization of these prejudices in black culture, while facing the challenges of discerning the dimensions of African American identity in the New South and the industrializing North.

The late nineteenth and early twentieth centuries in America were the great period of urbanization, immigration from southern and eastern Europe and Asia, and industrialization – three phenomena that were indelibly linked. Sidney H. Bremer explores the evolving literary representations of, and responses to, the transformation of American cities in this period, identifying a paradigm shift from what she terms earlier "cultural-city" novels to a new "economic-city" novel. She examines the literary histories of specific cities such as New York, Chicago, San Francisco, and New Orleans in the context of these two interacting literary perspectives and in the context of their changing demographics. During these years, the United States shifted from a "culture of character" to a "culture of personality," as massive changes led to a pervasive sense of disorientation that undermined the older belief in a coherent and unitary individual and national identity. Sarah Way Sherman analyzes this shift in the nature of subjectivity and the ways in which the relationship between surface and depth in the self was perceived. Identity, for many Americans, moved from being fixed and stable to becoming mutable and contextual – "a matter of performing as much as being." Class is all too often the silent partner in the academy's trinity of "race, class, and gender." Between 1865 and 1914, as wealth both grew at record rates and was distributed more and more inequitably, Americans became increasingly stratified, and class became especially significant. Christopher P. Wilson places class prominently before us by exploring the means by which social divisions, boundaries, and crossings were inscribed in the fiction of the period, and how the category of class intersected with other social parameters like race, gender, and ethnicity. If this period was a historical low point in the treatment of Native Americans and free African Americans, the same holds true for the diverse peoples of the New Immigration. Robert M. Dowling calls these years the nadir of ethnic relations in United States history and analyzes the emergence of current concepts of ethnicity during this time. He also explores the methods that ethnic authors employed to fashion their narratives in an attempt to understand their own groups, as well as their groups' relation to the larger American culture, employing a literary genre he terms "ethnic realism."

The impact of Charles Darwin on American literary culture in the late nineteenth and twentieth centuries is incalculable. Bert Bender explores the influence on American literature of Darwin's major works, showing the extent to which Darwinian ideas dominated American authors' understandings and representations of civilization, human nature, courtship, marriage, gender, the "New Woman," race, the role of the environment, heredity, sexual selection, and ecology. Another manifestly rich but, until recently, undeveloped area in literary studies is the relationship between narrative and law. William E. Moddelmog examines the engagement of fictional narrative with legal discourse, a phenomenon deeply revealing of American cultural anxieties in this period. He also demonstrates the ways in which developing concepts of law influenced literary notions of subjectivity, civil rights, and women's rights. The late nineteenth century was the heyday of a sub-genre of narratives far removed from the detailed referential world of realism and naturalism: utopian fiction, especially popular following the publication of Edward Bellamy's *Looking Backward* in 1888. Thomas Peyser analyzes the nature of utopian narrative: its goal of social justice, its dark underside of fascistic inclination, its inherent contradictions, and its historical influence. Although the scholarship on children's literature is large, it is rarely a topic for consideration in mainstream literary studies, and even in the histories of this literature the period covered by this volume has yet to receive its due. Gwen Athene Tarbox argues, however, that these years were of pivotal importance in the history of children's literature. Delineating three kinds of children's narrative – conventional, speculative, and insurgent – she shows how authors moved from didactic novels supporting the status quo to novels that questioned it, and then to novels that openly advocated social change, most especially with regard to gender roles, race, and class.

The final part of the volume is devoted to major authors – a subjective notion, to be sure, but one that we felt indispensable to such an enterprise. In addition to five authors whose works fall almost entirely within our period, we have also included essays on Edith Wharton and Theodore Dreiser – both of whom were productive well past 1914 – because of their obvious importance and the fact that both were products of the late nineteenth century. Another author whom we consider a major figure is Louisa May Alcott, who, although now acknowledged as significant, nevertheless still bears the inaccurate stigma of being "merely" a writer of children's books and has thus been relegated to the periphery of the canon. John Matteson explores the mind and art of Alcott within the biographical contexts of her atypical and complicated familial relationships, most especially that with her father, demonstrating how her complex feminism arose from her life and evolved over the course of her career. Mark Twain is arguably America's best known and least understood major author, his role in American culture so often appearing in soundbite assessments and his greatest novel almost universally misread and mistaught. Robert Paul Lamb examines some of Twain's literary achievements by focusing on six of his richest narratives, texts that feature his representations and critiques of race, identity, childhood, the South, the West, postbellum America, imperialism, and the myth of success. Although William Dean Howells is not well known outside of academia, and has even unaccountably vanished from volumes like *The Norton Anthology of American Literature*, there has never been (perhaps excepting Emerson) a more productive individual force in American literary history. He was the most influential critic of his day; the friend and promoter of such authors as Twain, James, Crane, Gilman, Norris, Chesnutt, Cahan, and Wharton; and a prolific, major novelist in his own right. Michael Anesko makes the case for Howells's significance, aesthetic and cultural, while telling the story of his gradual disillusionment with the failure of American ideals and with art's inability to affect society. Even among academic critics, there is probably no American novelist more redoubtable than Henry James, the artist *par excellence*; for students and general readers, the man known as "The Master" is even more formidable, especially in the complexities of his later works. John Carlos Rowe asks the question why we should read James, and answers it by examining how James's ambivalent responses to the ongoing process of modernization – which links his modern to our postmodern era – can help illuminate for us the commodified and globalized society in which we now live. Until relatively recently, James's friend and confidante Edith Wharton lived in his shadow in academic criticism, but, thanks mainly to feminist critics, we now have a much fuller understanding of her life and her achievements. Candace Waid and Clare Colquitt present Wharton's early life as providing her with the fictional concerns she would pursue throughout her career; they explore her interrelated critiques of gender in her novels of manners and her influence on later authors such as Cather and Faulkner. Stephen Crane is the Mozart of American literature, his virtuosity at so early an age gaining for him the admiration of such older masters as Henry James and Joseph Conrad, and his influence continuing to be felt down to our own day. William E. Cain analyzes the sources of Crane's aesthetic originality and power, his attempts to capture in his intense, compact prose the sensations of life as felt, the discordance between that life and the reifying processes of mind by which it is represented and understood, and the multiple ironies that ensue from such discordance. For the general reader, Theodore Dreiser is, along with Howells, the least well known of our canonical authors, but no one better captured the pulse of everyday life, of what it was like to live in the late nineteenth- and early twentieth-century United States. Clare Virginia Eby reads Dreiser's works against his recurring thematic concerns – poverty and wealth, class status, marginality, the relation of huge impersonal forces to the individual self and to its sense of identity, consumer culture, morality, criminality, sexuality, and the American myth of mobility.

We would like to express our profound gratitude to our contributors, the quality of whose work has exceeded our greatest hopes. It has been a humbling experience to watch the culmination of our original outline of topics in the outstanding essays they have produced, and it has been a genuine pleasure working with them. To a large extent, it's been their ship, and they have taken us on a wonderful intellectual journey. We hope and expect that the reader will experience something of the excitement and illumination that we have enjoyed while putting together this volume.

PART I
Historical Traditions and Genres

1

The Practice and Promotion of American Literary Realism

Nancy Glazener

Realist fiction is so familiar that it has been naturalized for many readers. We enter into it easily and willingly. Indeed, one of the signs that a work of fiction is realist is that we can ignore its technical crafting and become absorbed in the story. In the service of this absorption, the narrator of a realist work is generally either a plausible character or an unobtrusive stage manager; its symbolism is artfully worked into the fabric of its plot; and its characters give the impression of having minds of their own. A realist novel presents a social world that we can recognize (even if it isn't precisely our own), peopled by characters with whom we can identify (even though they give the impression of being unique), and, perhaps most importantly, the characters' thoughts and actions seem worthy of our attention. We do not mistake a realist novel for a work of history or journalism or sociology, but the very name "realism" makes a claim about the potential for fiction to capture something real about social life and perhaps even about the structure of our inner lives.

The more we take seriously the cultural value and social influence of realism's understanding of what is "real," the more we may be inclined to believe that realism (as a platform for literature and a set of novels) marked and perhaps helped bring about important historical transformations in how certain readers understood themselves and their worlds. Whereas American realism has often been treated as exclusively a development within American literary history (thereby reinforcing the tendency for American studies to consider the United States "exceptional" in relation to the rest of the world), this account will position American literary realism as an important episode within a larger history of the Anglophone novel. The development of the novel, in turn, was intertwined historically with a transnational set of historical changes known as modernity: changes by which people reorganized their lives around capitalism, democracy, and secular individualism rather than monarchy and feudalism. In their new roles as modern individuals, people have faced many challenging and contradictory experiences, including new forms of isolation and crowding, scarcity and consumeristic longing, responsibility and powerlessness.

These experiences have been registered and to some extent even shaped *as* experiences by the promoters and practitioners of literary realism.

The Onset of Realism

The earliest known usage of the word "realism" to designate a new kind of fiction occurred in 1853, in Britain's *Westminster Review* (Becker 1963: 7). However, the term "realism" provides only one index of the onset of literary realism in Europe and North America. For example, the strategy of contrasting a particular novel's verisimilitude with the artifice and conventionality of other kinds of fiction, dating back at least as far as Cervantes' *Don Quixote* (1605, 1615), signals a tendency toward realism, even though it is a strategy that can pave the way for a variety of fictional practices. Ian Watt argued in 1957 that realism had implicitly been the fundamental tendency of the English novel since the eighteenth century. He identified a beginning for novelistic realism in eighteenth-century works that depicted psychologically complex individual characters in plausible social worlds. In Watt's view, Henry Fielding's novels depicting characters who traveled through geographic and social expanses (*Tom Jones*, 1749) and Samuel Richardson's novels exploring the depths of individual experience and reflection (*Pamela*, 1740–1; *Clarissa*, 1747–8) were examples of two complementary tendencies in the novel, merged most successfully in the works of Jane Austen (Watt 1957: 297). Austen's novels, such as *Pride and Prejudice* (1813), featured complex, morally self-conscious characters who had to navigate densely meaningful familial and social relationships. Like Watt, most critics have drawn their models of fully developed realism from nineteenth-century European fiction. In addition to Austen's novels, mid- to late-century French and English novels – by Honoré de Balzac, George Eliot, Gustave Flaubert, Stendhal, the Goncourt brothers, and Anthony Trollope – provide the bulk of examples for Anglophone critics, although realist works from many other European literatures also circulated in Great Britain and the United States.

Because many of the novelistic techniques associated with realism predate realism's official recognition and can be found across a range of fictional works, it is impossible to identify a date – or even a decade – when realism was invented. Nevertheless, the mid-nineteenth century was the era when realism began to be noticed and promoted (or discouraged) as not only a specific way of writing fiction but also a specific understanding of fiction's social role and responsibilities. In the United States, realist fiction was most commonly defined in contrast with an earlier type of novel, the romance, which was loosely associated with the Romantic literary movement; William Dean Howells, one of the foremost promoters and practitioners of American realism, significantly distanced realism from "the mania of romanticism" which he saw afflicting even Eliot and Balzac (Howells 1967: 74). But Romanticism, which for Anglophone readers was primarily a British invention, had actually laid groundwork for literary realism. For example, William Wordsworth's "Preface" to *Lyrical Ballads*

(1800) anticipated – or inspired – realist ambitions, insofar as the object of that volume (co-authored by Samuel Taylor Coleridge) was "to choose incidents and situations from common life, and to relate or describe them, throughout, as far as was possible in a selection of language really used by men..." (Wordsworth and Coleridge 1967: 321). Realist fiction, too, would specialize in commonplace scenarios and characters and idiomatic speech.

The rest of Wordsworth's sentence marks an important difference between Romanticism and realism, though. He reports that he and Coleridge wished "at the same time, to throw over [these "incidents and situations from common life"]... a certain colouring of imagination, whereby ordinary things should be presented to the mind in an unusual aspect" (Wordsworth and Coleridge 1967: 321). Although American realists often insisted that their activity was artistic, not journalistic, because it relied on subtle forms of selection and transformation, public discussions of realism endowed it with the social mission of capturing something about Americans' shared reality. As this mission was construed, it was not compatible with the idea of imaginative coloring, nor with a penchant for the "unusual": the common, the typical, the everyday, and the ordinary were all bywords of realism. In this way, the writers and critics who promoted realism claimed an authority very close to that of empirical science, which was premised on the reproducibility – or typicality? – of experimental results. The artistic operations involved in realism were supposed to be harnessed to a project of representation, not fabrication. Accordingly, early nineteenth-century romance writers were deprecated by realists either for distorting reality (for which Mark Twain criticized both James Fenimore Cooper, in "Fenimore Cooper's Literary Offences" [1895], and Sir Walter Scott, in *Life on the Mississippi* [1883]), or for failing to try to capture it (in the case of Nathaniel Hawthorne, who was admired but often relegated to quaint social irrelevance [Brodhead 1986: 82] – unless he was reclassified as a realist [Howells 1967: 115]). In Scott's case, Twain faulted mainly the white American Southerners who willfully misperceived their own reality through Scott's historical fiction – a reminder that the promoters of realism were prescriptive about fiction because they believed that fiction-reading could have important social and political consequences (Brodhead 1986: 101).

It would have surprised realism's nineteenth-century supporters to learn that some twentieth-century critics came to admire romances precisely because they explored extraordinary scenarios and somewhat abstract philosophical issues. Indeed, in 1957 Richard Chase inaugurated a critical tradition that understood romances to comprise the main tradition of American literature, distinct from the realist tradition dominating British literature. Chase characterized romances as works in which abstract or symbolic modes of representation predominated. Nineteenth-century promoters of realism wanted literature to capture the possibilities and challenges of social integration; twentieth-century critics who followed Chase valued romances for highlighting the failures and costs of social integration. In the twentieth century, Hester Prynne's and Captain Ahab's metaphysical speculations (in Hawthorne's *The Scarlet Letter* [1850] and Melville's *Moby-Dick* [1851]), and the lavish symbolic possibilities of

Hester's embroidered "A" and Ahab's white whale and doubloon, came to seem like the very stuff of literature. The power of either Hester or Ahab to remake self or reality, far from being irrelevant and fantastic, could be linked to the power of the imagination or of language itself to make and unmake worlds. In keeping with the mid-twentieth century's new zeal for romance, any canonical works previously associated with realism came to be credited with incorporating certain qualities of romance. For example, Chase argued that James's Isabel Archer, the protagonist of *The Portrait of a Lady*, "sees things as a romancer does" (1957: 119), thereby counterpointing the more realist perspective of the narrator, and he proposed that Mark Twain's "real fictional province is . . . the borderland between novel and romance" (1957: 156).

Chase was only one of many critics to point out that realism and romance need not be incompatible. Moreover, outcroppings of not only romance but also sentimentalism, sensationalism, regionalism, naturalism, and non-literary genres such as ethnography run through works that have been associated with realism. Realism does not today seem like an exclusive generic label, and literary genres themselves seem less like blueprints for authors to follow than traces of how texts were positioned among an array of literary and extra-literary possibilities for narrative. Within the politics of literary history, however, it is important to recognize that realism was first promoted at the expense of romance as a more modern and more properly American literary form. As early as the 1850s, it is possible to trace the effects of this promotion on both authors and readers. For instance, each of Nathaniel Hawthorne's four major novels is prefaced with some discussion of the author's half-apologetic choice to pursue dreamy, moonlit romance. In his "Preface" to *The House of the Seven Gables* (1851) he claims that romance offers "a certain latitude, both as to its fashion and material," in contrast to the Novel, which aims "at a very minute fidelity, not merely to the possible, but to the probable and ordinary course of man's experience" (Hawthorne 1983: 351). An American reviewer writing in *Putnam's New Monthly Magazine* in 1857 epitomized the reaction against romance that prompted Hawthorne's defensiveness:

> I have passed the period of romance. Only children wait for adventures. I do not look for sudden wealth or poverty. I do not expect to fall in love with a princess, a beggar, or an opera-dancer. I can earn my bread, and am not exposed to great misery in any turn of the wheel of fortune. Is life, then, for me no longer worth living? . . . The right novel . . . will show the manhood, not the childhood, of the race. It will not need to elaborate a black background of misfortune to serve as a foil for doubtful happiness, but will exhibit an activity so splendid that it must shine in relief upon the dingy gray of ordinary circumstances, duties, and relations. (Anon. 1857: 96)

The version of romance presented here does not sound much like Hawthorne's, Scott's, or Cooper's novels, but the polemic exemplifies several of the ways in which realism came to be differentiated from romance. Indeed, the review is an early, especially clear example of the process by which respected US magazines helped to cultivate realist expectations in readers (Glazener 1997: 23–50). Romance is here linked to the old world and to old-fashioned or obsolete materials (princesses and beggars, presented as material for love plots). The presence of the opera-dancer associates romance with popular entertainments (opera not having yet been monopolized by elite urbanites, as Lawrence Levine has explained) and with the dime novels or story papers that might feature such a character. In short, the romance is associated with the immature, escapist pleasures of people who do not have serious middle-class responsibilities. The alternative to romance seems to be fiction that would help readers who are "not exposed to any great misery in any turn of the wheel of fortune" – readers who are at least comfortable and perhaps quite privileged – to see the importance and value of their daily routines and decisions.

The general mission of nineteenth-century realism was, then, to represent faithfully contemporary life and ordinary people (with "ordinary" taken to designate those who are neither very wealthy nor very poor); to depict characters with well-developed inner lives and situate them in thickly described social environments; and to simulate the language and interweavings of circumstance in the social worlds presented, avoiding conventionalized language and plot developments (or at least the conventions associated with the romance and other prior literary forms). Looking back at works associated with realism, we can connect this mission to some specific writerly practices, even though none of these practices is exclusive to realism. For explanatory convenience, I will combine nineteenth-century ideas about realism – found in prefaces, book reviews, and other essays – with the perceptions of some later literary critics. By "realism" I refer to the platform of the nineteenth-century literary movement that promoted realist fiction; by "realist fiction" I mean fictional works that have been associated with realism, even though I am suggesting that all fictional works cross genres.

Realist Fictional Practice

Realism has often been characterized by its avoidance of allegory and other forms of conspicuous symbolism, especially in contrast to the romance. (See e.g. Howells 1967: 23.) In keeping with the understanding that genres interweave and blend together in practice, this distinction is not airtight: most fiction offers symbolic possibilities, of course, and the symbols in both *The Scarlet Letter* and *Moby-Dick* could be read as furthering the realist project of characterization as well as embodying epistemological and semiotic problems. Hester's "A" accumulates meanings for the Puritans who see it, over time and in particular circumstances; Ahab's doubloon takes on a special meaning for several characters who mull over what it might bring to them, if they were lucky enough to win it by spotting Moby-Dick first. However, both Ahab and Hester question divine laws and prerogatives, and the textual signals that link them as metaphysical rebels to the charismatic Lucifer of Milton's *Paradise Lost* (1667) are very different from the sociological codings that distinguish realist characters.

Symbols are more self-effacing in realist works, which offer discerning readers the opportunity to pick out the symbolic potentials of details that are seamlessly incorporated into a believable fictional fabric. By way of contrast, consider a much earlier text: it is impossible to read John Bunyan's *Pilgrim's Progress* (1678, 1684) without recognizing that the Bible as a text and Christianity as a moral and metaphysical scheme are lovingly invoked and elaborated through the story of Christian's journey to the Celestial City. Bunyan's interrelated symbolic characters and landscapes constitute an allegory that operated – probably in Bunyan's time, perhaps in later times for certain communities of Christian readers – as a somewhat public understanding of a specific religion's model of faith. The fact that Bunyan's text was read by individuals, in other words, was either incidental to its communal purpose or slightly at odds with it. Conversely, a number of critics have suggested that the fact that realist novels are read by individuals is fundamental to their aesthetics. A reader's private pleasure of knowing that she might easily have missed a pattern of symbolism or a symbolic doubling or contrasting of characters – but that she didn't – makes a realist reader a connoisseur, manifesting her individual education or discernment rather than her participation in an interpretive community. Once discerned, even a biblical allusion functions very differently in a realist text from how it functions in Bunyan's work, because the cultural authority of the Bible is diminished in realism's secular textual milieu, regardless of an author's or reader's religious convictions. A devout reader of Bunyan may conclude that the Celestial City stands for heaven, in the sense that the only representational function of the Celestial City is to invoke the idea of heaven and give it a concrete form. However, the garden in which Isabel Archer spends happy time with Ralph Touchett and his father in *The Portrait of a Lady* (1881) may evoke Eden but is not devoted solely to that reference.

It is important to recognize that realist fiction does not exclude symbolism: realism reframes symbolism for the purposes of a secular, privatized readership. The discreet symbolism of realist fiction is one indication that realism is suspended between two kinds of authority: first, literary authority based on the text's appropriate citation and use of previous texts and literary traditions, and second, social authority based on the text's reliability as an account of contemporary life. The use of allusive symbolism is a bid for literary authority, whereas, as Roland Barthes has noted, the comparative resistance of certain realist details to familiar forms of thematic or symbolic interpretation creates the impression of empirical truth, validating the text's claim to represent a social reality (Barthes 1986). Literary authority indirectly carries social authority, but literary authority usually presumes a less direct routing of literature to society: not via representation of a social world or injunctions inculcating certain forms of behavior, but via the development of certain internal capacities of readers (imagination, judgment, and intellect, for example).

Literary historians have noted that in both Great Britain and the United States, by slightly different means, literature came to be sharply distanced from politics during the nineteenth century (Armstrong 1987; Brodhead 1986; Arac 1986, 1993). In contrast to literary works of previous centuries that were offered to a wealthy patron or ruler and shaped, for better and worse, by their authors' awareness of these recipients' political roles and policies, from the eighteenth century on literary works were produced for the public: in other words, for the markets constituted by those who would pay for works of literature as consumer goods. The British domestic novel evolved, famously, in tandem with conduct books aimed at middle-class citizens who were developing tastes and forms of authority very different from those of the aristocracy. Nancy Armstrong has detailed the process by which mainstream British novels came to focus on the psychological development and well-being of individuals rather than the political well-being of social groups, partly as a result of the powerful Enlightenment belief that the most valuable kind of knowledge would have "no particular political location" (1987: 35). The newly powerful position of the middle class underlay this belief, since only those who are seldom publicly challenged have the privilege of believing that their point of view can serve as the general reality. American fiction of the early nineteenth century was more openly political than the fiction Armstrong examines, but Jonathan Arac has suggested that from the 1850s, in the face of the national crisis presented by slavery, American literature, too, began to be valued for transcending political controversies rather than for entering into them (Arac 1986).

Viewed from this perspective, there was a tension between realism's simultaneous efforts to secure literary and social authority. On the one hand, realism's mission of informing middle-class readers about important issues and marginal populations, the source of its social authority, sent it careening into political minefields. On the other hand, realist fiction's development as a specifically literary form was incompatible with its endorsing any particular political position or analysis. The result was that realist novels took as their terrain the expanding domain of "society": a dimension of collective life separate from public political life, characterized instead by ongoing negotiation over behavioral norms (Arendt 1958: 38–49). Individual characters in realist novels might hold definite political views, but because reality itself did not conform to any system or program, realism ought not to rely on any either.

The height of nineteenth-century realism's claims to both social and literary authority might well have been reached in 1885, when the tory *Century Magazine* published excerpts from Twain's *Adventures of Huckleberry Finn* at the same time as it was serializing Howells's *The Rise of Silas Lapham* and James's *The Bostonians* (Arac 1997: 137). Howells, who was influential as editor of *The Atlantic Monthly* and as a literary reviewer and columnist for other prominent American magazines, was the foremost exponent of American realism, and he had explicitly endorsed Twain and James as model practitioners of realism. Therefore, the *Century* in 1885 brought together three authors whose works effectively defined the public's understanding of American realism at the time. All three novels took up easily identifiable social controversies. Twain's novel displaced contemporary racial tensions onto an antebellum plot in which white Huck Finn, son of the town drunk, befriends Jim, an escaped slave. Howells's novel, in which a provincial entrepreneur's financial success is ringed with thorny moral problems, turned its attention to business ethics and to the gap between true justice and the legal code. And *The Bostonians* rolled together spiritualism, women's rights, and Northern ambivalence about the post-Reconstruction South into a tense love triangle, one element of which was an erotically charged commitment between two women. Reading any of these novels, an American of 1885 might well have felt she had sampled a contemporary milieu in which certain divisive issues arose and operated. However, true to realism's charge, none of the three novels featured in the *Century* in 1885 took a clear political stand. Twain's novel might appear to espouse a reform, since Huck, the narrator, decides to aid and protect an escaped slave. As Jonathan Arac has pointed out, though, *Huckleberry Finn* is an anti-slavery novel written twenty years after slavery was abolished (Arac 1997). As a novel that might be read as commenting on the social integration or political inclusion of African Americans in 1885, *Huckleberry Finn* is much more slippery to interpret.

Perhaps the most prominent feature of realism is its devotion to complex – or "round" – characterization, which encourages readers to identify with characters and organize their interpretations around the moral and psychological qualities of significant individuals in the narrative. The novelistic emphasis on character has often been connected with the emergence of the peculiarly modern idea and experience of individualism. In historical scholarship, "modernity" designates the countless social and cultural transformations involved in the historical movement from primarily feudal economies, status-based societies, and centralized religious authorities – all characteristic of the Middle Ages – to primarily capitalist economies, class-based societies, the political authority of public opinion, and the dominance of secular, scientific knowledge. These transformations were gradually and unevenly underway during the eighteenth and nineteenth centuries in both western Europe and the United States.

The crucial integer of modernity is the modern individual, characterized by limitless potential (rather than a fixed place in society), endowed with independent economic interests, and committed to emancipating herself and others from whatever would prevent them from exercising their human rights and furthering their interests. Modern individuals tend to seek self-knowledge in the service of self-transformation, be the transformation moral improvement, social climbing, or the acquisition of more flattering consumer goods. And in the service of self-knowledge and self-transformation, the modern individual is willing to take on certain forms of self-monitoring and self-discipline that her society recommends, many of them oriented around the paradoxical task of determining whether she is, though different from anyone else who ever lived, "normal."

Realist characterization advanced both modern individualism and the equally modern project of producing knowledge about various demographic groupings. As individuals, leading characters in realist fiction tended to be capable of reflecting on their own private motives, interests, and moral capacities. They obligingly monitored (and sometimes disciplined) the inner lives that distinguished them as modern individuals. Deidre Lynch has suggested that nineteenth-century British fiction's attention to characterization resulted as much from readers' having been taught a new way to respond to literary characters as from writers' having found new ways to write them (1998: 126). "An ordinary-looking heroine, possessing an extraordinary, indescribable soul," presided over nineteenth-century British fiction, Lynch explains, and readers who were taught to value her over heroines devoted to external display were by the same process led to develop and value their own inwardness (p. 129). Huck Finn, Silas Lapham, and Verena Tarrant (a leading character in *The Bostonians*) do not much resemble Charlotte Brontë's title character Jane Eyre (1847), one of Lynch's key examples, but they all secure our interest by proving to be inwardly more complex than a lesser reader might expect. This development of literature around an aesthetic of seemingly innate personal value resulted in part, Lynch suggests, from writers' and readers' anxieties about the penetration of market relations and market-driven standards of value into social and cultural life (p. 128).

Moreover, realist characterization also produced social knowledge insofar as characters were connected to others as "types," even though writers such as Howells were careful to reject the most extreme forms of stereotyping (Howells 1967: 11). The sense of typicality – a floating cloud of social generalization in many realist works – was indispensable to the notion that realism presented plausible characters in plausible scenarios. "Mrs. March was one of those wives who exact a more rigid adherence to their ideals from their husbands than from themselves," remarks Howells's narrator in *A Hazard of New Fortunes* (1890), and a reader's understanding that this generalization is intended humorously doesn't keep it from evoking a world of knowable social types and familiar scenarios. As types, fictional characters embodied truths about certain groups of people, but these collective dimensions of characterization were not supposed to reinforce any recognizably political analysis of society. The perfect realist character, in other words, would be socially legible without tendentiously representing the interests of any politically significant social group. Reform novels, however admirable their political commitments, were commonly judged to be less literary than more purely realist novels because they sacrificed more enduring – therefore more literary – truths in order to expose and combat contemporary injustices.

Mediating between the psychology of individual characters and the fictional presentation of a social reality that exceeds them is free indirect discourse, a narrative technique widely used in novels but specially relevant to realism. Free indirect discourse results from the use of third-person narration that moves fluidly between directly representing characters' thoughts or words and commenting on them, perhaps through an interpretive summary. Between the quotation of a character's words or thoughts and the description of them by an observing narrator, free indirect discourse blurs the character's perspective and the narrator's (Bal 1997: 50). As an example of free indirect discourse at work in realism, consider Howells's early description of Bartley Hubbard in *A Modern Instance* (1882), whose title proclaims a realist commitment to probing contemporary social issues. A remarkably complex mode of narration is used to announce that Bartley, the editor of a newspaper in the Midwestern town of Equity, managed the office very economically, and by having the work done by girl-apprentices, with the help of one boy, he made it self-supporting. He modeled the newspaper upon the modern conception, through which the country press must cease to have any influence in public affairs, and each paper become little more than an open letter of neighborhood gossip. But while he filled his sheet with minute chronicles of the goings and comings of unimportant persons, and with all attainable particulars of the ordinary life of the different localities, he continued to make spicy hits at the enemies of Equity in the late struggle, and kept the public spirit of the town alive. (Howells 1984: 29)

In keeping with the difficulty of locating free indirect discourse in either narrator or character, it is virtually impossible to be sure whether the passage is loyally recounting Bartley's self-understanding, passing on a third-person view of Bartley that might surprise him, or moving between the two positions. A reader may have an opinion about whether Bartley, as presented in the novel as a whole, was capable of recognizing his own share in an innovation that resulted in watering down journalism, or about whether the narrator, as presented in the novel as a whole, was more likely to have observed this phenomenon independently. Nevertheless, the narrative instability of free indirect narration makes the narrator seem more authoritative – harder to locate and second-guess – and makes the character seem more complex and deep. Indeed, in the service of delineating a character capable of the development that is a hallmark of realism, free indirect discourse makes it hard to tell, at any given textual moment, what exactly the character understands and intends. The result is a remarkable linguistic structure, intricately weighted and balanced so that it permits movement but no stable resting-place.

Realist fiction is often pervaded by the sense that reality is messy, and its narrative authority depends on its ability to tackle this messiness. Michael Davitt Bell has argued that Howells and some later male realists – most notably, Ernest Hemingway – understood the capacity to tolerate and represent this messiness as a particularly masculine feat (1993: 37). Phillip Barrish further characterizes Bell's "realist masculinity" as requiring a "repeated turn towards, even taste for, insoluble social and personal difficulties" (2001: 47). Amy Kaplan has suggested that realist narratives often register indirectly the presence of the populations and problems that threaten their coherence (1988: 11–12); indeed, her analysis serves as a useful reminder that realism's allegiance to certain forms of social dominance was never completely stable. But Bell and Barrish accurately target the implicit sexism of the critical rhetoric that asserted realism's masculine control of unruly materials, rhetoric that often disparaged realism's competitors as feminine. Two of these competitors were sentimental fiction and reform novels, overlapping fictional forms which persistently took up "social and personal difficulties" but did not consider them insoluble. The foremost American example of their combination is *Uncle Tom's Cabin* (1852) by Harriet Beecher Stowe, which yoked together a Christian version of anti-slavery activism with politically double-edged support of African Americans' emigration to Liberia. As both Jane Tompkins and Kenneth W. Warren have emphasized, many of the sentimental novels that were derided by realists for their simplified characters and implausible plots nonetheless envisioned avenues of political action and concrete possibilities for historical change much bolder than anything to emerge from a mainstream realist novel (Tompkins 1985: 133; Warren 1993: 90).

Because novels end, but reality goes on forever, endings pose special compositional challenges in novels aspiring to realism (Kaplan 1988: 5). Many of the canonical novels associated with realism resist marriage plots or render them troubling, in spite of the fact that domestic fiction was an important crucible in which many realist techniques were fused – not only in Austen's novels, but in American works such as Caroline Kirkland's *A New Home, Who'll Follow?* (1839), Fanny Fern's *Ruth Hall* (1855), and Harriet Wilson's *Our Nig* (1859) (Warren 2000). A striking example of a marriage plot's undermining is the last sentence of Henry James's *The Bostonians* (1886), whose previously independent Northern heroine has been "wrenched . . . away" from a speaking engagement by her Southern lover's "muscular force" (p. 1218). The novel's ominous and unsettling concluding sentence is: "It is to be feared that with the union, so far from brilliant, into which she was about to enter, these [tears] were not the last she was destined to shed" (p. 1218).

Readers are forcibly reminded at the end of many realist works that the story that has engaged them is a simulation, often by tactics like James's that invoke but withhold a conventional form of closure. For example, both Edith Wharton's *The House of Mirth* (1905) and Kate Chopin's *The Awakening* (1899) end with the deaths of their central characters; but the deaths do not resolve the questions the novels have set in motion. In both cases, the deaths are suspended among several interpretive possibilities: a sentimental beatification of those who die innocent; a reformist indictment of any social world in which admirable characters cannot find a place; a social Darwinist account of evolutionary dead ends; or a tragic commemoration of noble persons brought down by the side-effects of their admirable ambitions. To pick out any one of these readings and privilege it would be to miss the ways in which these generic alternatives are cross-cut to produce the effect of realism. In this way, an overloading of interpretive possibilities can produce the effect of messy reality. In both Wharton's and Chopin's novels, as in *The Bostonians*, we are left with a profound sense of the eventfulness of human action, which might underline the significance of human agency. However, the complexity of the scenarios – in which choice is indistinguishable from accident and individual actions are amplified or neutralized unpredictably by circumstance – also points to the inadequacy of conventional understandings of individualized agency and accountability, both at the turn of the twentieth century and now.

Challenges to Realism

Widening the gap between individual actions and experiences and their social causes and consequences, naturalist fiction emerges at the turn of the century as both a development of realism and a dissenting literary movement. Indeed, perhaps because of the naturalists' tendency to privilege events that are too vast to be attributed to the operations of any individual, Frank Norris associated naturalism with a resurgence of the romance (Norris 1967). In the work of Norris, Stephen Crane, and Theodore Dreiser, naturalism focused on characters subject to precisely the sudden failures (as well as occasional successes) that the *Putnam's* reviewer had dismissed: California farmers are ruined in a battle against the railroad's high transportation costs in Norris's *The Octopus* (1901); the protagonist of Crane's *Maggie, A Girl of the Streets* (1893) is forced to become a prostitute; and Dreiser's *Sister Carrie* (1900) juxtaposes the fall of a Chicago businessman with the rise of a young actress. Further diminishing the scope of human action, naturalist works tend to present economic and biological processes as forces completely independent of human control. As June Howard has insightfully formulated, naturalist novels often distinguish the characters capable of social knowledge quite starkly from the characters capable of social action, with the result that naturalist fiction forecloses the optimistic possibility that fiction will equip its readers to participate more intelligently in social life (1985: 104–1).

Naturalism paved the way for the depiction of characters who did not understand themselves or their worlds, and frequently these were characters who were excluded from class privilege and its cultural competencies. Following the lead of Émile Zola, whose version of French realism made room for oppressed and marginal characters and catastrophic experience, Frank Norris lashed out at the gentility of nineteenth-century realism, especially as it was promoted and practiced by Howells:

> Romance, I take it, is the kind of fiction that takes cognizance of variations from the type of normal life. Realism is the kind of fiction that confines itself to the type of normal life.... Realism ... need not be in the remotest sense or degree offensive, but on the other hand respectable as a church and proper as a deacon – as, for instance, the novels of Mr. Howells. (Norris 1967: 280)

For reasons like Norris's, some readers would date the emergence of a more genuine literary realism from the era of this reaction against Howells: from *Sister Carrie* or *Maggie*. Although naturalism's penchant for invoking untamable social and economic forces made it peculiarly apolitical in spite of its sympathies with the have-nots, its broader social repertoire laid groundwork for the politically attuned realism of John Dos Passos's USA Trilogy (1930, 1932, 1936) and Richard Wright's *Native Son* (1940). And great as the distance might seem to be between Dreiser's world of tacky middling people and Edith Wharton's novels about the urban American upper crust, Wharton's work often conveys a naturalist sense that individuals are circumscribed by plots far too vast for them to resist effectively. Wharton's interest in anthropology led her to cast these plots as dense and intricate cultural webs rather than transhistorical forces, leaving room for human activity to be not utterly futile, merely incalculably slight in its effects.

Naturalist fiction often gives the impression that the social world – and characters' self-experience – is merely an illusion produced by forces that are not themselves social. A superb example of this decentering of social explanation is the narrator's sublime pronouncement, at the end of *The Octopus*, that the wheat itself has a destiny in relation to which farmers are incidental:

> *But the* WHEAT *remained*. Untouched, unassailable, undefiled, that mighty world-force, that nourisher of nations, wrapped in Nirvanic calm, indifferent to the human swarm, gigantic, resistless, moved onward in its appointed grooves. Through the welter of blood at the irrigation ditch, through the sham charity and shallow philanthropy of famine relief committees, the great harvest of Los Muertos rolled like a flood from the Sierras to the Himalayas to feed thousands of starving scarecrows on the barren plains of India. (Norris 1987: 651)

Such possibilities flicker in earlier more-or-less realist works, just as the possible madness of the governess-narrator flickers in James's *The Turn of the Screw* (1898) and just as a divine plan which will somehow improve the lot of millworkers flickers in the "promise of the dawn" at the end of Rebecca Harding Davis's *Life in the Iron Mills* (1861). The possibility that reasonable-sounding social descriptions and explanations might not be trustworthy or adequate is often raised in mainstream realist works, but not with the kind of ringing confidence emitted in *The Octopus*.

Another important offshoot of realism in the late nineteenth century was regionalist or local color fiction. To the extent that it was narrowly devoted to the social mission of representing particular subcultures of the United States, its literary authority was somewhat reduced. It thrived in literary magazines, though, perhaps because it served as an upscale version of the human interest story. Works such as Charles Egbert Craddock's *In the Tennessee Mountains* (1885) and Sarah Orne Jewett's *The Country of the Pointed Firs* (1896) examined the linguistic, geographic, and social distinctiveness of the residents of a particular region. Most regionalist narrative was driven by the need to catalogue a set of typical events and rituals; moreover, although some regionalist characters were quite memorable, they did not receive the heavily individualizing characterization common in realist fiction about white urbanites (sometimes depicted traveling or living abroad) and the white, mainly middle-class inhabitants of Midwestern towns. As Stephanie Foote has pointed out, "[T]he representation of regional characters allows us to look at how genres negotiated which persons would be granted character, personhood, status, and individuality" (2001: 36). In spite of the fact that the same word might be pronounced quite differently by a white native of Boston and a white native of Dayton, only rural characters, Southerners, immigrants, and African Americans were likely to have their speech rendered as dialect (marked especially by the nonstandard spelling of individual words). The imaginative centrality of cities in modernity and the social centrality of white Northern urbanites and townspeople are joined in the logic by which realism was distinguished from regionalism, and characters who spoke standard English were differentiated from characters whose speech had to be rendered as dialect.

Realism in Recent Literary History

It can be difficult to bear in mind both the generative potential of a genre and its constraints, especially since we late moderns are still struggling to imagine how frameworks such as literary genres might condition and discipline our creative actions without effacing them altogether. American literary realism promised authors a liberation from artifice and convention and the chance to present their personal visions of the life they saw around them and experienced within themselves. No doubt this promise was taken up gladly by many writers. It is equally true that realism bounded and constrained what authors could write about and how, and realism may even have shaped how writers and readers experienced the outside world and their inner lives.

To demystify realism is not to debunk it, but to take seriously its specific functioning in the social world in which it operated. The fact that regionalist writers were often not considered fully realist tells us something about the exclusivity of realism, even though we might not object that Thomas Nelson Page's nostalgic writings about the old plantation days were not as influential as more securely realist fiction. Another important index of realism's specificity was its relative inhospitality to African American writers. Charles Waddell Chesnutt, an African American fiction writer, complained revealingly in 1890 about criticisms he had received from Richard Watson Gilder, the editor of the *Century* who had published novels by Howells, James, and Twain concurrently in 1885:

> Mr. Gilder finds that I either lack humor or that my characters have a "brutality, a lack of mellowness, lack of spontaneous imaginative life, lack of outlook that makes them uninteresting." I fear, alas, that those are exactly the things that might have been expected to characterize people of that kind, the only qualities which the government and society had for 300 years labored faithfully, zealously, and successfully to produce, the only qualities which would have rendered their life at all endurable in the 19th century. I suppose I shall have to drop the attempt at realism and try to make them like other folks. (Farnsworth 1979: v)

Chesnutt's sardonic letter effectively claims that in pursuing genuine "realism" – truthful representation of African Americans in the wake of slavery and the throes of Jim Crow – he has run afoul of Gilder's notion of realistic characterization, which presumably worked better for the more privileged characters that realism made standard. Pauline E. Hopkins's preface to *Contending Forces* (1900), which repeatedly calls her novel a "romance" in spite of her use of the realist formulation that it is a "simple, homely tale, unassumingly told," might be another index of the ways in which realism offered African American writers a form of authority, but at a cost (Hopkins 1988: 13).

When Lionel Trilling railed in 1940 against the literary overvaluation of Theodore Dreiser's work, not because it was worthless but because "Dreiser's literary faults" were taken automatically to be "social and political virtues" (1950: 12), marking Dreiser's authenticity as a literary outsider, he identified a shift in the early twentieth-century construction of literary authority that opened fiction to new populations and their political projects. Many works of both modernism and postmodernism, the most prominent movements in twentieth-century literary fiction, have tried to demystify or unravel the kind of realism promoted in the late nineteenth century – signifying that literature is still bound up with realism, but not with its loyal practice. From the mid-twentieth century on, realism has thrived conspicuously (though by no means exclusively) as a commercial form, and realist works have not usually been granted the highest forms of literary authority.

Very likely Chesnutt's career was hindered by the fact that his reputation had been formed during the era of literary realism's dominance. Chesnutt himself may have identified the public value of his work with its legibility and acceptability to the realist literary establishment. Howells had praised Chesnutt's early, more convention-ally regionalist work, affirming that in literature "there is happily no color line" (Farnsworth 1979: vii), but he was clearly disappointed by Chesnutt's ambitious novel *The Marrow of Tradition* (1901), which depicted a white-instigated race riot. Calling the book "bitter," Howells argued that "There is no reason in history why it should not be so, if wrong is to be repaid with hate, and yet it would be better if it was not so bitter" (Farnsworth 1979: xv). Howells was sympathetic to Chesnutt, yet his stance implied that realist fiction precluded not only strong political convictions but also the exploration of certain politically charged realities. Chesnutt gave up writing fiction not long after *Marrow*'s publication, and when he claimed, in 1928, that his books had been written "a generation too soon," he gestured indirectly toward the possibility that African American writers who entered literature under later literary dispensations found greater opportunities (Farnsworth 1979: xvi). It is probably significant in this regard that the first more-or-less realist novel making use of an African American narrator and therefore inviting identification with a complex African American subjectivity was not written until 1912: James Weldon Johnson's *The Autobiography of an Ex-Coloured Man* (Boeckmann 2000: 175).

The academic canon of late nineteenth-century novels developed first as a canon of realism, even though these works were later reinterpreted through the lens of romance (and in some cases then repositioned in relation to new understandings of realism). A wave of late twentieth-century scholars who wished to open literary history and criticism to works that were never canonized, or that were fleetingly canonized, therefore brought to light a number of literary works that made use of realist subject matters, techniques, and forms of authority. Instead of letting Howells, James, and Twain monopolize realism – and, indeed, monopolize literary study after literary study that generalized grandiosely about the American novel, usually relying on a canon of realism far more restrictive than Howells's – critics of the 1970s and after made the case that Rebecca Harding Davis's *Life in the Iron Mills* might well count as the first American example of realism, or that Caroline Kirkland's *A New Home, Who'll Follow?*, Fanny Fern's *Ruth Hall*, and Harriet Wilson's *Our Nig* (which I cite, following Joyce W. Warren, as examples of domestic novels that deployed realist techniques) might be even earlier realist novels. As these examples suggest, many critics have found it important to acknowledge that women writers and African American writers of either sex offered their own treatments of the Woman Question and the Negro Question (as the political and social problems associated with gender and race were named in the nineteenth century). Elizabeth Stuart Phelps's *The Story of Avis* (1877), which detailed the obstacles encountered by a woman artist, ought not to take second place in authority and interest to James's account of female ambitions in *The Bostonians*, after all, nor should Chesnutt's *The House Behind the Cedars* (1900) be missed as a novel of passing at least as intelligent and valuable as Howells's *An Imperative Duty* (1891).

If realism is not understood as a genre or literary movement that any work could be securely "inside," though, or as a reliable index of current value, then there is no need to identify a text as realist in order to argue that it is worth reading and studying. Indeed, sentimental fiction, protest fiction, utopian fiction, and other significant nineteenth-century genres deserve study as much as realism does – if not more, given the inordinate attention the traditional realist canon has received. It may be more instructive to consider why Rebecca Harding Davis was the object of Henry James's realist boundary-patrolling, in an unsigned review that accused her of sentimentalism, and to reflect on the interplay between sentimentalism and realism in her work, than to privilege realism in Davis's work (Glazener 1997: 126–7). Similarly, it is important to question why Mark Twain was accorded a privileged relationship to realism in spite of the dense interweaving of melodrama and satire in his novels. In other words, rather than retroactively correcting the inflexibility of literary realism's arbiters, we may learn more from examining and understanding the many historical traces of the variable access and uneven opportunities it presented to authors (Brodhead 1993).

In the broadest of historical frames, as I have suggested, American realism can usefully be understood as playing a part in modernity's restructuring of life around capitalism. Homing in on the ways in which the crises in value precipitated by capitalism were manifested in the late nineteenth-century United States, a number of critics have taken up what Eric Sundquist calls "the romance of money" as an animating preoccupation of much realist fiction (1982: 19). This approach illuminates not only the prevalence of economic plots but also a host of ways in which late nineteenth-century Americans' fascination with money entered into fiction and structured literary meaning. Money itself was absorbing: for instance, Walter Benn Michaels has linked the late nineteenth-century debate over whether and how currency represented the nation's stockpile of gold to fiction's concern with the problem of what, if anything, words represent. The longings that realist characters have for things and for commodified versions of each other also registers the impact of the rapidly escalating commodity capitalism of the later nineteenth century: Henry James's fiction famously relies on economic metaphors to signal complex relationships of power and knowledge among the characters. The economic depressions of the time, along with well-publicized efforts to expand the use and power of corporations, the unexpectedly drastic gap between the poorest and richest Americans that loomed by the end of the century, and the sinister influences of monopolies and oligopolies, all presented new problems – and new ideas – to fiction writers, especially writers with a social mission. In this way the realists, like the critics who have studied them, were participating at once in the contemporary life they saw around them and in global historical transformations they had trouble grasping fully (Peyser 1998).

Modernity's reliance on scientific models of knowledge meant that the development of academic disciplines in the nineteenth century proceeded along strikingly scientific principles. During this period, anthropology, psychology, sociology, and a number of related humanistic disciplines were extricated from each other and installed in separate university departments whose disciplinary authority depended on their political disinterestedness. The joint constructions of society and the individual as objects of study that could be insulated from specifically political processes, actions, and convictions was taking place in tandem in the academic humanities and in realist fiction. Numerous critics have identified links between realist fiction, disciplinary professions, and academic disciplines. One can find striking thematic and linguistic continuities between more-or-less realist texts and anthropology (Elliott 2002), sociology (Mizruchi 1998), history (Hughson 1988; White 1973), law (Dimock 1996; Kearns 1996; Thomas 1997), and medicine (Rothfield 1992). The model of medical authority was especially congenial to many realists (and, indeed, many social scientists), who took up the role of sympathetic diagnosticians and could identify "diseases" of social life and gesture toward the desirability of cure without prescribing any specific course of treatment (Rothfield 1992). A character in *Life in the Iron Mills* who refers to a "world-cancer" (Davis 1985: 49) makes use of this trope. It makes sense that if realism was supposed to provide reliable social knowledge, it would share forms of authority and representational norms with the academic and professional disciplines that were granted authority to anatomize society and its component individuals.

It might seem paradoxical that a grand historical frame such as "modernity" or "capitalism" could lead critics to attend to the micro-level of texts, but the belief that these large formations took on distinctive and surprising local forms has led many critics to value realist texts for their detailed staging and exploration of the small-scale assumptions and transactions that made large-scale world-views and events imaginable. In this regard, it has been possible to learn a great deal from realist fiction about the barely perceptible movements of thought and language that create the preconditions for racial identities, gender identities, and sexualities. Precisely by *not* believing in the seamlessness of realist representation, but by presuming that textual renderings of social identities are riddled with linguistic tensions and paradoxes, critics have found more-or-less realist novels to be invaluable guides to the ways in which familiar social identities are invented. A case in point would be the burgeoning of criticism around Henry James – the mainstream realist most invested with literary authority rather than social authority – that has discovered traces in his novels of the ways in which race, gender, and sexuality were constructed in the social worlds he traversed (for example, studies by Sara Blair [1996] and Michael Moon [1998]). In the best of these studies, though, neither literature nor society – invisible institutions that were both invented in the nineteenth century and passed down to us – can have the last word about realism. The tension between literary authority and social authority that structures literary realism is part of the modern experience of literature and part of what serious readers need literature to help them understand.

AUTHOR'S NOTE

The author of this essay is grateful for careful readings and good advice provided by Jayne E. Lewis, Deidre Lynch, Susan Harris Smith, and Elizabeth Thomas.

PRIMARY TEXTS

Chesnutt, Charles Waddell. *The House Behind the Cedars*. 1900.

Chesnutt, Charles Waddell. *The Marrow of Tradition*. 1901.

Chopin, Kate. *The Awakening*. 1899.

Craddock, Charles Egbert [Mary Noailles Murfree]. *In the Tennessee Mountains*. 1884.

Crane, Stephen. *Maggie, A Girl of the Streets (A Story of New York)*. 1893.

Davis, Rebecca Harding. *Life in the Iron Mills; or, The Korl Woman*. 1861.

Dos Passos, John. *The Forty-Second Parallel*. 1930.

Dos Passos, John. *Nineteen Nineteen*. 1932.

Dos Passos, John. *The Big Money*. 1936.

Dreiser, Theodore. *Sister Carrie*. 1900.

Fern, Fanny. *Ruth Hall*. 1855.

Hawthorne, Nathaniel. *The Scarlet Letter*. 1850.

Hawthorne, Nathaniel. *The House of the Seven Gables*. 1851.

Hopkins, Pauline E. *Contending Forces: A Romance Illustrative of Negro Life North and South*. 1900.

Howells, William Dean. *A Modern Instance*. 1882.

Howells, William Dean. *The Rise of Silas Lapham*. 1885.

Howells, William Dean. *A Hazard of New Fortunes*. 1890.

Howells, William Dean. *Criticism and Fiction*. 1891.

Howells, William Dean. *An Imperative Duty*. 1891.

James, Henry. *The Portrait of a Lady*. 1881.

James, Henry. *The Bostonians*. 1886.

James, Henry. *The Turn of the Screw*. 1898.

Jewett, Sarah Orne. *The Country of the Pointed Firs*. 1896.

Johnson, James Weldon. *The Autobiography of an Ex-Coloured Man*. 1912.

Kirkland, Caroline. *A New Home, Who'll Follow?* 1839.

Melville, Herman. *Moby-Dick; or, The Whale*. 1851.

Norris, Frank. *The Octopus: A Story of California*. 1901.

Norris, Frank. *The Responsibilities of the Novelist*. 1903.

Page, Thomas Nelson. *In Ole Virginia*. 1887.

Phelps, Elizabeth Stuart. *The Story of Avis*. 1877.

Stowe, Harriet Beecher. *Uncle Tom's Cabin; or, Life among the Lowly*. 1852.

Twain, Mark. *Life on the Mississippi.* 1883.

Twain, Mark. *Adventures of Huckleberry Finn.* 1884.

Twain, Mark. "Fenimore Cooper's Literary Offences." 1895.

Wharton, Edith. *The House of Mirth.* 1905.

Wilson, Harriet. *Our Nig; or, Sketches from the Life of a Free Black, In a Two-Story White House, North. Showing That Slavery's Shadows Fall Even There.* 1859.

Wright, Richard. *Native Son.* 1940.

References and Further Reading

Anon. (1857). "Ideals in Modern Fiction." *Putnam's New Monthly Magazine*, July, pp. 91–6.

Arac, Jonathan (1986). "The Politics of *The Scarlet Letter*." In Sacvan Bercovitch and Myra Jehlen (eds.), *Ideology and Classic American Literature*, 247–66. New York: Cambridge University Press.

Arac, Jonathan (1993). "What is the History of Literature?" *Modern Language Quarterly* 54: 1, 105–10.

Arac, Jonathan (1997). Huckleberry Finn *as Idol and Target: The Functions of Criticism in Our Time.* Madison: University of Wisconsin Press.

Arendt, Hannah (1958). *The Human Condition.* Chicago: University of Chicago Press.

Armstrong, Nancy (1987). *Desire and Domestic Fiction: A Political History of the Novel.* New York: Oxford University Press.

Bakhtin, M. M. (1981). "Forms of Time and of the Chronotope in the Novel" (first publ. 1975). In *The Dialogic Imagination*, trans. Caryl Emerson and Michael Holquist, 84–258. Austin: University of Texas Press.

Bal, Mieke (1997). *Narratology: Introduction to the Theory of Narrative*, 2nd edn. Toronto: University of Toronto Press. (First publ. 1985.)

Barrish, Phillip (2001). *American Literary Realism, Critical Theory, and Intellectual Prestige, 1880–1995.* New York: Cambridge University Press.

Barthes, Roland (1986). "The Reality Effect" (first publ. 1984). In *The Rustle of Language*, trans. Richard Howard, 141–8. New York: Hill & Wang.

Becker, George J., ed. (1963). *Documents of Modern Literary Realism.* Princeton: Princeton University Press.

Bell, Michael Davitt (1993). *The Problem of American Realism: Studies in the Cultural History of a Literary Idea.* Chicago: University of Chicago Press.

Blair, Sara (1996). *Henry James and the Writing of Race and Nation.* New York: Cambridge University Press.

Boeckmann, Cathy (2000). *A Question of Character: Scientific Racism and the Genres of American Fiction, 1892–1912.* Tuscaloosa: University of Alabama Press.

Brodhead, Richard H. (1993). *Cultures of Letters: Scenes of Reading and Writing in Nineteenth-Century America.* Chicago: University of Chicago Press.

Brodhead, Richard H. (1986). *The School of Hawthorne.* New York: Oxford University Press.

Chase, Richard (1957). *The American Novel and its Tradition.* Garden City, NY: Doubleday.

Davis, Rebecca Harding (1985). *Life in the Iron Mills; or, the Korl Woman*, ed. Tillie Olsen. New York: Feminist Press.

Dimock, Wai Chee (1996). *Residues of Justice: Literature, Law, Philosophy.* Berkeley: University of California Press.

Doody, Margaret Anne (1996). *The True Story of the Novel.* New Brunswick, NJ: Rutgers University Press.

Elliott, Michael A. (2002). *The Culture Concept: Writing and Difference in the Age of Realism.* Baltimore: Johns Hopkins University Press.

Farnsworth, Robert M. (1979). "Introduction." In Charles Waddell Chesnutt, *The Marrow of Tradition*, v–xvii. Ann Arbor: University of Michigan Press (Ann Arbor Paperbacks).

Foote, Stephanie (2001). *Regional Fictions: Culture and Identity in Nineteenth-Century American Literature.* Madison: University of Wisconsin Press.

Franklin, Benjamin (1987). *Autobiography.* In *Benjamin Franklin: Writings*, ed. J. A. Leo LeMay, 1305–1469. New York: Literary Classics of the United States.

Glazener, Nancy (1997). *Reading for Realism: The History of a US Literary Institution, 1850–1910.* Durham, NC: Duke University Press.

Habermas, Jürgen (1991). *The Structural Trans-formation of the Public Sphere: An Inquiry into a Category of Bourgeois Society,* trans. Thomas Burger. Cambridge, Mass: MIT Press. (First publ. 1962.)

Hawthorne, Nathaniel (1983). *The House of the Seven Gables.* In *Nathaniel Hawthorne: Novels,* ed. Millicent Bell, 347–628. New York: Library of America.

Hopkins, Pauline E. (1988). *Contending Force: A Romance Illustrative of Negro Life North and South,* intr. Richard A. Yarborough. New York: Oxford University Press.

Howard, June (1985). *Form and History in American Literary Naturalism.* Chapel Hill: University of North Carolina Press.

Howells, William Dean (1967). *Criticism and Fiction.* In *William Dean Howells and Frank Norris, Criticism and Fiction/The Responsibilities of the Novelist,* 1–188. New York: Hill & Wang.

Howells, William Dean (1984). *A Modern Instance.* New York: Penguin.

Hughson, Lois (1988). *From Biography to History: The Historical Imagination and American Fiction, 1880–1940.* Charlottesville: University Press of Virginia.

James, Henry (1985). *The Bostonians.* In *Henry James: Novels 1881–1886,* ed. William T. Stafford, 801–1219. New York: Library of America.

Kaplan, Amy (1988). *The Social Construction of American Realism.* Chicago: University of Chicago Press.

Kearns, Katherine (1996). *Nineteenth-Century Literary Realism: Through the Looking-Glass.* New York: Cambridge University Press.

Levine, Lawrence (1988). *Highbrow/Lowbrow: The Emergence of Cultural Hierarchy in America.* Cambridge: Harvard University Press.

Lynch, Deidre (1998). *The Economy of Character: Novels, Market Culture, and the Business of Inner Meaning.* Chicago: University of Chicago Press.

Michaels, Walter Benn (1987). *The Gold Standard and the Logic of Naturalism: American Literature at the Turn of the Century.* Berkeley: University of California Press.

Mizruchi, Susan L. (1998). *The Science of Sacrifice: American Literature and Modern Social Theory.* Princeton: Princeton University Press.

Moon, Michael (1998). *A Small Boy and Others: Imitation and Initiation in American Culture from Henry James to Andy Warhol.* Durham, NC: Duke University Press.

Norris, Frank (1986). *The Octopus: A Story of California.* New York: Penguin.

Norris, Frank (1967). *The Responsibilities of the Novelist.* In *William Dean Howells and Frank Norris, Criticism and Fiction/The Responsibilities of the Novelist,* 193–320. New York: Hill & Wang.

Peyser, Thomas (1998). *Utopia and Cosmopolis: Globalization in the Era of American Literary Realism.* Durham, NC: Duke University Press.

Rothfield, Lawrence (1992). *Vital Signs: Medical Realism in Nineteenth-Century Fiction.* Princeton: Princeton University Press.

Sundquist, Eric J. (1982). "Introduction: The Country of the Blue." In Eric J. Sundquist (ed.), *American Realism: New Essays,* 3–24. Baltimore: Johns Hopkins University Press.

Thomas, Brook (1997). *American Literary Realism and the Failed Promise of Contract.* Berkeley: University of California Press.

Tompkins, Jane (1985). *Sensational Designs: The Cultural Work of American Fiction, 1790–1860.* New York: Oxford University Press.

Trilling, Lionel (1950). "Reality in America." In *The Liberal Imagination: Essays on Literature and Society,* 3–21. New York: Viking.

Warren, Joyce W. (2000). "Performativity and the Repositioning of American Literary Realism." In Joyce W. Warren and Margaret Dickie (eds.), *Challenging Boundaries: Gender and Periodization,* 3–25. Athens, Ga.: University of Georgia Press.

Warren, Kenneth W. (1993). *Black and White Strangers: Race and American Literary Realism.* Chicago: University of Chicago Press.

Watt, Ian (1957). *The Rise of the Novel.* Berkeley: University of California Press.

White, Hayden (1973). *Metahistory: The Historical Imagination in Nineteenth-Century Europe.* Baltimore: Johns Hopkins University Press.

Wordsworth, William, and Samuel Taylor Coleridge (1967). "Preface to the Second Edition of *Lyrical Ballads*" (first publ. 1800). In *English Romantic Writers,* ed. David Perkins, 320–31. New York: Harcourt Brace Jovanovich.

2
Excitement and Consciousness in the Romance Tradition
William J. Scheick

What, precisely, is meant by romance as a type of narrative has never been clear. During the Middle Ages the word accidentally became associated with French tales of chivalric knights, and later during the Renaissance the meaning of the term drifted to include long verse narratives that combined the subject matter of these medieval stories and the structure of classical epics. The definition of romance did not get any clearer with the rise of the novel during the eighteenth century, when romance was *generally* understood to refer to improbable, imaginative, and symbolic stories distinctly different from the novel. Such a broad distinction, critically impressionistic at best, was complicated by early nineteenth-century authors, especially Walter Scott and Nathaniel Hawthorne, whose hybrid fictions combined the factual properties of the novel and the imaginative reach of romance. By the end of the nineteenth century this hybrid form was very popular, despite the fact that some critics – fervid apologists for literary realism such as William Dean Howells – struggled in vain to distinguish between romance and the novel.

Characteristics of Romance

Notwithstanding the difficulties of exactly defining romance, certain of its features are generally recognized, the most common being the genre's extravagant manner. In general this quality refers to the abridgment of verisimilitude. In other words, romance settings, characters, and events are highlighted in a more elemental fashion than is typical of realistic novels, which provide complexly rendered psychological human interactions within densely detailed social milieux. Romance offers caricatures rather than deeply developed characters. These figures are defined by a few emphasized traits, such as the astonishing rational powers of Arthur Conan Doyle's Sherlock Holmes and the extraordinary intuitive capabilities of Gilbert K. Chesterton's Father Brown, both popular figures during *début-de-siècle* America. Like pen-and-ink caricatures, these sketched protagonists are rendered by wide strokes of description highlighting a few prominent traits or eccentricities, and they are defined by their plot effectiveness rather than by any complex psychological motives.

This feature of romance exhibits considerable variation. In the instance of domestic romances – usually sentimental works centering on young girls learning courtship rituals – both settings and characters are presented in a pared-down, more simplified manner than found in realistic fiction. Domestic romance plots often function by linking a few main sketch-like sentimental episodes that elicit the reader's memory of similar fictionally described situations. These unembellished episodes are like partially completed outlines, drawings that the reader may imaginatively enhance in various personal ways. Domestic romance protagonists, moreover, are rendered as "types," figures whose personal and class identities are designated by a limited number of distinguishing characteristics. Even Louisa May Alcott's *Little Women* (1868–9), a bestseller that in several respects modified the domestic romance formula, covers a short period of time, offers a few select episodes – Jo's staging of melodramas, John's successful courtship of Meg, Beth's near-death from scarlet fever – and presents characters identified chiefly by their vanity, shyness, or lack of femininity.

Both settings and protagonists were portrayed in greater detail in late nineteenth-century historical romances. Earlier such works, including Scott's fiction, especially *Ivanhoe* (1819), were very popular during the late nineteenth century – so much so, in fact, that in *Adventures of Huckleberry Finn* (1884) Mark Twain specifically targeted Scott's fiction as a baleful influence on Southern culture. Just how historically accurate these many fictional versions of historical figures and events were differed considerably from author to author, though many did diligently research their subjects. Such works included the larger-than-life portraits of Davy Crockett and General George Custer, Gertrude Atherton's romanticized portrait of Alexander Hamilton in *The Conqueror* (1902), and Sarah Orne Jewett's dramatic rendering of divided loyalties during the Revolutionary War in *The Tory Lover* (1901). Many historical romances were set during the Civil War, as typified by the clichéd local color stories of lovers essentially undergoing Romeo-and-Juliet tribulations in Thomas Nelson Page's *In Ole Virginia* (1887).

Research certainly informed Lewis Wallace's marketplace successes with *The Fair God* (1873), set during the Spanish conquest of Mexico, and *Ben-Hur* (1880), set during the late Roman empire. The immense sales of *Ben-Hur* became legendary, and in 1899 the book was also effectively dramatized by William Young. In such works, however, intricacies of historical circumstance and of human reactions to historical situations were regularly displaced by an emphasis on momentous events and actions. Instead of recognizable commonplace life experiences, these historical romances tended to depict grand sites of conflict with larger-than-life antagonists. The heroes of historical romance often possessed unusual mental or physical abilities, capacities that satisfied various fantasies of their audiences.

Even greater feats are attributed to the heroes populating late nineteenth-century adventure romances, exemplified by Richard Harding Davis's *Soldiers of Fortune*

(1897). In such works of intrigue, suspense, crime detection, Western frontier exploits, magic, science fiction, fantasy, and supernatural encounters, individuals engage in exciting events in exotic or enchanted locations. These tested heroes, usually young males identified by unique traits and at times motivated by jingois-tic/imperialistic aspirations, prevail (sometimes militaristically) over initially insur-mountable odds. Some adventure romances are like dreams, inhabited by caricatures who appear to be free from the constraints of social conventions, political forces, and occasionally even natural laws. Adventure romances can specifically involve alterna-tive worlds or supernatural realms, fantastic places where "reality" varies sharply from the reader's sense of the ordinary.

Most such romances are designed merely to entertain, but some authors creatively use this predictable medium to raise questions about the commonly perceived normalcy of everyday life. Utopian romances are a case in point, although (as we will see) there are more inventive experiments with the genre. At its best, romance indirectly suggests deep insights into a barely detected mystery underlying our ordinary lives. Its fictional world can embody truths that are, paradoxically, stranger than fiction. Through its disorienting strangeness, romance can critique our familiar world by intimating that our ordinary perception of reality has no authority or authenticity other than the simple fact that we customarily and subjectively experi-ence life a certain way.

Nevertheless, it is not always easy to distinguish romance from realistic fiction. Besides some domestic and historical romances, there are ghost stories that resist such a distinction. Ghost stories were enormously popular after the publication of Charles Dickens's *A Christmas Carol* (1843). Each issue appearing during the first year (1850) of *Harper's Monthly Magazine* included a ghost story, and by the end of the nineteenth century many periodicals routinely included such fiction in their December issues. In "Thurlow's Christmas Story" (1898) John Kendrick Bangs, a well-regarded satirist and staff member of *Harper's Monthly*, created an exceptionally clever ghost story precisely around this seasonal demand for such tales. Bangs's narrative, like other well-crafted ghost stories, is a hybrid fictional form. Its audience is left with the option of reading it either as a realistic work with a natural explanation for what occurs or as a romance with a supernatural explanation of its events. Does Thurlow only dream of a visitation by an admiring *doppelgänger*, a bizarre visit with starkly tangible consequences? Likewise, is the haunting in Henry James's *The Turn of the Screw* (1898) the result of the governess's deteriorating mental state or of actual malicious ghosts?

Since both of these stories could be classified as romance or as realistic fiction, their clever hybridity clouds any effort to differentiate perfectly between the two literary forms. It is pertinent to note that in *The Responsibilities of the Novelist* (1903) Frank Norris, who included elements of romance extravagance in his otherwise naturalistic fiction, makes a case for the legitimacy of romance and, as well, speaks of works of literary naturalism as romances. Generally, however, such hybrid works are best understood as romance when they tend to emphasize the events of the plot and, correspondingly, tend to curtail the sort of welter of experience, the depth of social and psychological portraiture, characteristic of complex examples of realistic fiction.

Morality and Readership

Definition is not the only source of contention concerning romance. Its morality is also a long-lived and heated issue. Many critics have been alarmed that the romance – understood as an antinomian imaginative extravagance with plots sometimes unrestrained by even the laws of nature – appeals to the deepest of human desires, and appears to do so without regard to possible consequences. Before the eighteenth century, romances were targeted by censorious Reformed clergy worried about the effect of this allegedly "sensual" genre on the social order. During the eighteenth century, the Age of Reason, romances were often denounced for their irresponsible promotion of dissipation – the supposed result of the genre's arousal of the sensationalistic pleasures of the imagination. Charges of falsehood, seduction, and subversion, particularly as perceived by acutely class-conscious critics, continued throughout the nineteenth century. In Charles Dickens's *Hard Times* (1854), for example, schoolmaster Thomas Gradgrind dismisses romances as "destructive nonsense."

The early twentieth century saw an abatement in the moral claims against romance and, at the same time, an intensification in the longstanding (if loosely defined) distinction between romance and the novel. While many writers were in fact practicing a hybrid form of romance, recognition of this distinctive practice was never widely appreciated as such by self-conscious realists, who relentlessly insisted upon the superiority of their own literary practice. The issue of characterization was paramount in their attack on romance. Compared to in-depth characters engaging in complex interior struggles – as found in, say, William Dean Howells's *A Hazard of New Fortunes* (1890) and Henry James's *The Ambassadors* (1903) – the two-dimensional typical caricatures of romance often seemed so slight as to be dismissed as juvenile.

Manner of characterization was not the only issue. In romance, ordinary locations are transformed into strange settings, places of adventure and mystery. Magic, wizardry, witchcraft, vanishing bodies, materializing spirits, demonic possession, disembodied voices, mental telepathy, levitation – hardly common matter in realist fiction – predominate in romance. Uncanny events in weird settings, or in ordinary settings suddenly made mysterious, seemed to many at the turn of the century more suitable for the immature imaginations of children.

In fact, even during the nineteenth century youth had long been a covert market for the publishers of romance. As these young readers matured during the early twentieth century, many recalled their own youthful reading and so identified romance with young audiences. Little changed in critics' rejection of the form as art, and there were occasional revivals of moral censure. But the genre that once was suspected as socially and morally subversive was now, at least in certain forms, generally thought to be appropriate children's fare. This period saw the publication of popular children's romances, including George Wilbur Peck's widely read *Peck's Bad Boy and His Pa* (1883) and Frank Baum's now classic *The Wonderful Wizard of Oz* (1900). With the Ragged Dick series, begun in 1867, Horatio Alger, Jr. launched a career that would produce more than a hundred commercially successful rags-to-riches novels. An admirer of these works, Edward Stratemeyer, would in 1899 publish the first of the Rover Boys books.

It is pertinent, as well, that earlier nineteenth-century romance favorites previously enjoyed by adults – works by Walter Scott and James Fenimore Cooper, for example – would eventually become shelved in the children's section of libraries. Nevertheless, not only were many adults still reading romances, but many authors worked in the genre with the expectation of a mature audience. This was the situation with Frank R. Stockton's whimsical fantasy *Rudder Grange* (1879) and his frequently anthologized "The Lady or the Tiger?" (1882). Publishers ranging from the *Century Magazine* to the more upscale *Atlantic Monthly* sometimes openly marketed certain romances for both children and adults, and by the end of the nineteenth century reader demand for romance was at an all-time high among youth and adults alike.

Increased literacy within every social class was one factor in this sizable demand, but equally important was the industrialization of mass printing, which encouraged growth in the number of magazines towards the end of the nineteenth century. There were so many magazines, a character in Ada Woodruff Anderson's *The Rim of the Desert* (1915) complained, that he found it difficult to single out one to purchase. A sign of the times was Frank A. Munsey's conversion of *The Argosy* in 1896 from a classy children's magazine into an inexpensive adult fiction periodical printed on coarse pulp paper stock. The proliferation of such markets encouraged authors to write romances, short stories or novella-length works suitable for both periodical publication and inexpensive book versions. These venues aimed at both youthful and mature audiences with modest earnings and limited expendable income.

With romance fiction prominent in such mass-marketed magazines, some self-appointed guardians of cultural standards revived older arguments about the detrimental effects of the genre. They specifically fretted over what they perceived as the pernicious influence of certain types of story on working-class and young readers. Fearful of dereliction in the workplace and of criminal behavior, for example, they railed against the violence and immorality of dime novels – thrilling tales often set in the West and published principally by the New York firm of Beadle & Adams between 1860 and 1895. The same fears would be expressed about the post-*Argosy* mystery, science-fiction, and erotic "pulps" launched in the 1920s.

As concerns about the moral and social effects of romance narrowed in focus to specific types of the narrative, the genre as a whole nonetheless remained stigmatized as an aesthetically deficient, lowbrow medium of cheap entertainment. Critics targeted what they viewed as the American version of the Penny Dreadfuls and Shilling Shockers, nineteenth-century mass-marketed British sensational tales increasingly (and mistakenly) identified as juvenilia. Frontiersman Deadwood Dick, sportsman Frank Merriwell, boy inventor Frank Reade, and detective Nick Carter were but four of American romance readers' popular heroes appearing weekly in dime-novel format. These stories emphasized plot – astounding puzzles, thrilling escapades, breathtaking escapes – designed solely to entertain the reader. Although serious authors of sophisticated historical romance, notably James Branch Cabell, appeared in Munsey's *Argosy*, this long-running New York-based periodical and its many imitators likewise perpetuated the dime-novel pattern of romance.

A Convenient Taxonomy

While more serious romance writers did from time to time vigorously defend their art against charges of immorality or of artistic slightness, they did not tend to undertake a taxonomy, a system of classifying the various types of the genre. Even practitioners of hybrid versions of romance rarely identified their work as such. They, like their readers, were generally aware of the easily recognized differences among domestic, historical, and adventure romances. The practice of sophisticated romancers, however, suggests a much deeper comprehension of the genre, an interest in exploring the artistic potential of the form in ways related to their influential predecessor Nathaniel Hawthorne earlier in the century.

For purposes of critical convenience, one way of observing this more sophisticated mode of romance is to identify three types of the genre: eventuary, aesthetic, and ethical. The boundaries dividing the three are fluid, a matter of degree of emphasis on certain elements of the genre and especially on implied audience disposition. Depending on these emphases, as we will see, a particular domestic, historical, or adventure romance may (for the purpose of discussion) be classified within one of these taxonomic types.

Eventuary romance

Eventuary romance is the most elementary form of the genre. This variety exhibits caricatures, settings, and plot action typical of dime novels. It primarily accentuates plot elements, exciting events. But what sets the type apart from other kinds of romance is its author's central commercial motive: to entertain in order to sell. For the author and publisher alike, the ideal reader of eventuary romance passively consumes a story and then desires similar plot-driven tales of action. Such an endlessly renewable demand would ideally lead to sequels, and indeed there are many such *fin-de-siècle* and *début-de-siècle* series presenting the "further adventures" of various popular fictional heroes. The intention behind these works is entirely commercial. These tales are not, at least not seriously, aimed at the production of any personally or socially productive thought in the reader.

Stockton's sensationally popular and frequently anthologized "The Lady or the Tiger?" is typically eventuary. Its narrative performance, including a surprise ending, seeks no higher goal than to thrill the reader. Another example of the type is Robert

W. Chambers's *The King in Yellow* (1895). This collection of romance stories was so popular in its day that Ellen Glasgow made an important allusion to it in *The Descendant* (1897) and railroad lines provided copies of it as free reading material for travelers. The early interrelated tales in this collection feature a verse play about a strange dimension, with twin suns and black stars, that exists behind our visible world. Readers of the play, which functions like a portal between worlds, become inexplicably haunted by some vague primordial memory that intermittently intrudes upon and fragments their minds. Chambers's sequence of tales, one of his many marketable entertainments, makes no real point and does not even yield an explanation. Its effect is only a commercially prompted mysteriousness designed as a transient pleasure for idle occasions – a perfect train book.

Frontier romances, cultivars of the dime novel, are at heart eventuary in manner. The best of them portray rugged individuals engaged in a Darwinian struggle for survival. In Zane Grey's many bestsellers, including the perennial favorite *Riders of the Purple Sage* (1912), the fittest are independent men whose loyalty to their families and comfort with an authorially contrived frontier code of ethics enable them to prevail over black-willed desperadoes. Notable, too, is Owen Wister's *The Virginian* (1902), which in several ways established the standard for the "Western." Set in late nineteenth-century Wyoming, Wister's story features the thrilling adventures of a cowboy caricatured as bold yet gallant.

Aesthetic romance

There were more serious artists who approached the medium of romance with greater expectations. While these writers were hardly averse to enjoying a commercial bonanza, their primary goal was to fashion a literary work true only to the ultimate dictates of artistic design. All the usual properties of the genre are featured in such narratives, but they serve aesthetic goals rather than audience desire. While this variety of the genre can be entertaining, as in Henry James's *The Turn of the Screw*, it evinces an indifference to the reader's comprehension or expectation. Like other artistic productions influenced by the late nineteenth-century Aestheticist movement, these romances marshal their generic properties in a mysterious self-referential manner that eludes final explication by the reader.

Such narratives are like a cube of mirrors. Whatever way they are turned, they reflect the viewer's perspective only from that particular transient angle. Like the timeless puzzles of existence that they artistically insinuate, aesthetic romances present themselves as exquisite art-for-art's-sake phenomena, a perfection of form exempt from immediate local issues. If they seem to reflect a moral, for instance, they do so only because the reader finds one, not because there necessarily is one. Authors of late nineteenth-century aesthetic romances claim complete moral indifference, whatever today we may think constitutes the inescapable ideological implications of their productions.

The Turn of the Screw, which James described as pure romance, is a masterpiece of the aesthetic type. It has fascinated and mystified readers from the first day of its appearance, and it persists as an enigmatic site of debate for today's critics. Pointing to both contextual and textual evidence, critics agree on virtually nothing about the story – not its meaning, not even its literal elements. Having meticulously combed through the novella, they have found nuances and clues in favor of basically two contrary readings: that the governess suffers from a mental disorder, or that she actually encounters evil apparitions.

James, who made a number of unreliable and contradictory observations about *The Turn of the Screw*, once referred to it as a *jeu d'esprit*. Jokes are in fact mentioned in the novella, which teases its readers into pondering textual mysteries resistant to definitive analyses. This and other aesthetic romances may indeed be read as inside jokes among practitioners of the genre. The beautiful technical design of such aesthetic romances invites the audience's admiration even as these narratives intrinsically dismiss this attention as completely irrelevant to their own self-referential artistic designs.

Ethical romance

If late nineteenth-century aesthetic romances such as Oscar Wilde's *The Picture of Dorian Gray* (1890) were more prominent in Britain than in America, the third "ethical" variety of the genre was truly a transatlantic phenomenon. Ethical romance often combines the narrative devices of eventuary narrative and the artistic strategies of the aesthetic version of the genre. This fruitful amalgamation potentially appeals to a wide audience but particularly targets the readers' conventional expectation of merely being entertained. More specifically, authors of ethical romance add a social conscience to their mixture of the commercial objectives of the eventuary variety and the artistic emphases of the aesthetic type. If, each in its own way, the unraveling plot of eventuary romance and the impenetrable puzzles of aesthetic romance bypass and resist their audiences' production of thought, in contrast the narrative performance of ethical romance is designed to stimulate reader awareness. Such a work may urge its audience to ponder some philosophical perspective on human life or to engage actively in some social or personal revision of current conditions.

Ethical romancers, it should be noted, may be either optimistic or skeptical on the subject of human choice in general or the capacity for meaningful change in particular. Even when skeptical, however, these works register a desire for change. Their authors wistfully contemplate a large, mysterious, or commonly unrecognized sector of human behavior where overlooked options *seem* to or *should* exist, whether in fact or in fantasy – the two categories routinely mingled in hybrid romances. This means, then, that domestic, historical, and adventure romances – often little more than eventuary in manner – can serve ethical romancers as vehicles for instruction through entertainment.

Describing the manner of ethical romances, for example, Jack London speaks of strategic narrative gaps or silences designed to produce a thought or a feeling in an audience. "What more is the function of art," London asks in *Revolution and Other Essays* (1910), "than to excite states of consciousness complementary to the thing portrayed?" (p. 231). Whereas authors of the eventuary and aesthetic types of romance conceive of their prospective readership as passive consumers of adventure stories or as passive admirers of brilliant art, ethical romancers boldly explore the capacity of the genre distinctly to provoke or engage an audience's thoughts. Such reflection implicates the reader in the advancement of the story's plot toward a greater resolution in the reader's world. In ethical romance there is, as it were, a suggestion that some undetected secret lies hidden within the seemingly superficial generic conventions of the narrative being read; and this suggestion, in turn, intimates that a parallel deep complexity apparently likewise lies behind the illusive mundane text-like conventions of the reader's world. Ethical romancers present audience, society, and romance as reciprocal imaginative narratives, each replete with "fantastic" or imaginative properties similar to dreams. That life is as mutable as a dream is, in fact, a recurrent point of reference in many of these tales. And this recurrent point suggests the power of the human mind to create alternative versions of reality not just imaginatively in books but creatively in the everyday world. Ethical romance encourages its audience to engage in detecting a mutually reinforcing relationship between the printed story, the audience's social milieu, and the reading self.

Utopia and Sentimentality

Ethical romances vary in their level of artistic sophistication. A substantial number of utopian romances published between 1880 and 1920 explicitly draw attention to various social issues of their time. Most, unfortunately, are as direct in their appeal as newspaper editorials or as hortatory in their manner as pulpit sermons. Feminist efforts at utopian romance include Alice Ilgenfritz Jones and Ella Merchant's *Unveiling a Parallel* (1892) and Charlotte Perkins Gilman's *Herland* (1915), both cogently satiric books marred, perhaps, by a preachy manner and a reticence on such important concerns as sexuality and class divisions. In its time Edward Bellamy's *Looking Backward: 2000–1887* (1888) was the most popular utopian work, selling a million copies in a few years and resulting in the formation of essentially socialistic clubs designed to promote the nationalization of industry and the redistribution of wealth.

Looking Backward does more than present its message. Julian West, the protagonist of the romance, serves as a surrogate for the book's reader. Like Julian, the reader encounters a series of related invitations to respond, to become enlightened, through encounters with strangeness. There are several features of this strangeness that are not resolved in Bellamy's futuristic narrative, including the issue of whether life is as mutable as a dream. Such irresolution potentially blurs the boundary between Bellamy's peculiar fictional text and its audience's quotidian text-like world. As a result of this fluid boundary, the reader may see the real world differently, possibly may become somewhat estranged from the customary perception of the status quo. Bellamy's utopian short story "To Whom This May Come" (1889), concerned with telepathic utopians, similarly employs narrative strategies designed to sensitize readers to the socially inhibiting limitations of ordinary language. In ways unusual for utopian fiction in general, both of these works by Bellamy exhibit the more sophisticated techniques of ethical romance. In their mutual fictionalized case for personal and societal reformation, they weaken the border between audience and story in a way that encourages readers to modify their thoughts and actions.

Besides most utopian stories, there were also a considerable number of sentimentally and moralistically rendered portraits of human behavior. Even when highly entertaining, these ethical romances excelled only at the lower levels of narrative potentiality. Bret Harte's early short fiction provides an excellent example of popular sentimental works that implicitly moralize. In "The Luck of Roaring Camp" (1868) a deceased prostitute's baby elicits the nobler capacities of hardened gold miners, who discover the beauty of human bonds. In "The Outcasts of Poker Flat" (1869) tough denizens of the western frontier make extraordinary humanitarian sacrifices. And in Harte's "Tennessee's Partner" (1869) a gambler and apparent thief serves as a foil for the exemplary behavior of his ill-treated friend, a man who exhibits saintly forgiveness and charity even after the gambler's death. There were many romances between 1870 and 1914 that achieved little more than sentiment, including widely read courtship stories and action tales in which seemingly unimportant people suddenly emerge as save-the-day heroes. Typical was Richard Harding Davis's immensely popular "Gallagher" (1890), in which a young newspaper stringer risks his life to expose corruption and as a result preserves the common good.

Satire and Allegory

There were, as well, ethical romances with satiric and broadly allegoric implications. Of this type, particularly outstanding are various works by Mark Twain (Samuel Langhorne Clemens). Twain's *The Adventures of Tom Sawyer* (1876) is replete with boyish fantasies fueled by romance stories of robbery and murder, but its entertaining, often satiric narrative high jinx have a dark undercurrent. The book, which was banned by several libraries as unfit for children, simultaneously registers an attraction and a resistance to the forces of civilization. Although the author finally asserts the need to restrain primitive or barbaric human impulses, he does so with so much ambivalence that the final meaning of his childhood romance remains ambiguous. More direct in its point, and far less enticing as a result, is Twain's *The Prince and the Pauper* (1882). Set in Tudor England and involving a temporary reversal of identities, this children's book heuristically satirizes class distinctions and particularly highlights injustices inflicted upon the poor. Hidden identity likewise informs *The Tragedy of Pudd'nhead Wilson* (1894), in which a slave plots to liberate her son by switching him for another child and then having him adopted by unsuspecting whites. The son turns out to be a murdering ne'er-do-well whose behavior results in bleak, tragic consequences, the meaning of which has been the subject of ongoing critical debate.

In contrast, there are many late nineteenth-century ethical romances less difficult to understand. As a revision of the destructive "ghostly" male legacy of *Hamlet*, for example, the supernatural manifestations in Pauline E. Hopkins's "The Mystery Within" (1900) call for a more present-minded, maternally communal collaboration that could therapeutically redeem the past. Likewise, the proliferating monsters in Louise J. Strong's "An Unscientific Story" (1903) implicitly admonish against male scientific appropriation of female generative powers: such an unnatural appropriation denies human community. Similarly, human discontent (suggested by the rise of anarchists, nihilists, socialists, and Levellers) becomes the "horror" in Sabine Baring-Gould's "A Dead Finger" (1904), which broadly predicts a communal and personal decomposition unless pertinent social changes occur. Such fiction, in its attempted provocation of the reader's reflection, is often more artistically accomplished than are its utopian and sentimental cousins. However, the dialectical nature of this fiction — its implied critique of some social malaise and its related intimation of an alternative possibility — is largely restricted to an implied audience's recognition of theme and subject matter.

More noteworthy are the romances of Sarah Orne Jewett, whose satire-tinged fiction often blends domestic, sentimental, and allegorical elements. Her frequently anthologized "A White Heron" (1886) features a young girl's conflict between her attraction to an ornithologist and her devotion to nature. Jewett's representation of Sylvia's personal sacrifices to save the heron from the collector's gun romantically moralizes against the urban displacement of rural life, the scientific displacement of natural sentiment, and the commercial displacement of human feeling. Jewett's "Fame's Little Day" (1895) is not merely a humorous and ironic account of a personal transformation resulting from a bored newspaper reporter's whimsical act, resulting in the mistaken impressions of a New England couple visiting New York City. The story also raises questions about the relationship between perception and reality and, as well, about the capacity of fiction, especially romance, to transform such perceptions.

Equally notable are the romances of another New Englander, Mary Wilkins Freeman. In such collections as *A Humble Romance and Other Stories* (1887) and *A New England Nun and Other Stories* (1891) sentimentality and objectivity mingle in accounts of aging and unmarried women undertaking acts that highlight their exemplary self-possession in spite of lives of hardship. The compassion of an impoverished woman in "Old Lady Pingree" (1887) is rewarded at the end of her life. "Christmas Jenny" (1891) features a paragon of charity, a spinster devoted to a deaf child. Freeman's "Silence" (1893) — an example of the capacity of historical romance to moralize — is more than a domestic story of two lovers united against great odds; it makes a feminist forecast of a future when the transformational power of female desire will emerge from the shadows of society's text-like conventions.

Gender

Many women found the ghost story particularly congenial in addressing ethical issues and simultaneously reaching the wide youthful audience of popular fiction. It is interesting to note, too, that depending on what emphasis the reader gives their supernatural elements, many of these works can be read as romance or as realistic fiction, as we noted about James's *Turn of the Screw*. In the realistic domestic setting of "A Woman's Fancy" (1903) Alice Maude Ewell adroitly revises the ghost-story genre to represent the spectral potentiality of female identity, which she associates with the creation of art. Edith Wharton's "A Journey" (1899) presents a protagonist who flees every opportunity for independence, even as she always complains that life is never fair to her. Her life's journey ends on a train where she is either fatally pursued by her deceased husband's spirit or is merely the victim of her attitudes and behavior. At the conclusion of the tale the reader is left to ponder more than an uncertainty over whether her head-damaging fall is caused by her husband's ghost and is fatal. Wharton, who criticizes the protagonist for longing to be rescued like Sleeping Beauty, leaves a final disturbing irresolution that latently provokes the reader's thought. The prospective female reader who expects to be passively entertained, one could say, is thereby rudely awakened by a narrative blow rather than rewarded with a gentle authorial kiss.

More well known today is Charlotte Perkins Gilman's "The Yellow Wall-paper" (1892), set in an inherited mansion described by the narrator as a haunted house. In this tale the repressed shadow behind the wallpaper symbolizes Gilman's assessment of the social situation of turn-of-the-century women. By the end of the narrative it is uncertain whether the female protagonist is possessed by a ghostly figure who has broken free from her wallpaper imprisonment or whether she is simply the victim of a misguided medical response to postpartum depression. The final paragraph of the story is not instantly comprehensible and requires thought, which ideally will revisit earlier innuendoes in the tale. The ethical romance narrative manner of "The Yellow Wall-paper" encourages the reader to ponder the reasons why the narrator (representing women generally) cannot occupy a room of her own – cannot achieve self-possession – except tragically through insanity.

Race and Class

Issues concerning both gender and race emerge in Helen Hunt Jackson's *Ramona* (1884), a historical romance with a half-blood heroine living in frontier California. Jackson's heroine and her murdered first love, a full-blood Native American, are rendered as racial types in the author's attempt to represent intolerance and injustice as the real culprits in the demise of an Indian presence in America. Native American traditions and romance techniques combine in Mary Austin's *The Basket Woman*

(1904). In the first of its tales a little boy's dream aligns his natural instincts with a Native American mother-figure who introduces him to a mythic perception of reality. Austin's romances in this book, the second edition of which was marketed as a school text, urge the cultural recovery of a childlike relationship to nature, a recuperation she associates with an appreciation of Native American values.

Racial issues inform romances by African American authors, who found the domestic, historical, mystery, supernatural, and even adventure varieties of the genre particularly congenial to their challenges to conventional white racial perceptions. Francis Watkins Harper's *Iola Leroy* (1892) is a historical romance in which a freed mulatta overcomes daunting obstacles, reunites her broken family, marries a black doctor, and becomes an advocate for her race. Pauline E. Hopkins's historical romances include *Contending Forces* (1900) and *Winona* (1902). The latter is a fast-paced sentimental work with a mulatta heroine whose experiences point to gender and racial injustice. The manner of the eventuary romance is revised in both Sutton E. Griggs's *Imperium in Imperio* (1899), a fantasy of a black secret society's plot to seize Texas, and Hopkins's *Of One Blood* (1902–3), a tale of a black explorer's discovery of an ancient civilization that proves the historical precedence of African civilization.

Hopkins especially relies on romance, and as we saw earlier she uses the ghost-story medium in "The Mystery Within," a preachy work notable primarily for its therapeutic paradigm of maternal nurture. Accounts of slaves magically escaping oppression through spells that transform them into animals and plants are related in Charles Waddell Chesnutt's *The Conjure Woman* (1899). The mystery genre underlies both Hopkins's *Hagar's Daughter* (1901–2) and John E. Bruce's *Black Sleuth* (1909–10), in both of which black detectives use their racial and social identity to solve crimes.

Concern for the welfare of working-class women and children informs nineteenth-century "factory literature," works revealing the impact of the later urban stages of the industrial revolution on human lives. Often these works are realist in manner, such as Rebecca Harding Davis's *Life in the Iron Mills* (1861), but many adopt the domestic romance tradition. Some are heavy-handed, as is evident in the beleaguered slave-of-the-loom heroine and the intrusively sentimental narrator of George W. Goode's *Kathie, the Overseer's Daughter* (1887). Goode ends his story with an insane woman's symbolic murder of a captain of industry, an act which facilitates Kathie's rescue through a happy marriage. Somewhat better is Maude Hilton's *Rose Michel* (1875), recounting the trials of a 17-year-old impoverished woman who gets mangled by a mill-wheel. At the conclusion of this romance, at least, the heroine marries a working-class rather than a patrician man.

Male interests are registered in Jack London's "A Thousand Deaths" (1899), a science-fiction horror tale that raises questions about patriarchy and imperialism. This tale of a scientist's willingness to torture his son in technological experiments has a distinctly Marxist cast. It suggests that the fathers of late nineteenth-century technology must be overthrown because they equate human life to machinery and imperialistically subjugate the rising generation. But if London holds a Marxist understanding of capitalistic class oppression, he also emphasizes the value of brute

Nietzschean individualism. Typical of this emphasis is the abandonment of the artificial inhibitions of civilization dramatized in London's *The Call of the Wild* (1903), a romance in which a sledge dog named Buck follows his instincts and becomes a leader of a wolf-pack after his master is murdered.

Philosophical Puzzles

Some authors fashioned sophisticated ethical romances apparently designed to examine, not resolve, difficult philosophical issues. Ellen Glasgow's "A Point in Morals" (1899), for instance, may at first seem little more than a satiric caricaturizing of aristocratic cruise passengers who indulge in facile conversation on the propriety of euthanasia. But allusions to Schopenhauer, a series of narrative reversals, a blurring of the boundary between fact and fiction, and an irresolution at several levels of the story all combine to unsettle the reader's conventional trust in a rational authority behind commonplace moral principles.

Stephen Crane's "The Blue Hotel" (1898) is equally radical in its skepticism toward conventional morality based on comfortable explanations of human existence. This satiric murder-mystery romance, which pertinently mentions dime novels, concludes with a reference to a "fog of mysterious theory." Crane's tale is a dime novel converted into an ethical romance of metaphysical detection. Specifically, the story puzzles over whether humanity perversely chooses or is hopelessly fated to acts of violent self-destruction. On the one hand, Crane dispassionately seems to suggest (as if he were a Darwinian naturalist) that violence is the pre-ordained condition of all life. On the other hand, he also appears to indicate that perhaps the life force is merely indifferent and that human violence emerges from a consciousness arrogantly preoccupied with its own interests. The story, which is replete with related ironically rendered conundrums, never resolves its metaphysical interrogation of the human experience of freedom and fate. Leaving the reader in a "fog of mysterious theory," both Crane's and Glasgow's narratives are clever ethical romances challenging the human ability to arrive at a firm code of ethics.

The Ethos of Storytelling

Crane's "The Blue Hotel" also reflexively entertains moral questions about the personal and societal consequences of art, of stories like itself. Crane's tale targets those critics who assert that social harm results from the pernicious influence of popular romance – dime novels, say, which in a widely publicized murder trial were specifically said to have prompted Jesse Pomeroy's sadistic acts of murder. All such fiction, Crane's story implies, merely reflects to the reader the propensities of the human mind, the origin of all tales. Given this circularity, what does it mean to attribute blame to such works? How subversive is any narrative that inevitably only reveals the mind to itself, the detecting audience to itself? "The Blue Hotel" effectively eradicates the moral boundary between cause and effect, a mainstay of a conventional understanding of the social order.

Clemens and Jewett disagree with Crane in this. As we saw, both maintain that fiction indeed has an impact on the world, for good or ill depending on how an audience responds. Most late nineteenth-century ethical romancers take a positive view of the circuit of their narratives between author and reader. In *The Basket Woman*, in which we noted an advocacy for a more fundamental appreciation of nature, prefatory comments indicate Mary Austin's deliberate use of romance, particularly its dreamlike quality, to stimulate an ever-present, childlike, myth-sensitive intuition in her readers. A boy's dream, a Native American woman's song, and a narrative of an encounter with a wolf, rendered collectively as stories within stories, coalesce in Austin's title narrative to suggest that language is a sacramental matrix connecting mind (spirit) and matter. Like the Transcendentalists she admires, Austin views storytelling as a therapeutic medium for the restoration of a healthy attitude toward life. In contrast to Crane's skepticism, Austin enthusiastically affirms a cause-and-effect feature to all stories. For her, as her ethical romances indicate, the freedom we imagine in dreamlike fiction can become the wonderful benign fate of our actual lives. Instead of a fogged understanding, Austin suggests, we can attain greater insight into the mystery of our being — can, in fact, through the imaginative stories we tell ourselves, actuate increasingly improved contingent versions of human reality.

Authorial and Cultural Intentions

As both Austin and Crane demonstrate, romancers were capable of considerable sophisticated deliberation about the nature of their art. Many romancers were well aware of the long history of social and aesthetic opprobrium heaped on the form. For example, in *Peeps at People* (1899) John Kendrick Bangs creates a mock interview with Rudyard Kipling, a *fin-de-siècle* British romancer *par excellence* who was also widely read in America; the humorous interview lampoons critics who devalue the romance genre as intellectually and aesthetically deficient. Bangs himself had been accused of achieving little more than buffoonery in his own romances.

While most romancers simply practiced their art, some defensively applied the word "journalism" to their work. It is true that many romancers were self-made individuals from outside the social elite and had a journalistic background. Moreover, a general case could be made for the affinity of romance with the sort of journalism practiced at the turn of the nineteenth century, especially the sensationalistic accounts characteristic of yellow journalism. Pertinent, too, were the many pseudo-newspaper accounts, only later identified as fiction, written by Joseph M. Mulholland under the name Orange Blossom. In short, romancers who had been trained as journalists often adapted elements of the newspaper medium in their fiction in order to appeal to the general reader.

There were, however, romancers – like Austin, Bangs, and London – who out-spokenly defended the artistic legitimacy of the genre. There were, as well, writers devoted to literary realism (including naturalism) who, like Norris, valued romance as a sophisticated art form. Many of these defenders may have learned important lessons in technique from Edgar Allan Poe but especially found support in the turn-of-the-century transatlantic popularity of Nathaniel Hawthorne's exemplary fiction. Anthony Trollope called Hawthorne a genius, while Leslie Stephen spoke of him as the tutor of romancers, whom R. H. Hutton likewise described as graduates from this great master's school. Julian Hawthorne, a popular romance author, spoke for others when he specifically pointed to his father's legacy of a hybrid literary form that combined the realistic and the imaginary. This Hawthornian hybrid type of romance was capable of simultaneously intimating and concealing the profound mystery of human existence, a capacity that potentially challenges our conventional perceptions of reality.

Turn-of-the-century authors such as Julian Hawthorne thought that the hybrid romance was a particularly American phenomenon, and during the 1950s Richard Chase advanced the argument to extend the romance tradition into the late twentieth century. Whatever the truth may be about the American-ness of the form, the hybrid romance was truly a transatlantic presence by the end of the nineteenth century. Trollope, Stephen, Hutton, and H. G. Wells were but a few of the British authors who praised Hawthorne's fiction as prominently influential. Whether socially conservative or radically skeptical in its implications, ethical romance was embraced as a substantial aesthetic medium by writers hoping to modify their readers' perspectives.

At this point we might pause in our consideration of authorial intentions and ask whether the performance of romance always conforms to these objectives. Problems in this regard can emerge, as is evident in the irresolvable debate over the meaning of Twain's *The Tragedy of Pudd'nhead Wilson*. One might also point to London's "A Thousand Deaths," in which the Marxist message is unwittingly undercut by the son's personal replication of his father's violence and absence of feeling. The point of Jackson's *Ramona* is likewise compromised when the heroine marries a Spanish gentleman and moves to Mexico, two narrative developments that in effect eradicate the Native American half of the heroine's mixed-blood identity. Authorial intentions may or may not be destabilized in any given romance, but the genre, like art generally, always conveys more than its creator intends.

This larger signification of romance has drawn the attention of recent critics who attempt to scrutinize the underlying cultural work of the genre and debate whether that performance primarily legitimates or resists consensus ideology. These critics focus on subtextual implications, especially cultural intentions that authors unconsciously and inevitably express simply because they live in a particular time or place. The seemingly simplest adventure romance, these critics argue, may reflect racist, sexist, classist, and imperialist attitudes not necessarily appreciated as such by its author. One might, for instance, find in the narrative performance of William Sydney Porter's episodic *Cabbages and Kings* (1904) an underlying national chauvinism, a pro-

American fervor, that reflects sympathy with the Manifest Destiny revival of the 1890s or with the much-publicized boyish exuberance of President Theodore Roosevelt, author of the widely read *The Rough Riders* (1899) and *African Game Trails* (1910).

These critics have a point. The quality of, as well as the demand for, romance during the late nineteenth and early twentieth centuries may reflect the reading public's sense of that period as an exuberant time when, for many, opportunities for national and personal expansiveness seemed to coalesce. Despite episodic economic setbacks, the middle class was awed by what appeared to be propitious times, as reflected in the (Frederick Jackson) Turner thesis (1893) defining American success in terms of frontier expansion, the US victory in the Spanish–American War (1898–9), the purchase of the Virgin Islands from Denmark (1902), the admission of many new states to the Union, and the appearance of the Brooklyn Bridge, skyscrapers, gasoline-powered automobiles, airplanes, hydroelectric power plants, incandescent electric lamps, telephones, and radio broadcasting, among other new wonders. To many Americans the Chicago World's Fair (1893) conveyed this very spirit of boundless national and personal prospects. But the technologically based atmosphere of dazzling expansiveness associated with the Fair hid shadows barely glimpsed by most of its enraptured visitors. Few contemplated the underside of the recent Oklahoma land grab and the Klondike gold rush, the migration of rural populations into cities, the proliferation of trusts and monopolies, or the concentration of wealth into the hands of a mere 1 per cent of the US population. And just below the twentieth century's horizon lurked the horror of World War I.

Primary Texts

Alcott, Louisa May. *Little Women*. 1868–9.

Anderson, Ada Woodruff. *The Rim of the Desert*. 1915.

Atherton, Gertrude. *The Conqueror*. 1902.

Austin, Mary. *The Basket Woman*. 1904.

Bangs, John Kendrick. "Thurlow's Christmas Story." 1898.

Bangs, John Kendrick. *Peeps at People*. 1899.

Baring-Gould, Sabine. "A Dead Finger." 1904.

Baum, Frank. *The Wonderful Wizard of Oz*. 1900.

Bellamy, Edward. *Looking Backward: 2000–1887*. 1888.

Bellamy, Edward. "To Whom This May Come." 1889.

Bruce, John E. *Black Sleuth*. 1909–10.

Chambers, Robert W. *The King in Yellow*. 1895.

Chesnutt, Charles Waddell. *The Conjure Woman*. 1899.

Crane, Stephen. "The Blue Hotel." 1898.

Davis, Rebecca Harding. *Life in the Iron Mills; or, The Korl Woman*. 1861.

Davis, Richard Harding. "Gallagher." 1890.

Davis, Richard Harding. *Soldiers of Fortune*. 1897.

Dickens, Charles. *A Christmas Carol*. 1843.

Dickens, Charles. *Hard Times*. 1854.

Ewell, Alice Maude. "A Woman's Fancy." 1903.

Freeman, Mary Wilkins. *A Humble Romance and Other Stories*. 1887.

Freeman, Mary Wilkins. "Old Lady Pingree." 1887.

Freeman, Mary Wilkins. "Christmas Jenny." 1891.

Freeman, Mary Wilkins. *A New England Nun and Other Stories*. 1891.

Freeman, Mary Wilkins. "Silence." 1893.

Gilman, Charlotte Perkins. "The Yellow Wallpaper." 1892.

Gilman, Charlotte Perkins. *Herland*. 1915.

Glasgow, Ellen. *The Descendant*. 1897.

Glasgow, Ellen. "A Point in Morals." 1899.

Goode, George W. *Kathie, the Overseer's Daughter*. 1887.

Grey, Zane. *Riders of the Purple Sage*. 1912.

Griggs, Sutton E. *Imperium in Imperio*. 1899.

Harper, Frances Ellen Watkins. *Iola Leroy; or, Shadows Uplifted*. 1892.

Harte, Bret. "The Luck of Roaring Camp." 1868.

Harte, Bret. "The Outcasts of Poker Flat." 1869.

Harte, Bret. "Tennessee's Partner." 1869.

Hilton, Maude. *Rose Michel*. 1875.

Hopkins, Pauline E. *Contending Forces: A Romance Illustrative of Negro Life North and South*. 1900.

Hopkins, Pauline E. "The Mystery Within." 1900.

Hopkins, Pauline E. *Hagar's Daughter*. 1901–2.

Hopkins, Pauline E. *Winona: A Tale of Negro Life in the South and Southwest*. 1902.

Hopkins, Pauline E. *Of One Blood*. 1902–3.

Howells, William Dean. *A Hazard of New Fortunes*. 1890.

Jackson, Helen Hunt. *Ramona*. 1884.

James, Henry. *The Turn of the Screw*. 1898.

James, Henry. *The Ambassadors*. 1903.

Jewett, Sarah Orne. "Fame's Little Day." 1895.

Jewett, Sarah Orne. "A White Heron." 1886.

Jewett, Sarah Orne. *The Tory Lover*. 1901.

Jones, Alice Ilgenfritz, and Merchant, Ella. *Unveiling a Parallel*. 1892.

London, Jack. "A Thousand Deaths." 1899.

London, Jack. *The Call of the Wild*. 1903.

London, Jack. *Revolution and Other Essays*. 1910.

Norris, Frank. *The Responsibilities of the Novelist*. 1903.

Page, Thomas Nelson. *In Ole Virginia*. 1887.

Peck, George Wilbur. *Peck's Bad Boy and His Pa*. 1883.

Porter, William Sydney. *Cabbages and Kings*. 1904.

Roosevelt, Theodore. *The Rough Riders*. 1899.

Roosevelt, Theodore. *African Game Trails*. 1910.

Scott, Sir Walter. *Ivanhoe*. 1819.

Stockton, Frank R. *Rudder Grange*. 1879.

Stockton, Frank R. "The Lady or the Tiger?" 1882.

Strong, Louise J. "An Unscientific Story." 1903.

Twain, Mark. *The Adventures of Tom Sawyer*. 1876.

Twain, Mark. *The Prince and the Pauper*. 1882.

Twain, Mark. *Adventures of Huckleberry Finn*. 1884.

Twain, Mark. *The Tragedy of Pudd'nhead Wilson*. 1894.

Wallace, Lewis. *The Fair God*. 1873.

Wallace, Lewis. *Ben-Hur*. 1880.

Wharton, Edith. "A Journey." 1899.

Wilde, Oscar. *The Picture of Dorian Gray*. 1890.

Wister, Owen. *The Virginian: A Horseman of the Plains*. 1902.

REFERENCES AND FURTHER READING

Bell, Michael Davitt (1980). *The Development of American Romance: The Sacrifice of Relation*. Chicago: University of Chicago Press.

Budick, Emily Miller (1989). *Fiction and Historical Consciousness*. New Haven: Yale University Press.

Chase, Richard (1957). *The American Novel and its Tradition*. Garden City, NY: Doubleday.

Dekker, George (1987). *American Historical Romance*. Cambridge, UK: Cambridge University Press.

Scheick, William J. (1994). *The Ethos of Romance at the Turn of the Century*. Austin: University of Texas Press.

Thompson, G. R., and Link, Eric Carl (1999). *Neutral Ground: New Traditionalism and the American Romance Controversy*. Baton Rouge: Louisiana University Press.

3

The Sentimental and Domestic Traditions, 1865–1900

Gregg Camfield

Despite about twenty years of serious work recovering the importance of sentimentalism in American literary culture, it is still necessary to begin an essay on sentimentalism in the post-Civil War period by pointing out many misconceptions. The term "sentimental" has taken on a negative connotation that makes it very difficult to recover the power it had in the late nineteenth century, although the history of the word's debasement can help us begin that process of recovery. For most of the twentieth century, literary critics disparaged American sentimental literature as little more than wisps crafted out of an unnaturally emotional literary style. For example, in *The Sentimental Novel in America, 1789–1860* (1940), Herbert Ross Brown opined that sentimentalists learned their trade from second-rate British novels, preferred to take their feelings "neat," and passed off justification for their emotionalism in naïve readings of British literature: "The sentimental formula was a simple equation resting upon a belief in the spontaneous goodness and benevolence of man's original instincts. It could point to what passed for philosophical justification in the admired writings of Shaftesbury, Hutcheson and Adam Smith" (Brown 1940: 176).

Brown got the sources partly right, but disparaged a manifestly rich intellectual heritage as an act of mere passing. For Brown and most of his contemporaries, sentimental literature was worth studying primarily as a backdrop to the ostensibly more important literature of the period, the works of the great Romantics, who crafted their masterpieces in defiance of the scribbling rabble whose popularity was explicable only in terms of the execrable taste of the masses.

No surprise, then, that literary historians noted a stylistic change, for the most part, after the Civil War, and, assuming that the important writers of the postbellum period were responding primarily to the Romantics of the antebellum years, described the years after 1865 as the years of an ascendant realism. Sentimentalism in this view is the quaint relic of, to use Santayana's influential term, the "genteel tradition," an ossified stylistic anachronism, once considered emotionally overwrought, now seeming rather prim. Literary historians assumed that sentimentalism died at Appomattox, the last casualty of the Civil War.

Certainly Fred Lewis Pattee's *The Feminine Fifties* (1940) is built on the supposition that sentimentalism reached its peak in the decade before the war. Perhaps more important is another of the erroneous interpretations that helped turn "sentimental" into a mildly derisive term. Pattee saw sentiment and femininity as synonymous, and the critical tradition of the first three-quarters of the twentieth century disparaged most women writers. The conjunction would prove propitious for the recovery of sentimental literature – and, ultimately, for the understanding that the ideas behind obviously sentimental literature persist to this day – because the rise of feminist criticism saw challenges leveled at any critical orthodoxy that disparaged women writers. It is now possible not only to study, but also to admire literature once dismissed as sentimental. In particular, feminist criticism has helped open up the study of realism, seeing interesting and accurate description of realities – realities seen neither by Romantics nor by those men traditionally called "realists" – in a literature once derided as naïve and idealistic.

Nonetheless, there remain three distortions not fully challenged by feminist criticism. First, sentimental literature was not the exclusive province of women writers. Second, it did not address exclusively domestic concerns; while domesticity was usually addressed through the terminology of sentimentalism, sentimentalism embraced almost every political, economic, religious, ethical, and aesthetic concern of American writers in the nineteenth century. Third, while the style that we can easily identify as sentimental had lost its cachet by 1865, sentimentalism did not disappear after the Civil War. While most literary critics working in this field still concentrate on the antebellum period, several argue quite persuasively that the impact of the ideas, forms, and patterns of sentimental literature persist in both high and low culture in America today. The last half of the nineteenth century witnessed the stylistic transformations that enabled such influence to persist despite at least seven decades of disparaging commentary.

Background

Sentimentalism began as an intellectual reaction to political and religious strife. John Locke, shocked by the excesses of the English Civil War of the seventeenth century, drafted his *An Essay Concerning Human Understanding* (1690) to explain the human propensity for error. In the process, he revolutionized Western models of human psychology, creating an image of the mind beginning at birth as a recording device that measures the world according to the external senses and a few internal faculties, such as memory and imagination. The mind he described was capable of reason, but motivated primarily by pleasure and pain, so that he described reason itself as deeply connected to feeling.

In the eighteenth century, two schools of thought developed out of Locke's psychology, in part reacting to two different bogeymen. On the one hand, Calvinism, which served as one of Locke's primary examples of error in reasoning, led Locke's realist followers to stress the importance of careful reasoning in order to avoid error. Followers such as Thomas Reid stressed the importance of the objective study of reality, pushing the empirical implications of Locke's psychology to the extreme. On the other hand, Thomas Hobbes, opposing Calvinism on similar political grounds to those postulated by Locke's political philosophy, had made an argument (in *Leviathan*, 1651) for an extremely authoritarian politics that was anathema to much of the English-speaking world. Furthermore, Hobbes's ideas were predicated on an atheism that was equally repugnant to most political and religious moderates who followed Locke. Ironically, they found their favorite version of Locke's philosophy in the writings of the Earl of Shaftesbury.

Shaftesbury, a student of Locke, felt that Locke's description of human faculties was incomplete. He felt that there were many distinct emotional impulses that pushed human beings toward fundamentally social, even altruistic behavior. He postulated several additions to the internal faculties, and asserted that these internal faculties were superior to, though dependent upon, the external senses. Thus he came up with a list of sensibilities, including the moral sense, that kept human beings from being the complete egotists that Hobbes had described. While Shaftesbury's deism diminished his popularity among English writers and thinkers, his solution to the problem of egotism proved quite important, with many extremely influential thinkers, including Francis Hutcheson, Adam Smith, and popularizers such as Archibald Alison, elaborating on sensibility and sympathy as the most important aspects of human psychology. These products of what Henry May calls the Didactic Enlightenment were enormously influential in America. They were heavily represented in the curricula of American colleges, and their ideas influenced everything from the Declaration of Independence to the practice and theory of all of the fine arts.

In this history, moreover, one sees that sentimentalism as a philosophy is a middle-ground philosophy, often called, referring to the mental capacities human beings share, "Common Sense" philosophy. It stands between the extremes of idealism and realism, between fundamentalist Christianity and atheism, between anarchy and totalitarianism. It addresses political and religious questions, epistemological questions, and aesthetic questions in a complex interplay. But, as a compromise philosophy, it is always pulled at the extremes. Whether to stress objectivity or subjectivity, whether to stress the communal pull of sympathy or the individualistic implications of philosophical voluntarism, whether to see sensibility as related to innate ideas and thus as a kind of idealism, or to see sensibility merely as a capacity that can be developed only in contact with an external world: these questions came up repeatedly in the philosophical tradition and had their echoes in *belles lettres*.

There are several corollaries that must be explored. First, as Locke and his followers grappled with the difficulty of finding "reality" but never doubted its existence, sentimental psychology is deeply implicated in literary debates over "realism."

Second, as Locke's ideas began in politics with an eye to religion, there were always political and religious elements at play in sentimental art. Third – a closely related point – sentimentalism posed a complex challenge to social class hierarchies, paradoxically providing a justification for class leveling while also providing a standard – refined sensibility – by which social class hierarchies could be judged and maintained. Fourth, the idea that the mind is a blank slate at birth put a new and very different emphasis on childhood as a time to develop moral adulthood by developing the sensibilities. Domesticity, while also a product of changes in economic organization, could not have developed as it did without this shift in understanding. Simultaneously, sentimentalism justified a different understanding of what a household should be: namely, a haven of love to protect from the pressures of the world. It was ideally to be based on affinities between men and women rather than on a man's power or on the economic organization of households. The gap between ideology and practice was one of the enduring themes of sentimental literature. Fifth, nostalgia became a moral imperative to retain the connection between childhood training and moral action. And finally, sentimentalists described a hierarchy of sensibilities, of course, but in so doing provided justification not only for the arts generally, but also for the most suspect kind of art – humor.

Realism

Sentimental realism now sounds like a contradiction in terms, but only because those who were explicitly sentimental in their writing lost the battle to define realism in the post-Civil War years. "Realism" is fundamentally paradoxical: no fictional account of reality can be anything but a radical abstraction. But "realism" in Locke's terms is honorific, and accordingly those who wanted to postulate a different kind of realism from that articulated by the antebellum standards of sentimentalism coopted the term. Sentimentalists at first engaged the debate explicitly, but went underground into local color realism after the war. The career of Harriet Beecher Stowe, America's premier sentimentalist and a writer who came on the literary scene in the 1850s but who wrote prolifically into the early 1870s, gives us an excellent window into the shift.

Uncle Tom's Cabin (1852) in part teaches its readers how to read sentimental literature as realistic. For Stowe, ultimate realities were emotional and moral, and pure sensibilities would allow any person to perceive moral truths. As she describes it – and her description is perfectly consonant with the moral philosophy of many of the Common Sense philosophers whose works she read – the daily grind can blunt sensibilities, driving a person away from truth. It is too easy, says Stowe, for the pursuit of something abstract, like money, to complicate our perceptions. In this way, Stowe's thought is very consonant with Locke's, working on the assumption that a faulty combination of simple ideas into complex ones leads to error; but, unlike Locke, Stowe argues that feelings offer the best way to cut through error. So her incessant pitch to feel right is predicated on an idea that unmediated perception will find truth. Her primary exponents of higher moral truth — Eva and Tom — get their peculiar clarity from unusual perceptive powers, powers not easily blunted by daily life.

But for most of us, Stowe says, the key to maintaining moral clarity is to develop habits of emotional perception and to support these through loving human relationships. Stowe best exemplifies this practice in the Halliday household, and Rachel Halliday is the model teacher. Her teachings work not simply through direct action, but through aesthetic associations, through complex memories of feelings that accrue through time. Consider Stowe's description of Halliday's squeaky rocking chair:

> as she gently swung backward and forward, the chair kept up a kind of subdued "creechy crawchy," that would have been intolerable in any other chair. But old Simeon Halliday often declared it was as good as any music to him, and the children all avowed that they would n't miss of hearing mother's chair for anything in the world. For why? for twenty years or more, nothing but loving words, and gentle moralities, and motherly loving kindness, had come from that chair. . . . (Stowe 1982b: 163)

For Stowe, then, mundane realities mediate moral truths. As she put it in *The Minister's Wooing* (1859):

> There is a ladder to heaven, whose base God has placed in human affections, tender instincts, symbolic feelings, sacraments of love, through which the soul rises higher and higher, refining as she goes, till she outgrows the human, and changes as she rises, into the image of the divine. At the very top of this ladder, at the threshold of paradise, blazes dazzling and crystalline that celestial grade where the soul knows self no more, having learned, through a long experience of devotion, how blest it is to lose herself in . . . eternal Love and Beauty. (Stowe 1982a: 579)

Stowe rejects the reality of neither spirit nor matter, but sees the human response to matter as having a profound impact on how well human beings are able to connect to truth. Specifically, the power of sympathy, the most important of the sentiments according to most sentimentalists, connects us, moving us from individual perceptions to transcendently communal ones, but always through experience.

Influential as Stowe's early work was, it did not go without challenge. Numerous critics of *Uncle Tom's Cabin* said she got all of her facts wrong, so her feelings could not be right. By her own standards, if her experience of daily life was wrong, she could not get to the truths behind it; so she wrote *A Key to Uncle Tom's Cabin* (1853) to prove that her story was grounded in fact. Yet all of this factual support deflected from her fundamental definition of truth. She, like her Hartford neighbor Charles Dudley Warner, did not really want to defend the plausibility of her plots; she wanted her readers to concentrate on the ideal feelings behind the stories. As Warner put it defensively in "Modern Fiction" (1883):

Art requires an idealization of nature.... When we praise our recent fiction for its photographic fidelity to nature we condemn it, for we deny to it the art that would give it value. We forget that the creation of the novel should be ... a synthetic process, and impart to human actions that ideal quality which we demand in painting.

Clearly, Warner worried that his position was losing ground. While he complained, other sentimentalists adapted sentimental realism to a new context.

The successful approach was to use the sketch to create local color realism, a realism grounded so narrowly and precisely in locale as to avoid criticism about plausibility, but one also so connected to emotion in its nostalgic intensity as to maintain the sentimental belief that emotions lead to higher truths. Stowe was one of the first to take this tack, in *Sam Lawson's Oldtown Fireside Stories* (1872). She avoids challenges to plausibility first by framing the stories, using an aged man, Horace Holyoke, to recall homey circumstances in which he was told stories by yarn-spinning ne'er-do-well Sam Lawson. The frame narrator's nostalgia and the inside narrator's unreliability buffer Stowe from criticism about the literal truth of the events she describes. She is able instead twice over to purify the stories of any inconsistent details in order to concentrate on clear moral questions or to create intense feelings. But in using the local color sketch, she is able to transcend the conventional high style of earlier sentimental works, moving toward a rougher, more realistic style under the relative freedom of the genre of the sketch, developed in the eighteenth century for its informality. Liberated from the absolute demands of plausibility and from a mannered high style, Stowe was able to craft very powerful sketches that addressed many of her fundamental themes about love, selflessness, the propriety of beauty, and the moral dangers of Calvinism, all under the pleasant and easy guise of childhood nostalgia for a New England that was long past.

There were other impulses for local color, of course, and not all writers of local color sketches were so self-consciously sentimentalists; nor were they all as well versed in the intellectual tradition as was Stowe. But the sketch as one of the genres most often used by sentimentalists made local color realism a good way to keep sentimental realism alive.

Many of Bret Harte's stories provide clear examples of this fusion of local color realism and sentimental impulses. "The Luck of Roaring Camp" (1868), for example, is replete with details of life in the California mining camps, but the tale is substantially about sympathy for the outcast. The illegitimate orphan child of a prostitute is adopted by the rough men of a mining camp. Their contact with the child softens them, revealing, in their domestic impulses, hearts of gold. Ultimately, in the face of a flood, one miner sacrifices his life in a vain effort to rescue the child. As a tale of sympathy dominant over self-seeking, the sketch found a large and enthusiastic audience and won Harte a fame that extended well into the 1870s. The style and approach are sufficiently maudlin by today's standards of taste for Harte's sketches to qualify as sentimental without question, but his lead influenced Mark Twain significantly. Often described as one of the most vigorous exponents of the new realism, Twain, in fact, also supported sentimental realism. For example, Huck's attitudes toward Jim in *Adventures of Huckleberry Finn* (1884) rely substantially on Twain's understanding of sentimental moral philosophy. Huck learns through concrete experience how to care for another person; altruism becomes real to him through "human affections, tender instincts, symbolic feelings, sacraments of love." Granted, Twain was a conflicted sentimentalist. *A Connecticut Yankee in King Arthur's Court* (1889) perhaps demonstrates Twain's greatest anxiety about sentimentalism, with the argument that altruism is a theory and Hank Morgan's declaration, "how empty is theory in the presence of fact." Nonetheless, the later "The Californian's Tale" (1893) returns vigorously to the sentimental stand; it is a local color sketch in which, once again, sacraments of love – this time in a domestic setting – reveal the transcendent reality of human sympathy.

Perhaps no other work better shows the subtle connection between local color realism and a symbolic "higher" realism than Sarah Orne Jewett's *The Country of the Pointed Firs* (1896). Jewett, a New Englander who was profoundly influenced by Stowe's work, began her writing career as a very explicit moralist, but as her career progressed she drew back from explicit moralizing to let her fiction make its points without the commentary. So, easy as it may be to see the sentimentalist behind "A White Heron" (1886), she is not so apparent behind *The Country of the Pointed Firs*. But in the context of Jewett's relationship to realism, it is clear that *Pointed Firs* mediates between the real and the ideal much as Stowe said "human affections, tender instincts, symbolic feelings, sacraments of love" should. The narrator builds her connection to the town of Dunnett Landing not as an outsider who merely wants to record local color details, but as one who sympathizes with the lives and spirits of those she comes to love. She can see the crude country woman in Almira Todd, but also can see the transcendent importance of her emotional life:

> She looked away from me, and presently rose and went on by herself. There was something lonely and solitary about her great determined shape. She might have been Antigone alone on the Theban plain. It is not often given in a noisy world to come to the places of great grief and silence. An absolute, archaic grief possessed this country-woman; she seemed like a renewal of some historic soul, with her sorrows and the remoteness of a daily life busied with rustic simplicities and the scents of primeval herbs. (Jewett 1981: 49)

Again, we see the sentimentalist's belief that the business of daily life can impede understanding of ultimate truth. The importance of literature is to open the sensibilities to fundamental realities, to strip away the distractions of "a noisy world" to get in touch with historic constants, with universal emotional truths.

The book's narrator is even capable of going further into the hearts of rural New Englanders than is Almira Todd herself. Only the narrator, with her careful sympathy, can find the reality of Elijah Tilley's emotional life. Todd sees no more than a "ploddin' man," but the narrator discovers a man whose domestic attachments run deep, as deep as his understanding of "nature and the elements" upon which his mind "seemed to be fixed...rather than upon any contrivances of man, like politics or theology" (Jewett 1981: 115). Ultimately, every detail in the book is both literally real and also symbolic of some emotional or transcendent truth, and the key is that a sentimental purification of feeling by stripping any mundane reality to its emotional core will enable the reader to feel fully the truth. Thus, Jewett's collection of sketches stands as a perfect example of the sentimental compromise between romantic idealism and materialistic realism.

When the matter is put in these terms, one begins to see even William Dean Howells's connection to the sentimental tradition. He worried that any artistic attempt to purify events to reveal their emotional cores would simply distort the emotional reality. As he put it in a letter to Mark Twain on 20 January 1882, "The ideal perfection of some things in life persuades me more and more never to meddle with the ideal in fiction: it is impossible to compete with the facts" (Howells and Twain 1960: 385). But he did not for a moment doubt that there was a connection, or that the way to reach the most important truths was through feelings generated by a sensitive contact with mundane reality. As he put it in *Criticism and Fiction* (1891), the realist "feels in every nerve the equality of things and the unity of men."

Sentimental Politics, Sentimental Religion

Sentimentalism is essentially liberal, predicated on the idea that human beings are born free and are endowed with the capacities to make decisions for themselves. Such philosophy from the outset defied not only the absolute monarchy of the Stuarts, but also the antithetical theocracy espoused by the Puritans who took over the reigns of British government during the Interregnum in the middle of the seventeenth century. Not surprisingly, sentimentalism remained true to this history when imported to the colonies, and by the time the United States was born, just about every religious or political reform movement drew on sentimental philosophy for justification and turned to sentimental art for rhetorical support. Certainly the pre-Civil War anti-slavery movement drew on sentimental tropes, arguing from sympathy that slavery dehumanizes fellow human beings, and arguing from the liberal point of view that slavery is incompatible with free will. At the same time, Calvinism came under attack in the United States in part because the doctrine of predestination violated a liberal sense of human dignity; without free choice to earn redemption, Christianity seemed crabbed and dogmatic. A more expansive sense of human choice militated for a sentimental version of Christianity, one in which Christian nurture provided a framework for moral freedom. Not surprisingly, then, most political crusades of the late nineteenth century were also religious crusades, at first working to undercut the harshness of Calvinism, then later using the successful battle against Calvinism to attack the new political conservatism and determinism of the Social Darwinists.

Consider, for example, Mary E. Wilkins Freeman's "A Conflict Ended" (1886). The action of the story is set in a town riven by an old-style doctrinal dispute between Calvinists and Arminians. Freeman assumes her audience will know the history of Christianity over the preceding 50 years. Her readers would understand that the older Calvinist orthodoxy that had had its last moment of glory in the 1830s believed that human fate was determined, that grace was given by God, not earned by men, and that good works were no more than a duty of obedience, not a road to salvation. Her readers would know that liberal Christianity substantially replaced Calvinism over the 1840s through 1860s, stressing free will over destiny, works over faith. On the one hand, this was a movement centered on domesticity, made up mostly of women, who turned to such books as the strange novel-*cum*-religious-treatise *The Gates Ajar* (1868), by Elizabeth Stuart Phelps, to satisfy their grief over the deaths of husbands and sons in the Civil War. Traditional Calvinism offered little solace, whereas Phelps's story, based substantially on Bishop Joseph Butler's *Analogy of Religion* (1750), offered a vision of a God who invited everyone to a heaven substantially like the earth they knew, and where all parted lovers, friends, and kin would be reunited. On the other hand, this was a political movement, led by such men as Joseph Cook, one of the founders of the social gospel, who saw Christianity as valid only if it was actively involved in stabilizing the political world, in part by mitigating the extremes of poverty. He called upon the wealthy and powerful to sympathize with the needy and weak.

While liberal Christianity was effective in diminishing the importance of fundamentalist religion, it was much less influential in the face of increasing economic disparities. In the 1880s and 1890s Social Darwinism advocated a new kind of determinism, a determinism of natural ability in which any intervention on behalf of the poor or weak would weaken the race. Naturalists like William Graham Sumner held sentiment to be an illusion, sympathy to be weakness, and competition to be a refining fire in which greatness would remain after the dross was driven off. As Richard Hofstadter puts it, Sumner

> tried to convince men that confidence in their ability to will and plan their destinies was unwarranted by history or biology or any of the facts of experience – that the best they could do was to bow to natural forces. Like some latter-day Calvin, he came to preach the predestination of the social order and the salvation of the economically elect through the survival of the fittest. (Hofstadter 1959: 66–7)

While some proponents of this kind of determinism were consistently naturalistic and rejected religion, others compartmentalized nicely, accepting Calvinist determinism as the other-worldly articulation of a naturalistic order on earth.

Freeman's "A Conflict Ended" draws an analogy between the conflict over Calvinism and the conflict over naturalism. She shows competition to be a dead end, and sympathy to be a power far superior to self-interest. In fact, it is Marcus Woodman's overweening pride, coupled with Esther Barney's hypersensitivity to her own, rather than to others', needs, that creates the story's central conflict. Not until the two work to satisfy each other do their lives become productive, fruitful, and happy. In this conclusion, Freeman suggests that naturalism is Calvinism revived, and that the appropriate answer to such a cold, hard, and fruitless philosophy is the same as it was to Calvinism proper.

In a similar vein, but with an explicitly pointed political agenda, is Charles Chesnutt's collection of stories *The Wife of His Youth and Other Stories of the Color Line* (1899). Within the collection are stories that are clearly sentimental, such as "Her Virginia Mammy," in which a girl's mother disowns her kinship with her daughter not only so that the girl can pass as white, but so that the girl never knows that her mother is black. This sacrifice is very much in the tradition of sentimental tales, but Chesnutt gives it two twists. For one, he makes it clear that the girl's fiancé can see the kinship that the girl cannot. Since it makes no difference to her fiancé, Chesnutt brings up his second twist – namely, that the girl's interest in her ancestry is in keeping with a racist Social Darwinism that would cause her fall from society.

The next story in the collection, "The Sheriff's Children," is a naturalistic tale in which a young man's destiny is absolutely determined by his station and race, but again the twist is that his white half-sister feels enough sympathy to make an effort to transcend determinism. After several more tales that blur the idea of a color line into an absurdity, the book ends once again with a counterpoint between an explicitly sentimental tale and an explicitly deterministic one. In "The Bouquet," a patrician white woman in a Southern town becomes a teacher in a school for black children. One of her charges dotes on her, so much so that when the teacher dies, the child insists on attending the funeral and wants to leave a bouquet on the grave. She cannot, because blacks are not allowed in the cemetery. Ironically, she can read the prohibition: "Sophy, thanks to Miss Myrover's painstaking instruction, could read this sign distinctly." But the dead teacher has a white dog that lies mourning at the grave site. Sophy calls the dog to her so that the dog can take the bouquet to the grave.

Excepting some sly, deliciously ironic counterpoint, this story has the heavy hand that earned sentimentalism its bad name. But the appearance immediately after it in the collection of the relentlessly naturalistic "The Web of Circumstance" makes it clear that Chesnutt is playing with styles as exempla of world-views. The run of the stories shows that he sees the sentimental formula in its pure form as naïve, but the last paragraph of "The Web of Circumstance" bespeaks a deeper, religious connection to sentimentalism:

> Some time, we are told, when the cycle of years has rolled around, there is to be another golden age, when all men will dwell together in love and harmony, and when peace and righteousness shall prevail for a thousand years. God speed the day, and let not the shining thread of hope become so enmeshed in the web of circumstance that we lose sight of it; but give us here and there, and now and then, some little foretaste of this

golden age, that we may the more patiently and hopefully await its coming! (Chesnutt 1968: 322–3)

While the rhetoric here is consonant with a Calvinist, though not a naturalistic, determinism, the twin emphases on love and hope recall the transcendent spiritual gifts promised in 1 Corinthians 13. These gifts, with the emphasis on love, were the passages to which liberal Christians often turned when arguing for the importance of a socially active form of religion. In this, Chesnutt gives his book's last word to a tradition that combines political activism in service of freedom with a hope for a millennium on earth. The hope for progress in human terms, seeing the earth as analogous to the divine, and the possibility of significant improvement on the path to salvation, was very much a part of the sentimentalist agenda; in closing his book with a fear of determinism and a plea for something else, Chesnutt expresses his affinities for a sentimental approach to politics.

Social Class

Of course, much of what Chesnutt addresses is the artificial social class distinction of race as marked by skin color; but his stories are equally alive to social class hierarchies within race. In the comic story "A Matter of Principle" (1899), Chesnutt shows a social class hierarchy that is articulated along the lines of color, but also along lines of wealth and deportment. The story begins with an ironic statement of principle: "'What our country needs most in its treatment of the race problem,' observed Mr. Cicero Clayton at one of the monthly meetings of the Blue Vein Society, of which he was a prominent member, 'is a clearer conception of the brotherhood of man.'" Clayton violates his fundamental principle ruthlessly, and ends up damaging his own interests with his hypocrisy. In relating this tale, Chesnutt supports the fundamental hope of sentimentalists that we are all created morally equal. As such, much sentimental literature explicitly reaches across class lines to extend sympathy to those in the bottom strata of society. As I mentioned above, sentimental interest in the lower social orders encouraged writers to explore the possibility of dialect speech as a form of art. But sentimentalism also provided a clear standard by which to judge social class hierarchies. Inasmuch as sentimentalism encouraged the development of refined taste not as a class exercise but rather as a moral exercise, sentimentalism encouraged slumming only to rescue the lower orders from the debilitating coarseness of their surroundings. Chesnutt's Blue Vein Society merely takes this agenda a step further, looking up to whiteness and to the refined habits of upper-class whites, while rejecting blackness as intrinsically lower class. Chesnutt portrays a group grotesquely mimicking upper-class white society, in which wealth is the first marker of status, but the origins of wealth in any kind of physical labor need to be hidden, and the embellishments of education provide the cover. Under these circumstances, as Chesnutt makes clear, the sympathetic inclinations of sentimentalism are often mere ornament, a part of the educated veneer that hides snobbery and money.

Edward Bellamy's *Looking Backward* (1888) makes much the same point regarding social class among whites. He divides society into "four classes, or nations, as they may be more fitly called, since the differences between them were far greater than those between any nations nowadays, of the rich and the poor, the educated and the ignorant." As the ensuing discussion makes clear, these classes often overlapped, but with the wealthy educated in particular exercising sympathy for those below them, and the ignorant wealthy merely despising them. In either case, however, "it was firmly and sincerely believed that there was no other way in which Society could get along." As the story unfolds, showing the new socialist utopia that would replace a class-based capitalism, Bellamy reveals his sentimentalist roots. His world is one in which all members of society engage in a portion of necessary work, but spend the bulk of their time cultivating their sensibilities. They all speak a rarefied high style; they all show delicate sensibility; they all show compassion developed into a political outlook. Bellamy's socialism is the logical extreme of sympathy as a fundamental principle, but his stylistic elegance shows the snobbery that says equality can be valuable only when the classes are leveled up. Precisely because Bellamy did not reject the stylistic elegance conventional to antebellum sentimentalists, he is easier to identify as a sentimentalist.

But it is important to remember that America's discovery of the artistic quality of the vernacular depended upon a sentimental interest in the lower classes. Those sentimentalists whose sympathies enabled them to embrace the poor or the powerless often found themselves entranced by the style of the uneducated. Nearly all of the writers I have mentioned so far used dialect writing to some degree in their works. Some, like Stowe and Jewett, distanced themselves from their dialect speakers through a refined narrator; others, like Twain, worked through the frame narrative to first-person dialect stories. *Adventures of Huckleberry Finn* is, among other things, a masterpiece of dialect, and it is arguable that Twain embraced the dialect in part because he had spent a career arguing with sentimentalist aesthetics and ethics.

Childhood and Domesticity

Locke's conception of the mind revolutionized child-rearing and family organization. If the mind is a blank slate at birth, it need not be controlled to restrict the power of original sin, but it must be protected and nurtured to keep it from pernicious influences and to develop beneficial ones. This concern dovetailed neatly with the liberal focus on amiable relationships rather than hierarchical status as the grounds of social organization. In fact, by the middle of the *eighteenth* century, moral philosophers were arguing that men had no right to rule over their families. As Francis Hutcheson put it in his influential *Moral Philosophy* (1755):

The tender sentiments and affections which engage the parties into this relation of marriage, plainly declare it to be a state of equal partnership or friendship, and not such a one wherein the one party stipulates to himself a right of governing in all domestick affairs, and the other promises subjection. Grant that there were generally superior strength both of body and mind in the males, this does not give any perfect right of government in any society. It could at best only oblige the other party to pay a greater respect or honour to the superior abilities. And this superiority of the males in the endowments of mind does not at all hold universally. If the males more generally excel in fortitude, or strength of genius; there are other as amiable dispositions in which they are as generally surpassed by the females. The truth is, nature shews no foundation for any proper jurisdiction or right of commanding in this relation; and, previous to some positive laws and customs, there is no presumption that the parties would stipulate about any. Where positive laws and customs have long obtained, and settled forms of contracting are received, no doubt there is an external right of superiority constituted to the husbands. But this shadow of right is no better than those which any insolent conqueror may extort from the vanquished; or any unjust sharper may obtain by some imperfection or iniquity of civil laws; or by the weakness, or ignorance, or inadvertence of one he is contracting with. To take advantage of such laws or forms, without regard to equity and humanity, must be entirely inconsistent with an honest character. . . . Domestic matters indeed seem to be divided into two provinces, one fitted for the management of each sex, in which the other should seldom interfere, except by advising. (Hutcheson 1755: bk III, ch. 1, sec. VII, 163–5)

As Hutcheson here describes it, families should be built on love, not power, but should be arranged according to the "dispositions" that predominate in each sex. Hence, he created the moral justification for a new kind of family arrangement, one that was not on the face of it hierarchical; but in establishing separate spheres for male and female activity, sentimental domesticity usually constrained women more than it did men.

These ideas helped justify – and the industrial revolution made economically possible – a radical reorganization of family life in the English-speaking world, with the shift in America taking place substantially between 1800 and 1860. As part of this change, the idea of separate spheres developed, with women being primarily responsible for domesticity and child-rearing and men primarily responsible for work outside the home. Even though this model rarely fully represented the way people in fact acted, it nonetheless had a powerful shaping influence on literature.

One of the most important impacts it had was in the development of a robust children's literature. Until about the 1830s, children were taught to read in primers, but beyond that there were no books graded to their abilities or to their ostensible intellectual and moral needs. With the development of McGuffy's readers, beginning in 1836, that changed. By the end of the Civil War, some of the bestselling books were targeted toward children. Eventually, children's magazines, like *St. Nicholas*, established in 1873 and edited by Mary Mapes Dodge (author of *Hans Brinker; or, The Silver Skates*, 1865), were among the more lucrative and influential literary markets.

St. Nicholas published work by Mark Twain, Rebecca Harding Davis, Louisa May Alcott, Frances Hodgson Burnett, Robert Louis Stevenson, Rudyard Kipling, William Dean Howells, and other stars of the postbellum period. It also published fiction by juvenile writers, many of whom – for example, Edna St. Vincent Millay, William Faulkner, F. Scott Fitzgerald, and E. B. White – were among the stars of the next literary generation.

The key to children's literature in the postwar period was the sentimental agenda of using fiction to inculcate moral values, much as Stowe suggested it should in *The Minister's Wooing*. The idea was to create situations of sufficient realism and excitement to attract the interest of young readers, but to show the readers situations of sufficient moral clarity that they would be able to learn, through sympathy with the characters, right from wrong. This was as true of the Horatio Alger stories and other formula fiction as it was of much better children's literature.

Louisa May Alcott was perhaps the most influential writer of children's fiction in the period. Her father, the eccentric educational reformer Bronson Alcott, advocated treating children according to their capacities through conversation, rather than through rote drilling, and his method of discipline was not to beat a child for transgressions, but instead to impress upon children how their ill behavior in fact causes psychological pain to others. As a system of inculcating intense sympathy and guilt, Alcott's was without parallel; not surprisingly, his daughter grew up with an intense sense of moral rectitude based on sympathy. At the same time, Bronson Alcott was economically incompetent; Louisa became the household breadwinner. First by taking on the editorship of a children's magazine, *Merry's Museum*, in 1867, and then in publishing *Little Women* over the following two years, Louisa May Alcott secured the fortune that had eluded her famous father.

Little Women (1868–9) serves as a fine exemplum of the genre of sentimental children's literature. On the one hand, the story tells how four girls grow into respectable womanhood, substantially by sublimating personal desires into other-regardingness. The novel's emphasis on propriety very much fits the stereotype of sentimental literature. It differs, however, in showing that propriety is hard-won. The character Jo, in particular, with whom most readers are expected to identify, finds the constraints of feminine roles galling. On the other hand, since much of the novel takes place with the father absent and all of it takes place in the context of the father's financial incompetence, the feminist implications of the novel lurk barely beneath the surface. Many critics now argue that the novel poses a significant challenge to the idea that women should be relegated to a separate sphere or that marriage should be the primary goal for women; instead, in Jo's rebelliousness and interest in the world outside the home, the novel argues that women should not only be considered the equals of men, but also be accorded the same freedoms. This paradox of propriety versus freedom, so central to most literature written by women in the late nineteenth century, is analogous to the sentimental paradox with respect to class – the liberal implications of the philosophy are in direct conflict with the impulse toward propriety and order.

Nostalgia

The tension between individual freedom and social coherence was not ignored by sentimentalists; indeed, sentimental philosophy developed to articulate ways to mediate this tension. The cultivation in childhood of tender sentiments was supposed to make a person's moral sense congruent with his sense of individual desires: that is, a child raised correctly should never desire to do ill. The world, however, in its tendency to blunt the higher sensibilities, would dim a person's memory of childhood if it were not for a regularly cultivated nostalgia.

The culture that could pine cheerily for "Home, Sweet Home," in the days before the war, certainly did not invent nostalgia after 1865; but the losses of the war itself deepened the literary trade in nostalgia. The tone was set, perhaps, by one of John Greenleaf Whittier's most influential poems, "Snow-Bound: A Winter Idyll" (1866). Coming immediately on the heels of the war, this poem by one of the most influential abolitionists spoke to a desire to live in a simpler moral universe. The emotional brilliance of the poem is to suggest, in fact, that abolition, the progressive consequence of the war, was in fact a return to the ideals and hopes of a plain New England childhood.

Deeply sentimental, this poem is in part a reply to the idealistic remoteness of Emerson's "The Snow-Storm" (1847). Whittier's response to Emerson shifts the focus from the antic power of nature outdoors to the community around the hearth indoors. Moral patterns, he suggests, are built in community and learned in childhood, and retain their intensity only insofar as adults stoke the fires of memory. He argues against a dispassionate and transcendent idea of morality or salvation, and makes a plea to honor the dead, not only those with whom we agreed but also those whose lives were troublesome and challenging to the status quo. In this plea, he seems to be rejecting not only transcendental idealism, with its contempt for weakness and error, but also a punitive reaction to the war itself. The poem refers directly to the war only once, but its popularity probably arose out of an exhausted nation's sense that turning backward was necessary for the nation to heal.

As the wounds of the war faded from memory, the impulse toward nostalgia did not slacken. Indeed, as Lincoln put it in his second inaugural address (1865), everybody expected "a result less fundamental and astounding," and the most fundamental and astounding aspect of the Civil War was industrialization. Industrialization in America had begun before 1861, but the war quickened its pace and encouraged concentration of power in various industries, changing the nation's economy forever. These economic conditions no doubt encouraged the nostalgia of local color. But the agenda of sentimental moral philosophy helps explain the persistence of a backward focus in a culture that relentlessly pushed progress, and also the continuing importance of domesticity in a highly mobile culture that put increasing pressure on families.

Not surprisingly, the sentimental tradition itself spawned a counter-literature that mocked the most utopian versions of the harmonious sentimental family. And, also not surprisingly, given that most sentimental children's literature was focused on the role of mothers and, to a lesser extent, daughters as moral paragons, that counter-literature tended to focus on male children. Thomas Bailey Aldrich's *The Story of a Bad Boy* (1870) makes the point explicitly in the title; but, that title notwithstanding, this is not the tale of a picaro. It is in fact a remarkably conventional story of a sentimental education, written nostalgically and implying that, while boys may not fit the sentimental stereotypes, they still evolve from childhood to be morally acceptable adults. Aldrich may have challenged the extremes of sentimental children's literature, but his ultimate conclusions, as well as his presentation, are fully in the sentimental tradition.

This is equally, though less obviously, true of Mark Twain's *The Adventures of Tom Sawyer* (1876). Described by an erudite and sophisticated adult narrator, Tom defies some of the characteristics of the stereotypical sentimental child. He is self-centered; he is usually unable to sympathize with others; he is willing to lie and cheat to serve his pleasures. But the story does show a significant moral growth *through* play. Eventually, Tom even demonstrates altruism in taking care of threatened femininity, both when he rescues Becky Thatcher from punishment for tearing her teacher's anatomy book, and later when he rescues her from the cave. Once again, we see the sentimental formula of childhood experiences inculcating moral improvement through a pursuit of pleasure, through "human affections, tender instincts, symbolic feelings, sacraments of love." Twain may challenge crude articulations of the sentimental agenda, but he does not challenge sentimentalism at its core.

Humor

The adjective "sentimental" now includes the idea of seriousness (though many modern readers find sentimental literature unintentionally funny). Again, this vision of sentimentalism is far too narrow. The very term "sense of humor" arose from sentimental moral philosophy, and it was sentimentalists who encouraged humor's value in the face of a deep history of disparaging laughter. In the classical tradition laughter was considered a form of aggression, and it was held suitable only to low-style occasions. In the Christian tradition it was considered worldly, working in opposition to the divine seriousness of redemption through pain and sacrifice. But sentimentalists argued that it was but one in a collection of sensibilities, and, like all sensibilities, could be cultivated to serve moral uplift.

In particular, the idea of amiable humor as a social bond capable of reaching across distinctions of class, gender, race, and nationality was a fundamental part of sentimental liberalism. The humorist was one who saw the incongruities of the world and encouraged us to celebrate them as part of the world's richness. This is a far cry from the classical tradition that scorn was designed to encourage conformity. Granted, the idea of satire as coercion never left the American literary scene, and granted, too, amiable humor could often be used as a mask for satire; yet the very idea of amiable humor as a healthy release of tension and as a bridge between people encouraged its use in a culture that had long been suspicious of humor. It is entirely plausible to argue that the flowering of American humor that budded in the years before the Civil War and that blossomed in the years after is substantially a product of sentimentalism.

Such a thesis again defies conventional literary history. According to two of the earliest and most influential critics of American humor, Constance Rourke and Walter Blair, American humor is a unique expression of the American character precisely because it resisted the Europeanized high culture promulgated by the elite classes of the eastern seaboard. The problem with this thesis is that the elite classes of the eastern seaboard were the very people who encouraged, published, and avidly read the humor of the American West, or the humor of American newspapers, a category often considered subliterary in the cultural hierarchies of the nineteenth century.

Consider, for instance, the newspaper columns of Sara Willis Parton, who wrote under the pen-name "Fanny Fern." Her career began in the 1850s and extended to her death in 1872. Many of her newspaper columns are quite conventionally sentimental as we have come to understand the term. She often wrote of angelic babies, sweet-tempered wives, and devoted husbands, all of whom inhabited domestic paradise because they rejected the strictures of Calvinism or the tyranny of the economic system. Other times she wrote satiric diatribes attacking pestilential and obstreperous children, termagant wives and tyrannical husbands. In such a mood she penned the famous saying, "The way to a man's heart is through his stomach." Occupying a middle ground between these two kinds of sketch were a number of humorous accounts of families trying to make domesticity work in spite of difficulties. The solution to difficulties, she repeatedly says, is to laugh in order to allow love to blossom. Her model was well followed — after all, her formula made her the most highly paid newspaper columnist of her day.

It is worth paying attention, then, to how often American humor endorsed sentimental attitudes even as it mocked them. For example, Marietta Holley's vernacular-speaking Samantha Allen is the antithesis of conventional sentimentality. Yet Holley's fiction uses this anti-sentimental comic character as the vehicle by which the author promotes women's rights, children's rights, temperance, marriage for love rather than money, and other causes dear to the hearts of sentimental reformers. Or take Mark Twain's account of Scotty Briggs and the parson in *Roughing It* (1872). Briggs, obviously occupying a far lower social class than the parson with whom he speaks, is a source of humor when his slang is impenetrable to the educated man. Then again, the high-flown and stale tropes used by the minister are equally impenetrable to Briggs. Construed as satire, this sketch could be seen as denigrating the lower classes or as subverting the upper classes. Yet as the sketch develops, the two find a capacity to put aside their differences. After all, both agree that it is a sign of Buck Fanshaw's virtue that he never, as Briggs puts it, "shook his mother." Having once found common ground, they work together to evangelize among the working class. As readers, we are to laugh at both, or rather laugh at the incongruities of their shared situation, and in the laughter to see a way out. Ultimately, the sketch embraces difference rather than arguing for the superiority of either position. In this respect, Twain very much worked out of the tradition of sentimental liberalism.

Of course, sentimentalism ultimately waned, both as a philosophy and as a common literary mode. Just as naturalism trumped sentimentalism in defining realism, so, too, it crowded out humor. By century's end and into the early twentieth century, naturalist definitions of laughter were once again being articulated, with theorists like Sigmund Freud and Henri Bergson essentially returning to the classical tradition in defining laughter exclusively in terms of aggression. Some writers tried to defend sentimental humor. Mary Wilkins Freeman's "A Conflict Ended" suggests something of the danger of an interpretation of humor as aggression in showing that Esther Barney's sensitivity to ridicule leads her into rigidity. And at tale's end, when the church audience doesn't know whether to laugh or cry, Freeman argues for the value of a sentimental version of laughter, one that can see the comedy as well as the pathos of human behavior. Similarly, her "A Poetess" (1890) argues that sentimental expression, though it may not be dignified, though it may even be comic, is nonetheless emotionally valuable. She encourages us to lay dignity aside and indulge pathos even if our sophistication judges it as bathetic. But Freeman was fighting a rearguard action by the 1890s. Styles and tastes were changing along with philosophy. As Western civilization turned toward racialism and militarism, as it engaged in an imperialistic trophy hunt throughout the world, as its arms race destabilized economies, and as nationalism challenged Enlightenment liberalism, sentimental ideas about sympathy and the innocent morality of childhood seemed naïve. Certainly the violence of the twentieth century seemed to seal the tomb of sentimentalism as a serious intellectual and artistic force.

But perhaps the fate of sentimentalism was built into its own philosophy. By requiring readers to focus on nostalgia, it left them no place to go. By focusing on the nuclear family, it put too much stress on primary relationships. And inasmuch as sentimentalism encouraged a purification of reality, it did not seem up to the task of describing the complexities of the modern world. Moreover, as a compromise philosophy, it constantly veered between one extreme and the other. Consider again Alcott's *Little Women*. Today's critics argue over the degree to which it expresses feminist ideas, especially in the character of Jo, but it can just as easily be seen as an attempt to turn women's equality as articulated in sentimental ideals into an ornamental alternative that in fact traps women. Both readings are implicit in the scene in which her returning father passes judgment on the Jo who has grown so during his wartime absence:

> "In spite of the curly crop, I don't see the 'son Jo' whom I left a year ago," said Mr. March. "I see a young lady who pins her collar straight, laces her boots neatly, and neither whistles, talks slang, nor lies on the rug, as she used to do. Her face is rather thin and pale, just now, with watching and anxiety; but I like to look at it, for it has grown gentler, and her voice is lower; she doesn't bounce, but moves quietly, and takes care of a

certain little person in a motherly way, which delights me. I rather miss my wild girl; but if I get a strong, helpful, tender-hearted woman in her place, I shall feel quite satisfied. I don't know whether the shearing sobered our black sheep, but I do know that in all Washington I couldn't find anything beautiful enough to be bought with the five-and-twenty dollars which my good girl sent me."

Jo's keen eyes were rather dim for a minute, and her thin face grew rosy in the firelight, as she received her father's praise, feeling that she did deserve a portion of it. (Alcott 2004: 176)

Here the sentimental doctrine that suffering creates a woman who knows her place confines any hint of nonconformity. The progressive potentials of sentimental liberalism are contained, especially when ratified by the self-satisfied tears of a young woman whose former rebellion has caused her much guilt. But the rebellion is merely contained, not gone. It's easy to see how such literature could have captured the imaginations of its young readers, who were struggling with the tension most Americans feel between individualism and community. Still, such articulations, with their resolution directed toward conventionality, dominated the primary literary markets. No wonder that young writers who felt constrained by such propriety tended to mock sentimental forms. Susan Glaspell, for example, who made her early mark through conventional domestic and sentimental stories, moved into a different artistic groove when she left Iowa for a bohemian life in New York City. Her most famous work, *Trifles*, or the non-dramatic version, "A Jury of Her Peers" (1917), uses many sentimental tropes ironically, and finds in a naturalistic subtext a new progressivism.

Yet the idea of sympathy guiding *political* as well as aesthetic or relational judgment remained at the heart of Glaspell's story. In this respect, sentimentalism has never died in American literature, even as it has gone underground through modernist and postmodernist forms. Perhaps in the work of no contemporary writer is this more true than in that of Barbara Kingsolver. The multiple points of view in the structure of, say, *Animal Dreams* (1990) imply the complexity of perspective, motivation, and causation implicit in so much modernist literature. But Kingsolver ultimately rejects the cynical sophistication of modernist thought in favor of a sentimental ending in which domesticity, community, political action, and individual freedom and happiness can be reconciled only by acknowledging feelings, not merely of grief and loss, but of love and joy.

Primary Texts

Alcott, Louisa May. *Little Women*. 1868–9.

Aldrich, Thomas Bailey. *The Story of a Bad Boy*. 1870.

Bellamy, Edward. *Looking Backward: 2000–1887*. 1888.

Chesnutt, Charles. *The Wife of his Youth and Other Stories of the Color Line*. 1899.

Cook, Joseph. *Conscience*. 1879.

Dodge, Mary Mapes. *Hans Brinker; or, The Silver Skates*. 1865.

Emerson, Ralph Waldo. "The Snow-Storm." 1847.

Fern, Fanny [Sara Willis Parton]. *Fern Leaves from Fanny's Port Folio.* 1853.

Fern, Fanny [Sara Willis Parton]. *Fern Leaves, Second Series.* 1854.

Fern, Fanny [Sara Willis Parton]. *Fresh Leaves.* 1857.

Freeman, Mary E. Wilkins. "A Conflict Ended." 1886.

Freeman, Mary E. Wilkins. "A Poetess." 1890.

Glaspell, Susan. "A Jury of Her Peers." 1917.

Harte, Bret. "The Luck of Roaring Camp." 1868.

Holley, Marietta. *My Opinions and Betsey Bobbet's.* 1872.

Holley, Marietta. *Josiah Allen's Wife as a P.A. and P.I.: Samantha at the Centennial.* 1878.

Holley, Marietta. *Poems, by Josiah Allen's Wife.* 1887.

Howells, William Dean. *Criticism and Fiction.* 1891.

Jewett, Sarah Orne. "A White Heron." 1886.

Jewett, Sarah Orne. *The Country of the Pointed Firs.* 1896.

Lincoln, Abraham. "Second Inaugural Address." 1865.

Phelps, Elizabeth Stuart. *The Gates Ajar.* 1868.

Stowe, Harriet Beecher. *The Minister's Wooing.* 1859.

Stowe, Harriet Beecher. *Uncle Tom's Cabin; or, Life among the Lowly.* 1852.

Stowe, Harriet Beecher. *Sam Lawson's Oldtown Fireside Stories.* 1872.

Twain, Mark. *Roughing It.* 1872.

Twain, Mark. *The Adventures of Tom Sawyer.* 1876.

Twain, Mark. *Adventures of Huckleberry Finn.* 1884.

Twain, Mark. *A Connecticut Yankee in King Arthur's Court.* 1889.

Twain, Mark. "The Californian's Tale." 1893.

Whittier, John Greenleaf. "Snow-Bound: A Winter Idyll." 1866.

REFERENCES AND FURTHER READING

Alcott, Louisa May (2004). *Little Women.* New York: Norton (Norton Critical Edition).

Alison, Archibald (1825). *Essays on the Nature and Principles of Taste,* rev. edn., 2 vols. Edinburgh: Archibald Constable and Co. (First publ. 1810.)

Atteberry, Phillip D. (1985). "Ellen Glasgow and the Sentimental Novel of Virginia." *Southern Quarterly* 23, 5–14.

Bader, Julia (1982). "The Dissolving Vision: Realism in Jewett, Freeman, and Gilman." In Eric J. Sundquist (ed.), *American Realism: New Essays,* 176–98. Baltimore: Johns Hopkins University Press.

Barnstone, Aliki (1984). "Houses within Houses: Emily Dickinson and Mary Wilkins Freeman's 'A New England Nun.'" *Centennial Review* 28: 2, 129–45.

Baym, Nina (1978). *Woman's Fiction: A Guide to Novels by and about Women in America, 1820–1870.* Ithaca, NY: Cornell University Press.

Bellamy, Edward (1888). *Looking Backward: 2000–1887.* Boston: Ticknor.

Bergson, Henri (1911). *Laughter: An Essay on the Meaning of the Comic,* trans. Cloudesley Brereton and Fred Rothwell. New York: Macmillan.

Berlant, Lauren (1992). "The Female Woman: Fanny Fern and the Form of Sentiment." In Shirley Samuels (ed.), *The Culture of Sentiment: Race, Gender, and Sentimentality in Nineteenth-Century America,* 265–81. New York: Oxford University Press.

Blair, Walter (1942). *Horse Sense in American Humor.* Chicago: University of Chicago Press.

Blair, Walter (1993). "Introduction to *The Sweet Singer of Michigan: The Collected Poems of Julia A. Moore*" (first publ. 1928). In W. Blair and H. Hill (eds.), *Essays on American Humor,* 104–13. Madison: University of Wisconsin Press, 1993.

Brand, Alice Glarden (1977). "Mary Wilkins Freeman: Misanthropy as Propaganda." *New England Quarterly* 50, 83–100.

Brown, Gillian (1990). *Domestic Individualism: Imagining Self in Nineteenth-Century America.* Berkeley: University of California Press.

Brown, Herbert Ross (1940). *The Sentimental Novel in America, 1789–1860.* Durham, NC: Duke University Press.

Butler, Bishop Joseph (1750). *The Analogy of Religion, Natural and Revealed, To the Constitution of Nature,* 4th edn. London: John & Paul Knapton.

Camfield, Gregg (1988). "The Moral Aesthetics of Sentimentality: A Missing Key to *Uncle Tom's Cabin*." *Nineteenth-Century Literature* 43, 319–45.

Camfield, Gregg (1991). "Sentimental Liberalism and the Problem of Race in *Huckleberry Finn*." *Nineteenth-Century Literature* 46, 96–113.

Camfield, Gregg (1992). "'I Wouldn't Be as Ignorant as You for Wages': Huck Talks Back to his Conscience." *Studies in American Fiction* 21, 169–72.

Camfield, Gregg (1994). *Sentimental Twain: Samuel Clemens in the Maze of Moral Philosophy*. Philadelphia: University of Pennsylvania Press.

Camfield, Gregg (1997). *Necessary Madness: The Humor of Domesticity in Nineteenth-Century Literature*. New York: Oxford University Press.

Camfield, Gregg (1999). "'I Never Saw Anything at Once so Pathetic and Funny': Humor in the Stories of Mary Wilkins Freeman." *American Transcendental Quarterly* n.s., 13: 3, 215–31.

Camfield, Gregg (2002). "Jewett's *Country of the Pointed Firs* as Gossip Manual." *Studies in American Humor* 3, 39–53.

Campbell, Donna M. (1994). "Sentimental Conventions and Self-Protection: *Little Women* and *The Wide, Wide World*." *Legacy* 11, 118–29.

Chapman, Mary, and Hendler, Glenn, eds. (1999). *Sentimental Men: Masculinity and the Politics of Affect in American Culture*. Berkeley: University of California Press.

Chesnutt, Charles W. (1968). *The Wife of his Youth and Other Stories of the Color Line*. Ann Arbor: University of Michigan Press.

Church, Joseph (1990). "Reconstructing Woman's Place in Freeman's 'The Revolt of "Mother."'" *Colby Quarterly* 26, 195–200.

Crane, Gregg D. (1996). "Dangerous Sentiments: Sympathy, Rights, and Revolution in Stowe's Antislavery Novels." *Nineteenth-Century Literature* 51, 176–204.

Cutter, Martha J. (1990). "Mary E. Wilkins Freeman's Two New England Nuns." *Colby Quarterly* 26, 213–25.

Cutter, Martha J. (1991). "Frontiers of Language: Engendering Discourse in 'The Revolt of "Mother."'" *American Literature* 63, 279–91.

Davidson, Cathy N., and Hatcher, Jessamyn, eds. (2002). *No More Separate Spheres! A Next Wave American Studies Reader*. Durham, NC: Duke University Press.

Dobson, Joanne (1997). "Reclaiming Sentimental Literature." *American Literature* 69, 263–88.

Donovan, Josephine (1983). "Rose Terry Cooke: Impoverished Wives and Spirited Spinsters." In *New England Local Color Literature: A Women's Tradition*. New York: Ungar.

Donovan, Josephine (1986). "Silence or Capitulation: Prepatriarchal 'Mothers' Gardens' in Jewett and Freeman." *Studies in Short Fiction* 23, 43–8.

Donovan, Josephine (1993). "Jewett and Swedenborg." *American Literature* 65, 731–5.

Douglas, Ann (1977). *The Feminization of American Culture*. New York: Knopf.

Farland, Maria Magdalena (1998). "'That Tritest/ Brightest Truth': Emily Dickinson's Anti-Sentimentality." *Nineteenth-Century Literature* 53, 364–89.

Fast, Robin Riley (1981). "'The One Thing Needful': Dickinson's Dilemma of Home and Heaven." *ESQ* 27, 157–69.

Fienberg, Lorne (1989). "Mary E. Wilkins Freeman's 'Soft Diurnal Commotion': Women's Work and Strategies of Containment." *New England Quarterly* 62: 4, 483–504.

Freud, Sigmund (1963). *Jokes and their Relation to the Unconscious* (first publ. 1905), trans. James Strachey. New York: Norton.

Freud, Sigmund (1987). "Humor" (first publ. 1928). In John Morreall (ed.), *The Philosophy of Laughter and Humor*, 111–16. Albany, NY: State University of New York Press.

Gardner, Kate (1992). "The Subversion of Genre in the Short Stories of Mary Wilkins Freeman." *New England Quarterly* 65: 3, 447–68.

Glasser, Leah Blatt (1984). "Mary E. Wilkins Freeman: The Stranger in the Mirror." *Massachusetts Review* 25: 2, 323–39.

Glasser, Leah Blatt (1987). "Legacy Profile: Mary E. Wilkins Freeman (1852–1930)." *Legacy: A Journal of Nineteenth-Century American Women Writers* 4: 1, 37–45.

Goshgarian, G. M. (1992). *To Kiss the Chastening Rod: Domestic Fiction and Sexual Ideology in the American Renaissance*. Ithaca, NY: Cornell University Press.

Graulich, Melody (1980). "'Women is my theme, and also Josiah': The Forgotten Humor of Marietta Holley." *American Transcendental Quarterly* 47–8, 187–98.

Gwathmey, Gwendolyn B. (1994). "'Who will read the book, Samantha?' Marietta Holley and the Nineteenth-Century Reading Public." *Studies in American Humor* n.s., 3: 28–50.

Haralson, Eric L. (1996). "Mars in Petticoats: Longfellow and Sentimental Masculinity." *Nineteenth-Century Literature* 51, 327–55.

Harker, Jaime (2001). "'Pious Cant' and Blasphemy: Fanny Fern's Radicalized Sentiment." *Legacy: A Journal of Nineteenth-Century American Women Writers* 18, 52–64.

Harris, Susan K. (1988). "Inscribing and Defining: The Many Voices of Fanny Fern's Ruth Hall." *Style* 22: 4, 612–27.

Harris, Susan K. (1991). "'But Is It Any Good?': Evaluating Nineteenth-Century American Women's Fiction." *American Literature* 63, 43–61.

Hartman, Matthew (1999). "Utopian Evolution: The Sentimental Critique of Social Darwinism in Bellamy and Pierce." *Utopian Studies* 10, 26–41.

Hedrick, Joan D. (1994). *Harriet Beecher Stowe: A Life*. New York: Oxford University Press.

Hendler, Glenn (1999). "The Structure of Sentimental Experience: Further Responses to Marianne Noble on Stowe, Sentiment, and Masochism." *Yale Journal of Criticism* 12, 145–67.

Hendler, Glenn (2001). *Public Sentiments: Structures of Feeling in Nineteenth-Century American Literature*. Chapel Hill: University of North Carolina Press.

Hirsch, David H. (1965). "Subdued Meaning in 'A New England Nun.'" *Studies in Short Fiction* 2, 124–36.

Hobbes, Thomas (1651). *Leviathan, or, The Matter, Form, and Power of a Common-wealth Ecclesiastical and Civil*. London: Andrew Crooke.

Hoeller, Hildegard (2000). *Edith Wharton's Dialogue with Realism and Sentimental Fiction*. Gainesville: University Press of Florida.

Hofstadter, Richard (1959). *Social Darwinism in American Thought*, rev. edn. New York: George Brazillier.

Howard, June (2001). *Publishing The Family*. Durham, NC: Duke University Press.

Howells, William Dean, and Twain, Mark (1960). *Mark Twain–Howells Letters*, ed. Henry Nash Smith and William Gibson. Cambridge. Mass.: Belknap/Harvard University Press.

Huf, Linda (1983). "Ruth Hall (1855): The Devil and Fanny Fern." In *A Portrait of the Artist as a Young Woman*. New York: Ungar.

Hutcheson, Francis (1755). *A System of Moral Philosophy*. Glasgow: R. and A. Foulis.

Hutcheson, Francis (1987). "Reflections on Laughter" (first publ. 1750). In John Morreall (ed.), *The Philosophy of Laughter and Humor*, 26–40. Albany, NY: State University of New York Press.

Jewett, Sarah Orne (1981). *The Country of the Pointed Firs*. New York: Norton.

Johnson, Wendy Dasler (1999). "Male Sentimentalists through the 'I-s' of Julia Ward Howe's Poetry." *South Atlantic Review* 64, 16–35.

Kelley, Mary (1978). "At War With Herself: Harriet Beecher Stowe as Woman in Conflict within the Home." *American Studies* 19: 2, 23–40.

Kelley, Mary (1984). *Private Woman, Public Stage: Literary Domesticity in Nineteenth-Century America*. New York: Oxford University Press.

Kete, Mary Louise (2000). *Sentimental Collaborations: Mourning and Middle-Class Identity in Nineteenth-Century America*. Durham, NC: Duke University Press.

Kingsolver, Barbara (1990). *Animal Dreams*. New York: HarperCollins.

Koppelman, Susan (1988). "About 'Two Friends' and Mary Eleanor Wilkins Freeman." *American Literary Realism* 21, 43–57.

Lasch, Christopher (1977). *Haven in a Heartless World: The Family Besieged*. New York: Basic Books.

Linkton, Sherry Lee (1993). "Saints, Sufferers, and 'Strong-Minded Sisters': Anti-suffrage Rhetoric in Rose Terry Cooke's Fiction." *Legacy: A Journal of Nineteenth-Century American Women Writers* 10, 31–46.

Locke, John (1690). *An Essay Concerning Human Understanding*. London: Eliz. Holt.

Lystra, Karen (1989). *Searching the Heart: Women, Men, and Romantic Love in Nineteenth-Century America*. New York: Oxford University Press.

Maik, Thomas A. (1990). "Dissent and Affirmation: Conflicting Voices of Female Roles in Selected Stories by Mary Wilkins Freeman." *Colby Quarterly* 26: 1, 59–68.

Marchalonis, Shirley, ed. (1991). *Critical Essays on Mary Wilkins Freeman*. Boston: Hall.

Martin, Terence (1969). *The Instructed Vision: Scottish Common Sense Philosophy and the Origins of American Fiction*. New York: Kraus Reprint Co. (First publ. 1961.)

May, Henry F. (1976). "The Didactic Enlightenment." In *The Enlightenment in America*. New York: Oxford University Press.

Meese, Elizabeth (1991). "Signs of Undecidability: Reconsidering the Stories of Mary Wilkins Freeman." In Shirley Marchalonis (ed.), *Critical Essays on Mary Wilkins Freeman*. Boston: Hall.

Morey, Ann Janine (1987). "American Myth and Biblical Interpretation in the Fiction of Harriet Beecher Stowe and Mary E. Wilkins Freeman." *Journal of the American Academy of Religion* 55: 4, 741–63.

Nelson, Dana D. (1999–2000), "'No Cold or Empty Heart': Polygenesis, Scientific Professionalization, and the Unfinished Business of Male Sentimentalism." *Differences* 11, 29–56.

Noble, Marianne (1996). "Dickinson's Sentimental Explorations of 'The Ecstasy of Parting.'" *Emily Dickinson Journal* 5, 280–4.

Noble, Marianne (1998). "An Ecstacy of Apprehension: The Gothic Pleasures of Sentimental Fiction." In Robert Martin and Eric Savoy (eds.), *American Gothic: New Inventions in a National Narrative*. Iowa City: University of Iowa Press.

Noble, Marianne (2000). *The Masochistic Pleasures of Sentimental Literature*. Princeton: Princeton University Press.

Pattee, Fred Lewis (1940). *The Feminine Fifties*. New York: Appleton-Century.

Pennell, Melissa McFarland (1991). "The Liberating Will: Freedom of Choice in the Fiction of Mary Wilkins Freeman." In Shirley Marchalonis (ed.), *Critical Essays on Mary Wilkins Freeman*. Boston: Hall.

Petry, Alice Hall (1984). "Freeman's New England Elegy." *Studies in Short Fiction* 21: 1, 68–70.

Phelps, Elizabeth Stuart (1964). *The Gates Ajar*, ed. Helen Smootin Smith. Cambridge, Mass.: Belknap/Harvard University Press.

Piepmeier, Alison (2001). "'Woman Goes Forth to Battle with Goliath': Mary Baker Eddy, Medical Science, and Sentimental Invalidism." *Women's Studies* 30, 301–28.

Pryse, Marjorie (1981). "Introduction." In Sarah Orne Jewett, *The Country of the Pointed Firs*. New York: Norton.

Pryse, Marjorie (1983). "An Uncloistered 'New England Nun.'" *Studies in Short Fiction* 20: 4, 289–95.

Reichardt, Mary R. (1987). "Mary Wilkins Freeman: One Hundred Years of Criticism." *Legacy: A Journal of Nineteenth-Century American Women Writers* 4: 2, 31–44.

Reichardt, Mary R. (1992). *A Web of Relationship: Women in the Short Stories of Mary Wilkins Freeman*. Jackson: University of Mississippi Press.

Romines, Ann (1992). *The Home Plot: Women, Writing and Domestic Ritual*. Amherst: University of Massachusetts Press.

Ross, Cheri L. (1989). "Nineteenth-Century American Feminist Humor: Marietta Holley's 'Samantha Novels.'" *Journal of the Midwest Modern Language Association* 22: 2, 12–25.

Rourke, Constance (1931). *American Humor: A Study of National Character*. New York: Harcourt, Brace.

St. Armand, Barton Levi (1984). *Emily Dickinson and her Culture: The Soul's Society*. Cambridge, UK: Cambridge University Press.

Samuels, Shirley, ed. (1992). *The Culture of Sentiment: Race, Gender, and Sentimentality in Nineteenth-Century America*. New York: Oxford University Press.

Santayana, George (1967). "The Genteel Tradition in American Philosophy" (first publ. 1911). In Douglas L. Wilson (ed.), *The Genteel Tradition: Nine Essays*, 37–64. Cambridge, Mass.: Harvard University Press.

Selinger, Eric (1991). "Aunts, Uncles, Audience: Gender and Genre in Charles Chesnutt's *The Conjure Woman*." *Black American Literature Forum* 25, 665–88.

Shaftesbury, Anthony Cooper, Third Earl of (1963). *An Inquiry Concerning Virtue or Merit*. In *Characteristicks*. Gloucester, Mass.: Peter Smith. (First publ. 1711.)

Showalter, Elaine (1991). "*Little Women*: The American Female Myth." In *Sister's Choice: Tradition and Change in American Women's Writing*. Oxford: Clarendon.

Smith, Adam (1969). *The Theory of the Moral Sentiments*. New Rochelle, NY: Arlington House. (First publ. 1759.)

Stadler, Gustavus (1999). "Louisa May Alcott's Queer Geniuses." *American Literature* 71, 657–77.

Stevens, J. David. (1997) "'She war a woman': Family Roles, Gender, and Sexuality in Bret Harte's Western Fiction." *American Literature* 69, 571–93.

Stowe, Harriet Beecher (1967). *Oldtown Folks and Sam Lawson's Oldtown Fireside Stories*, 2 vols. New York: AMS Press.

Stowe, Harriet Beecher (1982a). *The Minister's Wooing*. In *Stowe: Three Novels*, ed. Kathryn Kish Sklar, 521–876. New York: Library of America.

Stowe, Harriet Beecher (1982b). *Uncle Tom's Cabin; or, Life among the Lowly*. In *Stowe: Three Novels*, ed. Kathryn Kish Sklar, 1–519. New York: Library of America.

Sumner, William Graham (1972). *What Social Classes Owe to Each Other*. New York: Arno. (First publ. 1883.)

Tave, Stuart M. (1960). *The Amiable Humorist: A Study in the Comic Theory and Criticism of the Eighteenth and Early Nineteenth Centuries*. Chicago: University of Chicago Press.

Tompkins, Jane P. (1985). "Sentimental Power: *Uncle Tom's Cabin* and Politics of Literary History." In *Sensational Designs: The Cultural Work of American Fiction, 1790–1860*. New York: Oxford University Press.

Toth, Susan A. (1985). "'The Rarest and Most Peculiar Grape': Versions of the New England Woman in Nineteenth-Century Local Color Literature." In Emily Toth (ed.), *Regionalism and the Female Imagination: A Collection of Essays*. New York: Human Sciences.

Traister, Bryce (1999). "Sentimental Medicine: Oliver Wendell Holmes and the Construction of Masculinity." *Studies in American Fiction* 27, 205–27.

Walker, Nancy A. (1993). *Fanny Fern*. New York: Twayne.

Warner, Charles Dudley (1883). "Modern Fiction." *Atlantic Monthly* 51 (April).

Warren, Joyce W. (1992). *Fanny Fern: An Independent Woman*. New Brunswick, NJ: Rutgers University Press.

Welter, Barbara (1976). *Dimity Convictions*. Athens: Ohio State University Press.

Westbrook, Perry D. (1988). *Mary Wilkins Freeman*. Boston: Twayne.

Wild, Peter (1996). "Sentimentalism in the American Southwest: John C. Van Dyke, Mary Austin, and Edward Abbey." In Michael Kowalewski (ed.), *Reading the West: New Essays on the Literature of the American West*. Cambridge, UK: Cambridge University Press.

Winter, Kate H. (1984). *Marietta Holley: Life with "Josiah Allen's Wife."* Syracuse, NY: Syracuse University Press.

Wood, Ann Douglas (1972). "The Literature of Impoverishment: The Women Local Colorists in America 1865–1914." *Women's Studies* 1, 3–40.

4

Morality, Modernity, and "Malarial Restlessness": American Realism in its Anglo-European Contexts

Winfried Fluck

When William Dean Howells, the most influential American writer and critic in the "age of realism," tried to define the "new American school of fiction" in his essay "Henry James, Jr." (1882), his frame of reference was transatlantic. Howells argues that the new American school of fiction is up there with the most recent developments on the European continent, and that it promises to reinvigorate an Anglo-American tradition that was showing signs of exhaustion in England:

> The art of fiction has, in fact, become a finer art in our day than it was with Dickens and Thackeray. We could not suffer the confidential attitude of the latter now, nor the mannerism of the former, any more than we could endure the prolixity of Richardson or the coarseness of Fielding. These great men are of the past – they and their methods and interests; even Trollope and Reade are not of the present. The new school derives from Hawthorne and George Eliot rather than any others; but it studies human nature much more in its wonted aspects, and finds its ethical and dramatic examples in the operation of lighter but not really less vital motives. The moving accident is certainly not its trade; and it prefers to avoid all manner of dire catastrophes. It is largely influenced by French fiction in form; but it is the realism of Daudet rather than the realism of Zola that prevails with it, and it has a soul of its own which is above the business of recording the rather brutish pursuit of a woman by a man, which seems to be the chief end of the French novelist. This school, which is so largely of the future as well as the present, finds its chief exemplar in Mr. James; it is he who is shaping and directing American fiction, at least. (Cady 1973: 70–1)

In *Criticism and Fiction,* published nine years later, Howells repeats his claim that English fiction is outdated and blames English criticism, which "in the presence of the Continental masterpieces, has continued provincial and special and personal, and has expressed a love and hate which had to do with the quality of the artist rather than the character of his work" (Howells 1959: 38–9). The new standard in literature is provided by continental novels.

Henry James shared this opinion. In a letter to Howells in 1884, James writes about his Parisian encounters with the continental realists – Gustave Flaubert, Edmond de Goncourt, Ivan Turgenev, Émile Zola, Alphonse Daudet, and Guy de Maupassant – whom he called "the grandsons of Balzac" (Powers 1971: 1):

> ... there is nothing more interesting to me now than the effort & experiment of this little group, with its truly infernal intelligence of art, form, manner – its intense artistic life. They do the only kind of work, to-day, that I respect; & in spite of their ferocious pessimism & their handling of unclean things, they are at least serious and honest. The floods of tepid soap and water which under the name of novels are being vomited forth in England, seem to me, by contrast, to do little honour to our race. (James 1920: 104–5)

For Kate Chopin, who regarded American culture as stifling, the French school, and particularly Maupassant, opened up the prospect of approaching "modern topics" with new openness. In 1896 she gave a glowing account of her discovery of Maupassant: "About eight years ago there fell accidentally into my hands a volume of Maupassant's tales.... I read his stories and marvelled at them. Here was life, not fiction; for where were the plots, the old fashioned mechanism and stage trapping that in a vague, unthinking way I had fancied were essential to the art of story making" (Seyersted 1969: 51). Zola, in contrast, appeared technically clumsy and "continually irritated her" (Toth 1990: 168). In a review of Zola's *Lourdes*, Chopin wrote: "Not for an instant, from first to last, do we lose sight of the author and his note-book and of the disagreeable fact that his design is to instruct us" (Toth 1990: 250). Sarah Orne Jewett also thought little of the "Zola school of realism" and its ideal of scientific objectivity, but had two maxims by Flaubert tacked to her writing desk (Cary 1984: 201). Frank Norris took his inspiration for a new type of "romantic fiction" – and for the idea "that a series of thematically linked novels was the best means of encompassing a vast social or philosophical theme" (Pizer 1966: 115) – from Zola. Like Norris, Stephen Crane was strongly influenced by Zola's experimental method, but also by Flaubert and later by Tolstoy. As Robert Stallman observes, "*Maggie* was Crane's Bowery version of Zola and Flaubert" (1968: 73); but by the time Crane wrote *The Red Badge of Courage*, Tolstoy, especially in the novel *Sebastopol*, had become his main inspiration. As Crane himself put it: "I decided that the nearer a writer gets to life the greater he becomes as an artist, and most of my prose writings have been toward the goal partially described by that misunderstood and abused word, realism. Tolstoy is the writer I admire most of all" (Pizer 1990: 164–5). Theodore Dreiser "had long brooded over the aridity of American letters.... Even as late as 1911 his American literary admirations included only a few" (Hakutani 1964: 205). "When I go abroad," he said, "it is very different. Balzac, Zola, de Maupassant, Daudet, Flaubert, and Anatole France are great towering statues to me – the best in France" (Dreiser 1959: 121).

The claim that the American novel in the age of realism cannot be understood without its Anglo-European context appears to ignore the fact that American writers and critics of the period still seemed to pursue an exceptionalist agenda in their calls for the "Great American Novel." John William De Forest had revived the issue after the Civil War. His argument, however, was by no means exceptionalist in intention, for in his review of the state of American fiction he looked for "anything resembling the tableaux of English society by Thackeray and Trollope, or the tableaux of French society by Balzac and George Sand" (De Forest 1868: 27). With a national epic of its own, American society would finally be able to meet an international standard and thus arrive among the "cultured nations." In De Forest's view, the abolition of slavery had at last created the conditions for American society fully to realize its potential as an advanced civilization. What was still lacking were cultural achievements that would confirm this progress.

The challenge for the postwar generation, then, was to develop a literature that would gain international respect. But how could this be done? "Which way should a writer turn? Should he search for reality in the national scene, a 'daring Americanism of subject,' which, as Thomas Wentworth Higginson pointed out, had brought such success to Cooper and Mrs. Stowe?" (Falk 1953: 27). This looked like a recipe from the past. The postwar generation dismissed the historical novel in the style of Cooper because it failed to grasp the meaning of contemporary American life. Should novelists then "model themselves after the fashion of the French realists, Balzac, Flaubert, Zola, the Goncourts? Yet this path was an affront to morality and false to the 'higher decencies' of American life" (Falk 1953: 27). Even T. S. Perry, one of the strongest proponents of an international orientation, wrote about Zola: "his books, and notably his latest one, are more shameless and disgusting than anything in modern literature. . . . He knows very well that he secures his readers by covering his pages with so complete an assortment of indecencies that there is almost nothing left for those who come after him. . . . His position, then, may be held to be secured. He can glow with the infinite satisfaction of knowing that he has disgusted more readers than any man living" (Perry 2000b: 61–2).

The solution seemed to lie in a third way, a literature adapted to present-day American conditions. It would have to be modern, realistic, and democratic: it would have to focus on the present and not the past; on common, everyday life and not on the heroic or melodramatic exception; and it would have to be accessible to the common reader and not require a literary education in order to appreciate it. As Howells would later put it in *Criticism and Fiction* (1891):

> But let fiction cease to lie about life; let it portray men and women as they are, actuated by the motives and the passions in the measure we all know; let it leave off painting dolls and working them by springs and wires; let it forbear to preach pride and revenge, folly and insanity, egotism and prejudice, but frankly own these for what they are, in whatever figures and occasions they appear; let it not put on fine literary airs; let it speak the dialect, the language, that most Americans know – the language of unaffected people everywhere – and there can be no doubt of an unlimited future, not only of delightfulness but of usefulness, for it. (Howells 1959: 51)

This "third way" led to what would eventually be called American realism; but, contrary to a later view, realism was not conceived as a "literary reflection of the scientist's belief in objective truth" (Kirk and Kirk 1962: 121). To be sure, claims that the task of literature should be the truthful depiction of life abounded at the time and a promise of a truthful representation of reality became the central, most frequently used form of authorization for the new school of fiction. "Realism," Howells wrote in *Criticism and Fiction* in continuing his feud with English fiction, "is nothing more and nothing less than the truthful treatment of material, and Jane Austen was the first and the last of the English novelists to treat material with entire truthfulness" (Howells 1959: 38). "Truthful," however, is not to be confused with "factual" or "documentary." It refers to that which is considered truly representative of a society, including its "true" potential. This, in fact, is the meaning of an infamous, often ridiculed claim by Howells that, in contrast to a novel like Dostoevsky's *Crime and Punishment*, "our [American] novelists...concern themselves with the more smiling aspects of life" (Howells 1959: 62), because they are the more "truthful" as far as the potential of American civilization is concerned. Howells's first book about American society, *Their Wedding Journey* (1872) – half travel-book, half novel – is a proud, sometimes self-congratulatory inspection of contemporary American life. There may be excesses and many deplorable lapses of taste, but these do not describe the true possibilities of American society. The claim of truthful representation thus had the function of giving authority to a new – unsentimental, "modern," and basically optimistic – view of American society: "American realism might be most fruitfully described...as a cultural strategy to extend and modernize basic tenets of American Victorianism in order to gain influence on the definition of American society and culture after the Civil War" (Fluck 1992: 20).

   The fact that realistic modes of representation stood in the service of a larger goal, that of assessing the modern potential of American civilization, explains a surprising fact about American realism: until the mid-1880s, the term "realism" itself did not play any significant role in the critical legitimation of this new type of American fiction, although the European school of realism clearly provided the main inspiration for it. References to European realism can already be found in the 1850s, but uses of the term "realism" in American debates remain inconsistent and eclectic. Those American writers later considered the main writers of the "age of realism" – Howells, Henry James, and Mark Twain – shied away from the term. Of the three, only Howells would eventually adopt it. Even in his 1882 essay on James he does not yet use the term; and even after Howells began to use it programmatically, James continued to stay away from it. In an essay on Howells in *Harper's Weekly* in 1886, he takes great pains to avoid the word "realism," although, in setting up a contrast to the romance, he clearly refers to Howells as a realist:

> His work is of a kind of which it is good that there should be much to-day – work of observation, of patient and definite notation. Neither in theory nor in practice is Mr. Howells a romancer; but the romancers can spare him; there will always be plenty

of people to do their work. He has definite and downright convictions on the subject of the work that calls out to be done in opposition to theirs, and this fact is a source of much of the interest that he excites. (James 1956: 151)

Throughout his career, and even during the period in which he was most strongly influenced by French realism, James used the term "realism" infrequently and never accepted it as a description of his own work. After Howells had called him "the chief exemplar" of the new school of fiction, he strenuously tried to avoid being labeled, and, in his essay on "The Art of Fiction" (1884), denied the validity of a distinction between realism and romance altogether:

The novel and the romance, the novel of incident and that of character – these clumsy separations appear to me to have been made by critics and readers for their own convenience, and to help them out of some of their occasional queer predicaments, but to have little reality or interest for the producer, from whose point of view it is of course that we are attempting to consider the art of fiction. (James 1984a: 55)

American realism, then, was not a literary movement to realize an aesthetic program imported from Europe. Howells, James, and other American writers of the period did not want to copy European realism. They wanted to draw on realism's cultural capital as a "modern" movement in order to define modern life in American terms. Even the cosmopolitanism of James's later period still bears all the traces of this project.

II

The main influence on the American novel in the first half of the nineteenth century had been Walter Scott. Then Dickens became immensely popular and served as an important inspiration for Bret Harte and other regional writers. Elizabeth Stoddard was greatly influenced by the Brontë sisters, De Forest by Thackeray. For the young Howells, Jane Austen and George Eliot provided crucial inspiration. From Austen's novels of manners Howells took the central working premise of his early novels, confirmed and strengthened as a principle by Turgenev's novels: "I find I do not care for society, and that I do care intensely for people. I suppose, therefore, my tendency would always be to get my characters away from their belongings, and let four or five people act upon each other" (quoted in Howells 1928: 233). From George Eliot, on the other hand, Howells took the confirmation that these characters should be common people. But Howells strongly criticized the explicit "didacticism" of Eliot's novels: "The only observer of English middle-class life since Jane Austen worthy to be named with her was not George Eliot, who was first ethical and then artistic, who transcended her in everything but the form and method most essential to art, and there fell hopelessly below her" (Howells 1959: 39). The one novelist who, Howells felt, was worthy of Austen as such an observer was Anthony Trollope, "most like her in simple honesty and instinctive truth, as unphilosophized as the light of common day" (Howells 1959: 39). However, in search of a "commonplace realism" that was not overtly didactic, Turgenev became increasingly important:

> The business of the novelist is to put certain characters before you, and keep them before you, with as little of the author apparent as possible. In a play the people have no obvious interference from the author at all. Of course he creates them, but there is no comment; there can be none. The characters do it all. The novelist who carried the play method furthest is Tourguénief, and for a long time I preferred him to any other. (Howells 1959: 99)

In 1877 Howells called Turgenev "the man who has set the standard for the novel of the future" because of his distinct method of character portrayal; but three years earlier, T. S. Perry had already developed this argument in an influential essay on "Ivan Turgénieff": "He is a realist in the sense of hiding himself, and in the painstaking accuracy he shows with regard to everything his pen touches" (Perry 1874: 351). Robert Falk describes the crucial role Perry played in the discovery of Turgenev for the new school of fiction: "It was Perry who taught both James and Howells the importance of the Russian writer for American realists and who helped wean them away from the powerful influence of Hawthorne" (Falk 1953: 105). Daniel Lerner further notes that Turgenev served particularly well as a role model of the cosmopolitan writer for James: "It is clear that James found in Turgenev's situation and outlook striking similarities to his own. For James, Turgenev was a living embodiment of all that his education and up-bringing had taught him to consider admirable, of all that he had left home and country to find – 'Europe'" (Lerner 1941: 32).

Austen, Eliot, and Turgenev helped Howells to develop three key aspects of his novels: a conversational structure centered on a small group of characters; a focus on "commonplace" characters; and a dramatic method of narration that avoids authorial intrusion. Balzac, Flaubert, Maupassant, and Zola never assumed quite the same importance for Howells. Balzac he acknowledged as a pioneer: "Such a critic will not respect Balzac's good work the less for contemning his bad work. He will easily account for the bad work historically, and when he has recognized it, will trouble himself no further with it.... In César Birotteau, for instance, he will be interested to note how Balzac stood at the beginning of the great things that have followed since in fiction" (Howells 1959: 15–16). But, ultimately, Balzac is too melodramatic for Howells's taste and, hence, still "primitive": "It is very pretty; it is touching, and brings the lump into the reader's throat; but it is too much, and one perceives that Balzac lived too soon to profit by Balzac.... It is simply primitive and inevitable, and he is not to be judged by it" (Howells 1959: 16). Similarly, Zola is not the realist he fancied himself but a romantic at heart:

What Zola has done has been to set before us an ideal of realism, to recall the wandering mind of the world to that ideal, which was always in the world, and to make the reader feel it by what he has tried to do, rather than by what he has done. . . . Above all he has shown us what rotten foundations the most of fiction rested on, and how full of malaria the whole region was. He did not escape the infection himself; he was born in that region; the fever of romanticism was in his blood; the taint is in his work. (Howells 1959: 163)

When Howells finally began to aim at a more comprehensive social analysis that would go beyond the small group of interacting characters on which he had focused in his early novels, it was neither Balzac nor Zola but Tolstoy who provided the model. Howells's somewhat belated discovery of Tolstoy had all the force of a conversion experience. As Clara and Rudolph Kirk observe, "Turgenev taught Howells the art of novel writing; Tolstoy taught him to be impatient 'even of the artifice that hides itself' and to seek only 'the incomparable truth' beneath the tale" (Howells 1959: 166; for more on the influence of Tolstoy on Howells, see Lynn 1971; Goldfarb 1971; Walsh 1977).

The American writer who was most fully at home in a transatlantic culture of letters and most observant of European movements was Henry James. As Pierre Walker puts it, "James served, to an extent rarely fully acknowledged, as a spokesperson to the American and English reading public for contemporary French literary movements" (Walker 1995: xi; see also Grover 1973). James had, in fact, already used the term "realism" as early as 1865, when he advised Harriet Prescott to study the canons of the so-called realistic school (Falk 1953: 399). Throughout his interest in continental, and particularly French, realism, however, James remains somewhat ambivalent. He acknowledges that the continental novel sets the standards but, despite his professed cosmopolitanism, cannot quite overcome his concern about its lack of moral sense. Maupassant is a writer with whom it is impossible not to reckon, but his point of view "is almost solely that of the senses. If he is a very interesting case, this makes him also an embarrassing one, embarrassing and mystifying for the moralist" (James 1984b: 529). "Flaubert . . . is far from being a simple realist; but he was destitute of facility and grace" (James 1984b: 231). There is something ungenerous in the French author's genius. He is "cold." Art cannot be concerned merely with style. This is what is basically wrong with the French realists:

It would have been late in the day to propose among them any discussion of the relation of art to morality, any question as to the degree in which a novel might or might not concern itself with the teaching of a lesson. They had settled these preliminaries long ago, and it would have been primitive and incongruous to recur to them. The conviction that held them together was the conviction that art and morality are two perfectly different things, and that the former has no more to do with the latter than it has with astronomy or embryology. The only duty of a novel was to be well written; that merit included every other of which it was capable. (James 1888: 302)

James's extended comments on European literature – found, above all, in the collections *French Poets and Novelists* (1878), *Partial Portraits* (1888), and *Notes on Novelists* (1914) – show a clear development in his attitude. In his middle and later years, James's views of French realism underwent a number of revaluations. Balzac, at least from the distance of *Notes on Novelists*, now "stands signally apart" for James and "is the first and foremost member of his craft" (James 1984b: 90). James praises his immense hunger for facts, "the infinite reach in him of the painter and the poet" (p. 97), his thick local color, but then continues: "The prime aspect in his scene all the while, it must be added, is the money aspect" (p. 98): an interest so deep and all-embracing that James calls it "inscrutable, unfathomable" (p. 98) and, ultimately a failure of the imagination. "The imagination, as we all know, may be employed up to a certain point in inventing uses for money; but its office beyond that point is surely to make us forget that anything so odious exists" (p. 98). As Lyall Powers and others have pointed out, James's attitude toward Zola also changed during the course of his lifetime, although he never got entirely rid of his reservations:

> His initial response to Zola, in an essay of 1876, ranks him as "the most thorough-going" of the realist group but expresses little sympathy: "Unfortunately, the real for him, means exclusively the unclean, and he utters his crudities with an air of bravado, which makes him doubly intolerable." By the beginning of 1877, he can recommend Zola's latest novel to Howells – if his stomach can stand it. But the appearance of *L'Assommoir* later that year made an indelible and favorable impression on James, so that while he must still regret the grossness he can recommend it as "a literary performance; you must be tolerably clever to appreciate it." And so it went, until by the end of the decade James would exclaim, in an enthusiastic letter to Perry, that there is just nobody like Zola! Yet even in that letter the dubious distinction between earthiness and dirtiness raises its dusky head. "Zola's naturalism is ugly & dirty, but he seems to me to be *doing something* – which surely (in the imaginative line) no one in England or the U.S. is, – & no one else here." (Powers 1971: 37)

In an earlier review James had criticized Flaubert for being "cold." He praised Flaubert's insistence on the "impersonality" of his authorial stance but criticized his exclusive concern with style at the expense of the something else, beneath and behind, which gives art and life its meaning. By 1902, however, "James had accepted *Madame Bovary* as a classic" (Grover 1973: 72). He still criticized *Madame Bovary* for being "limited": "Our complaint is that Emma Bovary, in spite of the nature of her consciousness and in spite of her reflecting so much that of her creator, is really too small an affair" (James 1914: 81). David Gervais understands "too small" to mean "not representative enough" (1978: 51). But it also makes sense to relate "small" to Emma's consciousness. Despite the tragic things happening to her, she never quite reaches the stage of a "cultivated consciousness." As Philip Grover puts it: "The main subject of interest in a novel is always, for James, character; and character is consciousness.... So it is because of what Emma lacks in her points of contact with the world, her lack of a fine mind, that James finds *Madame Bovary* insufficient as a novel" (1973: 72–3). In describing the novel's problem this way, James has changed the terms of evaluation and transformed Emma into almost a Jamesian heroine: "That is the triumph of the book as the triumph stands, that Emma interests us by the nature of her consciousness and the play of her mind, thanks to the reality and beauty with which those sources are invested" (James 1914: 80). James could never quite overcome his criticism that French realism lacked a moral sense; but the moral sense still lacking is now that of a consciousness not yet sufficiently cultivated to turn a "small affair" into a source of heightened consciousness.

III

For American writers in the age of realism, Anglo-European fiction set new standards for "modern" literature but also illustrated pitfalls American fiction should avoid. Writers like Eliot, Balzac, Turgenev, Daudet, Flaubert, or Zola are praised but also criticized constantly. Hence, when American writers drew on European models, they did so selectively. James often appears to have written his novels in order to correct and revise his European sources (Tintner 1991: 2; see also Cargill 1961; Walker 1995). Discussing American fiction in an Anglo-European context thus should not be restricted to the faithful recording of influences: there were innumerable "germs," topics, plotlines, and characters that made their way into the American novel of the time, and it would go beyond the scope of this essay to make an effort to list them. But there are also influences that left a distinctive mark, by serving either as model for a new literary method or as point of departure for a major revision. If an Anglo-European context is to shed any light on American fiction, then we also have to focus on where and why the two movements differ and part company.

The influence of George Eliot is a case in point. References to Eliot are made throughout the period, but especially by Howells, for whom she provided a welcome legitimation for focusing on the representation of common, ordinary life. David Falk observes: "Like George Eliot who gladly turned away from angels, prophets, and heroic warriors 'to an old woman bending over her flower pot' while the softened light through the leaves 'just touches the rim of her spinning wheel and stone jug, and all those common things which are the precious necessities of life to her,' – so Howells in similar phrase found man in his natural and unaffected dullness to be 'precious'" (Falk 1953: 45). The passage refers to Howells's statement in *Their Wedding Journey* that "the sincere observer of man will not desire to look upon his heroic or occasional phases, but will seek him in his habitual moods of vacancy and tiresomeness. To me, at any rate, he is at such times very precious" (1968: 86–7). That Howells novel – the uneventful, decidedly unromantic story of a belated wedding journey ten years after the fact – provides an example of this realism of the commonplace. It tellingly begins:

Fortunately for me . . . in attempting to tell the reader of the wedding-journey of a newly married couple, no longer very young, to be sure, but still fresh in the light of their love, I shall have nothing to do but to talk of some ordinary traits of American life as these appeared to them, to speak a little of well-known and easily accessible places, to present now a bit of landscape and now a sketch of character. (1968: 1–2)

But the common life and common people Howells describes are far removed from Eliot's world. His characters are no longer representatives of a pre-industrial rural world filled with cottages, churches, and quaint workshops, but urban characters who enjoy – and occasionally indulge in – the amenities of modern life. In focusing on the commonplace, the purpose thus is not to give dignity to simple, common people whom modernity has left behind, but to depict representative modern Americans. The commonplace has become the representatively modern. If one wants to assess the progress of contemporary American society, then the "ordinary" pursuits of everyday characters should become the center of attention and the measure of that progress.

Hence characters, not plot, stand at the center of Howells's fiction. As we have already seen, the model for such a character-novel with minimized action was provided by Turgenev. But again, the transformation that Turgenev's method undergoes in the work of Howells is significant. For Turgenev, the lack of action on the part of his characters, as well as their brooding melancholy, is a device for revealing the paralysis of an aristocratic society. Strangely enough, this aspect of Turgenev's fictive world is hardly ever mentioned by American realists in their enthusiastic references to the Russian author. In contrast to Turgenev, Howells's novel is "eventless" not because his characters have no room for action, but because American society, as a prosperous and technologically advanced civilization, has taken the melodrama out of life. In its comforting prosperity, it has reduced the "plots" in which ordinary Americans live to the small, everyday dramas that Frank Norris would later call "teacup tragedies" and which even Howells occasionally presents with a dose of irony: "I suppose it is always a little shocking and grievous to a wife when she recognizes a rival in butchers-meat and the vegetables of the season" (1968: 13).

In their studies of the mid-career novels of James, critics like Oscar Cargill and Richard Brodhead have argued that with *The Bostonians* (1886) and *The Princess Casamassima* (1886) James finally aimed at a "public" novel in the manner of French realism. However, in an earlier novel, *Washington Square* (1881), James had already used a major work of French realism, Balzac's *Eugénie Grandet* (1833), as a source for "rewriting." The germ for James's novel obviously lay in a story told to him by the actress Sarah Kemble, but, as Richard Brodhead points out: "No James novel that I know points to a prior author as systematically as *Washington Square* points to Balzac." (Brodhead 1986: 116–17). Brian Lee has listed the striking parallels between *Washington Square* and *Eugénie Grandet*: "Both novels revolve around naive young girls who fall in love with more sophisticated suitors. In each case these prove to be shallow opportunists whose schemes are thwarted by the greater cunning of the girls' fathers. In both novels the heroines are depicted as being incapable of relinquishing their deep emotional attachments to their superficial lovers, and their lives are effectively ruined" (Lee 1984: 10). And yet, a striking difference remains: while *Eugénie Grandet* is a typically Balzacian study of single-minded, obsessive characters, *Washington Square* tells a story of self-development and, ultimately, self-empowerment in which the heroine, in a painful learning process, gradually moves toward a state of heightened awareness and the possibility of individual self-determination.

Grandet's obsession dominates Balzac's novel. He is the exemplary Balzacian Old World character who is ruled by only one passion, an insatiable hunger for money. In his single-minded pursuit of riches, however, he is merely more successful in doing what (almost) everybody else also wants to do. Sloper in *Washington Square*, on the other hand, is initially presented as an enlightened, cosmopolitan man whose "other side" is only gradually revealed and recognized by his daughter Catherine. For Grandet, money is everything; for Sloper, wealth is a given, so that his main interest lies in the art of cultivating life. Consequently, the central drama in *Washington Square* is not one of greed and the deforming effects of money: James focuses on a well-intentioned but suffocating form of guardianship, and an ensuing struggle for self-determination. *Eugénie Grandet* never develops during the course of Balzac's novel. She remains a victim throughout, whereas James's major interest, in *Washington Square* as well as in *The Portrait of a Lady*, lies in the challenge of how to get the heroine out of the status of a victim by developing her powers of consciousness. *Washington Square*, then, not only offers a far less bleak version of reality than *Eugénie Grandet*; it also rejects Balzac's analysis of modern life.

What the two novels have in common is the choice of a decidedly plain and unattractive heroine. This choice was daring, and reflects realism's goal of elevating the commonplace to the level of a legitimate topic for literature. Catherine Sloper must initially be one of the least interesting heroines of world literature. But whereas Balzac takes an almost sadistic pleasure in exploiting Eugénie Grandet's weakness by making it the ground for ever more shocking instances of deception and betrayal, James regards Catherine's plainness as a challenge to him, to transform (American) innocence into self-determination. The "truthfulness" at which Balzac's novel aims lies in an uncompromising analysis of bourgeois hypocrisy; the realism of James's novel lies in its attempt to overcome the melodramatic victimization plot. In this the novel played an important role in the realistic reorientation of the American novel in the late 1870s and early 1880s. But at the same time, it also moves away from European models by transforming a melodrama of deceit into a story of social apprenticeship. For this project, *The Portrait of a Lady* would provide the supreme example.

Like many novels in the age of realism, *The Portrait of a Lady* (1881) tells the story of a young woman who starts out with illusions about the world and then has to go through a series of painful experiences in order to shed these illusions. In most European versions – from Flaubert's *Madame Bovary* to Tolstoy's *Anna Karenina* and Theodor Fontane's *Effi Briest* – the heroine's search for self-fulfillment eventually leads to self-destruction. In contrast, James takes the melodrama out of the narrative by making his heroine single and wealthy. The adulterous heroines of European realism gain our sympathies because they are victims of seduction and social hypocrisy. But they do not grow in personality (least of all Emma Bovary). In *The Portrait of a Lady*, on the other hand, Isabel Archer goes through a process of inner growth that leads to her decision to go back to Gilbert Osmond. As in the case of Catherine Sloper – and in marked contrast to European realism – her disillusionment becomes a source of self-empowerment by leading her to accept her own responsibility as a guardian of Osmond's daughter, Pansy.

For Edna Pontellier, the heroine of Kate Chopin's *The Awakening* (1899), such a sense of social responsibility would have appeared as a trap. For Edna, adultery is only one experiment among many through which she tries to escape the imposition of social roles (including that of "mother"). The almost casual attitude Chopin takes toward adultery prompted several critics to call Edna the "American Madame Bovary," a comment not always intended as praise. Although Cyrille Arnavon, a Frenchman, in 1946 was the first to make the comparison, and used it to herald Chopin's novel as an important early American realist text, Willa Cather was less than impressed: "A Creole Bovary is this little novel of Miss Chopin's. Not that...Miss Chopin is a Flaubert – save the mark! – but the theme is similar....I shall not attempt to say why Miss Chopin has devoted so exquisite and sensitive, well-governed a style to so trite and sordid a theme" (Cather 1970: 687). As Per Seyersted points out, both heroines "become estranged from their husbands; neglect their children; have lovers; lose the sense of responsibility, and take their own lives....Mrs. Chopin did not use the French classic as a model, however, but only as a point of departure, giving the story an entirely new emphasis" (Seyersted 1969: 138–9). In Chopin's version, adultery is no longer the scandalous transgression that changes everything. It is only one (and by no means the final) step in a sequence of liberating acts that lead to Edna's gradual self-empowerment.

At first sight, Edna seems to resemble the European heroines of realist fiction in that she appears to be "defeated" at the end. But in contrast to the pitiful suicide of Emma Bovary, Edna's swimming out into the open sea bears the markings of a triumphant act of self-assertion in which she has finally cast off all remaining limitations on the self. Chopin adopts a "continental" subject matter but gives it a quasi-Transcendentalist reinterpretation. And, as Seyersed observes, in the short story "The Storm," Chopin presents an amazingly frank description of a joyful act of adultery:

> Kate Chopin not only outdistanced her compatriots, but also went a step beyond the Frenchmen. That her description of physical union is more open than theirs is a relatively minor point in this connection; what is important is its "happy," "healthy" quality.
>
> Flaubert, who once owned that he had been obsessed by the word "adultery," makes Emma Bovary's amatory exploits into a frantic flight from dreariness; Zola sees those of Nana as the vile expressions of a degenerating heroine. Kate Chopin was not interested

in the immoral in itself, but in life as it comes, in what she saw as natural – or certainly inevitable – expressions of universal Eros, inside or outside of marriage. . . . That "happy sex" should somehow be "indecent" . . . would be a completely foreign idea to the author of this story. In "The Storm," there is exuberance and a cosmic joy and mystery as Alcée and Calixta become one with another and with elemental nature. (Seyersted 1969: 168)

At about the same time, Theodore Dreiser carried the theme of adultery yet another step beyond European realism and even beyond the "cosmic" Transcendentalist vision of Chopin: he moves the subject matter to the level of the completely casual. In this respect, it seems more fitting to compare *Sister Carrie* (1900) with *Madame Bovary* than with any of Zola's novels. *Sister Carrie* and *Madame Bovary* not only share a similar subject matter but also aim at a new definition of the "commonplace." It was Flaubert's goal, after all, to demonstrate that the seemingly romantic was a mediocre affair and that mediocre, even vulgar, commonplace things were a legitimate topic of fiction; what mattered was not the "beautiful artistic subject" but the style in which it was presented: "What I am up against are commonplace situations and trivial dialogue. To write the *mediocre* well and to see that it maintains at the same time its appearance, its rhythm, its words is really a diabolical task, and I now see ahead of me thirty pages at least of this kind. Style is hard won! I am beginning over again what I did last week" (letter to Louise Colet, 12. Sept. 1853, quoted in Furst 1992: 41).

For Dreiser, on the other hand, the category of the "commonplace" has lost its programmatic thrust as an aesthetically innovative category. Whereas writers like Eliot, Flaubert, and Howells still work hard to capture the elusive quality of the commonplace, Dreiser is confidently at home in this world. For Howells, to write a novel of adultery would have meant to commit the "French mistake," that is, to join "the business of recording the rather brutish pursuit of a woman by a man, which seems to be the chief end of the French novelist," as he describes Zola's work in his essay on James. But in Dreiser's world, the legitimacy of the topic is no longer an issue. The result is not, however, a naturalist melodrama of a "fallen woman," but, quite to the contrary, the story of her rise to the top. Carrie's violations of official morality are "guilt-free." The only strong emotion she knows is the shame of not wearing the right clothes. Her inner "emptiness" is duly registered, but also described as a crucial precondition for her ability to fashion herself ever anew at various stages of her rise. What was formerly a moral scandal has become not only a fact of life but part of an ongoing series of acts of self-fashioning. In this sense, Carrie's "liberation" is the most superficial but also the most radical. Seyersted rightly stresses that for both Chopin and Dreiser, indifference toward bourgeois morality has taken the place of rebellion. They do not openly defy social convention but show a casual disregard for marriage and moral convention. *The Awakening* and *Sister Carrie* are thus the true American heirs to *Madame Bovary*; but while Emma's awakening is to the illusionary nature of her own dreams, Edna's and Carrie's awakening is to their own possibilities. Ironically, it was Kate Chopin and Theodore Dreiser who carried to a logical end what Howells and James had started. The realist revolution, imported from Europe, had reached a new but entirely unforeseen dimension of "modernity" in American fiction.

IV

In a wonderfully telling comment on Balzac's *Père Goriot*, Howells characterizes the novel as being "full of malarial restlessness, wholly alien to healthful art" (Howells 1959: 18). In another essay, he approvingly quotes the Spanish writer Armando Palacio Valdés:

> The French naturalism represents only a moment, and an insignificant part of life.... It is characterized by sadness and narrowness. The prototype of this literature is the Madame Bovary of Flaubert. I am an admirer of this novelist, and especially of this novel; but often in thinking of it I have said, how dreary would literature be if it were no more than this! There is something antipathetic and gloomy and limited in it, as there is in modern French life. (quoted in Howells 1959: 33)

These comments illustrate the central paradox of the new school of American fiction after the Civil War: on the one hand, it wanted to be "modern"; on the other hand, it disagreed with the European realists about what the representative, "truthful" characteristics of modern life were. One crucial issue in these debates is morality. American writers praised European realists for their "truthfulness," but then criticized them for going too far in presenting immorality as part of reality. That American fiction did not follow European realism "all the way" in this respect has often been criticized and is usually attributed to a lingering Puritanism. However, I want to suggest that the reasons lie somewhere else and, ultimately, have to be sought in two different views of modernity.

The major programmatic claim of realism was to be "truthful" to life. But what exactly does that mean? It means that the starting premise of realism (as it has been for a number of avant garde movements since then) was the goal of overcoming the separation of art and life. Howells put it succinctly:

> The light of civilization has already broken even upon the novel, and no conscientious man can now set about painting an image of life without perpetual question of the verity of his work, and without feeling bound to distinguish so clearly that no reader of his may be misled between what is right and what is wrong, what is noble and what is base, what is health and what is perdition, in the actions and the characters he portrays. (Howells 1959: 48)

All the writer has to do is to eliminate false, misleading views of reality; then reality will "speak for itself" and the novel will finally become relevant. Thus the realist project of "truthful representation" promises to turn the long despised genre of the novel into an avant garde medium.

In American realism, the goal of overcoming the separation of art and life by means of truthful literary representation rested on two premises. One is an almost metaphysical assumption that reality is governed by moral laws. Thus Howells can say: "We must ask ourselves before we ask anything else, Is it true? – true to the motives, the impulses, the principles that shape the life of actual men and women? This truth, which necessarily includes the highest morality and the highest artistry – this truth given, the book cannot be wicked and cannot be weak" (1959: 49). If vice is represented truthfully, it will recognize its true nature and recoil. As Howells wrote in a review of Hardy's *Jude the Obscure*: "Vice can feel nothing but self-abhorrence in the presence of its facts" (1959: 152). Consequently, if a literary work is truthful to life, it is, by definition, also great art: "In the whole range of fiction we know of no true picture of life – that is, of human nature – which is not also a masterpiece of literature, full of divine and natural beauty" (Howells 1959: 49). The truthful is the beautiful; "truly" truthful representation gives the literary text its aesthetic dimension: "But beauty, Señor Valdés explains, exists in the human spirit, and is the beautiful effect which it receives from the true meaning of things; it does not matter what the things are, and it is the function of the artist who feels this effect to impart it to others" (Howells 1959: 33–4).

For Howells, this is most obvious in the case of Tolstoy; in effect, it is the basis of Howells's great admiration for Tolstoy's work. Tolstoy has managed to achieve the seemingly impossible, namely to make the ethical and the aesthetic identical:

> It is usual to speak of the ethical and the aesthetical principles as if they were something separable; but they are hardly even divergent in any artist, and in Tolstoy they have converged from the first. He began to write at a time when realistic fiction was so thoroughly established in Russia that there was no question there of any other. . . . Then Tolstoy arrived, and it was no longer a question of methods. In Tourguénief, when the effect sought and produced is most ethical, the process is so splendidly aesthetical that the sense of its perfection is uppermost. In Tolstoy the meaning of the thing is so supreme that the delight imparted by the truth is qualified by no consciousness of the art. (Howells 1959: 172)

This "artless" art is literally "true art" and as such best suited to reveal the moral meaning of reality: "There had been many stories of adultery before 'Anna Karénina,' – nearly all the great novels outside of English are framed upon that argument, – but in 'Anna Karénina' for the first time the whole truth was told about it." Tolstoy's work proves that the truth can "never be anything but moral" (Howells 1959: 173). Yet, if so, then great art has to be deeply "ethical"; if it is not, the aesthetic gains dominance and we no longer have "truthful" art. Real art has to be "artless"; it can only be artless, however, if it is ethical, because it is the moral sense that transforms representation into art.

The case appears to be more complicated in the case of James, who disliked Tolstoy's novels and called them "very loose baggy monsters" (Jones 1985: 47). At the same time James insisted on the indispensability of a moral sense. However, the term "moral" covers a lot of ground in his critical comments, ranging from genuine indignation about the "immorality" of French realism to a term for the recognition of the complexity of human nature – as in James's "moral imagination." This is a term set up in contrast to the mechanical in reproduction, to *mere* fidelity in representation, to the merely photographic: its basic task is to preserve the idea that representation has to be made meaningful by going beyond the merely empirical. But it would be completely inadequate to conceive of the term as moralism. Although his use of attributes such as "unclean" indicates that James seems sometimes to have had an almost physical aversion to certain explicit descriptions of modern life, he cannot be pinned down to any particular ethical or philosophical position (so that his views of French realism could change and become more positive in his later years). The only criterion of the moral as the meaningful lies in the idea of a complexity that is the result of the work the imagination does with "reality." The privileged space for the development of such a consciousness is the work of art; this is why James can equate artistic value and morality and why, in the final analysis, he, too, can equate (a certain type of) "realistic" representation with moral meaning.

The second premise underlying American realism's project of overcoming the separation of art and life is that a literary method of truthful representation will reveal the true potential of American society. This belief is clearly held by Howells, but it is larger than his "more smiling aspects of life." What he had in mind was the democratic dimension of American life, which elevates the commonplace to a level that provides that life with its "distinction":

> Matthew Arnold complained that he found no "distinction" in our life, and I would gladly persuade all artists intending greatness in any kind among us that the recognition of the fact pointed out by Mr. Arnold ought to be a source of inspiration to them, and not discouragement. We have been now some hundred years building up a state on the affirmation of the essential equality of men in their rights and duties, and whether we have been right or wrong the gods have taken us at our word, and have responded to us with a civilization in which there is no "distinction" perceptible to the eye that loves and values it. Such beauty and such grandeur as we have is common beauty, common grandeur, or the beauty and grandeur in which the quality of solidarity so prevails that neither distinguishes itself to the disadvantage of anything else. (Howells 1959: 66)

"Distinction" is a term originally taken from aristocratic society. Democracy repudiates the conditions and characteristics of aristocratic class societies, such as, for example, the double standard that makes the novel of adultery possible. It was not merely a lingering Puritanism, then, but also a political interpretation of the social sources of "immorality" that explains why writers like Howells and James could not simply copy European realism. If realism was to be the truthful representation of reality, it could not focus on aspects of life that were leftovers from aristocratic societies. Instead, it had to focus on representative elements of democratic society. For Howells, this focus meant the commonplace not only in the sense of ordinary everyday life, but also as signifying what the members of a democracy have in common. In focusing on the commonplace, realism thus "is the only appropriate art for a democracy" (Lynn 1971: 285). "Men are more like than unlike one another: let us make them know one another better, that they may all be humbled and strengthened with a sense of their fraternity" (Howells 1959: 87). Ironically, at about the time Howells wrote these words, he himself began to doubt whether American society had really succeeded in establishing a democratic sense of fraternity or whether it needed a radical wake-up call.

"Fraternity" is a word that is unknown (and unthinkable) in the world of Balzac, Flaubert, or Zola – but also, one should add, in the world of James, Chopin, and Dreiser. Although they can all be considered significant representatives of the "age of realism," they offer radically different versions of "reality." James shows, both in his criticism and in his fictional texts, a Brahmin conviction "that democracy must mean provincialism" (Jones 1985: 22). But he also sets his hopes on the potential of his American characters to combine Old World and New World culture in order to create a new form of modern civilization. His realism is therefore one that initially continues the Victorian novel of apprenticeship and self-development and then begins to focus increasingly on processes of growth in consciousness. While Howells was "at least attempting to grasp America as a subject for fiction" (Jones 1985: 28), James was creating representative Americans and sending them to the Old World in order to see whether and how they would be able to transform it. Above all, it was the possibility of representing the individual imagination that made the novel interesting for James, so that realism, for him, was of interest mainly as a method for creating the illusion of encountering an interesting character. For Chopin, the goal was individual self-empowerment in the style of Emerson and Whitman; hers is a quasi-Transcendentalist view of the potential of American life. Finally, for Dreiser, American life consisted of an immense variety of different fates, all of which provide interesting instances of evolution. In each case, the view of modernity is further radicalized and individual-ized, from a Howellsian view of modern civilization as the final breakthrough of democracy to Dreiser's redefinition of democracy as the site of an evolutionary struggle. And yet a common factor connects these different versions: namely, the transformation of a realistic mode of representation into a narrative of empowerment designed to provide protection against the malarial restlessness of modern life.

PRIMARY TEXTS

Chopin, Kate. *The Awakening*. 1899.

Dreiser, Theodore. *Sister Carrie*. 1900.

Howells, William Dean. *Their Wedding Journey*. 1872.

Howells, William Dean. "Henry James, Jr." 1882.

Howells, William Dean. *Criticism and Fiction*. 1891.

James, Henry. *French Poets and Novelists*. 1878.

James, Henry. *The Portrait of a Lady*. 1881.
James, Henry. *Washington Square*. 1881.
James, Henry. "The Art of Fiction." 1884.

James, Henry. *Partial Portraits*. 1888.
James, Henry. *Notes on Novelists*. 1914.

REFERENCES AND FURTHER READING

Anon. (R.P.) (2002). "Novel-Writing as a Science" (first publ. 1885). In *Americans on Fiction*, ed. Peter Rawlings, vol. 3, 199–203. London: Pickering & Chatto.

Brodhead, Richard H. (1986). *The School of Hawthorne*. New York: Oxford University Press.

Cady, Edwin H. (1958). *The Realist at War: The Mature Years 1885–1920 of William Howells*. Syracuse, NY: Syracuse University Press.

Cady, Edwin H. (1971). *The Light of Common Day: Realism in American Fiction*. Bloomington: Indiana University Press.

Cady, Edwin H., ed. (1973). *W. D. Howells as Critic*. London: Routledge.

Cady, Edwin H., and Frazier, David L., eds. (1962). *The War of the Critics over William Dean Howells*. Evanston, Ill.: Row, Peterson.

Cargill, Oscar (1961). *The Novels of Henry James*. New York: Macmillan.

Cary, Richard (1984). "The Literary Rubrics of Sarah Orne Jewett." In Gwen L. Nagel (ed.), *Critical Essays on Sarah Orne Jewett*, 198–211. Boston: Hall.

Cather, Willa (1970). *The World and the Parish: Willa Cather's Critical Articles and Reviews, 1893–1902*, ed. William Curtin. Lincoln: University of Nebraska Press.

Daugherty, Sarah B. (1981). *The Literary Criticism of Henry James*. Athens, Ohio: Ohio University Press.

Davidson, Cathy, and Davidson, Arnold (1977–8). "Carrie's Sisters: The Popular Prototypes for Dreiser's Heroine." *Modern Fiction Studies* 23: 395–407.

De Forest, John W. (1868). "The Great American Novel." *The Nation* 6 (9 Jan.), 27–9.

Dreiser, Theodore (1959). *Letters of Theodore Dreiser*, ed. Robert Elias, vol. 1. Philadelphia: University of Pennsylvania Press.

Falk, Robert P. (1953). "The Rise of Realism 1871–1891." In Harry Hayden Clark (ed.), *Transitions in American Literary History*, 379–442. Durham, NC: Duke University Press.

Falk, Robert P. (1965). *The Victorian Mode in American Fiction 1865–1885*. Ann Arbor: Michigan State University Press.

Fluck, Winfried (1992). "Declarations of Dependence. Revising our View of American Realism." In Steve Ickingrill and Stephen Mills (eds.), *Victorianism in the United States*, 19–34. Amsterdam: VU University Press.

Furst, Lilian, ed. (1992). *Realism*. London: Longman.

Gervais, David (1978). *Flaubert and Henry James: A Study in Contrasts*. London: Macmillan.

Goldfarb, Clare R. (1971). "William Dean Howells: An American Reaction to Tolstoy." *Comparative Literature Studies* 8: 317–37.

Grover, Philip (1973). *Henry James and the French Novel*. London: Paul Elek.

Hakutani, Yoshinobu (1964). "Dreiser and French Realism." *Texas Studies in Literature and Language* 6: 200–12.

Howells, Mildred, ed. (1928). *Life in Letters of William Dean Howells*, vol. 1. Garden City, NY: Doubleday.

Howells, William Dean (1959). *Criticism and Fiction and Other Essays*, ed. Clara and Rudolf Kirk. New York: New York University Press.

Howells, William Dean (1968). *Their Wedding Journey*. Bloomington: Indiana University Press.

Howells, William Dean (1973). "Henry James, Jr.," in *W. D. Howells as Critic*, ed. Edwin Cady, 59–72. London: Routledge.

James, Henry (1888). *Partial Portraits*. New York: Haskell. (Repr. 1968.)

James, Henry (1914). *Notes on Novelists*. New York: Scribner.

James, Henry (1920). *The Letters of Henry James*, ed. Percy Lubbock, vol. 1. New York: Scribner.

James, Henry (1956). "William Dean Howells." In *The American Essays*, ed. Leon Edel. Princeton: Princeton University Press.

James, Henry (1984a). *Literary Criticism: Essays on Literature, American Writers, English Writers*, ed. Leon Edel. New York: Library of America.

James, Henry (1984b). *Literary Criticism: French Writers, Other European Writers, The Prefaces to the New York Edition*, ed. Leon Edel. New York: Library of America.

Jones, Vivien (1985). *James the Critic*. London: Macmillan.

Kirk, Clara, and Kirk, Rudolf (1962). *William Dean Howells*. New York: Twayne.

Leavis, F. R. (1961). "Foreword." In George Eliot, *Adam Bede*. New York: Signet.

Lee, Brian (1984). "Introduction." In Henry James, *Washington Square*, 7–23. London: Penguin.

Lerner, Daniel (1941). "The Influence of Turgenev on Henry James." *Slavonic and East European Review* 20: 28–54.

Lynn, Kenneth S. (1971). *William Dean Howells: An American Life*. New York: Harcourt Brace Jovanovich.

Matthiessen, F. O., and Murdock, Kenneth B., eds. (1947). *The Notebooks of Henry James*, vol. 1. New York: Oxford University Press.

Perry, Thomas Sergeant (2002a). "Ivan Turgénieff" (first publ. 1874). In *Americans on Fiction*, ed. Peter Rawlings, vol. 3, 346–58. London: Pickering & Chatto.

Perry, Thomas Sergeant (2002b). "Zola's Last Novel" (first publ. 1880). In *Americans on Fiction*, ed. Peter Rawlings, vol. 3, 61–7. London: Pickering & Chatto.

Pizer, Donald (1966). *The Novels of Frank Norris*. Bloomington: Indiana University Press.

Pizer, Donald, ed. (1990). *Critical Essays on Stephen Crane's* The Red Badge of Courage. Boston: Hall.

Pizer, Donald, ed. (1998). *Documents of American Realism and Naturalism*. Carbondale: Southern Illinois University Press.

Powers, Lyall (1971). *Henry James and the Naturalist Movement*. East Lansing: Michigan State University Press.

Rawlings, Peter, ed. (2002). *Americans on Fiction*, 3 vols. London: Pickering & Chatto.

Seyersted, Per (1969). *Kate Chopin: A Critical Biography*. Baton Rouge: Louisiana State University Press.

Stallman, Robert W. (1968). *Stephen Crane: A Biography*. New York: Braziller.

Stowe, William W. (1983). *Balzac, James, and the Realistic Novel*. Princeton: Princeton University Press.

Tintner, Adeline (1991). *The Cosmopolitan World of Henry James: An Intertextual Study*. Baton Rouge: Louisiana State University Press.

Toth, Emily (1990). *Kate Chopin*. New York: Morrow.

Walker, Pierre (1995). *Reading Henry James in French Cultural Contexts*. DeKalb: Northern Illinois University Press.

Walsh, Harry (1977). "Tolstoy and the Economic Novels of William Dean Howells." *Comparative Literature Studies* 14, 143–65.

5

American Literary Naturalism

Christophe Den Tandt

In the 1930s Vernon Louis Parrington defined naturalism as "a pessimistic realism, with a philosophy that sets man in a mechanical world and conceives of him as victimized by that world" (Parrington 1930: 325). Originating in France with Gustave Flaubert and Émile Zola, the naturalist school aimed to turn novelists into "men of science" able to analyze the interaction of individuals with their social environment (Zola, quoted in Parrington 1930: 324). Naturalist writers strove toward objectivity: they developed "an amoral attitude toward [their] material" (p. 323). Their fondness for behavioristic psychology led them to privilege "low-grade characters" or even "grotesques" (p. 325) at the risk of letting their fiction be ruled by a "'sex complex'" (p. 325). In terms of literary discourse, naturalist determinism gave rise to a non-Aristotelian form of tragedy focusing on the disintegration of protagonists who are neither noble nor afflicted with a tragic flaw: they are merely crushed by the urban industrial environment (see Parrington 1930: 326). This tragic world-view, Parrington argues, marks a pessimistic twist within a realist tradition which initially aimed to develop a "critical attitude" with regard to "the industrialization of America under the leadership of the middle class" (p. xxvi).

Parrington's argument ranks among the best of what might be called the orthodox descriptions of naturalism. It is echoed in many later essays (see Åhnebrink 1950: 21–33, 61–2; Kazin 1956: 66–7; May 1959: 169–71; Berthoff 1965: 226–7; Moers 1969: 143–6, 151–2; Conder 1984: 1–19; Pizer 1984: 9–11; Pizer 1995: 3–6; Mitchell 1989: 1–31). Since the 1980s, however, new scholarly approaches have challenged these views. The novels' politics, their contribution to the consolidation of a white male canon, the writers' relation to social and cultural institutions – all have been redefined almost beyond recognition. The present chapter starts off with a survey of naturalism from the point of view of orthodox readers. Revisionist approaches are discussed in the following section. I think it indeed useful initially to describe naturalism as it was perceived over the first century of its reception.

Although the earlier criticism may seem utopian in its judgment of naturalist politics, it captures a critical dimension in turn-of-the-twentieth-century fiction less often acknowledged by recent readers.

For orthodox scholars such as Parrington, Alfred Kazin, Lars Åhnebrink, Charles Child Walcutt, Warner Berthoff, Donald Pizer, and Ellen Moers, the most prominent naturalists are Stephen Crane, Frank Norris, Theodore Dreiser, and Jack London. Naturalism's secondary figures are Hamlin Garland, Harold Fredric, and Robert Herrick. That this corpus should be restricted to white males reflects the professional customs of a period in which canon expansion was not on the agenda. Yet we will see that this bias is also rooted in the naturalist writers' definition of their own practice. Naturalism, more than classical realism, established itself in opposition to literary traditions connoted as feminine – domestic fiction, sentimental romance, melodrama. It aimed at the literary appropriation of the public sphere: the exploration of the new metropolis. Writers, Norris argues, must "rough-shoulder [their] way among men" and find "healthy pleasure in the jostlings of the mob" (1964: 13). This cultural program presupposes a freedom from social restraints available only to empowered subjects. It was barely accessible to writers subjected to patriarchy and racism.

While gender and race are glossed over in orthodox criticism, class politics and the critique of corporate America play a polarizing role. Earliest comments on realism and naturalism – by the novelists themselves or by early twentieth-century critics such as H. L. Mencken – focused on the struggle against Puritanism (see Pizer 1995: 9). Left-liberal scholars – Parrington, Kazin, Berthoff – discuss fiction in broader social terms. They establish such narrow links between writing and its social context that their essays read like intellectual and political histories of the nineteenth and twentieth centuries. In their view, realism and naturalism embody the progressive momentum of US history. It challenges the dehumanizing aspects of capitalism. Still, left-liberal critics argue that naturalism compromises its literary integrity when it shifts to overt political commitment. For Parrington, the partisanship of Norris, London, Herrick, even Zola brought about their literary "failure" (1930: 325). Kazin condones the political commitment of Progressive-era novelists but believes that some writers of the 1930s (Michael Gold, Edward Dahlberg, James T. Farrell), by their endorsement of communism, forfeited the "deep and subtle alienation" from US society that naturalism requires (Kazin 1956: ix). Reservations about the political appropriations of naturalism by writers of the years preceding World War II form a tacit assumption of 1950s and 1960s criticism as well. Walcutt, Pizer, and Moers render naturalism accessible to the postwar readership by suggesting that it offers a "complex intermingling of form and theme," not mere documentary reportage (Pizer 1984: 30). They approach the texts from a New Critical angle, stress their affinities with the canonically prestigious American romance, and anchor them within a liberal humanist tradition highlighting the writer's "individual temperament" (Pizer 1984: 30).

II

In orthodox scholarship, the genesis of naturalism coincides with the fading of William Dean Howells's career. In this view, the generation of the 1890s – Crane, Norris, and Dreiser – broke free from the Howellsian novel of manners, which focused on the everyday rituals of the upper middle classes (see Kazin 1956: 7–8; Michaels 1987: 36; Parrington 1930: 250). Howells has often been ridiculed for endorsing the puritanical sentimentalism of the genteel tradition. Sinclair Lewis uncharitably described him as "a pious old maid" (quoted in May 1959: 8). His legacy had to be outgrown if one were to explore the truth of the social world. Yet Howells did anticipate naturalism. He defended realism against the post-Civil War craze for popular romances and sentimental fiction. Through his critical and editorial work, he introduced US readers to the European novels on which naturalism would feed. He also sponsored Crane's early works – the first naturalist texts to be published in the United States.

Above all, Howells was sensitive to changes in US society that only future novelists would address (see Parrington 1930: 242, 250–3; Kazin 1956: 6–8; Pizer 1984: 2–3; Michaels 1987: 41–2). By the end of his career, he realized that the future of the United States would be determined by class and ethnic inequalities, mass urbanization, and the exploitation of immigrant labor – the phenomena Alan Trachtenberg draws together as the "incorporation" of America (Trachtenberg 1982: 3). Howells had been one of the few US intellectuals to defend the anarchists accused of plotting the Haymarket riots of 1886 (see Michaels 1987: 35–6), and the Haymarket executions had rendered him skeptical of the course taken by the American republic. *A Hazard of New Fortunes* (1890) dramatizes this pessimism through the narrative of a failed publishing enterprise. It shows that, in socially and ethnically fragmented New York, characters from diverse backgrounds cannot pursue the same professional project. Gathering them physically in the same room already seems a breach of verisimilitude. When a strike breaks out, the group falls apart along class and ethnic lines, leaving a cluster of middle-class characters conscious of the failure of their utopian aspirations.

Howells was a Midwesterner who, after moving to Boston, identified so closely with the New England ruling classes that he became their cultural mentor. Naturalist writers positioned themselves further from the center of the literary field. Garland, another Midwesterner, wrote about impoverished frontier farmers. Norris, a California writer, described the urbanization and incorporation of the west coast. Crane's bohemian lifestyle seemed designed to frustrate the values of his Methodist parents. It included visiting prostitutes, rumors of drug addiction, and the peregrinations consequent on his work as a war correspondent (see Åhnebrink 1950: 90–102). Dreiser best embodies this off-center status. Born to German-speaking parents in an Indiana small town, he wrote English prose that proved the despair of editors. Complaints about the crudeness of Dreiser's style or about his indiscriminate handling of self-taught knowledge are commonplace (see Kazin 1956: 67; Berthoff 1965: 243; Moers 1969: xvi).

Early naturalist novels seem to take up the task of literary representation where Howells's *A Hazard of New Fortunes* left off. In *Hazard*, the character embodying the immigrant working classes is a literate German-born socialist. The uneducated immigrant masses are glimpsed only at a distance, as middle-class protagonists ride elevated trains and peep into tenement blocks (Howells 1990: ch. 9, 45). Crane's and Norris's texts, on the contrary, cross the barrier that keeps Howells's protagonists from actual contact with the poor. Crane's *Maggie, a Girl of the Streets* (1893) drags its readers into the "gruesome doorways" of the New York Bowery (Crane 1979: ch. 2, 6). The Irish families encountered there inhabit a world of alcoholism and brutality. Maggie Johnson is a "pretty girl" who "blossomed" in the Bowery's "mud puddle" (ch. 5, 16). Seduced and rejected by a neighborhood beau, she falls into prostitution. After her mother and brother chase her from the family tenement, she becomes a ghostly figure threading her way through New York crowds. Her death leaves her relatives wallowing in self-pity. Likewise, the inhabitants of San Francisco's Polk Street in Norris's *McTeague* (1899) are urban grotesques. The novel's eponymous figure is a barely literate dentist who competes with another suitor, Marcus Schouler, for the love and money of Trina Sieppe, the daughter of Swiss immigrants. McTeague, deprived of his dentist's practice by Marcus's political machinations, falls into poverty and murders Trina. He dies a fugitive in Death Valley, clutching Trina's gold, after an ultimate struggle with his rival.

Dreiser's *Sister Carrie* (1900) transgresses the norms of gentility in subtler ways. It allows its readers to share the experiences of a young woman from a Wisconsin small town who, with minimal soul-searching, becomes a kept woman and a Broadway star. This device allows Dreiser to describe as spectacles of wonder what puritanically minded readers might have viewed as visions of hell – a "gorgeous saloon" with "polished woodwork, colored and cut glassware and many fancy bottles" (Dreiser 1986: ch. 5, 42, 43), department stores perceived as "show place[s] of dazzling interest and attraction" (ch. 3, 22), or New York theaters with scantily clad chorus lines, featuring such plays as "'The Wives of Abdul'" (ch. 46, 444). Carrie's success story is paralleled by the grimmer account of Hurstwood, her second lover, who steals money from his boss, ends up in destitution, and dies alone in a flophouse. Through the narrative of his downfall, the novel provides extended descriptions of poverty.

As *Sister Carrie* reveals, naturalism, in addition to providing close-up depictions of slum life, outlines the large-scale features of the urban industrial world – crowds, corporations, the metropolitan sprawl. Howells's *Hazard* is, again, pivotal in that it anticipates novels staging what William Cronon calls the "cityward journey" – the discovery of the metropolis (1991: 9; see also Fisher 1985: 6–7). *Sister Carrie* is arguably the most famous among these, but it was preceded by Garland's *A Spoil of Office* (1892) and *Rose of Dutcher's Coolly* (1895), and followed by many others: Frank Norris's *The Pit* (1902); Upton Sinclair's *The Jungle* (1906) and *The Metropolis* (1907); James Weldon Johnson's *The Autobiography of an Ex-Coloured Man* (1912); Dreiser's

The Titan (1914) and *The "Genius"* (1915); Ernest Poole's *The Harbor* (1915); and Abraham Cahan's *The Rise of David Levinsky* (1917). The cities depicted in these texts allow their observers to experience what another novelist, Robert Herrick, in *Together*, calls "the realization of multitudinous humanity" (1962: ch. 11, 182). They are too large to be framed by the norms of realist local color (see Cronon 1991: 13; Den Tandt 1998: 3–4, 33–43). Accordingly, characters view them with ambivalence: they are "unfamiliar, immoral and terrifying," yet they also "challeng[e]" their inhabitants "with dreams of worldly success" (Cronon 1991: 13). Chicago's commercial streets are "wall-lined mysteries" to Carrie not only because they mystify customers but also because they genuinely embody the city's "strange energies and huge interests" (Dreiser 1986: ch. 2, 17). Urban masses appear simultaneously as "pleasure-loving throng[s]" and as lines of "broken, ragged" homeless men (ch. 48, 465, 467). In Norris's *The Octopus* (1901) and *The Pit*, crowds are made up both of righteous insurgent farmers (see Norris 1986: ch. 6, 272) and of aimless speculators, dazed by market fluctuations (see Norris 1971: ch. 10, 379). The corporate world is an octopus that keeps the country in its stranglehold; yet it is also a " sphinx," carrying enigmatic wisdom (Norris 1971: "Conclusion," 421).

Novels of the cityward journey appropriate mid-nineteenth-century pastoralism – Jefferson's, Emerson's, and Whitman's tradition – in complex ways, now debunking it, now endorsing it for their own ends. Pastoralist ideology paints nature in utopian terms and cities as a civic threat. Naturalism, on the contrary, partly deflates the claims of nature romanticism, thus acting as the fiction of the closing of the frontier (see Lawlor 2000: 71–109). Hamlin Garland depicts life on the farm unsentimentally. Nature in *Jason Edwards: An Average Man* (1892) is neither a philosophical backdrop for the realization of selfhood nor the locus of the yeoman's republic. The novel's protagonists are city people goaded by land speculators to move to a frontier farm. Their adventure ends in bankruptcy. *A Spoil of Office* narrates the unequal struggle of Grangers and Populists against Washington politicians and corporate lobbyists. On the other hand, when naturalist novels do celebrate urban vistas, they draw on the language of nature romanticism. Description of wheat speculation in Norris's *The Pit* echoes the rhetoric of Whitman: the flow of wheat spreads from the Chicago Board of Trade to "the elevators of Western Iowa" until "men upon the streets of New York [feel] the mysterious tugging of its undertow engage their feet" and "overwhelm them" (Norris 1971: ch. 5, 79–80). Likewise, Ernest Poole's *The Harbor* celebrates the US economy's capacity to turn "the raw produce of Mother Earth's four corners" (Poole 1915: bk II, ch 12, 177) into a flow of commodities – "toys, sofas, glue, curled hair" (p. 178) – streaming into New York.

As Parrington indicates, naturalist writers guarantee the truthfulness of their writing by flaunting their rejection of sentimentalism. Naturalism's relation to sentimentalism and romance is, we will see below, more complex than a sheer rejection of illusion for the sake of truth. Yet naturalist texts do stage a conflict between the voice of true experience and romance conventions. In Crane's *Maggie*, the voice of illusion is music-hall entertainment: Maggie is seduced by the performers providing Bowery audiences with a cheaper version of "the phantasies of the aristocratic theater-going public" (Crane 1979: ch. 7, 23). Naïvely, she believes that there is "transcendental realism" in melodramatic narratives displaying a "brain-clutching heroine...swoon[ing] in snow storms beneath happy-hued church windows" (ch. 8, 27).

The rejection of sentimentalism makes the pursuit of literary truth a gendered enterprise. Male writers challenge discourses of conformity they regard as feminized. In *McTeague* and *Carrie*, the inauthentic idiom is domestic or local realism. Dreiser's narrative of the breakup of Hurstwood's upper-middle-class marriage reads like a farewell gesture not only to Howellsian realism, but also to the domestic fiction the author of *Hazard* built on (Dreiser 1986: ch. 23, 212–13; see also Habegger 1982: viii–ix, 64–5). Hurstwood leaves his family for Carrie, who embodies a more vital field of experience. *McTeague* satirizes the sentimental representation of middle-class households by having its characters perform a grotesque mimicry of genteel conventions. McTeague and Trina's marriage ceremony is a painstakingly regulated affair where guests follow chalk marks on the floor (Norris 1985: ch. 9, 163). This attempt at discipline does not, however, prevent them from being tossed about by social and biological forces beyond their control.

Rejection of sentimental standards was most controversial in the representation of sexuality and, particularly, of women's desire. In Europe, Flaubert, Lev Tolstoy, Zola, Henrik Ibsen, and August Strindberg pointed out that the realistic portrayal of women's condition defied middle-class standards of propriety. To borrow Willa Cather's formula, mid- and late nineteenth-century European realism is the literature of lost ladies: heroines are frustrated, or, conversely, they display sexual behavior destructive to themselves and their surroundings. This context made the female protagonists' transgressions of sexual norms the benchmark of realistic radicalism – a situation epitomized in Europe by the trial for obscenity initiated against Flaubert's *Madame Bovary* (1857). Howells was aware of these developments yet was reluctant to write novels that might offend a readership composed partly of middle-class young women (see Pizer 1998: 8). American naturalist novelists flouted these restrictions, though they never attempted the frankness of Zola. Symptomatically, some of the first naturalist novels – *Maggie*, *Carrie* – are lost-lady narratives focusing on young women who live by prostitution or in promiscuous relationships. Other texts – Norris's *Vandover and the Brute* (1914), London's *The Sea-Wolf* (1904) – explore forms of masculinity ranging from primitive regression to homosocial desire. Norris in *A Man's Woman* (1899), London in *The Sea-Wolf* and *The Valley of the Moon* (1912), Poole in *The Harbor*, and David Graham Phillips in *Susan Lenox* (1917) specify how far they wish feminine empowerment to stretch. By twenty-first-century standards, however, the naturalist depiction of desire remains indirect: it is voiced through metaphors whose implications part of the naturalist readership may have ignored. Though daring for the time, it is still patriarchal.

The unsentimental gaze naturalism casts at social conditions is, according to the novelists, validated by science. Zola, in "The Experimental Novel," wishes the words "novelist" and "doctor" might become interchangeable (1963: 162; see also 187–96). US naturalists partly fulfill Zola's program: they echo the concerns of the nascent human sciences – studies of urban criminality such as Charles Loring Brace's *The Dangerous Classes of New York* (1872) or reform-minded investigation of poverty such as Jacob Riis's *How the Other Half Lives* (1890). They also indulge in philosophical reflections inspired by evolutionary thinkers – Herbert Spencer, predominantly. From this corpus, US naturalists retain the beliefs that human beings are shaped by their environment, not by idealist essences, and that Darwinian evolution is the historical manifestation of this socio-biological process. Humans are therefore not distinct from animals and are apt to revert to primitive behavior – to what Zola calls the human beast. Among US novelists, London most explicitly investigates this biological past. His companion novels *The Call of the Wild* (1903) and *White Fang* (1906) illustrate opposite evolutionary scenarios (see Lawlor 2000: 135–31). The former traces the path into the primitive of a dog who had first been cherished, then brutalized by humans. The latter shows a wolf evolving toward civilization by virtue of his human master's love. The novels do not specify which of the two options should prevail.

The thematics of atavism leads to a typically naturalistic form of dualistic characterization. Protagonists otherwise beholden to late-nineteenth-century decorum are overcome by primitive violence. In *McTeague*, a Sunday picnic degenerates into a wrestling match in which Marcus bites off a chunk of McTeague's ear and the dentist breaks his rival's arm. McTeague, metamorphosed, is animated by the "perverted fury of the Berserker" (Norris 1985: ch. 11, 235). His yelling is "no longer human"; it is "an echo from the jungle" (ch. 11, 234). Similarly, farmers in *The Octopus*, fired by political frenzy, turn into "human animal[s] . . . with bared teeth and upraised claws" (Norris 1986: ch. 6, 272). London's *Before Adam* (1907) drives atavistic characterization to extremes. The protagonist is an overcivilized weakling obsessed by dream visions of his Neanderthal ancestor "Big Tooth," fighting against "Red Eye," the tribe's alpha male (London 1984a: ch. 1, 2). Atavism, though ostensibly frightening, is a source of fascination in naturalist fiction: characters who revert to the primitive are Darwinian shamans, shifting from one plane of being to the other. In *The Sea-Wolf*, seal-schooner captain Wolf Larsen contemplates with relish the moment when his energy will turn into "strength and movement in fin and scale and the guts of fishes" (London 1984b: ch. 7, 68).

Admittedly, naturalist science is often comically outdated. Dreiser explains the chemistry of Hurstwood's depression by reference to "poisons in the blood . . . called katastates," counteracted by "helpful chemicals, called anastates" (Dreiser 1986: ch. 36, 339). He also compares the city's impact on Carrie to the "mesmeric operations of super-intelligible forces" (ch. 8, 78). Pizer offers an elegant method to reclaim such pseudoscience as literature. Some of it, he argues, is parasitical (see 1984: 64–8). Dreiser misleads his readers when he states that Carrie, as she ponders her surrender to Drouet, is a "wisp in the wind" wavering between "desire and understanding" (1986: ch. 8, 73). The passage aligns the novel with a Christian reading of Darwinian evolution and thereby covers up the fact that Carrie is eventually empowered by her assent to "the forces of life" (ch. 8, 73). On the other hand, naturalist science may be read metaphorically. Norris's *Vandover* tells the story of a young artist overcome by fits of lycanthropy. Vandover's behavior is explained in terms of such pseudoscientific concepts as "Life" and "Nature" (Norris 1978: ch. 14, 230). Yet the novel may also be viewed as an allegory of selfhood, pitting the artist's "life of the spirit" against his "demonic, self-destructive" tendencies (Pizer 1984: 62).

A few naturalist novels did endorse at least one metaphorical interpretation of Darwinian science: that which equates determinism with the law of capital, and evolutionary strife with what London calls "the group struggle over the division of the joint product," that is, the class struggle (1982b: 1124). The social question had been a recurrent subtext in late-nineteenth-century Darwinian sociology. Political economist David Graham Sumner regarded capitalism as the human species' biological destiny. He traced its origins "[a]mong the lower animals" (1961: 53). For Sumner, "Nature's forces know no pity" (p. 133). "[T]he victim" in the struggle for survival "is to blame" (p. 137). Sociologists Lester F. Ward and Thorstein Veblen showed, however, that Darwinism could articulate a less reactionary agenda. Evolution might aim to establish not primacy in the sociobiological scuffle, but instead rational collaboration. The Brutes of human history might be not slothful proletarians but the robber barons themselves (see Veblen 1934: 226–7).

Naturalist novels written from a Progressive or socialist viewpoint appropriate Darwinism along Ward's and Veblen's left-leaning lines. Sinclair's *The Jungle* narrates a sociobiological experiment leading to political liberation. The Rudkus family are transplanted from pre-industrial Lithuania to the Chicago meat-packing plants. Their ethos of family and village solidarity provides little support in this new environment. Chicago capitalism is a "slaughtering machine" performing meat-making "by applied mathematics" (Sinclair 1984: ch. 3, 44, 45). The industrial slaughterhouses turn animals – including, occasionally, the bodies of hapless workers – into packaged commodities. Biological fitness is crucial to this economic system, since foremen hire the strongest workers first and, as Jurgis Rudkus experiences, throw them to the streets when they are mangled. After the deaths of his wife and his son, Jurgis is rife for conversion to a more hopeful view of the future of the species: the novel ends as a pamphlet for socialist unionism.

Properly defining the future of humankind is the concern of London's *The Iron Heel* (1908) as well. Avis and Ernest Everhard, the protagonists of this socialist anti-utopia, wage guerilla warfare against a capitalist dictatorship whose members think of themselves as the crown of biological evolution. Avis and Ernest believe, however, that these self-styled supermen have "made a shambles of civilization" (London 1982a: ch. 5, 378). They let modern workers live "more wretchedly than the caveman" while human "producing power is a thousand times greater" than in prehistory (ch. 5, 377). Less optimistically than Sinclair, London predicts a temporary victory for capitalism. By co-opting the socialist activists, the dictatorship postpones the advent of the "Brotherhood of Man" for several centuries ("Foreword," 321). We have seen above that such political explicitness found little favor among critics – a disdain that

explains the lack of interest in the naturalist-oriented political fiction of the 1900s
and 1910s (Phillips; Charlotte Teller; Arthur Bullard; Poole). Yet a shift toward
politics seems logical for writers who investigated social life and were concerned with
the ends of human evolution. Parrington's and Kazin's skepticism notwithstanding,
the legacy of early naturalism consists partly in opening a field of possibilities for later
writers of political fiction – immigrant novelists such as Anzia Yiezerska and Mike
Gold, or African American writers such as Richard Wright and Ann Petry.

III

The belief that realism and naturalism are politically progressive was, however,
challenged in the 1980s and 1990s by neo-Marxist, neo-historicist, and feminist
critics, as well as by advocates of canon expansion. Eric Sundquist's critical collection
American Realism: New Essays (1982) served as manifesto for this new paradigm.
Ironically, as Michael Anesko remarks, the revaluation of realism and naturalism
thus initiated was facilitated by advances in textual bibliography performed by
orthodox scholars – the 1981 publication of the restored text of *Sister Carrie*, for
instance, or Donald Pizer's editions of turn-of-the-twentieth-century critical documents (see Anesko 1995: 86). The Marxist, feminist, and multiculturalist scholars
who write in the wake of Sundquist's volume – June Howard; Rachel Bowlby; Walter
Benn Michaels; Mark Seltzer; Philip Fisher; Elizabeth Ammons – highlight the
conspicuous, though previously overlooked, sexist and racist discourse of naturalist
writers (see Seltzer 1992: 31–5; Howard 1985: 85–6). As far as class politics go, they
debunk the left-liberal view of naturalism as a liberating force (see Howard 1985:
131–41; Michaels 1987: 48–58; Seltzer 1992: 40–4). Naturalists, in these views,
cannot be portrayed exclusively as crusaders for truth and justice, alienated from the
US mainstream. They are also literary professionals consolidating their position in a
burgeoning mass market (see Kaplan 1988: 80–7; Wilson 1985: 1–16). Far from
criticizing the trusts, they are fascinated by the opportunities of the consumer
economy (see Bowlby 1985: 1–17). Their class discourse fosters social control over
the disenfranchised (see Howard 1985: 146–7). Finally, the very logic by which the
concepts of realism and naturalism have been constructed is shown to privilege a
white male corpus that excludes similar works by women and minority authors (see
Ammons 1995: 95–7).

At the basis of these new readings lies a skeptical redefinition of naturalism's
relation to reality and social phenomena. Influenced by poststructuralism, the recent
critics no longer lend credence to what Erich Auerbach, after Aristotle, calls "mimesis" – realist representation (1946: 7). They contend that realism and naturalism
cannot capture ideologically neutral snapshots of the real. Instead, it carries out
ideological strategies described by such concepts as naturalization, surveillance,
management, or containment. Naturalization, as Roland Barthes defines it, implies
that realism passes off as natural what is historically and ideologically constructed (see

Barthes 1972: 141). Thus, Howells makes upper-middle-class domesticity the yard-stick of all social arrangements (see Michaels 1987: 40; Kaplan 1988: 9; Thomas 1997: 14). Likewise, when *The Sea-Wolf* suggests that overcivilized women should become the "mate of a cave-man," it promotes a patriarchal view of womanhood the more stringent as it is validated by Darwinism (London 1984b: ch. 36, 256). Surveillance is a concept borrowed from Michel Foucault. As applied to realism and naturalism, it means that novels contribute to an economy of power that anchors subjects in positions of supremacy and subordination. Realism and naturalism foster surveillance notably through the construction of what Irene Gammel calls a "panoptic city" – an urban scene subjected to a disciplinarian spectatorial gaze (1994: 64). Mark Seltzer argues similarly that the novels' mapping of the city "opens the way for . . . the emergence and dispersal of agencies of social training and social control" (1982: 103). Using the same logic, June Howard shows that naturalism sets' up a dichotomy between "the spectator and the brute" (1985: 115; also 70–102). The novels' mid-dle-class characters indulge in sociological slumming: they spy on proletarians or ethnic others depicted as subhuman. In this, they anticipate Progressive-era reformers.

Management refers to a more indirect implementation of power. Seltzer, drawing on Foucault, defines it as the naturalist text's capacity to create a total system of power that empties out the subject's potential for opposition. Norris's *Trilogy of the Wheat*, he argues, misleads its readers by setting up a pseudo-contrast between individual desire and corporate power – between "economic and sexual domains" (1992: 40). Yet it simultaneously makes these spheres interchangeable: by depicting economic processes in *The Trilogy of the Wheat* by means of sexual metaphors, Norris's text undercuts the subject's prerogative to challenge corporate power in the name of autonomous desire. Amy Kaplan, drawing on Fredric Jameson, suggests a less disciplinarian understand-ing of management. She contends that realist/naturalist texts are committed to what historian Robert Wiebe, in a discussion of Progressive-era reformers, called a "search for order" (1967: vii). Realist/naturalist novelists seek to construct "a cohesive social world to contain the threats of social change" (Kaplan 1988: 12, 160). Yet this social instability cannot be fully contained. In aiming for order, the novels "pose problems they cannot solve" (Kaplan 1988: 160).

The social turmoil that triggers ideological management in naturalism is, most recent critics contend, associated with the economic and cultural shift experienced by US society in its transition from the nineteenth to the twentieth century. This historical narrative had admittedly long been identified as naturalism's anchoring ground. Georg Lukács had argued that the passage from realism to naturalism marks the disappearance of the pre-1848 entrepreneurial bourgeoisie and its supersession by monopoly capitalism (1970: 118). US critics, when they describe the demise of Howellsian realism and the rise of naturalism in the 1890s, articulate an American variant of this scenario. Post-1980s scholars revisit this history either by judging it from a novel political angle or by focusing on its hitherto neglected dimensions. Unlike Parrington and Kazin, some fault naturalism for failing to resist capitalistic incorporation (see Howard 1985: 70–103; Bowlby 1985: 1–34; Seltzer 1992: 44).

Figure 5.1   The textile workers' strike in Lawrence, Massachusetts

In 1912, Lawrence, Massachusetts was the "worsted capital of the world," with 32,000 workers employed in its dozen cotton and wool mills. The laborers came from twenty-seven ethnic groups and spoke two dozen different languages. Corporate profits were high but wages were at the starvation level; workers lived in crowded, unlit rooms; infant mortality was over 17 percent; and disease, malnutrition, and death were widespread. When the state legislature passed a law reducing the work week for women and children from fifty-six to fifty-four hours, employers cut wages and 23,000 workers struck. The workers called upon the Industrial Workers of the World to organize the strike; IWW leaders Joe Ettor, Arturo Giovannitti, Big Bill Haywood, and Elizabeth Gurley Flynn arrived to take charge; and soon the New York *Sun* could report that "Never before has a strike of such magnitude succeeded in uniting in one unflinching, unyielding, determined and united army so large and diverse a number of human beings." Despite police intimidation, the presence of 2,500 armed militia, mass arrests of pickets and even of emaciated child workers, jail sentences, fines, and physical assaults on strikers, labor held firm. Three months later, employers capitulated and increased wages. But it would be the last victory for the IWW. In 1917 the Wilson administration suppressed IWW publications, raided its offices, and tried the entire leadership under trumped-up wartime espionage statutes. Bill Haywood – the legendary giant of the labor movement – was convicted, jumped bail, and ended up in the Soviet Union, where he died in 1928 as the IWW passed into legend. (Photograph by permission of Walter P. Reuther Library, Wayne State University.)

Conversely, others praise it for perceptively mapping the new corporate realm and for registering the supposedly irreversible passing of the producers' ethos on which classical realism relied (see Michaels 1987: 40–1).

Gender-focused approaches rewrite the turn-of-the-century transition as a psychosocial shift. Naturalism, in this view, signals the end of puritanical, work-ethic-oriented selfhood. It fosters indeed the advent of a more reckless form of masculinity, tuned to corporate capitalism and imperialism (see Lears 1981: 130–1; Michaels 1987: 198–213; Kaplan 1990: 667–71; Rotundo 1993: 227–32; Den Tandt

1998: 216, 223). Conversely, naturalism reveals the ability of the consumer market to structure the desire of its patrons – of urban women, particularly. The novels position their characters as urban *flâneurs*, contemplating quasi-pornographic displays of commodities (see Bowlby 1985: 52–65; Gammel 1994: 66–7; Gelfant 1995: 191–2; Fisher 1985: 162–9). These gender and economic changes are shown to interlink with new definitions of authorship. Naturalist writers have to fashion for themselves a cultural profile matching the destabilizing field of nascent mass literature. The naturalist discourse of masculinity, in this logic, helps male writers to shed the stereotype of the patrician dilettante and to style themselves as literary entrepreneurs, acting as journalists or social-scientist investigators (see Habegger 1982: 256–66; Howard 1985: 138–41; Wilson 1985: 17–39, 142–3; Trachtenberg 1982: 140–1). The construction of a naturalist writerly manhood requires that genres such as domestic fiction or local realism be branded as too feminized for turn-of-the-century conditions (see Campbell 1997: 48–74).

IV

While post-1980s criticism highlights naturalism's ideological work, it offers only fragmentary insights into genre definition. Circumscribing the nature and the boundaries of realist/naturalist writing has, admittedly, been a perennially unpopular task (see Pizer 1995: 1; Becker 1963: 36–8; Bell 1993: 4–5). Still, I believe the issue worth investigating. On the one hand, the new criticism occasionally foregrounds questions of classification previously left unanswered. On the other, by hesitating to embark on a remapping of the turn-of-the-twentieth-century field, recent essays have sometimes merely reinscribed previous corpus definitions that lacked adequate grounding.

Orthodox definitions of naturalism relied on two criteria: generational change (the 1890s) and specificity of philosophical outlook – naturalism as a realist sub-genre, inflected by "pessimistic materialistic determinism" (Becker 1963: 35). Late-twentieth-century criticism challenges the generational component of this definition. The generational narrative receives little backing from what June Howard calls naturalism's "generic text" – the writers' pronouncements on their own practice (1985: 10). Dreiser, the pivotal figure of US naturalism, still described himself as a realist. His European model was Balzac, not Zola (see Elias 1970: 73–7). The only first-generation novelist to endorse the naturalist label is Norris (see Norris 1964: 71–2). Turn-of-the-twentieth-century fiction might therefore be dominated by several variants of one single realist movement. Uncertainties about the novelists's self-characterization increase if one expands the corpus beyond the authors discussed in early essays. Less reputed canonical authors blur the logic of the generational paradigm: the so-called "Chicago realists," Henry Blake Fuller and Robert Herrick, appear after Howells, during the naturalist decade. Multiculturalist canon revision raises even thornier issues (see Ammons 1995: 105–11). The late nineteenth-century women, minorities, and radicals that are added to the corpus – Cahan, Cather, Charles Waddell Chesnutt, Kate Chopin, Sui Sin Far, Charlotte Perkins Gilman, Ellen Glasgow, Pauline Hopkins, James Weldon Johnson, Poole, Teller, Edith Wharton, and Zitkala Ša – fit in literary traditions that do not necessarily follow the chronology of canonical naturalism.

Recent criticism positions itself more ambiguously on the possibility of defining what, in Frederic Jameson's terminology, might be called naturalism's "semantic" genre (1981: 107) – its thematic unity. On the one hand, determinism loses its primacy as a defining parameter. It is still regarded as a symptom of social disintegration – indeed, as the nexus of a thematics of proletarianization (see Howard 1985: 95–103). Yet its dehumanizing pathos is less relevant to neo-Marxist/historicist approaches, which lend little credence to the autonomous self in the first place (see Howard 1985: 63–9; Seltzer 1992: 43; Gammel 1994: 79). On the other hand, we have seen above that the passage from mid- to late-nineteenth-century economic and cultural configurations does serve as covert support for a thematic definition: naturalism may be characterized as the fiction fitting the later stage of this historical transition.

Post-1980s scholars cannot, however, build a full-fledged literary classification on this historical basis. They face methodological barriers as well as obstacles inherent to the realist/naturalist corpus. First, the recent criticism's anti-mimetic stance makes it difficult to identify (sub)-genres within turn-of-the-twentieth-century literature. On the contrary, it fosters the intertextual dissemination of this literary field. Traditionally, realist/naturalist works marked themselves off from other forms of writing – Lew Wallace's *Ben-Hur* (1880), say – by their dedication to literary truth. Yet when concerns over referentiality are de-emphasized, genre definitions based on verisimilitude become porous. In Walter Benn Michaels's *Gold Standard*, for instance, Howells's, Dreiser's, and Norris's fiction is shown to have affinities with such diverse works as treatises on the Gold Standard and bimetallism, Populist tracts, late-nineteenth-century *trompe l'œil* painting, abstract expressionism, Richard von Krafft-Ebing's treatises on sexual pathology, and Leopold von Sacher-Masoch's *Venus in Furs* (see Michaels 1987: 115, 150, 161, 165). Within such variegated cultural constellations, naturalist novels can no longer be distinguished from non-realistic fiction (romance), referential non-fiction (late-nineteenth-century science), even non-fiction romance (the fantasy world of advertising and economic theory). Neo-historicism's unprecedented capacity to chart links among fictional and historical texts is based precisely on this flouting of generic divides.

Second, efforts at classification are defeated by the internal heterogeneity of naturalist texts. Georg Lukács wanted literary realism to be a discourse of cognitive authority expressing the whole of the world in one voice (see Lukács 1970: 142–3). Yet naturalism is, in Mikhail Bakhtin's terminology, more polyphonic than "monologic" (1981: 270). The novels lapse into a multiplicity of idioms (romance, sentimentalism, the gothic) that, as we have seen, they also ostensibly debunk. Whereas *Maggie* ridicules music-hall sentimentality, *Carrie* suggests without apparent irony that plays of "suffering and tears," graced with "tremolo music [and] long, explana-tory, cumulative addresses" (Dreiser 1986: ch. 17, 161), help Carrie "rise to a finer state of feeling" (ch. 17, 163). Small wonder, then, that Norris should argue as early as the 1890s that Zola, far from creating an "inner circle of realism" (Norris 1964: 72), fashioned himself into a "romantic writer" (p. 71). Later critics concur with Norris. Pizer points out that naturalism mixes the "commonplace" with the "sensational" (1984: 19; see also 34–8). Walcutt describes Norris's and Dreiser's idiom as a "divided stream," mingling realism with the literary tradition derived from mid-nineteenth-century Transcendentalism (1956: i).

Orthodox critics interpret naturalism's straying from classical realism as a breach of verisimilitude (see Berthoff 1965: 31, 246; Lukács 1970: 140) or, conversely, as a welcome return to the romance tradition – an idiom often characterized as more innate to American letters than realism itself (see Pizer 1984: 34–40; Walcutt 1956: i; Walcutt 1974: 10–11). Recent scholars reach similar conclusions through a different path. Naturalism is sometimes presented as the genre that precipitates the entropic "disintegration" of realism (Baguley 1990: 208). Against such non-referential inter-pretations, I think it useful to aim for a definition of realism and naturalism that makes allowances for the texts' polyphony without dismissing their ambition to map the social world. Anti-mimetic readings have admittedly enriched our sense of naturalism's internal make-up and of its complex cultural entanglements. Yet, as Jameson suggests, they miss their target if they fail to account for the prolonged success of realism and naturalism in making readers assent to its portrayal of social reality (Jameson 1991: 209).

A definition of realism and naturalism that balances out post-structuralist and referential concerns is sketched out in Amy Kaplan's discussion of *Carrie*. Kaplan adopts a logic reminiscent of Bakhtinian dialogism (see 1988: 158–60). She contends that *Carrie*'s interweaving of realism, sentimentalism, and romance does not amount to a surrender to fantasy. Instead, it sets up "a debate with competing definitions of reality" (p. 160). It would in this logic be misguided to expect Dreiser to depict a "more hard-boiled, dirty reality" (p. 160). His shifts into romance are not lapses but symptoms: they indicate that no single idiom in the text can express a totalizing truth. Dreiser's realism is meta-literary and pragmatically oriented: it comments on its own limits and pursues its goal through multiple discourses.

Kaplan, whose object of investigation is realism proper, sees no need for naturalism as a separate category, even in her characterization of Dreiser. Yet her dialogic model suggests how a differentiation may be traced out between literary discourses that more markedly embody respectively a realistic and a naturalistic practice. We should envisage realism and naturalism as overlapping discourses, developing side by side throughout the naturalist decades, and indeed coexisting within the same texts. Predominantly realist or naturalist works draw on a common stock of literary devices, though they do so in different proportions and to different ends. The novels that stand at the realist end of this continuum focus on what Kaplan, borrowing the term from Raymond Williams, calls "knowable communities" – circumscribed social spaces equivalent to the family settings of novels of manners (1988: 47). This is the universe of Lily Bart's Old New York in Wharton's *The House of Mirth* (1905), of Chesnutt's upper-middle-class African Americans, or of Zitkala Ša's Indian childhood on the Dakota prairie ("Impressions," 1900). Because of their local scope, such texts support a realism of demystification: they show observers who are well acquainted with a familiar universe uncovering its hidden logic. Lily resists the upper-class marriage market whose subtleties she perfectly masters. Mr. Ryder, the protagonist of Chesnutt's "The Wife of his Youth" (1899), exposes the African American bourgeoisie's class prejudices by acknowledging the wife he married under slavery. Zitkala Ša, as a child narrator, understands that the dignified life on the prairie is being threatened by the outside force of Anglo-American colonization. Yet this realist clear-sightedness remains bounded. The effort to dispel illusions encounters areas that resist elucidation. Lily Bart's exile from upper-class New York brings her "near the dizzy brink of the unreal" (Wharton 1986: ch. 13, 321). To Chesnutt's Mr. Ryder, slavery exists as a repressed, ghostly past. Young Zitkala Ša views both her tribe's rituals and the paleface's iron horse as awesome mysteries.

Novels where naturalist discourse predominates resort to romance in their attempt to represent the very objects realism cannot bring into focus – the realm *film noir* critic James Naremore calls "the social fantastic" (1998: 16). In these works, romance is an epistemological back-up: it offers a fuzzy map of what Norris calls the "secretest [*sic*] life" (1964: 77). In *The House of Mirth*, the switch to romance occurs when the author evokes the ill-understood forces shaping Lily's destiny. The heroine is dragged into death by "an invisible hand [making] magic passes over her in the darkness" (Wharton 1986: bk. II, ch. 13, 322). Such metaphors are infrequent in Wharton. They are systematically used in Norris's naturalistic *The Pit*. Here, the Chicago Board of Trade is a continental nexus where money and produce flow with "the appalling fury of [a] Maëlstrom" (Norris 1971: ch. 3, 80). The "Pit," the trading floor hub, is a "tremendous cloaca, the maw of some colossal sewer" (ch. 3, 79). Norris's novel does contain documentary essays on the mechanics of speculation. Yet the predominance of romance thwarts the depiction of determinate social relationships. The interaction of business and marriage is taken for granted, not analysed. Finance wrecks Jadwin's household merely because it possesses a power "coeval with the earthquake" (ch. 7, 259; ch. 10, 387).

Twentieth-century readers are tempted to dismiss Norris's rhetoric as heaps of "melodramatic cliché[s]" (Bell 1993: 81). Yet it constitutes a likely fallback solution for writers subjected to what Marxist theorists call reification – the dehumanizing illegibility of capitalist societies (see Kadarkay 1995: 233). Lukácsian Marxism prescribes that realistic fiction should portray society as a transparent, organic community of concrete human relations. Turn-of-the-twentieth-century novels suggest instead that the urban world cannot be captured in such rational terms. Logically, their romance idiom should remain an index of the limits of their realist vision. Yet it is also used as a medium of social mapping in its own right – as romance knowledge, so to speak. This paradoxical strategy can be traced back to the origins of urban fiction, indeed, as early as Balzac – Lukács's favorite realist and Dreiser's main European inspiration. It is central to the corpus of urban gothic from which naturalists derive their romance tropes – Eugène Sue's, Edgar Allan Poe's, and George Lippard's mid-nineteenth-century mysteries of the city (see Trachtenberg 1982: 103–5; Denning 1987: 85–117). It is also common in the turn-of-the-twentieth-century social sciences, which constantly allude to the dizzying abysses of atavism and evolutionary time. Herbert Spencer's sociology is backed by philosophical reflections on "the Unknowable" (Bannister 1979: 44). Dreiser, a Spencerian, launches Carrie in quest of the mysteries of "the other half of life, in which we have no part" (1986: ch. 19, 176).

The romance discourse of turn-of-the-twentieth-century novels differs from earlier equivalents in its deployment of a vitalist rhetoric. Naturalist writers make sense of the urban sphere by means of such quasi-mystical social Darwinian concepts as "forces" (*Sister Carrie*; Dreiser 1986: ch. 13, 118), "instincts" (*White Fang*; London 1987: 247), and "Life" itself (*The Titan*; Dreiser 1965: ch. 1, 12). This makes urban communities the locus of what Robert Herrick calls a mysterious "web of life" (1900: ch. 12, 348). Norris's biologically embodied economic metaphors (the "Wheat") or Sinclair's depiction of the life-grinding slaughterhouses of Packingtown are aspects of this urban vitalism (Norris 1986: ch. 8, 576; see Martin 1981: 160–1). Dreiser sums up its outlook in *The Titan*, when he writes that the building of Chicago is a process that allows "Life" to do "something new" (1965: ch. 1, 12). Poole's sprawling socialist novel *The Harbor* marks a late climax of this pre-World War I tradition. It locates the "rushing chaos of life" successively in the New York sex underworld, in "the homes of the Big Companies" on Wall Street (Poole 1915: bk II, ch. 10, 154), and in the "great spirit" of the "surging multitudes" of proletarian strikers (bk III, ch. 13, 315; bk III, ch. 12, 304).

Compared to the realistic practices of naturalization and surveillance, the specific ideological work of naturalist socio-vitalism is the construction of overdetermined mysteries. Urban crowds, sexuality, corporations, or the commodity market are made radically undecipherable by means of polysemic metaphors (see Den Tandt 1998: 146–50). Otherness in this corpus – whether racial, gender-based, or economic – is never self-contained. Any uncanny element interlinks with all other ill-understood energies of the urban field. Norris's portrayal of Lyman Derrick, the son of the insurgent farmers' leader in *The Octopus*, illustrates this device. A melodramatic villain who sells out the farmers to the railroad, Lyman is afflicted with a multilayered aura mingling economic, gender, and racial connotations. He is marked out as a mother's child, "a well-dressed, city-bred young man" who turned down the virile farmer's life for the corporate-identified legal profession (Norris 1986: ch. 4, 439). His feminized, citified status is signaled by his dark-complexioned "dago face" (ch. 4, 447) – a feature that in the novel's context associates him with unruly mobs of Mexican and Mediterranean farmhands. Social science texts cultivate uncanniness by similar means. Jacob Riis, in his survey of the New York slums, empathizes with several immigrant communities yet singles out the Chinese as the nexus of the city's disquieting complexity. In his text, immigrants from the Far East are associated simultaneously with white slavery and with the underground drugs economy (see Riis 1971: 78–80).

V

From what precedes, we may sketch out a literary-historical map of turn-of-the-twentieth-century fiction highlighting literary affinities and lines of fracture uncharted by previous periodizations. I contend that the novels traditionally ranked as naturalistic feed, with varying degrees of dominance, on three overlapping strands of writing: the realist and romance discourses described above, as well as an emergent modernist aesthetic. In the first place, this dialogic mapping highlights the continuity of a realist tradition through and beyond the naturalist 1890s. The latter current – the realism of knowable communities – includes authors previously studied as realists (Fuller, Wharton), local realists (Sarah Orne Jewett, Glasgow), African American writers (Chesnutt, Hopkins, Nella Larsen, Petry), muckrakers (Phillips), immigrant writers (Cahan, Yiezerska, Gold), 1920s and 1930s naturalists (Lewis, Steinbeck), or modernists (Fitzgerald). Through these writers, the realism of demystification perpetuates itself even in periods where it is no longer dominant.

Second, we may isolate the constellation of novels that I would be tempted to label naturalism proper, yet that should more accurately be called the fiction of sociological vitalism. This current includes works by canonical naturalists – Dreiser, Norris, and London – as well as quite a few lesser-known figures – Herrick, Johnson, Teller, and Bullard. Their works exist in constant interaction with realism. They are identifiable less by the self-contained consistency of a genre than by a recurrent pattern of dialogization – a specific way of playing out documentary discourse against romance and Darwinian tropes. Socio-vitalism largely dies out after World War I, as modernism becomes hegemonic. Dreiser's *An American Tragedy* (1925) and Dos Passos's fiction pursue its totalizing momentum, yet in an increasingly disenchanted mood stripped of romance intensities.

Third, the dialogic approach makes it easier to acknowledge the emergence of pre-modernist concerns such as the dedication to writing for its own sake, the exploration of inner selfhood, and the development of a bohemian scene of alienated intellectuals. Chief in this current is Henry James, who eludes classification by his plural allegiances to realism, naturalism, and (pre)-modernism (see Seltzer 1982: 96–7; Crowley 1995: 117–21; Wardley 1989: 639–42). Gilman, Chopin, and Cather fit in this category because they use the Darwinian tropes of socio-vitalism in ways that anticipate stream-of-consciousness modernism. Further, Cather is pre-modernistic in her predilection for narratives of artistic education – novels that, like *The Song of the Lark* (1915) (but also Johnson's *Autobiography*, Dreiser's *The "Genius"*, and Poole's *Harbor*), chronicle the development of turn-of-the-twentieth-century artists. In several respects, Crane, one of the earliest figures of US naturalism, ranks among the pre-modernists as well. He flaunts a detached narratorial stance that, though often regarded as the hallmark of naturalism, differs from the quasi-gothic affects of socio-vitalism. Also, unlike his peers, Crane favors a self-consciously patterned literary language: dialogues in *Maggie* are a carefully wrought imitation of the Irish American vernacular. In this, Crane, together with Sherwood Anderson, anticipates Hemingway's modernism – arguably the reason for his success among twentieth-century critics.

Finally, it is possible on this basis to define the relevance of naturalism to turn-of-the-twentieth-century women and minority writers. I indicate above that naturalism implies a level of writerly empowerment that seems accessible primarily to white males: it aims for a totalizing grasp of society and models itself on the paradigm of scientific authority. Howellsian realism, on the contrary, seems easier to appropriate: it focuses on community relations familiar to individuals subjected to the restraints of segregation and the domestic sphere (see Warren 1993: 13–14). The turn-of-the-twentieth-century corpus partially verifies this hypothesis. Chesnutt's stories of the color line and Cahan's *Yekl* (1896) portray community rituals. They are Howellsian texts whose focus has shifted from white middle-class parlors to the ballrooms of the African American "Blue Vein Society" (Chesnutt 1968: ch. 1, 1) or to Professor Peltner's dancing "academy" for East Side Jewish immigrants (Cahan 1896: ch. 2, 36).

Yet naturalism does share one key narrative pattern with women's and minority fiction: that which relies on picaresque narration and trickster characters. Johnson's *Autobiography* follows the itinerary of a light-skinned African American protagonist through locales embodying multiple facets of black middle-class experience. Cahan's *Levinsky*, unlike the locally focused *Yekl*, traces the development of a Jewish business-man from the yeshivas of tsarist Russia to the garment district of the Manhattan East Side. In Cather's *Song of the Lark*, Thea Kronborg becomes an opera singer after moving from Moonstone, Colorado to Chicago, the east coast, and Germany. Such stories cannot be narrated within the realist discourse of the knowable community: their successive climaxes occur when the protagonists experience the thrill or threat of unfamiliar worlds – black Harlem, the first glimpse of the New World's "magic shores" (Cahan 1960: bk 4, ch. 1, 67), or the discovery of Wagner at a Chicago opera. Structurally, they are similar to naturalist novels focusing on figures endowed with the trickster's ability to adapt to multiple environments – *Carrie*, London's *Martin Eden* (1912), or Phillips's *Susan Lenox*. In this light, naturalism would appeal to later minority authors – Wright or even Ralph Ellison – not only because of its concern for poverty, but also because it fits in a tradition of uprooted, mobile protagonists.

PRIMARY TEXTS

Bullard, Arthur. *Comrade Yetta*. 1913.

Cahan, Abraham. *Yekl: A Tale of the New York Ghetto*. 1896.

Cahan, Abraham. *The Rise of David Levinsky*. 1917.

Cather, Willa. *The Song of the Lark*. 1915.

Chesnutt, Charles W. *The Wife of His Youth and Other Stories of the Color Line*. 1899.

Chopin, Kate. *The Awakening*. 1899.

Crane, Stephen. *Maggie, A Girl of the Streets (A Story of New York)*. 1893.

Crane, Stephen. *The Red Badge of Courage; an Episode of the American Civil War.* 1895.

Dreiser, Theodore. *Sister Carrie.* 1900.

Dreiser, Theodore. *An Amateur Laborer.* Composed 1904.

Dreiser, Theodore. *The Financier.* 1912.

Dreiser, Theodore. *The Titan.* 1914.

Dreiser, Theodore. *The "Genius."* 1915.

Dreiser, Theodore. *Newspaper Days.* 1922.

Fuller, Henry Blake. *The Cliff-Dwellers.* 1893.

Fuller, Henry Blake. *With the Procession.* 1895.

Garland, Hamlin. *Jason Edwards: An Average Man.* 1892.

Garland, Hamlin. *A Spoil of Office: A Story of the Modern West.* 1892.

Garland, Hamlin. *Rose of Dutcher's Coolly.* 1895.

Gilman, Charlotte Perkins. "The Yellow Wallpaper." 1892.

Herrick, Robert. *The Web of Life.* 1900.

Herrick, Robert. *The Common Lot.* 1904.

Herrick, Robert. *Together.* 1908.

Howells, William Dean. *A Hazard of New Fortunes.* 1890.

Johnson, James Weldon. *The Autobiography of an Ex-Coloured Man.* 1912.

London, Jack. *The Call of the Wild.* 1903.

London, Jack. "The Scab." 1904.

London, Jack. *The Sea-Wolf.* 1904.

London, Jack. *White Fang.* 1906.

London, Jack. *Before Adam.* 1907.

London, Jack. *The Iron Heel.* 1908.

London, Jack. *Martin Eden.* 1909.

London, Jack. *The Valley of the Moon.* 1913.

Norris, Frank. *A Man's Woman.* 1899.

Norris, Frank. *McTeague: A Story of San Francisco.* 1899.

Norris, Frank. *The Octopus: A Story of California.* 1901.

Norris, Frank. *The Pit.* 1903.

Norris, Frank. *The Responsibilities of the Novelist.* 1903.

Norris, Frank. *Vandover and the Brute.* 1914.

Phillips, David Graham. *Susan Lenox, Her Fall and Rise.* 1917.

Poole, Ernest. *The Harbor.* 1915.

Sinclair, Upton. *The Jungle.* 1906.

Sinclair, Upton. *The Metropolis.* 1907.

Teller, Charlotte. *The Cage.* 1907.

Wharton, Edith. *The House of Mirth.* 1905.

Zitkala Ša. "Impressions of an Indian Childhood: The Big Red Apples." 1900.

REFERENCES AND FURTHER READING

Åhnebrink, Lars (1950). *The Beginnings of Naturalism in American Fiction: A Study of the Works of Hamlin Garland, Stephen Crane, and Frank Norris with Special Reference to Some European Influences, 1891–1903.* Cambridge, Mass.: Harvard University Press. A well-documented study of early US naturalism, containing an extended discussion of Garland.

Ammons, Elizabeth (1995). "Expanding the Canon of American Realism." In Donald Pizer (ed.), *The Cambridge Companion to American Realism and Naturalism: Howells to London*, 95–114. Cambridge, UK: Cambridge University Press. Examines the contribution of non-canonical authors to turn-of-the-twentieth-century realism.

Anesko, Michael (1995). "New Critical Approaches." In Donald Pizer (ed.), *The Cambridge Companion to American Realism and Naturalism: Howells to London*, 77–94. Cambridge, UK: Cambridge University Press. Surveys 1980s and 1990s criticism of realism and naturalism.

Auerbach, Erich (1946). *Mimesis: Dargestellte Wirklichkeit in der abendländische Literatur* [Mimesis: the representation of reality in Western literature]. Bern: A. Francke AG Verlag. A seminal study of the evolution of realism from antiquity to the early twentieth century.

Baguley, David (1990). *Naturalist Fiction: The Entropic Vision.* Cambridge, UK: Cambridge University Press. Describes naturalism as a generically heterogeneous discourse that brings about the deconstruction of realism.

Bakhtin, Mikhail (1981). *The Dialogic Imagination: Four Essays by M. M. Bakhtin*, ed. Michael Holquist, trans. Caryl Emerson and Michael Holquist. Austin: University of Texas Press.

Bannister, Robert C. (1979). *Social Darwinism: Science and Myth in Anglo-American Social*

Thought. Philadelphia: Temple University Press. Surveys the impact of Darwinism in late nineteenth-century philosophy, economic theory, and literature.

Barthes, Roland (1972). *Mythologies*, trans. A. Lavers. New York: Hill & Wang. (First publ. 1957.)

Becker, George J., ed. (1963). *Documents of Modern Literary Realism*. Princeton: Princeton University Press. A collection of key essays by writers and critics, spanning the development of European and US realism and naturalism from the nineteenth to the mid-twentieth century.

Bell, Michael Davitt (1993). *The Problem of American Realism: Studies in the Cultural History of a Literary Idea*. Chicago: University of Chicago Press. Discusses the construction of the concept of literary realism in the fiction and criticism of mid- and late nineteenth-century US writers.

Berthoff, Warner (1965). *The Ferment of Realism: American Literature 1884–1919*. New York: Free Press; republished 1981 by Cambridge University Press with a new preface by the author. A wide-ranging history of realism and naturalism in its socio-historical context.

Bowlby, Rachel (1985). *Just Looking: Consumer Culture in Dreiser, Gissing, and Zola*. New York: Methuen. In opposition to previous left-wing interpretations of naturalism, emphasizes Dreiser's involvement in the ideology of consumerism.

Brace, Charles Loring (1967). *The Dangerous Classes of New York and Twenty Years' Work among Them*. Montclair, NJ: Patterson Smith. (First publ. 1872.)

Bullard, Arthur (1913). *Comrade Yetta*. New York: Macmillan.

Cahan, Abraham (1896). *Yekl: A Tale of the New York Ghetto*. New York: D. Appleton and Co.

Cahan, Abraham (1960). *The Rise of David Levinsky*. New York: Harper & Row.

Campbell, Donna (1997). *Resisting Regionalism: Gender and Naturalism in American Fiction, 1885–1915*. Athens, Ohio: Ohio University Press.

Chesnutt, Charles W. (1968). *The Wife of his Youth and Other Stories of the Color Line*. Ann Arbor: University of Michigan Press.

Conder, John J. (1984). *Naturalism in American Fiction: The Classic Phase*. Lexington: University Press of Kentucky. Revisits the issue of determinism and defines naturalism on a philosophical basis.

Conn, Peter J. (1983). *The Divided Mind: Ideology and Imagination in America, 1898–1917*. Cambridge, UK: Cambridge University Press. Surveys the literary landscape of the Progressive years and discusses many previously overlooked authors.

Crane, Stephen (1979). *Maggie, a Girl of the Streets (A Story of New York): An Authoritative Text, Backgrounds and Sources, The Author and the Novel, Reviews and Criticism*, ed. Thomas A. Gullason. New York: Norton.

Cronon, William (1991). *Nature's Metropolis: Chicago and the Great West*. New York: Norton. This environmental history of nineteenth-century Chicago contains insightful remarks on realist and naturalist urban fiction.

Crowley, John W. (1995). "*The Portrait of a Lady* and *The Rise of Silas Lapham*: The Company They Kept." In Donald Pizer (ed.), *The Cambridge Companion to American Realism and Naturalism: Howells to London*, 117–37. Cambridge, UK: Cambridge University Press. Analyzes James and Howells as founding figures of American realism.

Denning, Michael (1987). *Mechanic Accents: Dime Novels and Working-Class Culture in America*. London: Verso. Brings to light the working-class appropriations of mid- and late nineteenth-century popular fiction.

Den Tandt, Christophe (1998). *The Urban Sublime in American Literary Naturalism*. Urbana and Chicago: University of Illinois Press. Discusses naturalism's use of romance rhetoric for the exploration of unfamiliar aspects of the urban industrial metropolis.

Dreiser, Theodore (1965). *The Titan*. New York: New American Library.

Dreiser, Theodore (1986). *Sister Carrie*. Harmondsworth: Penguin (Pennsylvania Edition).

Elias, Robert H. (1970). *Theodore Dreiser: Apostle of Nature*. Ithaca, NY: Cornell University Press. (First publ. 1949.) An introduction to Dreiser's life and works.

Fisher, Philip (1985). *Hard Facts: Setting and Form in the American Novel*. New York: Oxford University Press. Analyzes Dreiser's contribution to the representation of the urban experience.

Gammel, Irene (1994). *Sexualizing Power in Naturalism: Theodore Dreiser and Frederic Philip Grove*. Calgary: University of Calgary Press. Drawing on Foucault, discusses naturalism's gendered construction of urban space.

Gelfant, Blanche H. (1995). "What More Can Carrie Want? Naturalistic Ways of Consuming Women." In Donald Pizer (ed.), *The Cambridge Companion to American Realism and Naturalism: Howells to London*, 178–210. Cambridge, UK: Cambridge University Press. Discusses desire and consumerism in Dreiser and links these issues to naturalist determinism.

Habegger, Alfred (1982). *Gender, Fantasy, and Realism in American Literature*. New York: Columbia University Press. Discusses the shift from domestic fiction to realism.

Herrick, Robert (1900). *The Web of Life*. New York: Macmillan.

Herrick, Robert (1962). *Together*. Greenwich, Conn.: Fawcett.

Howard, June (1985). *Form and History in American Literary Naturalism*. Chapel Hill and London: University of North Carolina Press. Describes naturalism's contribution to the anti-proletarian politics of middle-class Progressive-era reformers.

Howells, William Dean (1990). *A Hazard of New Fortunes*. Oxford: Oxford University Press.

Jameson, Frederic (1981). *The Political Unconscious: Narrative as a Socially Symbolic Act*. Ithaca, NY: Cornell University Press.

Jameson, Frederic (1991). *Postmodernism, or, the Cultural Logic of Late Capitalism*. Durham, NC: Duke University Press.

Kadarkay, Arpad, ed. (1995). *The Lukács Reader*. Oxford: Blackwell.

Kaplan, Amy (1988). *The Social Construction of American Realism*. Chicago: University of Chicago Press. Against proponents of the romance tradition, demonstrates the importance of realism in late-nineteenth-century letters and provides a reading of realism as a socially constructed discourse.

Kaplan, Amy (1990). "Romancing the Empire: The Embodiment of American Masculinity in the Popular Historical Novel of the 1890s." *American Literary History* 2, 659–90. Highlights the construction of imperialistic masculinity in popular romances.

Kazin, Alfred (1956). *On Native Grounds: An Interpretation of American Prose Literature*. New York: Reynal & Hitchcock. (First publ. 1942.) Remarkable for its broad range, this classic essay describes realism and naturalism as vital traditions in the social and intellectual history of the United States.

Lawlor, Mary (2000). *Recalling the Wild: Naturalism and the Closing of the American West*. New Brunswick, NJ, and London: Rutgers University Press. Describes the shift from a romantic to a naturalistic vision of the West (Crane; Norris; London).

Lears, T. J. Jackson (1981). *No Place of Grace: Antimodernism and the Transformations of American Culture 1880–1920*. New York: Pantheon. Discusses the shift in gender ideology underlying the romance components of naturalist writing.

London, Jack (1982a). *The Iron Heel*. In Donald Pizer (ed.), *Jack London: Novels and Social Writings*, 319–553. New York: Library of America.

London, Jack (1982b). "The Scab." In Donald Pizer (ed.), *Jack London: Novels and Social Writings*, 1121–35. New York: Library of America.

London, Jack (1984a). *Before Adam*. Mattituck, NY: Amereon House.

London, Jack (1984b). *"The Sea-Wolf" and Other Stories*. London: Penguin.

London, Jack (1987). *The Call of the Wild, White Fang, and Other Stories*. New York: Viking Penguin.

Lukács, Georg (1970). "Narrate or Describe." In *Writer and Critic and Other Essays*, 110–48. New York: Grosset & Dunlap. Discusses the status of realism and naturalism with regard to the changes in nineteeenth-century capitalism.

Martin, Ronald E. (1981). *American Literature and the Universe of Force*. Durham, NC: Duke University Press. Analyzes the social Darwinian discourse of naturalism and its metaphysics of force.

May, Henry F. (1959). *The End of American Innocence*. Chicago: Chicago University Press. Surveys US intellectual and literary life from the 1890s to World War I.

Michaels, Walter Benn (1987). *The Gold Standard and the Logic of Naturalism: American Literature at the Turn of the Century*. Berkeley: University of California Press. An iconoclastic neo-historicist rereading of naturalism and turn-of-the-twentieth-century culture, this essay highlights the pro-corporate aspects of Norris's and Dreiser's works.

Mitchell, Lee Clark (1989). *Determined Fictions: American Literary Naturalism*. New York: Columbia University Press. Focuses on the philosopical aspects of determinism and selfhood.

Moers, Ellen (1969). *Two Dreisers*. New York: Viking. An in-depth discussion of Dreiser's life and works.

Naremore, James (1998). *More Than Night: Film Noir in Its Contexts*. Berkeley: University of California Press. Highlights the legacy of realism and naturalism in Hollywood crime films.

Norris, Frank (1964). *The Responsibilities of the Novelist*. In *The Literary Criticism of Frank Norris*, ed. Donald Pizer, 81–98. Austin: University of Texas Press.

Norris, Frank (1971). *The Pit*. Cambridge, Mass.: Robert Bentley.

Norris, Frank (1978). *Vandover and the Brute*. Lincoln: University of Nebraska Press.

Norris, Frank (1985). *McTeague: A Story of San Francisco*. Harmondsworth. Penguin.

Norris, Frank (1986). *The Octopus: A Story of California*. New York: Viking Penguin.

Parrington, Vernon Louis (1930). *The Beginnings of Critical Realism in America, 1860–1920*. New York: Harcourt, Brace. This classic history of realism and naturalism portrays the two genres as voices of protest against puritanism and corporate culture.

Pizer, Donald (1984). *Realism and Naturalism in Nineteenth-Century American Literature*, 2nd edn. Carbondale: Southern Illinois University Press. (First publ. 1966.) A post-World War II vindication of realism and naturalism, this collection of essays draws on the methodology of the New Criticism and of myth criticism in order to underline the two genres' literary qualities.

Pizer, Donald, ed. (1995). *The Cambridge Companion to American Realism and Naturalism: Howells to London*. Cambridge, UK: Cambridge University Press. Collects recent essays covering most aspects of scholarship on realism and naturalism.

Pizer, Donald, ed. (1998). *Documents of American Realism and Naturalism*. Carbondale and Edwardsville: Southern Illinois University Press. A collection of essays on realism and naturalism by US writers and critics from the late nineteenth century to the present.

Poole, Ernest (1915). *The Harbor*. New York: Macmillan.

Riis, Jacob (1971). *How the Other Half Lives: Studies among the Tenements of New York*. New York: Dover. (First publ. 1890.) A pioneering social sciences survey of social conditions in New York, illustrated by famous photographs of tenement life.

Rotundo, E. Anthony (1993). *American Manhood: Transformations of Masculinity from the Revolution to the Modern Era*. New York: Basic Books/HarperCollins. Highlights the plurality and historicity of definitions of masculinity in US culture.

Seltzer, Mark (1982). "*The Princess Casamassima*: Realism and the Fantasy of Surveillance." In Eric J. Sundquist (ed.), *American Realism: New Essays*, 95–118. Baltimore: Johns Hopkins University Press. Reads Henry James in the light of Foucault's analysis of power and surveillance.

Seltzer, Mark (1992). "The Naturalist Machine." In *Bodies and Machines*, 25–44. New York: Routledge. Describes the politics of Norris's naturalism as pro-corporate and totalitarian.

Sinclair, Upton (1984). *The Jungle*. Harmondsworth: Penguin.

Sumner, William Graham (1961). *What Social Classes Owe to Each Other*. Caldwell, Idaho: Caxton Printers. (First publ. 1883.)

Sundquist, Eric J., ed. (1982). *American Realism: New Essays*. Baltimore: Johns Hopkins University Press. Introduced neo-Marxist and neo-historicist reading paradigms to the field of realism and naturalism.

Thomas, Brook (1997). *American Realism and the Failed Promise of Contract*. Berkeley: University of California Press. Differentiates realism from naturalism by arguing that the former is based on a democratic ethos relying on contractual practices.

Trachtenberg, Alan (1982). *The Incorporation of America: Culture and Society in the Gilded Age*. New York: Hill & Wang. Surveys the cultural currents that marked the transition of the United States towards a corporate economic system.

Veblen, Thorstein (1934). *The Theory of the Leisure Class*. New York: Modern Library. (First publ. 1899.) This pioneering analysis of consumerism reverses the premises of social Darwinism by making modern capitalists the embodiment of archaic, obsolete human traits.

Walcutt, Charles Child (1956). *American Literary Naturalism: A Divided Stream*. Minneapolis: University of Minnesota Press. Influenced by myth criticism, highlights the affinities of naturalism with the romance tradition and transcendentalism.

Walcutt, Charles Child, ed. (1974). *Seven Novelists in the American Naturalist Tradition*. Minneapolis: University of Minnesota Press. (First publ. 1963.) Collects chapters by separate scholars on canonical naturalists.

Ward, Lester Frank (1970). *The Psychic Factors of Civilization*. New York: Johnson. (First publ. 1893.) Develops a of theory of evolution oriented toward social collaboration instead of strife.

Wardley, Lynn (1989). "Woman's Voice, Democracy's Body and *The Bostonians*." *English Literary History* 56, 639–65. A neo-historicist reading of Henry James's gender politics.

Warren, Kenneth W. (1993). *Black and White Strangers: Race and American Literary Realism*. Chicago: University of Chicago Press. Examines the racial discourse of canonical realists and evaluates the relevance of realism and naturalism to African American literature.

Wharton, Edith (1986). *The House of Mirth*. New York: Penguin.

Wiebe, Robert (1967). *The Search for Order: 1977–1920*. New York: Hill & Wang. Provides a positive appraisal of the efforts of Progressive-era reformers to adapt American capitalism to twentieth-century conditions.

Wilson, Christopher P. (1985). *The Labor of Words: Literary Professionalism in the Progressive Era*. Athens, Ga.: University of Georgia Press. Describes the efforts of American literary naturalists to secure their place in the developing market of mass literature.

Zola, Émile (1963). *The Experimental Novel* (first publ. 1880). In G. J. Becker (ed.), *Documents of Modern Literary Realism*, 161–96. Princeton: Princeton University Press. The seminal essay in which the French novelist defines naturalism as a scientifically informed variety of realism.

6

American Regionalism: Local Color, National Literature, Global Circuits

June Howard

In the third decade of the nineteenth century the United States was already considered a place where thought circulated incredibly rapidly. During his travels in America, the prescient French observer Alexis de Tocqueville crossed part of Michigan in an uncovered cart that followed "scarcely cleared paths through immense forests of green trees" to deliver bundles of mail to cottages serving as post offices (2000: 290). He marveled at how many letters Americans sent and received, at the informed interest in national affairs shown by people who were (to his eye) living in a wilderness, and at the number and circulation of newspapers. After the Civil War, the rate of increase in the volume of printed matter produced and distributed in the United States surged even higher. More publishers produced more copies of more books, and they cost less to buy. The number of magazines being published, according to estimates by the historian Frank Luther Mott, more than tripled in the fifteen years between 1865 and 1880.

It takes a leap of imagination to grasp the power that print must have had then, before the other media that constantly compete for later generations' attention had come into existence. Knowledge of other places came either by word of mouth or from words on paper. So did stories. Magazines printed far more fiction than they do now; by Mott's calculations, in the early 1870s a third of their pages were filled with serialized novels and short stories, and that percentage increased in the decades that followed. New technologies for printing illustrations meant that more and more images were circulating through that medium too. Not everyone had access to printed materials, of course. It is no easy matter to establish literacy rates, but it is estimated that in 1850 less than 11 percent of the white population (of both genders) could not read; that rate had fallen to 6.2 percent by 1900, in which year the self-reported rate of illiteracy in the non-white population was 44.5 percent (Kaestle et al. 1991: 25). But for people of all classes print was becoming inescapable – in making purchases, in traveling, at church, on the job, and at leisure. Historical studies of reading practices suggest that those who could not read might still listen to stories read aloud and thereby actively participate in a local literary culture that was linked both to the institutions of national literature and to global forces.

Regionalism, I want to suggest, is not only about place but also about the relations between places. Local color fiction emerges as a response to a modern world in which, wherever we are, we encounter traces of other localities: people whose lives have been shaped by voluntary or coerced movement, trans-local institutions, commodities produced elsewhere – including images and ideas. The relational orientation of this literary form, and its seemingly paradoxical connection to national and global literatures, also follows from the very nature of place. It is so fundamental that we often take it for granted, as a stable, inert background. Yet the smallest neighborhood is shaped by oppositions – by what it means to me that I am standing in my house and not the one next door or down the street, by the line between this district and that one. Any dot on a map takes its meaning from its relation to the region depicted and to the whole globe that (through our knowledge of the practice of mapping) implicitly surrounds it. As the geographer Doreen Massey puts it, "the particular mix of social relations which . . . defines the uniqueness of any place is by no means all included within that place itself" (1994: 5). The region is constructed not only by the boundary drawn around it, but also by its particular mix of connections – on many different scales – to what is beyond the boundary. Many local colorists write about the relations between places in subtle and sophisticated ways. And some of the most intriguing intricacies of regionalism, as we shall see, involve multiplying rather than choosing between identities. The vogue for local color fiction can be appreciated only in this historical framework of rapidly increasing connectedness, and increasing awareness both of national and global connections and of the distinctiveness of American "places."

West and East: Beginning the Local Color Vogue

In the summer of 1868 the new California magazine *Overland Monthly* published an anonymous story entitled "The Luck of Roaring Camp." Locally, this tale of a mysteriously blessed child born to a mixed-race prostitute in a mining camp was controversial. In the East and elsewhere in the country it became enormously popular and was praised by critics as well. By the fall everyone knew that the author of the story was Bret Harte, who was also the editor of the *Overland Monthly*. The fiction and poetry he published over the next two years exemplified the rapid circulation of printed material and thought. Harte's writings sold copies of the magazine both in the West and in the East, ensuring its success, and the stories were sometimes reprinted all across the country within days of their appearance. (It took slightly longer for his work to appear in England.) Soon Harte accepted an offer of $10,000 to write exclusively for the distinguished Boston magazine the *Atlantic Monthly* for a year. Harte was neither the first nor the biggest literary celebrity of the era (Charles Dickens's reception in America has been compared to that of the Beatles), but the lavish contract itself was news, and his railway trip across the country with his family generated publicity at every stop. Their host for their first week in Boston, the eminent author and critic William Dean Howells, wrote later that Bret Harte's journey from the Pacific to the Atlantic had been "like the progress of a prince, in the universal attention and interest which met and followed it" (1911: 290).

The appeal of Harte's work was inseparable from the fascination of the *place* he wrote about: California in the era of the Gold Rush. Accounts of regionalist fiction between the Civil War and the First World War often begin with his explosive entry onto the literary scene, because it marks a moment when the writerly strategy of focusing on particular places became highly visible. All literature arguably has some sort of relation to place, but for several decades in this period attention to locality played an especially powerful role in how people wrote and read both prose and poetry. The form shaped not only how writers marketed their material, but also how they visualized it, and influenced both how readers selected and how they interpreted literature. By 1886 James Lane Allen could open an article titled "Local Color" like this: "One everywhere meets with this phrase in current criticism of fiction" (Allen 1886: 13).

Local color fiction was not, of course, a wholly new invention. Its salient sources vary depending upon the authors one examines. For Harte, the most influential form was Western humor, an oral tradition that entered into print in the 1830s and 1840s through sketches and anecdotes appearing in newspapers and "sporting" journals catering to men's interests. Mark Twain's early publications also emerged through this form – his tall tale of the "jumping frog of Calaveras County" is the most familiar example. Years later, looking back at his own place in literary history, Harte described this humor as distinctively American, praised it as irreverent and original, and implied its link to later fiction by writing that it "voiced not only the dialect, but the habits of thought of a people or locality" (1899: 3).

However, though Harte declined to acknowledge them, there were other places to find representations of locality in nineteenth-century American writing. Their publication venues were quite distinct from those of Western humor, although their readership probably overlapped. Sketches of village life – influenced both by earlier American writings such as Washington Irving's *Sketch-Book* (1819–20) and by the popular works of English writer Mary Russell Mitford – appeared in annuals, gift books, and magazines during the 1820s and 1830s, and occasionally in book form as well. Their episodic form, foregrounding atmosphere and a web of relationships rather than plot, links them to many later regional fictions. Humble characters engaged in everyday activities, often speaking in dialect, could also be found in the domestic fiction of the mid-nineteenth century. For example, Susan Warner's immensely popular novel *The Wide, Wide World* (1850) weaves long passages of quotidian detail into its didactic and dramatic narrative; her character Aunt Fortune would be quite at home in a local color story.

These bodies of work, Northeastern in focus and oriented strongly although not exclusively to women's concerns, are influential sources for New England local color writers. Harriet Beecher Stowe stands at the confluence of these traditions and, indeed, others: she makes Cotton Mather a precursor of regionalism when she cites his history of Christianity in New England, *Magnalia Christi Americana* (1702), with its "wonderful stories" of "the very ground I trod on," as one of the books that shaped her imagination (Fields 1898: 28). Like Mark Twain, Stowe is often discussed as a major author without reference to regionalism, but her work, like his, is deeply informed and engaged by it. Stowe had published New England sketches before she became the author of the nineteenth century's most successful didactic novel, *Uncle Tom's Cabin* (1852), and her 1862 novel *The Pearl of Orr's Island* was set in an actual location on the Maine coast. That novel contributed crucially to the development of local color, and subsequent works such as *Oldtown Folks* (1869) helped to confirm folkloric material, humorous rural characters, and dialect as conventions of the form.

Of Time and Place: Some Terminological Discriminations

Local color stories about the West and New England by Harte, Stowe, and others are often interpreted as commentaries on "America." In the United States and globally, regionalist fiction has a complex, even seemingly paradoxical relation to national literatures. Writing about a region, whether that writing is celebratory or critical, articulates its distinctiveness and announces its importance, explicitly or implicitly resisting assimilation of particular places into a vision of the nation as a whole. Yet from the time of its emergence, American readers understood local color fiction as contributing to an aggregate picture of the nation. Even representations of a particular place that contested prevailing notions of America seemed to ratify the whole by participating in a dialogue about it. In literary history, volumes like the present one display regionalism as one among many elements of an American literature, similarly suggesting that the natural and proper unit of literary history is the national tradition.

Regionalism may, however, also indicate a geographical constellation larger than a single country – as, for example, in a formulation like "Latin American literature." Here too the category is both opposed to and thoroughly entangled with the nation. It examines continental continuities and trends, challenging the national model by organizing literary history on a different scale; yet any discussion of it depends on the names of particular countries and contributes to their definition. Scholarship on the United States rarely considers that perspective – a neglect exemplified in our appropriation of the term "American" for the literature of a single nation. Regionalism has in fact been a very important genre in Latin America, although it became prominent later than the period considered here. It figures in the literary histories of Canada, the Caribbean, and the Pacific, as well, and some critics have argued for a hemispheric approach to regionalism.

Regionalism may also be considered as part of the transatlantic realist movement. James Lane Allen's analysis of local color emphasized its response to the tints of specific natural landscapes, an element prominent in his own stories of Kentucky, and praised the American contribution to this development in literature – but he began by citing the work of Balzac. William Dean Howells's criticism also placed local color writing in the broad context of European literature. Whether in the United States or elsewhere, regionalism and realism are not so much wholly different genres as different ways of reading complexly connected bodies of work. As the British critic Raymond Williams has pointed out, the standard definitions assume that some places are regional and others are not: regional fiction takes place in Wales (his own birthplace) and not in London.

Williams's implicit distinction between a metropolitan and a non-metropolitan setting involves a persistent element in the history of the term "realism." James Lane Allen had mentioned Howells's New England fiction as a contribution to local color, but Howells is generally considered a "realist" not only because of his reiterated philosophical allegiance to the concept of literary realism current in Europe and America, and his own work's highly specified social locations, but also because it primarily portrays privileged people in metropolitan places. "Local color" fiction about New York City or Chicago, such as Abraham Cahan's or Edith Wyatt's, is more often set in immigrant neighborhoods. The distinction reflects, as Williams put it, "centralized cultural dominance" (n.d.: 230).

Value judgments weave unsystematically through most efforts to distinguish genres from one another, and in this case they create considerable confusion. Realism has sometimes been defined as literature of general significance, and regionalism as limited. On the other hand, "regionalism" has sometimes been defined as geographically specific literature that also illuminates the general human condition (Faulkner is the usual example), with the term "local color" reserved for work considered narrow, quaint, and minor. Embedded in this latter usage is the mid-twentieth century's critical preference for the regionalists who wrote between the world wars, with an accompanying prejudice against the earlier writers who are the focus of this essay.

I would argue, instead, that movements, genres, and forms offer opportunities to authors, not outcomes, and that narratives often mobilize conventions affiliating them with multiple genres and traditions. Howells juxtaposed Cahan's stories and Stephen Crane's *Maggie* (1893) as stories of New York "low life"; critics today more often read them as contributions to, respectively, Jewish American literature and literary naturalism. Although Edith Wharton and her contemporaries may have thought of her stories of New England as local color, they probably would not have used that term for her fiction about elite New Yorkers. Yet both are portraits of strictly delimited social worlds. We do not need to value one genre over another, or to decide whether or not a given work "belongs" to a genre. It is more helpful – both for interpreting individual texts and for understanding literature's historical significance – to consider how reading a work in relation to a form or practice illuminates both.

In this essay I use the terms "local color" and "regionalism" interchangeably in referring to the literature of the United States from the latter nineteenth through the early twentieth century, but limit the former to that particular period. It was a historical moment in which there was good reason for Americans to focus their attention on the scale of social relations. It was difficult for anyone to ignore sectional tensions, which had so recently erupted into the Civil War; national unity had been affirmed by force. But in the decades that followed, improvements in transportation and communication knitted different regions of the country ever more closely together.

Continental Expansion: Unifying and Differentiating Forces in the Print Market

Between the end of the Civil War and 1890 the miles of railroad track in operation in the United States more than quadrupled. Perhaps the most visible symbol of national integration was the completion of the transcontinental railroad in 1869. Consider too that in 1883 the railroad companies instituted something we now take for granted – standard time zones – and shortly thereafter they completed the project of standardizing the tracks themselves, so that the same gauge was used all over the country. The reach of markets and the size of the most successful businesses were constantly being enlarged; more and more of the economy was national. The scale of labor organization similarly increased: in 1877 the first national strike stopped the trains and deeply alarmed the privileged classes. Not only goods and money but people were circulating: inhabitants of rural areas migrated to the cities, African Americans moved from the South to the North, and millions of immigrants arrived from eastern and southern Europe. The nation appeared at once more closely connected and larger, even distended; both regional identity and coherence seemed threatened.

The increasing, and increasingly rapid, circulation of newspapers, magazines, and books was an important part of this process of national integration. As the market for print expanded, it also became more differentiated. The *Atlantic Monthly*, in particular, succeeded in creating a self-consciously elite, cultivated forum for American letters. This elevated literary realm distinguished itself from the domestic, didactic culture of letters (to use Richard Brodhead's term) only gradually, but so effectively that a century after the *Atlantic*'s first issue, in 1857, it seemed surprising that it had included work by Harriet Beecher Stowe. Published in Boston, the journal was strongly affiliated with New England, but increasingly aspired to a national audience and to define American literature at its best. What is notable about this "high" culture is not just the elaboration of privileged practices, which can be found in any hierarchical society, but their emergence within the realm of commercial culture. Subscriptions to the "quality" national magazines (*Atlantic*, *Harper's Monthly*, *Scribner's*) were an emblem of cultivation – publicly on offer, to anyone who could afford them.

The local color movement is closely associated with these magazines. The best-known writers of the day published in them; most of the regionalists we still read today did so as well, and published their books with the houses that owned the magazines or with other Northeastern publishers. In that sense their representations of local behavior, dialect, and landscapes were directed to metropolitan eyes. Perhaps more precisely, they were directed to metropolitan editors – and through them to readers both in the cities and the countryside, all over the nation.

But there were multitudes of local and regional magazines, and literary works were printed in newspapers, as well. Those forums were also important for local color writers. Bret Harte, for example, began his career as contributor and compositor for a newspaper in northern California, and then played the same dual role – sometimes composing sketches and poems while setting type – for the San Francisco weekly *The Golden Era*. As his work gained recognition, he contributed to other local publications and succeeded in placing one story in *Atlantic Monthly*, co-founded a literary periodical called *The Californian*, and then became editor of *The Overland Monthly*. Only then was he summoned to the East, to write for the *Atlantic* (and, eventually, to end his career writing from England). Most local color writers, like most writers, found outlets for their work in varied sorts of publication. Recent research has shown that two of the writers most identified with particular magazines – Mary E. Wilkins Freeman, with *Harper's Monthly* and *Harper's Bazaar*, and Sarah Orne Jewett, with the *Atlantic Monthly* – also placed stories with a syndicate for newspaper publication. The nationalizing literary culture existed in a constant interplay not only with the oral worlds of particular localities, but with local newspapers and magazines, regional periodicals, and the small number of book publishers scattered in cities outside the Northeast.

When in 1894 the Midwestern regionalist Hamlin Garland articulated the principles of his work, he wrote that "Local color in a novel means that it has such quality of texture and background that it could not have been written in any other place or by any one else than a native" (Garland 1894: 64). Like many other definitions of the genre, this statement contains a value judgment; it is a prescription for what local color ought to be, stated as a description of what it is. But by this time local color had been popular for several decades, and it was clear that many non-natives had contributed to the movement. To take just one example (of a writer well known in her day, although not in ours), Constance Fenimore Woolson sojourned in and wrote about the Great Lakes states, the South, and Europe as well.

The question of whether regionalism entails an insider's or an outsider's perspective is still debated by critics. Some agree with Garland, valuing it for its authenticity, how it offers interpretations that emphasize the intimacy and accuracy of its representations of particular places. Others – especially recently – emphasize its orientation toward national print culture and treat local color as, in effect, literary tourism: a genre that nostalgically preserves regional culture and by that very gesture places it in the past. We can incorporate the insights of both perspectives by acknowledging that all sorts of people wrote about all sorts of places, and that local color stories and poems circulated in many different kinds of publications, addressing multiple overlapping audiences. On the one hand, local color writers contribute to the social construction of regional identities. On the other, they *place* those identities as parts of a national culture, and in many cases contribute to the national economy precisely by circulating those representations as information commodities – by putting them into print.

By the time Hamlin Garland published his assertion that local color must be a local product – in fact, long before then – he had left his native rural Wisconsin and moved to Boston. He had recently returned to the Midwest, not to his original home but to Chicago. Garland is unquestionably a native, in the sense in which he uses the word, but his perspective is not exclusively or simply local. His story "Up the Coulé" (1891) depicts the interplay of provincial and metropolitan perspectives through an encounter between two brothers. The central character has stepped away from his successful life in the city to make a long-deferred visit home; his brother has spent his life on the farm. In this account of the "return of the native" (to quote the title of a novel by the English regionalist Thomas Hardy) Garland writes as both insider and outsider.

Other regionalists occupy similarly complex positions. The Tennessee writer Mary Noailles Murfree was a native of the state, but was far more genteel than the mountain folks who appear in her stories (and seems to be disowned by present-day residents of the region). Sarah Orne Jewett was born and bred, lived and died, in Maine, but she was also a cosmopolitan who traveled in Europe and as an adult spent part of each year in Boston with Annie Fields, widow of one of the early editors of the *Atlantic Monthly*. Her work linked New England to the nation but looked beyond the nation, invoking the classics and her racialized vision of Anglo-Norman civilization. Abraham Cahan read Russian literature and was a prominent, prolific writer in Yiddish before he turned his hand to fiction in English; his East Siders are also, visibly and importantly, European Jews. New Orleans as portrayed by George Washington Cable and Alice Dunbar-Nelson is profoundly Creole – a cultural affiliation that is variously Caribbean, French, Spanish, and African, and is implicitly or explicitly contrasted with being American. Writings about locality may counterbalance the national not by turning inward, but by creating an alternative set of connections.

Sectional Groupings: The Complexities of Regionalism

Regional writing is so various that from this point I will proceed by looking at a few writers and texts in terms of how they are loosely and provisionally grouped by the sections of the country with which they are usually associated. Such groupings must be heuristic, not only because authorial identities are complex and works are hetero-geneous, but also because of the fluid, relational nature of place. I follow a common practice in discussing "Appalachia" as part of "the South." Yet that region – arguably one of the most saliently self-defined in the United States today and certainly one of the most clearly defined, since the establishment of the Appalachian Regional Commission in 1965 – stretches from New York through Pennsylvania and Ohio to Mississippi. The southeastern Ohio counties that are part of Appalachia might also seem to be subsumed in a discussion of "the Midwest"; and Michigan might figure there or under the quite different rubric "Great Lakes." Indeed, every American place can be considered not only as part of one or more regions but also as a component of a state. For example, the Midwestern or alternatively "Great Plains" state of Iowa has (in its quite cosmopolitan university town, Iowa City) a "Literary Walk" celebrating "its" writers with bronze plaques embedded in the sidewalks. And states have officially established Humanities Councils invested in promoting "their" literature. The scale of solidarities is endlessly negotiable.

I begin with Northeastern authors, whose status clearly and powerfully demon-strates the fluidity of the relation between regional and national literature. The works that for much of the twentieth century were considered to define American literature were mainly New England books. This was true of Barrett Wendell's 1900 *Literary History of America*: the critic Fred Lewis Pattee humorously suggested that the volume should have been titled "A Literary History of Harvard University, with Incidental Glimpses of the Minor Writers of America." It was true as well in the influential notion of an "American Renaissance" that F. O. Matthiessen established in his 1941

Figure 6.1   Internal improvements
In 1846, long before he built the more famous Brooklyn Bridge (completed 1883), the century's premier designer and builder of suspension bridges, John Augustus Roebling, proposed the first permanent bridge over the Ohio River, connecting Cincinnati, Ohio with Covington, Kentucky. The only privately funded project during the Civil War, the Cincinnati–Covington Bridge was begun in 1856, completed in late 1866, and dedicated on January 1, 1867 (the year of this photograph). At 1,057 feet – 2,252 feet counting the approaches – it was the largest suspension bridge in the world. Linking the industrializing North with the colonized South, the bridge was one of many internal improvements in the late nineteenth century that were also connecting East and West. These developments, which radically reduced the times of travel and communication, included improved roads and canals, the telegraph, and of course the railroad. Under the direction of his son, Roebling's company later built the Williamsburg Bridge, Manhattan Bridge, Bear Mountain Bridge, George Washington Bridge, Golden Gate Bridge, and Tacoma Narrows Bridge, among others. In 1983, the Cincinnati–Covington Bridge was renamed the John A. Roebling Bridge. (Photograph by permission of Cincinnati Museum Center–Cincinnati Historical Society Library.)

study of Emerson, Hawthorne, Melville, Thoreau, and Whitman under that title. In fact, it is precisely in relation to these provincial "normative" visions of the national literature that the local color writers discussed in this chapter were found wanting by "standard" literary historians: the topics and texts of regionalists were considered too slight to be significant.

The term "New England" dates back to the seventeenth century, and it still evokes the colonial era. Both in schools and in popular culture, representations of Pilgrims and colonial villages are pervasively (although often seasonally) offered. They automatically symbolize American history, but such images respond to their own historical moments at least as much as they imply continuity with the past. The notion of America as an exemplary nation relies upon patriotic veneration of a democratic past, and is very much alive in the present. John Winthrop's frequently cited oration "A Model of Christian Charity," with its vision of loving communal life and New England as a godly city upon a hill with the eyes of the world on it, was delivered in 1630 on the ship *Arbella* at the end of the voyage to the New World. Yet it was first published two hundred years later, its version of the nation polemically quoted by a regional elite whose power was contested in Jacksonian America. And the Thanksgiving holiday that today's Americans imagine connects them with the Pilgrims was not federally established until 1863, by Abraham Lincoln, after a long effort by cultural politician Sarah Josepha Hale.

Increasingly, in that period after the Civil War, writers, visual artists, historical preservationists, and investors in tourism busied themselves creating what came to be called "Old New England." The image of a rural, exclusively white, harmonious world of farms and villages is mostly inaccurate even as an image of the past. Certainly it purposefully disregarded its own industrializing, ethnically various present. But the success of this invention of a pastoral past for America is attested by its persistence even today. That simplified past is itself an integral part of modernity, not only as a narrative, but also as embodied in institutions like tourism and the market for antiques. New England local color writers actively participate in the invention of that tradition, but they also often complicate it and challenge it.

Let us take as an example Rose Terry Cooke, a popular and respected writer during the latter half of the nineteenth century, although little read now. She was, with Stowe, one of only two women whose work was featured in the inaugural issue of the *Atlantic Monthly*. Her story, "Sally Parson's Duty" (1857), is the tale of a woman who, at the outset of the Revolutionary War, refuses to marry the man she loves until he changes his allegiance from the Tory to the Yankee side. It portrays a sturdy New England patriotism and explicitly affirms an important role for women in the battle for the new nation. As Augusta Rohrbach shows, however, in its moment the story was less comfortably nostalgic than worrisomely immediate, implicitly invoking the tensions between North and South that would soon lead to another war. The story is both personal and political, both local and national. The title of one of Cooke's later collections, *Somebody's Neighbors* (1881), in similarly exemplary fashion asserts the realism of local color and epitomizes its paradoxically general intimacy. These characters, it suggests, must be recognized as real actors in the life of a particular place; affection and distance are simultaneously implied in the reminder that these people are somebody's neighbors, although not yours. Yet, with neighbors as with family, closeness can imply conflict as easily as unity (as in "Sally Parson's Duty"). Cooke's stories are often intensely critical of New England ways: of Calvinism, of narrow-mindedness and miserliness, and especially of men's cruelty to women. Rohrbach argues that Cooke, drawing on the vocabulary of the abolition movement throughout her career, links slavery and women's bondage in marriage, in effect giving a counter-history of the region.

The work of an even more celebrated writer, Mary E. Wilkins Freeman, is similarly complex. Many of her stories that focus closely on village life imply a sophisticated commentary on regional and national culture. For example, "A Poetess," first published in *Harper's Monthly* in 1890, portrays the life of a spinster in a small village. Freeman conveys Betsey Dole's constrained circumstances through imagery and explicit description but shows too that she is imaginative and intensely serious about the poetry she writes. At the request of a neighbor whose small son has died, Betsey writes an elegy; and she is very proud when Mrs. Caxton (whose name alludes to the man who, in the fifteenth century, introduced printing into England) has the poem typeset and two dozen copies printed. That increased local circulation, however, leads the minister (whose own poetry has been printed in a magazine) to speak disparagingly of Betsey's sentimental verses. His remarks are repeated to Mrs. Caxton, who repeats them to Betsey. Devastated, Betsey burns her work in the stove, enters into a decline, and eventually dies. She demands of her empty room, "Had I ought to have been born with the wantin' to write poetry if I couldn't write it – had I?... Would it be fair if that canary bird there, that ain't never done anything but sing, should turn out not to be singin'?" There are no villains here. Mrs. Caxton is incapable of understanding what is at stake for Betsey. The minister has no inkling of the role he has played; he is not a privileged snob, but merely "a country boy who had worked his way through a country college," a sincere aspirant to virtue and culture. The story reaches no simple conclusions but asks us to reflect on the fatality of temperament and situation, the contingent nature of literary value, the subjective and historical implications of print. Freeman dramatizes the limited circulation of the poetess's work and thereby gains a national audience for the story of her life.

The stories and novels Freeman produced during her long and successful career strike many different notes, from the realist pathos of "A Poetess" through more light-hearted and humorous tales to gothic ghost stories. She even satirized the condescension of the metropolitan to the regional, and the construction of the pastoral image of Old New England, in a short novel titled *The Jamesons* (1899). This tale of summer visitors from the city is narrated by one of the residents of Linville, and here the locals have the cognitive advantage: Mrs. Jameson's patronizing attitude and efforts to reform her neighbors and beautify the village are absurd, although they are indulged or resisted with unfailing courtesy. She does not persuade the villagers that hens should (for hygienic reasons) sit on hard-boiled eggs, and her efforts to plant vines around their houses are merely tolerated. But one of her projects does succeed; at her suggestion, Linville holds a celebration of the centennial of its founding. The process of re-creating a colonial house and organizing the procession and banquet reveals the past as largely an urban fantasy – virtually a tourist attraction, to which Mrs. Jameson invites "every celebrity whose grandfather ever drove through Linville." But the successful event also embodies reconciliation between the locals and the summer people, and enables the resolution of the novel's marriage plot.

These works are strikingly self-conscious treatments of themes found frequently in New England local color fiction. Many stories are set in the past and both interrogate and commemorate its meaning. Alice Brown's "The Flat-Iron Lot" (1899) dramatizes the struggles of an elderly local man to preserve traces of the past against what he considers the creeping commercialism of the present; he gains a hearing among his neighbors through his contribution to a centennial celebration. Similarly, Sarah Orne Jewett's "Decoration Day" and "The Flight of Betsey Lane" (published in book form in *A Native of Winby*, 1893) present characters participating in national observances. The few veterans of the Civil War in the village of Barlow organize a procession that renews both the community's sense of its cohesion and its allegiance to the nation. Betsey Lane uses an unexpected gift of money to travel to the national centennial in Philadelphia and comes home to the Byfleet poorhouse full of stories to tell, satisfied to have seen, in effect, the "world." Whereas in "A Poetess" an encounter between different kinds of cultural practice is destructive, in Jewett's work it is more likely to be enriching for both sides. These works are not only about particular places, but also about connections between places and about the politics of knowledge.

Jewett is one of the most critically esteemed local color writers. The bulk of her work is short stories, but she wrote several novels, including one, *The Country of the Pointed Firs* (1896), often considered a masterpiece. This subtle account of the coastal Maine community of Dunnet Landing, seen through the eyes of an unnamed summer sojourner, is structured not so much by events as by the narrator's developing web of intimate and social connections. As I have noted already, Jewett invokes a deeply hierarchical and specifically racialized vision of social order. Yet her work also implies a kind of epistemological and spiritual democracy, in which everyone's perspective is infinitely valuable. Jewett's first and widely read novel, *Deephaven* (1877), contains a remarkable moment in which the condescending interest taken by the two girls who are its protagonists in a circus performance is transformed. A fat lady on exhibit proves to be a former acquaintance of a companion; and our perspective necessarily shifts as her voice enters the text. Here and elsewhere in Jewett's early work she invokes Christianity as the source of her values. Later, as aesthetic ideologies changed, her writing becomes less openly didactic, more broadly allusive, and even more polished. In *The Country of the Pointed Firs* Jewett's prose not only describes, but also stylistically enacts acts of perception that enable sympathy and ensure mutually respectful relations. "Tact," her narrator affirms, "is after all a kind of mindreading."

Not all New England local color writers published in literary journals or women's magazines. The stories of the Vermont writer Rowland Robinson, for example, frequently appeared in *Field and Stream*. His narratives of community are untidily diverse but filled with carefully crafted dialect speech. Robinson, although virtually ignored in the academy, is remembered in his own region. For example, the contemporary poet David Budbill named his own French Canadian character Antoine, in homage to Robinson's "outrageous and delightful" recurring character (Robinson 1995: xi). Indeed, in New England and elsewhere, the concerns of regionalism remain vital to this day. The local color fiction of an earlier period makes a place for local knowledge. For example, the relation of utterly unpicturesque locals to more prosperous newcomers – in effect, tourists – is a central topic in Ernest Hebert's 1979 novel *The Dogs of March*. Zoe Cutter buys her farmhouse because of "a picture discovered thirty years ago in a *National Geographic*": a picture of a New Hampshire village, complete with birches and a church steeple, which for her embodies peace, perfection, and the antithesis of unsatisfactory modernity. Of course, she sets out immediately to make the landscape conform to her fantasy. Her neighbor Howard Elman has no vocabulary for talking about beauty, although he loves the land. His harsh history counters the pastoral image of the village; yet, as a child without family, he named himself after an elm tree. The novel allows him to negotiate a provisional, limited space for the things he cares about – very much in the tradition of earlier local color fiction.

I have mentioned only a fraction of the authors who were considered, in their day, New England local colorists; and the category "the Northeast" also takes in a wider region than is now thought of as "New England." Philander Deming, an author rarely read today, wrote stories of the Adirondacks; Margaret Deland's popular fiction included narratives of community set in a Pennsylvania town called Old Chester; and so on. As mentioned, writers as well known as William Dean Howells and Edith Wharton also set important works in New England and addressed regionalist themes. Harold Frederic, now more often read as a naturalist, also wrote about upstate New York; so did Stephen Crane, in his *Whilomville Stories* (1900). Pauline Hopkins has been recovered from the files of early twentieth-century magazines for the tradition of African American literature; she was born in Maine and educated in Boston, and the critic Elizabeth Ammons has included some of her short stories set in New England in an anthology of local color fiction.

Abraham Cahan, whose stories of Jewish immigrants in New York City I have earlier mentioned, is a particularly interesting example of a writer whose work intersects with but substantially exceeds the category of regionalism. American literary history to date has been written almost exclusively about publications in English, but increasingly we recognize that there is an enormous body of work in other languages. As the national framework is complemented by a comparative one, and we examine a wider range of literature on the continent as well as beyond it, we will become better able to understand the relation between the two versions of *Yekl* (1896), first written in English, translated and first published in Yiddish as *Yankel der Yankee* (see Taubenfeld 1998).

This perspective will make a difference in other regions as well. For example, the Polish publishing industry, which produced hundreds of short stories, novels, poems, and plays, was centered in the Midwest. According to Karen Majewski, the tension between the local and the national is key to this body of work. In the nineteenth century Poland did not exist as an independent state, and in the century's latter years there was an active effort to repress Polish culture (the official languages of the region were Russian and German). Intellectuals writing in Polish in the United States strove to instill a sense of nationalism in their audience; they wanted immigrants to imagine themselves returning not only to their villages, but also to *Poland*. These works too are part of the story of American regionalism.

The Midwest also had its early narratives of community. Alice Cary was a native of Ohio who began publishing in Cincinnati, where there was a strong literary community, in the 1830s. Eventually she relocated to New York and transformed herself, as Judith Fetterley puts it, from "a volunteer poet with a local reputation" into "a writer capable of establishing a national reputation and earning her living by her pen." Cary's work appeared not only in Cincinnati and New York, but also in Harte's *Overland Monthly*, although her popular sketches of Clovernook preceded the vogue for local color and her early death prevented her from taking advantage of it.

The second bestseller of the movement, however, was a product of the Midwest. Edward Eggleston's novel *The Hoosier School-Master*, set in rural Indiana during the 1850s, was published in *Hearth and Home*, a magazine that combined articles on agricultural and domestic topics with literature, during 1871. The tale had been conceived as a short series, but was so popular it was extended. Like Harte's work, it buoyed the fortunes of the journal in which it appeared (though in this case not for long). Eggleston's attention to folkways and dialect was widely praised (his interest in documenting social life led him to become, in later life, an eminent historian), though he was also criticized for caricaturing his subjects. In this novel the central figure of the schoolteacher is an insider to the region, who grew up only a few miles from the district of "Flat Crick" where the action takes place. But as an educated man and a teacher, he is also the representative of metropolitan information and standards. Indeed, there are almost as many teachers as tourists in local color fiction, and here as in other works and other regions they mediate between local knowledge and book learning.

Later in the century, Hamlin Garland's stories of the Midwest were also initially published outside the established literary magazines, in his case in the reform journal *The Arena*. He then found a hearing in the most politically and topically oriented member of the Harper family of magazines, *Harper's Weekly*. His strongest work, stories collected as *Main-Travelled Roads* (1891), offers powerful portraits of the hardships of rural life, with a particular focus on the lives of farm women. They also evoke trans-local connections as a shaping element of local life (as in "Up the Coolly"). Garland's widely read "The Lion's Paw," directly based on populist political ideas, presents the farmer's economic difficulties as being rooted in the national system of finance capital. Carrie Tirado Bramen (2000) shows, in fact, that Garland's affirmation of local color in *Crumbling Idols* (1894) is part of a claim that we apprehend the universal through the particular – a vision of America as a pluralist nation. In her view, regionalism is part of an intellectual history that has led us to think of diversity as a distinctively American value, although it is manifestly more widespread.

The term "Midwest" is (like "Northeastern") a place-keeper, meant as a relatively neutral designation for places that would have been identified variously. Garland in fact subtitled the first edition of *Main-Travelled Roads* "Six Mississippi Valley Stories," and he refers in a later preface to the prairie and the midland wilderness; other people might say the "Middle West" or simply the "West." Alice French (who wrote under the name of Octave Thanet) titled one of her books about owners and workers, of various ethnicities, *Stories of a Western Town* (1893). The region includes the Great Lakes, which conjure up a rather different image, and Chicago as well as small towns and farms.

In the Midwest, as in other areas, there were not only regionalists like Alice Cary who wrote both poetry and fiction, but also many who fall entirely outside the scope of this essay because they wrote only poetry. Dialect poetry was both published and performed locally, and we do not yet have a good understanding of its social and cultural significance. Some of these authors also gained a national audience. For example, the Hoosier poet James Whitcomb Riley, whose work first appeared in the Indianapolis *Journal* and other Midwestern newspapers, became so widely read that some of his poems, especially "When the Frost is on the Punkin'," are still familiar today.

"The South" is not so old a designation as "New England," but it became a very powerful one. The states that compose what we now call the South had their antebellum traditions, of course. Especially relevant for local color are the historical fictions (published from the 1830s through the 1850s) of South Carolina author William Gilmore Simms, and John Pendleton Kennedy's Virginia sketches in *Swallow Barn* (1832). The literary history of the region must reckon, however, with the fact that throughout the century almost all the institutions of publishing, with the exception of newspapers, were located elsewhere; after the economic devastation of the Civil War, even regional magazines struggled. In the late 1860s and early 1870s the Philadelphia magazine *Lippincott's* took the lead in publishing sympathetic accounts of the white South; other magazines, such as *Scribner's* and the *Harper's* publications, soon followed. The local color fiction that appeared in their pages was one of the important sites of a discourse of reconciliation between North and South in the postbellum era.

Oral traditions were an important influence on local color writing and a key element of its appeal to readers. The popular "Uncle Remus" dialect stories, still a nursery staple today, were first printed in the newspaper *The Atlanta Constitution*; Joel Chandler Harris then moved on to the familiar periodicals, mainly the *Century*, and to books published with Houghton Mifflin. Of course, the "ownership" of those tales, written by the white son of an Irish immigrant based on tales he had heard from enslaved people during his childhood, is a complex matter. "Negro" dialect is also fundamental to the work of Thomas Nelson Page, whose first published work was the poem "Uncle Gabe's White Folks" (1877). His short-story collection *In Ole Virginia* (1887) offers tales of heroic, aristocratic plantation dwellers adhering to an inflexible code of honor and hospitality and virtually worshipping exquisite white ladies. To narrate these stories, Page frequently invents characters who are freedmen still loyal to their former owners and longing for the happy, orderly days of slavery. This fiction, like the works already mentioned, undertakes the re-creation of a regional past that implies a vision of the nation. Page's portrait of the Old South was perhaps the most unequivocally affirmative, but regionalist reconciliation often entailed a narrative in which neither the North nor the South was criticized. Writers from other regions also sometimes embraced this perspective (Jewett's story "A War Debt" [1895] is a notable example).

But the local color movement also included important writers who took a critical view of the South. Soon after George Washington Cable's first sketches appeared in the *New Orleans Picayune*, he moved on to journals and books published in the Northeast and eventually found it advisable, because of local responses to his advocacy of the rights of African Americans, to move his residence outside the region as well. The African American writer Charles W. Chesnutt, born and later resident in Ohio but raised in North Carolina, cast his early "conjure tales" as dialect fiction, with a white narrator reporting the picturesque speech of a former slave. His subtle portraits of the characters in the frame stories and the content of Uncle Julius's tales encode double meanings into this conventional form. The narratives taken as a whole convey both a powerful view of the horrors of slavery and the resilience of the enslaved within an uncompromising view of the racism of his present-day South. Chesnutt went on to write more openly critical stories and novels that, although they earned the respect of perspicacious readers like William Dean Howells, did not receive a favorable reception from the mostly white reading public. His reputation declined, and only in recent years has he been understood as a major figure of the period; some of his late work, in fact, is now being published for the first time.

It is not possible in the confines of a short essay to represent fully the diversity of the region or the range of writers who fall into the category of Southern local color. The distinctive city of New Orleans is treated not only by Cable but also by Grace King, Alice Dunbar-Nelson, and Kate Chopin. In their engagement with Creole life these authors demonstrate, as I have suggested, that locality can point beyond national boundaries. Increasingly, some of the works of the international intellectual W. E. B. Du Bois have been linked to the local color movement. Appalachian literature is a topic in itself. Mark Twain is both a Southern and a Western writer. As the example of Twain reminds us, there is also a fluid boundary between Southern and Western literature; as noted above, Twain as a "major" American author is not always considered in those terms, but their conventions and perspectives deeply inform his work. Western writing was important early in the local color movement, as we have seen, and that did not change. Some of the most interesting writers from this region, in fact, appeared late in the era. I can do no more here than mention the westward course of regionalism in the context of race, ethnicity, and the increasing "globalization" of regionalist issues; a few brief examples will have to suffice.

The work of the Yankton Sioux author Zitkala Ša (also known as Gertrude Bonnin) was published in *Harper's* and *Atlantic Monthly* in the first years of the twentieth century, but much of it was not collected in book form until 1921. Her writings provide a powerful account of the local world into which she was born, the new locality of the mission boarding-school that initiates her into the white world, and the complexities of their relation, including the dilemma of the native who tries to return home. Mary Austin sold her first story to the *Overland Monthly* in 1892 and published many books over the next few decades. Her writings about the Southwest, such as *The Land of Little Rain* (1903), engage explicitly and critically the local color tradition (one chapter of the book is titled "Jimville – A Bret Harte Town") and, more unusually, Native American culture. They focus strongly on the land itself – an element within regionalist writing that is receiving, and deserves, increasing attention.

The Southwest became part of the United States only in 1848, when Mexico ceded it at the end of the Mexican–American War – in other words, precisely in the moment Bret Harte located his stories, and only two decades before he wrote them. María Amparo Ruiz de Burton's regional novel *The Squatter and the Don* (1885), set mainly in California in the 1870s, takes up the relation of dialect and class, race and region, section and nation from the perspective of the newly incorporated population. Zitkala Ša, Austin, and De Burton have radically different values and politics, and each brings those explicitly into her literary works. But what they have in common is their recognition of the West as an *occupied* landscape: military conquest has become settlement. The local color tradition also includes white writers whose sense of entitlement to the land is absolute: for example, Alfred Henry Lewis, whose tales of Wolfville (published under the pseudonym Dan Quin and illustrated by Frederic Remington) pioneered the popular genre we think of as the "Western." In each case – and one could add the works of Helen Hunt Jackson, especially her novel *Ramona* (1884) – everyday life is a contact zone for different peoples.

Some of the most intriguing intricacies of regionalism are embodied in the work of the Chinese Canadian writer Sui Sin Far, who, characteristically multiplying rather than choosing between identities, also used her birth name, Edith Eaton. She was born in England, to a Chinese mother and an English father, and raised mainly in Montreal. She also lived briefly in the Caribbean and on the east and west coasts of the United States. Many of the stories in her *Mrs. Spring Fragrance* (published in Chicago in 1912) are set in the West, but her work is identified with that region in large part because in the American imagination the diasporic space of "Chinatown" belongs there. Not only Sui Sin Far's biography, but also her vision of nationality, put the simplicity of such an identification into question; her work offers a complex and cosmopolitan interrogation of the relation of race, culture, and citizenship. Sui Sin Far was never a very well-known writer, and after their initial publication her works disappeared for decades. In recent years, however, she has attracted the attention of scholars and, gradually, other readers. For example, in her novel of San Francisco's Chinatown, *Bone* (1993), Fae Myenne Ng gives the institution where her narrator attended classes and now teaches the name "Edith Eaton School."

Although in this essay I have been able to mention only a small portion of the local color works that are still read, I have tried to suggest some of the main themes and emerging directions in the study of regionalist writing of the period between the Civil War and the First World War. The body of texts that have entered American literary history is itself, of course, only a tiny fraction of the fiction that was published. The map of this field has been radically redrawn in recent years, and new discoveries may lie ahead. What might be waiting, untouched by professional readers, in the local library's files of a local newspaper? From its emergence, regionalist writing has been one way in which Americans narrated their local, national, and global identifications and affiliations. Those stories of solidarity and conflict are still being told and retold today.

PRIMARY TEXTS

Allen, James Lane. "Local Color." 1886.

Allen, James Lane. *A Kentucky Cardinal: A Story.* 1894.

Austin, Mary. *The Land of Little Rain.* 1903.

Austin, Mary. *The Basket Woman: A Book of Fanciful Tales for Children.* 1904.

Brown, Alice. "The Flat-Iron Lot." 1899.

Cable, George Washington. *Old Creole Days.* 1879.

Cahan, Abraham. *Yekl: A Tale of the New York Ghetto.* 1896.

Cahan, Abraham. *The Imported Bridegroom and Other Stories of the New York Ghetto.* 1898.

Chesnutt, Charles W. *The Conjure Woman.* 1899.

Chesnutt, Charles W. *The Wife of His Youth and Other Stories of the Color Line.* 1899.

Chesnutt, Charles W. *Mandy Oxendine.* c.1896–7.

Chesnutt, Charles W. *The Marrow of Tradition.* 1901.

Chopin, Kate. *Bayou Folk.* 1894.

Cooke, Rose Terry. "Sally Parson's Duty." 1857.

Cooke, Rose Terry. *Somebody's Neighbors.* 1881.

Craddock, Charles Egbert [Mary Noailles Murfree]. *In the Tennessee Mountains.* 1885.

Crane, Stephen. *Maggie, A Girl of the Streets (A Story of New York).* 1893.

Crane, Stephen. *Whilomville Stories.* 1900.

Deland, Margaret. *Old Chester Tales.* 1898.

Deming, Philander. *The Best Short Stories of Philander Deming.* 1880–1907.

Du Bois, W. E. Burghardt. *The Souls of Black Folk.* 1903.

Dunbar-Nelson, Alice. *The Goodness of St. Roque and Other Stories.* 1899.

Eggleston, Edward. *The Hoosier School-Master.* 1871.

Frederic, Harold. *Seth's Brother's Wife, a Study of Life in Greater New York.* 1887.

Freeman, Mary E. Wilkins. "A Poetess." 1890.

Freeman, Mary E. Wilkins. *A New England Nun and Other Stories.* 1887–1916.

Freeman, Mary E. Wilkins. *The Jamesons.* 1899.

Garland, Hamlin. *Main-Travelled Roads.* 1891.

Garland, Hamlin. "Up the Coulé." 1891.

Garland, Hamlin. *Crumbling Idols: Twelve Essays on Art Dealing Chiefly with Literature, Painting and the Drama.* 1894.

Hardy, Thomas. *The Return of the Native.* 1878.

Harris, Joel Chandler. *Uncle Remus, His Songs and His Sayings.* 1880.

Harte, Bret. "The Luck of Roaring Camp." 1868.

Harte, Bret. "The Rise of the 'Short Story.'" 1899.

Hopkins, Pauline. *Contending Forces: A Romance Illustrative of Negro Life North and South.* 1900.

Howells, William Dean. *Annie Kilburn.* 1889.

Howells, William Dean. "New York Low Life in Fiction." 1896.

Howells, William Dean. *The Landlord at Lion's Head.* 1897.

Howells, William Dean. *Literary Friends and Acquaintance: A Personal Retrospect of American Authorship.* 1901.

Howells, William Dean. *The Vacation of the Kelwyns; An Idyl of the Middle Eighteen-Seventies.* 1920.

Irving, Washington. *The Sketch Book.* 1819–20.

Jackson, Helen Hunt. *Ramona.* 1884.

Jewett, Sarah Orne. *Old Friends and New.* 1870.

Jewett, Sarah Orne. *Deephaven.* 1877.

Jewett, Sarah Orne. *A Native of Winby and Other Tales.* 1893.

Jewett, Sarah Orne. *The Life of Nancy.* 1895.

Jewett, Sarah Orne. "A War Debt." 1895.

Jewett, Sarah Orne. *The Country of the Pointed Firs.* 1896.

Kennedy, John Pendleton. *Swallow Barn, or, A Sojourn in the Old Dominion.* 1832.

King, Grace. *Balcony Stories.* 1892.

Lewis, Alfred Henry. *Wolfville.* 1897.

Mitford, Mary Russell. *Our Village.* 1824–32.

Page, Thomas Nelson. *In Ole Virginia, or, Marse Chan, and Other Stories.* 1887.

Ruiz de Burton, María Amparo. *The Squatter and the Don.* 1885.

Simms, William Gilmore. *Guy Rivers: A Tale of Georgia.* 1834.

Stowe, Harriet Beecher. *The Mayflower; or, Sketches of Scenes and Characters Among the Descendants of the Puritans.* 1843.

Stowe, Harriet Beecher. *Uncle Tom's Cabin; or, Life among the Lowly.* 1852.

Stowe, Harriet Beecher. *The Pearl of Orr's Island: A Story of the Coast of Maine.* 1862.

Stowe, Harriet Beecher. *Oldtown Folks.* 1869.

Sui Sin Far [Edith Eaton]. *Mrs. Spring Fragrance.* 1912.

Thanet, Octave [Alice French]. *Stories of a Western Town.* 1893.

Tocqueville, Alexis de. *Democracy in America.* 1835, 1840.

Twain, Mark. *The Celebrated Jumping Frog of Calaveras County and Other Sketches.* 1867.

Warner, Susan. *The Wide, Wide World.* 1850.

Wendell, Barrett. *A Literary History of America.* 1900.

Wharton, Edith *Summer.* 1917.

Wharton, Edith. *Old New York: Four Novellas.* 1924.

Woolson, Constance Fenimore. *For the Major and Selected Short Stories.* 1875–95.

Wyatt, Edith. *Every One His Own Way.* 1901.

Zitkala Ša [Gertrude Bonnin]. *American Indian Stories.* 1921.

Later Collections

Austin, Mary (1999). *The Basket Woman: A Book of Indian Tales.* Reno: University of Nevada Press, 1999. (First publ. as *The Basket Woman: A Book of Fanciful Tales for Children*, 1904.)

Brown, Alice (1967). *Tiverton Tales.* Ridgewood, NJ: Gregg.

Cahan, Abraham (1970). *Yekl and The Imported Bridegroom and Other Stories of Yiddish New York*, intr. Bernard G. Richards. New York: Dover.

Cary, Alice (1987). *Clovernook Sketches and Other Stories*, ed. Judith Fetterly. New Brunswick, NJ: Rutgers University Press.

Chesnutt, Charles W. (1993). *The Conjure Woman and Other Conjure Tales*, ed. Richard H. Brodhead. Durham, NC: Duke University Press.

Chesnutt, Charles W. (1968). *The Wife of His Youth and Other Stories of the Color Line.* Ann Arbor: University of Michigan Press.

Wharton, Edith (1995). *Wharton's New England: Seven Stories and Ethan Frome*, ed. Barbara A. White. Hanover, NH: University Press of New England. (First publ. 1895–1937.)

Woolson, Constance Fenimore (1967). *For the Major and Selected Short Stories*, ed. Rayburn S. Moore. New Haven, Conn.: College and University Press.

REFERENCES AND FURTHER READING

Allen, James Lane (1886). "Local Color." *The Critic* 8: 106 (9 Jan.), 13–14.

Ammons, Elizabeth, ed. (1998). *American Local Color Writing, 1880–1920*. New York: Penguin.

Austin, Mary (1903). *The Land of Little Rain*. Boston: Houghton.

Ayers, Edward L.; Onuf, Peter S.; Limerick, Patricia Nelson; and Nissenbaum, Stephen (1996). *All Over the Map: Rethinking American Regions*. Baltimore: Johns Hopkins University Press.

Bramen, Carrie Tirado (2000). *The Uses of Variety: Modern Americanism and the Quest for National Distinctiveness*. Cambridge, Mass.: Harvard University Press.

Brodhead, Richard H. (1993). *Cultures of Letters: Scenes of Reading and Writing in Nineteenth-Century America*. Chicago: University of Chicago Press.

Brown, Dona (1995). *Inventing New England: Regional Tourism in the Nineteenth Century*. Washington DC: Smithsonian Institution Press.

Campbell, Donna M. (1997). *Resisting Regionalism: Gender and Naturalism in American Fiction, 1885–1915*. Athens, Ohio: Ohio University Press.

Fields, Annie, ed. (1898). *Life and Letters of Harriet Beecher Stowe*. Boston: Houghton Mifflin.

Folsom, Marcia McClintock (1984). "'Tact is a Kind of Mind-Reading': Empathic Style in Sarah Orne Jewett's *The Country of the Pointed Firs*." In Gwen L. Nagel (ed.), *Critical Essays on Sarah Orne Jewett*, 76–89. Boston: Hall. (First publ. 1982.)

Garland, Hamlin (1894). *Crumbling Idols: Twelve Essays on Art Dealing Chiefly with Literature, Painting and the Drama*. Chicago: Stone & Kimball.

Harte, Bret (1899). "The Rise of the 'Short Story.'" *Cornhill Magazine* n.s., 7: 37 (July), 1–9.

Hebert, Ernest (1995). *The Dogs of March*. Hanover, NH: University Press of New England. (First publ. 1979.)

Howard, June, ed. and intr. (1994). *New Essays on The Country of the Pointed Firs*. New York: Cambridge University Press.

Howells, William Dean (1911). *Literary Friends and Acquaintance: A Personal Retrospect of American Authorship*. New York: Harper & Bros.

Howells, William Dean (1993). "New York Low Life in Fiction." In Donald Pizer et al., *Selected Literary Criticism*, vol. 2: *1886–1897*, 274–78. Bloomington: Indiana University Press.

Johannigsmeier, Charles (1997). "Sarah Orne Jewett and Mary E. Wilkins (Freeman): Two Shrewd Businesswomen in Search of New Markets." *New England Quarterly* 70 (March), 57–82.

Jordan, David M. (1994). *New World Regionalism: Literature in the Americas*. Toronto: University of Toronto Press.

Kaestle, Carl F.; Damon-Moore, Helen; Stedman, Lawrence C.; Tinsley, Katherine; and Trollinger, William Vance, Jr. (1991). *Literacy in the United States: Readers and Reading since 1880*. New Haven: Yale University Press.

McHenry, Elizabeth (2002). *Forgotten Readers: Recovering the Lost History of African-American Literary Societies*. Durham, NC: Duke University Press.

Majewski, Karen (1998). "Crossings and Double-Crossings: Polish-Language Immigrant Narratives of the Great Migration." In Werner Sollors (ed.), *Multilingual America: Transnationalism, Ethnicity, and the Languages of American Literature*. New York: New York University Press.

Massey, Doreen (1994). *Space, Place and Gender*. Minneapolis: University of Minnesota Press.

Matthiessen, F. O. (1941). *American Renaissance: Art and Expression in the Age of Emerson and Whitman*. New York: Oxford University Press.

Mott, Frank Luther (1930–68). *A History of American Magazines*, 5 vols. Cambridge, Mass.: Harvard University Press.

Ng, Fae Myenne (1993). *Bone*. New York: HarperCollins.

Pattee, Fred Lewis (1925). *Tradition and Jazz*. New York: Century.

Pawley, Christine (2001). *Reading on the Middle Border: The Culture of Print in Late-Nineteenth-Century Osage, Iowa*. Amherst: University of Massachusetts Press.

Riley, James Whitcomb (1982). *The Best of James Whitcomb Riley*, ed. Donald C. Manlove. Bloomington: Indiana University Press, 1982. (First publ. 1870–1907.)

Robinson, Rowland E. (1995). *Danvis Tales: Selected Stories*, ed. David Budbill. Hanover, NH: University Press of New England. (First publ. 1887–97.)

Rohrbach, Augusta (2002). *Truth Stranger than Fiction: Race, Realism, and the US Literary Marketplace*. New York: Palgrave.

Ruiz de Burton, María Amparo (1992). *The Squatter and the Don*, ed. Rosaura Sánchez and Beatrice Pita. Houston: Arte Público.

Scharnhorst, Gary (2000). *Bret Harte: Opening the American Literary West*. Norman: University of Oklahoma Press.

Simms, William Gilmore (1834). *Guy Rivers: A Tale of Georgia*. New York: Harper & Bros.

Sollors, Werner, ed. (1998). *Multilingual America: Transnationalism, Ethnicity, and the Languages of American Literature*. New York: New York University Press.

Sui Sin Far [Edith Eaton] (1912). *Mrs. Spring Fragrance*. Chicago: C. McClurg.

Taubenfeld, Aviva (1998). "'Only an "L"': Linguistic Borders and the Immigrant Author in Abraham Cahan's *Yekl* and *Yankel der Yankee*. In Werner Sollors (ed.), *Multilingual America: Transnationalism, Ethnicity, and the Languages of American Literature*. New York: New York University Press.

Tocqueville, Alexis de (2000). *Democracy in America*, trans. Harvey C. Mansfield and Delba Winthrop. Chicago: University of Chicago Press.

Truettner, William H., and Stein, Roger B., eds. (1999). *Picturing Old New England: Image and Memory*. New Haven: National Museum of American Art–Smithsonian Institution/Yale University Press.

Warner, Susan (1987). *The Wide, Wide World*. New York: Feminist Press.

Wendell, Barrett (1900). *A Literary History of America*. New York: Charles Scribner's Sons.

Williams, Raymond (n.d.). "Region and Class in the Novel" (first publ. 1982). In *Writing in Society*, 229–38. London: Verso.

Zagarell, Sandra A. (1988). "Narrative of Community: The Identification of a Genre." *Signs* 13, 498–527.

7

Women Authors and the Roots of American Modernism

Linda Wagner-Martin

In the usual attempt to "define" American modernism, the single most significant aesthetic movement of the twentieth century, the critic begins assessment at its heart. Any discussion of modernism must include the texts of William Faulkner, Ernest Hemingway, John Dos Passos, Gertrude Stein – as well as the highly influential modernist poets Ezra Pound, T. S. Eliot, Robert Frost, William Carlos Williams, Wallace Stevens, and Marianne Moore, among others. Yet nearly all of these writers began publishing after 1914. Literary definitions are often a matter of induction: these works have come to exist; therefore, the assumption goes, the qualities in common that shaped them must have been *a*, *b*, and *c*.

Working towards a definition of American modernism from its points of origin, however, reveals a somewhat different pattern. The critic is made more conscious of the connections between nineteenth-century American letters and the currents of unrest, of interrogation of principles, that led to the development of modernism. For basic to most American literature was the aim of creating an eloquent new language in order to speak about themes germane to the rich promise of the New World. The American language – highly colloquial, privileging an easy naturalness rather than a by-the-book formality – served as the vehicle to express the American themes of the individual both at odds with a culture and a community and enfolded in it. Even as the fascination with America as physical space was diminishing – the frontier becoming as mythic in actuality as it had been imaginatively – more and more writers turned for their subject matter to the range of varied American character.

Mark Twain gave readers one set of perspectives; Henry James provided another. Between the two, late-nineteenth-century American writers saw their culture whole, through the lens of a realism that would not disguise people's motives. The heart of literature was character, and the ideal subject for United States fiction was the American character. Because Samuel Langhorne Clemens drew from his own wide experiences as reporter, miner, Confederate soldier, printer, riverboat pilot, and lecturer, and published much of his writing in the popular press, his sometimes humorous work tended to bridge the chasm between popular and elite, even if the themes of that work were frequently intellectual.

Revered by Ezra Pound and other contributors to the 1918 special edition of *Little Review* that memorialized his fiction, Henry James brought a deftly new representation of the American voice, and its experience, into narrative. Meticulously inventive, James's texts drew on the sometimes unheard language of the inexpressible – for much of what occurred in this strangely unpolished United States culture was often halting, even lame. If realism became the marker for all writing American, then Henry James was a frequently mute realist: he conveyed character by what a persona did not say as often as through what was said, and his complex narrative action was frequently so unplotted as to seem static.

Henry James's theorizing about successful fiction provided one of the linchpins of a truly American narrative; it also conveyed, if suggestively, ideas that were to become central to the evolution of modernism. Reading James's "The Art of Fiction" (1884) in conjunction with Ezra Pound's (and F. S. Flint's) "Imagiste Manifesto" in Harriet Monroe's 1913 *Poetry* is to chart the aesthetic currents shaping thirty years of late nineteenth-century and early twentieth-century American letters. As James had wisely said, "the good health of an art which undertakes so immediately to reproduce life must demand that it be perfectly free." Only this freedom will make fiction "interesting," its sole criterion for excellence. That Pound and Flint tried to provide specific principles for his prolegomenon did not diminish its effects.

Unfortunately, because the reading public was so convinced that the quality of a narrative depended upon its story (i.e. the long-established moral purpose of literature), Henry James's novels and stories were viewed as episodes in the lives of upper-class American characters who yearned to experience Europe. By limiting the influence of James's fiction to the international theme, critics failed to understand that the reason Gertrude Stein, John Peale Bishop, Ellen Glasgow, F. Scott Fitzgerald, Edith Wharton, T. S. Eliot, Ezra Pound, and Willa Cather – among others – so admired James was the sheer precision of his selection in both word and structure. For these and other writers, no matter what the rubric for a literary mode or period, the excellence of the craft was always the primary consideration.

The Force of Realism

Part of the prestige of realism grew from the prominence of newspapers in America's everyday culture. When in 1893 Stephen Crane privately published his *Maggie* (later subtitled *A Girl of the Streets*), a fictional treatment of the life of a young woman who becomes a prostitute, he signaled that capturing the real was the significant aesthetic. Even if Crane's verisimilitude was fictional, as it would be in his next work, *The Red Badge of Courage* (1895), the effect was the realism praised by Émile Zola, Gustave Flaubert, and the American writers Hamlin Garland and Frank Norris.

When Hamlin Garland coined the term "veritism," he furthered James's notion of the writer ideally being free to create. For Garland, veritism "puts aside all models, even living writers" (1894) and is particularly influenced by the individualized environment of the writer. Local color, as a positive descriptor, was just a short step ahead. For Norris, writing in "Simplicity in Art" (1901), the American writer owed a debt to literature to pare away the rhetorical, leaving "not one word unessential." Both men were poised to combine accuracy through the observed with the integrity of the honestly real.

If this new mode of modeling the lower-class and less well-educated figures of American life satisfied an artistic need, it sold fewer books than the realism that was a compromise between the aesthetically new and the conventional. Norris's *Moran of the Lady Letty* (1898) and even his *McTeague* (1899) sold fewer copies than did most of Henry James's or William Dean Howells's novels of the nineteenth century. But the books that were earning more money were those written by women authors – Sarah Orne Jewett, Mary E. Wilkins Freeman, and, a decade later, Kate Chopin, Edith Wharton, and Ellen Glasgow.

Women writers did not always write about women protagonists; that may be one area in which literary traditions (that "literature" was about a self-determined male character, free to make choices and move with impunity in the world) helped these authors to gain a readership. Especially in the cases of Edith Wharton and Ellen Glasgow, readers found male protagonists (such as Lawrence Selden in Wharton's *The House of Mirth*, 1905, or Nicholas Burr in Glasgow's *The Voice of the People*, 1900) to whom they could relate. Even in Freeman's and Jewett's fiction, strong men were familiar, common. The concept of gendered roles was still remote for nineteenth-century readers. Yet, even as women readers continued to be pleased with such male characters, culturally, interest in the New Woman and the continuing battle for women's rights enhanced the reputation of women writers: a kind of gender pride influenced what women readers found, read, enjoyed.

These women writers, regardless of their ostensible subjects, were uniformly interested in characters and the psychological motivation for their actions. Because they focused on motivation, these authors often chose to use a narrator who was more of an observer than a participant in the narrative: the story, as it were, spotlighted the protagonist. Style, accordingly, could be reportorial, objective, and therefore "realistic." For the aim of the serious woman writer was to escape being labeled "woman" or "feminine." Women writers wanted to be Henry James, William Dean Howells, Hamlin Garland; they did not want to be categorized as different because of their sex. Above all, they wanted to be received into the community of serious writers.

This required a particular subtlety on the part of women writers, because there would be clear differences between the way Ellen Glasgow might see a narrative about an abused woman character, and the way Howells might portray that same kind of character. It was this need to disguise that made the stories and novels by Sarah Orne Jewett, for example, and Willa Cather, her friend through relationships with Annie Fields and Susan Glaspell, more suggestive than representative fiction by James.

Heavily symbolic, Jewett's entire story sequence in *The Country of the Pointed Firs* (1896) coalesces through a few repeated details of the natural setting, and the home within that country. Similarly, for Charlotte Perkins Stetson Gilman, the narrative of the unnamed protagonist in "The Yellow Wall-paper" (1892) has a plotline that is so fanciful, so oblique to the real, that the reader is forced to stay within that character's inner consciousness: Gilman's "story" subtracts the element of plot entirely. As is true of both these examples, much fiction by women writers failed to end conclusively. The open ending, leaving the reader to draw what conclusions seemed likely or at least palatable, became a feature of late nineteenth-century women's writing – and of nearly all modernist writing to follow.

One illustration of the way women writers needed to walk a tenuous, and often unclear, line between the new and the traditional was the way Kate Chopin's 1899 novel, *The Awakening*, disturbed readers. Chopin, too, utilized the open ending – but not quite subversively enough. When Edna Pontellier disrobes and walks into the sea, swimming off to what we presume is her chosen death, she violates the incipient "women's novel" plot – a heterosexual family romance narrative, one that more than likely ends with either a betrothal or a marriage. Within the patriarchal system, the fragile woman goes from the protection of her father's house to that of her husband's. Chopin, however, varied that plot immensely. In *The Awakening*, Edna was already a married woman, already the mother of two young boys, already a prominent member of her husband's society. To describe the novel as a female bildungsroman (treating Edna's actual age as subordinate to her psychological age, in which she remains an adolescent who is subject to crushes and unrealistic fixations on eligible men) is to change definitions for a readership that thought it already knew the story Chopin wanted to tell. Discounting the book's title – for what kind of an "awakening" would the novel of manners tell? – these readers felt angry at Edna's search for sexual satisfaction outside the boundaries of marriage, angry at her leaving her children to the care of either maids or grandmothers, angry at her abandoning her prosperous household to live among the lower class – for these readers, too much within Edna's psyche remained inexplicable.

That Kate Chopin, who had tested some of these narrative lines in her short stories but never before in a novel-length fiction, misread her readership served as a warning to Edith Wharton, whose first bestseller was the story of Lily Bart, a woman who led a much less adventurous life but who died, it might be argued, accidentally. In *The House of Mirth*, Wharton emphasized Lily's inabilities (her failure to stand up to her aunt, her women friends; her willfulness in not marrying; her gambling; her pride in being poor) and made her a character far different from Wharton herself. Unlike either the men in that novel or her creator, Lily Bart became a sacrifice to the patriarchal system, and many readers had sympathy for Lawrence Selden's bereaved anguish at the end of the novel. That the work was extremely open, that Selden's grief could easily be read as ironic, as a calculated appeal for more than usual sympathy for the beautiful (and dead) Lily, made *The House of Mirth* a key text in the progress toward such modernist novels as F. Scott Fitzgerald's *The Great Gatsby*

(1925) – another interrogation of social values, another validation of characters' right to be free, another open-ended work.

Study of the production of Ellen Glasgow's long list of novels, nearly all of them bestsellers, shows that her work eventually became importantly feminist, but that it was not until her 1913 novel *Virginia* that she was consciously using women characters as protagonists. She considered *Virginia*, the novel ostensibly about her beloved mother and sister – traditional women who had given all for love, and reaped unhappiness – the first of her trilogy about women's lives; it was followed in 1916 by *Life and Gabriella*, her only work set in the metropolis of New York (where she herself had lived after the end of her life-changing romance) rather than in some part of her home state of Virginia. Known as the chronicler of Virginia, in fact, Glasgow struggled throughout her long writing life with the burden of writing historically accurate novels, in working through a series of romance plots, from the first narrative of Michael Akershem (*The Descendant*, 1897; published anonymously, it was sometimes attributed to the controversially irreverent Harold Frederick) and the Civil War romance, *The Battle-Ground* (1902) with Betty Ambler, its imperious and impractical woman character, to the two novels that created lower-class heroes (*The Romance of a Plain Man* [1909] and *The Miller of Old Church* [1911]). Educated at home, Glasgow wanted to be seen as a young disciple of John Stuart Mill and Malthus, a proponent of free will and other iconoclastic beliefs: she tried to write as if she were an educated man. Although she had drawn interesting women characters in these early novels, they existed, largely, to complete the romance plots that venerated the male heroes.

With the completion of *Virginia*, however, Glasgow turned to novels that focused on strong women characters – and became increasingly modernist in their execution. The deft descriptions of relationships in *Life and Gabriella*, which grew more heavy-handed and more anti-male in her 1925 *Barren Ground*; the over-the-top heroism of *One Man in His Time* (1922), countered by the short stories – especially the ghost stories – published from 1905 to 1923 in *The Shadowy Third*; the outright feminist and ironic Queenborough novels of *The Romantic Comedians* (1926) and *They Stooped to Folly* (1929); and the bitter denunciation of patriarchal power in each of the male characters of *The Sheltered Life* (1932): this sequence of works charted Glasgow's own immense change from a writer who wanted to trace the important intellectual challenges of the early twentieth century to a writer who wanted to make the world attend to the lives of its valuable women participants in their quickly changing modern existence. As Glasgow grew more feminist, her style grew more elliptical and suggestive; her novels included more dialogue (all voices – though mostly of white speakers – appropriately colloquial); and her narrative lines moved further from the family romance. Either Glasgow's women characters are unmarried, or they are the stronger of the married couple. That such a range of powerful women characters exists regardless of social or financial class may be Glasgow's largest contribution to the evolution of the modern American novel.

It may seem idiosyncratic to link the three women protagonists of Gertrude Stein's 1909 *Three Lives* (entitled in manuscript *Three Deaths*) with Glasgow's achieving Ada

Fincastle (*Vein of Iron* [1935]) or her women characters of *In This Our Life* (1941). But Stein, like the later Glasgow, was insistent on using women characters as the subjects of her writing. Whether in her later *The Mother of Us All* (mid-1940s), the novel *Ida* (1941), the portrait poems, or her longest and most important work, *The Making of Americans* (1925), Stein chose to write about the magnificence of women protagonists.

In 1909, at the time of its publication, such an emphasis was difficult to see in *Three Lives*. "The Good Anna" and "Gentle Lena" appeared to be nonentities whose deaths did not diminish the community. With her inherently superb irony, played with a straight-faced demeanor, Stein showed the centrality of both these women, both undermined by cultural assumptions (that really "good" women married and produced children, that "gentle"ness was a virtue, that selfless giving was every woman's aim). But she presented both sides of that inherent irony, and rather than simply criticizing patriarchal power, found ways to insist that Anna and Lena were complicit in their victimization. Convoluted in sentence patterns as well as in the structure of each story, the three segments of *Three Lives* gave readers a conundrum of characterization rather than a linear presentation of cause-and-effect development. Far removed from Hamlin Garland's works in *Main-Travelled Roads* (1891), Stein's achievement in *Three Lives* was an appropriately complex rendering of the varied forces – social, psychological, biological, national – that played upon any developing woman in the United States. The book was meant to be admonitory.

Like "The Good Anna," Stein's treatment of "Melanctha," the central and longest story of the three, and the most radical in that it dealt with an African American woman, was also sexually controversial. Both these characters were sexually deviant (using the terminology of the early twentieth century). Anna loved one of her women friends in her life, yet she behaved as if in a courtship with the men for whom she worked: her social skills were dominated by the family romance. The more complex Melanctha, however, knew that her ability to survive depended on her marrying a suitable man, and consequently she gave an inordinate amount of time and energy to her relationship with the young black doctor. Melanctha, however, loved a woman; and the failure of that relationship led to her indiscriminate sexual exploits.

Of these important stories and novels by women writers, perhaps Stein's *Three Lives* comes the closest to being a conventional "realistic" work. No reader was tempted to see these characters as surrogates for their author, as might have been the case with Lily Bart's story read as a clear parallel to the pre-marriage life of Edith Wharton, or with Dorinda Oakley's renunciation of men after Ellen Glasgow's recovery from her several broken engagements. The inherent distancing of the lives of Anna, Lena, and Melanctha from the life of Gertrude Stein, the favorite student of William James and other professors at Harvard, an honors graduate of Radcliffe, an author published in medical journals, a woman completing Johns Hopkins medical training, was automatic. Free from the possibility of being read as autobiographical, *Three Lives* then took its place among the classics of realist American fiction, marked by its colloquial rhythms, its lower-class characters, and its commonplace settings.

The Force of Modernism

It goes without saying, however, that Stein's *Three Lives* simultaneously became a forerunner of modernism. Not only were the colloquial sounds of the American language to be heard clearly in the stories, but those sounds were repeated from dialogue to description, rather than being isolated in dialogue: Stein's prose was like none other in English. She was content to mimic the brokenness of the German character's mastery of the American idiom, and that hesitation, that repetition which she called "insistence," dominated her prose in this work from sentence to sentence, page to page. Influential among key modernists like William Carlos Williams, Sherwood Anderson, Kay Boyle, and many others, Stein's *Three Lives* grew to become an underground classic, abetted by the 1914 publication of her poem collection, *Tender Buttons*, so that her writings were considered standpoints of American modernism. Stein's approach to fiction and all other genres was a true redefinition of the way words could be used, as well as a redefinition of what constituted a "word."

Much less stylistically experimental, Theodore Dreiser's *Sister Carrie* (1900) also took on iconic value. The successful outcome of the naïve actress, her relative fame set against the downfall of her lover and mentor, Hurstwood, provided a shocking counterpoint to the stories of women who lived adventurously, who broke out of the family romance pattern, but then paid their debts to society with their deaths. Alive and prosperous at the end of the novel, Carrie Meeber seems to suffer no regret for her sexual promiscuity, her morally abhorrent climb to stardom. Dreiser left the ending of his novel open, however, so as to provide readers the same kind of room to mourn that Wharton was to offer at the end of *The House of Mirth*. The ambivalence of the American concept of "success" – a theme that was to dominate American modernist fiction – was firmly entrenched here. Dreiser's linearity in composing the novel comforted readers who might otherwise have been disoriented from the start by Carrie's shocking approach to the uses of sexuality.

The same kind of judicious balancing was clear in Willa Cather's second novel, the 1913 *O Pioneers!* As she had in stories, and as she was to do in, particularly, *My Ántonia* (1918) and *A Lost Lady* (1923), Cather was able to draw compelling women characters who never spoke for themselves: in the latter two novels, she chose to use naïve male narrators who seldom understood the full implications of the story being related, but rather used their narration as a means of self-identifying. Perhaps the most structurally complex of the seemingly "traditional" women writers of these years, Willa Cather brought to the progression into modernism a reasoned calm, a fiction woven from the textures of American daily life that were, taken separately, inoffensive, even predictable. Yet the impact of her total achievement in each novel was so far-reaching that the reader was left to question every premise that being "American" in the early years of the twentieth century had accepted. It is this kind of subversive simplicity that the acclaimed modernists from Sherwood Anderson, Ernest Hemingway, and

F. Scott Fitzgerald to John Dos Passos, Djuna Barnes, and Jean Toomer recognized, borrowed, and tailored to fit their own narratives.

Coda

Even as T. S. Eliot's long poem *The Waste Land* (1922) has come to serve as an icon of American modernism – cited for its fragmented structure, its allusive reference system, its organic rhythms, and its mixed texture of somber comedy and tragic sobriety – so Robert Frost's "Mending Wall" (1914) is an apt metaphor for this premodernist era. What the historical backward glance shows is that artists in search of the innovative were never far from their traditions, both national and literary. The step toward the modern was more of a glide than a kick, as the dancer's skirt continued to cover her ankles.

In this quietly subversive poem, Frost too veered away from the acknowledged sources of convention. The crux of the dialogic narrative is the maxim to be challenged: "Good fences make good neighbors." Just as the poem's speaker argues against this bit of folk wisdom, so the poem replicates a seemingly nineteenth-century poetic convention – the strongly accented blank verse, end-rhymed and yet colloquially inflected, breaks into shorter groups of lines that fit – organically – with the meaning of each discrete segment. The complexities of getting along in rural America here give texture to Frost's aimed-for simplicity.

The resulting combination of acute ambivalence with the sure polish of conclusion mirrors the most accomplished works of American modernism – the acerbic vision expressed through simple and colloquial language, shaped in patterns that force the reader into a second reading; and with that reading comes the understanding that aesthetic truth – at least, modern aesthetic truth – is often illusive.

PRIMARY TEXTS

Cather, Willa. *O Pioneers!* 1913.

Cather, Willa. *My Antonia*. 1918.

Cather, Willa. *A Lost Lady*. 1923.

Chopin, Kate. *The Awakening*. 1899.

Crane, Stephen. *Maggie, A Girl of the Streets (A Story of New York)*. 1893.

Crane, Stephen. *The Red Badge of Courage; an Episode of the American Civil War*. 1895.

Dreiser, Theodore. *Sister Carrie*. 1900.

Eliot, T. S. *The Waste Land*. 1922.

Fitzgerald, F. Scott. *The Great Gatsby*. 1925.

Frost, Robert. "Mending Wall." In *North of Boston*. 1914.

Garland, Hamlin. *Main-Travelled Roads*. 1891.

Garland, Hamlin. *Crumbling Idols: Twelve Essays on Art Dealing Chiefly with Literature, Painting and the Drama*. 1894.

Gilman, Charlotte Perkins Stetson. "The Yellow Wall-paper." 1892.

Glasgow, Ellen. *The Descendant*. 1897.

Glasgow, Ellen. *The Voice of the People*. 1900.

Glasgow, Ellen. *The Battle-Ground*. 1902.

Glasgow, Ellen. *The Romance of a Plain Man*. 1909.

Glasgow, Ellen. *The Miller of Old Church*. 1911.

Glasgow, Ellen. *Virginia*. 1913.

Glasgow, Ellen. *Life and Gabriella*. 1916.

Glasgow, Ellen. *One Man in His Time*. 1922.

Glasgow, Ellen. *The Shadowy Third*. 1923.

Glasgow, Ellen. *Barren Ground*. 1925.

Glasgow, Ellen. *The Romantic Comedians*. 1926.

Glasgow, Ellen. *They Stooped to Folly*. 1929.

Glasgow, Ellen. *The Sheltered Life*. 1932.

Glasgow, Ellen. *Vein of Iron*. 1935.

Glasgow, Ellen. *In This Our Life*. 1941.

James, Henry. "The Art of Fiction." 1884.

Jewett, Sarah Orne. *The Country of the Pointed Firs*. 1896.

Norris, Frank. *Moran of the Lady Letty*. 1898.

Norris, Frank. *McTeague: A Story of San Francisco*. 1899.

Norris, Frank. "Simplicity in Art." In *The Responsibilities of the Artist and Other Literary Essays*. 1901.

Pound, Ezra. "Imagiste Manifesto." 1913.

Stein, Gertrude. *Three Lives*. 1909.

Stein, Gertrude. *Tender Buttons*. 1914.

Stein, Gertrude. *The Making of Americans*. 1925.

Stein, Gertrude. *Ida*. 1941.

Stein, Gertrude. *The Mother of Us All*. Mid-1940s.

Wharton, Edith. *The House of Mirth*. 1905.

8

The Short Story and the Short-Story Sequence, 1865–1914

J. Gerald Kennedy

The short story emerged in the United States as a feature of the literary magazines that proliferated after 1825. A long though discontinuous tradition of short fiction in English had included fables, parables, and Oriental tales, but not until the rise of periodicals was there a market to encourage and sustain its production. Noting that "[t]he whole tendency of the age is Magazine-ward," Poe observed in 1846 that "the curt, the condensed, the pointed, the easily diffused" was taking the place of "the verbose, the detailed, the voluminous, the inaccessible" (Poe 1984: 1414–15). The "tale" (as it was then called) epitomized this new style of writing which demanded brevity and condensation; it privileged incident over character development or social panorama. In the United States, where nation-building drove the formation of culture, short fiction seemed well adapted to the limited leisure of a practical, industrious people. But an economic factor also spurred the production of short fiction: periodicals offered cash for stories, providing a market for writers hindered from book publication by the absence of an international copyright law. Because foreign works lacked this protection, American publishers routinely "pirated" novels by popular British authors and reissued them in US editions, thus purveying established talent at minimal expense. Although they also printed American novels to demonstrate national loyalty, the need to offer US authors royalties made their works relatively less profitable. This situation, so disadvantageous to native authors, persisted until 1891 and partly explains the affinity for short fiction that marked US literature during the nineteenth century and persisted as a cultural tradition after the resolution of the copyright problem.

During the 1850s, two further developments affected short fiction. One was the appearance of the great literary monthlies (still in circulation) that would become the twin pillars of the American magazine world in the later nineteenth century: *Harper's Monthly Magazine* (1850) and the *Atlantic Monthly* (1857). Harper & Brothers also launched a separate, illustrated magazine in 1857, *Harper's Weekly*. These three journals greatly influenced the reconstruction of a postwar national literary culture and the shaping of reading tastes and critical standards in the wake of Romanticism.

They became important venues for short fiction in transition from the idealized, fanciful, or symbolic tale of the antebellum period to the more realistic "short story." Analyzing this second development, Robert F. Marler has argued that Melville's "Bartleby the Scrivener," published by *Putnam's* in 1853, marks the crucial shift toward a fiction attuned to social reality and informed by a psychological realism that resists character simplification (Marler 1974: 153–69). But Rebecca Harding Davis's "Life in the Iron Mills," published in the *Atlantic* (1861), perhaps even more dramatically embodied this new realism in its attention to lower-class life, labor injustice, and the abuses of capitalism. Davis's shocking depiction of the squalor in which mill workers lived (and the inferno where they worked) was so advanced, in fact, that a comparably grim realism did not resurface until Stephen Crane and Hamlin Garland began publishing short stories around 1890. Nevertheless, Davis's candid tone and her focus on the conditions of everyday life, on ordinary human beings engaged in mundane activities within an actual social milieu, signaled a fundamental shift in the object of much postwar short fiction.

This new, modern form did not acquire the name "short story" until 1885, when critic Brander Mathews published his "Philosophy of the Short-story" in *Lippincott's Magazine*. For two decades, however, short fiction in American periodicals had largely avoided dreamy or fantastic plots and aberrant, supernatural, or idealized types, taking instead as its usual subject the contemporary real world and often the distinctive conditions of life in different regions of the United States. William Dean Howells, who at different times edited both the *Atlantic* and *Harper's Monthly*, wrote in *Criticism and Fiction* (1891) that the writer's task was to represent the "real grasshopper" as opposed to an ideal or heroic simulacrum. His dictum applied to both novels and short fiction, and his advocacy of realism was less an avant-garde manifesto than an endorsement of an aesthetic already established on the European continent and gaining influence in the United States. The rise of realism coincided with, and to some extent reflected, the growth of urban culture, the emerging authority of science and social science, and the development of modern technology. One technological innovation – photography – has much to do with the realist aesthetic: it epitomized exact representation, the effort to make art reflect the ordinary, everyday world of lived experience. Yet this aesthetic never entirely transformed the American novel or the short story, for cultural idealism, romantic provincialism, and Victorian gentility all checked the evolution of realism as social critique. As short stories proliferated between 1865 and 1914, the form thus reflected the ambivalence of a culture that on the one hand revered pragmatism and frankness, and on the other refused to examine too closely unpleasant social realities that marked taboos or contradicted national ideals of freedom, equality, and justice.

Regionalism

The politics of sectionalism that brought the Civil War also reshaped literary culture during Reconstruction and its aftermath. But it did so by sublimating old hostilities and recent indignities, producing a quietist regionalism that encouraged postwar reconciliation by presenting local narratives in which social conflicts served mainly to complicate love plots. While notable exceptions come to mind – regional stories that expose injustice or hypocrisy – the predominant purpose of such writing was to entertain rather than reform. The great literary magazines of the Northeast purveyed "local color" as a palliative, an escape from political resentment and contemporary scandal. Regional short fiction became fashionable in the late 1860s and directed American writing for three decades. Its hallmark was an ostensibly realistic attention to local dialects and folkways, to distinctive place and family names, to local characters and customs, and to representative landscapes. In place of strict objectivity, however, sentiment or pathos often crept in, producing a hybrid, empathetic realism. Such writing was self-consciously provincial in perspective, rarely concerning itself with matters of national, much less transnational, significance; it restricted its focus to small towns and rural scenes enfolded by the local landscape.

With the exception of such urban writers as George Washington Cable, Henry Blake Fuller, or Abraham Cahan, exponents of local color tended to avoid cities and their attendant social problems; in its various manifestations, regional writing marks a studied resistance to modernism and cosmopolitanism. As Richard H. Brodhead has observed, writers depicted life in the provinces for largely metropolitan, educated readers who defined their cultural superiority in relation to the semi-literate backwaters that provided literary (and touristic) diversion. On another level, he adds, the movement amounted to a "cultural elegy" for regional cultures then already being engulfed by an increasingly homogeneous national culture (Brodhead 1993: 120). Stephanie Foote contends that in the face of heavy foreign immigration in the late nineteenth century, regional writing underscored "the role of difference in the creation of an American character"; it challenged nativism by revealing "distinctly foreign" elements of native life (Foote 2001: 14, 179). Mass-circulation magazines such as *Harper's Weekly*, *Harper's Monthly*, the *Atlantic*, *Galaxy*, the *Nation*, *Scribner's Monthly*, and its successor, the *Century*, became primary outlets for regional short fiction, thus implicitly sponsoring an ideology of diversity, dismantling residual sectionalism with a self-conscious provincialism that putatively affirmed both regional difference and national unity.

Historically the regional mode evolved from antebellum frontier humor by A. B. Longstreet, Johnson J. Hooper, George Washington Harris, and others. These writers popularized sketches, yarns, and anecdotes that incorporated colorful dialect and portrayed backwoods types engaged in outlandish schemes, contests, or feuds. No short-story writer of the post-war era knew this tradition better than Mark Twain, whose early piece, "Jim Smiley and his Jumping Frog" (1865; later entitled "The Celebrated Jumping Frog of Calaveras County"), captured the vernacular of California mining towns as well as the male boasting, betting, competition, and trickery featured in tales of the Old Southwest. Twain's Western short fiction includes a handful of other pieces, including "Buck Fanshaw's Funeral," "The Story of the Old Ram," and "A Trial" (all from *Roughing It* [1872]), as well as "What Stumped the Bluejays" (from *A Tramp Abroad* [1880]). These rambling narratives show little regard for either conventional short-story form or locodescriptive detail; rooted in oral storytelling, they aim mainly for dialect humor and colorful characterization. Conversely, Twain's late, conventional piece, "The Californian's Tale" (1893), begins in topography and ends in sentiment, revealing an old miner's delusional attachment to his dead wife and thus signaling Twain's debt to his erstwhile mentor, Bret Harte.

Often regarded as the inventor of local color, Harte preceded Twain as a writer of Western stories by five years. Not until his *Overland Monthly* featured "The Luck of Roaring Camp" (1868), though, did Harte become a literary celebrity, hitting upon a clever formula soon adapted by other regionalists. Reprinted in magazines across the nation, his most famous story appeals blatantly to sentiment: when "Cherokee Sal," the only woman in Roaring Camp, dies in childbirth, miners raise young "Luck" and become comic nannies, but a flash flood takes the life of the baby and his hirsute, unlikely protector, "Kentuck." Harte's blend of humor and pathos, coupled with superficial glimpses of the Sierra landscape and colorful characters ostensibly representative of Gold Rush towns, ensured the popularity of his collection, *The Luck of Roaring Camp and Other Sketches* (1870). In the year of its publication he returned to the East, signed a lucrative contract with the *Atlantic*, and turned the writing of Western stories into an industry. In reality Harte had spent little time in the mining camps, gathering material instead from prospectors visiting San Francisco. Reflecting his wide reading and gift for imitation, Harte's style contrasts narratorial suavity with local slang. Another story of disaster, "The Outcasts of Poker Flat" (1869), has become his most anthologized work, principally because the gambler John Oakhurst's ironic reflections on chance and fate, as he calculates the odds of surviving a blizzard, give the story a philosophical heft and quasi-naturalistic feel as they prefigure his suicide. Harte soon filled a second collection of mining-camp stories, *Tales of the Argonauts* (1875), and many others followed. Even after moving to Europe in 1878, he continued to produce California novels, plays, poems, and stories, exhausting the materials of his early work. Briefly the most imitated writer in America, Harte created a demand for regional short fiction and blazed the way for such later Western regionalists as Joaquin Miller, Alfred Henry Lewis, and Mary Austin.

If Harte popularized local color stories in the early 1870s, he was not, however, their first exponent. The New England writer Rose Terry Cooke began supplying the *Atlantic* with regional short fiction in 1857, a decade before Harte came to prominence. Her modest, loosely plotted narratives make her an improbable precursor of a widespread literary movement. Though certain of her early pieces savor of outmoded Romanticism, narratives such as "Ann Potter's Lesson" or "Lizzie Griswold's Thanksgiving" reflect an emerging focus on the life-choices faced by ordinary rural New England women. For three decades Cooke contributed regularly to the *Atlantic* and *Harper's Monthly*, with occasional appearances in *Putnam's* and *Galaxy* as well. Chronicling the homely dramas of simple villagers and farm folk, she portrayed her native Connecticut with a keen ear for dialect and a sharp eye for what she called "domestic tactics," the negotiations of power between husbands and wives; she focused especially on the hardships of women in loveless marriages and the gratifications of female friendship, although she also produced numerous love stories about couples thwarted by parental authority. The late narrative "How Miss Celia Changed Her Mind" (1892) recapitulates these main themes: having helped young Rosabel Stearns defy her father by eloping, the "old maid" Celia Barnes escapes spinsterhood by wedding frugal Deacon Everts; but after four years of marital misery she celebrates his decease with a Thanksgiving dinner attended by "every old maid in town." Cooke's fiction also laments the dwindling of spiritual devotion in Protestant New England or, conversely (as in "Root-Bound"), celebrates the "active Christian life," although her fine story "Too Late" (1875) portrays a woman to whom a repressive Calvinism has given a "heart of granite." Cooke brought her best magazine stories together in three later collections — *Somebody's Neighbors* (1881), *The Sphinx's Children and Other People's* (1886), and *Huckleberries Gathered from New England Hills* (1891). Although she lacked Harte's flamboyance, Cooke nevertheless merits recognition as the true foremother of the regional short story.

Another early practitioner of New England regionalism, Harriet Beecher Stowe, has often overshadowed Cooke. Yet if we exclude two early New England sketches, Stowe did not turn from anti-slavery fiction to regional writing until her novels *The Minister's Wooing* (1859), *The Pearl of Orr's Island* (1862), and *Oldtown Folks* (1869). Nor did she attempt provincial short fiction until her 1872 collection, *Sam Lawson's Oldtown Fireside Stories*, a transparent effort to boost sales of her most recent novel after critical attacks by Harte and others. Using the persona of Oldtown blacksmith Sam Lawson, Stowe stitched together ten tales in homespun vernacular, many incorporating bits of superstition and legend. More consonant with the stories of Cooke, "The Minister's Housekeeper" presents a widower's dilemma: the Reverend Carryl's decision to wed the cheerful young housemaid who attended his dying wife thwarts the ambitions of widow Pipperidge and quiets his gossiping congregation. "Mis Elderkin's Pitcher" also treats a recent event, the discovery of gold coins secreted in a pitcher inherited by a long-suffering daughter. Stowe added five more Oldtown stories to later editions of *Fireside Stories*, including "The Parson's Horse-Race," but did not significantly expand her regionalist repertoire.

The most gifted New England regionalist, Sarah Orne Jewett, discovered the provincial subject by reading Stowe's *The Pearl of Orr's Island*. She too became a frequent contributor to the *Atlantic*, placing her first story there in 1868 and gaining critical attention with the serialized regional sketches collected as *Deephaven* (1877). Jewett's first volume of short stories, *Old Friends and New* (1879), was followed by nine subsequent collections, including *A White Heron and Other Stories* (1886) and *The King of Folly Island and Other People* (1888). She wrote mostly about the poor, isolated villages of coastal Maine and the friendships between single women in depopulated communities where men had either gone to sea or emigrated to the West — the gendered, geographical antithesis of Harte's predominantly male California boom towns. Her much-admired story "A White Heron" dramatizes the dilemma of a girl torn between her attraction to a handsome stranger, an ornithologist collecting bird specimens, and her attachment to a beautiful heron she has spotted from a tall tree. Probing the subtleties of "A White Heron," Louis A. Renza has rightly challenged the critical disposition to regard regional writing as a "minor" literature (Renza 1984: 3–42). Other Jewett stories sometimes reprinted include "The Dulham Ladies," an exquisite satire of class pretension and female vanity that yet offers an understanding view of spinsterhood, and "Miss Tempy's Watchers," the story of a night vigil in which two women unburden their hearts at the home of a deceased friend. Another fine story, "Marsh Rosemary," traces the unraveling of Nancy Floyd's marriage. Determined to expose her estranged husband as a bigamist, Nancy then glimpses his happiness with a younger woman and chooses renunciation: "She could not enter in and break another heart; hers was broken already, and it would not matter." Jewett's sensitivity to psychological nuance and her careful balancing of detachment and sympathy also inform the connected sketches and stories that make up *The Country of the Pointed Firs* (1896).

A fourth New England regionalist, Mary E. Wilkins Freeman, began publishing stories in the early 1880s and collected her best work (some of which was featured in *Harper's Bazaar*) in *A Humble Romance and Other Stories* (1887) and *A New England Nun and Other Stories* (1891). Like Cooke and Jewett, Freeman (who did not marry until her fiftieth year) wrote often about solitary women in declining communities or about the complications of female friendships; she was particularly attentive to the buried life, the repressed feelings and thwarted desires of her subjects, treated unsentimentally and at times wryly. Her unaffected style and direct method match the straitened lives of the plain folk she depicted; these qualities grace her most celebrated stories, "The Revolt of 'Mother'" and "A New England Nun." In the former, a long-suffering wife protests her husband's construction of a spacious barn by making it her home, installing (in her husband's absence) their meager domestic furnishings, while in the latter, Louisa Ellis overhears her fiancé's conversation with another woman and releases him from marital obligation, despite her own fourteen years of waiting, "prayerfully" taking up an ordered life as "an uncloistered nun." Like most of her cohort, Freeman drifted away from provincial fiction after the turn of the century, but many of her stories from the 1880s retain subtle appeal.

In the South, regionalism often served a deeply reactionary purpose: to justify the Lost Cause retroactively by evoking a romanticized version of slavery and plantation life. Both Thomas Nelson Page's collection *In Ole Virginia* (1887) and James Lane Allen's *Flute and Violin* (1891) use sentimentalism to arouse nostalgia for a chivalric antebellum South. Page's best-known story, "Marse Chan," ostensibly reproduces the black dialect of eastern Virginia as the narrator, a former slave, recollects the gallantry and death of his kindly former master. In Allen's "Two Gentlemen of Kentucky," Colonel Fields's servant Peter in effect refuses emancipation, becoming an honorary "gentleman" through dog-like loyalty. Efforts by Page and Allen to reassert racial hierarchy in the face of Reconstruction and the Thirteenth and Fourteenth Amendments were to some extent mirrored by Ruth McEnery Stuart, whose *In Simpkinsville:*

Character Tales (1897) plays off comic blacks against ignorant poor whites in rural Arkansas.

Other Southern regionalists took different approaches to race. Mississippi-born (Katherine) Sherwood Bonner drew upon her travels in the South to produce *Dialect Tales* (1883) and *Suwanee River Tales* (1884), which sketch Southern blacks as objects of white ethnographic interest. A better-known and more controversial case is that of Joel Chandler Harris, the Georgia journalist who popularized a white version of African American folklore, assuming a black voice for his *Uncle Remus: His Songs and His Sayings* (1880). Harris also built several poignant short stories, such as "Free Joe and the Rest of the World," around the vicissitudes of slaves or former slaves, walking a fine line between commemoration and caricature. In addition, he produced stories of Southern mountain folk, such as "Trouble on Lost Mountain," thus traversing fictional terrain mapped by Bonner and by Tennessee writer Mary Noailles Murfree. Under the pen name of Charles Egbert Craddock, Murfree published *In the Tennessee Mountains* (1884), a collection of eight *Atlantic* stories, and a subsequent volume, *The Mystery of Witch-Face Mountain and Other Stories* (1895). Her upland South, populated mostly by Scots-Irish, Cumberland types, is haunted less by race and Reconstruction than by folklore and superstition, as in her best-known story, "The 'Harnt' that Walks Chilhowee."

If the South generated more regional fiction than elsewhere, Louisiana became its most evocative site, a place where diverse cultures converged and class status hinged on degrees of racial mixture. George Washington Cable examined the colorful history of New Orleans in a somewhat romanticized collection, *Old Creole Days* (1879), and in a regional novel, *The Grandissimes* (1880), both of which dealt openly with miscegenation, exploring the social, racial, and ethnic mix of his native city. Between 1873 and 1876, six of the seven stories originally included in *Old Creole Days* appeared in *Scribner's Monthly*, which under editor J. G. Holland promoted reconciliation between North and South. In such pieces as "Madame Délicieuse" Cable made Louisiana exotic for Northern readers by contrasting Creole and American cultures. In the face of local resentment of his progressive racial views he moved to Massachusetts in 1885, but he continued to write about Louisiana and especially New Orleans; later collections included *Strange True Stories of Louisiana* (1889) and *Strong Hearts* (1899). Aiming to correct Cable's putative exaggerations of Creole culture, the part-Creole Grace King composed her *Balcony Stories* (1893), a linked sequence of fourteen narratives supposedly recounted by a circle of refined New Orleans women. "La Grande Demoiselle" typifies her theme, the decline of the Creole aristocracy: while Union troops occupy the Reine Sainte Foy plantation, a fire destroys the house and the family's wealth, leaving the once-formidable Mademoiselle Idalie a pathetic figure at the end, teaching at "the colored public school." Other writers also helped to elaborate a Louisiana regional narrative. Lafcadio Hearn published journalistic sketches of Creole life during his stay in New Orleans and penned a regional novel, *Chita: A Memory of Last Island* (1889); Alice Dunbar-Nelson, a Creole woman of color, elided race but emphasized ethnic difference in the dialect pieces featured in *The Goodness of St. Rocque and Other Stories* (1899); and Ruth McEnery Stuart portrayed the New Orleans she had known as a young wife in *A Golden Wedding and Other Tales* (1905).

But no one wrote about Louisiana more compellingly than Kate Chopin. Returning to her native St. Louis after fourteen years as the wife of a Creole cotton merchant and planter, Chopin began writing piquant, ironic stories influenced by Maupassant. She conceived as her broad subject the convergence of Acadian, Creole, African American, and Anglo-Saxon cultures in Louisiana. Having lived both in New Orleans and in Cajun bayou country, Chopin used her perspective as an outsider to write insightfully about paternalism and gender relations in Catholic, French Louisiana. Between 1889 and 1899 she composed almost one hundred stories, many for *Vogue* and *Youth's Companion*, and most featuring the distinctive French patois of southwestern Louisiana. Chopin collected many of her best pieces in two volumes, *Bayou Folk* (1894) and *A Night in Acadie* (1897). As in her provocative novel *The Awakening* (1899), the recurrent theme of her short fiction is desire, complicated by boredom, neglect, jealousy, infidelity, or emotional confusion and circumscribed by such biological inevitabilities as pregnancy, childbirth, aging, and death. Her most brilliant story, "Desirée's Baby," turns on the problem of miscegenation and describes proud Armand Aubigny's tragic repudiation of his wife when their baby proves of mixed race; after Desirée departs, presumably to kill herself and the child, Aubigny finds a letter from his mother revealing that he himself "belongs to the race that is cursed with the brand of slavery." Cultural and class differences complicate both "At the 'Cadian Ball" and the torrid, long-suppressed sequel, "The Storm." Though Chopin deftly managed longer narratives – and "Athenaïse" is one of her best – her gift for verbal compression and apt detail reveals itself best in such brief fictions as "Regret," where Mamzelle Aurélie, who had "never thought of marrying," is pressed into child care by a desperate neighbor and unexpectedly grieves her childlessness. Chopin's tightly wound plots, her nuanced representation of racial, class, and cultural differences, and her insight into underlying motivations transcend the regional formula.

Sustained by magazines serving a metropolitan elite, provincialism thus had the unintended effect of democratizing literary production. As Brodhead astutely remarks, "regionalism made the experience of the socially marginalized a literary asset, and so made marginality itself a positive authorial advantage" (Brodhead 1993: 117). No career better illustrates this insight than that of Charles W. Chesnutt, who returned from Ohio to North Carolina with his half-black parents and educated himself to become a teacher, a school principal, and finally a writer. He entered the domain of regional fiction specifically to counter the blackface impersonations of Page and Harris. Because "The Goophered Grapevine" (1887) and "Po' Sandy" (1888) superficially resembled the derisive black dialect pieces that pleased Northern audiences, the *Atlantic* welcomed Chesnutt's first contributions. In these stories the former slave Julius McAdoo entertains the newly arrived Northern landowner John with amusing local lore, his vernacular style subtly revealing the power of "conjure" as both a folk practice and a rhetorical strategy. Although Uncle Julius's revelation that a vineyard has been "goophered" (cursed) does not prevent John from buying it, his story encourages the new owner's indulgence of local blacks who eat his grapes. After publishing two more dialect pieces ("The Conjurer's Revenge" and "Dave's Neckliss"), Chesnutt turned to the controversial subject of mixed blood, but met with editorial reluctance. At the request of Houghton Mifflin he wrote a handful of new Uncle Julius stories in 1898, from which the publisher chose six for *The Conjure Woman and Other Conjure Tales* (1899). In the same year Chesnutt published *The Wife of His Youth and Other Stories of the Color Line*, a story sequence that pondered prejudice and racism in the postwar era.

Unlike the South, the more sparsely settled Midwest produced relatively little regional writing. Apart from novels by Edward Eggleston and Edgar Watson Howe, only the farm stories of Hamlin Garland and certain narratives by Constance Fenimore Woolson still command critical attention. Garland knew farm life intimately and lived in Wisconsin, Iowa, and the Dakota territories before going east in 1884 to become a teacher; but his reading in Boston of such social theorists as Herbert Spencer and Henry George radicalized his understanding of land use and economic survival. After visiting the Midwest he began to write the stories collected in *Main-Travelled Roads* (1891), delivering not nostalgia but rather candid images of the wearying labor and harsh conditions of rural life. In Garland's view the villains of the Midwestern regional narrative were the predatory land speculators bent on getting rich by exploiting farmers, and in "Under the Lion's Paw" he exposed the tactics of Jim Butler, who rents a farm to Steven Council, lets him make improvements, and then adds the value of the renovations to the inflated sale price he demands. Garland produced two subsequent volumes of stories, *Prairie Folks* (1893) and *Other Main-Travelled Roads* (1910), but wrote increasingly from formula, curbing the indignation that gave an edge to his first collection.

Constance Fenimore Woolson grew up in Ohio and spent summers in Michigan; later she resided in Florida, Georgia, and North Carolina before becoming an expatriate in Italy. She came to the regional short story early in its vogue, and her literarily self-conscious method produced two volumes of regional short fiction: *Castle Nowhere: Lake-Country Sketches* (1875), set mostly in Ohio and the upper Great Lakes, and *Rodman the Keeper: Southern Sketches* (1880), depicting the mountain, Piedmont, and tidewater South. "The Lady of Little Fishing," from her first collection, reflects the influence of Harte in its witty yet finally sentimental account of one woman's civilizing influence on a rowdy community of trappers on an island in Lake Superior. Woolson's peripatetic life gave her a sharp sense of regional differences and a range of experiences in diverse landscapes that she cannily parlayed into rapid fame. Yet when she left for Italy in the late 1870s, she put American regionalism behind her and wrote about the European scene, deploying a psychological realism encouraged by her friendship with Henry James in the 1880s.

Another writer from the Midwest, Dayton-born Paul Laurence Dunbar, achieved prominence mainly as a poet but produced nearly one hundred stories, most in the tradition of black regional dialect pieces. From his parents, Dunbar heard about the Southern slave life he represented in *Folks from Dixie* (1898) and *In Old Plantation Days*

(1903). The latter volume, a composite novel, includes two stories, "The Conjuring Contest" and "Dandy Jim's Conjure Scare," that unmistakably reflect Dunbar's awareness of Chesnutt's work. Dunbar also traced the migration of Southern blacks to the North in stories set in New York. Jay Martin and Gossie H. Hudson have argued that Dunbar's short fiction concerns itself with "the relations between regions" and thus provides a "representative and coherent picture" of "the fate of black men before and after emancipation" (Martin and Gossie 1975: 64–5). Dunbar's version of the antebellum South in *Old Plantation Days* should be read against the "moonlight and magnolias" tradition popularized by Page.

Realism

No absolute demarcation separates literary regionalism from realism, and indeed several exponents of local color produced "realistic" stories, while several so-called realists (for example, Twain) made conscious use of regional material. But one distinction can be made: while literary regionalism replicated itself through definable conventions, the concept of realism resists neat explanation. Michael Davitt Bell has even suggested that the authors and works commonly yoked under the rubric "American realism" do not comprise "*any* coherent formal tradition" (Bell 1993: 4). Writers who practiced what Bell calls "realist thinking" (p. 15) produced markedly different kinds of fiction – a disparity nowhere more evident than in the contrast between Twain's loosely structured yarns and James's tightly wound studies of psychological motive. Whereas regionalism emphasizes a *particular subject* (the distinctive features of a cultural enclave), realism has been understood variously as a *style* of representation, "the documentary rendering of external detail"; as a *method* of impersonal "objectivity" or "impartiality"; or as a *general subject*, the normative or "typical" as opposed to the "unique" and exceptional (Lee 1987: 26). Although Howells led a high-minded campaign for literary realism in *Harper's Monthly*, beginning in 1886, there was no consensus about the nature of realism, much less a conventionalized "realistic" short story that could be reproduced in magazines as was the regional story. What emerged from the "ferment of realism" – to invoke the title of Warner Berthoff's landmark study – was a group of writers who, despite their diverse interests and approaches, endeavored to represent the real world rather than the purely subjective or imaginary, dramatizing what they conceived to be universal (that is, non-localized) truths about human nature. This smaller contingent nevertheless produced some of the most consequential short fiction of the era.

Though often overlooked in critical summaries, Rebecca Harding Davis warrants recognition not just for "Life in the Iron Mills" but also for her efforts in later novels and short stories to advance a more truthful fiction, reflective of social reality. Her 1862 *Atlantic* story "John Lamar" proffers, in Sharon Harris's view, "a devastatingly realistic depiction of slavery," manifesting depths of "psychological awareness... staggering for the time" (Harris 1991: 77). After 1868 Davis became a mainstay contributor to *Peterson's*, and while many of her stories were unremarkably conventional, some possessed unusual frankness and freshness. Harris identifies "'In the Market'" (1868) as pivotal in its examination of women's issues related to the economics of marriage and to class issues embedded in matrimonial choices. Another study of the snares of gender, "Two Women," appeared in *Galaxy* in 1870; the story contrasts two key types, according to Harris, "the domestic woman and the woman who seeks work outside her home" (Harris 1991: 160). Davis remained a prolific writer of stories and essays, contributing during the 1870s and 1880s to nearly every important magazine in the United States. The late collection *Silhouettes of American Life* (1892) shows her evolving realism engaging key social issues.

More conspicuous than Davis as a champion of realism, William Dean Howells deserves brief attention here as a short-story writer. Ruth Bardon's "annotated story list" includes forty-six pieces (including children's stories) dating from 1853 to 1917; her inventory shows two periods of productivity – the "early realism" and "later psychological realism" – interrupted by three decades of consular and editorial work as well as novel writing (1861–93), during which the author completed only seven stories (Bardon 1997: xvii, 239–62). Howells's pre-Civil War stories about the fictional town of Dulldale led him toward an operative realism of the commonplace, yet he retained from his early work (as in the 1861 story "A Dream") an interest in psychology and the paranormal that would increasingly complicate his realism. His later stories reflected the influence of his friend Henry James in their attentiveness to perception – conventional and extra-sensory. His fine Hawthornesque story "A Difficult Case" (1900) contemplates the soul's afterlife, and "The Eidolons of Brooks Alfred" (1906) stages the psychic struggle of a man afflicted by unbidden visions. Howells's most admired, most anthologized story, "Editha" (1905), portrays a romance complicated by an ideological clash over the Spanish–American war: Editha's blind patriotism pushes the fated George Gearson into enlistment, but after a disconcerting encounter with George's mother (who blames the girl for her son's death in combat) Editha recovers her equanimity and "idealism." Howells's later stories recurrently represent a realistic, bourgeois milieu in which characters suffer psychic traumas or become fixated upon uncanny phenomena.

While defying literary classification, Howells's friend Mark Twain focused relentlessly as a writer of short stories on the base motives of individual conduct and the hypocrisies of social behavior. Unless he was mocking rhetorical pretension, he wrote in a plain, direct style and created characters who spoke in a colloquial, folk idiom. Twain did not worry, as some realists did, about representativeness or plausibility, and indeed often relied on the sort of preposterous exaggeration seen in "Cannibalism in the Cars" (1868), where the narrator dispassionately reports the decorous process by which passengers on a snowbound train are elected for consumption – and then ranked in palatability. In his much-cited essay "How to Tell a Story" (1895), Twain explained the "humorous story" as a distinctly American genre dependent upon "the *manner* of the telling," an essentially oral form contingent upon the well-timed pause. As a humorist he poked fun at conventional literary genres; such pieces as "An Awful

Terrible – Medieval Romance" (1870), "A Ghost Story" (1870), and "A Double-Barrelled Detective Story" (1902) instantly identify the parodied forms. The literature of religious moralism became a favorite target, as Twain turned narrative patterns upside-down in spoofs such as "The Story of the Bad Little Boy" (1865), "The Story of the Good Little Boy" (1870), and "Edward Mills and George Benton: A Tale" (1880). The more ambitious satire "Was It Heaven? Or Hell?" (1902) savages the sentimental memoir which moralized on faith, suffering, and death. In a number of stories – and notably in the three extant versions of his late, unfinished novella, *The Mysterious Stranger* (posthumously published in 1969) – Twain challenged the most hallowed beliefs of orthodox Christianity and evinced a deepening skepticism.

Of the sixty-odd stories Twain wrote, few match the seriousness of "A True Story" (1874). Anticipating the post-Reconstruction vogue for black dialect pieces, Twain transcribed a story related by his cook, Mary Cord, adding a brief account of her experience as a slave and adopting the African American voice of "Aunt Rachel." Uncharacteristically, as Tom Quirk observes, the storyteller "does not ramble," and Twain's own "persona in the story is clearly altered to enhance Rachel's dignity and to emphasize his own unfeeling stupidity" (Quirk 1997: 59). Indeed, the naïve assumption of "Misto C" that Rachel has never known trouble because she laughs so much allows her to overturn a stereotype as she reveals her heartbreaking separation from her children. The story was published in the *Atlantic* in 1874, marking Twain's first appearance in that journal, and the following year he included "Aunt Rachel" in *Mark Twain's Sketches, New and Old*, his most substantial collection of stories and anecdotes. From then on his work appeared frequently in the *Atlantic*, *Galaxy*, *Harper's Monthly*, *Century*, and *Cosmopolitan*. His inventive use of the folk idiom – what Andrew Hook has called the "most lasting and memorable" of Twain's accomplishments: "his transformation of American vernacular speech into a creative and aesthetically satisfying literary medium" – gives freshness and realism to his most improbable short narratives (Hook 1985: 116).

Especially after the Panic of 1893, Twain focused his satire on the tyranny of money; several stories hinge on a craving for affluence and expose the materialism of the Gilded Age (an era he helped to name). Deep in debt, Twain composed "The £1,000,000 Bank-Note" (1893), which as Peter Messent notes, wryly depicts "the conditions and contradictions of capitalist exchange" in the social power conferred by unspendable currency (Messent 2001: 124). "The $30,000 Bequest" (1904) traces the ruination of the Fosters, a quiet couple from a "pleasant little town" in the Far West: expecting an inheritance, they entertain "dizzying" fantasies of wealth, but a market crash wipes out their hypothetical fortune just as they discover that their relative died penniless. A similar premise informs his celebrated "The Man That Corrupted Hadleyburg" (1899), in which a stranger tempts a small town's leading citizens by promising gold to the person who has done a good deed – and can complete a test phrase. On the surface "Hadleyburg" resembles a regional short story, and Twain's narratorial candor, ordinary characters, and insights into the psychology of cupidity add realism. Shifts in tone, viewpoint, and narrative method, however, undermine that effect, and Twain gives the story universal significance by exposing the dishonesty endemic to humankind. The author's increasing cynicism about "the damned human race" and the value of life itself colored such later pieces as "The Five Boons of Life" (1902), which leads to a disturbing revelation: "Pleasure, Love, Fame, Riches: they are but temporary disguises for lasting realities – Pain, Grief, Shame, Poverty." Twain's fictional meditations on the ultimate nature of reality produce a realism altogether different from that of his contemporaries.

While Twain played the irreverent innocent abroad during his several tours of Europe, the Anglophile Henry James personified the sophisticated expatriate. After taking up life abroad in 1875, he produced a body of short fiction nearly as accomplished as the brilliant, mannered novels for which he is best known. James's first signed story appeared in the *Atlantic* in 1865 ("The Story of a Year") and before his definitive departure from the United States he had already published more than two dozen short narratives, including two lengthy short stories prefiguring the direction of his later work: "A Passionate Pilgrim" (1871) and "Madame de Mauves" (1874). The former introduces the international theme as it traces the dying American Clement Searle's romantic attachment to his ancestral English homeland. The latter anticipates James's extensive treatment of American innocence victimized by European cunning, as the idealistic American Longmore, James's "central consciousness," teases out the story of Euphemia de Mauves, an American heiress unhappily married to a treacherous French baron. James included both pieces in his first collection, *A Passionate Pilgrim and Other Tales* (1875).

Assessing James's short fiction, Richard Hocks counts 112 such narratives, although he concedes the difficulty of distinguishing in the James canon among short stories (or "anecdotes"), "nouvelles" (long short stories), and "tales" (novellas) (Hocks 1990: xiv–xv). James's realism hinges, Hocks adds, on "the psychology of individual character" (p. 8) and on his attention to the manners, gestures, and rituals of *fin de siècle* polite society. One of his best-known stories, "Daisy Miller" (1878), illustrates social realism in its depiction of national and class distinctions through differences of manner or sensibility. Daisy's susceptibility to Giovanelli, the suave Italian fortune-hunter, stems in part from her origins as a member of the American *nouveaux riches*, a status betrayed by her mother's hopeless vulgarity. With remarkable ingenuity James worked variations on the problem of cultural difference, typically portraying Americans like Daisy (or Bessie Alden in "An International Episode") as too frank, naïve, or independent to negotiate the subtleties of the European scene. The later story " 'Europe' " (1899) also probes the international subject that would impel his late, great novels *The Wings of the Dove* (1902), *The Ambassadors* (1903), and *The Golden Bowl* (1904).

During the 1880s James also turned to ironic, self-reflexive narratives about the life of the artist or writer. His 1873 *Atlantic* story "The Madonna of the Future" anticipates this interest in its anatomy of an expatriate painter's failure: established in Florence, the perfectionist Theobald laments his American cultural origins and realizes too late that he has missed his opportunity for creativity. The 1884 story "The

Author of 'Beltraffio,'" which portrays the private torment of writer Mark Ambient, heralds a succession of fine narratives about the life of writing, including "The Lesson of the Master" (1888), "Greville Fane" (1892), and "The Middle Years" (1893). Consistently cited as one of James's greatest stories, the 1888 nouvelle "The Aspern Papers" pits a scheming biographer keen to penetrate the secret life of the dead American poet Jeffrey Aspern against a formidable old woman who had been his lover. Another superb story of literary obsession, "The Figure in the Carpet" (1896), dramatizes the anguish of a critic intent on puzzling out the master trope that will explain the secret subject of Hugh Vereker's fiction. Several related stories focus on dilemmas faced by painters, including "The Liar" (1888) and two frequently anthologized narratives, "The Real Thing" (1892) and "The Tone of Time" (1900). In such works James typically concerned himself with the perplexing relationship between life and art, or between an idea and its realization, with the artifact paradoxically revealing and concealing the truth of lived experience.

The concept of realism articulated in James's criticism and displayed in his short fiction concerned itself primarily with the meticulous elaboration of character, which, rather than plot, was in his view the engine of narrative. Although his stories often unfold in an identified place and within a plausible social milieu, James provides few localizing particulars, emphasizing instead interactions between characters, nuances of personality revealed by comments, expressions, or gestures. His aim was to illuminate the "psychological reason" (as he said in "The Art of Fiction" [1884]) animating private and social behavior. This impulse led to the complex psychological realism of his work after the mid-1880s and to his late predilection (shared with Howells) for credible narratives of visionary experience. Among such works, the 1898 nouvelle "The Turn of the Screw" stands apart as one of James's most dazzling creations. The story's carefully balanced ambiguities complicate the question of whether young Miles and Flora have been possessed by the ghosts of two former servants, or whether the Governess, James's "central consciousness," has through her own repressed desires fantasized the haunting that she reports. Another much-admired ghost story, "The Jolly Corner" (1908), dramatizes Spencer Brydon's spectral encounter, in his vacant childhood home, with his alter ego, the monstrous American self he might have become had he not lived his life abroad. Similar ghostly effects figure in "The Way It Came" (1896; later entitled "The Friends of the Friends"), "The Real Right Thing" (1899), and "The Great Good Place" (1900). Two additional stories that briefly evoke phantasmic presences are "The Altar of the Dead" (1895) and "The Beast in the Jungle" (1903). In the former, James describes the candle-lighting ritual by which George Stransom marks the passing of his earthly acquaintances and gradually withdraws from the world of the living. The latter, regarded as among James's best stories, unfolds the queer, unrealized romance between May Bartram and John Marcher, a man so consumed by the notion that something strange will befall him that he misses the extraordinary thing, May's love. The story first appeared in the collection *The Better Sort* (1903), one of the twenty-odd volumes of short fiction James published during a long and distinguished career.

By contrast, the career of Stephen Crane was pathetically brief, yet during the 1890s he produced a handful of short stories that confirmed his lasting importance. Crane left Syracuse University to become a writer and published his first significant work, the novella *Maggie, A Girl of the Streets* (1893), at the age of twenty-two. As a freelance writer in New York he produced numerous sketches of street and tenement life that recall the photographic work of Alfred Stieglitz. Crane's Civil War novel, *The Red Badge of Courage* (1895), made him famous and led to a collection of related stories, *The Little Regiment and Other Episodes of the American Civil War* (1896). Journalistic assignments took Crane to the West and Mexico, to Greece, and to Cuba twice. When Crane's ship sank en route to Cuba in early 1897, he underwent an ordeal like the one recounted in his finest story, "The Open Boat." That deeply ironic narrative combines attention to the natural elements – sharks, gulls, clouds, waves – with stylized language (the "seven mad gods" refrain) and enigmatic emblems (the light-house) to produce a story of survival that questions the significance of human life in a blank, indifferent universe epitomized by "a high cold star on a winter's night." During a sojourn in England and Ireland in 1897–8, Crane wrote his novella *The Monster*, about a black man disfigured by fire and acid, and two stories of the West, "The Bride Comes to Yellow Sky" and a longer, darker narrative, "The Blue Hotel." Set in Nebraska during a blizzard, the last piece dramatizes the transformation of the Swede from coward to bully before he is stabbed by a gambler, producing the observation that "a human body, this citadel of virtue, wisdom, power, was pierced as easily as if it had been a melon." Crane here creates the memorable metaphor of the earth itself as a "space-lost bulb." He returned to Cuba in 1898 and covered the Spanish–American War for Pulitzer's *World*, producing a number of sketches and stories of combat. Crane spent the last eighteen months of his life abroad, where in an English manor house he wrote the linked narratives of childhood collected in *Whilomville Stories* (1900). Contesting the view that Crane was a naturalist, Bell has argued that he "used formal strategies associated with literary naturalism" to undermine its assumptions and assert a "transcendental realism" (Bell 1993: 134, 148). Arthur Voss has aptly remarked that "Crane's best work does not bulk large, but it makes an impression out of all proportion to its quantity" (Voss 1973: 167).

During the same decade in which Crane achieved a brief celebrity, Edith Wharton began publishing well-crafted short fiction in *Scribner's Magazine* and *Century*. The first of her eighty-five short stories, "Mrs. Manstey's View," appeared in *Scribner's* in 1891 and reflects, according to Donna Campbell, a "veiled critique" of the regionalists – principally Freeman and Jewett – whose provincial view Wharton set out to transcend but to whose work she was nevertheless indebted (Campbell 1997: 151–4). A more important influence was Henry James, whom Wharton admired and later befriended. Like James, Wharton grew up in privileged circumstances and wrote often, though not exclusively, about the domestic and social entanglements of the leisured class. Many Wharton stories employ an international theme (as in "The Last Asset" [1904] or "Les Metteurs en Scène" [1909]), and like James, she pondered the complications of the artistic life, depicting in "The Recovery" (1901), for example, the epiphany of an American painter who in the Louvre realizes the provincialism of his own work and envisions an international career. In "The Pelican" (1898) she satirized the declining popularity of Mrs. Amyot, a literary lecturer purveying "second-hand ideas," and in "The Angel at the Grave" (1901) she produced a wry yet moving account of a granddaughter's paralyzing devotion to the memory of a minor Transcendentalist. Wharton also produced a spate of ghost stories around the turn of the century, of which her 1910 story "The Eyes" has commanded greatest interest. Too much can be made of Jamesian parallels, and in her treatment of marriage and divorce Wharton surpassed James in candor if not in sensitivity, converting her own unhappy experience (she divorced Teddy Wharton in 1907) into trenchant narratives exposing the sometimes hidden cruelties of the matrimonial state. Her most brilliant early story, "Souls Belated" (1899), elaborates the dilemma of Lydia Tillotson, newly divorced and determined to remain unmarried yet compelled by circumstance to pose as the wife of the man with whom she is traveling in Europe. In "The Other Two" (1904), Waythorn unexpectedly meets his twice-divorced wife's previous spouses, accepts them as figurative "partners in the business," and comes to regard his wife as "a shoe that too many feet had worn." The less confident Mrs. Ransom in "The Pretext" (1908) resists the temptation of an adulterous affair but comes to see her uneventful married life as a "desert." In addition to the novels for which she is better known, Wharton published five collections of short stories prior to 1914, including *The Greater Inclination* (1899), *Crucial Instances* (1901), and *Tales of Men and Ghosts* (1910); during and after the war six more such volumes followed. Wharton had little interest in proletarian subjects and generally avoided naturalistic themes but hewed to an objectivity and frankness in her narratives of marriage, divorce, adultery, and female entrapment. Amy Kaplan has convincingly described her as a "realist" whose work is located "at the complex intersection of class and gender" (Kaplan 1988: 66).

Another writer of realistic short fiction whose career straddled the Great War was Willa Cather, whose Nebraska prairie origins and admiration for Sarah Orne Jewett created the regional emphasis in novels such as *O Pioneers!* (1913) and in certain of her stories. But Cather also moved beyond the provincial subject; after teaching in Pittsburgh she relocated in New York, where she edited *McClure's* and wrote short stories. Like Wharton, she too came under the influence of James, as the story "Flavia and Her Artists" (1905) unmistakably reveals. The best known of her thirty-odd short stories, "Paul's Case," anatomizes the suicide of a sensitive and possibly homosexual young man who seeks in the glamour of New York the beauty absent from his dreary life in Pittsburgh. Cather collected "Paul's Case" in *The Troll Garden* (1905) and later refurbished it for *Youth and the Bright Medusa* (1920).

Naturalism

Of the distinction between realism and naturalism, Christophe Den Tandt has described their development as a "parallel" process, "two interdependent, overlapping forms of discourse" (Den Tandt 1998: 18). Donald Pizer has supplemented the usual understanding of naturalism – as "realism infused with a pessimistic determinism" – by elucidating tensions within naturalism between "controlling force" and "individual worth" (Pizer 1993: 85, 100). Whatever the linkage between realism and naturalism, relatively few US writers produced short fiction emphasizing deterministic causality. Among those associated with naturalism, Frank Norris, its major proponent, wrote relatively few magazine tales, and these as a group prove surprisingly tame, conventional, and even romantic. The pieces collected in *A Deal in Wheat and Other Stories* (1903) include sketches and fragments; the title story reads like the synopsis of a novel. Stephen Crane, another figure sometimes labeled as a naturalist, produced short stories that subvert their naturalistic premises by affirming human will and ethical responsibility. The only writers of short stories plausibly identifiable as naturalists were Theodore Dreiser and Jack London, and Dreiser was better known as a novelist.

Like Crane, Dreiser came to fiction from journalism, having been a reporter in Toledo, Cleveland, and Pittsburgh before coming to New York in the mid-1890s. About the time that he wrote *Sister Carrie* (1900), Dreiser surveyed the short stories then being promulgated in *Century*, *Scribner's*, and *Harper's* and (as he noted in *A Book about Myself*) detected a genteel conspiracy to exclude "the coarse and the vulgar and the cruel and the terrible." He aimed to rectify that omission with stories that examined previously suppressed topics, bringing to the task a social consciousness sharpened by his reading of Herbert Spencer and a determination to capture broad truths about human psychology and modern experience. He did not complete many stories, but two early efforts included "Old Rogaum and His Theresa" and the unhappily titled "Nigger Jeff," both published in *Ainslee's* in 1901. The former piece, set in a New York ethnic milieu, presents the conflict between a German butcher and his teenaged daughter who defies her curfew; Dreiser juxtaposes Theresa's misadventure (she is locked out and later arrested) against that of a suicidal prostitute who dies on Rogaum's doorstep. The latter story, told from the viewpoint of a reporter, chronicles the lynching of a black man by a white mob, whose collective psychology Dreiser perceptively analyzes. As June Howard notes, the story portrays the "ambivalent" reporter as both "emotionally involved" and a "spectator" Howard 1985: 106). Another early piece, "McEwen of the Shining Slave Makers," presents a Kafkaesque daydream in which a man becomes an ant, experiences hunger and warfare, and then wakes to the truth that "necessity" governs all of life. Dreiser collected these three stories and eight others (including "The Lost Phoebe") in *Free and Other Stories* (1918), in the preface to which Sherwood Anderson hailed him as the "pioneer" of a "movement toward greater courage and fidelity to life in writing."

In contrast to Bret Harte's spectatorial view of California mining, Jack London participated in the Klondike Gold Rush of 1897, in the process surviving harsh wilderness conditions and collecting vivid material for the many Northland stories and novels he published around the turn of the century. Shaped by his study of Spencer, his readings in Marx, his admiration for Kipling, and his attraction to

Nietzsche, London evolved a contradictory proletarian naturalism concerned less with social equality than with an ethos of indomitability. He launched his literary career with "To the Man on Trail," the first of eight stories initially featured in the *Overland Monthly*, and, after the *Atlantic* published "An Odyssey of the North," gathered his stories into *The Son of the Wolf* (1900). Survival is the quintessential theme of London's Northland narratives, as exemplified memorably in his best-known story, "To Build a Fire" (1908). With the appearance of his novel *The Call of the Wild* (1903), London became the most sought-after writer of his generation; in the short seventeen years of his literary career, he published nineteen novels and more than one hundred and fifty stories, collected in eighteen separate volumes. Other volumes of Yukon tales included *Children of the Frost* (1902) and *Lost Face* (1910). In later collections, such as *South Sea Tales* (1911) and *The House of Pride and Other Tales of Hawaii* (1912), London depicted both the life he had known as a merchant sailor and the exotic places he had visited while cruising the South Pacific aboard his schooner *Snark*. Neither widely read nor deeply philosophical, London wrote quickly and devised adventure plots set against striking natural landscapes, insistently dramatizing scenes of injustice in a starkly naturalistic order where only the fittest and fiercest survive.

Innovators and Others

In addition to the regionalists, realists, and naturalists cited above, many other authors contributed to the profusion of American short fiction between the Civil War and the Great War. By the end of the century the short story had become a matter of formula and venues for such publications so numerous that a veritable industry emerged. Writers such as F. Hopkinson Smith and Richard Harding Davis (son of Rebecca) enjoyed contemporary renown and published numerous volumes of collected periodical stories. Another writer of formula stories, Frank Stockton, attained brief fame on the basis of a single, tantalizing narrative, "The Lady or the Tiger?" (1884). In the first decade of the new century, only Jack London rivaled the popularity of William Sydney Porter, who under the pen name of O. Henry produced a dozen volumes of ingenious, entertaining stories culled from the pages of *Everybody's Magazine*, *Munsey's*, *McClure's*, and others. After serving a term in prison for embezzlement, Porter moved to New York, assumed his famous persona, and began writing weekly stories for the *New York World*. He learned his craft from Harte, Kipling, and Maupassant, carrying plot ingenuity to a new level of proficiency, often deploying the surprise ending for which he became famous. Setting his narratives typically in Texas or New York, O. Henry combined humor and pathos with puns and malapropisms, creating clever, entertaining tales about colorful but uncomplicated characters. His best-known story, "The Gift of the Magi" (1906), shows the influence of Maupassant in its ironic plot twist which turns on the mutual sacrifices of a husband and wife buying Christmas gifts for each other. Collections such as *Cabbages and Kings* (1904) and *The Four Million* (1906) made O. Henry a household name, and the subsequent creation of the O. Henry Memorial Award elevated him posthumously to the status of a cultural icon, despite the relative superficiality of even his best stories.

While the sheer volume of magazine fiction encouraged facile conventionality, a few writers of the time produced stories unusual in content and method, reflecting a resistance to the call for realism. One such maverick was Ambrose Bierce, author of the lurid, fantastic Civil War stories collected in *Tales of Soldiers and Civilians* (1891; later entitled *In the Midst of Life* [1898]) and the supernatural narratives published as *Can Such Things Be?* (1893). Trained as an engineer, Bierce served in the Union army and then worked as a journalist during three different stints in San Francisco, where he published his first story in the *Overland Monthly*; he also spent three years abroad writing acerbic squibs for the London press and worked in the Dakota Territory as a mining engineer. He published his best stories between 1888 and 1893, and his war stories reveal Poesque horrors in riveting battlefield episodes. His most celebrated tale, "An Occurrence at Owl Creek Bridge," anticipates Borges' "The Secret Miracle" in its elaboration of a fantasy at the moment of a planter's execution. "Chickamauga" contrasts the make-believe war games of a deaf child playing in the woods with the ghastly retreat of gory Union soldiers. Herbie Butterfield describes the paradigmatic war story by Bierce as representing "a man either physically or morally alone" facing a test of "conscience or nerve" (Butterfield 1985: 144). The author's sardonic humor, his predilection for terror, and his stunning, graphic imagery set him apart from writers of more conventional war fiction such as Harold Frederic. The pieces collected in *Can Such Things Be?* are no less unsettling: in the Poe-inspired "Moxon's Master," an exercise in science fiction, a chess-playing automaton murders its creator, while in "The Realm of the Unreal," the narrator never fathoms the motive or method of Dr. Dorrimore, the mysterious hypnotist who confounds him with terrible illusions. In his 1897 essay "The Short Story," Bierce endorsed Poe's theory of brevity while savaging Howells, realism, and the fiction of "probability." His late, mordant *The Devil's Dictionary* (1911) appeared just two years before his strange disappearance in Mexico.

Known primarily as a reformer, Charlotte Perkins Gilman published short stories, novels, and non-fictional works to advance equitable gender relations, especially as they pertained to labor, economics, and domestic responsibilities. Yet her autobiographical short story "The Yellow Wall-paper" (1892), first published in the *New England Magazine*, now occupies a privileged place in anthologies as a touchstone of contemporary feminist theory. Initially hailed for its gothic effects, "The Yellow Wall-paper" delivers a devastating critique of patriarchal attitudes through a complex representation of the constraints placed upon nineteenth-century women. Gilman's method recalls Maupassant's "The Horla": her unreliable first-person narrator suffers from depression and becomes increasingly delusional. The author presents the story as a clandestine journal, produced by the wife in defiance of her doctor-husband's ban on mental exertion. Confined to a former nursery, the woman becomes preoccupied by the "horrid" wallpaper, finally attempting to strip it off to liberate her alter ego, the imagined woman trapped behind its arabesque design. In 1893 Gilman produced a brief sequel, "Through This," which resumes the flow of the woman's disconnected thoughts, but her later stories were less autobiographical, adopting more conventional forms to elaborate didactic, sometimes utopian narratives depicting enlightened gender relations. Gilman published many of her roughly two hundred stories in *The Forerunner*, the monthly she edited from 1909 to 1916. Janet Beer writes that "the development of a coherent aesthetic was never her concern"; this insouciance allowed her to move "in and out of fantasy, fable, detective, romance, melodrama, homily, parable, and legend with ease and expediency" (Beer 1997: 150–1). Gilman aimed to educate in stories such as "When I Was a Witch" (1910), "The Widow's Might" (1911), and "If I Were a Man" (1914) and consequently never again approached the unsettling intensity of "The Yellow Wall-paper."

The Short-Story Sequence

With few exceptions, the volumes of short stories published in the United States prior to the 1890s were single-author anthologies: collections of previously published pieces (or mostly so) selected with some regard for arrangement but little concern for collective effect. The standard format fixed the title of the pre-eminent story as the collection's title, with the phrase "and Other Stories" added to signal the heterogeneity and supplemental status of the accompanying narratives. Although such anthologies inevitably reflected a continuity of imaginative habit (of style, situation, or theme), they rarely revealed an overarching design and instead juxtaposed stories written over time under different pressures and promptings. Regionalism may have given the first impetus to organized story collections or sequences, for the representation of a specific community demanded the collocation of discrete narratives that implied local commonalities. And while few regionalists seem to have planned collections from the outset or self-consciously composed stories to fill out an emerging pattern, the practice of reading regional anthologies by Harte, Woolson, Jewett, and Murfree gradually disclosed the potential collective mimesis of the story collection. As a form between the novel and the individual short story, it could articulate a community narrative, a weave of separate stories that would complement each other as they illuminated the larger story of a peculiar people living together under certain distinctive conditions.

Stowe's *Oldtown Fireside Stories* (1871) may not be the first identifiable American short-story sequence, but it is difficult to name an earlier collection of explicitly linked short narratives. The question of "linkage" is of course crucial to the genre, and sequences may be linked in different ways. But Stowe's focus on a particular place ("Oldtown," or Natick, Massachusetts), her use of a recurrent narrator, Sam Lawson, and his retelling of legends that shape community identity give the volume formal cohesiveness. That Stowe devised the volume (as noted earlier) to give fresh life to her novel *Oldtown Folks* embeds the stories in an already established communal narrative. Stowe emphasizes the cultural function of folk-tales in her opening pages:

> In those days, chimney-corner story telling became an art and an accomplishment. . . . Then the aged told their stories to the young, – tales of early life; tales of war and adventure, of Indian captivities and escapes, of bears and wild-cats and panthers, of rattlesnakes, of witches and wizards, and strange and wonderful dreams and appearances and providences.

She thus identifies storytelling as a ritual crucial to the transmission of history; her stories define both a local community and the imagined community of the nation in a way that asserts the New England origins of the American self. As Lawson evokes strange, comic, or supernatural events from the past, he alludes repeatedly to Cotton Mather, to the Indians of New England, and to the Revolution. "Colonel Eph's Shoe-Buckles" one-sidedly summarizes Indian depredations against colonists, alluding to Mary Rowlandson's captivity and her husband's anguish. Forgetting the Anglo decimation of native tribes, Lawson calls Indians "the horridest, paintedest, schree-chin'est, cussedest critters" imaginable. "The Widow's Bandbox," which recounts a bizarre British plot to hijack an American sloop, refers to Commodore Tucker's role in transporting Benjamin Franklin to France and (after the war) John Adams to England. Repeatedly emphasizing the work of Providence, Lawson offers his young male listeners lessons in cultural heritage that affirm the virtue of religion and assume white dominance over Indians (such as the forlorn Ketury) and blacks (figured as servants and "niggers" in several stories); he inculcates a sense of history consonant with the exceptionalist vision of the oft-cited Mather. The antebellum setting of the storytelling permitted Stowe to elide both New England abolitionism and the Civil War, appealing to nostalgia for a putatively more innocent Anglo-American past.

Quite a different sense of community emerges in *Old Creole Days* (1879), whose title indicates George Washington Cable's effort to reconstruct the epoch of Creole influence in New Orleans. He saw his stories as implicitly connected, writing to his mother: "My papers [on New Orleans] have somehow taken a form which must make a book if they are fit to make anything" (Turner 1966: 51). Yet to speak of *Old Creole Days* as a story sequence raises nagging formal questions, for Cable's publisher (*Scribner's*) determined the order of the seven original stories, and his novella *Madame Delphine* (1881) was added in 1883 as an introductory piece. The volume nevertheless sprang directly from Cable's research into the history of New Orleans and reflected his shrewd awareness that Creole culture was then being effaced and transformed by Anglo-Americans. As Arlin Turner has pointed out, the author wanted to arrange the stories chronologically and to affix specific dates, for "to his mind, the exact historical context he had given them was important" (Turner 1966: 84). Although Cable did not prevail on either score – and was moreover forced to accept the title assigned by his publisher – the collection's cultural and historical specificity nevertheless asserts the author's controlling purpose. So too does his insistent emphasis on outcasts or loners, characters set apart by racial, ethnic, or cultural identity, a theme underscored by the refugee milieu of "Café des Exilés" but present virtually everywhere, even in the comic "Posson Jone," wherein a Creole "heathen" corrupts an outsider, a preacher from west Florida on his first visit to New Orleans. Despite the fact that *Madame Delphine* was inserted belatedly, Alice Hall Petry has called it "the ideal introductory tale" for the collection, noting that Cable wrote it in response to a reader's complaint that another Creole story, "Tite Poulette," had disingenuously obscured the stigma of being a quadroon (Petry 1988: 25). Dramatizing the complications faced by Olive and her mother, Madame Delphine, Cable thus sums up the dilemma of mixed blood for New Orleans and for the nation itself. Like Harte's stories of natural disaster, "Belles Demoiselles Plantation" creates an idyllic image of Colonel de Charleu's great mansion in order to stage its tragic destruction: when a river bank caves in, the house collapses into the Mississippi, taking with it de Charleu's seven lovely daughters. The transition from Creole to American cultural dominance finds its clearest expression in "Jean-ah Poquelin," which contrasts Jean's dilapidated, remote dwelling with the neat abodes of American entrepreneurs. The fact that Jean has remained a hermit to conceal his brother's leprosy makes the stunning conclusion – in which Jean's coffin is borne to the land of the lepers – a prefiguration of Creole cultural displacement in New Orleans. Cable's subtle analysis of cultural conflict, inflected by ethnic and racial differences, gives *Old Creole Days* surprising cohesiveness as a story sequence despite its problematic arrangement.

But Cable's work did not immediately popularize a new genre. The decade of the 1880s saw the appearance of many fine collections of stories, but no discernible effusion of sequences. The case of Rose Terry Cooke's *Somebody's Neighbors* (1881) is typical: cultural commonalities link her character studies, yet the dozen stories (written over a span of twenty-two years) do not circumscribe a particular community – as the book's title coyly admits – nor do they reflect by thematic specificity a definite, collective purpose. As with most collections of that era, the volume served a frankly commercial function, repackaging diverse periodical stories for resale in the book trade. Late in the decade, however, Hamlin Garland conceived the idea of a connected series of stories, a purposive sequence to illustrate his progressive ideas about farming and land use, and between 1888 and 1890 he had published four such stories, three of them in *Harper's Weekly*. He added two previously unpublished stories to complete the original edition of *Main-Travelled Roads* (1891), in which homecoming forms a dominant motif, reflecting the effects of Garland's own bittersweet return visits in 1887 and 1889. The powerful opening story, "A Branch-Road," juxtaposes two episodes, Will Hannan's angry departure from the Midwest after a misunderstanding with Agnes, the girl he loves, and his penitent return seven years later to rescue her from a grim life of spousal abuse. In "Up the Coulé" an actor and theatrical producer returns to the Midwest to visit his mother and brother but finds the latter crushed by "circumstances." The cultured son suffers exquisitely, contrasting the glories of nature with the tragedy of hopeless labor, but when he offers to repurchase the family homestead (which had been sold), his morose brother declares himself "too old to make a new start" and "a dead failure." In the closing lines of "Return of the Private," a tale of postwar homecoming, the conclusion of Edward Smith's "war with the South" marks the resumption of his "daily running fight with nature"; it will be a "hopeless battle," Garland concludes, waged until God grants a "furlough." The "Herculean toil" of Haskins to improve his farm intensifies the cruelty of Butler's financial exactions in "Under the Lion's Paw." Even the two lighter stories – the courtship tale "Among the Corn Rows" and the semi-comic rebellion of a farm wife in "Mrs. Ripley's Trip" – confirm the impossibility of escaping the rigors of farm life. In its collective effect, the sequence confirms the truth of Garland's opening inscription: "The main-travelled road in the West . . . is traversed by many classes of people, but the poor and the weary predominate."

By the century's last decade, collections of patently linked stories had become more numerous. Grace King's *Balcony Stories* (1893) reflect a concerted effort to produce an ensemble effect, and the same may be said of Mary Catherwood's collection, *The Spirit of an Illinois Town* (1897). The notion of representing a community through connected, individual narratives also impelled Jewett's *The Country of the Pointed Firs* (1896), though here a chronological storyline – the writer–narrator's discoveries about local folk – connects interdependent segments or chapters, turning the volume into a composite novel rather than a story sequence. A radically different principle connects the nine stories of Chesnutt's *The Wife of His Youth and Other Stories of the Color Line* (1899). Typifying the volume as "an anthology gleaned from more than a dozen 'problem stories' and didactic tales" written over the previous "fifteen years," William L. Andrews concludes that *Wife* "defies analysis as a single entity" (Andrews 1980: 74). Yet Chesnutt himself asserted that the "backbone" of the collection was the "great problem" of the "color line," which W. E. B. Du Bois soon after prophetically characterized as the defining dilemma of twentieth-century America (Andrews 1980: 74–5). An examination of the volume's composition history, as reconstructed by Andrews, indicates moreover that Chesnutt completed the collection in a flurry of work, as if self-consciously limning permutations of the "race problem." The consecutive composition of such stories as "The Wife of His Youth," "A Matter of Principle," "Uncle Wellington's Wives," "Her Virginia Mammy," and "Cicely's Dream" reveals a writer intent upon a compelling subject: the agonizing consequences of racial prejudice and segregation for all persons of color and especially for those of mixed blood and ambiguous racial identity. Even while he was writing "conjure" stories in the late 1880s, Chesnutt had been pointing toward another series focused on interracial desire, miscegenation, and racial indeterminacy. "The Sheriff's Children" (1889) had broached the subject of the "color line" by turning the conventional sheriff-and-lynch-mob story into an unexpected encounter between a courageous lawman and his long-forgotten son by a former slave – a son whose escape is foiled, ironically, by his white half-sister. Chesnutt flanked "The Sheriff's Children" in *Wife* with "Her Virginia Mammy," the story of a young woman tormented by uncertainty about her racial identity, and "A Matter of Principle," a Reconstruction-era comedy of manners about the hypocrisy of Mr. Clayton, a respectable mulatto who contrives a preposterous hoax to prevent a congressman alleged to be "very black" from courting his daughter. Like "A Matter of Principle," the opening story, "The Wife of His Youth," portrays a light-skinned protagonist, a member of the Groveland "Blue Vein Society" who is obsessed with maintaining racial aloofness from full-blooded African Americans. His anticipated triumph, a public proposal to an attractive young widow "whiter than he," proves humiliating when the black woman to whom he had been married before the war makes a surprise appearance. A similar tension complicates "Uncle Wellington's Wives," in which a mulatto leaves his black wife in North Carolina, marries a white woman in Ohio, and then, abandoned himself, comes crawling back to his first wife. The volume closes with "The Web of Circumstance," Chesnutt's bleak indictment of Southern justice in the post-Reconstruction South. Despite their diversity, the nine stories in *Wife* collectively illuminate the cruelties of the color line in a race-conscious nation.

By contrast, the nine stories of London's *The Son of the Wolf* (1900) cohere around Malamute Kid (who figures in six tales) and the idea, repeated in scene after scene, of Darwinian struggle – man against man, man against animal, man against the elements. In the opening story, "The White Silence," the Kid puts a wounded trail companion out of his misery, sending Mason's Indian wife on ahead to spare her a gruesome memory. The phrase "White Silence" pertains to the inscrutable impassivity of London's natural world, about which Mary Lawlor has observed: "For all of its unavailability and indifference to the human subjects whose fate it determines, the silent pressure of nature manifests itself as a brute, inimical companion, and thus acquires the presence and agency of an unnamed, mystified character" (2000: 117). London's title story, "The Son of the Wolf," embodies a troubling racism, as Scruff Mackenzie claims an Indian bride by flaunting his superiority as a Wolf (white man) and discouraging tribal reprisal by reciting "the Law of the Wolf": "*Whoso taketh the life of one Wolf, the forfeit shall ten of his people pay.*" At the center of the sequence, "To the Man on Trail" finds Malamute Kid briefly harboring a fugitive, Jack Westondale, whose "rugged pertinacity and indomitability" identify him as a Northland super-man. In a volume of violent episodes, "In a Far Country" reaches an extreme as two men, refusing to trek in frigid weather, consign themselves to horrifying deaths. London's closing story, "An Odyssey of the North," recounts the epic quest of an Indian to find his betrothed and the massive Nordic who took her from him. London adopts the Indian's point of view to enforce the irony that, even after Alex Gunderson dies from exposure, Unga refuses to follow Naass back to the "dirty huts" of their village, preferring death to a life of racial inferiority. Malamute Kid personifies Darwinian adaptability and acts as a moral force in the amoral wilderness, repeatedly articulating an intuitive wisdom about natural law.

By the turn of the century, writers were increasingly embracing the conceptual challenges and commercial advantages of organized story sequences. Appealing to a younger audience, Stephen Crane stitched together episodes from childhood in his *Whilomville Stories* (1900), and Mary Austin achieved formal cohesion in *The Land of Little Rain* (1903). Willa Cather's *The Troll Garden* (1905) featured seven ingeniously linked stories depicting unusual individuals (as in "The Sculptor's Funeral") who pursue the arts to escape their drab origins. Zona Gale's *Friendship Village* (1908) assembled twenty portraits of local types sketched by a central narrator, producing a prewar bestseller, while Gertrude Stein adapted the model of Flaubert's *Trois Contes* to create *Three Lives* (1909), a triptych of novellas using experimental repetition to depict in stories such as "Melanctha" the inner lives of ordinary women. As Richard Hocks has shown, Henry James's *The Finer Grain* (1910), a collection reflecting "the tangential, fragmentary nature of modernity itself," marked the author's first "short story sequence proper" after a succession of "miscellanies" sometimes disguised (as in *Terminations*) by resonant volume titles (Hocks 1995: 6, 16). The emergence of the story sequence as an attractive and innovative arrangement of discrete stories integrated by locale, motif, or recurrent characters made possible the memorable collections by Sherwood Anderson, Jean Toomer, and Ernest Hemingway that followed soon after the cataclysm of the Great War.

References and Further Reading

Andrews, William L. (1980). *The Literary Career of Charles W. Chesnutt*. Baton Rouge: Louisiana State University Press.

Bardon, Ruth, ed. (1997). *Selected Short Stories of William Dean Howells*. Athens, Ohio: Ohio University Press.

Beer, Janet (1997). *Kate Chopin, Edith Wharton, and Charlotte Perkins Gilman: Studies in Short Fiction*. New York: St. Martin's.

Bell, Michael Davitt (1993). *The Problem of American Realism: Studies in the Cultural History of a Literary Idea*. Chicago: University of Chicago Press.

Berthoff, Warner (1965). *The Ferment of Realism: American Literature, 1884–1919*. New York: Free Press.

Brodhead, Richard H. (1993). *Cultures of Letters: Scenes of Reading and Writing in Nineteenth-Century America*. Chicago: University of Chicago Press.

Butterfield, Herbie (1985). "'Our Bedfellow Death': The Short Stories of Ambrose Bierce." In A. Robert Lee (ed.), *The Nineteenth-Century American Short Story*, 134–49. London: Vision.

Campbell, Donna M. (1997). *Resisting Regionalism: Gender and Naturalism in American Fiction, 1885–1915*. Athens, Ohio: Ohio University Press.

Den Tandt, Christophe (1998). *The Urban Sublime in American Literary Naturalism*. Urbana: University of Illinois Press.

Foote, Stephanie (2001). *Regional Fictions: Culture and Identity in Nineteenth-Century American Literature*. Madison: University of Wisconsin Press.

Harris, Sharon M. (1991). *Rebecca Harding Davis and American Realism*. Philadelphia: University of Pennsylvania Press.

Hocks, Richard A. (1990). *Henry James: A Study of the Short Fiction*. New York: Twayne.

Hocks, Richard A. (1995). "Henry James's Incipient Poetics of the Short Story Sequence: *The Finer Grain* (1910)." In J. Gerald Kennedy (ed.), *Modern American Short Story Sequences*, 1–18. New York: Cambridge University Press.

Hook, Andrew (1985). "Reporting Reality: Mark Twain's Short Stories." In A. Robert Lee (ed.), *The Nineteenth-Century American Short Story*, 103–19. London: Vision.

Howard, June (1985). *Form and History in American Literary Naturalism*. Chapel Hill: University of North Carolina Press.

Kaplan, Amy (1988). *The Social Construction of American Realism*. Chicago: University of Chicago Press.

Lawlor, Mary (2000). *Recalling the Wild: Naturalism and the Closing of the American West*. New Brunswick, NJ: Rutgers University Press.

Lee, A. Robert, ed. (1985). *The Nineteenth-Century American Short Story*. London: Vision.

Lee, Brian (1987). *American Fiction 1865–1940*. London: Longman.

Marler, Robert (1974). "From Tale to Short Story: The Emergence of a New Genre in the 1850s." *American Literature* 46, 153–69.

Martin, Jay, and Hudson, Gossie H., eds. (1975). *The Paul Laurence Dunbar Reader*. New York: Dodd, Mead.

Messent, Peter (2001). *The Short Works of Mark Twain*. Philadelphia: University of Pennsylvania Press.

Petry, Alice Hall (1988). *A Genius in his Way: The Art of Cable's "Old Creole Days."* Rutherford, NJ: Fairleigh Dickinson University Press.

Pizer, Donald (1984). *Realism and Naturalism in Nineteenth-Century American Literature*, 2nd edn. Carbondale: Southern Illinois University Press. (First publ. 1966.)

Pizer, Donald (1993). *The Theory and Practice of American Literary Naturalism*. Carbondale: Southern Illinois University Press.

Poe, Edgar Allan (1984). "Marginalia – December 1846." In *Edgar Allan Poe: Essays and Reviews*, ed. G. R. Thompson. New York: Library of America.

Quirk, Tom (1997). *Mark Twain: A Study of the Short Fiction*. New York: Twayne.

Renza, Louis A. (1984). *"A White Heron" and the Question of Minor Literature*. Madison: University of Wisconsin Press.

Sundquist, Eric, ed. (1982). *American Realism: New Essays*. Baltimore: Johns Hopkins University Press.

Turner, Arlin (1966). *George W. Cable: A Biography*. Baton Rouge: Louisiana State University Press.

Voss, Arthur (1973). *The American Short Story: A Critical Survey*. Norman: University of Oklahoma Press.

White, Barbara A. (1991) *Edith Wharton: A Study of the Short Fiction*. New York: Twayne.

PART II
Contexts and Themes

9
Ecological Narrative and Nature Writing
S. K. Robisch

No prose is written out of place. Even the most abstract, symbolic, or conceptual work is dependent upon certain laws that locate us. As such, writers inevitably incorporate in their work the relationship between place and all other elements of craft, with varying degrees of ecological consciousness. The inclusion of a biotic environment (that is, not only the office building but also the land on which it is built), full paragraphs describing a region, the presence of a non-human species – these demand the attention of both writer and reader as beings in relation to their own environments. The ubiquity of place and interspecificity in the craft of literature should by now be a given topic in pedagogy and literary scholarship. And yet, nature writing is still the single most neglected genre in the literature curricula of American universities.

Two types of prose sharply demonstrate a writer's expression of his or her ecological consciousness: the first and more obvious is nature writing, which follows certain conventions I will address in a later section of this essay; the second is ecological narrative – prose (usually fiction) that does not necessarily foreground its ecological concerns but contains and reveals them nonetheless (for other, more elaborate, classification systems, see Scheese 1996; Lyon 2001; Glotfelty and Fromm 1996; Finch and Elder 1990; Armbruster and Wallace 2001). Two social and literary movements in America distinguished nature writing from other literatures without subordinating nature writing in the process. The first was the realist movement, especially through regionalism, which bloomed in response to industrialization after Reconstruction and lasted into Theodore Roosevelt's presidency. The second, called "the environmental movement," flourished in the 1960s and early 1970s, then formalized for literary criticism in the 1990s. The Romantic period, often cited for the influences of Thoreau and Emerson, is certainly important, but because this essay focuses only on the latter part of the nineteenth century, the Romantic and postmodern periods of environmental awareness must be relegated to historical context. For their success, both movements (realism/regionalism and the environmental movement) depended upon both the specialization of the biological sciences beyond natural philosophy and the ascendance of the empirical method as a means of disseminating knowledge.

Nature writing is most often based on observation and rumination, offering the reader a view of a place and/or species that includes both research and personal response. The work demands the reader's participation – to go and see, to experience, to negotiate the writer's perception with the reader's own. Ecological narrative, on the other hand, is less apparently driven by activist or scientific concerns, even by particularly ecological ones. The reader finds and emphasizes the influence of the nonhuman world on all aspects of the text. Such an approach certainly applies as well to other textual forms, poetry being the most obvious, but this essay concentrates on prose (for ecocritical approaches to poetry, see Kroeber 1994; Bryson 2002).

Ecological thought is systemic; by definition, ever since Ernst Haeckel coined the term in 1866 (along with the famous, and now questionable, phrase "ontogeny recapitulates phylogeny"), ecology is the study of an organism's relation to its biotic and abiotic environment (Haeckel 1992). Where biology is concerned largely with individual and anatomical study, ecology favors – both metaphorically and literally – context over text, interdependence over isolation. The principles of scientific ecology developed during the late nineteenth century had a significant effect on the lexicon and canonization of literature. Both intellectual elevation (evolutionary theory) and social oppression (Spencerianism) resulted from the interpretations and misinterpretations of Charles Darwin's work. Science's striking out on its own from philosophy may well be why the word "naturalism" became so plausibly multifarious in its application during the early twentieth century, and why literary taxonomy has chosen to follow some of the same rules as Linnaean taxonomy. Melville's "folio whale" is a rubric for the ensuing synthesis of American art and science.

Context as a key feature of text formation is a given – no more a nineteenth-century phenomenon than a postmodern one. The debate over how realism, regionalism, local color, and literary and philosophical naturalism should be arranged greatly depends upon three matters of readers' and writers' ecological awareness: familiarity with place; the behavior of other species; and the subject's relation to its biotic and abiotic environment. Ecosystemic thought constitutes the canopy under which every one of those literary movements resides. Instead, literary history shows us how place has been relegated to mere "setting," a canvas in front of which the anthropocentric action occurs (Cooper's grand rock in *The Prairie*). Interspecific encounters have traditionally been read, and often written, either as overt foreshadowings or as symbols of supposedly more important human concerns (Steinbeck's dog in *Of Mice and Men*, or Norris's bird in the gilded cage in *McTeague*).

Canonical Movements and Ecological Literature

Scholarship must better define American literary history with regard to ecological thought. Three major movements of this genre correspond roughly with three of

America's traditionally canonized literary periods (the romantic, realist, and modernist/postmodernist), although some of the watershed dates may differ: the turn toward realism in ecological literature, for instance, might be said to have occurred in 1859 with Darwin's *The Origin of Species by Means of Natural Selection* or in 1863 with George Perkins Marsh's *Man and Nature*, rather than with the beginning or end of the Civil War.

The romantic environmental tradition of the 1830s–1860s is known especially for its Transcendental vein. Transcendentalism considered the nonhuman world in ethereal terms, and generally looked askance at scientific methodology even as it embraced such forms of empiricism as direct and repeated observation in the field. Emerson's theory in his 1836 *Nature* and Thoreau's practice (perhaps less so in *Walden* than in "Ktaadn") argued with great pedagogical force for the correlation between material facts and spiritual truths. This established an ethical system for how humanity should function in what was then more broadly and freely called "Nature" (Emerson 1991). Emerson's doctrine remains a major topic of environmental discourse, traceable from the debates over Darwin's atheism to the deep ecology movement (Browne 1995; Desmond and Moore 1991; Devall and Sessions 1985: 63, 223, 245ff.).

Granted, the shades of realism reach back into the very beginnings of romanticism – Cooper certainly attempted verisimilitude – but Spencerian thought would in practice govern the industrial era's politics and ideology, marginalizing the poet-naturalist (Arnold 2003). Thoreau had at once maintained the romance of the Jeffersonian yeoman farmer, championed the qualities of wilderness, and demanded the reformation of the cities. In part because of America's changing identity during Reconstruction, realists and naturalists would consider his project at least unfashionable or hypocritical, if not obsolete, to lasting effect. Paradoxically, Thoreau would become the repository for nearly all critical references to nature writing's role in American literature. Some ideas assumed to be Thoreauvian are probably better attributed to John Muir or Rachel Carson, who employed, respectively, far-ranging wilderness observation and scientifically determined evidence for their positions, but movements require heroes, and Thoreau is a fine one.

The second major movement of ecological literature corresponds with Gilded Age literary realism and peaks in the 1910s. It is born of Roosevelt's popularization of the hunter-conservationist ethic, a revived expeditionary impulse, and reactionary "naturalisms" (literary, philosophical, and to some extent life-scientific, especially botanical, ornithological, and geological). This movement both challenged industrial boosterism and received some patronage from the robber barons. Its terminus could be considered World War I, the scale of which created profound changes in Western environmentalism.

But one thread of it continued, lasting through the 1920s and into the 1940s, during which the modes of military production strongly dictated the modes of land management. This was the "new regionalism" espoused by Carey McWilliams, Walter Prescott Webb, and Lewis Mumford, among others. An early and rough manifestation of bioregionalism almost entirely passed over in literary-historical study, the new regionalism reconsidered the efficacy of the nation's four major geopolitical regions: New England, the Midwest, the South, and the West (McWilliams 1930; Wilson 1998). The better choice of catalyst than war for the change from romanticism to realism in American ecological literature is probably the industrialized control of major waterways – particularly the damming of Hetch Hetchy and the cutting of the Panama Canal during 1913–14 – a major concern of the new regionalists.

Except for works by a few writers such as Aldo Leopold and Konrad Lorenz, ecological prose waited for the rise of its third wave until the 1960s and 1970s. This is commonly called "the environmental movement," a phrase that suffers from its singularity. The environmental movement corresponds less with the literary conventions of postmodernism than with a neo-Transcendentalism that flourished between the Wilderness Act of 1964 and the Endangered Species Act of 1973, after which the combined forces of the energy crisis and the ensuing new conservatism brought about sufficient factionalism to change its cohesion. Its brands of activism, as Roderick Nash has noted (1989), reflected those of the civil rights movement, and this is certainly one of the principal reasons for Thoreau's continued canonization. The environmental movement also took on the daunting project of countering C. P. Snow's declaration in 1959 that the sciences and humanities would always remain divided by an unbridgeable chasm (Snow 1998). This work has culminated in Glen A. Love's convincing demonstration of how ecological literature is grounded in the life sciences, and his call for a "practical ecocriticism" (Love and Love 1970; Love 2003).

The strange bedfellows of the Reagan administration and academic postmodern theory created another Scylla and Charybdis for ecological thought. In response, a parent organization for scholars interested in ecocriticism, the Association for the Study of Literature and the Environment (ASLE), grew up out of the Western American Literature conferences and has managed the discipline's independence (Waage 1985; Glotfelty and Fromm 1996: intro.).

The romantic era lent its platform to deep ecology and neo-pagan environmentalisms; the industrial era, especially given its combined revolutions in thought begun by Darwin and Marx, lent its platform to social ecology and radical environmentalism (see Marx 1964; Nash 1976). Over the decades of its refinement, psychoanalysis and its tendency to symbolize and internalize nature would prompt a reapplication of Jung and primitivism. This resulted in the revisionist discipline called ecopsychology (Roszak et al. 1995). To some extent, both romanticism and industrialism spawned modern ecological feminism (See Starhawk 1997; Merchant 1990, 1994; Kolodny 1984; Jensen and Limerick 1995).

Over all three periods of American literature, nature writing consistently cycles back to the attempted reconciliation of scientific knowledge with spiritual enlightenment, often in terms of atheistic or agnostic struggle (see Hay 2002). The radical activism of Edward Abbey and the metaphysics of Annie Dillard inherit respectively the radical activism of John Muir and the metaphysics of Ralph Waldo Emerson. The revision of assumptions that nature needed to be tamed in full – and so the revision of environmental ethics toward what Leopold called "The Land Ethic" (1987:

201) – contributed to the mass-market demand for this genre, especially for recreational narratives and handbooks.

That second literary movement of ecological consciousness in America demands an informed historicity and critical method. Such various writers as John Burroughs, Sarah Orne Jewett, Frederick Jackson Turner, and Jack London call for no less. David Mazel captures a number of missives from turn-of-the-century nature writers themselves in his collection *A Century of Early Ecocriticism*. For instance, Fannie Eckstorm, a writer for *Field and Stream* reviewing Thoreau's *The Maine Woods* in 1908, remarks that Robert Louis Stevenson considered the book to be "not literature," and Eckstorm at once concedes and negotiates the point by calling it a "fair substitute." She then demands of Stevenson some credibility based on experience: " . . . had Robert Louis worn [*The Maine Woods*] next to the skin he might have perhaps absorbed enough of the spirit of the American forest to avoid the gaudy melodrama which encloses *The Master of Ballantrae*" (Mazel 2001: 165). Here we see the canonical narrative, not the nature writing text, being criticized for its retrograde romantic sensibilities and subjected to a critical method founded on environmental awareness.

The Chronological, Geopolitical, and Bioregional

Scholars of literature recognize the permeability, momentum, and arbitrariness of periodicity. Sharp representations of this permeability are found in nature writing, particularly in writings about geology, because of the burden to address epochal time and the web of life. Even Clarence King, friendly as anyone to humanity as the great alchemistic race turning dirt to gold, ends his *Mountaineering in the Sierra Nevada*:

> Travelling to-day in foot-hill Sierras, one may see the old, rude scars of mining; trenches yawn, disordered heaps cumber the ground, yet they are no longer bare. Time, with friendly rain, and wind and flood, slowly, surely, levels all, and a compassionate cover of innocent verdure weaves fresh and cool from mile to mile. While Nature thus gently heals the humble Earth, God, who is also Nature, moulds and changes Man. (King 1989: 262).

King's passage resonates with much of the writing of the 1870s and 1880s, including the combination of divinity with natural process. Such disparate writers as William Cullen Bryant in *Picturesque America* (1872), Muir in *The Mountains of California* (1894), Louis Agassiz in his lectures (1863), Roosevelt in *Ranch Life and the Hunting Trail* (1896), and Mary Austin in *The Land of Little Rain* (1907) all articulated this marriage of the spiritual and material. At stake and at odds was the responsibility or absolution of the human actant.

If we follow the chronological approach that governs traditional literary classification, we can see the symbiotic relationships among ecological narrative, nature writing, and the political events during which they unfolded. Darwin is certainly the touchstone, although his act of literature cannot be separated from his quite public competition with Lamarck, Wallace, and Lyell for the theoretical lock on a subject in wide parlance before its publication (Browne 1995). After evolutionary theory was unveiled, an ecological literary history developed as complex and significant as any tracking race, class, or gender, and quickly developed its own subcategories. In the 1860s Samuel Hammond's works led to Roosevelt's popularization of the hunter-conservationist ethic. *Forest and Stream* magazine began under George Bird Grinnell, who wrote widely read accounts of Indian language and lore in campfire settings invoking the importance of wilderness to several tribes (Grinnell 1972; 1995). In this decade we have also Thoreau's famous last words ("moose... Indian"); Marsh's *Man and Nature*, with its emphasis on forest preservation and soil and water conservation, and its diction accommodating both scholars and lay people; and John Burroughs's first essay, "With the Birds," appearing in the *Atlantic Monthly* to superlative reviews. Burroughs sets the mark for Muir as the writer of the wilderness, a man driven to articulate the nonhuman world as realistically as possible (see Stewart 1995: 51–76).

Hayden's 1867–78 survey and others of the West coupled with the growing popularity of nature writing to reform the American perception of wilderness as a place of evil and suffering. It became for many a place of respite, healing, beauty, and/or adventure (Nash 1976). The naturalist expeditionary journal medium of Lewis and Clark was revisited, and connected the explorer's essay with nature writing to as great a degree as with "travel writing" (see Thwaites 1904–7). In the year of the golden spike, 1869, John Wesley Powell took his expedition down the Colorado River. Both events affected American literature by combining a commercial transcontinental sensibility with a close-to-the-bone pioneer sensibility – exactly the same competing mythic impulses that would contribute to the heated arguments over dams, deforestation, and the loss of biodiversity. Not to be diminished is the fact that the recreational impulse would be made more palatable over the next forty years at the expense of scores of American Indian tribes, and at the expense of whole species rendered extinct through human action.

The national perception of Western and regional America was also complicated by the purchase of Alaska from Russia (from under the Tlingit and other tribes), which immediately resulted in two things that generated a substantial body of nature writing: the industrial mass destruction of land and species; and the reportage of gold miners, journalists, mushers, and amateur naturalists – such as those culminating in the famous Harriman expedition of 1899 (Goetzmann and Sloan 1982; Burroughs et al. 1986; Grinnell 1995). America had to account for both its enchantment by and its treatment of the new wild far North. For example, Russia had instituted controls on fur seal hunting, but America did not, resulting in the near-extinction of the population until slow and minimal government intervention. The fur seal issue would be one of several (oil drilling, cannery pollution and salmon decline, strip mining, and deforestation being others) that would last for a hundred years in one high-level debate after another. These pervade the literature of Alaska since its addition to the American republic (Servid and Snow 1999; Haycox 1990; Ford 1966; Howe 1992; Gharst 1995).

With Bret Harte's mining narratives and Mark Twain's *Roughing It*, the West as a region fully enters the American literary consciousness. *Roughing It* appears in 1872, the year in which Ulysses S. Grant designates Yellowstone as a national park, J. Sterling Morton establishes Arbor Day, and William Cullen Bryant produces *Picturesque America* (a seminal work in the future of the nature coffee-table book). This is also the red-hot center of Reconstruction, during which the identities of both the South and the West would gather their mythic force. What follows in the next decades – contextualizing all but the most urban American literature of the time – is a series of timber acts, bag limits and other hunting laws, water rights litigation given the misnomer "reclamation," and scientific discoveries that at once demand environmental responsibility and increase its difficulty (see Worster 1993).

While regionalism and local color flourish (particularly in New England) during the 1880s, ornithology becomes one of the specialized sciences to boom in post-Darwin America, especially in the form of bird-watching guides written by the new ornithologists. Ellen Swallow Richards leads the movement to pass pure food laws in Massachusetts, and the muckraking tradition begins twenty years before Upton Sinclair contributes perhaps its most famous example, *The Jungle* (serialized in 1905 and published in 1906). Critiques of the so-called advances of scientific development during this era sometimes did not surface until many decades later. For example, German graduate student Othmar Zeider discovered the chemical formula for DDT in 1874, but the rebellion against its use on the basis of its destructive environmental effects (and carcinogenic content) did not really ignite until 1962 with Carson's *Silent Spring*.

And when the fruition of realism occurs – when *Life on the Mississippi* (1883), *Adventures of Huckleberry Finn* (1884), *The Rise of Silas Lapham* (1885), and "A White Heron" (1886) appear – American literature is infused with a new ecocritical sense, although such a phrase is not employed for more than another century, until the birth of ecocriticism. By 1900, the Boone and Crockett Club (a Roosevelt project) and the Audubon Society (a Grinnell project) are formed; the first acts are passed to preserve Alaskan salmon and to federally manage Western forests; and perhaps the defining battle of the West is begun in earnest – the battle over water (Limerick 1987: 293–322; Reisner 1993; Stegner 2002, Powell 1997; Webb 1981). When we refer to regionalist literature as a late nineteenth-century phenomenon, we refer as well to the admission of the American territories as states, to the very concept of South as a region in a unified nation, and to the West as a manifestation of nationhood markedly different from the East. The hair-splitting distinctions in literary handbooks between local color and regionalism belie the terms by which late nineteenth-century writers such as Cable, Jewett, Twain, Austin, and Muir were defining those regions for other writers, and residents, to follow.

The next two modes of study after the chronological are the geopolitical and the bioregional – each concerned with space over time, but each distinct from the other in the means by which the space is defined. In the geopolitical mode, we refer to a New England, a South Dakota, a "four corners." We assume a Southern literature and then have difficulty determining which texts belong, or which texts may be rooted in the High or Deep South, or for which it particularly matters that they were composed in this South (Francisco et al. 2001). And so we follow certain politically drawn lines to create a manufactured system that often defies the natural system on which it depends. The Ohio river's geopolitical importance in the slave narrative transcends the time of its writing (say, from Twain to Morrison). But finally, behind both the geopolitical and chronological lies its bioregional importance.

Bioregionalism, the third mode of the study of ecological literature, is a useful critical method that looks at the mapping of land (and so the formation of place in literature) in terms of its geological, topological, and climatic features, rather than only in terms of human politics (Garreau 1989; Sale 1991; Berg 1995). From a bioregionalist perspective, a river may often indeed determine a political border, but not always; and sometimes that coincidence produces more irony than efficacy. The "bug line" between North and South is more real, bioregionally speaking, than the Mason–Dixon line. The isohyetal lines marking western aridity, the expanse of the Bering Strait, the changing banks of the Mississippi – such hard facts of geography determine regionalism more profoundly than geopolitics can. And because the confrontation with, for instance, western aridity was largely an event of the late nineteenth century, the concept of regionalism had to be altered from its early New England conventions.

We may classify texts according to what they share of ecological systems. Although they are not coined as such until the 1980s, both geopoliticism and bioregionalism are transparently demonstrated in such writers as Mary Austin (the Great Basin), Kate Chopin (the northern Gulf coast), Gene Stratton-Porter (the Midwestern wetlands), George Washington Cable (the Mississippi banks), Charles Chesnutt (the agricultural High South), and Bret Harte (the Sierra mining country). There are anthologies of river and mountain literature, collections of forest tales, desert readers, lake journals – and in these, the genres of nature writing, conventional fiction, and poetry are often presented on equal terms (Durham and Jones 1969; Hedges and Hedges 1980; Kittredge and Smith 1988). In coming to understand a riparian or Gulf or ecotone literature, we will find that the chronological value of canonization exists only in proportion to its ecological value. The place dictates the terms of plausibility, verisimilitude and mimesis, narrative relevance, and the human vernacular. Twain, Cable, Powell, and Muir all gave rivers (respectively, the upper Mississippi, lower Mississippi, Platte and Colorado, and Tuolumne) the significance they deserved as physical facts acting upon plot and character, rather than treating them as mere setting or backdrop. Austin directly addressed aridity as the characteristic trait of her region, and consequently her narratives of the desert are, quite reasonably, obsessed with water.

One means by which nature writing negotiates the relationships among romance, realism, regionalism, and naturalism is its concern with presenting the "common" in an attempt to break from the fantastic worlds of Transcendental and symbolic romanticism. In human-centered studies of these movements, the effort to represent the mundane or common as worthy fictional material was focused on the individual under the pressure of a stratified society in terms of race, class, and gender. But realists found that commonness also depended upon the nonhuman environment. We might accept that realism poured the foundation of naturalism, but we must then accept that both movements – perhaps inadvertently to some degree – constructed a new perception of the environment in their distinction between garden and desert, city and farm, boxed watercolor and raw mineral paint.

In *The Rise of Silas Lapham*, resource extraction and value determined by labor and self-reliance (see Horwitz 1991) meet with the Brahmin sensibilities of the landed gentry. Bromfield Corey may criticize the Laphams only on aesthetic grounds, because he must accept that industrialism has provided access to wealth for those who work the earth, versus those who merely purport to own it. Silas Lapham finds his mineral paint and pulls the raw material from the land to which he is connected. However, even in the context of industrial America, the only way for him to reconcile his social and material successes is to refine that material and own its end product, a situation that Howells himself mines for metaphoric value. This results in Lapham's reach exceeding his grasp, largely because the doctrine of social progress is inextricably bound with the course of material progress – both of which depend entirely upon the good fortune of "owning" a piece of land containing valuable resources (see Michaels 1987).

Therefore, Corey's assertion of an aesthetic rubric of value is conducted in the context of formative sensibilities about the natural world and its yield. As well as a Howellsian departure from the Transcendental romantic vision, this is the prologue to the naturalist aesthetic of an environment devoid of character or moral, an earth to be used by the struggling laborer until, in its ultimate detachment, it destroys that laborer. Howells entertains the courtship of these two schools of thought, in a manner resonant of Norris's later efforts, when he places Silas Lapham in the midst of a shady business deal involving the sale of his factory – which Howells then resolves in Lapham's return to the rural (Howells 1983: 352). Similarly, Fitzgerald would pick up this theme when he sends Nick Carraway back to Minnesota, away from the corruption of Long Island. This literary theme of return to the rural is multifaceted. Lapham's and Carraway's retreats to the comfort of the country are in sharp contrast to Huck's "lighting out for the territories," which is a move toward greater mystery and potential danger.

The realist commitment to preserving the low or common thus defaults to the raw or natural. This in turn adds to the criteria for classifying regions. Someone like Wright Morris's Timothy Scanlon had to be constructed of the material of "a West," whereas Twain's white Southerners had to be made of the stuff of a plantation South, and the New England domestic sphere depended upon the permeability of its bounds with the green and blue world outside the domestic space. The influence of environmental features finally bioregionalizes character and plot beyond the abilities of traditionally defined realism to account for them. Realism's necessary, if only partly recognized, attunement to the environment articulates ecosystemic diversity: Chopin's South is not Twain's, nor is Twain's South his West. In fact, I might argue that *Roughing It* is a lesser work than much of Twain's corpus because it pulls too much of Twain's Southernism westward, and because it is actually Richard Irving Dodge's West in revision. Twain knew the Mississippi better – his efforts in the West were, quite literally, often speculative. In point of fact, Morris's West is now the Midwest, since the combination of chronological, geopolitical, and bioregional modes of study finally recognizes that west is a direction, and movement in that direction leads to definition of what space is entered (Eliade 1971). Perhaps no one better articulated this than Frederick Jackson Turner in 1893, when he waved the checkered flag over the movement that turned the West into the Midwest (Turner 1996).

Some Tenets of Ecological Literature

Among the long list of traits that we might identify, a few have particular bearing on industrial-era nature writing. They are:

1. *The subordination of narrative to place in the text's construction.* The conventional textbook method of reading prose is to emphasize narrative and (human) characterization. A heightened ecological consciousness, however, especially one shared by the writer and reader, puts place at the text's helm. In some cases (Powell, Van Dyke) narrative seems interposed merely to hold the interest of less ecologically mature readers. The subordination of narrative to place contradicts the assumption that narrative and character govern story, and that the environment is merely a vehicle, usually symbolic, for human fulfillment. Such a challenge is certainly present in Gilbert White, Thoreau, and the Hudson River School painters – even despite the latter's proclivities for art indicating divinely ordained human progress. But the literary naturalists greatly aided the transference of this trait to fiction, largely through tenet number two.

2. *The humbling, even the humiliation, of the human subject in the face of the nonhuman world.* This is a form of biocentrism, a bit like the decentered subject of some postmodern schools of criticism (Devall and Sessions 1985; Tomashow 1996). Where the Romantic sublime is found during a reverent silence in the midst of divine maelstrom, the sublime of the industrial era – to which nature writing responds and reacts – is found during the mind-numbing fatigue in the midst of mechanical maelstrom. In the Romantic ecological narrative, "every atom found in nature has its cunning duplicate in mind," while in the realist mode, as the Reverend Sewell tells Silas Lapham, "We can trace the operation of evil in the physical world . . . but I'm more and more puzzled about it in the moral world. There its course is so often very obscure; and often it seems to involve, so far as we can see, no penalty whatever" (Melville 1992; Howells 1983: 364).

3.   *Observation/rumination motivated by the belief in intrinsic value – that geographical or interspecific contributions to literature are found in their active presence in the text.* To consider it an end, rather than a means, that a heron is catching fish in a riparian ecological system, without our control over the heron's actions, simply has not penetrated the general approach to literary study. And yet, the literal presence and intrinsic value of sex, violence, even faith, are all regularly paired with (rather than removed from) their symbolic value, even sometimes in postmodern critical theory. The observations and ruminations of a John Burroughs demonstrate that sex, violence, and faith are all biological features functioning in relation to their biotic and abiotic environments. The balance struck in the realist method is therefore between the objectifying eye–thing relationship and the phenomenological eye–thing relationship (see Abram 1996).

4.   *The natural sciences are taken seriously and have a stake in the text, whether under critique, employed as method, or (in the most useful works) both.* Nature writing depends upon interdisciplinarity beyond the scope of the humanities; it directly confronts the C. P. Snow dilemma. As such, all of its manifestations during the late nineteenth century converged on an issue as central to American literature as any of the last two centuries: the matter of veracity. The concerns of realism were as well articulated during the "nature fakers" controversy by Burroughs, Roosevelt, London, and Long as they were by Howells and James (Stewart 1995: 131–56) – and perhaps more significantly argued because they reached the nation beyond the capacity of academic discourse. If nineteenth-century nature writers shared anything, it was their attraction (whether genuine or opportunistic) to the representation of that which could not be crafted by human effort, and consequently eluded the human lexicon.

The Nature Fakers Controversy

If there is a signature event for early twentieth-century nature writing, it would be the "nature fakers" controversy. Theodore Roosevelt coined the term, but the episode was initiated in 1903 by John Burroughs, speaking against those who he felt were misrepresenting the natural, particularly the animal, world. This was not the first time the matter of verisimilitude was argued by American nature writers – Audubon had written in his *Ornithological Biography* about "closet naturalists" in the 1830s – but the nature fakers debate was singular in that it was rooted in literature, and had for the first time a lexicon, supplied by the realist literary movement and the new sciences, that gave it teeth (Lutts 1990).

Burroughs wrote to the *Atlantic Monthly* in reaction to a glowing review of William J. Long's work, asserting that what passed for realistic nature writing among those who knew nothing about it was not necessarily realistic nature writing (Lutts 1990: 3). At stake were no less than the definition of Ruskin's pathetic fallacy; the classification of nature writing as a genre based on both observable and repeatable (empirical) occurrence; and two of the core elements of realism: verisimilitude and mimesis. These matters taken together, and in the context of Reconstruction, marked veracity as the key element distinguishing nonfiction from fiction, realism from romance, nature writing from snake oil. It would provide a vocabulary for similar arguments to follow, from Farley Mowat's claims in *Never Cry Wolf* to the rumor of Annie Dillard's pilfered opening of *Pilgrim at Tinker Creek*.

Following Burroughs's letter, several prominent authors who fell into the major categories of nature writing (Ernest Thompson Seton, Burroughs, Roosevelt) and ecological fiction (London, Long) divided into factions. The fiction writers defended their right to speculate on the ethology and psychological states of animals, based on evidence from both their own experience and the current science (e.g. London's time in the Yukon and the dubious taxonomies of canids). In the other faction were those who demanded absolute fidelity to biological fact as well as to personal experience. The defenders of speculation had their doubts about how wildly one could guess, and the objectivists had their hypocrisies, which sufficiently complicated the debate to reduce it at times to a shouting match. London's and Seton's works have lasted longest, London dodging the bullet Seton could not by writing literature beyond the animal tale. Burroughs remarked that Seton's *Wild Animals I Have Known* should have been titled "Wild Animals *I Alone* Have Known" (Lutts 1990: 39), while London is still considered a lesser canonical author whose animal fiction is taught for its metaphoric social commentary. The full study to read regarding the nature fakers controversy is by Ralph Lutts (1990).

Two other complexities of naturalism that stir the matter of nature faking are atavism and bestial decline. These are perhaps best demonstrated in London's dog books and in Frank Norris's *McTeague* (1899). If anthropomorphism was the bane of scientific naturalism, then zoomorphism was the boon of its literary version. What London boldly attempted was the resolution of Spencerianism (which he perceived as Darwinism), first with Nietzschean übermensch psychology (which he misread in large part because of his interpretation of Darwinian competition), then with political socialism. In this tumultuous center where the three great schools of thought to grow in London's day – evolutionary theory, psychoanalytic philosophy, and socialist politics – converged, he may perhaps be expected to have sought some iconic figure to preserve his own sanity and relative comfort. He did so in most of his work and in his own life, and chose as his vehicle atavism (his nickname, referencing many of his characters, was "Wolf"). However obviously the animal cognition story is subject to failure, London's efforts – particularly *The Call of the Wild* (1903) and *White Fang* (1905) – attempted to articulate the complex relationships between civilization and wilderness, survival and comfort, struggle and comfort, love and instinct, hate and instinct (Wilcox 1973; Labor et al. 1988).

Frank Norris drew the lines between these pairs in the field of wheat (in *The Octopus* and *The Pit* – and, had he lived to finish it, in the third novel of the series, *The Wolf*), and in Death Valley. McTeague fails to reconcile each pair, and so he is consumed by what the literary naturalists took to be the product of genetic human nature – an animal of their own invention. We see the importance of ecological narrative as an exchange between writer and reader in the moments of speculation about animal and human behavior, psychology, and causality, because those moments fail the most spectacularly and guess the most boldly (see Allen 1983; Howard 1985). Norris posits that McTeague's downfall is to the condition of "a caged brute;" even his tobacco has "come down" from "Yale mixture" to "Mastiff" (Norris 1990: 203, 215ff.). One of the first questions we should ask of the text is what this says about "the animal," and which animal our author means, not only to better understand the metaphor, but to better understand the raw material of its creation – some living, thinking animal implied to be mean, base, lesser, even irredeemable.

If the nature fakers controversy was so significant, then why was it not as popular a topic of study in conventional surveys on the turn of the century as was muckraker writing? We might entertain the possibility that the muckrakers lived in cities, wrote for city papers, and reached the audience that had control over both publishing and cultural discourse in America, while nature writers, as they still do, spent a bit too much time out in the bush. In the era of big publishing and the proliferation of universities, nature writing somehow came to seem too homespun for the urbane intellectual.

It bears mention that in the midst of the serious debates over veracity, the nonhuman world's relationship with America's new capitalist industrial mentality was also ripe for parody. In 1892 Twain's *The American Claimant* appeared – a sequel to *The Gilded Age* that begins with a characteristic disclaimer:

> THE WEATHER IN THIS BOOK
> No weather will be found in this book. This is an attempt to pull a book through without weather. It being the first attempt of the kind in fictitious literature, it may prove a failure, but it seemed worth the while of some dare-devil person to try it, and the author was in just the mood.... Many a reader who wanted to read a tale through was not able to do it because of delays on account of the weather. (Twain 1997: 1)

To stave off such interruptions, Twain declares that he will place all the weather in the novel's appendix. There is indeed an appendix, consisting of a Melvillian epigraph collection about weather ending with, "It rained for forty days and forty nights." Also in characteristic fashion, Twain uses weather several times in the narrative. However, he limits its use to an overt metaphor for Sally's mercurial love of Tracy, and avoids any mention in the text of physical climate or its conditions. Acting as both realist and Gilded Age confidence man, Twain means "no real weather," so he is both truthful (there's no real weather) and playing us (weather is invoked in the narrative).

Representative Writers: Jewett and Muir

In order to give some depth to this survey of industrial-era ecological narrative and nature writing, I have chosen to look more closely at two of its exemplary texts: Sarah

Orne Jewett's story "A White Heron" (1886) and John Muir's first book, *The Mountains of California* (1894). Each brief explication demonstrates the chronological, geopolitical, and bioregional possibilities inherent in these works.

While John James Audubon shot many of the birds he painted, he nevertheless exhibited an intelligence of and concern for conservation. His significant contribution to ornithology was conducted according to a nineteenth-century hunter–conservationist ethic that satisfied his desire to capture a species in a painting in order to educate a wider audience as to that species' beauty and importance. As is also true for the lepidopterist, the dead subject is easier to represent, finally controllable, and demands only ritual responsibility from the one studying it. Unfortunately, while the illusion of life is sufficient to the great work of expanding a reader's capacity for empathy, the passenger pigeon is now only an image with captions in books.

The hunter who comes to call on Sylvia and her grandmother is an Audubon figure (Allen 1991: 47), and so the feminist conflation of male seduction and repression (hunting as metaphor) with the hunter's desire to kill and therefore possess the bird is both obvious and justified. In the reading of "A White Heron" as a gendered text (and in the context of recovery work that brought recognition to women's regionalism), the exchange of money for favor, the pine tree and/or gun as phallic symbols, and the linkage of the heron's whiteness with Sylvia's purity are emphasized. An ecological reading of the story both supports this position, partly through ecofeminism, and questions its primacy as an avenue into the text.

The first two and a half pages of an eleven-page story take place outdoors, with a girl, transparently named Sylvia (i.e. "sylvan"), and a cow walking through a shadowed wood with the western light at their backs (Jewett 1956: 162). From the beginning, the conventional critic is enticed to fall into the old habits of reading this moment in terms of "mood" or "setting." And so, at the very start, the conventional reading denies that the story is primarily about the shadowed wood and its inhabitants. Sylvia has come from "a manufacturing town" and feels "as if she never had been alive before she came to live at the farm" (p. 162). She is connected twice in the story with the grandeur of the planet, and marked as inhabiting a liminal space, barely the agricultural zone in the midst of a forest (pp. 163, 169).

When the encounter with the hunter/ornithologist occurs, there is the frisson of Red Riding Hood to it, an intrusion, a potential violation. Here, we've been trained, is the real drama: we've moved from one character to two, from isolation to politics. So it is, but Sylvia's social life is more with other species than other human beings. "Afraid of folks," they say of her in town (Jewett 1956: 162), while the birder is "charming," an imposing but sociable figure with an interesting life that he apparently lives in the city (he is "on vacation": p. 166). At one point, his classification of "this New England wilderness" divides the low, dirty folk from the neat, tidy folk like Sylvia and Mrs. Tilley; his perception is filtered by a civilized (i.e. masculine) sense of "housekeeping" as the gauge of proper conduct for women, for his convenience (p. 166).

That the hunter is an ornithologist contributes a great deal to the plot and sharpens the story's dilemma. When he explains how he stuffs and preserves the birds he studies, he reveals himself as poured from Audubon's mold (Jewett 1956: 165), and Jewett follows through by having him speculate as to why the "little white heron" might be in New England. His speculations are themselves highly questionable. "Migrating" or "chased from its region by a bird of prey" seem odd (perhaps hopeful) explanations, depending on what kind of bird this actually is and how far it may have traveled. The white heron is not native to New England unless there is an assumed conflation with the snowy egret. The very sub-classification of herons has long been debatable – that is, whether color should make a significant difference in classification (Allen 1991: 35). This white heron could be a phase color of another subspecies of heron, could be an albino blue heron, could be a snowy egret (far more common to New England), or could be, as the hunter calls it, "the little white heron," a possible subspecies of its own (Jewett 1956: 165; Allen 1991: 25). Jewett's Audubon figure explains that he has come to see the bird because it is so rare, and exudes the confidence of a man who knows his business. We are to assume that this bird is a visitor, like the hunter, and that the human visitor is interested in valuing it according to terms not shared by our protagonist – a pure and satisfying situation for good fiction.

The story takes its dramatic turn when Sylvia climbs the oak to the pine and achieves a perspective that prompts her not to reveal the whereabouts of the bird. Several elements in this passage seduce the reader toward its gendered symbolism, but just as many problematize that approach. There are two trees, not one, so the phallic imagery is questionable, although the language of the climbing certainly has this resonance. Jewett knows her trees, though; the white oak, with its low, wide branches, would be far easier to climb than a tall pine, especially for a small person. Both trees stand in the clearing of a cut, where Jewett says, "the woodchoppers had felled [the pine's] mates" (1956: 167). The pine in the clearing reveals what kind of a world Sylvia inhabits – not just a symbolically sylvan one, but an actual forest in New England that is being cut, into which has flown a rare species whose motivation is its own, outside human ken, and who, for its effort, is about to be killed.

In the late 1800s, egret and other bird feathers were so frequently used in women's hats that bag limits had to be placed and industry conservation laws instituted in order to maintain the bird populations (Allen 1991: 10, 30–1). If Sylvia is not giving in to the purchase of her sexual identity, then she also isn't giving in to the purchase of her ecological one. She is not selling out to the consumerism that has put the birds of her region in danger for the sake of fashion. When Sylvia spots the heron, she identifies it as (or assumes it to be) a male, and finds that it also has a mate (Jewett 1956: 170). If Sylvia's purity in the midst of all this coupling symbolism is to be connected with both the heron's whiteness and its victimization, then the heron's *maleness* creates a scramble in the gendered reading that is irrelevant to the ecological one. Perhaps the male pronoun for the heron emphasizes its role as bird over its role as symbol, and directs our attention to its individuality, as well as to Sylvia's.

Her credibility in woodcraft is all we have by which to conclude that the bird is male; the story's climax relies on our trust of both her experience and her principles, and so her power as naturalist at least coexists with her dilemma as feminist. The white heron has a symbolic connection to Sylvia, yes; but that is of little consequence if we find the story's power and value to be in whether or not she possesses a sound land ethic, as Aldo Leopold would say. It matters whether or not the bird dies in the course of the narrative, regardless of whether or not Sylvia achieves her epiphany in the story and refines her ethics.

The story only benefits the more that she does both. Her growth is profound and poignant, its epiphanic moment revealed expositionally at the base of the oak: "Alas, if the great wave of human interest which flooded for the first time this dull little life should sweep away the satisfactions of an existence heart to heart with nature and the dumb life of the forest!" (Jewett 1956: 168). It is fully formed in the final sentences: "Were the birds better friends than their hunter might have been – who can tell? Whatever treasures were lost to her, woodlands and summer-time, remember! Bring your gifts and graces and tell your secrets to this lonely country child!" (p. 171). As Jewett presents them, "dumb" and "lonely" are not necessarily negative, any more than the frequently mentioned shadows in the forest are evil. Shadows are in forests. Life in the liminal space is for Sylvia as it was for Thoreau, beautifully lonely. The dumb brutes of the forest are Sylvia's teachers – and who would say that her decision not to reveal the secret of the heron is a bad one? Indeed, Jewett asserts that it makes Sylvia a wise listener, one to whom we should tell our secrets, not one from whom we should try to extract them – one who hears both the birds (in several passages identifying them by call) and the human voice, and can properly decipher their messages.

Notice that the story follows three of the four tenets of ecological literature listed previously. It can be challenged only in regard to the first one – the subordination of narrative to place – and that because this is an ecological narrative, not a work of nature writing. While it has a narrative arc, because it is a realist story, it humbles the human subject in the author's biocentric framework; it uses observation and rumination to assert value in sheer presence and transcendence of human manufacture; and it invokes the natural sciences to pose its dilemma. It also demonstrates that Jewett's ecological consciousness was more sophisticated and informed than that of the bulk of critics who have considered her work under even the most reformed doctrines of canonization.

In chronological terms, we see a regionalist narrative produced during the boom of ornithology handbooks and studies, troping Audubon and critiquing the rising industrial mores of America – a text universally designated as realist and regionalist. In geopolitical terms, we have an examination of rural New England occupied by a cultured hunter naturalist who desires to study a rarity of that New England. The vernacular, the idiomatic exchanges, the rules and boundaries of Sylvia's existence, are all in keeping with the traits we would assume to be part of village Maine. In bioregional terms, we have a rare species nesting in a northern coastal and arboreal region – a domestic moment more important to the bird than to anyone – one of the many members of the *ardea* family in the sights of a hunter who wishes to study its corpse. The plotline depends upon the dilemma of the protagonist, whose kinship with her bioregion finally determines her decision. This story might be best understood by a tree climber. Its lesson to the critic is stated in its first paragraph: "They were going away from the western light, and striking deep into the dark woods, but their feet were familiar with the path, and it was no matter whether their eyes could see it or not" (Jewett 1956: 161).

To one degree or another, all human civilizations are composed of three major zones – the city, the field, and the wilderness – each with an expansive canon of literature. The last of the three constitutes what Leopold called "the raw material out of which man has hammered the artifact called civilization" (1987: 188). Ecological narrative and nature writing share the need to arbitrate the relationships among those zones, and during America's industrial period, the early proliferation of sprawl, mechanization of agriculture, and simultaneous awakening to and destruction of wilderness gave that arbitration a color very different from prior eras in American history.

If such relationships were put on a line, with the metropolitan center to the far left and the untrammeled wilderness (to use the language of The Wilderness Act) on the far right, then *The Jungle* (1906) or Steffens's *The Shame of the Cities* (1904) would mark hard on the left end; *Walden* and *The Country of the Pointed Firs* would likely be located on the line between the town and the field; *Of Mice and Men* (1938), *My Ántonia* (1918), and Liberty Hyde Bailey's *The Country-Life Movement in the United States* (1911) would fall into the agricultural center, and Van Dyke's *The Desert* (1901), Austin's *The Land of Little Rain* (1907), and Isabella Bird's *A Lady's Life in the Rocky Mountains* (1880) would all slide along the line into the wilderness zone, depending on how we define "trammeled." We may certainly find in wilderness writers plenty of civilization, but their concerns are for that which is not yet given over to, for instance, a national infrastructure. Their vision is toward the experience of what is neither city nor field. The extent to which they romanticize this is mitigated sufficiently by their experiences, which validate the change in textual space from cultivated to uncultivated, from manufactured to beyond the capacity for fabrication.

John Daniel has called the propensity for people to limit their views of the natural world a struggle between the cult of beauty and the cult of utility (1992: 42), and since the industrial era this binary has been a major subject of inquiry in nature writing. Some writers negotiate the binary with great complexity, and John Muir is such a writer. His field studies of glaciology, conducted after approximately one year's worth of college training, changed the accepted textbook theories, and themselves became textbook material (Turner 1997: 199–200; Muir 1961: x–xi). He was a consummate inventor – a noble profession during the Gilded Age – but left that pursuit after a factory accident that blinded him for two weeks and prompted him to spend the bulk of his life in the direct experience of wilderness. After the accident, he saw the world through a spiritual lens ground fine from the thick glass of his abandoned Calvinism. Academic resistance to the language of his faith has in part marginalized Muir's work, the result of an institution disinclined to celebrate the Dickensian style outside the Dickensian mode, to the loss of a fuller bioregional knowledge of American literature.

The Mountains of California, like Muir's other work, is filled with the kind of exuberance that sometimes wears out even other nature writers. It often so subordinates the human narrative as to raise the issue of the text's continuity, until we find that the age of a mountain, the girth of a sequoia, the song of the Tuolumne, or the characteristics of sub-alpine ecosystems constitute the plot, characters, themes, and denouements of Muir's text. Taken as a body, his work presents a bold challenge to those who would approach ecological narrative from their offices, as Lawrence Buell has said, "Bartleby-like" (Buell 1995). Thoreau may well have instigated this approach to constructing ecologically conscious prose in terms of direct action, but Muir pushed the form as far as it would go.

In the tradition of Louis Agassiz and other scientists who followed Darwin's science but not his atheism, Muir embraces a creationist evolution: the empirical method was a way to get at what God had created and to track its function, in reconciliation with the Romantic impulse. He defies regressive anthropocentrism founded on the idea that the earth was composed of resources ordained by God for human use, although he is apt to employ anthropomorphism, even mechanical analogy, designed to laud the creation: "God's glacial mills grind slowly, but they have been kept in motion long enough in California to grind sufficient soil for a glorious abundance of life, though most of the grist has been carried to the lowlands, leaving these high regions comparatively lean and bare" (Muir 1961: 44). Muir articulates his knowledge through miniature narratives throughout a book devoted to regional description (chapters are titled "The Snow," or "The River Floods"). In the end, we learn about glacial activity's regional effects and its effects on our narrator.

An advocate of experience over abstraction, Muir was purportedly dragged into writing first articles and then *The Mountains of California* by Robert Underwood Johnson, editor of the *Century* magazine, and others who had loved hearing his stories. He gained no less than the approval of Emerson; a varied but friendly relationship with Theodore Roosevelt; consequently, the backing of an American public freshly taken with the once preposterous notion of excursions out of the city as offering both recreation and healing; the success of the Sierra Club beyond the many environmentally concerned clubs of the day; the passage of forest management policies that would continue to be echoed for decades (Turner 1997: 246–7); the popularization of the national park system and several peaks such as Rainier, Shasta, and Whitney (each of which may have been climbed by Muir before those who claimed them); and the elevation of such smaller, less mesmerizing species as the Douglas squirrel and the water ouzel (both given chapters in *The Mountains of California*) to positions of greatness equal to those accorded the sequoia and the grizzly bear (Muir 1961).

This last accomplishment is a reminder of the importance Muir gave to craft; he devoted little time to the high-profile megafauna, and spent more ink on small, resourceful animals that he felt taught us, in the tradition of both Gilbert White and

T. H. White, lessons about our own sense of value. Understanding our own sense of value is certainly not, for Muir, the goal of being in the presence of nonhuman life – his work is a constant demonstration of the possibilities of intrinsic value – but even Muir had his biases. He detested sheep, although he doesn't seem to have extended this distaste more broadly to the domestic animal as a category (Muir 1987); he developed a great fondness, for instance, for a little dog he called Stickeen (after the Alaskan river), and about whom he wrote a book that contains a fiery activism and catholicism about animal life in a romantic man-and-his-dog narrative (Muir 1990). Until the end of his life he was embroiled in the water rights issues of the West that for him would end tragically in the damming of Hetch Hetchy in 1913.

Unlike Twain, Muir's skill was forthrightness, not parody. His book is mostly weather. His biographers, as well, are obligated to load their tales with storms, white-outs, clouds, rain, intense heat and sunshine – because these made up Muir's working days, formed the skin of the hand that held his pen. *The Mountains of California* contains one of Muir's more famous incidents, the chapter "A Wind-Storm in the Forests." During a December hike to a peak above the Yuba river, he becomes what most of us would call "caught" in a storm (Muir 1961: 190). He decides to climb a Douglas spruce to its top and feel the storm as the tree would feel it:

> Though comparatively young, they were about 100 feet high, and their lithe, brushy tops were rocking and swirling in wild ecstasy. Being accustomed to climb trees in making botanical studies, I experienced no difficulty in reaching the top of this one, and never before did I enjoy so noble an exhilaration of motion. The slender tops fairly flapped and swished in the passionate torrent, bending and swirling backward and forward, round and round, tracing indescribable combinations of vertical and horizontal curves, while I clung with muscles firm braced, like a bobolink on a reed. (p. 193)

Muir is often this transported figure, a man who seems oblivious to the politics of humanity, literally above them, but the beginning and ending of his final chapter, "The Bee Pastures," reveal his savvy and diplomacy. He opens with a one-sentence paragraph: "When California was wild, it was one sweet bee-garden throughout its entire length, north and south, and all the way across from the snowy Sierra to the ocean" (Muir 1961: 259). He ends the chapter and book with this sentence: "In short, notwithstanding the widespread deterioration and destruction of every kind [of forest] already infected, California, with her incomparable climate and flora, is still, as far as I know, the best of all the bee-lands of the world" (p. 289).

His was the West of bees, not of the Newlands Act or the ensuing Pinchot/Ballinger affair. Neither the Division of Biological Survey nor the damming of the Western rivers could dissuade him from the value of wilderness beyond its mere beauty or use, exploited for the comfort of American nationalism (Axelrod and Philips 1993). He had lived and worked through the age of barbed wire and Colt pistol and territorial dispute that defined Western America (Slotkin 1985), and he had risen above it in his practice as no Transcendentalist had in theory.

After the turn of the century, while Muir was in his sixties, he would travel to Alaska with Harriman, Curtis, Burroughs, and Grinnell, and contribute to an "Album of Chronicles and Souvenirs" toward the promotion of preservation. He would fight the United States government in a precedent-setting battle over San Francisco water use in the Hetch Hetchy valley that would lay the foundation for the 1960s fight against Lake Powell (McPhee 1990). In the time of the muckrakers such as Sinclair and Norris, writing for food acts and better working conditions and the reformation of Wall Street and the mines — writing that instigated legislation just as Carson's would later on, when Swedish chemist Svante Arrhenius argued that the greenhouse effect from coal and petroleum use was warming the globe — when Ford's assembly line began, when desperate efforts were undertaken by the government to manage the wilderness — during this crucial time Muir's life waned. He held out for long enough to see the battle for Hetch Hetchy lost, not quite long enough to see us cut North America from South America through Panama. *The Mountains of California* is his first book, and in it we see his commitment as clearly as we see it in *A Thousand Mile Walk to the Gulf*. In the midst of an era of great environmental turmoil and the production of a literature deeply concerned with that turmoil, Muir delivered his own thesis, quoted here by his best biographer, Frederick Turner: "His retirement from the world for wilderness, he said, 'was no solemn abjuration of the world. I only went out for a walk, and finally concluded to stay out till sundown, for going out, I found, was really going in'" (Turner 1997: 350).

Muir's experience in the Douglas spruce differs too much from Sylvia's in the pine to draw a direct and tidy equation; his coast, for instance, is not Jewett's, and a spruce is not a pine. But the connection of character and author as tree climbers, physically familiar with their places of epiphany, makes it possible to entertain their contrasting narratives as of the same order: their separate places keep the two stories from being the same retold. Although Sylvia and John's ethics are the same, their evergreens are not, and in ecocritical considerations of regionalism and realism, that has made all the difference.

Primary Texts

Agassiz, Louis. *Methods of Study in Natural History.* 1863.

Audubon, John James. *Ornithological Biography, or the Account of the Habits of the Birds of the United States of America.* 1831–9.

Austin, Mary. *The Flock.* 1906.

Austin, Mary. *The Land of Little Rain.* 1903.

Bryant, William Cullen. *Picturesque America.* 1872.

Burroughs, John. *Birds and Poets, with Other Papers.* 1895.

Cable, George Washington. *Old Creole Days.* 1879.

Darwin, Charles. *On the Origin of Species by Means of Natural Selection.* 1859.

Emerson, Ralph Waldo. *Nature.* 1836.

Fitzgerald, F. Scott. *The Great Gatsby.* 1925.

Haeckel, Ernst. *The Riddle of the Universe.* 1899.

Howells, William Dean. *The Rise of Silas Lapham.* 1885.

Jewett, Sarah Orne. "A White Heron." 1886.

Jewett, Sarah Orne. *The Country of the Pointed Firs.* 1896.

King, Clarence. *Mountaineering in the Sierra Nevada.* 1872.

London, Jack. *The Call of the Wild*. 1903.

London, Jack. *White Fang*. 1905.

London, Jack. "The Other Animals." 1909.

Melville, Herman. *Moby-Dick; or, The Whale*. 1851.

Muir, John. *The Mountains of California*. 1894.

Muir, John. *Our National Parks*. 1901.

Muir, John. *Stickeen*. 1909.

Muir, John. *My First Summer in the Sierra*. 1911.

Muir, John. *Travels in Alaska*. 1915.

Muir, John. *A Thousand Mile Walk to the Gulf*. 1916.

Norris, Frank. *McTeague: A Story of San Francisco*. 1899.

Norris, Frank. *The Octopus: A Story of California*. 1901.

Norris, Frank. *The Pit*. 1903.

Norris, Frank. *The Responsibilities of the Novelist*. 1903.

Norris, Frank. *Vandover and the Brute*. 1914.

Powell, John Wesley. *Exploration of the Colorado River of the West and its Tributaries*. 1875.

Roosevelt, Theodore. *The Winning of the West: From the Alleghenies to the Mississippi 1769–1776*. 1889–96.

Roosevelt, Theodore. *Ranch Life and the Hunting Trail*. 1896.

Sinclair, Upton. *The Jungle*. 1906.

Steffens, Lincoln. *The Shame of the Cities*. 1904.

Stratton-Porter, Gene. *A Girl of the Limberlost*. 1909.

Thoreau, Henry David. *Walden*. 1854.

Thoreau, Henry David. "Ktaadn." 1864.

Thoreau, Henry David. *Cape Cod*. 1865.

Thwaites, Ruben Gold, ed. *Early Western Travels, 1748–1846: a series of annotated reprints of some of the best and rarest contemporary volumes of travel, descriptive of the aborigines and social and economic conditions in the middle and far west, during the period of early American settlement*. 1904–7.

Turner, Fredrick Jackson. "The Significance of the Frontier in American Literature." 1893.

Twain, Mark. *Roughing It*. 1872.

Twain, Mark. *Life on the Mississippi*. 1883.

Twain, Mark. *Adventures of Huckleberry Finn*. 1884.

Twain, Mark. *The American Claimant*. 1892.

References and Further Reading

Abram, David (1996). *The Spell of the Sensuous: Perception and Language in a More-than-Human World*. New York: Vintage.

Agassiz, Louis (1970). *Methods of Study in Natural History*. Ayer.

Allen, Hayward (1991). *The Great Blue Heron*. Northword.

Allen, Mary (1983). *Animals in American Literature*. Southern Illinois University Press.

Armbruster, Karla, and Wallace, Kathleen R., eds. (2001). *Beyond Nature Writing: Expanding the Boundaries of Ecocriticism*. University of Virginia Press.

Arnold, Jean (2003). "'From so Simple a Beginning': Evolutionary Origins of US Nature Writing." *ISLE: Interdisciplinary Studies in Literature and Environment* 10: 1 (Winter), 11–26.

Axelrod, Alan, and Phillips, Charles, eds. (1993). *The Environmentalists: A Biographical Dictionary from the 17th Century to the Present*. New York: Facts on File.

Berg, Peter (1995). *Discovering Your Life-Place: A First Bioregional Workbook*. Planet Drum.

Browne, Janet (1995). *Charles Darwin: Voyaging*. Princeton: Princeton University Press.

Bryson, J. Scott (2002). *Ecopoetry: A Critical Introduction*. Salt Lake City: University of Utah Press.

Buell, Lawrence (1995). *The Environmental Imagination: Thoreau, Nature Writing, and the Formation of American Culture*. Cambridge, Mass.: Belknap/Harvard University Press.

Burroughs, John (2001). *Birds and Poets, with Other Papers*. NL: Fredonia.

Burroughs, John; Muir, John, et al. (1986). *Alaska, the Harriman Expedition, 1899*. New York: Dover.

Calicott, J. Baird, ed. (1998). *The Great New Wilderness Debate*. University of Georgia Press.

Clarke, Graham, ed. (1994). *The American Landscapes: Literary Sources and Documents*, 3 vols. New York: Routledge.

Conron, John (1974). *The American Landscape: An Anthology of Prose and Poetry*. Oxford: Oxford University Press.

Daniel, John (1992). "The Impoverishment of Sightseeing." In *The Trail Home: Essays*. New York: Pantheon.

Desmond, Adrian, and Moore, James (1991). *Darwin: The Life of a Tormented Evolutionist.* New York: Norton.

Deutsch, Sarah (1987). *No Separate Refuge: Culture, Class, and Gender on an Anglo-Hispanic Frontier in the American Southwest, 1880–1940.* Oxford: Oxford University Press.

Devall, Bill, and Sessions, George, eds. (1985). *Deep Ecology: Living as if Nature Mattered.* Gibbs M. Smith.

Durham, Philip, and Jones, Everett L., eds. (1969). *The Frontier in American Literature.* Bobbs-Merrill.

Eliade, Mircea (1971). *The Myth of the Eternal Return.* Princeton: Princeton University Press.

Finch, Robert, and Elder, John, eds. (1990). *The Norton Book of Nature Writing.* New York: Norton.

Ford, Corey (1966). *Where the Sea Breaks its Back: The Epic Story of a Pioneer Naturalist and the Discovery of Alaska.* Boston: Little, Brown.

Francisco, Edward; Vaughan, Robert; and Francisco, Linda, eds. (2001). *The South in Perspective: An Anthology of Southern Literature.* Prentice-Hall.

Garreau, Joel (1989). *The Nine Nations of North America.* Avon.

Gharst, Michael, ed. (1995). "The Klondike Journal of William Mann." *Pacific Northwest Forum* 8 (Winter/Spring), 5–28.

Gifford, Terry (1996). *John Muir: His Life and Letters and Other Writings.* The Mountaineers.

Glotfelty, Cheryll, and Fromm, Harold, eds. (1996). *The Ecocriticism Reader: Landmarks in Literary Ecology.* University of Georgia Press.

Goetzmann, William, and Sloan, Kay (1982). *Looking Far North: The Harriman Expedition to Alaska.* New York: Viking.

Grinnell, George Bird (1972). *Cheyenne Indians: Their History and Ways of Life.* University of Nebraska Press. (First publ. 1923.)

Grinnell, George Bird (1995). *Alaska 1899: Essays from the Harriman Expedition.* Seattle: University of Washington Press. (First publ. 1901.)

Haeckel, Ernst (1992). *The Riddle of the Universe.* Prometheus.

Hay, Peter (2002). *Main Currents in Western Environmental Thought.* Indiana University Press.

Haycox, Stephen W. (1990). "Economic Development and Indian Land Rights in Modern Alaska: The 1947 Tongass Timber Act." *Western Historical Quarterly* 21: 1 (Feb.), 21–47.

Hedges, Elaine, and Hedges, William, eds. (1980). *Land and Imagination: The Rural Dream in America.* Hayden Publishing.

Horwitz, Howard (1991). *By the Law of Nature: Form and Value in Nineteenth-Century America.* Oxford: Oxford University Press.

Howard, June (1985). *Form and History in American Literary Naturalism.* Chapel Hill: University of North Carolina Press.

Howe, Doris (1992). *Bibliography of Research and Exploration in the Glacier Bay Region, Southeastern Alaska, 1798–1992.* US Dept. of the Interior, US Geological Survey.

Howells, William Dean (1983). *The Rise of Silas Lapham.* New York: Penguin.

Jensen, Joan M., and Limerick, Patricia Nelson, eds. (1995). *One Foot on the Rockies: Women and Creativity in the Modern American West* (Calvin P. Horn Lectures in Western History and Culture). Albuquerque: University of New Mexico Press.

Jewett, Sarah Orne (1956). *The Country of the Pointed Firs and Other Stories.* New York: Anchor/Doubleday.

King, Clarence (1989). *Mountaineering in the Sierra Nevada.* New York: Penguin.

Kittredge, William, and Smith, Annick (1988). *The Last Best Place: An Anthology of Montana Writing.* Montana Historical Society Press.

Kolodny, Annette (1984). *The Land Before Her: Fantasy and Experience of the American Frontiers, 1630–1860.* University of North Carolina Press.

Kroeber, Karl (1994). *Ecological Literary Criticism: Romantic Imagining and the Biology of Mind.* New York: Columbia University Press.

Labor, Earle; Leitz, Robert C., III; and Shephard, Milo, eds. (1988). *The Letters of Jack London,* 3 vols. Stanford, Calif.:Stanford University Press.

Leopold, Aldo (1987). *A Sand County Almanac, and Sketches Here and There.* Oxford: Oxford University Press. (First publ. 1949.)

Limerick, Patricia Nelson (1987). *The Legacy of Conquest: The Unbroken Past of the American West.* New York: Norton.

Love, Glen A. (2003). *Practical Ecocriticism: Literature, Biology, and the Environment.* University of Virginia Press.

Love, Glen A., and Love, Rhoda M., eds. (1970). *Ecological Crisis: Readings for Survival.* Harcourt.

Lutts, Ralph H. (1990). *The Nature Fakers: Wildlife, Science, and Sentiment*. Golden, Colo.: Fulcrum.

Lyon, Thomas J. (2001). *This Incomparable Land: A Guide to American Nature Writing*. Milkweed.

McPhee, John (1990). *Encounters with the Archdruid*. Noonday.

McWilliams, Carey (1930). *The New Regionalism in American Literature*. Seattle: University of Washington Press.

Marx, Leo (1964). *The Machine in the Garden: Technology and the Pastoral Idea in America*. Oxford: Oxford University Press.

Mazel, David (2001). *A Century of Early Ecocriticism*. University of Georgia Press.

Melville, Herman (1992). *Moby-Dick; or, The Whale*. New York: Penguin.

Merchant, Carolyn (1990). *The Death of Nature: Women, Ecology, and the Scientific Revolution*. San Francisco: Harper.

Merchant, Carolyn (1994). *Ecology: Key Concepts in Critical Theory*. Humanity Books.

Michaels, Walter Benn (1987). *The Gold Standard and the Logic of Naturalism: American Literature at the Turn of the Century*. University of California Press.

Muir, John (1961). *The Mountains of California*. New York: Doubleday.

Muir, John (1987). *My First Summer in the Sierra*. New York: Penguin.

Muir, John (1990). *Stickeen*. Heyday.

Muir, John (1999). *To Yosemite and Beyond: Writings from the Years 1863–1875*, ed. Robert Engberg and Donald Wesling. University of Utah Press.

Nash, Roderick, ed. (1976). *The American Environment: Readings in the History of Conservation*, 2nd edn. New York: Knopf.

Nash, Roderick (1982). *Wilderness and the American Mind*, 3rd edn. New Haven: Yale University Press.

Nash, Roderick (1989). *The Rights of Nature: A History of Environmental Ethics*. Madison: University of Wisconsin Press.

Norris, Frank (1990). *McTeague: A Story of San Francisco*. New York: Vintage.

Powell, John Wesley (1997). *Exploration of the Colorado River of the West and its Tributaries*. New York: Penguin.

Reisner, Marc (1993). *Cadillac Desert: The American West and its Disappearing Water*. New York: Penguin.

Roszak, Theodore; Gomes, Mary E.; and Kanner, Allen D., eds. (1995). *Ecopsychology: Restoring the Earth, Healing the Mind*. San Francisco: Sierra Club.

Sale, Kirkpatrick (1991). *Dwellers in the Land: The Bioregional Vision*. University of Georgia Press.

Scheese, Don (1996). *Nature Writing: The Pastoral Impulse in America*. New York: Twayne.

Servid, Carolyn, and Snow, Donald, eds. (1999). *The Book of the Tongass*. Milkweed.

Slotkin, Richard (1973). *Regeneration through Violence: The Mythology of the American Frontier, 1600–1860*. Middletown, Conn.: Wesleyan University Press.

Slotkin, Richard (1985). *The Fatal Environment: The Myth of the Frontier in the Age of Industrialization: 1800–1890*. New York: Atheneum.

Slotkin, Richard (1992). *Gunfighter Nation: The Myth of the Frontier in Twentieth-Century America*. New York: Atheneum.

Smith, Henry Nash (1950). *Virgin Land: The American West as Symbol and Myth*. Cambridge, Mass.: Harvard University Press.

Snow, C. P. (1998). *The Two Cultures*. Cambridge, UK: Cambridge University Press. (First publ. 1959.)

Starhawk (1997). *Dreaming the Dark: Magic, Sex, and Politics*. Boston: Beacon.

Stegner, Wallace (1987). *The American West as Living Space*. University of Michigan Press.

Stegner, Wallace (2002). *Where the Bluebird Sings to the Lemonade Springs*. Modern Library.

Stewart, Frank (1995). *A Natural History of Nature Writing*. Washington DC: Island Press.

Thwaites, Ruben Gold, ed. (1904–7). *Early Western Travels, 1748–1846: a series of annotated reprints of some of the best and rarest contemporary volumes of travel, descriptive of the aborigines and social and economic conditions in the middle and far west, during the period of early American settlement*, 32 vols. A. H. Clark.

Tomashow, Mitchell (1996). *Ecological Identity: Becoming a Reflective Environmentalist*. Cambridge, Mass.: MIT Press.

Turner, Frederick Jackson (1996). *The Frontier in American History*. New York: Dover. Originally "The Significance of the Frontier in American Literature," a lecture given in 1893.

Turner, Frederick (1997). *John Muir, from Scotland to the Sierra*. Edinburgh: Canongate.

Twain, Mark (1997). *The American Claimant*. Oxford: Oxford University Press.

Waage, Frederick O. (1985). *Teaching Environmental Literature: Materials, Methods, Resources*. Modern Language Association.

Webb, Walter Prescott (1981). *The Great Plains*. University of Nebraska Press. (First publ. 1934.)

Wilcox, Earl (1973). "'The Kipling of the Klondike': Naturalism in London's Early Fiction." *Jack London Newsletter* 6, 1–12.

Wilson, Charles Reagan, ed. (1998). *The New Regionalism*. University of Mississippi Press.

Worster, Donald (1993). *The Wealth of Nature: Environmental History and the Ecological Imagination*. Oxford: Oxford University Press.

Zola, Emile (1970). *The Experimental Novel and Other Essays*. Haskell House. (First publ. 1880.)

10

"The Frontier Story": The Violence of Literary History

Christine Bold

The 1893 World's Columbian Exposition in Chicago has been widely analyzed as an iconic moment in the cultural maturation of the United States. The fair also serves as a nice paradigm of the nation's frontier story, in terms of both the emergence of that narrative and its reconstruction in literary and cultural history. The most dominant feature of the fair was its centerpiece "White City," a symmetrical plaza of towering white classical simulacra that both symbolically announced America's cultural power and betrayed the vestiges of European mimicry. Tucked away in another part of the fairground was another, much more modest structure, equally redolent of mythologies-in-the-making but in this case distinctively homegrown. This was the log cabin erected by the Boone and Crockett Club, an exclusive enclave of wealthy Easterners, "gentlemen hunters" who sought to extend their influence into the management of Western lands. Among the members who converged on the fair that summer were Theodore Roosevelt, co-founder of the club in 1887, a rising political figure who would become President of the United States in 1901 and would eventually author twenty-four volumes, many of them devoted to the American West; Owen Wister, who was beginning to publish stories of the ranching West in the *Harper's* magazines and who would produce in 1902 the bestselling novel *The Virginian*; and Frederic Remington, who had already begun to illustrate Roosevelt's writings, would soon illustrate Wister's, and was emerging as America's best-known artist of Western cowboys, cavalry, and Indians. Meanwhile, in another order of club at the fair – the meeting of the scholarly American Historical Association – Frederick Jackson Turner, a professor of history at the University of Wisconsin, delivered his famous "Frontier Thesis." And just beyond the gates was William Cody, who was attracting audiences of thousands with Buffalo Bill's Wild West, a new kind of entertainment that converted Western history and skills into commercial spectacle. Together, these five men are generally credited with forging the definitive image of the frontier West.

Yet, within and beyond the fairgrounds, there were intimations of other presences, equally significant to the cultural emergence of the American West yet excluded – by race, gender, class – from the influence of the frontier club or the commercial reach of the entrepreneur. There were, for example, the Native peoples, who were most visible at the exposition as "Show Indians" but were struggling for a degree of autonomy and self-representation in their displays of traditional community. African Americans made a distinct mark on the West as cowboys, settlers, and authors but were reduced to racist stereotypes in the show's coverage. Hispanics worked the cattle ranges but provided little more than exotic "color" at the fair. And women's work as mothers, prostitutes, entrepreneurs, artists and writers had contributed to making the West what it had become but was invisible at the exposition (Bank 2002: 591 and *passim*). All these cultural presences were subordinated in the fair's organizational rhetoric to the vision of Anglo-American male triumphs; and only recently, as scholars have excavated new evidence and asked new questions, has the picture begun to change. Similarly with the frontier story. While the received lineage of Western fiction – in both scholarly and popular parlance – remains dominated by members of the frontier club in this period, more recent scholars have begun to bring forward literary fragments – recovered voices, "lost" publications, newly interrogative analysis – that complicate the record exponentially. This essay tells both these stories, tracing the lines of the established, still influential literary history and attending to some of the re-emerging fragments and tensions which defy scholarly closure.

The Frontier Club

The best-known version of the American West's literary history is a nicely coherent narrative revolving around the five figures named above who – in their complementary cultural roles as politician, author, artist, historian, and showman – harnessed the West rhetorically and symbolically to nationalist and imperialist ends. By this understanding, this group crystallizes the modern Western at a point midway between the American Civil War and the onset of World War I. Everything prior becomes positioned as precursor to this culmination, and everything subsequent simply plays the changes on this definitive model: an adventure-filled version of the interior West of Rocky Mountains and open-range ranching of the late nineteenth century, figured as the climactic meeting point of civilization and savagery.

Although the importing of the American frontier into narrative can be traced back variously – to Puritan captivity narratives, to James Fenimore Cooper's Leatherstocking cycle – it is generally agreed that its decisive incorporation into American popular culture came in 1860, with mass-produced dime novels. The first dime novel house was started by the Beadle brothers, who soon joined with Robert Adams to found Beadle & Adams, with their famous editor Orville J. Victor. Although the West was never the exclusive setting for dime novel adventures, it did provide the first and dominant background for Beadle's thirty-eight years of cheap publications. Number One of Beadle's Dime Novels was *Malaeska, the Indian Wife of the White Hunter*, by Mrs. Ann S. Stephens, a reprint from an 1839 story paper. Set in the early wilderness of the Hudson valley, the action focuses on a Native woman who bears a child to her white husband, then, after his death at the hands of her people, loses her son to his aristocratic New York City relatives, retaining contact only by serving as his nurse-maid. Not until adulthood does the boy learn of his mixed racial heritage, and the knowledge leads him to suicide. The novel ends with Malaeska's death, broken-hearted on her son's grave, and the vow of celibacy by his sweetheart, who has been robbed of a happy future by these events.

Although this work sold at least half a million copies, it did not become the dominant formula for dime novel Westerns. What Orville Victor pronounced "the perfect Dime Novel" arrived on his desk later in 1860, and he went about giving it the editorial push and advertising resources that would ensure its success (Smith 1950: 93). With *Seth Jones; or, The Captives of the Frontier*, Edward S. Ellis brought to the Beadles a plot much more closely modeled on Fenimore Cooper's Leatherstocking Tales, in terms of the focus on captivity, chase, and rescue as white men pursued white women captured by Mohawks in the wilds of western New York State. But Ellis also resolved a central problem of Cooper's work: the tension between the wilderness adventure and the romance imperative. In Cooper's creation Natty Bumppo, or Leatherstocking, remains permanently stranded in that contradiction, lacking the niceties of Eastern social class to attract the woman he desires, locked in his lonely role as the skilled frontiersman necessary to America's western expansion. Ellis's Seth Jones, in contrast, manages to fulfill both roles by the simple device of disguise. For most of the novel, Seth is the uncouth wilderness fighter leading less experienced Easterners in pursuit of their women. At the end, he discards his lowly posture and vernacular speech to reveal himself an aristocrat, well suited for marriage to one of the young captives. The resolution is unbelievable at the level of verisimilitude but satisfying in terms of playing out wilderness adventure in the safety of an Eastern, socially based, happy ending. This was the formula that Victor pronounced perfect. Beadle & Adams roused popular interest with large-scale newspaper notices, bill-boards, and handbills carrying the tantalizing question: "Who Is Seth Jones?" followed by widely circulated lithographs of a coonskin-capped hunter declaring "I am Seth Jones" (Johannsen 1950: vol. 1, 32). The tactics were eminently successful, and this model dominated the growing mass literature market, as a proliferation of series and publishing houses spawned more and more Western narratives. Even when dime novel production shifted largely into juvenile products – around 1898, partly because of strictures imposed by the Postmaster General – clean-cut Western boys such as Deadwood Dick Jr., Young Wild West, and Ted Strong were fashioned to the same design: the Western hero with sufficient measure of Eastern refinement to serve as a love interest; the basic action of captivity, chase, and rescue; and the western-moving frontier, from New York to the Great Lakes, to the west coast and back to the open-range frontier of the Rocky Mountain states.

This was the point at which Roosevelt, Wister, Remington, Turner, and Cody came together – a cultural convergence that converted the dime and nickel Western into a form straddling cultural hierarchies. One context was a cultural panic among Eastern social circles in relation to the West, a reaction both prompted and reflected by Frederick Jackson Turner in his 1893 address at the Columbian Exposition, published the next year as "The Significance of the Frontier in American History." Turner argued that the frontier line, as it advanced westward across America, provided the nation with its distinctive character, separating its identity off decisively from Old World models (which, until Turner, had been argued as the seeds of American culture). On the moving frontier, according to Turner, occurred a repeated regenerative movement, as American men regressed into the savagery necessary to conquer wilderness conditions and then built back up to a state of civilization. The kicker in Turner's argument was that, in the wake of the 1890 census, the open spaces necessary to this distinctive movement were gone. The frontier was officially closed.

Simply put, this vision threatened Anglo-American hegemony. The apparent shrinking of spacious, available land was a further blow to "the Eastern Establishment," already dismayed at the assault on their power by the influx of east European immigrants, uncontrolled urbanization, and unbridled industrialization. One response was to find cultural forms which reasserted that power and integrated it into larger patterns of nationalism, imperialism, and modernity. Owen Wister's reactions were typical of his class and represent the literary edge of the discourse promoted by the frontier club. Himself a wealthy, Harvard-educated Easterner, Wister first encountered the West in 1885, when his doctor sent him to Wyoming as a restorative for his failing health. In this setting, Wister saw regeneration not just for himself but for the nation as a whole. To Wister's eyes (as to those of his club companions) the West retained the freedom from social and legal niceties that could enable the perpetuation of white patriarchal power. Back in the Philadelphia Club one "Autumn evening of 1891, fresh from Wyoming and its wild glories," he began to rewrite the "Alkali Ike" image of the West with stories that bring East and West together on the frontier to forge a new America. His emphasis came partly through the perspective of an Eastern tenderfoot who learns to appreciate the West, partly through romance between Western cowboys and Eastern women, and partly through a discursive philosophizing (by Eastern and Western voices) that rationalizes the Anglo-Saxon masculinism enacted in stories of adventure and violence (Wister 1930: 29).

Intriguingly, the first of these stories, "Hank's Woman" (published in *Harper's Weekly* in 1892), is atypical of Wister's *œuvre*. It focuses on an Austrian woman, Willomene, trapped in marriage to a degenerate cowboy, "little black Hank," in the wilds of Wyoming. The situation ends in tragedy when he shoots the crucifix she refuses to surrender, and she kills him with an axe, then throws herself down the desolate Pitchstone Canyon. From then on, Wister's focus shifted to the adventures of vigorous cowpunchers, among them Lin McLean, Scipio LeMoyne, and, most heroically and most famously, the Virginian – all introduced to the reader by the Eastern tenderfoot narrator and all perpetuating, in fiction, the ways of life and values that seemed threatened by modernizing America. Wister's most explicit bulwark against the disappearing frontier was his 1895 essay "The Evolution of the Cow-Puncher," which opens with the meeting of an English lord and a Western cowboy and proceeds to demonstrate that the latter figure is a direct descendant of the chivalric knight, the essential (but vaguely defined) "Anglo-Saxon," an eternal type who will live on in the true American. The ultimate unification of East and West, past and future, takes place in his bestselling novel *The Virginian* (1902), in which the eponymous cowboy forges a relationship with the Eastern narrator, wins the hand of the Eastern school-ma'am, wipes out rustlers and other criminal elements, then carries essential Western values into the post-frontier age with his elevation to rancher and businessman.

The images produced by Roosevelt, Remington, and Cody in their various ways complemented Wister's writing, but also directly fed print forms of Western narrative. Roosevelt was closest to Wister in terms of both his social network and his vision of the West. Roosevelt, too, had gone west as the result of personal distress – fleeing to his ranch in North Dakota in 1884, after the death of his wife and his mother – and he too saw the open range as a powerful site of renewal: personal, national, and political. In his writings on "the strenuous life" in North Dakota, as in the political rhetoric and campaign paraphernalia that he developed in public office (as Governor of New York State, Vice-President, and, from 1901, President), Roosevelt represented the Western hunter and cowboy as the ideally vigorous, Anglo-Saxon American type who would save the nation from racial impurity, corporate greed, and political corruption. Roosevelt also yoked this idealized image of the open-range West to American imperialism, using the image of the "Rough Rider" – an amalgam of Western cowboy and Eastern gentleman – to justify America's imperial adventures in Cuba, the Philippines, and Puerto Rico. "Rough Riders" was the nickname of the 1st US Volunteer Cavalry put together by Roosevelt at the outbreak of the Spanish–American War in 1898. By extrapolation, the name served a new imperialist heroics that avoided conflation with Old World forms of imperialism, ostensibly anathema to the American political order. The Rough Rider motif also served, in 1904, as the model of a juvenile weekly produced by Street and Smith: *The Young Rough Riders Weekly*, later retitled *Rough Rider Weekly*, with its hero Ted Strong ("tread softly but carry a big stick") clearly crafted in homage to the man who had recently begun his second term in the White House. In this way, Roosevelt's rhetoric was directly written into the popular dissemination of Western adventure stories.

Frederic Remington also came out of the East, though his origins were less moneyed than Wister's and Roosevelt's, and he was never as securely positioned within the club circuit. Like them, he went west in the face of personal difficulties (in 1881 to Montana, then in 1883 to a Kansas sheep ranch). By 1885 he was back in New York with sketches of cowboys, cavalry, and Indians in the Southwest which Eastern periodicals, beginning with *Harper's Magazine* and *Outing*, were keen to publish. He became the pre-eminent artist of the West, in great demand as an illustrator (for Roosevelt and Wister, among others) and a prolific producer of drawings, paintings, and sculpture for the next twenty years. His visual art consistently focuses on the cowboy work, cavalry engagements, and Indian ways that predate the denser settlement of Western lands. His representations can be understood, like Roosevelt's and Wister's, as a means of securing the wild West from encroaching social forms. Remington discovered the limits of this heroic vision, however, when he accompanied the Rough Riders to Cuba: the squalid trenches and technological horrors seemed entirely disjunct from frontier glory, and his writings and drawings from the front reflect his reservations. When he reluctantly painted a canvas of the Rough Riders' charge up Kettle Hill, at Roosevelt's prompting, he showed the men (accurately) on foot in foreboding poses, either actually falling or rushing into great danger. The effect is very different from the dashing "Bronco Buster" sculpture of 1895, which the Rough Riders presented to Roosevelt at the close of their service. For Remington, frontier imagery was not transferable to overseas imperial adventure. A cognate fissure is explicit in his writings: the essays, short stories, and novel which also revolved around cowboys, cavalry, and Native peoples in the nineteenth-century West. Particularly in *John Ermine of the Yellowstone* (1902), Remington dwelt on the dark side of the encounter between East and West, the losses represented by the frontier's inevitable disappearance and the violence accompanying the triumph of Eastern social rule, much more emphatically than Wister. Significantly, Remington's visual art, so much easier to read as celebrating a heroic West, remains famous and instantly recognizable, while his writings are now little known.

William F. Cody came out of a different milieu from the three Easterners, but his contribution was crucial. Born in Iowa, Cody worked all across the Western plains, as a Pony Express rider, stagecoach driver, buffalo hunter, and cavalry scout. Written into numerous dime novels and theatrical pieces as "Buffalo Bill" (first by Ned Buntline from 1869, then by Prentiss Ingraham), Cody subsequently seized control of his own image-making with his invention in 1883 of Buffalo Bill's Wild West, a massively successful spectacle that toured until 1916. Like Wister's fiction, Roosevelt's speeches, and – to a point – Remington's images, the Wild West show re-presented frontier adventure to fit the causes of nationalism and imperialism. At first a type of rodeo demonstrating the traditional skills of Western horsemen, the show became a much more ambitious display of frontier mythology, put together in Turnerian sequences which, the program claimed, re-enacted America's development: from, for example, Pocahontas saving John Smith, through a Plains Indian attack on the Deadwood Coach repulsed by Buffalo Bill and a replay of "Custer's Last Stand" in 1876, up to imperialist conflicts such as the storming of San Juan Hill (actually, Kettle Hill) by Roosevelt's Rough Riders in 1898 and the "Boxer Rebellion" of 1900. Such spectacles were organized into what Richard Slotkin calls the "mythic space" of the show: a rising arc of American triumphalism in which historical and contemporary modes, frontier and imperialist adventures are seamlessly joined (Slotkin 1981: 36). It was no accident that the name coined for the show's 1893 staging outside the Columbian Exposition – the Congress of Rough Riders – was readily adopted for jingoistic use in the Spanish–American War. Cultural imperialism was also foreshadowed when this vision traveled overseas; from 1887 until 1906, the show toured to enthusiastic European audiences that often included royalty, most famously Queen Victoria.

By this account, then, these image-makers together represent the culmination of America's Western narrative, the constellation that produced the nation's dominant and most useful mythology. From that period onwards, all frontier adventure narratives can be read as essentially formulaic repetitions. Perhaps the best-known of the next generation of writers is Zane Grey, who began publishing Westerns in 1910, set a record by appearing in the top ten bestseller list nine times from 1915 to 1924, and ultimately produced fifty-nine Western novels (as well as thirty-three books of Eastern fiction, outdoor adventure, and juvenile stories) (Bold 1987b: 76). Grey emphasized sexual attraction more than Wister, and his settings are more luridly described, but the scenario is familiar, with an Eastern-inflected Western hero standing at the meeting point of savagery and civilization, conquering the one to enable the other and taking the heroine in the process. Thousands of pulp magazines, dozens of writers (such as Max Brand, Jack Schaefer, Louis L'Amour) and, from Edwin S. Porter's 1903 "The Great Train Robbery," movies perpetuate this central storyline. The political climate may change, but the reaffirmation of Anglo-American masculine power in the pre-civilized wilderness continues to serve the national interest.

This, in outline, is the version of literary and cultural history produced by the "big books" of scholarship. Henry Nash Smith's *Virgin Land* (1950) was the first to bring attention to the significance of dime novels to the development of America's Western mythology, but interest in turn-of-the-century Western literature really took off only in the 1960s and 1970s, when Leslie Fiedler, John Cawelti, and others began to trace the formulaic elements and cultural uses of Western narratives. In 1968 G. Edward White – in a key event for Western studies – produced a deeply researched study of the political and social networks out of which Wister, Roosevelt, and Remington emerged, showing how America's most powerful mythology originated in the class relations of the East. The most thorough treatment was Richard Slotkin's, in three massive volumes that trace the patterns and uses of frontier narratives from 1860 to the Cold War: *Regeneration through Violence* (1973), *The Fatal Environment* (1985), and *Gunfighter Nation* (1992). Slotkin's great contribution was to show not only how the dominant frontier myth organizes perceptions of the West but also how thoroughly and broadly the formulaic Western narrative is tied into multiple discourses of American public life and how the formula's starkest version has provided a vocabulary of justification for onslaughts on human rights. In the later nineteenth century, for example, while the key creators were developing their written and visual images, newspapers used the language of frontier conflict to represent striking industrial laborers as "savages" akin to Western Indians who had to be exterminated if civilization were to flourish (Slotkin 1985: 480–9).

Other Voices, Other Wests

So what does this account – like the Columbian Exposition – subordinate or erase? There are many writers who could be added to the record for this period. There were novelists whose combination of Western adventure and romance was similar to Wister's: Emerson Hough, for example, was preferred by critic Douglas E. Branch.

There were also nonfiction writers such as Andy Adams, whose *Log of a Cowboy* (1903) was considered more powerful than any fictional Western by the historian Walter Prescott Webb. Then there were those authors whose sights were trained on geocultural areas quite different from the open-range ranches: the Southwestern desert of Mary Austin's meditations; the very different West Coast of Mark Twain, Bret Harte, Gertrude Atherton, and Sui Sin Far; the Middle Border farmland of Hamlin Garland; the ironic frontier of Stephen Crane; and the cross-country journeys documented in numerous diaries, letters, and journals by female and male travelers. In today's cultural climate, however, what seems most urgently to demand attention is the range of culturally diverse voices – Native peoples, African Americans, Hispanics, women of varied ethnicity – who took on the popularized West and yet were long omitted from the record. Recently, there has begun the recovery and analysis of voices from the period that, together, powerfully expose and challenge the assumptions and exclusions of the frontier club while richly multiplying the West's cultural meanings. Although these voices tell a range of stories, they share a common difference: while their West is a place of adventure and challenge, it is not the ultimate testing ground on which white men prove their own, and by extension the nation's, dominance by subduing land, animals, women, and people of other races. In these accounts, the West is rarely a safety valve or a culmination: it is more often a starting place, a temporary labor opportunity, an area deeply implicated in national issues of slavery, Native peoples' rights, equality for women. In other words, the West is not the frontier.

An early work by Houston A. Baker, Jr. challenges "the vested interests" of white America (including its scholars and intellectuals) to realize the distinctiveness of black American culture: "When the black American reads Frederick Jackson Turner's *The Frontier in American History*, he feels no regret over the end of the Western frontier. To black America, *frontier* is an alien word; for, in essence, all frontiers established by the white psyche have been closed to the black man" (1972: 2). One of the first debates among the New Western historians, when that field took off in the 1980s, concerned the nationalism, racism, and ethnocentrism of the very term "frontier," as well as the fictiveness of its "closing" (Limerick 1991: 85–6). Certainly, the voices considered in this section do not articulate space as a wave of movement, from East to West, mowing down wilderness and regressive types in order to open up opportunity, freedom, individualism for true Americans. Native peoples found themselves hemmed in by white settler-invaders on all sides, their space of possibility shrinking in the inexorable process of genocide. Many Mexican Americans found themselves trapped on the wrong side of a newly established national border after the Treaty of Guadalupe Hidalgo in 1848. Black pioneers experienced the frontier as a closed society to which they struggled to gain entrance in search of their rightful "share of the nation's wealth" (Baker 1972: 4). All of these racial groups "stole" what power they achieved, in forays that were often furtive and sporadic and had none of the formalist shape or teleological trajectory of frontierism.

Figure 10.1 Chinese workers building the Central Pacific Railroad

Chinese immigrants comprised 90 percent of the laborers who built the Central Pacific Railroad – the western part of the transcontinental line. Between 1865 and 1869 the 12,000 Chinese workers used great ingenuity in laying track, leveling roadbeds, blasting through mountains, and boring tunnels. On May 10, 1869, at Promontory Summit, Utah, the Central Pacific line that began in Sacramento, California joined with the Union Pacific line that started in Omaha, Nebraska. Together, the two lines consisted of 1,776 miles of new tracks. The lines were attached with a golden spike in a famous photograph that showed dignitaries, company officials, and the mostly Irish immigrant laborers from the Union Pacific – but the Chinese workers of the Central Pacific were not invited to the ceremony. Thirteen years later, in 1882, Congress passed the Chinese Exclusion Act, which prohibited Chinese immigrants from entering the country and declared the Chinese ineligible for American citizenship – a ban that would last until 1943.

In this photograph, workers transport dirt by carts to fill in the Secrettown Trestle in the Sierra Nevada Mountains. (Photograph by permission of Union Pacific Historical Collection/Union Pacific Railroad Museum.)

Despite the immense obstacles for Native peoples in the West in gaining access to print publication, several managed to publish powerful works that spoke from their distinctively located perspective. Sarah Winnemucca (Hopkins) (Piute) was the first Native woman in print with a mixture of personal narrative and tribal ethnography, with *Life among the Piutes; Their Wrongs and Claims* in 1883. Although this work is more historical than fictional, her representation of her own adventures in Nevada seems shaped by recognizable dime novel techniques of suspense and sensationalism. She shows from the inside the terror of white colonization and the injustices of government officials and policies. Similar mixtures of autobiography, history, and traditional tales – and similar critiques of government – inform the writings of Charles Eastman (Sioux), who collaborated with his non-Native wife Elaine Eastman from 1894 to 1921. The first full-fledged novel about Native life by a Native author was *O-gî-mäw-kwe Mit-i-gwä-kî, Queen of the Woods* (1899) by Simon Pokagon (Pota-watomi). Although many of these works are situated in the same geographical regions as the works of Wister and Remington, the Native perspectives shift the dynamic of Western expansion, demonstrating its costs to community life. The triumphs are those of survival rather than conquest.

In 1971 William Loren Katz issued a stirring call for attention to long-neglected black Westerners, and set about reconstructing the contributions of historical black cowboys and settlers. There is now increasing recovery of African American stories of the West, which explicitly sought a popular audience and used familiar geographical settings and motifs of adventure. The centrality of black figures in these works rings the changes in at least three ways: heroism is no longer the preserve of the Anglo-American; cowboy work is comparable with other forms of labor; and property and marriage – staple components in the Western hero's success – are experienced as social problems. Even in the African American works most akin to the formulaic fictions of the frontier club, the West is not a utopian land set off from the nation – a vision most famously popularized by Zane Grey's *Riders of the Purple Sage* (1912), which ends with the male and female protagonists cutting themselves off from the world in a hidden valley.

Take, for example, *The Life and Adventures of Nat Love* (1907), the ostensibly autobiographical tale of a black cowboy on the Western plains, and *The Conquest* (1913) by Oscar Micheaux (better known as a film-maker), the somewhat fictionalized experiences of black pioneer Oscar Devereaux in South Dakota. In many ways, the action of Love's narrative is highly formulaic. This account of his pursuit by members of Yellow Dog's tribe across the Texas plains – a scene familiar from countless dime novels and, later, "B" movies – is typical of his representation of his own prowess and of Native people:

> as I had considerable objection to being chased by a lot of painted savages without some remonstrance, I turned in my saddle every once in a while and gave them a shot by way of greeting, and I had the satisfaction of seeing a painted brave tumble from his horse and go rolling in the dust every time my rifle spoke.

It is all the more startling, then, that Love's narrator documents a thoroughly unfamiliar racial scene, not only regularly pointing to his own blackness but enumerating the black cowboys whom he encounters – "several" in the Texas outfit, six in the roping contest in Deadwood. Similarly, Oscar Devereaux insistently remarks on his status as the sole colored person on the South Dakota frontier, with the attendant problems of this racial isolation. Structurally, neither work positions the West as a narrative climax. Both protagonists intertwine their Western work with jobs as Pullman porters. For Love, indeed, the Pullman job is the acme of his career and ultimate symbol of the nation's progress; Devereaux returns to Pullman stints every time his settlement plans go awry. Their relationship to property is also disorienting for the reader accustomed to the formulaic signs of success, such as the ranches that the Virginian and Ted Strong come to own. Both Love and Devereaux begin life *as* property, that is, within the category of the nonhuman: Love describes his birth as an enslaved person who is unrecorded property, then his childhood experiences of being treated like a horse, a cow, or at best "like a pet dog." The stakes in these journeys west are much higher than for the white adventurers; these narrators seek to be recognized as fully human members of an American community. Part of the complication in that search revolves around the romantic interest – the second signal of frontier success. Micheaux's narrator, in a familiar move, says that romance is the motive force of his account. In this case, however, color changes everything: as an isolated black on South Dakota's frontier, Devereaux cannot marry the white woman with whom he enjoys a mutual attraction. Instead, he returns to Chicago to find a black wife, setting in motion a spiral of unhappiness and despair. The novel ends abruptly, with a stillborn child, the wife fleeing to her father, and the pioneer's crops failing.

More obviously heroic resistance was offered by Mexican American *corridos*, fast-paced ballads of adventurous struggle against Anglo colonization which circulated mainly in Spanish. Around the turn of the century, one of the most popular concerned Gregorio Cortez, a Mexican-born *vaquero* persecuted by southern Texas lawmen. Especially in light of the casual racism afforded Hispanics in many popular Western narratives, the *corridos'* glorification of the fast-shooting, hard-riding hero reads like a writing back to the dominant culture: "He represents an attempt by Mexican-Americans to reclaim the most admired qualities of *vaquero* culture – horsemanship, marksmanship, courage, and endurance – which Anglo-Americans had appropriated. The *corrido* Cortez is, quite simply, a John Wayne in brownface" (Paredes 1987: 1084). The emerging Hispanic writings in English of the period – for example, the stories and sketches of María Cristina Mena in the *Century* and *American* magazines of the 1910s – are seen as paler and more genteel than the vigorous *corridos*.

And what of white women's contributions to this most masculinist of genres? Among the many who wrote of the open range in this period – Molly Moore Davis, Caroline Lockhart, Honoré Willsie Morrow, among others – the most prolific was B. M. Bower. She produced over seventy Westerns, which appeared between 1904 and 1953, the best known of them making up the "Flying U" series set on a Montana ranch. Again, many of Bower's adventures are conventional: calamities and hair-raising rescues on cattle drives, pitched battles with rustlers and outlaws, romance between Western cowboys and Eastern women. Yet her narratives also distinctively emphasize community (particularly the "Happy Family" of ranch workers), independent women workers, and the comic. For example, in *Chip of the Flying U* (serialized by Street and Smith in 1904), Della Whitemore comes west to visit her rancher brother. A trained physician, she defeats various attempts to undermine her authority as a "girl doctor," including shooting a coyote from a swaying wagon within an hour's arrival in the West, saving the hero's fallen horse from slaughter by setting its broken leg, and persuading Chip to exhibit his talents as an artist. Lynching in this story is a joke – performed with a stuffed dummy to frighten the "old maid" from the East; shades of good and bad complicate easy moral distinctions; and, although the ending devolves into the recognizable romantic resolution between Chip and Della, chapter headings such as "Love and a Stomach Pump" undermine the sentimentalism.

We do not yet have "big books" shaping this diverse output into the explanatory patterns and causal narratives that would produce an alternative history of the literary West. What we have are fragments of recovery and analysis: scholars such as P. Jane Hafen (Taos Pueblo) and Sally Zanjani expanding access to Native women's voices of the period, Blake Allmendinger analyzing Nat Love's writings as black cowboy and Pullman porter, M. K. Johnson reconsidering Oscar Micheaux's African American take on frontier mythology, Vicki Piekarski and Norris Yates excavating long-lost women writers, Jane Tompkins repositioning nineteenth-century women from the sidelines to the centre of the genre, as the motive force of the modern Western written by men to rebuff women's newfound power in the literary and public spheres. It has been nearly forty years since Philip Durham and Everett L. Jones called on the academic establishment and cultural producers to open up "the heritage of the West" to "all Americans" (Durham and Jones 1965: 229–30), yet cultural diversity has to date neither made much of a dent on the popular image nor cohered into a pattern. Perhaps that is as good a place as any to start – without pattern, but with fragments and a sense of urgency. The less familiar names cited in this essay (along with dozens which remain uncited) did not belong to the frontier club, but they are there for the finding, writing their own Wests, if we look for them.

Around 1902

The difference that this revisionist literary history might make to how we read Westerns can be suggested by focusing on a particular moment within the period: 1902. This was the year in which Owen Wister's *The Virginian* appeared and soon took on bestselling status: reprinted fifteen times in its first year, it notched up sales of 300,000 in its first two years (Frantz and Choate 1955: 5–6; Meyer 1974: 667/25). There is a longstanding tendency to figure that success as the genre's sole point of crystallization. As Lee Clark Mitchell noted, "Choose any history of the Western, and Owen Wister's *The Virginian* (1902) will invariably be cited as *the* transitional text – responsible all by itself for making the restrained, soft-spoken, sure-shooting cowboy into a figure worthy of sustained popular interest" (1996: 95). A one-man-genre narrative of literary history has been particularly evident since the 1960s in the work of Leslie Fiedler, John Cawelti, Richard Etulain, Ray Allen Billington, and others.

This version of literary history now seems both simplistic and ideologically fraught, a tale of heroic individualism that mimics the emphases of the novel. This history promotes the "faith in a single authority" that Susan Rosowski has worried about ideologically with popular Westerns (1999: 289): "It is a claim to authority in the most basic sense, that is, to author an identity for a nation" (p. 290). This historical narrative also erases difference or the presence of minority voices in American culture. G. Edward White's analysis, for example, is marked by repeated elisions of the values of Wister's social class with the values upheld in Wister's fiction and with the values that structure White's own literary history. For example, White's case for Wister as a cultural synthesizer partly depends upon a characterization of his readership as universal: those who read *The Virginian* become "the American reading public" *tout court*. White repeatedly claims that "the idealized traits" of Wister's hero matched "the aspirations of Americans at the close of the nineteenth century" (1968: 140) – which Americans? we need to ask. At the same time, he treats "Americans" and "immigrants" as separate categories, as does the rhetoric of the frontier club. Ultimately, this is literary and cultural history incorporated into the nation-building exercise, supporting the hegemony that it documents.

In fact, 1902 saw numerous fictions that grappled with the modernization of the West. Among them were Frances McElrath's *The Rustler*, Frederic Remington's *John Ermine*, and Mary Hallock Foote's *The Desert and the Sown*. The Yankton Sioux Zitkala Ša published "Why I Am a Pagan" in the *Atlantic Monthly* and "A Warrior's Daughter" in *Everybody's Magazine*. Novels by black authors included Pauline Hopkins's *Winona* and Sutton E. Griggs's *Unfettered*. The Mexican American broadside *corrido* about Gregorio Cortez's 1901 adventures was circulating. And cheap fiction – including Frank Tousey's new juvenile nickel series *Wild West Weekly* – proliferated. All this and more was on the market simultaneously. Considering just a few examples shows the competing stories, character relations, and ideological systems in play at the same moment.

Some works read almost like direct refutations of *The Virginian*. Wister's plot, told intermittently in the voice of an Eastern narrator, focuses on a cowboy as skilled with words as he is with cattle and guns, who rises to ranch foreman, then partner, then landowner and local businessman. His crossing of class barriers is particularly signified by his ability to woo and wed the cultured schoolma'am from the East, Molly Stark, who initially rebuffs his approaches but eventually is won over not only to him but to his entire code of conduct, which includes lynching rustlers and gunning down his longstanding nemesis, Trampas.

Almost the same scenario in Frances McElrath's *The Rustler* leads to diametrically opposite results. As Victoria Lamont has discussed, *The Rustler*, like *The Virginian*, is a fictionalization of the Johnson County War – the struggle of large, often Eastern stockmen against small ranchers and cowboys in Wyoming that culminated in 1892 with the stockmen murdering two suspected rustlers, and the army removing the stockmen and ultimately protecting them from prosecution. In Wister's hands, right is clearly on the side of the large ranchers: much of the Virginian's philosophizing is aimed at defending his own violent eradication of rustlers, action that he takes explicitly on the orders of his employer Judge Henry (a fictionalized version of a Wyoming rancher). McElrath gives us access to another perspective, showing the damage done by the importation of Eastern social mores to the West. Jim, a foreman on a ranch – this time in Montana, though the action moves later to Wyoming – is

Figure 10.2   The revolution in agriculture
After the Civil War, the rise of large cities and the increasingly global economy led to an expanded market and
the adoption of labor-saving technology on the farm. The revolution began in the 1860s and 1870s with the
shift from human to horse and mule power, as in this early 1900s photograph in which thirty-three mules pull
a combine across a Pacific wheat field. In 1870, agricultural workers comprised 52 percent of the American
workforce, but by 1900 this figure had fallen to 40 percent. At the same time, the value produced per
agricultural worker rose sharply – by 43 percent between 1870 and 1900. In 1830, it took 250–300 labor
hours to produce one hundred bushels of wheat; by 1890, that had been cut to 40–50 labor hours, and the
United States had become the breadbasket of the world. By the 1910s horses and mules were being replaced by
gas-powered engines, leading to even greater economies of scale, further displacement of rural populations, the
rise of corporate agriculture, and the eventual demise of the family farm. (Photograph courtesy of Caterpillar
Inc. Corporate Archives.)

attracted to a high-society Eastern visitor, Hazel Clifford. She leads him on, posing as
a humble teacher, only to humiliate him at the moment when he believes marriage is
possible. In reaction, he becomes a rustler, stealing from the landed class whose
condescension is symbolized in Hazel's treatment of him and building his fiefdom
in Wyoming's notorious Hole-in-the-Wall. Just as Jim repents and returns his ill-
gotten gains to the state, he is gunned down. Hazel, whom he has kidnapped to his
outlaw hideout, cares for him on his deathbed. Subsequently she releases her Eastern
fiancé from their engagement and dedicates her future to the education and nurturing
of the former outlaws' children. In this romance plot, class emerges as "the impassible
barrier of natural difference" – no matter how talented and hardworking the humble
cowboy, he can never reach across the class differences signaled by costume, language,
money, and geocultural alliances.

Frederic Remington's *John Ermine* dramatizes similar impossibilities, although this time the eponymous protagonist attempts to reach across racial as well as class lines. John Ermine, who is biologically of white parentage, has been raised in the wilds of Montana by the Crow or Absaroke, who train him in wilderness skills. Attempting to rejoin "the brotherhood of the white kind," he begins to scout for the US cavalry and at their military outpost meets Katherine Searles, the major's daughter on a visit from the East. Again, the Western man believes that the Eastern woman is attracted to him, only to have his marriage proposal humiliatingly rejected. When Katherine's fiancé, Lieutenant Butler, confronts Ermine with a drawn gun, demanding the return of her photograph, Ermine shoots him in the arm and flees. Later, as he returns to kill Butler, Ermine is killed from ambush by a Crow scout who bears a grudge. This denouement demonstrates not only that there can be no integration of East and West but that indigenous Westerners like John Ermine (and, earlier, James Fenimore Cooper's Natty Bumppo) who lend their skills to Eastern settlement inevitably bring about their own destruction. Both novels carry direct echoes of *The Virginian*, especially in the romantic action: when Jim "does his toilet" prior to proposing to Hazel he acts out the same nervous ritual as the Virginian; when John Ermine offers to "make a good camp in the mountains" with Katherine, he is proposing exactly the same honeymoon as the Virginian provides for Molly. The difference is that Katherine laughs in Ermine's face.

Relatively close to these works in geographical setting, but a chasm apart in cultural location, are the writings of Zitkala Ša, a Yankton Sioux. Zitkala Ša's work appeared in some of the same periodicals as Wister's, but her adventures come from the other side of the white myth of progress; it was a myth whose costs she intimately knew. The two pieces that appeared in 1902 are typical of this author's range: one, in a first-person voice, reflects on the narrator's resistance to a Christianity that is colonizing her people and fracturing their spiritual relationship with the land; the other tells the adventures of a fierce young Sioux girl rescuing her warrior lover from captivity by an enemy tribe. The balance of interest here is all with Native peoples – especially Native women – who are never offered power or agency. They have to seize it through initiative and courage. In the context of a genocide erasing her people from national narratives, Zitkala Ša's insistence on voice and centrality was a powerful strategy for cultural survival.

Most distant, geographically and generically, from *The Virginian* is Pauline Hopkins's *Winona*. This serialized novel was part of an attempt to create a popular black press by a "colored co-operative" of writers and editors in Boston at the turn of the century. They began *The Colored American Magazine*, priced it at fifteen cents an issue and attempted a circulation to rival the Euro-American slicks currently filling the market. Although the experiment was only partly successful – with the magazine going to New York City as an organ of the National Negro Business League after four years – it does offer a fascinating insight into the uses to which popular American iconology and mythology were put by a politicized black community (Carby 1988: xxx). *Winona* uses recognizable dime-novel techniques of characterization, setting, and action (as analysed by Nicole Tonkovich) to tell the story of a young woman in the mid-nineteenth century who is the product of an aristocratic European-gone-Indian and his African American wife. Winona lives an idyllic life in the wilds of the borderland between New York State and Canada with her father and her African American friend Judah – until her father is suddenly killed by a Missouri plantation owner and his overseer. They steal Winona and Judah back to their plantation – a legal move under the recently passed fugitive slave law – there to subject the boy in particular to a series of violent and demeaning experiences designed to break his spirit. Eventually the two are rescued by Warren Maxwell, an English lawyer searching for Winona as the rightful heir to a landed estate. After a thrilling escape back across the border to Canada, Warren marries Winona and takes her and Judah back to England, where Judah marries into a rich English family.

This tale exists in rich counterpoint to Wister's, particularly in its treatment of the South. *The Virginian* repeatedly severs connections between South and West: the hero has cast off his Southern family specifically to find freedom of opportunity and action in the West; Judge Henry delivers a long speech to Molly clarifying the ways in which lynching in the West is entirely unrelated to and untainted by lynching in the South. The two cultural regions are linked primarily in the niceness of the Virginian's manners. In *Winona*, in contrast, West and South are inextricably intertwined. Not only does the action insistently move back and forth between frontier and plantation, but the characters' heritage is a mixture of both regions, and the nation's laws arise from and affect regional power struggles. One compelling scene shows Judah demonstrating his manly credentials by breaking a bucking bronco by means of the whip, then almost immediately himself being seized and whipped brutally by the white overseer intent on breaking his spirit. The violent assertion of manliness in both cases – the one so paradigmatic of frontier stories, the other of Southern slave tales – is pointedly similar.

With the geographical linkages comes, also, a racial mixing that is repudiated in *The Virginian*. The ruling class of that novel consistently argues for whiteness and racial purity, while the setting demarcates a "pure" West, separate and distinctive. The legacy of *The Virginian* remains highly visible, in reductive form, in run-of-the-mill movie Westerns: the white hat always wins. *Winona* celebrates the cross-racial heritage of the heroine who can marry the Anglo-Saxon, the African American who thrives in English society. It is the white supremacists who lose, morally and actually, in this adventure story. *Pace* Wister, Remington, Roosevelt, and especially Turner, the authorial voice in *Winona* declares there is no "line" in the frontier West:

> Many strange tales of romantic happenings in this mixed community of Anglo-Saxons, Indians and Negroes might be told similar to the one I am about to relate, and the world stand aghast and try in vain to find the dividing line supposed to be a natural barrier between the whites and the dark-skinned race. No; social intercourse may be long in coming, but its advent is sure; the mischief is already done. (Hopkins 1988: 287)

Attending to these very different cultural voices makes one alive to their presence –
in highly repressed form – in *The Virginian*. Toni Morrison has argued that an
"Africanism," deeply suppressed within literary works and national discourses, "provided the staging ground and arena for the elaboration of the quintessential American
identity" (1992: 44). Especially when we compare Wister's cast to Nat Love's roll-call
of black working cowboys, we begin to detect the traces of black presence in the
Virginian's racist jokes and songs and in "little black Hank," Scipio LeMoyne, and
the Virginian himself, all of whose ambiguous coloring and naming lead them to
insist repeatedly on their own whiteness. Similarly, reading Zitkala Ša brings us alive
to the startling absence of Native characters in *The Virginian*. Although the hero is at
one point critically injured by what is implied are Indian warriors, they never appear,
and there is no sense of Native agency in this Western scene. All that can be glimpsed
are stolid "Indian chiefs" in blankets, silent witnesses to the cowboys' fun. Following
Toni Morrison's analysis, it becomes clear that in *The Virginian* the triumph of the
Anglo-Saxon Western hero depends on a network of racialized others – black cowboys,
black Pullman porters, Native American inhabitants and guides, Chinese railroad
workers, Jewish salesmen, women entrepreneurs. All of them were necessary –
historically, to the popularization of the West and fictively, to the dynamics of
Wister's novel – yet their participation is doubly obscured: first dispelled to the
margins of *The Virginian*, then further erased by cultural and literary histories
insistent on that novel's paradigmatic status. If we want to record who authored the
popular West, we have to pay attention to these figures too.

That such an exclusive cultural narrative is not inevitable is suggested by other
disciplinary methods. When theatre historian Roger Hall, for example, discusses the
dramatization of *The Virginian*, adapted by Wister and Kirk La Shelle and first staged
in 1904 with Dustin Farnum in the lead role, he does not treat it as a singular or a
culminating event. This production figures as one of a constellation of turn-of-the-
century popular frontier dramas – including Augustus Thomas's *Arizona*, Edwin
Milton Royle's *The Squaw Man*, and David Belasco's *The Girl of the Golden West* –
credited with creating a public appetite for the modern Western, a decidedly collaborative process from Hall's disciplinary perspective. Similarly, John Dorst has worked
through visual and material culture studies to reconfigure "the Wister moment" in
the cultural history of the American West. Dorst's terms represent a generational
shift. Where White or Cawelti characterized Wister's writing as masterfully joining
East and West in a triumph of synthesis, Dorst discusses it as a visually charged
"nexus" (1999: 41), "the primary conduit" through which nineteenth-century materials and twentieth-century conventions met in an emerging consumer culture (1999:
218, n. 5). A similarly reconstructed literary history would return Wister's writing to
the company it once kept, centering those very many voices currently being recovered,
not as "also-rans" – precursors to or imitators of – Wister, but as participants in the
process of writing the West. Even limiting the focus to the turn of the twentieth
century there is, as we have seen, a multitude of culturally diverse writers to be
reckoned with.

Such a variegated reconstruction would also allow us to ask the crucial question: *why*, out of all the possibilities, was the impact of *The Virginian* on both popular readership and academic scholarship so distinctive? Why, for example, has it taken a century to return Frances McElrath to print, and why are her life and career still smothered in such obscurity? What does this case tell us about how popular and academic reputations are made? About the constitutive force of the material conditions of production and circulation? It seems less than a coincidence, for example, that of all the voices considered here, Wister was the one with the most prestigious Eastern connections, the one, indeed, who belonged to the same club as his original publisher. How much do our accepted mythologies of the West continue to go under the sway of the frontier club?

Conclusion

And so we are on the cusp of new literary histories, as more and more forgotten works are recovered, enabling different connections and mythologies to be made. The false starts and muffled echoes are intriguing: the lengthy history of dime novels, starting with a long-neglected woman-centered Western whose concerns echo eerily in the ending of *The Rustler* and are answered in another key by *Winona*; Wister, who acknowledged a primary debt to Mary Hallock Foote, beginning his writing career with an Eastern woman who refuses to bow to Western male domination and pays the price; Remington unable to illustrate his only female character; women's collision with Montana ranch culture echoing through Bower and McElrath right to the present day with Judy Blunt. The importing of the US frontier into narrative during the 1865–1914 period increasingly seems a highly managed exercise. First, a constellation of public voices – publisher, writer, visual artist, politician, scholar, showman – came together to popularize a vivid and heroic version of the American West. Some time later, academic forces conjoined to canonize that version as the dominant literary history of the Western narrative. As a result, there is today an established history of the frontier narrative that is nicely arced, complete, and closed in its internal coherence. There are also, dimly and coming recently to light, glimmerings of other stories and another, less coherent and hegemonic version of how, by whom, and for whom frontier narratives of the period were produced. This essay has attended to both those stories. They tell us as much about our time and our progressive narratives of "modernity" as they do about the turn of the last century.

AUTHOR'S NOTE

The research for this essay was made possible by a generous grant from the College of Arts Research Enhancement Fund, University of Guelph.

PRIMARY TEXTS

Adams, Andy. *The Log of a Cowboy: A Narrative of the Old Trail Days*. 1903.

An Old Scout [Cornelius Shea]. *Young Wild West: The Prince of the Saddle*. 1902.

Bower, B. M. *Chip of the Flying U*. 1906.

Bower, B. M. *The Lonesome Trail*. 1909.

Bower, B. M. *The Happy Family*. 1910.

Bower, B. M. *Flying U Ranch*. 1912.

Buntline, Ned [E. Z. C. Judson]. "Buffalo Bill, the King of Border Men! The Wildest and Truest Story I Ever Wrote." 1869–70.

Davis, Molly F. Moore. *The Wire-Cutters*. 1899.

Ellis, Edward S. *Seth Jones; or, The Captives of the Frontier*. 1860.

Foote, Mary Hallock. *The Led-Horse Claim: A Romance of a Mining Camp*. 1883.

Foote, Mary Hallock. *The Desert and the Sown*. 1902.

Grey, Zane. *The Heritage of the Desert*. 1910.

Grey, Zane. *Riders of the Purple Sage*. 1912.

Griggs, Sutton E. *Unfettered: A Novel*. 1902.

Hopkins, Pauline. *Winona: A Tale of Negro Life in the South and Southwest*. 1902.

Hopkins, Sarah Winnemucca. *Life among the Piutes; Their Wrongs and Claims*. 1883.

Hough, Emerson. *The Girl at the Halfway House: A Story of the Plains*. 1900.

Hough, Emerson. *Heart's Desire: The Story of a Contented Town, Certain Peculiar Citizens and Two Fortunate Lovers*. 1905.

Ingraham, Prentiss. *Buck Taylor, King of the Cowboys; or, The Raiders and the Rangers: A Story of the Wild and Thrilling Life of William L. Taylor*. 1887.

Ingraham, Prentiss. *Buffalo Bill's Bodyguard; or, The Still Hunt of the Hills: The Story of the "Robber of the Ranges."* 1892.

Lockhart, Caroline. *"Me—Smith."* 1911.

Lockhart, Caroline. *The Lady Doc*. 1912.

Love, Nat. *The Life and Adventures of Nat Love*. 1907.

McElrath, Frances. *The Rustler: A Tale of Love and War in Wyoming*. 1902.

Micheaux, Oscar. *The Conquest: The Story of a Negro Pioneer*. 1913.

Morrow, Honoré Willsie. *The Heart of the Desert*. 1912.

Morrow, Honoré Willsie. *Still Jim*. 1914.

Pokagon, Simon (Potawatomi). *O-gî-mäw-kwe Mit-i-gwä-kî, Queen of the Woods*. 1899.

Remington, Frederic. *Pony Tracks*. 1895.

Remington, Frederic. *Crooked Trails*. 1898.

Remington, Frederic. *Sundown Leflare*. 1899

Remington, Frederic. *John Ermine of the Yellowstone*. 1902.

Remington, Frederic. *The Way of an Indian*. 1906.

Roe, Vingie E. *The Heart of Night Wind*. 1913.

Roosevelt, Theodore. *Hunting Trips of a Ranchman*. 1885.

Roosevelt, Theodore. *Ranch Life and the Hunting Trail*. 1888.

Roosevelt, Theodore. *The Rough Riders*. 1899.

Roosevelt, Theodore. *The Winning of the West*. 1889–95.

Stephens, Mrs. Ann S. *Malaeska; The Indian Wife of the White Hunter*. 1839.

Taylor, Ned [St. George Rathborne]. *Ted Strong's Rough Riders; or, The Boys of Black Mountain*. 1904.

Wheeler, Edward L. *Deadwood Dick, the Prince of the Road; or, the Black Rider of the Black Hills*. 1877.

Wister, Owen. "Hank's Woman." 1892.

Wister, Owen. "The Evolution of the Cow-Puncher." 1895.

Wister, Owen. *Red Men and White*. 1895.

Wister, Owen. *Lin McLean*. 1897.

Wister, Owen. *The Jimmyjohn Boss and Other Stories*. 1900.

Wister, Owen. *The Virginian: A Horseman of the Plains*. 1902.

Wister, Owen. *Members of the Family*. 1911.

Zitkala Ša. "A Warrior's Daughter." 1902.

Zitkala Ša. "Why I Am a Pagan." 1902.

REFERENCES AND FURTHER READING

Allmendinger, Blake (1998). *Ten Most Wanted: The New Western Literature*. New York: Routledge.

Baker, Houston A., Jr. (1972). *Long Black Song: Essays in Black American Literature and Culture*. Charlottesville: University Press of Virginia.

Bank, Rosemarie K. (2002). "Representing History: Performing the Columbian Exposition." *Theatre Journal* 54: 4, 589–606.

Billington, Ray Allen (1981). *Land of Savagery, Land of Promise: The European Image of the American Frontier in the Nineteenth Century*. New York: Norton.

Boatright, Mody (1951). "The American Myth Rides the Range." *Southwest Review* 36: 3, 157–63.

Bold, Christine (1987a). "The Rough Riders at Home and Abroad: Cody, Roosevelt, Remington and the Imperialist Hero." *Canadian Review of American Studies* 18: 3, 321–50.

Bold, Christine (1987b). *Selling the Wild West: Popular Western Fiction, 1860 to 1960*. Bloomington: Indiana University Press.

Bold, Christine (1996). "Malaeska's Revenge; or, the Dime Novel Tradition in Popular Fiction." In Richard Aquila (ed.), *Wanted Dead or Alive: The American West in Popular Culture*, 21–42. Urbana: University of Illinois Press.

Branch, Douglas (1926). *The Cowboy and His Interpreters*. New York: D. Appleton.

Carby, Hazel V. (1988). Introduction. In *The Magazine Novels of Pauline Hopkins*, xxix–l. New York: Oxford University Press.

Cawelti, John G. [1971]. *The Six-Gun Mystique*. Bowling Green, Ohio: Bowling Green University Popular Press.

Cawelti, John G. (1976). *Adventure, Mystery and Romance: Formula Stories as Art and Popular Culture*. Chicago: University of Chicago Press.

Dorst, John D. (1999). *Looking West*. Philadelphia: University of Pennsylvania Press.

Durham, Philip, and Jones, Everett L. (1965). *The Negro Cowboys*. New York: Dodd, Mead.

Etulain, Richard W. (1973). *Owen Wister*. Boise, Idaho: Boise State College. (Boise State College Western Writers Series no. 7.)

Etulain, Richard W. (1996). *Reimagining the Modern American West: A Century of Fiction, History, and Art*. Tucson: University of Arizona Press.

Fiedler, Leslie (1968). *The Return of the Vanishing American*. New York: Stein & Day.

Frantz, Joe B., and Choate, Julian Ernest, Jr. (1955). *The American Cowboy: The Myth and the Reality*. Norman: University of Oklahoma Press.

Graulich, Melody, and Tatum, Stephen, eds. (2003). *Reading* The Virginian *in the New West*. Lincoln: University of Nebraska Press.

Hall, Roger A. (2001). *Performing the American Frontier 1870–1906*. Cambridge, UK: Cambridge University Press.

Hopkins, Pauline (1988). *Winona: A Tale of Negro Life in the South and Southwest*. In *The Magazine Novels of Pauline Hopkins*, intr. Hazel V. Carby, 285–437. New York: Oxford University Press (The Schomburg Library of Nineteenth-Century Black Women Writers.)

Johannsen, Albert (1950, 1962). *The House of Beadle and Adams and its Dime and Nickel Novels: The Story of a Vanished Literature*, 2 vols., with supplement. Norman: University of Oklahoma Press.

Johnson, M. K. (1998). "'Stranger in a Strange Land': An African American Response to the Frontier Tradition in Oscar Micheaux's *The Conquest: The Story of a Negro Pioneer*." *Western American Literature* 33: 3, 229–52.

Johnson, Michael K. (2002). *Black Masculinity and the Frontier Myth in American Literature*. Norman: University of Oklahoma Press.

Katz, William Loren (1987). *The Black West*, 3rd edn. Seattle: Open Hand Publishing. (First publ. 1971.)

Katz, William Loren (1997). *Black Indians: A Hidden Heritage*. New York: Simon & Schuster/Aladdin Paperbacks. (First publ. 1986.)

Lamont, Victoria (2001). "The Bovine Object of Ideology: History, Gender, and the Origins of the 'Classic' Western." *Western American Literature* 35: 4, 373–401.

Lee, L. L., and Lewis, Merrill (1980). *Women, Women Writers, and the West*. Troy, NY: Whitston.

Limerick, Patricia Nelson (1991). "What on Earth Is the New Western History?" In Patricia Nelson Limerick, Clyde A. Milner II, and Charles E. Rankin (eds.), *Trails: Toward a New Western History*, 81–8. Lawrence: University Press of Kansas.

Lyon, Thomas J., ed.-in-chief (1997). *Updating the Literary West*. Fort Worth: Texas Christian University Press.

Meyer, Roy W. (1974). "B. M. Bower: The Poor Man's Wister." In Richard W. Etulain and Michael T. Marsden (eds.), *The Popular Western: Essays toward a Definition*, 667/25–679/37. Bowling Green, Ohio: Bowling Green University Popular Press.

Mitchell, Lee Clark (1996). *Westerns: Making the Man in Fiction and Film.* Chicago: University of Chicago Press.

Morrison, Toni (1992). *Playing in the Dark: Whiteness and the Literary Imagination.* (The William E. Massey Sr. Lectures in the History of American Civilization 1990.) New York: Vintage/Random House.

Paredes, Raymund A. (1987). "Early Mexican-American Literature." In J. Golden Taylor et al. (eds.), *A Literary History of the American West,* 1079–1100. Fort Worth: Texas Christian University Press.

Piekarski, Vicki, ed. (1984). *Westward the Women: An Anthology of Western Stories by Women.* Garden City, NY: Doubleday.

Piekarski, Vicki, ed. (2003). *No Place for a Lady: Western Stories by Women.* Waterville, Me.: Gale/Five Star.

Remington, Frederic (1979). *The Collected Writings of Frederic Remington,* ed. Peggy and Harold Samuels. Garden City, NY: Doubleday.

Roosevelt, Theodore (1923–6). *The Works of Theodore Roosevelt,* 24 vols., ed. Hermann Hagedorn. New York: Charles Scribner's Sons.

Rosowski, Susan J. (1999). *Birthing a Nation: Gender, Creativity, and the West in American Literature.* Lincoln: University of Nebraska Press.

Rydell, Robert W. (1984). *All the World's a Fair: Visions of Empire at American International Expositions, 1876–1916.* Chicago: University of Chicago Press.

Scheckel, Susan (2002). "Home on the Train: Race and Mobility in *The Life and Adventures of Nat Love.*" *American Literature* 74: 2, 219–50.

Slotkin, Richard (1973). *Regeneration through Violence: The Mythology of the American Frontier, 1600–1860.* Middletown, Conn.: Wesleyan University Press.

Slotkin, Richard (1981). "The 'Wild West.'" In *Buffalo Bill and the Wild West.* Brooklyn: Brooklyn Museum.

Slotkin, Richard (1985). *The Fatal Environment: The Myth of the Frontier in the Age of Industrialization 1800–1890.* New York: Atheneum.

Slotkin, Richard (1992). *Gunfighter Nation: The Myth of the Frontier in Twentieth-Century America.* New York: Atheneum.

Smith, Henry Nash (1950). *Virgin Land: The American West as Symbol and Myth.* Cambridge, Mass.: Harvard University Press.

Taylor, J. Golden, ed.-in-chief (1987). *A Literary History of the American West.* Fort Worth: Texas Christian University Press.

Tompkins, Jane (1992). *West of Everything: The Inner Life of Westerns.* New York: Oxford University Press.

Tonkovich, Nicole (1997). "Guardian Angels and Missing Mothers: Race and Domesticity in *Winona* and *Deadwood Dick on Deck.*" *Western American Literature* 32: 3, 241–64.

Turner, Frederick Jackson (1894). "The Significance of the Frontier in American History." In *Annual Report of the American Historical Association for the Year 1893.* Washington DC: Government Printing Office.

Webb, Walter Prescott (1931). *The Great Plains.* New York: Grosset & Dunlap.

White, G. Edward (1968). *The Eastern Establishment and the Western Experience: The West of Frederic Remington, Theodore Roosevelt, and Owen Wister.* New Haven: Yale University Press.

Wister, Owen (1930). *Roosevelt, The Story of a Friendship, 1880–1919.* New York: Macmillan.

Yates, Norris (1995). *Gender and Genre: An Introduction to Women Writers of Formula Westerns, 1900–1950.* Albuquerque: University of New Mexico Press.

Zanjani, Sally (2001). *Sarah Winnemucca.* Lincoln: University of Nebraska Press.

Zitkala Ša (Sioux) (1902a). "A Warrior's Daughter." *Everybody's Magazine* 4: 4, 346–52.

Zitkala Ša (Sioux) (1902b). "Why I Am a Pagan." *Atlantic Monthly* 90, 801–3.

Zitkala Ša (Sioux) (1985). *American Indian Stories,* foreword Dexter Fisher. Lincoln: University of Nebraska Press. (First publ. 1921.)

Zitkala Ša (2001). *Dreams and Thunder: Stories, Poems, and The Sun Dance Opera,* ed. P. Jane Hafen (Taos Pueblo). Lincoln: University of Nebraska Press.

Zitkala Ša (2003). *American Indian Stories, Legends, and Other Writings,* ed. Cathy N. Davidson and Ada Norris. New York: Penguin.

11

Native American Narratives: Resistance and Survivance

Gerald Vizenor

What boy would not be an Indian for a while when he thinks of the freest life in the world? This life was mine. Every day there was a real hunt. There was real game. Occasionally there was a medicine dance away off in the woods where no one could disturb us, in which the boys impersonated their elders. (Charles Alexander Eastman, *From the Deep Woods to Civilization*, 1916)

Natives of Appomattox

The Civil War ended with the surrender of General Robert E. Lee at Appomattox Court House in Virginia on April 9, 1865. The carnage was horrific, but the republic survived, albeit with a wounded spirit. Four days later Abraham Lincoln, the sixteenth president, was assassinated. Native American Indians have been riven, disunited, and removed by constant colonial, cultural, and territorial conflicts, but the total, bloody war between the Union and the Confederacy forever abated a Native sense of presence, sovereignty, and continental liberty.

Francis Paul Prucha pointed out in *American Indian Treaties* (1994) that at the end of the Civil War the federal government was "intent on dealing strongly" with those Natives who had "disowned their treaty obligations" and "formed alliances" with the Confederacy (p. 264). An estimated 20,000 Natives fought in the Civil War, slightly more for the Confederacy than for the Union.

Prucha argued in *The Indian in American Society* (1971) that by the time Natives were "crushed militarily, they had already lost status as independent political entities" to negotiate treaties with the United States. Ely S. Parker, the first Native to serve as Commissioner of Indian Affairs, insisted that the "treaty system be scrapped, since it falsely impressed upon the tribes a notion of national independence. 'It is time,' Parker said, 'that this idea should be dispelled, and the government cease the cruel farce of thus dealing with its helpless and ignorant wards'" (Prucha 1971: 42). Native "dependency increased," observed Prucha, "as the traditional means of survival were weakened and destroyed in the passage of time" (p. 41). The military, however diminished, moved against Natives on the western frontier at the end of the Civil War. Railroads were soon built across the continent, Natives were deceived by treaties and removed to reservations, and bison, their primary source of food and income, were slaughtered by the millions in the hide trade.

The Civil War was not the first act of savagery to rouse a Native sense of *survivance* — the sensibilities of diplomatic, strategic resistance, and aesthetic irony. The new warriors of survivance, however, had a vision of futurity. Natives created many spirited narratives in the very ruins of racist and chauvinistic crusades on the elusive frontier of a constitutional democracy. Colonel Ely S. Parker, for instance, a Seneca sachem of the Iroquois Confederacy, was military secretary to General Ulysses S. Grant, and transcribed the actual surrender terms that ended four years of war. Parker was born in 1828 at Indian Falls on the Tonawanda Reservation in New York. Thirty-seven years later he was present for the surrender of Robert E. Lee at Appomattox Court House. Robert Utley wrote in *The Indian Frontier of the American West* that Parker "loyally served his chief as adjutant, military secretary, and aide-de-camp," and two years later directed a "comprehensive plan of Indian management, including transfer of the Indian Bureau to the War Department." The plan "won strong support in the Congress" (Utley 1984: 130, 131). Jay Winik noted in *April 1865* that after the two generals had "signed the preliminary papers, Grant proceeded to introduce Lee to his staff. As he shook hands" with Parker, "Lee stared for a moment and finally said, 'I am glad to see one real American here.' If this account is true, Parker responded to the general, 'We are all Americans'" (Winik 2001: 189). There is, of course, "some debate as to whether this exchange ever actually happened," observed Winik. "It has also been speculated that Lee at first may have thought Parker was a black man" (p. 419). The irony is doubled either way.

Grant was elected president three years later and appointed Parker the commissioner of Indian Affairs. Parker wrote that General Grant "showed his love for his military family by doing kindness for them whenever he could." As President "he sought them out, and without solicitation on their part, provided for many of them." Grant "never forgot a favor rendered him when he was poor and he was kind to such people when he had the power" (Grant n.d.).

Appomattox, the actual place of the surrender, is derived from a Native word. The name was first recorded about four centuries ago and has now become a part of a national narrative history. John Smith observed in "The Description of Virginia," his seventeenth-century adventure stories, the "pleasant river of *Apamatuck*," and some thirty "fighting men" of that name.

Brigadier-General Stand Watie is another significant name in the history of the Civil War. Cherokee by birth and politics, educated at the Moravian Mission School in Georgia, he was the only Native general in the Confederacy. Praised and promoted for his raids on federal supply lines, he was the last officer to surrender his forces in June 1865. He supported the removal of the Cherokee to Indian Territory in what is now Oklahoma. Utley pointed out that Stand Watie "set up a rival Cherokee government with himself as chief" (1984: 75). Several tribes were divided by their loyalties to the Union and the secession of the Confederacy. Watie supported slavery and was a member of the Knights of the Golden Circle, an association that countered the abolition movement. Many Southern Natives were slavers and enlisted in the cause of the Confederacy.

Native American Indians served as scouts for colonial regimes, and much later for the army on the frontier and in other countries. For them, entering military service was an obvious escape from the reservation. Thomas Britten argued in *American Indians in World War I* that Native veterans were more experienced, and "more effectively" resisted the "encroachments on their lands, cultures, and liberties" (1997: 25). Natives served in the military to ensure their survivance, however ironic, and as warriors to "obtain security, honor, prestige, and wealth, and to enact revenge on enemies" (p. 11). Most Natives served in integrated military units. Britten pointed out that the War Department "continued its policy of conscious assimilation of Indians into white units." Natives fought in integrated units in the Spanish–American War, the Filipino Revolution, and the Boxer Rebellion in China (Britten 1997: 26). The narratives of their service as common soldiers were seldom included in war histories.

Ten thousand Natives served in the American Expeditionary Force during World War I. Britten wrote that many Native soldiers returned with "emotional scars" and memories of horror, but "others gained a sense of purpose, discipline, and pride" (1997: 186). The Society of American Indians and many Native progressives of the time supported the war and encouraged Natives to serve their country to "win respect and high valuation in the estimation of the world" (p. 61). Meanwhile, Natives were forever burdened by the corruption and bureaucratic abuses of federal agents at home on the reservations. A Lakota elder told an ironic story about the war and torment of reservation policy. The German Kaiser, said the elder, should be confined on a reservation, and the federal agent should say to him, "Now you lazy bad man, you farm and make your living by farming, rain or no rain; and if you do not make your own living don't come to the Agency when you have no food in your stomach and no money, but stay here on your farm and grow fat till you starve" (p. 185).

Newspaper Indians

"The Civil War changed American journalism," declared John Coward in *The Newspaper Indian*. The number of readers increased, there was more "competition between urban newspapers," and there were new economic incentives to report the news promptly. Coward pointed out that the "telegraph helped put speed ahead of accuracy" (Coward 1999: 16). News reports of Indian affairs were "distributed more efficiently and consistently," and, as a consequence of speed and consolidation, the news was standardized (Coward 1999: 17). Native cultures, diplomacy, resistance, wars, and removal were reported in simplistic, descriptive, and romantic narratives. Many news stories contributed to the simulation of Native images in the dominant culture.

The Civil War "set a pattern for news coverage of the Indian wars," noted Coward. "In both cases, reporters sometimes resorted to inventing sensational or dramatic details in order to improve the copy" (p. 129). Charles Sanford Diehl, for instance, reported on the surrender of the Nez Perce for the Chicago *Times*. Many newspapers at the time reported daily on the military pursuit of the Nez Perce by General Nelson Miles, and covered the surrender of Chief Joseph on October 5, 1877, at the Bear Paw Mountains in Montana. On this occasion Chief Joseph, the Nez Perce diplomat and political leader, was reported to have said: "Hear me, my chiefs. I am tired. My heart is sick and sad. From where the sun now stands, I will fight no more forever" (Utley 1984: 193). That eloquent statement was reported widely, and has become a romantic signifier of a Native vanishing point in art, literature, and history. However, while Lieutenant Charles Erskine Scott Wood may have construed the speech, there is no secure record or document to explain how or when the actual surrender sentiment was transcribed and translated from an emotive oral expression to a written language. Wood, an acting aide-de-camp at the time of the surrender, was named the transcriber, but the handwritten evidence does not support his story. Mark Brown noted in *The Flight of the Nez Perce* (1967) that the "story that Joseph surrendered his rifle with this touching little speech, while Wood stood by 'with a pencil and a paper pad' to record it does not have a word of truth in it." Brown observed that the "formal surrender took place near evening" and only a "small group were present to receive the surrender" (1967: 407).

Thomas Sutherland, a correspondent for several newspapers, including the San Francisco *Chronicle* and the New York *Herald*, described the scene of surrender in somber, tragic metaphors. "As the sun was dropping to the level of the prairie and tinging the tawny and white land with waves of ruddy lights, Joseph came slowly riding up the hill," wrote Sutherland. Joseph raised his head and "with an impulsive gesture, straightened his arm toward General Howard, offering his rifle, as if with it he cast away all ambition, hope and manly endeavors leaving his heart and his future down with his people in the dark valley where the shadows were knitting about them a dusky shroud" (Brown 1967: 408).

Bruce Hampton argued in *Children of Grace* that Lieutenant Wood later disavowed an earlier account and claimed that Chief Joseph had delivered the surrender notes. "Still, there is a resonance to the speech that closely resembles other declarations attributed to Joseph. If not his explicit words, Wood – probably with some literary polish – seems to have captured their gist" (Hampton 1994: 307).

"Diehl was not with General Miles and was not a witness to the surrender of the Nez Perce," wrote Coward. "I wrote my story, by candlelight, in a cold army tent," explained Diehl, "and dispatched it by courier to Helena, Montana." Diehl was a respected war reporter because he created a sense of "action and excitement." Coward pointed out that the "job of the Indian reporter was to find excitement, even when it was inspired by fiction" (1999: 131).

Chief Joseph, the august native diplomat Yellow Bull, and Ad Chapman, an interpreter, visited Washington DC in January 1879, two years after their surrender, to argue for tribal recognition and the return of the exiled Nez Perce to their homeland in the Pacific Northwest. Members of Congress, the Cabinet, diplomats, and commercial leaders listened to a memorable, heartfelt entreaty for liberty. Chief Joseph heard a standing ovation at the end of his speech. Bruce Hampton pointed out that "Washington newspapers praised the speech and several philanthropic organizations, including the Indian Rights Association and, strangely enough, the Presbyterian Church, began to show an interest in the exiles" (1994: 325). Chief Joseph's purported speech – and there are several versions – was published as an article a few months later in the *North American Review* (Joseph 1879).

> If the white man wants to live in peace with the Indian he can live in peace. There need be no trouble. Treat all men alike. Give them all the same law. Give them all an even chance to live and grow. All men were made by the same Great Spirit Chief. They are all brothers. The earth is the mother of all people, and all people should have equal rights upon it. You might as well expect the rivers to run backward as that any man who was born a free man should be contented penned up and denied liberty to go where he pleases.
>
> When I think of our condition my heart is heavy. I see men of my race treated as outlaws and driven from country to country, or shot down like animals. I know that my race must change. We cannot hold our own with the white men as we are. We only ask an even chance to live as other men live. We ask to be recognized as men. We ask that the same law shall work on all men.
>
> Whenever the white man treats the Indian as they treat each other, then we shall have no more wars. We shall be all alike – brothers of one father and one mother, with one sky above us and one country around us, and one government for all. Then the Great Spirit Chief who rules above will smile upon the land, and send rain to wash out the bloody spots made by brothers' hands upon the face of the earth. For this time the Indian race are waiting and praying. I hope that no more groans of wounded men and women will ever go to the ear of the Great Spirit Chief above, and that all people may be one people. (Joseph 1879: 432, quoted in Hampton 1994: 326)

Congress received fourteen petitions of support for the cause of Chief Joseph. Otis Halfmoon noted in the *Encyclopedia of North American Indians* that on "May 22, 1885, the Nez Perce boarded railroad cars in Arkansas City to return home to the reservation. The charisma and diplomacy of Chief Joseph had prevailed." Sadly, the Nez Perce were not allowed to return to the Wallowa valley in Oregon. They were removed to the Colville Reservation in Washington, where Chief Joseph died on September 21, 1904 (Hoxie 1996: 311). Robert Utley pointed out in *Frontier Regulars* (1973) that Chief Joseph "refused to give up hope of returning to his beloved Wallowa Valley in Oregon." Once more, in 1897, "he journeyed to Washington and urged his cause on President McKinley." General Nelson Miles and other military leaders supported his initiative, but the "whites of the Wallowa refused to part with any land for Indian occupancy."

The Nez Perce created a great narrative of resistance, tragic retreat, surrender, and survivance. Utley wrote, "Their just cause, their unity of purpose and action, their seemingly bottomless reservoirs of courage, endurance, and tenacity, their sheer achievement and final heartbreaking failure when on the very threshold of success, have evoked sympathy and admiration for almost a century" (1973: 324). The Nez Perce are truly the patriots of a continental Native liberty.

Higher Civilization

"The novelty of a newspaper published upon this reservation may cause many to be wary in their support, and this from a fear that it may be revolutionary in character," announced Theodore Beaulieu, the Native editor of *The Progress*, the first newspaper published on the White Earth Reservation in northern Minnesota, March 25, 1886.

> We shall aim to advocate constantly and withhold reserve, what in our view, and in the view of the leading minds upon this reservation, is the best for the interests of its residents. And not only for their interests, but those of the tribe wherever they now are residing.
>
> We may be called upon at times to criticize individuals and laws, but we shall aim to do so in a spirit of kindness and justice. Believing that the "freedom of the press" will be guarded as sacredly by the Government on this reservation as elsewhere, we launch forth our little craft, appealing to the authorities that be, at home, at the seat of government, to the community, to give us moral support, for in this way only can we reach the standard set forth at our mast-head.

The Progress was dedicated to "A Higher Civilization: The Maintenance of Law and Order" (Vizenor 1984: 78).

The United States Indian Agent confiscated the press and ordered the editor and Augustus Beaulieu, the publisher, both of whom were tribal members, removed from the White Earth Reservation. The agent alleged that *The Progress* printed "false and malicious statements concerning the affairs of the White Earth Reservation, done evidently for the purpose of breaking down the influence of the United States Indian Agent with the Indians" (Vizenor 1984: 80).

The second issue of *The Progress* was published more than a year later on October 8, 1887, after a hearing in the federal court and a government investigation. Theodore Beaulieu observed that "we began setting type for the first number of *The Progress* and were almost ready to go to press, when our sanctum was invaded by T. J. Sheehan, the United States Indian Agent, accompanied by a posse of the Indian police. The composing stick was removed from our hands, our property seized, and ourselves forbidden to proceed with the publication of the journal." Beaulieu continued,

> We did not believe that any earthly power had the right to interfere with us as members
> of the Chippewa tribe, and at the White Earth Reservation, while peacefully pursuing
> the occupation we had chosen. We did not believe there existed a law which should
> prescribe for us the occupation we should follow. We knew of no law which could compel
> us to become agriculturists, professionals, "hewers of wood and drawers of water," or per
> contra, could restrain us from engaging in these occupations. Therefore we respectfully
> declined obeying the mandate, at the same time reaching the conclusion that should we
> be restrained we should appeal to the courts for protection.
>
> We were restrained and a guard set over our property. We sought the protection of the
> courts, notwithstanding the assertion of the agent, that there could be no jurisdiction in
> the matter. The United States district court, Judge Nelson in session, decided that we
> were entitled to the jurisdiction we sought. The case came before him, on jury trial. The
> court asserted and defended the right of any member of the tribe to print and publish a
> newspaper upon his reservation just as he might engage in any other lawful occupation,
> and without surveillance and restrictions. The jury before whom the amount of damage
> came, while not adjudging the amount asked for, did assess and decree a damage with a
> verdict restoring to us our plant. (Vizenor 1984: 92)

The Progress was the first newspaper published on the White Earth Reservation, and
it was the first Native newspaper seized by federal agents in violation of the
Constitution of the United States. *The Progress* was published weekly for two years;
the newspaper was enlarged and the name was changed to *The Tomahawk*. The Native
editor and publisher remained the same; both newspapers published reservation, state,
and national news stories, and critical, controversial editorials. The newspapers
opposed the federal act that allotted collective Native land to individuals. One article,
for instance, carried this headline on the front page: "Is it an Indian Bureau? About
some of the freaks in the employ of the Indian Service whose actions are a disgrace to
the nation and a curse to the cause of justice. Putrescent through the spoils system"
(Vizenor 1984: 94).

Messiah of Survivance

Wovoka was a shaman, an envoy of the sacred world. His concise narrative envisioned
the resurrection of Native reason and a sense of presence. He revealed new, crucial
ceremonies that would exalt ancestors to return, revive the bison to the prairie, and
restore a Native continental liberty.

Wovoka, or Jack Wilson, a Northern Paiute who was born near Smith Valley,
Nevada, inspired thousands of Natives by his direct, temperate, and humane instruc-
tions to wear sacramental paint, dance in a circle for five days, bathe in the river, feast,
and do "not refuse to work for the whites and do not make any trouble with them

until you leave them. When the earth shakes do not be afraid." The Native dead would be resurrected by the dance, and the "great change will be ushered in by a trembling of the earth, at which the faithful are exhorted to feel no alarm," observed James Mooney in the *Ghost-Dance Religion and the Sioux Outbreak of 1890.* "The moral code inculcated is as pure and comprehensive in its simplicity as anything found in religious systems from the days of Gautama Buddha to the time of Jesus Christ" (Mooney 1991: 782). Wovoka asked Mooney to present a copy of his narrative to government officials in Washington. The purpose was "to convince the white people that there was nothing bad or hostile in the new religion" (Mooney 1991: 776).

The Arapaho version, the first transcription of the narrative, begins with the direct advice of the messiah of survivance: "What you get home you make dance, and will give the same. When you dance four days and one day, dance day time five days and then fift, will wash for every body." Wovoka told the concise stories of his vision to several Native translators. Casper Edson, an Arapaho who had studied at the federal Carlisle Industrial Indian School, translated and transcribed the first narrative into English, and that became the ironic lingua franca of the Ghost Dance Religion. That original narrative was later translated into other Native oral languages on reservations, but the initial doctrine and other renditions were communicated in English. More than 20,000 Natives in some thirty Western tribes actively participated in the Ghost Dance. "No white man had any part, directly or indirectly," in the first translation and production of the narrative. Nor was the doctrine of the messiah "originally intended to be seen by white men," wrote Mooney. "In fact, in one part the messiah himself expressly warns the delegates to tell no white men."

Mooney, who had several conversations with Wovoka, years after his shamanic vision, pointed out in a rather reductive manner that while the messiah was "sick there occurred an eclipse of the sun, a phenomenon which always excites great alarm among primitive peoples. In their system the sun is a living being, of great power and beneficence, and the temporary darkness is caused by an attack on him by some supernatural monster which endeavors to devour him, and will succeed, and thus plunge the world into eternal night unless driven by incantations and loud noises" (Mooney 1991: 773). Wovoka stated that he was "stricken down by a severe fever" and experienced an ecstatic, shamanic vision. "When the sun died," a reference to a solar eclipse, he was entranced and taken to heaven. Later he returned from the spirit world with a revelation. Wovoka was probably in his early thirties at the time of his vision, a cosmic ideation, and a total eclipse on January 1, 1889.

Mooney pointed out that there were three early versions of the translated narrative in English: Arapaho, Cheyenne, and the third, a free rendering, the most familiar version of the transcribed narrative. Here is the free rendered version of the entire narrative. The "good cloud" probably refers to rain, and "each tribe there" suggests reservations and Native country. The reference to a "young man" is probably the first translator of the narrative, Casper Edson.

When you get home you must make a dance to continue five days. Dance four successive nights, and the last night keep up the dance until the morning of the fifth day, when all must bathe in the river and then disperse to their homes. You must all do in the same way.

I, Jack Wilson, love you all, and my heart is full of gladness for the gifts you have brought me. When you get home I shall give you a good cloud which will make you feel good. I give you a good spirit and give you all good paint. I want you to come again in three months, some from each tribe there.

There will be a good deal of snow this year and some rain. In the fall there will be such a rain as I have never given you before.

Grandfather says, when your friends died you must not cry. You must not hurt anybody or do harm to anyone. You must not fight. Do right always. It will give you satisfaction in life. This young man has a good father and mother.

Do not tell the white people about this. Jesus is now upon the earth. He appears like a cloud. The dead are all alive again. I do not know when they will be here; maybe this fall or in the spring. When the time comes there will be no more sickness and everyone will be young again.

Do not refuse to work for the whites and do not make any trouble with them until you leave them. When the earth shakes do not be afraid. It will not hurt you.

I want you to dance every six weeks. Make a feast at the dance and have food that everybody may eat. Then bathe in the water. That is all. You will receive good words again from me some time. Do not tell lies. (Mooney 1991: 781)

Many Natives wrote letters to the messiah of survivance. The letters were translated from dictation by the first generation of Natives who had attended federal and mission schools. Several letters were published in *I Wear the Morning Star*, the catalogue of an exhibition on the Ghost Dance published by the Minneapolis Institute of Arts (1976). Cloud Horse, for instance, sent his letter to the messiah on April 11, 1911, from Pine Ridge, South Dakota:

Jack Wilson,
Dear Father: Why do you not write to me. I sit with you and I write to you this letter. I hope I will come to see you. I send you a dollar bill. Why dont you answer me?

When you get this letter answer soon, Father. This man writing a letter for me but he lives far and this man write for me this letter.

This man a good man write for me this letter. I sit with Cloud Horse and we write this letter.

Your loving son, I shake hands with you, Answer quick when you get this letter.
Cloud Horse
Address answer to Red Star
Pine Ridge, So. Dak.

The English language and the postal service became the primary means of communicating the Ghost Dance Religion. Cloud Man Horse wrote this letter to Jack Wilson from the Kyle Post Office, South Dakota, on December 13, 1911:

Dear Father:

Your letter has been received and I was very glad indeed to hear from you dear father

Now I am going to send you a pair of mocissions but if they are not long enough for you when you write again please send me you foot measure from this day on – I will try to get the money to send to you. I wish I had it just at present I would send it wright away.

I think I might get the money soon enough to send it so that is why I say that so. I will get it just as soon as possible and be sure to send it so if you get a letter from me I may have the money in that letter so dear Father this will be all. I can answer you so for your sake all the Indians out here make fun of me but I allways think dear Father that around me you would give me strength. so if you get the money I want that medican and some good feathers & that paint so that is what I want you to send me.

So this is all for this time. I give a good & hard shaking of the hands to you I hope you have pity on me

I remain your son

Cloud Man Horse (18)

Wovoka was a storier of transcendence, a clairvoyant of the weather, and, in at least one instance, an apparent seer of familial futurity. Harlyn Vidovich, his grandson, became a pilot and fulfilled a prophecy.

Michael Hittman wrote in *Wovoka and the Ghost Dance* that the messiah said his grandson would attend school, become a "credit to his people," and fly. Harlyn, born in 1919, was the son of Andrew Vidovich, a Death Valley Shoshone, and Alice Wilson, the illegitimate daughter of Jack Wilson. Wovoka said at the baptism, according to Andrew, that Harlyn would be "flying in the skies." Andrew pointed out that there were few airplanes at the time of his prophecy. Wovoka continued, "And then he's going to join the United States Flying" and "lead the white men in the skies. He will become a great captain" (Hittman 1997: 163).

Hittman reported that Harlyn Vidovich was "posthumously awarded" the "Distinguished Flying Cross" as a fighter pilot in the Flying Tigers (1997: 163). Captain Vidovich was indeed listed in official Air Force records as a pilot in the 74th Fighter Squadron, Flying Tigers, in China, but not the earlier Flying Tigers, the American Volunteer Group established in the late 1930s under the celebrated command of General Claire Lee Chennault.

Wounded Knee

Wovoka, Charles Alexander Eastman, Luther Standing Bear, and Sophia Alice Callahan were born in the era of migrations, treaty reservations, and moral duplicities of the Civil War. They matured at a time of monstrous cultural burdens, military vengeance, and state violence; a Native generation forsaken at the end of a great continental liberty, they yet created narratives of chance and survivance.

Lakota Ghost Dancers were on the move that winter with visions of Native survivance. Big Foot and his escorts had resisted removal to reservations and were

Figure 11.1   Chief Tatanka Iyotanka of the Hunkpapa Lakota Sioux

Tatanka Iyotanka (1831?–90), known in white culture as "Sitting Bull," was one of history's greatest champions of human liberty. He rose to prominence in the early 1860s when he led the Lakotas against federal troops sent to "pacify" tribes in the Dakotas and Montana. After the Treaty of Fort Laramie in 1868, the Lakota tribes split into two factions: those who acquiesced in US authority, moved to the Great Sioux Reservation in western Dakota, and were given government rations; and those who refused to accept white authority and continued to roam the buffalo hunting ranges. When white settlers, railroads, gold miners, and federal troops encroached on the hunting grounds and sacred lands of the Dakotas, Tatanka Iyotanka was the force behind an alliance of the northern plains tribes, principally the Sioux and Cheyenne, that resisted their trespass. His coalition destroyed General George Custer's Seventh Cavalry at the Battle of Little Bighorn in 1876, but within a year the alliance fell apart and he was forced to flee to Canada, and eventually, in 1881, to surrender. After an illegal two-year incarceration and a brief tour with "Buffalo Bill" Cody's Wild West in pursued with a vengeance by the military. Fourteen years after the defeat of General George Custer at the Little Bighorn River, the Seventh Cavalry massacred destitute men, women, and children at Wounded Knee Creek, South Dakota, on December 29, 1890. "No one on either side that morning had any thought of a fight. Certainly not the Indians, as the army later charged; they were outnumbered, surrounded, poorly armed, and had their women and children present," argued Utley. "Wounded Knee assumes a larger significance, for it marks the passing of the Indian frontier" (1984: 256, 257).

The bodies of the dreamers were frozen in the snow; some three hundred natives were slaughtered, and more than a hundred of the dead were buried in a mass grave. Big Foot, the traditional elder, weakened by pneumonia, was wounded but did not survive the massacre. His frozen head, shoulders, and arms were raised and braced in the snow, an enervated simulation by a mercenary photographer.

William Coleman wrote in *Voices of Wounded Knee* that Dewey Beard saw the soldiers murder the Ghost Dancers. Beard was wounded and "surrounded by soldiers." He "fought his way toward the ravine." Beard said,

> I saw my mother standing and singing. She was waving a pistol. She told me to take it, she was dying. I cried and helped her sit down. I felt like I couldn't get up, I looked down and saw I had been shot again, in the lap.
>
> I was badly wounded and pretty weak too. While I was lying on my back, I looked down the ravine and saw a lot of women coming up and crying. When I saw these women, little girls, and boys coming up, I saw soldiers on both sides of the ravine shoot at them until they had killed every one of them. (Coleman 2000: 309)

Turning Hawk said, "Those who escaped that first fire got into the ravine, and as they went along up the ravine for a long distance they were pursued on both sides by the soldiers and shot down, as the dead bodies showed afterwards" (Coleman 2000: 312).

Celene Not Help Him survived the massacre. She said, "My grandfather was shot in the back; it went through his lung in the first volley of gunfire. He was again shot

---

which he shrewdly observed the white man's ways, he returned to the Standing Rock Reservation. In 1890 he became prominent in the Ghost Dance religion that had spread among the Sioux. Fearing that the Ghost Dance would lead to an uprising, the army sent forty-three Lakota policemen to arrest Tatanka Iyotanka; he was murdered along with his son and twelve others while defending himself, on December 15, 1890, two weeks before the massacre of the Lakota families at Wounded Knee.

Tatanka Iyotanka – whose name represents a buffalo bull sitting intractably on its haunches, thus immoveable – was a great and wise chief, a warrior of legendary courage, and a revered medicine man. Throughout his life he was adamantly opposed to any form of assimilation, disdainful of white men's promises, and contemptuous of paternalist government programs, insisting instead on maintaining the traditional Lakota way of life. As he rhetorically asked, "Is it wrong for me to love my own? Is it wicked for me because my skin is red? Because I am Sioux? Because I was born where my father lived? Because I would die for my people and my country? God made me an Indian." (Photograph by permission of the Custer Battlefield Museum, Garryowen, Montana.)

in the right calf and in the hip. He was coughing blood. He had lost a lot of blood. He could hear someone singing a death song. Whenever someone moved, the soldiers shot them" (Coleman 2000: 309).

The Seventh Cavalry returned to the Pine Ridge Agency with their dead and wounded soldiers. Most of them had been shot "by their own comrades, who had encircled the Indians." Very few of the Natives had guns, wrote Charles Alexander Eastman in *From the Deep Woods to Civilization*. "A majority of the thirty or more Indians wounded were women and children, including babies in their arms." There were not enough tents, so the mission chapel, "in which the Christmas tree still stood," was offered as a "temporary hospital. We tore out the pews and covered the floor with hay and quilts. There we laid the poor creatures side by side in rows, and the night was devoted to caring for them as best we could. Many were frightfully torn by pieces of shells, and the suffering was terrible." Eastman, a medical doctor, was placed in charge. The army surgeons were ready to assist, but the "tortured Indians would scarcely allow a man in uniform to touch them" (Eastman 2001: 234).

Eastman, Santee Dakota, was born in 1858 near Redwood Falls, Minnesota. Many Lightnings, his father, was imprisoned for his active resistance in the Dakota Uprising of 1862. Seth Eastman, his maternal grandfather, was a graduate of West Point. Later he was the commander of Fort Snelling in Minnesota. Charles attended the Santee Normal Training School, Beloit College, Knox College, Dartmouth, and graduated from the Boston Medical College as one of the first Native medical doctors (two others of the same time were Susan LaFlesche Picotte and Carlos Montezuma). Eastman had been in practice for about a month when he treated the survivors of the Wounded Knee Massacre. His Dakota nicknames were Hakadah, The Pitiful Last, and Ohiyesa, The Winner.

Wounded Knee was buried in snow. Eastman, who searched for survivors after the storm, wrote:

> Fully three miles from the scene of the massacre we found the body of a woman completely covered with a blanket of snow, and from this point on we found them scattered along as they had been relentlessly hunted down and slaughtered while fleeing for their lives. Some of our people discovered relatives or friends among the dead, and there was much wailing and mourning. When we reached the spot where the Indian camp had stood, among the fragments of burned tents and other belongings we saw the frozen bodies lying close together or piled upon one another. I counted eighty bodies of men who had been in the council and who were almost as helpless as the women and babes when the firing began, for nearly all their guns had been taken from them. A reckless and desperate young Indian had fired the first shot when the search for weapons was well under way. Immediately the troops opened fire from all sides, killing not only unarmed men, women, and children but their own comrades who stood opposite them, for the camp was entirely surrounded.
>
> It took all of my nerve to keep my composure in the face of this spectacle and of the excitement and grief of my Indian companions, nearly every one of whom was crying

aloud or singing his death song. The white men became very nervous, but I set them to examining and uncovering every body to see if any were living. Although they had been lying untended in the snow and cold for two days and nights, a number had survived. Among them I found a baby of about a year old warmly wrapped and entirely unhurt. I brought her in, and she was afterward adopted and educated by an army officer. One man who was severely wounded begged me to fill his pipe. When we brought him into the chapel, he was welcomed by his wife and daughters with cries of joy, but he died a day or two later. (Eastman 2001: 237–8)

Luther Standing Bear, or Plenty Kill, was in the first class of Native students to attend the Carlisle Indian School, a former military barracks, in 1879. He survived the extreme experience with distinction and was hired to teach in the government school on the Rosebud Reservation. Later, he moved to the Pine Ridge Agency.

Standing Bear noted in *My People the Sioux* (1928) that the soldiers were sent to escort and protect Big Foot and the Ghost Dancers. "The following morning the news arrived of the terrible slaughter of Big Foot's whole band. Men, women, and children – even babies were killed in their mothers' arms!" he wrote many years later.

When I heard this, it made my blood boil. I was ready myself to go and fight then. There I was, doing my best to teach my people to follow in the white man's road – even trying to get them to believe in their religion – and this was my reward for it all! The very people I was following – and getting my people to follow – had no respect for motherhood, old age, or babyhood. Where was all their civilized training?

Days later he visited the site of the massacre. The bodies had been buried. "The place of death was forsaken and forbidding. I stood there in silence for several minutes, in reverence for the dead, and then turned and rode toward the agency" (Standing Bear 1975: 223, 224, 226).

Indian agents were determined to turn Natives into "citizen farmers," observed L. G. Moses in *The Indian Man: A Biography of James Mooney*. The "Ghost Dance religion would not be permitted to challenge the tidiness of the process." Natives watched the military parades in silence. Grievously, "faith in the prophet was no longer enough to inspire armed resistance to the combined forces of civilization" (Moses 1984: 54).

Fictional Shoulders

Sophia Alice Callahan had almost completed her novel *Wynema* (1891) at the time of the war crimes at Wounded Knee Creek. She included a descriptive, omniscient scene about the "day of the skirmish," one of the first fictional notices of the massacre.

Wounded Knee is introduced at the very end of the novel by two characters in a passive, romantic conversation about a singular newspaper editorial: "The great

Indian war is over – nothing was done except what was intended to be done."
Defenseless "Indians were murdered; the Indian agents and contractors reaped a rich
harvest; that's all."

> "I think the editor is rather bitter," said Genevieve.
> "Yes dear," answered Robin, "but if you had seen the Indians slain on the battle-field
> as we did, and could have heard the groans of the wounded you would not think so."
> Robin placed his hands over his eyes and said, "I shall never forget that battle-field all
> strewn with dead and dying men and women and children, and the three little babies
> resting sweetly and unconsciously in their dead mothers' bosoms." (Callahan 1997: 101)

Callahan created Wildfire, a noble warrior of omniscience, who maintained that he
would never surrender his arms, and "my followers shall not. They are ours to use for
our pleasure, or defense if need be." Carl Peterson, a missionary, counsels Wildfire to
surrender on a reservation and assume a "submissive attitude": then the government
"will protect you; you will not be starved again, for those criminal agents have been
discharged and better ones employed" (Callahan 1997: 80). "May the Great Father
hear me say, let this arm wither, let these eyes grow dim, let this savage heart still its
beating, when I stand and make peace with a Government whose only policy is to
exterminate my race," said Wildfire. This is "not a policy to live by," said Peterson.
"Then let it be a policy to *die* by," declared Wildfire. "If we cannot be free, let us die.
What is life to a caged bird, threatened with death on all sides?" (Callahan 1997: 81).
Big Foot and the Ghost Dance are not directly named, for the fictional Natives,
revised in sentimental conversations, are an absence, not a presence, in the novel.

Callahan died at age twenty-six in 1894. *Wynema* is one of the first novels written
by a Native, and the first published by a Native woman. Apparently the novel was not
widely read in the first edition. A. LaVonne Brown Ruoff pointed out in the historical
introduction to *Wynema* that the only notice of the original publication was in *Our
Brother in Red*, which noted that Callahan "is an intelligent Christian lady and we look
forward with pleasure to a time when our other duties will permit us to read the
book" (Callahan 1997: xvii). "Callahan combines the themes of domestic romance and
protest novel" and "uses multiple voices and perspectives, Indian and non-Indian,
female and male, to educate her readers," observed Ruoff. The last section of the novel,
"Sioux hostilities, the murder of Sitting Bull, and the massacre at Wounded Knee, is
such an abrupt departure from the earlier romance plot that it was probably added to
an almost completed novel" (Callahan 1997: xxvi, xxvii).

Pagan Sentiments

Gertrude Simmons was eight years old when she left the Yankton Reservation for the
first time to attend White's Indiana Manual Labor Institute in Wabash, Indiana,
sponsored by the Society of Friends. "The first turning away from the easy, natural

flow of my life occurred in an early spring," she wrote in *Atlantic Monthly*. "At this age I knew but one language, and that was my mother's native tongue." Gertrude spied the missionaries that morning and heard the promises of "red, red apples" (Zitkala Ša 1900: 46). Her mother resisted but then agreed that her daughter would "need an education when she is grown, for then there will be fewer real Dakotas, and many more palefaces. This tearing her away, so young, from her mother is necessary, if I would have her an educated woman" (p. 47).

Gertrude was indeed an educated woman. She assumed a Native literary name, Zitkala Ša, and wrote traditional and autobiographical stories for several magazines at the time. She taught at the Carlisle Indian School, played the violin with the band, and performed as a soloist at the Paris Exposition in 1900. Zitkala Ša left the Carlisle School in 1902, returned to the Yankton Reservation, ended her engagement to Carlos Montezuma, the medical doctor, and married Raymond Bonnin, a Native who worked for the Indian Service. Later she transcribed Native melodies and collaborated on the production of *The Sun Dance Opera* that was performed in Salt Lake City, Utah, in 1913. She became a Native activist, was elected secretary of the Society of American Indians, and, with her husband, founded the National Congress of American Indians in 1926.

"Controversial to the end, Gertrude Bonnin remained an enigma," observed Dexter Fisher in "Zitkala Sa: The Evolution of a Writer." She was

> a curious blend of civilized romanticism and aggressive individualism. Her own image of herself eventually evolved into an admixture of myth and fact, so that by the time of her death in 1938, she believed, and it was erroneously stated in three obituaries, that she was the granddaughter of Sitting Bull, though the Yankton tribal rolls indicated that her own mother was older than Sitting Bull. (Fisher 1979: 238)

Ruth Heflin wrote in *"I Remain Alive": The Sioux Literary Renaissance* that Gertrude Bonnin, like Charles Alexander Eastman, "at first wrote both autobiographical essays and short stories, later merging her literary talents with political rhetoric." She wrote blatant political "essays and appeals, seeking equity and suffrage for Indians" (Heflin 2000: 106). Zitkala Ša published "Why I Am a Pagan" in the *Atlantic Monthly* (1902). Having returned to the reservation, in this essay she responded to the criticism of missionaries. "I prefer to their dogma my excursions into the natural gardens where the voice of the Great Spirit is heard in the twittering of birds, the rippling of mighty waters, and the sweet breathing of flowers. If this is Paganism, then at present, I am a Pagan."

Ely Samuel Parker, Chief Joseph, Theodore Beaulieu, Wovoka, Charles Alexander Eastman, Luther Standing Bear, Sophia Alice Callahan, and Gertrude Bonnin, and many other Natives were neither pagans nor evangelists of dominance; they were by visions, words, and actions, the new warriors of survivance between the Civil War and World War I. Their narratives have inspired many generations of Natives.

Primary Texts

Callahan, Sophia Alice. *Wynema: A Child of the Forest*. 1891.

Eastman, Charles Alexander. *From the Deep Woods to Civilization*. 1916.

Grant, Ulysses S. *The Papers of U. S. Grant*. n.d.

Joseph. "An Indian's View of Indian Affairs." 1879.

Mooney, James. *The Ghost-Dance Religion and the Sioux Outbreak of 1890*. 1896.

Standing Bear, Luther. *My People the Sioux*. 1928.

Zitkala Ša. "Impressions of an Indian Childhood: The Big Red Apples." 1900.

Zitkala Ša. "Why I Am a Pagan." 1902.

References and Further Reading

Abel, Annie Heloise (1992). *The American Indian in the Civil War, 1862–1865*. Lincoln: University of Nebraska Press.

Britten, Thomas A. (1997). *American Indians in World War I*. Albuquerque: University of New Mexico Press.

Brown, Mark H. (1967). *The Flight of the Nez Perce*. New York: G. P. Putnam's Sons.

Callahan, S. Alice (1997). *Wynema: A Child of the Forest*. Lincoln: University of Nebraska Press.

Coleman, William S. E. (2000). *Voices of Wounded Knee*. Lincoln: University of Nebraska Press.

Coward, John M. (1999). *The Newspaper Indian: Native American Identity in the Press, 1820–90*. Urbana: University of Illinois Press.

Eastman, Charles Alexander (2001). *From the Deep Woods to Civilization*. Chicago: Donnelley.

Fisher, Dexter (1979). "Zitkala Sa: The Evolution of a Writer." *American Indian Quarterly* 5: 3, 229–38. Repr. in Janet Witalec (ed.), *Native North American Literature*, Gale Research, 1994, 171–4.

Grant, Ulysses S. (n.d.). *The Papers of U. S. Grant*. Microfilm, Series 7, reels 32, 33. Repr. on the internet at www.mscomm.com/~ulysses/page63.html.

Halfmoon, Otis (1996). "Joseph (Heinmot Tooyalakekt)." In Frederick Hoxie (ed.), *Encyclopedia of North American Indians*, 309–11. New York: Houghton Mifflin.

Hampton, Bruce (1994). *Children of Grace: The Nez Perce War of 1877*. New York: Holt.

Heflin, Ruth J. (2000). *"I Remain Alive": The Sioux Literary Renaissance*. Syracuse, NY: Syracuse University Press.

Hittman, Michael (1997). *Wovoka and the Ghost Dance*. Lincoln: University of Nebraska Press.

Hoxie, Frederick, ed. (1996). *Encyclopedia of North American Indians*. New York: Houghton Mifflin.

Jensen, Richard E.; Paul, R. Eli; and Carter, John E. (1991). *Eyewitness at Wounded Knee*. Lincoln: University of Nebraska Press.

Joseph (1879). "An Indian's View of Indian Affairs." *North American Review*, April.

Minneapolis Institute of Arts (1976). *I Wear the Morning Star: An Exhibition of American Indian Ghost Dance Objects* (exhibition catalogue). Minneapolis: Minneapolis Institute of Arts.

Mooney, James (1991). *The Ghost-Dance Religion and the Sioux Outbreak of 1890*. Lincoln: University of Nebraska Press, 1991.

Moses, L. G. (1984). *The Indian Man: A Biography of James Mooney*. Lincoln: University of Nebraska Press.

Prucha, Francis Paul (1971). *The Indian in American Society*. Hinsdale, Ill.: Dryden Press.

Prucha, Francis Paul (1994). *American Indian Treaties*. Berkeley: University of California Press.

Standing Bear, Luther (1975). *My People the Sioux*. Lincoln: University of Nebraska Press.

Utley, Robert (1973). *Frontier Regulars: The United States Army and the Indian, 1866–1891*. Lincoln: University of Nebraska Press.

Utley, Robert (1984). *The Indian Frontier of the American West, 1846–1890*. Albuquerque: University of New Mexico Press.

Vizenor, Gerald (1984). *The People Named the Chippewa: Narrative Histories*. Minneapolis: University of Minnesota Press.

Vizenor, Gerald (1998). *Fugitive Poses: Native American Indian Scenes of Absence and Presence.* Lincoln: University of Nebraska Press.

Vizenor, Gerald (1999). *Manifest Manners: Narratives on Postindian Survivance.* Lincoln: University of Nebraska Press.

Winik, Jay (2001). *April 1865: The Month that Saved America.* New York: HarperCollins.

Zitkala Ša (1900). "Impressions of an Indian Childhood: The Big Red Apples." *Atlantic Monthly* (Jan.). Repr. on the internet at Electronic Text Center, University of Virginia Library.

Zitkala Ša (1902). "Why I Am a Pagan." *Atlantic Monthly* (Dec.). Repr. on the internet at The Online Archive of Nineteenth-Century US Women's Writings, ed. Glynis Carr.

12

Representing the Civil War and Reconstruction: From Uncle Tom to Uncle Remus

Kathleen Diffley

In the immediate aftermath of the Civil War, which had rocked older allegiances between 1861 and 1865, Rebecca Harding Davis opened *Waiting for the Verdict* (1867) with a scene at the Philadelphia ferry that should have been about a girl. Ross Burley and her grandfather heave into sight of the wharf in the white and red Conestoga wagon that regularly carries them from field to market and that must now, bells jingling, be driven onto the boat. It is the herb-girl's yellow hair and brown eyes that catch the departing light of the November evening and the attention of an aging Alabama planter, who makes her a gift of the yellow dog she wrestles in play as the ferry moves into the river. But the dog is not altogether his to give; by right of possession, Luff belongs to the slave boy who has nursed a neglected puppy back to health. Rather than see his dog lick the hand of another, the mulatto Sap hugs him ("He wur all I had") and takes his life. The red ooze on the ferry's deck unexpectedly puts the slave boy at the scene's center and makes longing and ownership, race and blood, the novel's recurring concerns.

The literature of the Civil War and Reconstruction was similarly preoccupied with promise and danger, and had been since the first momentous stirrings in *Uncle Tom's Cabin* (1852), the runaway bestseller that Harriet Beecher Stowe began serializing in Washington's *National Era* during 1851. For hundreds of thousands of readers, Stowe made the Compromise of 1850 with its Fugitive Slave Law suddenly wrenching, just as she made sentimental tropes the path of choice into a decade of growing anti-slavery protest and sectional divide. The success of Stowe's little Eva, the ailing Southern child who longed to teach slaves and slave-owners how to love, effectively explains the gendered appeal of Ross Burley and the several engraved illustrations in *Waiting for the Verdict* that favor Ross's domestic peace, especially as the years pass. But the fate of Sap and a more broadly masculine ethos of duty and entitlement increas-ingly challenged antebellum conventions and a feminine lien on the country's imagined life. As early as the dramatizations of *Uncle Tom's Cabin*, which would transform American theater during the 1850s and beyond, the literature of civil crisis reveals a gendered tension that carried readers from the Christian sacrifice of Uncle Tom at the beginning of sectional splintering to the Brer Rabbit audacity of Uncle Remus as Reconstruction waned, especially after Joel Chandler Harris published his recollected "songs and sayings" in 1880. During the years of upheaval in between, the country's writers would be so mindful of political events that literary texts became generically unstable and hybrid, formal confirmation of disruption and a new national identity in the making. It is striking how much that redefinition apparently owed to revolutionary promises and how often the language of freedom and independence, bound as it was to the Founding Fathers, was invoked by everyone in the midst of tumult. For the sake of a nation "dedicated to the proposition that all men are created equal," as Abraham Lincoln recalled at Gettysburg, it is also striking how repeatedly independence was linked to property and ownership, even by those once enslaved.

The significance of property had been acknowledged since the country's founding commitment to life and liberty, especially when the pursuit of happiness was caught up in the promise of property that marriage delivered through mutual consent. Consensual ties were so fundamental to the commencement of both family life and the new republic, in fact, that "union" served as a common term for both and marriage was soon reckoned the most appropriate social forum for new citizens, what Nancy Cott calls "a training ground of citizenly virtue" (2000: 18). Initially, those most likely to benefit from the domestic responsibilities that seemed to begin at home were the adult white males in whose names family property was vested by law, an arrangement that made for unequal "partnerships" in addition to dependants without public standing. But as the nineteenth century unfolded, particularly in the North, the ascendancy of urban market forces separating home and work helped to redefine domestic relations. What Peter Bardaglio has termed an "undifferentiated individualism" (1995: 35), one based on the marketplace premise of self-ownership, slowly recast bourgeois households as bound by affective ties and increasingly encouraged the feminized rhetoric in which their political agendas could be couched. Nowhere was the resulting domestic sphere more compelling than in the outcry over the Fugitive Slave Law, part of the mid-century compromise that forced free citizens to aid slave masters in returning "property" to bondage. It was enough to send one particular writer into a white heat.

While Lincoln may not actually have greeted Harriet Beecher Stowe as "the little woman who wrote the book that made this great war," there is little question that Stowe wrote the book that made great war literature for decades to come. The success of *Uncle Tom's Cabin* was quick and phenomenal: as Thomas Gossett has documented, 10,000 copies of the book were sold within a few days, 300,000 within the first year (1985: 164). Prompted by the Fugitive Slave Law, Stowe intended to focus her novel on the nature of property; her first subtitle, "The Man that Was a Thing," suggests not only the humanity Uncle Tom could never claim as a slave but also the cabin he could never legally own and the marriage with Aunt Chloe to which he could never legally consent. It is therefore worth noting that Stowe changed her subtitle after it had been announced. When the novel's first installment appeared during June 1851,

Uncle Tom's Cabin shifted attention to "Life among the Lowly," in no small measure because the anti-slavery *National Era* was directly aimed at Southerners whom the newspaper and authors like Stowe were hoping to persuade. For that reason, among others, many key scenes are communal, like the early cabin and parlor gatherings that aim to instruct as much as the assemblage of anti-slavery articles in the newspaper itself. The return to such gatherings over forty-one weeks suggests the manner in which serialized literature could imitate what Susan Belasco Smith calls "the complicated conversations and exchanges of false starts, distractions, and breaks that occur within the family circle" (1995: 71). Read as a magazine venture that situated political protest in such feminizing precincts instead of a finished novel that Stowe's own *Key* (1853) would help to document, *Uncle Tom's Cabin* was formally open-ended and politically shrewd. Its steady attention to "the lowly" added working-class urgency to issues of cabin property and Christian grace, especially for potential converts who were kept waiting for weekly installments and then encouraged by the *National Era* to write back.

That invitation to respond was more acutely felt in mid-century theaters. Even before serialization of Stowe's novel concluded dramatic versions were beginning to appear, and they would multiply throughout the decade that led to civil war. But theater houses of the 1850s catered to a different audience from anti-slavery newspapers. Although *Uncle Tom's Cabin* would lure respectable families to see one of the first full-length American productions to graft a moral cause onto a sentimental story, they shared the spectacle each week with the rowdy "b'hoys" they had previously scorned. As Eric Lott has observed, those longtime frequenters of the pits expected even more conventional melodrama than Stowe had serialized. To suit mechanic audiences as well as the more heavily male companies of the period, dramatizations of *Uncle Tom's Cabin* curbed Stowe's influential matrons, expanded her novel's verbal humor, and orchestrated a succession of special effects and tableaux that would become "Tom" hallmarks: living pictures that could be read even by the illiterate. Where serialization mimicked the interruptions of parlor life and thus quietly merged anti-slavery zeal with the rhythms of bourgeois households, melodramatic tableaux made grown b'hoys cry, and in record numbers. "For every one of the three hundred thousand who bought the novel in its first year," Lott observes, "many more eventually saw the play" (1993: 212). The size of that audience reveals how significant the theater of spectacle would prove to be in reckoning with the competing claims of property and self-ownership, as the political events of the 1850s accelerated.

The dramatization of *Uncle Tom's Cabin* that was closest to Stowe's novel, written by George Aiken during 1852 and brought to New York's National Theater in 1853, featured many of the same scenes and was thus generically agile in setting representational norms. The mulatta Eliza still escaped with her son on the ice floes of the Ohio River ("Courage, my child! – we will be free – or perish!"), her husband George still declared his independence in the language of the country's founders ("I'll fight for my liberty, to the last breath I breathe! You say your fathers did it, if it was right for them, it is right for me!"), and Uncle Tom himself still insisted on his longing to be free ("I'd rather have poor clothes, poor house, poor everything, and have 'em *mine*, than have the best, if they belong to somebody else"). On the stage, freedom was again tied to ownership for men, to domestic sanctuary for women, often in language that the War of Independence had made familiar. But in the play's heavenly conclusion, a visual departure from Stowe's final gesture toward Africa, the beaten Uncle Tom kneels beside his former master while above them, amid clouds and sun, little Eva appears robed in white on the back of a dove. She is the picture of piety rather than property, of housebound innocence rather than breakaway independence. In a heaven without the rambunctious Topsy, white virtue seemingly trumped black aspiration as the national "family" grew.

The spectacle's powerful shorthand made drama a political vehicle of moment as the Civil War neared, particularly when fiction's narrative sway could be made visually arresting and ideologically charged in the wake of events. The spectacle that concludes Dion Boucicault's *The Octoroon* (1859), which opened within days of abolitionist John Brown's execution at Harper's Ferry, focuses like *Uncle Tom's Cabin* on the loss of youth. As if to stymie slave uprising once more, Boucicault's beautiful octoroon does not finally escape; she breathes her last in George Peyton's Louisiana home, where she is surrounded on stage by the white and black plantation family. But that concluding tableau barely replaces the screams of the overseer turned owner who has been chased offstage by an Indian with a tomahawk. As Bluford Adams has observed, Boucicault's red and black characters join to make slave insurrection a counterpoint to the "self-annihilating octoroon" (1997: 155) and to make the drama of savage revenge a threatening alternative to the failed romance of amalgamation.

The sharp edge of liberty was similarly insistent in William Wells Brown's play *The Escape; or, A Leap for Freedom* (1858), the first drama written and published by an ex-slave. Where Stowe's George ultimately makes for Liberia with his family and Aiken's George disappears from the play with Eliza and their child, Brown foregrounds the narrative of black agency, which follows this play's mulatto couple to Niagara Falls and the boat they grab for freedom. Against the backdrop of iconic tumble and mist, the representative Mr. White ("I'll fight for freedom!") also sees the error of little Eva's self-satisfaction and learns the lesson in true equality that Boucicault's George never taught. Although *The Escape* was never fully mounted or performed, Brown's dramatic readings did more to win support for abolition than the lectures he delivered to the Mr. Whites of the anti-slavery North, particularly after the Dred Scott decision in 1857 found that black men had no rights which white men were bound to respect. *The Escape* literally gave Brown a voice, especially in its unmounted opportunities to "leap for freedom" through the differing voices of his cast.

The question of who could inherit the revolutionary legacy of freedom and property, also the central question of Boucicault's *The Octoroon* and of later wartime emancipation, was formulated as well in novels by African Americans during the 1850s, although the grounds of their responses to Stowe and thus their claims to legitimacy varied significantly. In his single work of fiction, *The Heroic Slave* (1853), Frederick Douglass reimagined the reports of an 1841 revolt aboard a slave ship that granted "cargo" the stature of colonial patriots. The consequence, as Maggie Sale has observed, is more than "a founding father in blackface" (1995: 45); instead, Douglass effectively reconceives the Revolution as an emancipatory fight for all sons of liberty, though not for liberty's daughters. While Douglass's Marcus Washington returns for his wife only to be captured by a slave-gang ("humanity converted into merchandise"), the slave story of female promise and danger was more incisively told by Hannah Crafts in *The Bondwoman's Narrative*, a recently recovered manuscript from the 1850s that hinges on the malediction of an aging slave as she hangs from a linden tree. Her curse leads to a concubine's escape and the autobiography of a semi-fictional character that includes sufficient verifiable reference for Henry Louis Gates, Jr. (2002) to document its author's probable race. But the "undeviating happiness" Hannah says she finds in the North was undone in principle by Harriet E. Wilson's *Our Nig* (1859), another recovered novel whose subtitle is crucial: "Sketches from the Life of a Free Black, In a Two-Story White House, North. Showing That Slavery's Shadows Fall Even There." Where Douglass posited new sons of liberty and Crafts followed new black families into the land of the free, Wilson portrayed the corrosive domesticity of black female servants in Northern households ("Faugh! to lodge one; to eat with one; to admit one through the front door; to sit next to one; awful!"), servants whose "undifferentiated individualism" was a mirage and whose freedom lay ambiguously in the blackness of print.

During the years of growing sectionalism, the South made little pretence of broadening the claim to freedom and property, and not simply because investments in chattel could not readily be set aside. Industrializing less rapidly, Southern states maintained a largely rural emphasis on the household as a site of production and thus a patriarchal stronghold rather than a feminine sphere. A wholly different domestic order emerged in the region over time, a conservative ethos bound by laws and customs that the North was leaving behind. As Peter Bardaglio has put it, "A distinctive variation of republicanism developed in the household of the Old South, one based more on hierarchy and dependence than on egalitarianism and consent" (1995: xi). Buttressing that social order were the lingering priorities of coverture, which had at one time more pervasively established men as heads of household who "covered" their women. By the eve of the Civil War, the persisting subordination of Southern wives and even single women made marriage a fitting analogy for a solely masculine claim to independence, especially when slavery was deemed a similar "domestic relation" overseen by a benevolent patriarch. As Stephanie McCurry has astutely observed, the principle of hierarchy extended as well to yeoman households, which aligned their interests with planter control more thoroughly than has been acknowledged. "The yeomanry's passionate commitment to independence and equality," writes McCurry, "betrayed an equally passionate commitment to dependence and desperate inequality. That was the nature of slavery republicanism" (1992: 37). Southern advocates of slavery were thus hostile to abolition not only because they demanded a secure labor force but also because they approved what Emily Field Van Tassel calls "the organic bonds of dependency" (1995: 883), which were fostered and preserved in patriarchal households by slavery and coverture.

Domestic fiction in the South therefore undergirded a remarkably different paradigm of social order, even in the hands of women writers. If Stowe's *Uncle Tom's Cabin* was the clarion call of the free labor North, Augusta Jane Evans's *Macaria; or, Altars of Sacrifice* (1864) was the South's most substantial response in kind. A Confederate bestseller first printed on wrapping paper, the book was read by men as well as women, in camps and hospitals as well as parlors, in the North as well as the South; a copy smuggled through the lines prompted a New York edition, though Jan Bakker points out that Union officers prohibited their men from reading the novel's enticing case for Southern independence and sectional self-possession (1987: 132). Curiously, it is not a final marriage but *Macaria's* paired female protagonists, one a well-educated aristocrat studying astronomy ("I am a free-born American") and the other a less moneyed artist ("I must depend upon myself"), who champion the "Freedom – Independence" of the Confederacy after the man they both love has enlisted and the unencumbered future they anticipated has been sacrificed. While both subsequently refuse loveless marriages, they elect instead "the broad highway of Duty," which appears to be less a tribute to individual choice than an acknowledgment of inevitable hierarchy. After all, both suspend their studies for hospital work and later teaching. In the course of the novel, Evans merely nods to "the perpetuity of the institution of slavery" and avoids coverture altogether in setting marriage aside; but the "macaria" or sacrifice cum blessing her protagonists choose underlines the "Womanly Usefulness" they accept rather than the Yankee market they revile. The protracted speeches they make, a generic burden of a more philosophical sort, ultimately set the terms of their submission to the Southern novel's organic bonds and the Southern novelist's sense of woman's place, which only flirts with Stowe's domestic insurgency.

Other Southern women were less self-abnegating in their narratives, but the war they regularly chronicled as "the battle of Southern independence" was rarely the avenue to personal liberty that Stowe's Eliza found on the ice floes or Douglass's revolutionary sailors claimed for themselves. Constance Cary, who conceived a series of letters between "Secessia" in Baltimore and "Refugitta" in Richmond printed as "Blockade Correspondence" in 1864, also published other short fiction in Southern periodicals, including a three-part story entitled "A Summer Idyl" in the *Southern Illustrated News* toward the end of 1862. Set in rural Virginia during the war's second summer, the story follows the retreat of Bel Peyton from Richmond's wartime hardships to the Virginia mountains, though the narrative progresses by intercutting correspondence with the city so that the "horrors" of the Confederate capital intrude on the "abrupt green hill-sides" of "Bumpkindom." The counterpoint in locales is picked up in the story's verbal froth, especially the military metaphors that run through Bel's mountain romance: when her bickering sweetheart asks that they "let the white flag be hung out," his wit suggests the difficulty of separating the war's advance from the heroine's retreat, or his liberty as an officer on leave from her "shame-faced" acquiescence in marriage.

Bel's early feistiness brought to heel is in keeping with the brash intelligence of Mary Boykin Chesnut's diary, which has long been praised as a quotidian entrée to the upper reaches of Confederate Richmond but turns out to be fiction of an unusual sort. Although it is true that the well-connected Chesnut kept a private journal during the war, C. Vann Woodward (1981) has shown that the forty-eight notebooks of her "wartime diary" were actually crafted several decades and several novels later (1881–4): good reason for Daniel Aaron to have described her pages as "a fictional memoir" that "presented herself and the War novelistically" (2003: 251). Certainly the diary is narratively adroit and relentlessly candid; so much so that Suzy Clarkson Holstein sees Chesnut postponing publication for decades because she was struggling with "the ideal, dependent woman" she chafed at becoming (1991: 126). As Chesnut put it, "there is no slave, after all, like a wife." Much more customary during the war years, when men could be patriarchs in absentia, was Mrs. Mary Jones's journal lament as Sherman marched through Montevideo, Georgia, on his way to the sea. "Oh, if my country was but free and independent," Jones wrote on December 22, 1864, "I could take joyfully the spoiling of my goods!" (Jones et al. 1995). The subservience of Southern wives translated readily into the patriotism of Confederate matrons, even as revolutionary liberties receded with the impending fall of Richmond.

In the hands of men, Southern fiction of the 1860s was far more likely to assume the willing subservience of Mary Jones than the irrepressible challenge of Mary Chesnut. But domestic dependency shaped a masculine fiction of Confederate nationalism in other ways, particularly for citizens who saw themselves continuing what Drew Gilpin Faust calls "the struggle of 1776" (1988: 14). William Gilmore Simms, for instance, had already produced a series of revolutionary romances tied allegorically to the political events of the 1850s, as Charles Watson (1992) has pointed out. In 1858 Simms projected a final volume meant to link the impending conflict to the causes of the first war between "rebels" and "loyalists." The manuscript progressed during the early 1860s, but for want of a publisher Simms did not complete *Joscelyn: A Tale of the Revolution* (1867) until New York's *The Old Guard* agreed to serialize installments after the war. In this late novel from an aging virtuoso, the threat of "a dreadful war" is set against "home delights" in two sharply drawn characters who suggest the rhetorical weight of parlors in winning a revolution. The cause of the Crown is most forcefully argued by a yeoman loyalist so outspoken and, at length, so tarred and feathered that he becomes itinerant, stranded in "an almost contemptuous heedlessness" that Simms associates with the imperial North. Simms figures the wiser policy of home maintenance in the maiden aunt whose apparent dependence upon a bullying patriarch masks sound judgment and the wisdom that "Liberty Boys" in backwater Georgia and South Carolina needed to learn. Even before Lee's surrender at Appomattox prompted Simms to consider Reconstruction strategies, he imagined the cause of national independence tied to domestic negotiation as much as stump invective, to the preservation of homes (and black waiting maids) as much as the risks of sacred honor.

Those priorities shifted when the fighting began and writers from the war's battlefields emerged to celebrate Southern honor. Though lauded more often for his poetry, Sidney Lanier tried his hand at a single novel entitled *Tiger-Lilies* (1867), which he began mid-war during his service as a Confederate scout in the Signal Corps and then his months in federal prisons. Written sporadically in three distinct "books," his novel is uneven and generically awkward, what biographer Aubrey Harrison Starke terms "a fairly close autobiographical record" (1933: 98) as well as "an allegorical account" (p. 100) and "almost a literary scrapbook" (p. 103). As Lanier himself admits in his preface, his principal narrative difficulty was balancing the experience of a veteran with the imagination of a writer, "facts" with "truth," which helps explain the generic blur that reads sometimes like a loosely philosophical German romance and sometimes like a wartime chronicle. Still, key early scenes like the deer hunt, the musical performance, the college pranks, and the duel belong to men, whereas most of the novel's women (even those with significant property) are unnamed and ineffectual. Once the war begins, Lanier is at his best far from patrician romance in contrasting well-schooled officers with less moneyed volunteers and conscripts, some of whom resent the Confederacy's demands. Where the heroines of *Macaria* sacrificed science and art for duty, the yeoman brothers of *Tiger-Lilies* lose the honor of their mountain family when one deserts ("what did they drag me from hoam and fambly for?"), only to discover he has lost the cabin and kin he returns to claim. The burnt earth he finds instead, "the charred remains of his kingdom," obliterates wife and child amid the stumbling eloquence of his dismay. His revenge on the rich man who had him drafted similarly confirms the persistent Southern assumption of wifely subordination: the bullet that kills the planter through an open window also kills the planter's wife, as she lays her head on his.

Although the title of Lanier's novel was meant to join a crouching masculine passion to a delicate womanly virtue as they had flowered together in war, *Tiger-Lilies* sees the planter's wife as an acquisition, the yeoman's wife as a grave. What might be called the male world of blood and regiments predominates, as was common in the fiction of other Confederate veterans even when it was less severe. William H. Kemper, writing for Baltimore's *Southern Magazine*, later set "The Sergeant's Little Story" (October 1873) in the midst of the euchre and decanters of camp life, where "licker" brings messmates together to hear the tale of a scout. "Confederate Gray" set "T. J.'s Cavalry Charge" (April 1870), a comic story published in Baltimore's *New Eclectic Monthly*, among the "hardy mountaineers" with whom T.J. has long caroused and sometimes shared the occasional "stag dance" with its substitute girls. John Esten Cooke was more preoccupied with authenticating his scenes in *Surry of Eagle's-Nest* (1866), the autobiography of a fictional officer that trips over more footnotes ("his words," "an actual occurrence," "a real incident") than fiction can readily absorb. But he memorably pictures enemy soldiers captured in northern Virginia and put in their place when they are made to carry black babies. "A long line of Federal prisoners were marching on foot over the dusty high road to Winchester, accompanied by a guard of cavalry," Cooke writes; "each one of the blue-coats carried in his arms a negro child!" Since Cooke further reports that the guard was savoring "this compulsory dry nursism," his peculiar scene suggests nothing so much as an inverted Southern household, a patriarchal order turned upside down for Union prisoners. Cooke also notes the "disgust" of Yankee invaders made to "carry the darkey," the most revealing touch in his momentary portrait of the "late Revolution" as yet another veteran defense of home and family whose women have disappeared and whose slaves have yet to find their footing.

Significantly, the fiction of Confederate veterans and fellow travelers like Simms appeared after the war ended, though its composition often began earlier. Just as significantly, Southern writers by that time looked almost immediately to publishing houses in the North. Lanier traveled to New York in 1867; Simms went in 1866, as did Cooke, who found he could scarcely tolerate "the Yankees," as Steve Davis notes (1978: 68), but could make an exception for Northern editors. Simms's career reveals why; for decades, the older writer had complained about the inadequacy of Southern publishers, who knew little about what biographer John Caldwell Guilds calls "merchandising" (1992: 289). As a magazine editor himself, Simms had also fretted that Southern subscribers did not pay and that Southern planters did not subscribe, another reason why his novels had long been published in New York. Following the war and his trip north, Simms was willing to settle for simple serial publication in *The Old Guard*, a stridently oppositional journal (anti-Lincoln, anti-war, anti-abolitionist) that paid poorly but had found an audience since 1862. That was more than any Southern literary magazine could claim; none lasted past 1865, and those that were founded later rarely paid their contributors. A few writers like Evans and Cary could still afford to rely on Southern publishing opportunities and could hold fast to a settled patrician order in the face of wartime upheavals. But Southern novelists in need of an income after the war ended had to look north, which meant acclimating their fiction to the evolving domestic priorities, the premium on self-ownership, and the dynamic social relations that the marketplace favored and emancipation confirmed.

While Southern printing presses were ailing for want of replacement parts or rendered useless by advancing armies like Sherman's, Northern publishing houses were booming, fueled by what Alice Fahs calls "the complex synergy between patriotism and commerce" (2001: 15). Lanier would rail against such vulgar "Trade" when he defended the "Chivalry" of the South, as Daniel Aaron has pointed out (2003: 270), but the war was indisputably good for expanding Northern business in new directions, like George Palmer Putnam's *Rebellion Record*, the United States Christian Commission's traveling loan libraries, Root and Cary's illustrated song sheets, and James Redpath's "Books for the Camp Fires" series. Several of these ventures were aimed at military men often bored enough for long stretches to read for pleasure as they never had previously; more than four out of five were literate, according to David Kaser, and that was more than enough to encourage the series and libraries that only grew in number after Appomattox (Kaser 1984: 4). The increasing capacity to read, soon shared by freed slaves, bespeaks a distinctive Northern individualism through schooling. As William Charvat has put it, "education was the social foundation on which the region was building a culture radically different in quality, depth, and extent from the patrician culture which had prevailed in the old urban centers and in the South" (1992: 303). Of course, catering to camps and hospitals as well as cabins did not mean abandoning Northern parlors or, for that matter, neglecting the homes for which soldiers had fought or the "house divided" their war was beginning to redefine. In the North as well as the South, the adventure of war was never far from the summons of home; north of the Mason–Dixon line, the gendered differences in Confederate fiction were echoed and curiously amplified.

The most remarkable distinction in the first Northern fiction about the Civil War came with the greater liberty of the war's women, no matter what their race. Given the Southern mainstay of female dependency, it is noteworthy that Louisa May Alcott, for instance, could not stay put. While she would make her postwar fame with the domestic fiction par excellence of *Little Women* (1868–9), her wartime service as a Union nurse took her out of her father's home in Concord for a wayward journey to Washington DC, and a decidedly wayward novella. Based on letters she wrote to her family during the latter half of 1862, *Hospital Sketches* (1863) was assembled for serial publication in Boston's *Commonwealth*, an anti-slavery newspaper, before book publication that same year and later republication with further stories in 1869. Each reappearance added to the fictional patina of Tribulation Periwinkle, the hospital nurse at Hurly-burly House who displaces the masculine ethos of warfare to privilege the feminine territory of recovery and the jubilation of New Year's Day 1863, when Lincoln's proclamation took effect and freedmen "tooted and tramped" through Washington's streets. Consistently, Alcott ties the latitude of her protagonist to the liberation of slaves; when Nurse Periwinkle passes the capitol building under construction, she sees the new dome's "statue of Liberty" waiting in the mud without a pedestal, much as the country was waiting for the pedestal that emancipation would provide. In Liberty's hand she also spots a bird's nest, as though domesticity in *Hospital Sketches* were held high in the name of freedom. But since the claims of home literally appear beyond the reach of freedmen in the capital's muddy streets, Nurse P's "omen" suggests an unspoken hierarchy among the rebellious, what Elizabeth Young describes as "an allegorical fantasy of white maternal leadership" (1999: 93). Having found her place in an army of female volunteers, Nurse P chronicles the hurly-burly promise of her "house" away from home without *Our Nig*'s disdain but without bringing the premises any closer to black ownership.

Although Alcott herself saw waves of the wounded, particularly after the Union's calamitous loss at Fredericksburg in mid-December 1862, the story of how Northern soldiers fell and whose union they fought to defend came more regularly from veterans, who were less likely to notice cunning nests than to report on wartime damage. Of the many such accounts that began appearing once the war had ended, few have remained as intriguing as John W. De Forest's *Miss Ravenel's Conversion from*

Secession to Loyalty (1867), which interweaves battlefield trauma (the "scattering musketry of broken lines," the coward's "ghastly backward glare of horror," the "great pools of clotted blood") with intricate affairs of the heart. Therein lay one of the novel's problems. When Harper and Bros. bought the manuscript, begun in late 1864 after De Forest was mustered out of the Twelfth Connecticut, their intention was to serialize the novel in New York's *Harper's Monthly*. But the Harpers eventually demurred: the novel was thought too bracing for family consumption, and not because of De Forest's sharp battlefield reports. After all, his military accounts (like "The First Time Under Fire" and "The Battle of Cedar Creek") had been appearing in the same magazine since 1864. Nor were the Harpers worried that families in the victorious North would be appalled by Lillie Ravenel's titular conversion, the verbo-ten change of heart that would never have occurred to Cary's Bel Peyton and that arguably kept Mary Chesnut's diary out of print. The sticking point proved to be De Forest's cynical revision of Southern honor through two characters: the novel's charismatic Colonel Carter, a southerner in the Union army who cannot control his appetites, and an even more wily Creole widow who joins nonchalant adultery to business acumen completely "unchecked by conscience" or narrative censure. If the colonel was unacceptable to the Methodist Harpers in his patrician indulgences, the widow was disquieting in her readiness to convert, meanwhile accommodating distracted husbands and acquiring real estate. As Thomas Fick writes of De Forest's novel, "The stable world of property and patriarchy was giving way to the risky one of capital investment" (1992: 488). For the Harpers as cultural gatekeepers, De Forest's ambitious widow amounted to an uncavalier "tiger lily," a new woman amiably ready to pounce in a war that was at once heroic and corrupt.

How much the abolition of slavery figured in that new social order depended on whose story of the war got told in print. While De Forest was largely content with the occasional happy darkey in his conversion narrative, which dwelled instead on the complexities of gender, the stories circulated in Northern periodicals ranged more widely and half-assimilated those "created equal" with distinct formal adjustments. "Buried Alive" (7 May 1864) in New York's *Harper's Weekly* reported the recent slaughter of colored regiments at Fort Pillow through the voice of a slave volunteer, whose short narrative reprints the last letter of a butchered fellow soldier. By contrast, "Believe in Ghosts!" (3 November 1870), a short anecdote published anonymously in Washington's *New National Era*, described a ruined Virginia mansion and the night-time "column of flame" that glides spectrally toward it without mentioning the Union picket's race, even to "the Colored People of the United States" who read Frederick Douglass's postwar newspaper. Constance Fenimore Woolson's "Wilhel-mina" (January 1875) in Boston's *Atlantic Monthly* grafted service and race onto one another imaginatively by tallying the cost of the war to an Ohio separatist community in three consecutive endings, in the course of which an adopted "Nubian" daughter ultimately dies unloved after her Gustav leaves her for a nearby regiment and then the gilt beads and "new ways" of Cincinnati. "Thomas Elliott's Speculations" (February 1863), published like De Forest's battle reports in *Harper's Monthly*, anticipated the appeal of Cincinnati's surging commerce by catching the euphoria of New York's commission merchants when the port of New Orleans opened to Northern trade ("Allonthesquare!" "honorbright!") in 1862, without a word about slavery or a twitch in its headlong dialogue for anyone more significant than the boss's daughter. Although author Fred B. Perkins was the nephew of Harriet Beecher Stowe and the father of Charlotte Perkins Gilman, neither the fate of the slaves nor the self-possession of yet another Lily keeps his hero from becoming the "proprietor" of a willing wife and the junior partner in a thriving business. That hunger for commercial enterprise encouraged a postwar magazine neglect of "Nubian" opportunity and instead favored ex-states over ex-slaves, particularly once black veterans won voting rights in 1870.

The literary elision of slavery as the war's spur can be seen even earlier in the Northern focus on the conflict of comrades, a substitute focus that Kirk Savage sees ultimately privileging "a normative white soldier and citizen" (1997: 167) over black volunteers or emancipated slaves in later public monuments. Commemorating the war in their own fashion, Herman Melville and Walt Whitman each published a volume of war poetry within months of Union victory, and each included at least one long poem that nods to the pull of narrative, the shiver of setting, and the instructive choice of essential characters. In Melville's *Battle-Pieces and Aspects of the War* (1866), the "Conflict of Convictions" in the collection's opening pages gives way to a volley of battle poems as verse experiments that culminate in "A Scout toward Aldie," a near-ballad about Virginia's John Singleton Mosby and his harrying guerrilla success in the shadow of the capitol's new iron dome. Fleetingly in the poem's several haunted scenes, the rancor of the occupied South takes the form of a veiled lady and her slave; but Melville's black man seems to shrug at freedom, and the proud lady may be Mosby in disguise, a measure of masculine usurpation in the territory that the "shark" Mosby patrols and the "boyish" Northern colonel loses during a fatal ambush. In what Edward Goggin describes as "a world of misperceptions, mistaken identities, fatuous notions, and lethal misunderstandings" (1993: 5), Melville reveals that Mosby's "homily" ("*Man must die*") leaves little room for mercy.

This is the world Whitman sought to ease in *Drum-Taps* (1865), where his own wartime experience as a nurse in Washington hospitals lay the ground for the "wound dresser" he limned and the elegy to Lincoln he added in "When Lilacs Last in the Dooryard Bloom'd." More lyric than Melville's stern reckoning, Whitman's "Lilacs" at one point follows the journey of the President's coffin across the country to Illinois, though Whitman's Lincoln is not named any more than Melville's Mosby is seen. Where Melville underlines clash in a perpetual "or" that trades "the Founder's dream" for "Dominion," however, Whitman imagines joining the spring smell of lilacs to the promise of the evening star and the dark swamp of the hermit thrush in a perpetual "and," one born out of a "serenade" to death. It is the poet's recuperative gift, his own echoing song like a sprig of lilac placed on the passing coffin, that transfigures the "convulsiveness" of the war years into joy, what M. Wynn Thomas calls a "redemptive anguish" that scarcely acknowledges emancipation or the "racially inclusive" agenda of Reconstruction (1997–8: 103–4). Even as early as 1865, "comrades" were becoming the war's replacement cast in the bivouacs and hospitals that could serve as model homes for the reconstructing years to come.

Wartime photographs reveal that those temporary havens were not inevitably white. Fugitive slaves serving white officers and colored troops serving the Union cause were also entitled to the rewards of duty and homes of their own, at least in print. But black women, who had served as wartime cooks, laundresses, spies, and teachers in some numbers, were not regularly photographed or pensioned. During the years following emancipation, they had to find a narrative substitute for the fugitive wandering of Hannah Crafts and often a new genre to encompass the sense of self they were suddenly free to fashion. For dressmaker Elizabeth Keckley in *Behind the Scenes; or, Thirty Years a Slave, and Four Years in the White House* (1868), that was part slave narrative with emancipation coming early, part autobiography with more attention to Lincoln than to 'Lizabeth, and part sentimental novel with next to no place for Keckley's own family, though plenty of room for publisher James Redpath to include copies of Mrs. Lincoln's letters without permission. What holds this hybrid narrative together is not the antebellum role of the suffering slave, as Jennifer Fleischner has pointed out (1996: 93–132), but the acquisition of property, what Keckley attributes to "youth's important lesson of self-reliance" and Frances Smith Foster describes as an early genius for transforming herself "from capital to capitalist" (1992: 49). Keckley nevertheless surrendered her lucrative dressmaking business to oversee Mrs. Lincoln's muddled post-assassination finances, just as she surrendered her recollecting voice to Mrs. Lincoln's letters and her publishing venture to Robert Lincoln's rage at her seeming revelations about his mother. When he halted distribution of *Behind the Scenes*, Keckley saw her narrative bid for freedom and property fail and her lessons of self-reliance evaporate.

The uncertain postwar ground of female self-fashioning was considerably less treacherous for Belle Boyd, the Confederate spy whose *Belle Boyd in Camp and Prison* (1865) reveals a deft impersonator repeatedly inventing herself as gender roles became a disguise. Where Keckley's chief verbal maneuver was an enigmatic silence, Boyd's was a tantalizing ventriloquism in remembered scenes with Stonewall Jackson and then a shrewd acquiescence when her husband's narrative voice interrupted her own. His interpolated journal might appear to reassert domestic dependency through narrative displacement, a verbal claim to this tandem autobiography's final word. But as a result of his concluding chapters the prose burden of Southern defeat is borne by an emasculated Confederate officer, a "Mr. Belle Boyd" who declines like the Confederacy as his wife survives with greater panache. Boyd's memoir went through two editions and was flourishing in 1868 when Keckley's was so furiously attacked by Robert Lincoln, persuasive evidence that the cultural negotiations of Reconstruction allowed more play to renegade Confederate patriotism than to deliberate black assimilation.

This was not a foregone conclusion or an uninterrupted lesson in whose rights Reconstruction was bound to respect. With the number of magazines and their readers on the rise, the market for competing visions of a more perfect union grew apace, even if book publication proved as elusive for others as it had for Simms. Tucked into a neglected corner of postwar print was Philadelphia's *Christian Recorder*, the organ of the African Methodist Episcopal Church in which Frances E. W. Harper serialized *Minnie's Sacrifice* (1869) for the largely black middle-class audience that the church had long shepherded. Harper's recently recovered novel skewers white benevolence and eventually mulatto accommodation when the titular heroine is killed in the unsettled postwar South of Ku Klux terror. In her place, Harper's novel champions the enduring freedmen Minnie had begun to teach and the near-white husband who insists on the importance of owning land, what Harper calls "earth hunger." It is as though the spectacle of little Eva were replaced by Uncle Tom with a hoe, or Alcott's statue of Liberty had tossed its nest into the mud that freedmen could reach. Since *Minnie's Sacrifice* includes parts of Harper's speeches and occasional open letters, the novel's structure itself favors the principle of redistribution, with the result that what Farah Jasmine Griffin terms the "cross-class alliances between blacks and free people of color" (2001: 312) crowd out the onerous privileges of whiteness.

As Radical Reconstruction foundered after 1870, however, it was much more likely that the privileges of whiteness would obliterate the gains Harper wrote to enable as well as the "white maternal leadership" of Alcott's women. When Mark Twain and Charles Dudley Warner collaborated to produce *The Gilded Age* (1873), the only hints of emancipation were a defeated congressional scam for educating freedmen and a "scowl" on the face of a black cadaver that female medical students hesitate to dissect. The imagined outrage of the "persecuted black man" even after death is palpable; but in a novel whose delirious graft would give the postbellum period its name, the questions briefly prompted are set aside as quickly as "the new one" can be covered up again. Female ambition fares little better: medical studies lead to collapse as well as the joy of "dependence on another's nature" for a girl from Pennsylvania, while a girl from Missouri who shrewdly lobbies Washington congressmen is stranded by a sensational murder and "heart trouble." In this collaborative novel, what Ellen Goldner calls "the strategy of the joint venture" (1993: 69) simultaneously characterizes both the book's composition and its contrapuntal challenge to gendered expectations, as though the epidemic logic of the market could reduce liberty's daughters as well as the war's freedmen to scam and slab.

The hopes of liberated slaves and liberating women were also associated in Albion Tourgée's *A Fool's Errand* (1879), particularly when the novel's resolute carpetbagger is saved from a North Carolina lynching by the "plucky" midnight ride of his daughter Lily. With her subsequent marriage to a Southern scion, however, the "fool" abandons the state for a capitalist venture in Central America, his plan for black schools, black houses, and black land titles demolished by what Tourgée calls "the triumph of the ancient South." Although *A Fool's Errand* electrified the North during the campaign year of 1880, when Tourgée added an account of the Ku Klux Klan entitled *The Invisible Empire*, sales lapsed during 1881, as Edmund Wilson has noted (1994: 536); and genuine reconstruction in Tourgée's North Carolina lapsed even earlier with the return to power of "a people who did not regard the colored man as having any *inherent* right to liberty and self-government." That was not Reconstruction's last hurrah or liberty's keenest challenge: in George Washington Cable's *The Grandissimes* (1880), an enslaved African prince finally demands more from his master so thunderously that Barbara Ladd sees the regal Bras-Coupé as "a locus for black defiance" (1991: 73) and Robert Allen Alexander further credits his insurgency as a "resistance to commodification" (2002: 130). But Cable could not sell his unpicturesque story to Northern magazines during the 1870s, and the novel that eventually grew up around the thrice-told tale of Bras-Coupé's demand was evidently more pleasing for its Creole romance set in the days of the Louisiana Purchase and its eventual exile of both the fierce voodoo priestess who dreams of insurrection and the free man of color who enters the novel a diffident man of property and leaves it a haggard suicide. More intent than Twain and Warner on emancipation's radiating tremors, Tourgée and Cable could not sustain their reconstructed casts, and their novels break instead into multiple endings as flagging characters die.

Instead of the black land titles that Tourgée asserted and Cable delivered, the most saleable version of black desire after 1877, when federal troops were recalled to their barracks and ex-Confederates moved into Southern statehouses, was the lure of the briar patch that Joel Chandler Harris recalled from the cabins of his youth. As the first of several Harris collections, *Uncle Remus: His Songs and His Sayings* (1880) assembled a genre-busting thirty-four legends, twenty-one sayings, ten songs, a clutch of proverbs, and a reconstructed "Story of the War" that together located plantation life, as Stowe once had, in the slave quarters. After nearly thirty years, however, it was nostalgia and sass that made Harris's compilation what David Blight terms the year's "number one best-selling book" (2001: 228). Two weeks after publication, the first two printings of 1,500 had both sold out; as Joseph Griska has noted, sales would thereafter average 4,000 copies a year through the end of the century and beyond (1981: 32–5). Northern magazines like the *Critic* and the *North American Review* invited Harris to make further contributions, and *Scribner's Monthly* in a regular column about "Topics of the Times" championed the South for its "new literary era" based on a "broad sympathy and catholic culture" that New England could no longer claim (Anon. 1881: 786). As Walter Brasch has noted, Harris accepted his New York publisher's title but had favored "Uncle Remus's Folk-Lore" (2000: 66): an acknowledgment that the cabins of the South had stories worth telling as much as souls worth saving.

For his part, Harris popularized a seemingly playful world of "de animils en de beastesses" in what he called a "curiously sympathetic supplement" to *Uncle Tom's Cabin*. On this Georgia plantation after the war, however, it is the comradeship of an aging black "uncle" and a little white boy that invites stories by the cabin fire, not the good girl summons of Little Eva on the wings of a dove. While the redemptive affection that Stowe aimed to teach still frames the tales that Harris retells, the plantation loyalty of Uncle Remus fades before the briar-patch liberty of Brer Rabbit and the lessons in "lopin' up de big road," more often shared with little boys than

Figure 12.1 A new kind of bondage

The postwar failure to give the freed slaves any land, not even the forty acres and a mule they had been promised, meant a new form of economic dependence – sharecropping, often on land owned by the former master. The plantation was divided into small plots farmed by individual families; the landlord supplied the land, tools, seed, mules, and food in return for a contractually agreed upon price or a portion of the harvested crop. The landlord usually supervised the operations and marketed the crop. Because of the crop lien system, usurious interest rates, exorbitant prices on food and supplies, and swindling on the part of store owners and landlords, most sharecroppers fell into heavy debt. During Reconstruction, courts adjudicated conflicts between landlords and credit merchants, on the one hand, and sharecroppers, on the other. But after 1877 both the state legislatures and the courts tilted their support to the landlords and merchants, leaving sharecroppers with no means of redressing grievances. Combined with other legal forms of discrimination and disenfranchisement, and extralegal forms of terrorism, sharecropping was one of the institutions of the New South that prevented African Americans from becoming citizens in any meaningful way. Eventually, the lack of economic opportunity, social equality, and political rights led to the great migration of African Americans to Northern cities in the twentieth century.

In this 1875 photograph, an unidentified white man on a horse, perhaps the former master or overseer, ominously looks on as a family of sharecroppers harvests cotton. (Photograph by permission of Picture History.)

little girls. Harris genteelly blunted their instructive edge for the unwary; as he put it in his introduction, "it is not virtue that triumphs, but helplessness; it is not malice, but mischievousness." While the trickster's spunk is temperate enough when he is "smokin' his seegyar," especially in a plank-and-rock house with the "lookin'-glass," "chist," "rockin'-cheer," and "terbarker" he can call his own, Brer Rabbit also demolishes what little Eva would gather round: he boils Brer Wolf in scalding water, watches Brer Possum get roasted alive for his own theft, and sends Brer Fox's head to the Fox children for dinner. What Robert Hemenway calls a "liberating sense of anarchy" (1982: 30) Stowe might have called a heartless independence, one surprisingly close to the malevolence of Legree when Brer Rabbit can "slap de spurrers into Brer Fox flanks" and ride him like the family horse. As an exercise in a veritable "Give me liberty or die," *Uncle Remus: His Songs and His Sayings* repeatedly portrays the big road of Reconstruction as ornery, acquisitive, and male.

Arguably, that post-emancipation road was more regularly traveled by freedmen, whose voting rights the Fifteenth Amendment was meant to secure and whose military service was thereby rewarded. As veterans in a late-century culture that would witness the expansion of the Grand Army of the Republic (founded 1866) and the emergence of magazines like the *Southern Bivouac* (founded 1882) and the *Confederate Veteran* (founded 1893) as well as the *Century's* ambitious series "Battles and Leaders of the Civil War" (1884–7), freedmen would become the very sons of liberty Frederick Douglass once imagined, even at the expense of Frances Harper's Minnies. As wartime soldiers, they also had access that freedwomen did not to the more immediate camaraderie of militia units and fraternal societies in addition to the unusual assistance of the United States Christian Commission in learning how to read, particularly after a call went out on behalf of colored troops for the primers, spelling books, and blackboards that David Kaser has noted (1984: 109). As ex-slaves, whatever their military standing, they finally became "heads of household" as soon as the war's end could bring the Freedman's Bureau to the South and a substitute system of domestic dependency could be established. "Bureau agents," writes Nancy Cott, "construed the freedman's command over the persons and labor of his wife and children as a reward of his free status and an evidence of his citizenship" (2000: 93). Certainly the postwar move of freedpeople from the centralized slave quarters to more scattered housing brought the work of black women in their inner yards under the supervision of their men, an example of what Eric Foner describes as "the increasingly patriarchal quality of black family life" (1988: 88). And yet Foner is one of many historians who also notes how quick freedpeople were to confirm their marriages once the abolition of slavery made such vows legal and once the war's end made black family reunions possible and joyous. Those renewed marriages and restless migrations gave unexpected meaning to the pursuit of happiness after freedpeople could claim life and liberty at last. Because the featherbeds, wagons, patch crops, and livestock that slaves had quietly accumulated were not legally "owned," as Dylan Penningroth (2003) has pointed out, their sense of property was always less acquisitive or individualistic than bound to the family and social ties that Penningroth examines and that the hybrid literature of the Civil War and Reconstruction fitfully sought to explore.

For Rebecca Harding Davis in 1867, the enterprise of freedmen was heroic but fraught with difficulties. In *Waiting for the Verdict*, her slave boy Sap is adopted and educated by a Quaker matron; he becomes a sought-after surgeon with a well-appointed hospital, a sprawling estate, and the comforts of the wealthy. Because he is light enough to pass, he even wins the heart of the white woman he loves, though not her hand, since social custom and her own prejudice intrude. When he dies at the head of a black regiment entering Richmond, yet another black man of property who falls before the final curtain, he may not have rescued his race from their "balked, incomplete lives" but he has publicly acknowledged his slave brother Nathan, who is searching for his lost wife and child. In the last chapters of Davis's novel, Nathan's black family is brought together by Ross Burley in a New Jersey home of their own at least as good as Brer Rabbit's. Still, it is Nathan's restored Anny, a "born house-keeper," who probes the book's ultimate truth: that the longing for liberty and the chance to own property are insufficient when the verdict on four million ex-slaves ("waitin' for de whites to say which dey shall be – men or beasts") has yet to come in. "De blood's different," says Anny, as she wonders what her son's "birthright in dis country" will be. All Sap wanted on the long-ago Philadelphia ferry was to keep his dog. In the aftermath of the Civil War, Davis saw a generation of freedmen antici-pating the promise of education and work, while freedwomen like Anny looked down the big road of Reconstruction to the domestic dangers that lay ahead.

Primary Texts

Aiken, George L. *Uncle Tom's Cabin; or, Life among the Lowly, A Domestic Drama, in Six Acts.* 1852.

Alcott, Louisa May. *Hospital Sketches.* 1863.

Alcott, Louisa May. *Little Women.* 1868–9.

Anon. "Buried Alive." 1864.

Anon. "Believe in Ghosts!" 1870.

Boucicault, Dion. *The Octoroon; or, Life in Louisiana.* 1859.

Boyd, Belle. *Belle Boyd in Camp and Prison.* 1865.

Brown, William Wells. *The Escape; or, A Leap for Freedom.* 1858.

Cable, George Washington. *The Grandissimes: A Story of Creole Life.* 1880.

Cary [Harrison], Constance. "A Summer Idyl." 1862.

Chesnut, Mary. *Mary Chesnut's Civil War.* 1881–4.

Confederate Gray. "T. J.'s Cavalry Charge." 1870.

Cooke, John Esten. *Surry of Eagle's-Nest; or, The Memoirs of a Staff-Office Serving in Virginia.* 1866.

Crafts, Hannah. *The Bondwoman's Narrative.* 1850s.

Davis, Rebecca Harding. *Waiting for the Verdict.* 1867.

De Forest, John W. *Miss Ravenel's Conversion from Secession to Loyalty.* 1867.

Douglass, Frederick. *The Heroic Slave.* 1853.

Evans, Augusta Jane. *Macaria; or, Altars of Sacri-fice.* 1864.

Harper, Frances E. W. *Minnie's Sacrifice.* 1869.

Harris, Joel Chandler. *Uncle Remus, His Songs and His Sayings.* 1880.

Jones, Mary, et al. *The War the Women Lived: Female Voices from the Confederate South.* 1995 (written 1860s onwards).

Keckley, Elizabeth. *Behind the Scenes; or, Thirty Years a Slave, and Four Years in the White House.* 1868.

Kemper, William H. "The Sergeant's Little Story." 1873.

Lanier, Sidney. *Tiger-Lilies.* 1867.

Lincoln, Abraham. "The Gettysburg Address." 1863.

Melville, Herman. *Battle-Pieces and Aspects of the War.* 1866.

Perkins, Fred B. "Thomas Elliott's Speculations." 1863.

Simms, William Gilmore. *Joscelyn: A Tale of the Revolution.* 1867.

Stowe, Harriet Beecher. *Uncle Tom's Cabin; or, Life among the Lowly.* 1852.

Stowe, Harriet Beecher. *A Key to* Uncle Tom's Cabin; *Presenting the Original Facts and Documents upon which the Story is Founded. Together with the Corroborative Statements Verifying the Truth of the Work.* 1853.

Tourgée, Albion W. *A Fool's Errand: A Novel of the South during Reconstruction.* 1879.

Twain, Mark, and Warner, Charles Dudley. *The Gilded Age: A Tale of To-Day.* 1873.

Whitman, Walt. *Drum-Taps.* 1865.

Wilson, Harriet E. *Our Nig; or, Sketches from the Life of a Free Black, In a Two-Story White House, North. Showing That Slavery's Shadows Fall Even There.* 1859.

Woolson, Constance Fenimore. "Wilhelmina." 1875.

REFERENCES AND FURTHER READING

Aaron, Daniel (2003). *The Unwritten War: American Writers and the Civil War.* Tuscaloosa: University of Alabama Press. (First publ. 1973.)

Adams, Bluford (1997). *E Pluribus Barnum: The Great Showman and the Making of US Popular Culture.* Minneapolis: University of Minnesota Press.

Alexander, Robert Allen, Jr. (2002). "The Irreducible African: Challenges to Racial Stereotypes in George W. Cable's *The Grandissimes.*" In Suzanne Disheroon-Green and Lisa Abney (eds.), *Songs of the Reconstructing South: Building Literary Louisiana, 1865–1945,* 123–33. Westport, Conn.: Greenwood.

Anon. (1881). "Topics of the Times: Southern Literature." *Scribner's Monthly* (Sept.), 785–6.

Bakker, Jan (1987). "Overlooked Progenitors: Independent Women and Southern Renaissance in Augusta Jane Evans Wilson's *Macaria; or, Altars of Sacrifice.*" *Southern Quarterly* 25: 2 (Winter), 131–42.

Bardaglio, Peter W. (1995). *Reconstructing the Household: Families, Sex, and the Law in the Nineteenth-Century South.* Chapel Hill: University of North Carolina Press.

Blight, David W. (2001). *Race and Reunion: The Civil War in American Memory.* Cambridge, Mass.: Belknap/Harvard University Press.

Brasch, Walter M. (2000). *Brer Rabbit, Uncle Remus, and the "Cornfield Journalist": The Tale of Joel Chandler Harris.* Macon, Ga.: Mercer University Press.

Charvat, William (1992). *The Profession of Authorship in America, 1800–1870,* ed. Matthew J. Bruccoli. New York: Columbia University Press. (First publ. 1968.)

Cott, Nancy F. (2000). *Public Vows: A History of Marriage and the Nation.* Cambridge, Mass.: Harvard University Press.

Crafts, Hannan (2002). *The Bondwoman's Narrative,* ed. Henry Louis Gates, Jr. New York: Warner.

Davis, Steve (1978). "John Esten Cooke and Confederate Defeat." *Civil War History* 24, 66–83.

Fahs, Alice (2001). *The Imagined Civil War: Popular Literature of the North and South, 1861–1865.* Chapel Hill: University of North Carolina Press.

Faust, Drew Gilpin (1988). *The Creation of Confederate Nationalism: Ideology and Identity in the Civil War South.* Baton Rouge: Louisiana State University Press.

Fick, Thomas H. (1992). "Genre Wars and the Rhetoric of Manhood in *Miss Ravenel's Conversion from Secession to Loyalty.*" *Nineteenth-Century Literature* 46, 473–94.

Fleischner, Jennifer (1996). *Mastering Slavery: Memory, Family, and Identity in Women's Slave Narratives.* New York: New York University Press.

Foner, Eric (1988). *Reconstruction: America's Unfinished Revolution, 1863–1877.* New York: Harper & Row.

Foster, Frances Smith (1992). "Autobiography after Emancipation: The Example of Elizabeth Keckley." In James Robert Payne (ed.), *Multicultural Autobiography: American Lives,* 32–63. Knoxville: University of Tennessee Press.

Gates, Henry Louis, Jr. (2002). Introduction. In Hannah Crafts, *The Bondwoman's Narrative,* ed. Henry Louis Gates, Jr. New York: Warner.

Goggin, Edward W. (1993). "Confusion and Resolution in 'The Scout toward Aldie.'" *Melville Society Extracts* 92 (March), 5–9.

Goldner, Ellen J. (1993). "Tangled Webs: Lies, Capitalist Expansion, and the Dissolution of the Subject in *The Gilded Age.*" *Arizona Quarterly* 49: 3 (Autumn), 59–92.

Gossett, Thomas F. (1985). Uncle Tom's Cabin *and American Culture*. Dallas: Southern Methodist University Press.

Griffin, Farah Jasmine (2001). *"Minnie's Sacrifice*: Frances Ellen Watkins Harper's Narrative of Citizenship." In Dale M. Bauer and Philip Gould (eds.), *Cambridge Companion to Nineteenth-Century American Women's Writing*, 308–19. New York: Cambridge University Press.

Griska, Joseph M., Jr. (1981). "Uncle Remus Correspondence: The Development and Reception of Joel Chandler Harris' Writing, 1880–1885." *American Literary Realism* 14, 26–37.

Guilds, John Caldwell (1992). *Simms: A Literary Life*. Fayetteville: University of Arkansas Press.

Hemenway, Robert (1982). "Author, Teller, Hero." In Joel Chandler Harris, *Uncle Remus: His Songs and His Sayings*, ed. and intr. Robert Hemenway, 7–31. New York: Penguin.

Holstein, Suzy Clarkson (1991). "'Offering Up Her Life': Confederate Women on the Altars of Sacrifice." *Southern Studies* n.s., 2: 2 (Summer), 113–30.

Jones, Mary, et al. (1995). *The War the Women Lived: Female Voices from the Confederate South*, ed. Walter Sullivan. Nashville: J. S. Sanders.

Kaser, David (1984). *Books and Libraries in Camp and Battle: The Civil War Experience*. Westport, Conn.: Greenwood.

Ladd, Barbara (1991). "'An Atmosphere of Hints and Allusions': Bras-Coupé and the Context of Black Insurrection in *The Grandissimes*." *Southern Quarterly* 29: 3 (Spring), 63–76.

Lott, Eric (1993). *Love and Theft: Blackface Minstrelsy and the American Working Class*. New York: Oxford University Press.

McCurry, Stephanie (1992). "The Politics of Yeoman Households in South Carolina." In Catherine Clinton and Nina Silber (eds.), *Divided Houses: Gender and the Civil War*, 22–38. New York: Oxford University Press.

Penningroth, Dylan C. (2003). *The Claims of Kinfolk: African American Property and Community in the Nineteenth-Century South*. Chapel Hill: University of North Carolina Press.

Sale, Maggie (1995). "To Make the Past Useful: Frederick Douglass' Politics of Solidarity." *Arizona Quarterly* 51: 3 (Autumn), 25–60.

Sánchez-Eppler, Karen (1993). *Touching Liberty: Abolition, Feminism, and the Politics of the Body*. Berkeley: University of California Press.

Savage, Kirk (1997). *Standing Soldiers, Kneeling Slaves: Race, War, and Monument in Nineteenth-Century America*. Princeton: Princeton University Press.

Smith, Susan Belasco (1995). "Serialization and the Nature of *Uncle Tom's Cabin*." In Kenneth M. Price and Susan Belasco Smith (eds.), *Periodical Literature in Nineteenth-Century America*, 69–89. Charlottesville: University Press of Virginia.

Starke, Aubrey Harrison (1933). *Sidney Lanier: A Biographical and Critical Study*. Chapel Hill: University of North Carolina Press.

Thomas, M. Wynn (1997–8). "Weathering the Storm: Whitman and the Civil War." *Walt Whitman Quarterly Review* 15: 2–3, 87–109.

Van Tassel, Emily Field (1995). "'Only the Law Would Rule between Us': Antimiscegenation, the Moral Economy of Dependency, and the Debate over Rights after the Civil War." *Chicago Law Review* 70, 873–926.

Watson, Charles S. (1992). "Simms and the Civil War: The Revolutionary Analogy." *Southern Literary Journal* 24: 2 (Spring), 76–89.

Wilson, Edmund (1994). *Patriotic Gore: Studies in the Literature of the American Civil War*. New York: Norton. (First publ. 1962.)

Woodward, C. Vann (1981). "Diary in Fact — Diary in Form." In C. Vann Woodward (ed.), *Mary Chesnut's Civil War*, xv–xxix. New Haven: Yale University Press.

Young, Elizabeth (1999). *Disarming the Nation: Women's Writing and the American Civil War*. Chicago: University of Chicago Press.

13
Engendering the Canon:
Women's Narratives, 1865–1914
Grace Farrell

The recovery of nineteenth-century women's narratives over the past generation not only has produced bibliographies of lost works and details about lost lives, but has also uncovered the processes by which important women were erased from the American literary tradition. Furthermore, in recontextualizing our reading of nine-teenth-century literature, feminist scholarship has added to the complexity of genres and period concepts. No longer, for instance, can students be taught that realism began in the last quarter of the nineteenth century. Lionel Trilling could distinguish between American and British novelistic traditions on the basis of the former's lack of social realism mainly by ignoring women's literature, which was very much *in* the tradition of social realism. Literary fictions by and about women make it abundantly clear that the entire nineteenth century was an age of reform.

Post-Civil War women writers boldly addressed the issues of industrialization and changing race relationships. For example, with *John Andross* (1874) Rebecca Harding Davis continued the critique of capitalism and corruption that she had begun in *Life in the Iron Mills* (1861) and *Margret Howth* (1862), both of which addressed the economic oppression of industrialization. Abolitionist lecturer Anna Dickinson (*What Answer?* [1868]) and Harding Davis (*Waiting for the Verdict* [1868]) explored postwar racism, while Lydia Maria Child dealt with three interracial marriages in *A Romance of the Republic* (1867). Lillie Devereux Blake's *Fettered for Life* (1874) voiced the sexual exploitation of seamstresses; Frances Ellen Watkins Harper's *Iola Leroy* (1892) exposed the systematic rape of slave women and the racism of Reconstruction; Sui Sin Far's *Mrs. Spring Fragance* (1912) disrupted ethnic and nationalistic stereotypes in Chinese/Caucasian cultural exchanges and, in "Wisdom of the New," articulated the violence arising from racial and sexual oppression.

The Civil War, as well as industrialization, immigration, and an increasing urban population, brought profound changes to the lives of women and to the culturally coded notions of the feminine. Restrictions on women's use of public space, whether on the lecture circuit, on public streets, or in newspapers; issues of women in the workforce, their housing arrangements, and their limited vocational options; the various forms of sexual harassment to which women were subjected, their educational options, and the push for reform in matters of property rights and marriage and of female attire and exercise – all were subject to question and revision in reform movements and in women's fiction of the period.

Bold as women writers were in addressing the oppression of others, they were, at first, more tentative in their approach to changes in the middle-class lives of women who were most like themselves. Immediately after the war, a surfeit of single women produced calls for greater opportunities in education and work. Louisa May Alcott's postwar "Happy Women" (1868) presents life options for four unmarried women, each from a different class, with different talents and different careers. "Happy Women" does not question nineteenth-century middle-class ideas about women; rather, it describes careers – physician, teacher, missionary, and writer – that allow women to bring the nurturing qualities of the domestic sphere out into the world. These women share the attributes of "true womanhood," especially abnegation of the self. They never talk of themselves, they never complain, they do not admit to ambition, and the success of each is measured by how beloved they are. Despite Alcott's protestations that single womanhood can be a "beautiful success," an aura of sadness and failure hovers over her women. Their happiness is both a fragile compensation for their failure to find mates and a requirement for true womanhood. The nineteenth-century Hartford-based poet Lydia Sigourney had advised that women should "endeavor to preserve cheerfulness of deportment, under the pressure of disappointment or calamity" (1835: 183). A chapter on "Cheerfulness" follows those on "Domesticity," "Obedience," and "Submission," in *The Young Wife; or, Duties of Woman in the Marriage Relation* (1837), an advice manual by William Alcott, Bronson Alcott's first cousin.

Pairing works from early and late in the period reveals striking transformations in thinking about women. By the end of the century Rose Terry Cooke, popular writer of short stories, one of which was published in the inaugural issue of the *Atlantic Monthly*, was charging head-on into the issue of unmarried women: " 'If there's anything on the face of the earth I *do* hate, it's an old maid!' " declares the old maid of "How Celia Changed Her Mind" (1891). The married woman to whom Celia utters these words feels the loneliness of her own life and thinks that perhaps unmarried women, in the words of St. Paul, "doeth better." But Celia is aware of the contempt with which society looks upon an old maid and is determined to marry. She accepts the proposal of a widowed deacon in need of a housekeeper and soon comes to wish that his first wife had been his last. She bears the yoke of marriage for four years, but is finally saved by widowhood and, "so thankful to be an old maid ag'in!", celebrates each Thanksgiving Day with all the old maids of her little town of Bassett.

Louisa May Alcott's need to domesticate her public women is indicative of the postwar dis-ease with which the middle class approached any change in the status of women. Alcott's *Work: A Story of Experience* (1873) provided a survey of various professions available to middle-class women. Alcott's insistent interpretation of women's work in the public world as a continuation of their duties in the home reasserts the notion that woman's essential nature is connected to a separate domestic sphere and skirts the issue of the appropriateness of women working outside that sphere. Only when Alcott's heroine, Christy, sacrifices herself to save another can the reader begin to answer Alcott's central question: "A fine actress perhaps, but how good a woman?" We watch as illness and misfortune bring about a passivity in Christy, and we are told that her better self is emerging. When Christy looks back over her life, her proof of its success is her dead husband's presumed approval, her subordination of her own work to his, and the self-sacrificial nature of her endeavors.

Almost thirty years after *Work* was published – although women, not men, were still faced with making choices between love and work – Mary Hunter Austin's *A Woman of Genius* (1912) imagined the possibility of a woman making a decidedly different choice from that made by Christy. Octavia Lattimore is a talented and an ambitious actress who attempts to integrate her career with marriage and mother-hood. Neither her husband nor, subsequently, her lover can appreciate her commit-ment to the theater. But unlike Christy, who becomes a true woman by sacrificing her profession, or Edna Pontillier in Kate Chopin's *The Awakening* (1899), who is unable to admit to ambition and who is devastated when she realizes that the man she loves cannot fathom the depth of her unconventionality, Octavia chooses her passion for the theater over her passion for her lover and later finds companionship with a man who will support her artistic life.

II

Writing about women and work constituted one way of entering an intense social debate over the changing status of women in postwar America. A prominent thread of this debate followed women into the medical profession, where they were seen as unconventional and undesirable. In the 1850s, white males at Harvard were outraged when three black men and a white woman were admitted to the medical school. The pressure was such that the woman withdrew. In 1859, the Philadelphia County Medical Society passed a resolution that excommunicated any member physician (all of whom were male) who consulted with a female physician. Not until after the war, in 1869, were "the Drs. Blackwell... accepted as members of a voluntary 'Medical Library and Journal Association.'" Harvard, however, was a holdout: "On Oct. 9, 1879, an editorial in the *Boston Medical and Surgical Journal* says: 'We regret to be obliged to announce that, at a meeting of the councilors on Oct. 1, it was voted to admit women to the Massachusetts Medical Society'" (Jacobi 1891: 187).

In 1873 Fanny Fern, the highly popular social satirist Sara Willis Parton, wrote a piece on "Lady Doctors" that plays on stereotypes of the supposed petty envy and vanity of women: "Before swallowing her pills (of which she would be the first), I should want to make sure that I had never come between her and a lover, or a new bonnet.... If I desired her undivided attention to my case, I should first remove the looking-glass." Fern concludes, "while I am in my senses I will never exchange my gentlemanly, soft-voiced, soft-stepping, experienced, intelligent, handsome doctor, for all the female M.D.s who ever carved up dead bodies or live characters – or tore each other's caps." Mark Twain and Charles Dudley Warner's *The Gilded Age* (1873) also spoofs women who go into medicine with dreams of supporting a practice of $10–20,000 a year "and a husband besides," yet never get beyond "practice in hospitals and in their own nurseries, and it is feared that some of them were quite as ready as their sisters, in emergencies, to 'call a man.'" Ultimately *The Gilded Age*'s medical student Ruth Bolton collapses from overwork and fever contracted in a hospital. Attended by a male physician and her fiancé, she awakens to the joy of helplessness and dependence: "It was new for Ruth to feel this dependence on another's nature, to consciously draw strength of will from the will of another. It was a new but a dear joy, to be lifted up and carried back into the happy world. . . ."

Michel Foucault has made of madness and the clinic a particularly sharp surgical instrument for extracting specific discourses and bringing them to the foreground of our knowledge of the past, where they press upon the constrictive frameworks of our "Grand Narratives." William Dean Howells's *Doctor Breen's Practice* (1881), however, rehearses what had come to be standard fare in the novelistic treatment of women physicians, who were seen as stunted emotionally because of their inability to find husbands. Howells's Grace Breen enters medicine "in the spirit in which other women enter convents" – that is, in response to an unhappy love affair, her fiancé having married her best friend. She is seen as strong only when she admits to her failure in love and allows herself to be rescued, through marriage, from the ridiculous predicament of having a profession. Only then can she complete her "arrested development" and fully mature into a married woman.

Sarah Orne Jewett's *The Country Doctor* (1884) answers the question of how to balance marriage with career by determining that it simply cannot be done. Her Nan Prince chooses to fulfill herself in medicine, but not in marriage. Two years earlier, Elizabeth Stuart Phelps's *Doctor Zay* (1882) depicted a fully mature, self-possessed professional, a new type of women who "demands a new type of man" if the conflict between marriage and a woman working is to be resolved. Phelps, daughter of a president of Andover Theological Seminary who railed against woman suffrage, always wrote from the standpoint of women: *The Gates Ajar* (1868) focuses on women's bereavement in the face of civil war; *The Silent Partner* (1871) addresses issues of women factory workers; *The Story of Avis* (1879) draws upon her novelist mother's struggle to find her voice amid her roles as wife and mother. The title character of *Doctor Zay* represents the New Woman of the last quarter of the century who threatened the gender hierarchies of the ideal middle-class home. Phelps traces the growth of her male protagonist, Waldo Yorke, who is at first a spoiled, rich male whose stereotypical view of women continually leads him to misread Dr. Zay as someone in need of rescue or wooing rather than as a professional who can take care of herself and with whom he must negotiate a partnership of equals. In a gender role reversal, Waldo, as Dr. Zay's patient, is an invalid who "lay there like a woman, reduced from activity to endurance, from resolve to patience," while Dr. Zay has "this exquisite advantage over him." In a riff on Howells who portrayed his Dr. Breen as suffering from what the nineteenth century often referred to as "arrested development," Waldo Yorke finds that he is "cherishing a host of feminine virtues . . . I am *not* a woman, unfortunately. I am only an arrested development."

Phelp's insistence that her Dr. Zay is a homoeopathic rather than an allopathic physician is a clear shot against the male medical establishment. It was the male allopathic physicians who, in the 1860s and 1870s, "began systematically to transpose the Cult of True Womanhood into a medical and scientific dogma. . . . Gender distinctions were rooted in biology, and so, therefore, was the patriarchal world order" (Smith-Rosenberg 1985: 23, 47). Disorderly women attempting to break out of their circumscribed world were deemed mentally unbalanced. The narrator of Charlotte Perkins Gilman's "The Yellow Wall-paper" (1892) is a woman made mad by a culture that treats her like a child and constrains her in a nursery. In Kate Chopin's *The Awakening*, Edna Pontellier's husband consults a doctor about his wife's "odd" behavior, which seems to be related to "some sort of notion in her head concerning the eternal rights of women." The doctor's first task is to rule out any hereditary mental illness, before proceeding to explain to Mr. Pontellier that "Woman" is a "very peculiar and delicate organism."

Leonce Pontellier's connection of his wife's odd behavior with the push for women's rights is a telling one. At a time when large numbers of women were joining the suffrage movement and questioning all aspects of "true womanhood," the medical and educational establishment counterthrusted by confining women within the strictly defined limits of their own biology. In the nineteenth century all female ailments, including problems of "mental hygiene," were connected to the female reproductive organs, and medical men based their opposition to the education of girls on female biology. Writing in 1873, Edward H. Clarke, M.D., former Professor of Medicine at Harvard and Fellow of the American Academy of Arts and Sciences, wrote that the growth of the female reproductive system unfortunately coincides with a girl's education: "The growth of this peculiar and marvelous apparatus, in the perfect development of which humanity has so large an interest, occurs during the few years of a girl's educational life." Overtaxing the system by trying to develop the brain while Nature is developing the reproductive organs, Clarke reports, has resulted in the growth of many an excellent female scholar with undeveloped ovaries. "Later they married, and were sterile," or, worse still, they suffered progressive invalidism and even consignment to lunatic asylums. In *Plain Talk About Insanity* (1872), T. W. Fisher, M.D. cites incidents of girls studying to the point of insanity.

Even rest and avoiding the stresses of educational opportunities did not always create sufficient submissiveness on the part of women. The solution to the threat of truly unruly women – such as feminists, midwives, or bloomer-wearers – consisted of various forms of "female castration." Americans pioneered the use of ovariotomy, hysterectomy, and clitoridectomy as the "solution" to mental disorders in women.

In such cases, from the late 1860s until 1904, clitoridectomy was the operation of choice (Barker-Benfield 2000: 89).

While Sarah Orne Jewett may have skirted these issues in *The Country Doctor*, she revisited them twelve years later in *The Country of the Pointed Firs* (1896). When read against the polemics of other writers of the period, *The Country of the Pointed Firs* seems apolitical, but deeply submerged in its luscious prose is a systematic critique of nineteenth-century medical ideology. In Jewett's world both men and women go crazy — usually from loss and loneliness, not from the delicacy of their reproductive apparatus: Captain Littlepage, obsessed by his stories of a world beyond the North Pole; Elijah Tilley, whose mourning for his wife is never-ending; Santin Bowden, turned down by the army, who cannot pass a crowd without trying to get them into marching formation; "Poor Joanna" who, self-exiled on an island, is quite capable of living an independent life, even if, in another day, she would have been sent "up to Massachusetts" — a reference to the many asylums springing up in western Massachusetts during the last quarter of the nineteenth century.

The development of commercial medical schools in the midcentury had resulted in an overproduction of doctors and in increased competition with midwives and female medical practitioners. Jewett's rhetoric puts stress on the market economy that leads the male establishment, under the rubric of professionalism, to eliminate female business rivals. The magnificent Almira Todd, who dominates Jewett's narrative from beginning to end, has a medical practice that is consistently referred to as a business, and the opportunistic village doctor can only hope with "suggestive jokes" that she will fail in her remedies, leaving him with an edge in the medical market. Mrs. Todd towers over the shadowy doctor of Dunnet Landing, who is encountered toward the beginning and the end of the narrative. In both instances, his competitiveness with Mrs. Todd and his superior attitude are established at the same time that he is dismissed by her from any serious regard. At their second encounter, she sends him on an errand to ask a neighbor to close her front door, apparently not having enough confidence in the doctor to rely on him to do the deed himself. She does remark that he is too busy now to take the time to talk to the patients who come to a healer's door for the very purpose of talking. Interaction on the personal level is Mrs. Todd's forte, so she and the doctor have become partners of a sort. Perhaps such partnerships would have been Jewett's solution to the battle against the midwives raging in America. But it was not to be. In the early twentieth century, midwives were effectively eliminated from practice via licensing regulations and legislation. In Massachusetts, in 1913, midwives were outlawed and were prosecuted if they practised (Barker Benfield 2000: 66).

While Dunnet Landing's men of authority look upon women with an amusement born of a sense of superiority, the doctor is not the only victim of Almira Todd's disdain. When the minister sails with Mrs. Todd to visit "Poor Joanna," he, "but a little man," insists on taking lead in the sail, fails to manage the wind, and begins screaming for help in the midst of a vacant sea. To save her life — and his — Mrs. Todd is obliged to knock the little minister down into the bottom of the boat while she sets the sails aright. Even after this humiliation, the minister "put[s] on his authority" when attempting to deal with Joanna, who dismissively sends him off hunting for arrowheads as if he were "a boy." He is ineffectual in dealing with human depth; Mrs. Todd, who has potions and lotions and syrups and cordials and cough-drops, puts it damningly: the minister "seems to know no remedies."

Mrs. Todd knows remedies, and is, like Atalanta Zay, a homoeopathic healer. Like many a midwife, Mrs. Todd is a herbalist, a cultivator of a "rustic pharmaco-peia . . . [that] might once have belonged to sacred and mystic rites, and have had some occult knowledge." The association of midwifery with the cultivation of herbs and with witchcraft continued throughout the nineteenth century (see Ulrich 1991: 374 n. 12), and Almira Todd, part domestic woman/part witch, is a sibyl of gigantic and mysterious proportions who mixes her brews in a kitchen caldron.

Mrs. Todd collects pennyroyal, which Elizabeth Ammons has identified as "used in childbirth to promote the expulsion of the placenta; it is also . . . used to induce or increase menstrual flow. . . . pennyroyal suggests . . . the central awesome power of women . . . to give or not to give life" (1983: 91). Not giving life is the operative phrase when it comes to pennyroyal, which, along with savine and tansy, was probably used as an abortifacient (Ulrich 1991: 56; 378 n. 47). The inducement of early miscarriage with the use of herbs was an important part of midwifery, and "by the 1840s and the 1850s, ads for abortifacients filled [the] pages" of urban newspapers (Smith-Rosenberg 1985: 225). But the link of midwives with abortion and with the freedom of women to direct their own sexual lives was yet another reason why the male medical establishment sought to eliminate its rival female profession. Between 1860 and 1880 the newly formed American Medical Association, made up of allopathic physicians, successfully lobbied against abortion, and, as Carroll Smith-Rosenberg puts it, "a practice [abortion] that had once existed quite unselfconsciously within the private female world of wives and midwives [was precipitated] into the public and commercial world of men" (1985: 218, 226). Between 1870 and 1890, for the first time, abortion became illegal throughout the United States.

By 1896 Sarah Orne Jewett could only imply that Mrs. Todd's medical practice is involved in abortion. Not only does Mrs. Todd collect pennyroyal, but some of her "suffering neighbors" come to her "at night as if by stealth." Sometimes she proffers "whispered directions" or mutters "long chapters of directions, and kept up an air of secrecy and importance to the last." Mrs. Todd takes the narrator to Green Island, her girlhood home. Flagging our attention, Jewett entitles this chapter "Where Penny-royal Grew," and while pennyroyal still grows on Green Island, and Mrs. Todd and the narrator go out to pick it, the chapter title's past tense situates the narrative focal point in the past. So, in a secret spot, Mrs. Todd shares a secret of her past with the narrator and with her readers. For the first time she speaks of her husband, who, shortly after their marriage and in sight of the headland of pennyroyal, died at sea: " . . . he died before he ever knew what he'd had to know if we'd lived long together." Mrs. Todd whispers "as if she were at confession – . . . My heart was out o' my keepin' before I ever saw Nathan . . . he never knew. But this pennyr'yal always reminded me, as I'd sit and gather it and hear him talkin' – it always would remind me of – the other one." In a spot of "great grief and silence," Mrs. Todd, possessed of "an absolute, archaic grief," has had what by 1896 could only be whispered or confessed. She is reminded, by a field of pennyroyal, of her own abortion.

Mrs. Todd's hidden story, told in secret in a secret spot, is emblematic of the abortive lives of women in late nineteenth-century America. Towards the end of *The Country of the Pointed Firs*, aware of the power of Mrs. Todd's presence, the narrator muses: "I was full of wonder at the waste of human ability in this world, as a botanist wonders at the wastefulness of nature, the thousand seeds that die, the unused provision of every sort. . . . a narrow set of circumstances had caged a fine able character and held it captive."

III

While the agenda of controlling women by controlling female sexuality is clearly articulated in the medical literature of the period and in the politics of abortion and of mental hygiene, there had long existed in American culture a plethora of seamy adventure stories filled with sex and violence (see Reynolds 1989). In 1871 the Free Love movement became a celebrated cause when Victoria Woodhull, or "Mrs. Satan" as she was dubbed, briefly insinuated herself into the suffrage movement; but she was edged out when the identification of woman suffrage with free love became so strong that many supporters of suffrage retreated from the movement. In *My Wife and I* (1871) Harriet Beecher Stowe characterized Woodhull as the "bold[ly] intrus[ive] . . . Miss Adacia Dangyereyes." In 1872 Woodhull became the first woman nominated for President of the United States. That same year she threatened to expose one of the biggest sex scandals of the nineteenth century, that of Revd. Henry Ward Beecher's affair with Elizabeth Tilton. Woodhull demanded of Beecher – Harriet Beecher Stowe's brother and the most famous clergyman in America at the time – a public apology for adultery or a declaration that he, like Woodhull, was an advocate of free love. In 1875, when Elizabeth Tilton's husband Theodore Tilton brought civil charges against Beecher, Woodhull published transcripts of the 112-day civil trial. Woodhull declared that she and Theodore Tilton had become lovers in 1871, when the infatuated Tilton was writing an adoring biography. Tilton denied the affair, explaining that he had on at least one occasion spent the night at Woodhull's only because, exhausted from working on the biography (a 33-page essay), he had fallen asleep on the couch.

Clearly sex and desire, male and female, were not taboo subjects in the popular press of late nineteenth-century America. But sex in middle-class women's narratives, like desire in middle-class women themselves, was a topic forbidden by the pervasive ideology that defined the "true woman" as asexual. Women writers went underground when it came to discussions of sex. Jewett's Mrs. Todd confesses her secret story in a secret spot. Kate Chopin's *The Awakening* may have been shocking in its time, but its portrayal of a middle-class woman who wants to direct her own sex life is so subtly coded that present-day students, accustomed to explicit renditions of sex, have difficulty noticing Edna Pontillier's sexual encounters. With oblique language, Lillie Devereux Blake's *Fettered for Life* (1874) explores the realities of sexual exploitation. As a consequence of abduction and rape, or in a parallel scenario of seduction and betrayal, Blake's working-class women are forced by upper-middle-class men into prostitution. The wives of those same men suffer similar violations of their bodily integrity because they do not possess the right to refuse marital sex, a topic hotly debated by suffragists, some of whom felt that such a right – referred to as "self-ownership" – would be the downfall of marriage itself. When *Fettered for Life*'s Ferdinand LeRoy tells his reluctant bride Flora that he has the right of entrance to all parts of his house, the sexual implications and the pervasiveness of control are clear: a married woman did not belong to herself. Reflecting the struggle of women for personal autonomy, Blake presents femaleness itself as a fetter that, in a patriarchal social order, enchains a woman for life, limiting her fulfillment as it circumscribes her freedom. Hidden in Blake's novel is the story of a man who is a woman. Blake's gender switch implies that gender itself is a surface detail, and that the profound differences between the sexes, used to create a hierarchy and to justify social inequities, are themselves not preordained givens but social constructions.

The freedom to respond to their own sexuality and to love where they would was an issue in women's writing throughout the period following the Civil War, from Lydia Maria Child's interracial marriages in *A Romance of the Republic* (1867) to Edith Wharton's *Ethan Frome* (1911), that tale of truncated adultery which transforms the idealized domestic space of the nineteenth century into a twentieth-century hell where a kitchen-bound love triangle plays out its endgame. In "The Yellow Wall-paper" Gilman's narrator is confined to an attic room furnished only with a bed – the site, Elizabeth Ammons points out, of "male sexual privilege and dominance" (1992: 37). Harriet Prescott Spofford's "The Wages of Sin" (1900) features a heroine who lives with but refuses to marry her lover. "I have no voice in making the law," she reasons, "why should I obey it?" The sexuality of Wharton's Lily Bart (*The House of Mirth*, 1905), so aroused by Laurence Selden, is confiscated by a social system that requires that she snag a wealthy husband. Lily Bart is caught within conflicting desires. The socially constructed desire, so useful to regulating female sexuality and to which she fully subscribes, leads her toward moneyed men. Her sexual desires lead her consistently to undermine her success in the marriage market. She can neither free herself from social restrictions nor embrace the freedom of her own sexuality.

Self-ownership meant something entirely different to black women slaves, who owned neither their bodies nor their right to refuse their owner's sexual advances. Indeed, their bodies were commodities sold for sex and for the increase of an owner's capital stock. Frances Ellen Watkins Harper's *Iola Leroy*, published in the same year as "The Yellow Wall-paper," gives voice to the sexual exploitation of slave women by their owners. The novel is formed against a background of prewar plantation life,

Northern compromises and prejudices, the brutality of Jim Crow laws, and the movement for education by a rising postwar black middle class. *Iola Leroy* questions the construction of racial divides, which the widespread existence of mulattoes makes problematic. "'Isn't it funny,'" remarks one of Harper's characters, "'how these white folks look down on colored people, an' then mix up with them?'" Her blue-eyed, pale-skinned heroine, a product of generations of such mixing, is sold into slavery when her white father dies and her mother's mixed race is revealed.

Harper, an abolitionist lecturer, postwar activist for African American education, and poet, was well aware that the anti-miscegenation laws passed during Reconstruction outlawed a practice that had long been sanctioned by a system that trafficked in the bodies of black women. The widespread rape of slave women was twisted into a stereotype of the sexually promiscuous African. At a time when middle-class white women were fighting for their sexual lives, Harper was caught in a racial bind. She could not give her heroine a sex life without giving rise to the stereotype that she fought against. To undermine that racial stereotype, Harper presents Iola Leroy as a pure, asexual "true woman." Iola fights off her rapacious master, telling him she would rather die than submit to him, and, later, as a lecturer for negro education, she declares that "after the war we were thrown upon the nation a homeless race to be gathered into homes, and a legally unmarried race to be taught the sacredness of the marriage relation. We must instill into our young people that the true strength of a race means purity in women and uprightness in men." Freed black women found themselves restrained by the requirements of "true womanhood."

The story of Iola's transformation from a privileged, white, untouchable "true woman" into a sexually available slave seems not to have been an unusual incident. It was common enough to have fictional precedents in, among others, Child's *Romance of the Republic* and Harriet Beecher Stowe's *Uncle Tom's Cabin* (1852). There, Cassy tells a similar story of a childhood of white privilege before her appropriation as the bitter and battered sex slave of Simon Legree. In contrast, despite the assaults upon her, Iola Leroy is never the tragic mulatta. Iola makes clear that not she but her owners are debased, and that her strength arises from her choice to align herself with her black heritage.

In a different way, Mary Wilkins Freeman's "Old Woman Magoun" (1909) complicates the issue of female self-ownership. Hers is a disturbing story of a grandmother who kills Lily, her fourteen-year-old granddaughter. Lily, whose name, of course, denotes her virginal innocence, is a commodity fought over by her father, who would barter her to pay a gambling debt, and her grandmother, who fears the child's sexual maturity. Mrs. Magoun, the matriarch and enforcer of morals in the tiny hamlet of Barry's Ford, reproduces the patriarchy's protection of female sexuality, demanding death rather than sexual violation. Twice Lily complains that her grandmother holds her hand too tightly, and, as often, she expresses a yearning for the handsome Jim Willis. But both grandmother and father collude in denying Lily self-ownership.

IV

Women's lives changed dramatically during the period between the Civil War and World War I, and women's narratives traced and promoted those changes, but they did so in the face of fierce opposition from the medical and educational hierarchy. The idea that sexual difference might be the reason why women writers have been lost to our literary traditions has seemed a difficult notion to accept, although one would have to wonder why the literary establishment would be immune to the pervasive belief in female inferiority or to the politics of power that insisted upon female subordination. It has been far easier to believe versions of the story that the narrator of Constance Fenimore Woolson's "Miss Grief" (1880) gives out, a story that purports to answer a hypothetical question asked about women's writing – "But is it any good?" – a question that contains the unstated conclusion that only the inferior are ever lost, and presumes upon the supposedly unbiased judgments of credentialed "literary men" to ensure that only the best are represented on the publication lists or in the academy's canon.

Many women's narratives tell a different story about the fate of female artists. For example, the protagonist of Augusta Jane Evans's novel *St. Elmo* (1867) is an acclaimed novelist whose new husband declares, "There shall be no more books written!...You belong solely to me now..." In Lillie Devereux Blake's *Fettered for Life*, although Laura Stanley wins first prize in the Academy of Design's annual show, economic forces reduce her to flower painting on commission. The artist of Charlotte Perkins Gilman's "The Yellow Wall-paper," like Gilman herself, undergoes S. Weir Mitchell's famously infantilizing rest cure, forbidding women any creative activity because it might upset the delicate female nervous system. In Kate Chopin's *The Awakening*, Edna Pontellier's artistic proclivities are stirred only as she is sexually awakened, but she must struggle against an ideology that links female sexuality only with motherhood, not with art. Women's art is suppressed, then, by marriage, limited economic opportunities, the narrow confines of "normal" female behavior, the infantilizing of women, and restrictions on women's own self-empowerment. In *Fettered for Life*, Lillie Devereux Blake, who makes the writing of male cultural stories and the erasure of female voices her central political statement, adds an indictment of the male literary establishment to this list of ways in which women were eliminated from literature's ranks: the burning of a woman's manuscripts by her husband becomes a trope both for the erasure of women's attempts to write their own lives and for the suppression of women's literary tradition. It is a trope that defines much of the fiction written by women between 1865 and 1914.

A battle of the sexes in Woolson's "Miss Grief" delineates the politics engaged in by women writers of the period. "An authoress!" exclaims with disgust the successful male novelist who narrates Woolson's story. "You, *you* – YOU literary men!" spits the aunt of the impoverished authoress under discussion. The disdain with which women and their work are dismissed and the attendant rage at that disdain and that dismissal define the gender politics that lie at the heart of "Miss Grief." The thoroughly misogynist narrator takes the liberty of renaming Aaronna Moncrief "Miss Grief" and presumes that she – "eccentric and unconventional – qualities extremely tiresome in a woman no longer young or attractive" – is a seller of old lace. But, reading her manuscript, he learns that she possesses "the divine spark of genius," and that her gifts go well beyond his own. After a half-hearted effort to place her manuscript and a vain attempt to revise it for a conventional marketplace, he acknowledges the brilliance, integrity, and superiority of her accomplishment. Like Moncrief's fictional "profligate and commonplace man," the narrator leads "the authoress" to believe, on her death-bed, that her manuscript has been sold. Instead, he keeps it locked away and orders it destroyed upon his death. Does he do this, as he would have it, because it is flawed and he wants no one to "cast so much as a thought of scorn" upon her or because, as Aaronna Moncrief's aunt had avowed, he, as all "literary men," is a "vampire" who "take[s] her ideas and fatten[s] on them, and leave[s] her to starve"? The narrator is well aware of the difference between his writing and Moncrief's: "She, with the greater power, failed – I, with the less, succeeded. The want of one grain made all her work void, and that one grain was given to me." The one grain of difference, Woolson makes clear, is sexual.

At the time of "Miss Grief's" publication, toward the end of the nineteenth century when there was a concerted move to construct a distinctly American literary history, its framers, whether professors or critics, essayists or editors, explicitly distanced themselves from women's writing. Susan Harris finds a "revulsion from the feminine" at the heart of American literary criticism (1990: 2–8). Certainly the feminine was seen as a threat to male hegemony, and William Dean Howells's agenda in his manifestoes on realism concerned making literature real men's work rather than, as Alfred Habegger contends, a sissy, womanish activity (1982: 57). While realism established itself against sentimentality, naturalism established itself against realism, and each used the female to denigrate its predecessor. The naturalists referred to Howells himself as an old maid, and women's realistic writings were dismissed as "teacup tragedies." Novel-writing was called the most virile of the arts, not the "affair of women and aesthetes" (Norris 1967: 158–9).

Howells's late nineteenth-century pronouncements on realism were drawn against the sentimentality of domestic fiction, which, while certainly not written only by women, was derisively associated with them and their issues. In *Country of the Pointed Firs*, after her narrator muses on the "narrow set of circumstances" that cages capable women, Sarah Orne Jewett moves her readers' attention to a figure who epitomizes the wasted talent of women writers – the sentimental poetess – with whom so many women writers of the nineteenth century have been associated as a prelude to their dismissal. So powerful is the scorn heaped upon the sentimental that even Mrs. Todd, the embodiment of feminine power in the face of male denigration of it, finds it somewhat difficult to appreciate the long-windedness of "the poetess" who recites at the Bowden family reunion.

Perhaps the most memorable parody of sentimental literature in its stereotypically female form is Mark Twain's creation of Emmeline Grangerford in the *Adventures of Huckleberry Finn* (1884). Like a nineteenth-century Edward Gorey, without the irony, Emmeline draws funereal pictures with such titles as "Shall I Never See Thee More Alas": "One was a woman in a slim black dress, belted small under the arm-pits, with bulges like a cabbage in the middle of the sleeves, and a large black scoop-shovel bonnet with a black veil, and white slim ankles crossed about with black tape, and very wee black slippers, like a chisel, and she was leaning pensive on a tombstone on her right elbow. . . . " A poetess, Emmeline would "slap down" lines for every dead person in town and "be on hand with her 'tribute' before he was cold. . . . it was the doctor first, then Emmeline, then the undertaker. . . . "

Mary Wilkins Freeman's "A Poetess" (1891) literally dies from humiliation after her minister, a published poet, ridicules her funereal verses. Because the poetess absorbs the scorn heaped upon sentimentality, no one needs to burn her manuscripts; she does it herself and places the ashes in, appropriately enough, a sugar-bowl. Before dying, the poetess manipulates the doubly authoritative minister–poet by exacting a promise that he will recite an original verse over her coffin. Freeman transfers the burden of sentiment onto him and in so doing complicates her title with gentle irony: "The minister stood holding the sugar-bowl; he was quite pale with bewilderment and sympathy." At the story's end, a bird in a cage "trill[s] into a triumphant song." The minister holds the sugar-bowl: *he* will become a poetess.

Like Constance Fenimore Woolson, Jewett and Freeman, while keeping their politics underground, hold within their fiction "the elements of revolution" (Freeman, "A Village Singer" [1891]). Their fiction is engaged in undermining the inferiority of their position as literary women. "'I'd like to know if it's fair,'" says Freeman's poetess; "'Had I ought to have been born with the wantin' to write poetry if I couldn't write it – had I? Had I ought to have been let to write all my life, an' not know before there wa'n't any use in it?'" Early in the twentieth century, with an echo of Woolson's narrator's disdainful "an authoress!", an essay in the *Yale Review* dismissed women writers with the sneering titular comment, "The Female Nuisance in American Literature." Frederick Pattee expressed the misogyny of the critical process in his *Feminine Fifties*, characterizing the 1850s with ten words, not meant as compliments – "fervid, fevered, furious, fatuous, fertile, feeling, florid, furbelowed, fighting, and funny" and the "single adjective which combines them all" – feminine (Pattee 1940: 3–4).

The most denigrated form of literature, nineteenth-century women's fiction, went unrecognized by the twentieth-century educated elite who were taught to ignore it as (to add a word outside the confines of Pattee's f-word list) didactic. However, American literature has a tradition of didacticism going back to its Puritan roots, shifting over time from sermons and poetic prescripts into novels, which proved to be perfect vehicles for conveying social values. In the nineteenth century, critics reviled Poe for neglecting to conclude his stories with pithy moral tags, while Longfellow was canonized for his didactic verse.

Rhetorical changes favoring the anti-didactic can be detected as nineteenth-century America transformed itself into a secular society, and twentieth-century criticism tended to place aesthetic value above all other, having no place in its dicta for others' didacticism. The modernist "make it new" came to be seen as a universal aesthetic, but in fact it is part of an ideology quite particular to its post-Darwinian moment, in which time is seen as always evolutionary and the new as always a move to a progressively higher plane. Thus the novel "rises" and American literature "develops" as it casts off the inferiority of its immature and feminine past, lowers its pitch, and becomes more manly. As Alexander Cowie put it: "The voice of our prose has lowered its pitch and become more husky. The sentence is now shorter, with a lower centre of gravity. Understatement and deliberate de-emphasis have become habitual with many writers. Befrilled locutions are out; diction has gone into denim" (1951: 754). Assumptions about gender in American culture are reflected in a representative theme in canonized fiction – the escape from woman. In prototypical tales from "Rip Van Winkle" to *Huckleberry Finn* and beyond, males are the good-hearted bad boys of a social order dominated by female forces that aggressively seek to domesticate them. Their escape into adventure is a flight from women who seek to keep them, too, for ever at home. Both canonized plots and the critical rhetoric which removed women from a central position in American fiction reflect this flight from the female. As Leslie Fiedler put it, "the typical male protagonist of our fiction has been a man on the run ... [avoiding] the fall into sex, marriage and responsibility" (1966: 26). Josephine Donovan writes that America has

> a cultural identity and a canon that have been narrowly defined according to the chauvinistic thematics of male culture. It is one that privileges (in the case of American literature) hybristic juvenile fantasies of escape and redemption through violence, notions that still pervade popular culture. Reconceiving American literature, and indeed Western culture, to include women's masterpieces might help to establish new bases for that culture's identity, away from one characterized by dominance, escapist violence, competition, and exploitation toward one governed by a sense of humility, humanity, and compassion, born of the realization that ... the deaths and resurrections of everyday life, the wresting of story from infirmity, are the stuff of great literature. (2000: 6)

V

The recovery of women writers and their introduction into the canon of American literature has destabilized period concepts that had been defined either in the absence of women's work or in a rejection of what was figured as feminine. This chapter has abjured the effort of fitting woman writers into period constructs that were formed in an effort to eliminate them from the canon. Elements common to what have been defined as realism, sentimentality, or naturalism blur the distinctions among these categories. Traces of each can be found variously recombined in women's narratives. The realism of everyday life fills the thickly plotted narratives of sentiment. Empathic connections are as important to naturalism as they are to sentimentality. Christian piety and elements of the romance crop up within otherwise realistic narratives.

Exemplifying such eclecticism is the work of Pauline Elizabeth Hopkins, a prolific writer who earned her living as a stenographer, but published several novels at the turn of the century. In *Winona: A Tale of Negro Life in the South and Southwest* (1902), through the eyes of a young man from England who seeks to free two Native American children sold into slavery, we see the hypocrisies of slavery in a free society and mob violence within a democracy. Along with sentimental revelations proving one of the enslaved children to be an heiress of a British aristocratic family, Hopkins integrates realistic details of John Brown and his men into scenes of battle with the "Rangers" who sought to keep the Western territories free of abolitionists, and even gives her readers a fleeting glimpse of the sodomizing of an imprisoned black man.

Hopkins uses the sentimental trope of revealed identity to expose the fragile construction of racial divides: *Of One Blood* insists the title of a 1902–3 serial, while the subtitle of her 1901–2 *Hagar's Daughter: A Story of Southern Caste Prejudice* makes a rhetorical shift from race – a term too malleable to be meaningful – to caste. *Hagar's Daughter*, set first in 1861, tells a familiar story. The evil St. Clair Enson, through his slave-trader friend, Walker, discovers that his older brother's wife, Hagar, has negro blood. Ellis Enson's love for his wife and their child overcomes his prejudice; he buys her and his child and plans to live in Europe. Before carrying out his plan, however, he, it would seem, is found dead. Hagar is sent to be sold, but escapes from a slave pen and, clutching her babe, throws herself into the Potomac. Flash forward twenty years. Hopkins employs disguises galore. In 1881 St. Clair Enson passes himself off as General Benson, while his slave-trader pal is now a business associate named Madison. They cook up a scheme whereby Madison's daughter, the siren Aurelia Madison, will steal away the fiancé of Jewel Bowen, daughter of a deceased US senator, so that General Benson can marry her for her money. But, lo and behold, a detective named Henson discovers not only that Senator Bowen's widow and Jewel's stepmother is really Hagar, who was unwillingly rescued from the Potomac, but that Senator Bowen and his first wife had also rescued Jewel from a floating log in the same river. As in fairy tales – or sentimental novels – proofs found in a locket and a little chest reveal that Hagar and Jewel are mother and daughter, rather than stepmother and step-daughter. They are reunited with Ellis Enson, who never had died, but instead had become the detective, Hensen.

Enson, Benson, Henson – a linguistic drift from one identity to another is analogous to the fluidity of blackness and whiteness. Like Harper's *Iola Leroy*, Hopkins uses the existence of "white" slaves, such as Hagar and Jewel, to explode the notion of racial divides. All the elements of sensational literature – sirens, evil younger brothers, abductions, imprisonments, disguises, reappearances, and reunions – are brought to bear on the weighty issue of identity, specifically of racial identity.

Hopkins camouflages her radical challenge to the notion of race with sentimental tropes and sensational designs.

VI

No canon is inevitable. There is only that which fits the common dogma of a particular moment. Foucault reminds us that the overwhelming predominance of the "Grand Narrative" of paternal authority has sacrificed, marginalized, or ignored altogether the development of discourses that might have questioned both the validity and predominance of ingrained canons. Feminist critics – female and male – have been intent not just on expanding the American canon to make room for women, but on challenging its inevitability. The loss of female voices from the community of American writers denied full context to literary canons. As we recover more works and enrich the social context that produced them, we can begin to see the ways in which our cultural memory has been anesthetized by the inflexibility of our canonical tradition or the constructed seamlessness of our grand narratives.

PRIMARY TEXTS

Alcott, Louisa May. "Happy Women." 1868.

Alcott, Louisa May. *Work: A Story of Experience.* 1873.

Alcott, William. *The Young Wife; or, Duties of Woman in the Marriage Relation.* 1837.

Austin, Mary Hunter. *A Woman of Genius.* 1912.

Blake, Lillie Devereux. *Fettered for Life.* 1874.

Child, Lydia Maria. *A Romance of the Republic.* 1867.

Chopin, Kate. *The Awakening.* 1899.

Clarke, Edward H. *Sex in Education; or, A Fair Chance for Girls.* 1873.

Cooke, Rose Terry. "How Celia Changed Her Mind." 1891.

Davis, Rebecca Harding. *Life in the Iron Mills; or, The Korl Woman.* 1861.

Davis, Rebecca Harding. *Margret Howth.* 1862.

Davis, Rebecca Harding. *Waiting for the Verdict.* 1867.

Davis, Rebecca Harding. *John Andross.* 1874.

Dickinson, Anna. *What Answer?* 1868.

Evans, Augusta Jane. *St. Elmo.* 1867.

Fern, Fanny [Sara Willis Parton]. "Lady Doctors." 1873.

Fisher, T. W. *Plain Talk About Insanity.* 1872.

Freeman, Mary Wilkins. "A Poetess." 1891.

Freeman, Mary Wilkins. "Old Woman Magoun." 1909.

Gilman, Charlotte Perkins. "The Yellow Wallpaper." 1892.

Harper, Frances Ellen Watkins. *Iola Leroy; or, Shadows Uplifted.* 1892.

Hopkins, Pauline Elizabeth. *Hagar's Daughter: A Story of Southern Caste Prejudice.* 1901–2.

Hopkins, Pauline Elizabeth. *Winona: A Tale of Negro Life in the South and Southwest.* 1902.

Hopkins, Pauline Elizabeth. *Of One Blood.* 1902–3.

Howells, William Dean. *Doctor Breen's Practice.* 1881.

Jewett, Sarah Orne. *A Country Doctor.* 1884.

Jewett, Sarah Orne. *The Country of the Pointed Firs.* 1896.

Phelps, Elizabeth Stuart. *The Gates Ajar.* 1868.

Phelps, Elizabeth Stuart. *The Silent Partner.* 1871.

Phelps, Elizabeth Stuart. *The Story of Avis.* 1879.

Phelps, Elizabeth Stuart. *Doctor Zay.* 1882.

Sigourney, L. H. *Letters to Young Ladies.* 1835.

Spofford, Harriet Prescott. *Old Madame and Other Tragedies.* 1900.

Stowe, Harriet Beecher. *Uncle Tom's Cabin; or, Life among the Lowly.* 1852.

Stowe, Harriet Beecher. *My Wife and I.* 1871.

Sui Sin Far [Edith Maud Eaton]. *Mrs. Spring Fragrance.* 1912.

Twain, Mark. *Adventures of Huckleberry Finn.* 1884.

Twain, Mark, and Warner, Charles Dudley. *The Gilded Age: A Tale of To-Day.* 1873.

Wharton, Edith. *The House of Mirth.* 1905.

Wharton, Edith. *Ethan Frome.* 1911.

Woolson, Constance Fenimore. "Miss Grief." 1880.

Later Collections

Austin Hunter, Mary (1987). *Stories from the Country of Lost Borders*, ed. and intr. Marjorie Pryse. New Brunswick, NJ: Rutgers University Press.

Cooke, Rose Terry (1986). *"How Celia Changed Her Mind" and Selected Stories*, ed. and intr. Elizabeth Ammons. New Brunswick, NJ: Rutgers University Press.

Fern, Fanny [Sara Willis Parton] (1873). *Fanny Fern: A Memorial Volume*, ed. James Parton. New York: Carleton & Co.

Freeman, Mary Wilkins (1891). *A New England Nun, and Other Stories.* New York: Harper & Bros.

Freeman, Mary Wilkins (1974). *The Revolt of Mother and Other Stories.* New York: Feminist Press.

Hopkins, Pauline (1988). *The Magazine Novels of Pauline Hopkins*, intr. Hazel V. Carby. New York: Oxford University Press (The Schomburg Library of Nineteenth-Century Black Women Writers). Includes *Hagar's Daughter, Of One Blood,* and *Winona.*

Jewett, Sarah Orne (1994a). *Sarah Orne Jewett: Novels and Stories.* New York: Library of America.

Jewett, Sarah Orne (1994b). *The Country of the Pointed Firs and Other Stories*, intr. Marjorie Pryse. New York: Norton.

Spofford, Harriet Prescott (1900). *Old Madame and Other Tragedies.* Boston: Badger.

Sui Sin Far [Edith Maud Eaton]. (1995). *Mrs. Spring Fragance and Other Writings*, ed. Amy Ling and Annette White-Parks. Urbana: University of Illinois Press.

References and Further Reading

Ammons, Elizabeth (1992). *Conflicting Stories: American Women Writers at the Turn of the Century.* New York: Oxford University Press.

Ammons, Elizabeth (1983). "Going in Circles: The Female Geography of Jewett's *Country of the Pointed Firs.*" *Studies in the Literary Imagination* 16: 2 (Fall), 83–92.

Avallone, Charlene (1997). "What American Renaissance? The Gendered Genealogy of a Critical Discourse." *PMLA* 112 (Oct.), 1102–20.

Banta, Martha (1987). *Imagining American Women: Idea and Ideals in Cultural History.* New York: Columbia University Press.

Barker-Benfield, G. J. (2000). *Horrors of the Half-Known Life.* New York: Routledge.

Baym, Nina (1981). "Melodramas of Beset Manhood: How Theories of American Fiction Exclude Women." *American Quarterly* 33, 123–39.

Repr. in Nina Baym, *Feminism and American Literary History: Essays* (New Brunswick: Rutgers University Press, 1992), 3–18.

Bell, Michael Davitt (1993). *The Problem of American Realism: Studies in the Cultural History of a Literary Idea.* Chicago: University of Chicago Press.

Bell, Michael Davitt (1994). "Gender and American Realism in *The Country of the Pointed Firs.*" In June Howard (ed.), *New Essays on The Country of the Pointed Firs*, 61–80. Cambridge, UK: Cambridge University Press.

Bercovich, Sacvan, ed. (1986). *Reconstructing American Literary History.* Cambridge, Mass.: Harvard University Press.

Berthoff, Warner (1994). *American Trajectories: Authors and Readings, 1790–1970.* University Park: Pennsylvania State University Press.

Blake, Lillie Devereux (1996). *Fettered for Life, or, Lord and Master: A Story of Today*, with afterword by Grace Farrell. New York: Feminist Press.

Boyd, Anne E. (2004). *Writing for Immortality: Women and the Emergence of High Literary Culture in America*. Baltimore: Johns Hopkins University Press.

Buhle, Mari Jo (1981). *Women and American Socialism, 1870–1920*. Urbana: University of Illinois Press.

Campbell, Donna M. (1997). *Resisting Regionalism: Gender and Naturalism in American Fiction, 1885–1915*. Athens, Ohio: Ohio University Press.

Cott, Nancy (1977). *The Bonds of Womanhood: "Woman's Sphere" in New England, 1780–1835*. New Haven: Yale University Press.

Cowie, Alexander (1951). *The Rise of the American Novel*. New York: American Publishing Co.

Cuddy, Lois A., and Roche, Claire M., eds. (2003). *Evolution and Eugenics in American Literature and Culture, 1880–1940*. Lewisburg, Pa.: Bucknell University Press.

Cutter, Martha J. (1991). "Frontiers of Language: Engendering Discourse in 'The Revolt of "Mother."'" *American Literature* 63 (June), 279–91.

Dobson, Joanne (1993). "The American Renaissance Reenvisioned." In Joyce W. Warren (ed.), *The (Other) American Traditions: Nineteenth-Century Women Writers*, 164–82. New Brunswick, NJ: Rutgers University Press.

Donovan, Josephine (2000). "Women's Masterpieces." In Joyce W. Warren and Margaret Dickie (eds.), *Challenging Boundaries: Gender and Periodization*, 26–38. Athens, Ga.: University of Georgia Press.

Douglas, Ann (1977). *The Feminization of American Culture*. New York: Knopf.

Farrell, Grace (2002). *Lillie Devereux Blake: Retracing a Life Erased*. Amherst: University of Massachusetts Press.

Fetterley, Judith, and Pryse, Marjorie, eds. (1992). *American Women Regionalists, 1850–1910*. New York: Norton.

Fetterley, Judith, and Pryse, Marjorie, eds. (2003). *Writing Out of Place: Regionalism, Women, and American Literary Culture*. Urbana: University of Illinois Press.

Fiedler, Leslie (1966). *Love and Death in the American Novel*. New York: Stein & Day.

Fisher, Philip (1985). *Hard Facts: Setting and Form in the American Novel*. New York: Oxford University Press.

Gilbert, Sandra, and Gubar, Susan (1988). *No Man's Land*. New Haven: Yale University Press.

Habegger, Alfred (1982). *Gender, Fantasy, and Realism in American Literature*. New York: Columbia University Press.

Harris, Sharon M. (1991). *Rebecca Harding Davis and American Realism*. Philadelphia: University of Pennsylvania Press.

Harris, Susan K. (1990). *Nineteenth-Century American Women's Novels: Interpretive Strategies*. New York: Cambridge University Press.

Hedges, Elaine (1994). "Introduction. Repositionings: Multiculturalism, American Literary History, and the Curriculum." *American Literature* 66: 4 (Dec.), 769–829.

Hedrick, Joan D. (1994). *Harriet Beecher Stowe: A Life*. New York: Oxford University Press.

Hergesheimer, Joseph (1921). "The Female Nuisance in American Literature." *Yale Review*, 10 (July), 716–25.

Howard, June (1985). *Form and History in American Literary Naturalism*. Chapel Hill. University of North Carolina Press.

Howard, June, ed. and intr. (1994). *New Essays on The Country of the Pointed Firs*. Cambridge, UK: Cambridge University Press.

Jacobi, Mary Putnam (1891). "Women in Medicine." In Annie Nathan Meyer (ed.), *Women's Work in America*, 195–6. New York: Henry Holt & Co.

Kaplan, Amy (1988). *The Social Construction of American Realism*. Chicago: University of Chicago Press.

Karcher, Carolyn L. (1994). *The First Woman in the Republic: A Cultural Biography of Lydia Maria Child*. Durham, NC: Duke University Press.

Kelly, Joan (1984). "Did Women Have a Renaissance?" In *Women, History and Theory: The Essays of Joan Kelly*, intr. Catherine Stimpson et al., 19–50. Chicago: University of Chicago Press.

Kolodny, Annette (1985). "The Integrity of Memory: Creating a New Literary History of the United States." *American Literature* 57, 291–307.

Lauter, Paul (1991). *Canons and Contexts*. New York: Oxford University Press.

Norris, Frank (1967). *Complete Works of Frank Norris*, ed. Charles Norris, vol. 7. Port Washington, NY: Kennikat.

Pattee, Fred Lewis (1940). *The Feminine Fifties.* New York: Appleton–Century.

Pizer, Donald (1984). *Realism and Naturalism in Nineteenth-Century American Literature*, 2nd edn. Carbondale: Southern Illinois University Press. (First publ. 1966.)

Reynolds, David (1989). *Beneath the American Renaissance: The Subversive Imagination in the Age of Emerson and Melville.* Cambridge, Mass.: Harvard University Press.

Sherman, Sarah Way (1989). *Sarah Orne Jewett: An American Persephone.* Hanover, NH and London: University Press of New England.

Showalter, Elaine (1986). "Piecing and Writing." In Nancy K. Miller (ed.), *The Poetics of Gender*, 222–47. New York: Columbia University Press.

Showalter, Elaine (1990). *Sexual Anarchy: Gender and Culture at the Fin de Siècle.* New York: Penguin.

Sigourney, L. H. (1835). *Letters to Young Ladies.* Hartford, Conn.: W. Watson.

Smith-Rosenberg, Carroll (1985). *Disorderly Conduct: Visions of Gender in Victorian America.* New York: Knopf.

Spacks, Patricia (1972). *The Female Imagination.* New York: Avon.

Sundquist, Eric, ed. and intr. (1982). *American Realism: New Essays.* Baltimore: Johns Hopkins University Press.

Tompkins, Jane (1985). *Sensational Designs: The Cultural Work of American Fiction, 1790–1860.* New York: Oxford University Press.

Twain, Mark, and Warner, Charles Dudley (1873). *The Gilded Age: A Tale of To-Day.* Hartford, Conn.: American Publishing Co.

Ulrich, Laurel Thatcher (1991). *A Midwife's Tale; The Life of Martha Ballard, Based on Her Diary, 1875–1812.* New York: Knopf.

Warren, Joyce W., and Dickie, Margaret, eds. (2000). *Challenging Boundaries: Gender and Periodization.* Athens, Ga.: University of Georgia Press.

Welter, Barbara (1966). "The Cult of True Womanhood: 1820–1860," *American Quarterly* 18 (Summer), 151–74.

Wharton, Edith (1990). *The House of Mirth*, ed. Elizabeth Ammons. New York: Norton.

Wharton, Edith (1995). *Ethan Frome*, ed. Kristin O. Lauer and Cynthia Griffin Wolff. New York: Norton.

Woolson, Constance Fenimore (1988). *Women Artists, Women Exiles: "Miss Grief" and Other Stories*, ed. and intr. Joan Myers Weimer. New Brunswick, NJ: Rutgers University Press.

Young, Elizabeth (1999). *Disarming the Nation: Women's Writing and the American Civil War.* Chicago: University of Chicago Press.

14
Confronting the Crisis: African American Narratives
Dickson D. Bruce, Jr.

The years between 1865 and 1914 comprise an important period in the history of African American narrative. Major works by African American writers had begun to appear near the close of the antebellum period, mainly within the context of the abolition movement; nevertheless, the impact of emancipation and Reconstruction, from 1865 to 1877, helped to create new conditions for African American literary activity. The post-Reconstruction period, beginning about 1877, saw changes in American life that were to affect African American authors, by the early twentieth century, in complex and far-reaching ways.

The Reconstruction period represents something of a lost era in the study of African American literature, in part because much of the work of recovering literary activity remains to be done. Although scholars have identified several important works from the period, including novels and stories appearing in newspapers and in such influential journals as the African Methodist Episcopal Church's *Christian Recorder*, the number of known works remains small.

Still, enough has survived to indicate some major directions in Reconstruction-era writing. One is a focus on problems of race and racial discrimination and a continuing adaptation of anti-slavery traditions from the first half of the nineteenth century to address them. Such adaptations are especially visible in narratives that draw on what is sometimes called the "tragic mulatto" tradition, a staple of anti-slavery fiction. Such tales depict genteel young men and women, knowingly or unwittingly passing for white, who are revealed to have "African" ancestry, forcing them to suffer the horrors of racial oppression, often epitomized by a tragic frustration of love across the color line. The use of such protagonists served to highlight the evils of discrimination while dramatizing the artificial, arbitrary nature of racial distinctions.

One early post-Civil War example of the tragic mulatto tale is "The Curse of Caste" (1865), an incomplete novel by Julia C. Collins, serialized in *The Christian Recorder*. A white man from New Orleans marries a beautiful quadroon, fleeing with her to New England. Unfortunately, business requires him to return to his home, and, during his absence, his wife dies. Their daughter, educated, refined, and unaware of her mother's ancestry, goes to New Orleans years later, and is employed as a governess in her father's family. When she plans marriage to a young white man, her secret is exposed. Her ultimate fate remains a mystery, since Collins died before she could finish the story. But Collins's use of the tragic mulatto tradition is typical in its exposure of both the absurdity and the tragic consequences of race.

This tradition also informs the first known novel by a more prominent author, Frances Ellen Watkins Harper, who began her literary career as an abolitionist writer and activist. *Minnie's Sacrifice*, rediscovered by Frances Smith Foster (1994), was serialized in the *Christian Recorder* in 1869. It, too, is the story of a refined young woman who appears white but who, having been sent from the South to the North for education, must confront a revelation that she has African ancestry. Minnie does not react with despair, but seizes on the knowledge with pride, dedicating her life to the improvement of African Americans, founding a school for freedpeople in the Recon-struction South. There she displays her courage and virtue, even as she is forced to confront the challenges posed by racist whites. Although the story ends tragically with Minnie's death (in a yet to be recovered installment), Harper is not entirely focused on the tragedies of race. As Minnie embraces her identity, she also provides an object lesson in racial improvement, one Harper uses to address a range of issues, from woman suffrage to community building, as well as the demand for racial equality.

Such an approach is apparent in many of Harper's works. Shortly before the end of Reconstruction she published another serialized novel, *Sowing and Reaping* (1876–7), again in the *Christian Recorder*. In this novel, Harper ignored racial issues as such to focus on her strong interests in Christian morality and, especially, temperance. Such a focus on "uplift" was itself to be an important element in Reconstruction-era fiction, as writers sought to inculcate what they saw as necessary virtues in developing African American communities.

This focus is also apparent in at least some of the writing of Thomas Detter, a businessman who had made his career in California and Nevada since the 1850s. Detter wrote a number of short pieces, some in the abolitionist "tragic mulatto" tradition. He also produced a pioneering short story, "Uncle Joe," a literary setting of an African American folk-tale. His most ambitious work, however, was a novella, *Nellie Brown; or, the Jealous Wife* (1871). The story focuses primarily on white characters, although Detter includes a few black servants who play an essential role in the plot. As the title indicates, the main character is Nellie Brown, a woman whose jealousy, combined with the bad influence of corrupt friends, nearly destroys both her marriage and her husband. A morality tale, the work joins Harper's as an effort to dramatize ideals of domestic virtue, despite its relative indifference to racial concerns.

Perhaps the most ambitious work of fiction from the Reconstruction period – and the most unusual – is Lorenzo Dow Blackson's lengthy book *The Rise and Progress of the Kingdoms of Light and Darkness; or, the Reign of Kings Alpha and Abadon* (1867). It is a retelling of world history from the creation account of Genesis through the prophecies of the book of Revelation as a story of continuing conflict for world supremacy between the two key kingdoms. Filled with mythological elements and personified forces, the narrative also sets the historical fight against slavery and prejudice, even denominational rivalries, within the rubric of the larger cosmic battle Blackson sets forth.

Given the relatively small number of recovered works, it is difficult to generalize about Reconstruction-era literary activity on the part of African American writers. It is possible, however, to note at least a few characteristics that help to connect it to the period and to explain its writers' concerns. The Reconstruction era itself was a period of high hopes and real achievement for African Americans. Under the aegis of Reconstruction policies, African Americans had found many reasons for optimism. Participating effectively in politics, especially in the liberated Southern states, they could also perceive signs, at least, that prejudice was weakening. A wave of institution-building gave reason for hope, and helped to create the foundation for a growing middle class. Reconstruction-era literature reflected those hopes and achievements. Its ultimate goal was racial equality, and the assimilation of African Americans into the American mainstream. That goal underlay what might be called the genteel protest inherent in the kinds of characters and stories such writers as Collins and Harper created, and the emphasis on ideals of virtue in their works, and those of Detter.

The post-Reconstruction period, from 1877 to 1914, was to see both new possibilities and new complications for African American literature. For a variety of reasons, literary production began to expand rapidly. At the same time, Reconstruction policies at the national level were being steadily abandoned after 1877, initiating a significant decline in the fortunes of African Americans through the early years of the twentieth century. In the South, where most lived, this decline was marked by disfranchisement and the development of a "Jim Crow" society in which virtually all institutions and facilities came to be segregated by law. Campaigns of violence and intimidation, including riots and the most gruesome forms of lynching, helped enforce the emerging segregated social and political order.

So did forms of intellectual and popular culture. Academic, scientific racism and notions of "Social Darwinism," which reached their highest level in the late nineteenth century, celebrated white superiority while asserting the innate intellectual and moral inferiority of nonwhite peoples. Trends in popular culture did much to reinforce such a view. Especially important was that body of literature known as the "plantation tradition," including works by such writers as Thomas Nelson Page, Irwin Russell, and Joel Chandler Harris. Making broad use of dialect – a burlesque representation of African American folk speech – it helped to create images of African Americans as a simple-minded, dependent, childlike people, and of an Old South in which black people, loyal and devoted to their masters, had been happy and content as slaves.

All these developments did much to shape the content and trajectory of African American writing. For one thing, however inauspicious these trends may appear, they probably did much to encourage literary activity by increasing African American writers' sense of the importance of their work as a response to the era's racist practices and conventions. Literary activity was also encouraged by the continuing growth of a middle-class community of readers and writers, despite the forces arrayed against it. This community helped support the creation of new publication outlets for African American writers, including such journals as the short-lived *Howard's Negro-American Magazine* (1890) and the longer-lasting *A.M.E. Church Review* (1884–), a new and influential publication of the African Methodist Episcopal Church.

Changes in historical conditions did not lead immediately to new forms and new directions; many of the earliest post-Reconstruction narratives continued to draw heavily on older traditions. James H. W. Howard's *Bond and Free* (1886), for example, was essentially an abolitionist novel in the "tragic mulatto" tradition, placing a beautiful, pale-skinned young slave woman in a typically brutal plantation setting. Much writing also continued to use genteel conventions in order to engage, as had Frances Ellen Watkins Harper and others, in a dual project of protest and uplift.

Harper's own novels from this period continued to embody this dual project. Her third serialized novel for the *Christian Recorder*, *Trial and Triumph* (1888–9), is little more than a series of dramatized dialogues conveying messages of virtue, and the need to resist temptation, for what Watkins took to be an African American audience. But her most famous novel, *Iola Leroy* (1892), was particularly important for the ways in which it brought together traditions of uplift with those of protest. Harper again drew on older forms by featuring a light-skinned, genteel heroine and introducing a story of interracial romance. Opening during the Civil War, the novel describes Iola's escape from slavery. Joining in the Union war effort by working in a field hospital, she meets a young white officer who proposes marriage to her, suggesting that she pass for white. Iola, however, refuses, proudly accepting her black identity and, like Minnie before her, dedicating herself to a life of service. Iola's decision brings down upon her all the cruelties that racist whites can inflict. But Iola, no tragic mulatto, is strong, and Harper uses her life and dedication to create both a testimony to and a model for African American virtue, gentility, and activism in the challenging post-Reconstruction world. Moreover, as if to reinforce the denial of racist views, Harper also introduces one of the first major dark-skinned characters in African American fiction, Lucille Delany, whose virtue and gentility, equal to Iola's, further affirm that culture and refinement know no color line.

The dual project in which Harper engaged underlies a substantial number of post-Reconstruction works. Many writers who took part in it did so, like Harper, by juxtaposing African American virtue with accounts of virulent racism, proving African American capabilities while disproving racist ideas. But the project is also apparent in a variety of works that made only minimal direct references to race as such. Katherine Davis Tillman's serialized novella "Beryl Weston's Ambition" (1893–4), appearing initially in the *A.M.E. Church Review*, superficially shields its characters, as Claudia Tate has noted, "from the extreme resurgence of racism in the 1890s" (1992: 193). But it also uses their refinement and achievements both to provide a model for her readers and to deny, dramatically, widely held racist images.

A few works in this vein even feature protagonists whose race is left unspecified and immaterial to the story. These include such novels as *Clarence and Corrine; or, God's Way* (1890) and *The Hazeley Family* (1894) by Amelia E. Johnson, and *Megda* (1891) and *Four Girls at Cottage City* (1898) by Emma Dunham Kelley. Each offers images of domestic virtue and female gentility, dramatizing the key orientation of uplift ideas at the close of the nineteenth century. Nevertheless, even without direct references to race, dimensions of protest are at least implicit as the characters stand in tacit contradiction to racist ideas.

Despite these apparent continuities, however, there began to be some signs by the late 1880s and early 1890s that many African American writers, in the face of worsening conditions, were also beginning to raise questions about the dual project of what might be called "genteel protest." Such questioning is to be seen, for instance, in the novel *Appointed* (1894) by Walter H. Stowers and W. H. Anderson (writing under the pseudonym "Sanda"). This novel follows the popular model in many ways, offering refined characters and a message of uplift. It is, however, one of the first novels to focus on lynching, its black protagonist, Saunders, a University of Michigan engineering graduate, suffering at the hands of a mob inflamed by a trumped-up charge against him. The novel is not entirely pessimistic – Saunders receives support and aid from a white friend throughout the story, suggesting at least the possibility of a permeable color line. But it offers less assurance that achievement and gentility can fully overcome prejudice.

A subtler but no less important move away from genteel protest may be seen in the first significant attempts by African American writers to adapt and rearticulate elements of the plantation tradition. This included using folk characters and even employing, as did most writers in the tradition, literary versions of African American folk speech, or dialect. Earlier writers, including Harper, had used such characters but had done so mainly to highlight their protagonists' gentility, proving that plantation tradition stereotypes did not represent the only possibility for African Americans. Now they would occupy center stage.

One early effort to create such a protagonist came from the prominent civic activist Victoria Earle Matthews. Although she had written several pieces in the framework of genteel protest, her "Aunt Lindy," published initially in the *A.M.E. Church Review* in 1891 and reissued as a pamphlet in 1893, was one of the first attempts to create a folk protagonist. "Aunt Lindy" is the story of an old ex-slave called to nurse a dying white man who turns out to be her former owner. During her time in slavery he had sold off her children, and now she sees the possibility of taking revenge. In the end, however, her religious scruples overcome her anger, and she nurses him back to health. In gratitude, he restores her surviving son to her, and provides handsomely for her family for the rest of their lives. Despite the happy ending, it should be stressed that Aunt Lindy is hardly the contented slave of the white plantation tradition. Her unwillingness to harm her former owner has nothing to do with loyalty or affection; it is her faith, not gratitude, that provides the focus for the story. Her moral superiority is the story's most important message.

Ultimately, however, the most prominent writers to work with plantation tradition conventions were Paul Laurence Dunbar and Charles W. Chesnutt. Publishing in such "mainstream" periodicals as *Century* magazine and the *Atlantic Monthly*, they were the first black writers since emancipation to gain a large national audience. They were also the writers who most profoundly addressed the critical developments in post-Reconstruction race relations.

Of the two, Dunbar was in many ways the more influential. Bursting on the scene in 1896, largely as a result of a tribute from America's leading critic, William Dean Howells, he made his career primarily as a poet. But he was always interested in fiction, and early in his career began to produce a body of short stories and novels that added to his fame. Like his most popular poetry, much of Dunbar's fiction, particularly his short fiction, grew out of efforts to work with conventions of the plantation tradition, including an extensive use of dialect.

Dunbar published four collections of short stories – *Folks from Dixie* (1898), *The Strength of Gideon* (1900), *In Old Plantation Days* (1903), and *The Heart of Happy Hollow* (1904), each including a number of plantation tradition pieces. His approach to that tradition was complex. Some of his stories do little more than mirror the writings of such white authors as Thomas Nelson Page and Joel Chandler Harris. "Aunt Tempe's Triumph," from *In Old Plantation Days*, for example, is little more than a patronizing look at an old slave's devotion to her master and his family, and there are many other stories like it. But Dunbar was also able to adapt genuine folk motifs in ways that subverted plantation tradition complacencies. Thus, "The Case of C'a'line," from *The Strength of Gideon*, draws on trickster traditions found in African American folklore as it presents a black cook who fools her employer into giving her a raise.

Dunbar was himself ambivalent about his efforts to use the plantation tradition. He was proud of his craft; but, fiercely opposed to racism and discrimination, he was also, as Gavin Jones has said, "highly aware of the racial ramifications of any repetition of white cultural forms" (1999: 191). At the same time he was a multifaceted writer, and his plantation tradition efforts represented only a part of his output. Some of his fiction was directly concerned with protest, and had little to do with genteel ideals. Thus, two of his stories – "The Tragedy at Three Forks," from *The Strength of Gideon*, and "The Lynching of Jube Benson," from *The Heart of Happy Hollow* – take on the timely subject of racial violence in a harsh, realistic way. Deeper and subtler forms of protest underlie his four novels, *The Uncalled* (1898), *The Love of Landry* (1900), *The Fanatics* (1901), and *The Sport of the Gods* (1902).

Dunbar's first novel, *The Uncalled*, is in many ways the most revealing. Avoiding specifically racial themes – the novel never indicates whether its protagonists are black or white – it is the story of a young Midwesterner's search for an identity of his own, despite the constraints others try to place on him. Challenging narrowness and the power of tradition, it is, for all its avoidance of race, a novel that calls into question the kinds of received categories informing dominant American racial ideas, and the kinds of constraining categories Dunbar himself had to face as a writer. This is a theme that also dominates *The Love of Landry*, despite the novel's ostensible setting among white characters in Colorado.

It is also a concern that frames his last two novels, which do address specifically racial themes. *The Fanatics* portrays white citizens in a town so blinded by racial hatred that they allow their community to be torn apart. *The Sport of the Gods*, one of the first works to deal seriously with the migration of African Americans from the South to the North, dramatizes the extent to which the brutality of American racism turns human beings into human toys, as the title implies. The novel focuses on the family of Berry and Fanny Hamilton, faithful employees of the white Oakleys. When Berry is falsely accused of theft and imprisoned, Fanny and their children are driven from their home and escape to New York. The urban environment corrupts the children, and, though Berry is released and seeks to restore his family life in the North, the family has been destroyed. In what Dunbar makes clear is desperation, Berry and Fanny return to the South. The novel expresses what seems to have become, for Dunbar, a near-fatalism about African American prospects, perhaps reflecting the era's worsening racial conditions.

Those worsening conditions are similarly apparent in the work of Charles Chesnutt. Chesnutt occupies a complex place in African American literary history. Although he actually began his career in the late 1880s, before Dunbar, he was not widely known, initially, to be an African American writer. As a result, his influence did not begin to be felt until fairly late in the 1890s. As with Dunbar, much of his important early fiction was at least superficially connected to the era's popular plantation tradition. These were stories that began to appear in such magazines as the *Atlantic* by 1887, ultimately to be collected in his 1899 volume, *The Conjure Woman*. Framed by the reportage of an upper-class Northern white man who has just bought an abandoned North Carolina plantation, they center on dialect tales of the plantation's long-time resident, ex-slave Uncle Julius McAdoo, and draw on folk traditions of magic — "conjuration" — as Julius hopes to play on superstitious fears to preserve an autonomy to which he has become accustomed. Julius's trickery never really works; his efforts are more amusing than effective.

But, more than Dunbar, even as Chesnutt used conventions of the plantation tradition he often did so in ways that subverted them, presenting a more realistic view of slavery and race than the plantation tradition normally allowed. Violence, not paternalism, characterizes Chesnutt's representation of the plantation regime. Julius's stories tell of family separations and brutal beatings; even, in some cases, of slaves wreaking havoc on their masters.

There is thus a strong element of protest in Chesnutt's plantation fiction. It is apparent in the conjure tales and also in such a story as "The Passing of Grandison," from his second major collection of short fiction, *The Wife of His Youth* (1899). This story satirizes that plantation-tradition staple, the loyal slave, as its title character, Grandison, uses superficial displays of loyalty to trick his master and gain freedom for himself and his family. Trickery and antagonism characterize Chesnutt's plantation world; these were hardly the stuff of white plantation-tradition fiction.

Protest also dominated Chesnutt's work as he, like Dunbar, moved away from the plantation tradition into other narrative forms. This is especially clear in the three novels published during his lifetime: *The House Behind the Cedars* (1900), *The Marrow of Tradition* (1901), and *The Colonel's Dream* (1905). The latter two are among the first overtly political novels within the African American narrative tradition: *The Marrow of Tradition* is based on an ugly 1898 race riot in Wilmington, North Carolina, while *The Colonel's Dream* describes an effort at community-building frustrated by racism. Both provide strong if pessimistic indictments of the racist social and economic order of the emerging "New South."

The House Behind the Cedars, on the other hand, shows the appeal for Chesnutt of the "tragic mulatto" tradition, with its familiar motifs of passing and love across the color line. The novel focuses on a story of love between a white Southern young man and a beautiful young woman, Rena Walden, with a touch of African ancestry. When her secret comes out, their planned marriage is cancelled, even though each retains a love for the other. Rena makes an effort to fit into the African American community, but confronts enormous hardships. In the end, she goes insane and finally dies, her white lover feeling an almost overwhelming remorse.

The novel is one of several of Chesnutt's narratives to deal with the arbitrariness of race through motifs of passing and interracial love. A recently published novel from about 1896 or 1897, *Mandy Oxendine*, tells the story of a supercilious young woman's attempt to pass, rejecting her black lover for a white one. Her effort produces tragic results for all concerned. *The Wife of His Youth* included some of Chesnutt's most important pieces along these lines, especially "The Sheriff's Children" (originally published in the New York *Independent* in 1889). This is the story of a young African American criminal who turns out to be the son of the white sheriff who arrested him, a son born during the era of slavery. The young man dies just as the sheriff begins to acknowledge both the guilt and the responsibility his fatherhood entails.

No less important is the title story, "The Wife of His Youth," originally published in the *Atlantic* in 1898: a story that takes a somewhat different tack in confronting the color line. A wealthy, very light-skinned man is surprised at a social occasion by the appearance of the "wife of his youth," an old, very black woman to whom he had been married in slavery. Publicly acknowledging her, he challenges a color line within the African American community that, Chesnutt indicated, was itself an ugly legacy of slavery and racism.

As "The Wife of His Youth" suggests, the real tragedy of race for Chesnutt, as for Dunbar, lay in the extent to which it made people unable to see through color to individual character. He made this point especially well in one of his few stories in which racial themes appears on the surface to be wholly absent, his comic "Baxter's Procrustes." Published in the *Atlantic* in 1904, it is a story about a book collectors' club whose members focus their interest primarily on beautifully produced volumes. Baxter, in a fit of cynicism, introduces a particularly fine volume to be distributed, sealed, among the members. When a visitor opens the wrappings, he discovers that the volume's pages are blank. The apparently familiar message that one should not judge a book by its cover seems particularly pointed when viewed in light of Chesnutt's other works.

After about 1905 Chesnutt's literary efforts decreased dramatically, for reasons that are not entirely clear. He did, however, publish one of his most striking stories, "The Doll," in 1912. It appeared in the *Crisis*, a magazine edited by W. E. B. Du Bois as the official organ of the National Association for the Advancement of Colored People (NAACP). A brief story, it centers on the inner turmoil a black barber suffers when he learns that the white customer in his chair was the murderer of his father. The barber must decide whether to take revenge – he is holding a razor preparing to shave the murderer's neck – or, given the violent retribution he would certainly suffer, to resist the temptation in the interest of fulfilling his responsibilities to his family. He chooses the latter, his nonviolence presented by Chesnutt as evidence not of the barber's submissiveness but rather of his moral character.

The works of Dunbar and Chesnutt help to highlight several emphases in turn-of-the-century African American narratives. For one, their very success seems to have further encouraged a vogue for dialect and local color writing among African American authors. Some of this work followed Dunbar and Chesnutt by exploiting the plantation tradition. Dialect tales found special favor among African American authors; even a few of the more genteel writers also tried their hands at dialect.

Some writers, however, departed significantly from the plantation tradition by moving more toward realism in their depiction of black folk life. Alice Moore Dunbar, Paul Laurence Dunbar's wife, made an important contribution along these lines. She published two collections of short stories in the 1890s. The first, *Violets* (1895), appeared prior to her marriage and is firmly within the framework of gentility. Her second, *The Goodness of St. Rocque* (1899), went in a very different direction, creating realistic portrayals of folk characters and customs in southern Louisiana. Another writer who began in the genteel tradition, Katherine Davis Tillman, produced two works, the serialized "Clancy Street" (1898–9) and the short story "The Preacher at Hill Station" (1903), both appearing in the *A.M.E. Church Review*, which offer similarly realistic portrayals of African American folk communities. "Clancy Street" actually anticipated Dunbar's *Sport of the Gods* in its use of an urban setting. Particularly radical was the Kentucky teacher Joseph Seamon Cotter, whose *Negro Tales* (1912) captures some of the improvisational character of African American (as of most) oral traditions.

Not everyone approved of the vogue for a literature evoking African American folk life. Critics worried, as had Dunbar, about the tendencies of such works to echo, as Eric Sundquist has noted, the worst excesses of "vaudeville and minstrelsy" (1992: 47). This concern underlies one of the more significant turn-of-the-century novels, James D. Corrothers's *The Black Cat Club* (1902). Another pioneer in using an urban setting, Corrothers also drew on genuine folk traditions to tell the story of the Black Cat Club, a Chicago "literary society" established by a group of men of less-than-elite background. Their gatherings are boisterous; they constantly prove their ignorance of respectable ideals. The central character in the novel is the society's president, and poet laureate, Sandy Jenkins (an apparent reference to a treacherous figure in Frederick Douglass's autobiographies). As the novel progresses, Sandy Jenkins is attaining a growing reputation as a dialect poet, recognized not only by his club mates but also by middle-class people who are making him a literary celebrity. The book makes heavy use of dialect, and Corrothers himself had made a reputation as a dialect poet. But, like Dunbar, he had always been uncomfortable with the form, and it is not difficult to see in the novel both a certain reflexivity and a negative commentary on the fashion for dialect writing and folk portrayals. As Corrothers follows Sandy's escapades, especially among his adoring audiences, he condemns both Sandy as a charlatan and the audiences as too uncritical to understand the harm Sandy's writing can do.

The vogue for dialect and folk portrayals, and the concerns they raised, may also be seen as elements in a larger set of processes influencing tendencies in African American literature in the late nineteenth and early twentieth centuries. One, reflecting the increasing power of racism and segregation in post-Reconstruction America, involved a kind of turning inward, evidenced by a growing interest on the part of African Americans in what appeared to be the distinctive characteristics of black communities. The emphasis on distinctiveness was reinforced by the broad currency of white racial ideas, denying to African Americans any genuine creative potential. Many writers and thinkers felt a need to assert distinctive African American achievement, despite the barriers posed by a Jim Crow America. The heightened interest in folk traditions was a measure of these impulses, as writers sought to rescue folk communities from the racist portrayals of the white plantation tradition while offering positive portrayals of distinctively African American ways of life.

The celebration of folk traditions was not, however, the only way in which African American writers began to stress distinctiveness. A minor example of the same trend may be seen in an otherwise unremarkable 1896 novel by Kenneth M. Young, *Selene*. A story of the eternal triangle, it revolved around a female protagonist who, like Harper's Lucille Delany, departed from the older, light-skinned norm. But in describing Selene, Young went beyond what Harper did with Delany, emphasizing not only the quality but also the distinctiveness of her beauty.

Another writer, John S. Durham, went in a very different direction in *Diane: Priestess of Haiti* (1902). *Diane* is a story of international intrigue, set in Haiti, involving a conspiracy to bring the island under the control of a German syndicate. The plot is foiled by the combined efforts of the German ambassador and the Haitian president, assisted by the brave young soldier Alcide. But within the novel is also a love story involving Alcide and the title character, Diane, one of the first truly exotic heroines in African American literary tradition. Although Diane, the daughter of a voodoo priest, maintains the vogue for light-skinned heroines, she is also presented as passionate and erotically sensuous, departing significantly from older, more genteel models.

The early years of the twentieth century thus saw increasing diversity in African American fiction, as writers facing the complex problems posed by a Jim Crow society explored a variety of literary directions in addressing those problems. As was the case for Dunbar and Chesnutt, many writers also continued to identify the real tragedy of the post-Reconstruction era in the power of entrenched racial categories. They confronted that tragedy through re-elaborations and re-articulations of older motifs, including, as with Chesnutt, stories of passing and interracial love. The earlier dual project of uplift and protest, however, has little significance for writers from this era. They are chiefly concerned to address an environment where racial categories and racial lines had become both pervasive and increasingly reified.

Stories of passing and interracial love showed up in a variety of ways. Thus, J. McHenry Jones, in *Hearts of Gold* (1896), found it useful to couple his novelistic exposé of Southern labor conditions with a tale of a young woman's confrontation with the potential demands of passing and the implications of an African American identity, reinforcing his indictment of prejudice and discrimination. George Marion McClellan's stories collected in his *Old Greenbottom Inn* (1906) also focused on changing conditions in the turn-of-the-century South and used motifs of passing and interracial love to decry, as had Chesnutt, the cruel choices that racism handed to African Americans.

The motifs of racial mixture, passing, and love across the color line were to play an especially significant role in periodical fiction by African American authors during this time. Several important periodicals appeared during the early twentieth century, including the *Colored American Magazine* (1900–9), the *Voice of the Negro* (1904–7), and *Alexander's Magazine* (1905–9). Also influential were three magazines edited by W. E. B. Du Bois: *Moon* (1905), *Horizon* (1907–10), and, especially, the NAACP's *Crisis* (1910–), which Du Bois edited from its inception to 1934. Each published a wide variety of narrative pieces by African American authors, from sentimental love stories to political satires to dialect pieces and evocations of folk life and traditions. A number of stories addressed the problem of white racial violence; a few offered visions of black violent resistance. "The Returning Road of Dreams" (1904) by William Stanley Braithwaite – then the leading African American man of letters – was a pioneering satire taking on the debate over Booker T. Washington's approach to racial questions. There were even experimental works such as Angelina Grimké's dream tale, "Black Is, as Black Does" (1900), initially published in the *Colored American*, offering a vision of the retribution racist whites would suffer at the judgment seat of God.

This periodical fiction was to be particularly marked, however, by the prevalence of tales using motifs of passing and love across the color line. Such stories were especially common in the *Colored American* – which published more fiction than any other magazine during the tenure of its outstanding literary editor, Pauline Elizabeth Hopkins, who was associated with the magazine from 1900 to 1904.

Hopkins herself produced some of the most significant narratives using such motifs. She wrote numerous short stories – some under the pen-name Sarah Allen – and three serialized novels for the magazine. She also published a novel independently of the periodical, *Contending Forces* (1900), which offers one of the most original uses of traditional motifs. The novel features the descendants of an elegant woman, Grace

Montfort, who had been married to a wealthy planter when she was rumored to have African ancestry. She was subsequently betrayed by perfidious local whites who murdered her husband and forced her into slavery, leading to her suicide. The rest of the novel focuses on her grandchildren, Dora and Will Smith, who, with slavery's end, are making their lives in the North. Hopkins spins a complex story of love and betrayal as Dora and Will encounter an array of questionable characters, white as well as black, while confronting racism and discrimination. In so doing, she evokes a strongly ironic view of white pretensions to racial superiority. At the same time, hers was not, on the surface, so tragic a view as that taken by Chesnutt and many other writers who pursued themes of passing and interracial love. Grace Montfort's husband had not abandoned her, despite the rumors about her ancestry. Moreover, the novel ends happily when Dora and Will are rediscovered and acknowledged by a white descendant of their grandfather's family and set on their way to prosperous futures.

A similar approach informs much of Hopkins's other work. Two of her serialized novels, *Hagar's Daughter* (1901–2) and *Winona* (1902), resemble *Contending Forces* in holding out the possibility of successful marriages across the color line, as does her 1900 murder story "Talma Gordon." These plots should not be read as an advocacy of interracial marriage. As Hazel Carby has emphasized, nothing could be farther from Hopkins's views on race and race relations (1987: 140–1). Rather, as Hopkins portrays the possibility of genuine love, and even marriage, across the color line, she illuminates, by contrast, the nature of white America's infatuation with the color line. Hopkins's works thus envision a better world in order to dramatize the meaning of racial categories in the world her works confront.

But perhaps the most unusual narratives of the color line are the novels of Baptist minister Sutton E. Griggs. Griggs wrote five novels: *Imperium in Imperio* (1899), *Overshadowed* (1901), *Unfettered* (1902), *The Hindered Hand* (1905), and *Pointing the Way* (1908). All employ themes of racial mixture and interracial romance to address issues of racial identity while protesting racial prejudice. Griggs, however, frames those themes in unanticipated ways, combining them with political concerns and with a degree of pessimism that exceeds even that of Dunbar and Chesnutt.

Griggs's most striking novel of the color line is his fourth, *The Hindered Hand*. Revolving around a debate over racial strategies between two characters, the conservative Ensal Ellwood and the more militant Earl Bluefield, the novel puts that debate in perspective through the lives and fates of two light-skinned young women, Tiara and Eunice. Tiara values her black identity and, marrying Ensal, is put on course to a happy future. Eunice seeks to pass, but, challenged, she is found by a court to be of African ancestry. She promptly goes mad. At this point, the novel could be taken, like many, as an object lesson in being true to one's race. Griggs, however, undercuts such a reading as he concludes with Ensal and Tiara making contingent plans to emigrate to Africa, "should the demented Eunice prove a wiser better prophet than the hopeful, irrepressible Earl."

Griggs's first and best-known novel, *Imperium in Imperio*, is, if anything, more pessimistic. It is the story of the birth and death of a black revolutionary movement, the "Imperium," which attempts to create a separatist state. The movement fails mainly because of the raw ambition of its leaders. Even here, however, Griggs inserts a tragic tale of the color line to emphasize the desperation that drives his characters into the movement, and the inescapable power of race in their lives and their society. Dramatizing both the significance and the arbitrariness of the color line, Griggs portrays a world in which alienation appears the most likely outcome of any attempt to overcome a racist America.

Griggs's work helps to highlight the dilemmas African American writers faced at the opening of the twentieth century. These were challenges revolving around the question of how to create a satisfying identity – for oneself and one's community – in the context of a pervasively racist and racially segregated society. Although, for the most part, these questions remained below the surface in African American fiction from the period, at least a few writers did confront them directly, and by a variety of means.

In some ways, the most traditional approach to these dilemmas may be seen in stories that, following Chesnutt's "Wife of His Youth" or Harper's *Iola Leroy*, call for a rejection of an internal color line. Ruth Todd's "The Folly of Mildred" (1903), about a young woman who throws away her life by pursuing only men of light complexion – whatever their character – is one example. So is "Emmy" (1912 13), by Jessie R. Fauset – later to become a leading figure in African American literary life. This is the story of a young engineer given every inducement to pass for white. He refuses to do so out of his love for the dark-skinned Emmy, even if it means the loss of his career. Such stories, while remaining within the framework of gentility, not only decry what their authors, and others, saw as a problem within African American communities; they also suggest the possibility of finding happiness within an African American world and through an African American identity.

A more elaborate approach to dilemmas of identity may be seen in Pauline Hopkins's final novel, *Of One Blood* (1902–3). Much of the story, as in her other works, revolves around interracial love and passing, but this time the setting is more fantastic. In the course of the novel, its protagonist, the young doctor Reuel Briggs, not only confronts his African ancestry but, on an archaeological expedition, also learns of his descent from the ancient kings of Ethiopia. The novel concludes with his marriage to the beautiful Ethiopian Queen Candace, consummating an African identity that he had earlier refused to accept. Drawing on a tradition of ancient African celebration going back to the early nineteenth century, Hopkins uses it here to convey a distinctive identity and a historical source of racial pride that transcended the trials posed by racism in America.

A no less influential understanding of what dilemmas of identity entailed resulted from the impact on African American thought and letters of W. E. B. Du Bois. His thinking since the 1890s, given broad publicity by the publication of his collection of essays *The Souls of Black Folk* (1903), did much to encourage an interest in African American distinctiveness and in possibilities for creating uniquely African American forms of art and literature. For Du Bois, the key to African American distinctiveness lay in such "African" attributes as an innate spirituality and a capacity for feeling that stood as powerful alternatives to the materialistic American mainstream. Du Bois did not reject that mainstream, but, encapsulating the dilemma many writers portrayed, argued that a truly African American identity could emerge from a synthesis of the African with the American, drawing on the best that each had to offer.

In outlining what was specifically African in America, Du Bois, simultaneously capturing significant literary tendencies of his day and giving them an ideological base, looked particularly at African American folk communities and traditions. These, he suggested, offered the purest realization of those distinctive African American attributes. He argued that such communities and traditions could serve as important sources for distinctively African American literary and artistic efforts.

Du Bois put his ideas into practice in *The Quest of the Silver Fleece* (1911). It is a complicated novel. On the one hand, it is a political work telling the story of the efforts of some white Southerners and their Northern comrades to establish a monopoly in the cotton trade. On the other, it is a love story involving the two protagonists, Bles and Zora, who seek to resist those efforts. Zora, however, described by Du Bois as dark and primitive, embodies the virtues he celebrated as uniquely African. Becoming, by the end of the novel, an educated, politically sophisticated young woman, she nevertheless draws her strength from those virtues, giving substance to the synthesis of Africa and America that Du Bois believed could create a satisfying African American identity.

A more profound dramatization of Du Bois's ideas, and of the dilemmas out of which they grew, may be seen in what is certainly the most accomplished African American novel from the early twentieth century, James Weldon Johnson's *Autobiography of an Ex-Coloured Man* (1912). It was originally published anonymously, purported to be the autobiography of a man who has decided to pass for white. Much of the novel appears at first, however, to tell a different story as the narrator, who speaks anonymously, describes his increasing efforts to create an African American identity. He is a musician who develops a growing interest in African American traditions and ultimately decides to go to the South to discover more about them. The South, however, turns out to be a horrible place, the narrator's horror reaching its apogee when he is forced to witness a lynching. In shock and dismay he flees from the South, from his quest, and, finally, from any kind of African American identity. He becomes white, marries (though his bride knows his secret), and assumes a new life. The ending is not happy. The narrator, Johnson concludes, has gained comfort at the cost of his soul. Building on Du Boisian themes, Johnson stresses the integrity and heroism of an African American cultural and historical experience. But he also expresses deep concern about the possibilities for creating a wholly positive African American identity in a bifurcated, segregated American world.

Johnson's *Autobiography of an Ex-Coloured Man* forms a capstone to the history of African American narratives from emancipation to the coming of World War I. In many ways, it helps to summarize a history of growing unease about prospects and possibilities in an increasingly racist environment. It is also a capstone in the way it looks toward issues of identity as such, grappling profoundly with dilemmas of distinctiveness and what Du Bois influentially described as "double consciousness," a sense of, among other things, being American and not American at one and the same time. Such themes would come to dominate African American narratives in the post-World War I period, continuing through much of the twentieth century.

PRIMARY TEXTS

Blackson, Lorenzo Dow. *The Rise and Progress of the Kingdoms of Light and Darkness; or, the Reign of Kings Alpha and Abadon*. 1867.

Braithwaite, William Stanley. "The Returning Road of Dreams." 1904.

Chesnutt, Charles W. *Mandy Oxendine*. cg. 1896–7.

Chesnutt, Charles W. *The Wife of His Youth and Other Stories of the Color Line*. 1899.

Chesnutt, Charles W. *The Conjure Woman*. 1899.

Chesnutt, Charles W. *The House Behind the Cedars*. 1900.

Chesnutt, Charles W. *The Marrow of Tradition*. 1901.

Chesnutt, Charles W. "Baxter's Procrustes." 1904.

Chesnutt, Charles W. *The Colonel's Dream*. 1905.

Chesnutt, Charles W. "The Doll." 1912.

Collins, Julia C. "The Curse of Caste; or, the Slave Bride." 1865.

Corrothers, James D. *The Black Cat Club: Negro Humor and Folklore*. 1902.

Cotter, Joseph Seamon. *Negro Tales*. 1912.

Detter, Thomas. *Nellie Brown; or, the Jealous Wife, with Other Sketches*. 1871.

Du Bois, W. E. B. *The Souls of Black Folk*. 1903.

Du Bois, W. E. B. *The Quest of the Silver Fleece*. 1911.

Dunbar, Alice Moore. *Violets and Other Tales*. 1895.

Dunbar, Alice Moore. *The Goodness of St. Rocque*. 1899.

Dunbar, Paul Laurence. *Folks from Dixie*. 1898.

Dunbar, Paul Laurence. *The Uncalled*. 1898.

Dunbar, Paul Laurence. *The Love of Landry*. 1900.

Dunbar, Paul Laurence. *The Strength of Gideon and Other Stories*. 1900.

Dunbar, Paul Laurence. *The Fanatics*. 1901.

Dunbar, Paul Laurence. *The Sport of the Gods*. 1902.

Dunbar, Paul Laurence. *In Old Plantation Days*. 1903.

Dunbar, Paul Laurence. *The Heart of Happy Hollow*. 1904.

Durham, John S. *Dianne: Priestess of Haiti*. 1902.

Fauset, Jessie R. "Emmy." 1912–13.

Griggs, Sutton E. *Imperium in Imperio*. 1899.

Griggs, Sutton E. *Overshadowed*. 1901.

Griggs, Sutton E. *Unfettered: A Novel*. 1902.

Griggs, Sutton E. *The Hindered Hand; or, the Reign of the Repressionist*. 1905.

Griggs, Sutton E. *Pointing the Way*. 1908.

Grimké, Angelina. "Black Is, as Black Does." 1900.

Harper, Frances Ellen Watkins. *Minnie's Sacrifice*. 1869.

Harper, Frances Ellen Watkins. *Sowing and Reaping*. 1876–7.

Harper, Frances Ellen Watkins. *Trial and Triumph*. 1888–9.

Harper, Frances Ellen Watkins. *Iola Leroy; or, Shadows Uplifted*. 1892.

Hopkins, Pauline E. *Contending Forces: A Romance Illustrative of Negro Life North and South*. 1900.

Hopkins, Pauline E. "Talma Gordon." 1900.

Hopkins, Pauline E. *Hagar's Daughter: A Story of Southern Caste Prejudice*. 1901–2.

Hopkins, Pauline E. *Winona: A Tale of Negro Life in the South and Southwest*. 1902.

Hopkins, Pauline E. *Of One Blood*. 1902–3.

Howard, James H. W. *Bond and Free; a True Tale of Slave Times*. 1886.

Johnson, Amelia E. *Clarence and Corinne; or, God's Way*. 1890.

Johnson, Amelia E. *The Hazeley Family*. 1894.

Johnson, James Weldon. *The Autobiography of an Ex-Coloured Man*. 1912.

Jones, J. McHenry. *Hearts of Gold*. 1896.

Kelley-Hawkins, Emma Dunham. *Megda*. 1891.

Kelley-Hawkins, Emma Dunham. *Four Girls at Cottage City*. 1895.

McClellan, George Marion. *Old Greenbottom Inn and Other Stories*. 1906.

Matthews, Victoria Earle. *Aunt Lindy: A Story Founded on Real Life*. 1893.

Stowers, W. H., and Anderson, W. H. ["Sanda"]. *Appointed. An American Novel.* 1894.

Tillman, Katherine Davis. "Beryl Weston's Ambition." 1893–4.

Tillman, Katherine Davis. "Clancy Street." 1898–9.

Tillman, Katherine Davis. "The Preacher at Hill Station." 1903.

Todd, Ruth D. "The Folly of Mildred, a Race Story with a Moral." 1903.

Young, Kenneth M. *Selene.* 1896.

Later Collections

Ammons, Elizabeth, ed. (1991). *Short Fiction by Black Women, 1900–1920.* New York: Oxford University Press.

Dunbar, Paul Laurence (2003). *In his Own Voice: The Dramatic and Other Uncollected Works of Paul Laurence Dunbar,* ed. Herbert Woodward Martin and Ronald Primeau. Athens, Ohio: Ohio University Press.

Harper, Frances Ellen (1994). *Minnie's Sacrifice, Sowing and Reaping, Trial and Triumph: Three Rediscovered Novels by Frances E. W. Harper,* ed. Frances Smith Foster. Boston: Beacon.

Hopkins, Pauline E. (1988). *The Magazine Novels of Pauline Hopkins,* intr. Hazel V. Carby. New York: Oxford University Press (The Schomburg Library of Nineteenth-Century Black Women Writers). Includes *Hagar's Daughter, Of One Blood,* and *Winona.*

Tillman, Katherine Davis Chapman (1991). *The Works of Katherine Davis Chapman Tillman,* ed. Claudia Tate. New York: Oxford University Press.

References and Further Reading

Andrews, William L. (1980). *The Literary Career of Charles W. Chesnutt.* Baton Rouge: Louisiana State University Press.

Bell, Bernard W. (1987). *The Afro-Amerian Novel and its Traditions.* Amherst: University of Massachusetts Press.

Bloom, Harold, ed. (1994). *Black American Prose Writers before the Harlem Renaissance.* New York: Chelsea House.

Bruce, Dickson D., Jr. (1989). *Black American Writing from the Nadir: The Evolution of a Literary Tradition, 1877–1915.* Baton Rouge: Louisiana State University Press.

Campbell, Jane (1986). *Mythic Black Fiction: The Transformation of History.* Knoxville: University of Tennessee Press.

Carby, Hazel (1987). *Reconstructing Black Womanhood: The Emergence of the Afro-American Woman Novelist.* New York: Oxford University Press.

Elder, Arlene A. (1978). *The "Hindered Hand": Cultural Implications of Early African-American Fiction.* Westport, Conn.: Greenwood.

Foster, Frances Smith (1993). *Written by Herself: Literary Production by African American Women,* *1746–1892.* Bloomington: Indiana University Press.

Gaines, Kevin Kelly (1996). *Uplifting the Race: Black Leadership, Politics, and Culture in the Twentieth Century.* Chapel Hill: University of North Carolina Press.

Gruesser, John Cullen, ed. (1996). *The Unruly Voice: Rediscovering Pauline Elizabeth Hopkins.* Urbana: University of Illinois Press.

Hull, Gloria T. (1987). *Color, Sex, and Poetry: Three Women Writers of the Harlem Renaissance.* Bloomington: Indiana University Press.

Jackson, Blyden (1989). *A History of Afro-American Literature: The Long Beginning, 1746–1895.* Baton Rouge: Louisiana State University Press.

Jones, Gavin (1999). *Strange Talk: The Politics of Dialect Literature in Gilded Age America.* Berkeley and Los Angeles: University of California Press.

Logan, Rayford W. (1965). *The Betrayal of the Negro from Rutherford B. Hayes to Woodrow Wilson.* New York: Collier.

McElrath, Joseph R., Jr., ed. (1999). *Critical Essays on Charles W. Chesnutt.* New York: Hall.

Martin, Jay, ed. (1975). *A Singer in the Dawn: Reinterpretations of Paul Laurence Dunbar*. New York: Dodd, Mead.

Rampersad, Arnold (1976). *The Art and Imagination of W. E. B. Du Bois*. Cambridge, Mass.: Harvard University Press.

Rodgers, Lawrence R. (1997). *Canaan Bound: The African-American Great Migration Novel*. Urbana: University of Illinois Press.

Sundquist, Eric J. (1992). *The Hammers of Creation: Folk Culture in Modern African-American Fiction*. Athens, Ga.: University of Georgia Press.

Sundquist, Eric J. (1993). *To Wake the Nations: Race in the Making of American Literature*. Cambridge, Mass.: Harvard University Press.

Tate, Claudia (1992). *Domestic Allegories of Political Desire: The Black Heroine's Text at the Turn of the Century*. New York: Oxford University Press.

Williamson, Joel (1984). *The Crucible of Race: Black/White Relations in the American South since Emancipation*. New York: Oxford University Press.

Wonham, Henry B. (1998). *Charles W. Chesnutt: A Study of the Short Fiction*. New York: Twayne.

Yarborough, Richard Alan (1980). "The Depiction of Blacks in the Early Afro-American Novel." Ph.D. diss., Stanford University.

15

Fiction's Many Cities

Sidney H. Bremer

The end of the Civil War ushered in the United States' most concentrated half-century of urbanization. During the fifty years preceding World War I, the number and size of the nation's cities increased hugely, the percentage and ethnic diversity of Americans living in cities multiplied, mechanical transportation and utility systems transformed the urban infrastructure, and industry moved from upstream rural watermills to dockside urban coal supplies, distribution hubs, and financial centers. Of course, different cities incorporated these changes differently, some gradually, some dramatically. Fiction's cities also changed in various ways, as different authors experienced particular dimensions of city life and brought diverse creative visions to bear on them, and as literary realism increased attention to socio-economic issues generally. Nearly all fictions with city settings explored the changing relationship of private and public "spheres." Some city settings, especially those embodying the nation's most dramatic urban changes, became themselves subjects of fiction. Others stayed closer to pre-Civil War urban imagery, the focus kept more closely on residential dimensions of urban life.

Pre-Civil War fiction depicted US cities mostly as overgrown towns. John Winthrop's 1630 image of "the city on the hill" initiated a long literary tradition of city-towns shaped by human choice and expressive of human capacities – for good or for evil, for various psychological states, for different manners and interests. Their physical spaces are built on a human scale and domesticate nature in parks and gardens. Primarily "walking cities" also in historical fact (Weber and Lloyd 1975: *passim*), city-towns offer room to move around on one's own both physically and through social groups, in a community extending organically from private families into the more public "polis" (Phillips and LeGates 1981: 81–105). Although pre-Civil War fictions show European cities constrained by historical accumulations of people, inequities, and decay – such as London in Edgar Allan Poe's "The Man of the Crowd" (1840), Liverpool in Herman Melville's *Redburn* (1849), and Rome in Nathaniel Hawthorne's *The Marble Faun* (1860) – on American soil, their city-town settings often point toward open-ended futures – as in James Fenimore Cooper's image of an inclusive, promising town on its way to becoming a city in *The Pioneers* (1823) or Nathaniel Hawthorne's retrospect of revolutionary Boston as a "little metropolis" of family history and individual choice in "My Kinsman, Major Molineux" (1832). Even the deceptive masquerades and willful privacy of midcentury Boston in Hawthorne's *The Blithedale Romance* (1852) and the stony egotism in Herman Melville's *Pierre: or, the Ambiguities* (1852) and "dead-wall reveries" in his "Bartleby the Scrivener: A Story of Wall Street" (1853) depict cities as creative expressions of human culture – as cultural cities.

Throughout the post-Civil War period, fiction wrestled with the changing relationship between private and public life in America's growing cities, although it proved slow to recognize the increasing dominance of industry and technology in them. Even Rebecca Harding Davis, whose *Life in the Iron Mills* (1861) had pioneered the theme of urban industry on a small West Virginian scale, downplayed the impact of industry and mechanization on Philadelphia in *Waiting for the Verdict* (1867). Her post-Civil War novel presents a port city bound to its mercantile past and old-family elites. Its "steep manufactories" and "rushing trains" are relatively peripheral, and its industrial sector is mentioned only once. While "swarming" urban crowds recur several times – in a metaphoric breakthrough that would later become standard code for cities' immigrant and poor populations – they have no impact on Davis's plot; instead, such crowds serve to establish the personalities of major characters observing them. Despite Davis's thematic concern with discrimination as a public issue, her plot depends on private attitudinal changes. Her fictional Philadelphia is a cultural expression of private family associations. Its ruling irony is that the "Quaker City" of brotherly love has turned socially exclusionary; those who can find no place there are social outcasts who lack "good blood": a mulatto physician and a white artisan of illegitimate birth. True to the cultural city's openness to its regional surroundings, moreover, *Waiting for the Verdict*'s outcasts find a good life in the nearby countryside.

During the next decade, Washington DC provided a compelling fictional contrast to elitist Philadelphia. The nation's capital city is an open society defined by its political system in Henry Adams's aptly named *Democracy* (1880), as also in *The Gilded Age* (1873) by Mark Twain and Charles Dudley Warner and in *Honest John Vane* (1875) by John W. De Forest. These three novels even use the same set of devices to expose the rough cultural edges of Washington's openness: an awkward calling-card exchange among provincial ladies and polished diplomats, at least one speech-filled session of Congress against a background of lobbying and bribery, prying newspaper stories, and private interests perverting public policy. As indicated by Adams's subtitle "An American Novel," these novels offer Washington DC as a national epitome – its "POWER" explicitly contrasted to Philadelphia's elitism, New York's commerce, and Boston's intellectualism by *Democracy*'s heroine. Nonetheless, Madeleine Lee finds no personal power in Washington – either for herself in women's limited social sphere, nor for its supposed political leaders, who lose communal grounding by betraying the "public good." *Democracy* describes Washington at several points as a "great machine" with "automata" for leaders, but also as a "wilderness" of "trees" stuck in "mire." Logically antithetical, Adams's machine and wilderness metaphors both emphasize the powerlessness of men to govern this urban society. Like *Waiting for the Verdict*'s "swarming" crowds, they make an important break-through in urban imagery. They point ahead a quarter-century to fiction's economic city of Chicago, where workers are both machine cogs and beasts in *The Jungle* (1906) by Upton Sinclair. But Washington DC in 1870s fiction is too devoid of any urban industrial machinery, too unremitting in its raw political power, and too ephemeral as a residence to epitomize the nation's changing cities.

Boston looks like a promising contender for status as a national urban center in William Dean Howells's *The Rise of Silas Lapham* (1885). Its title figure is a paint manufacturer introduced as the new " 'type of the successful American' " in the public newspaper interview that begins the novel. But it focuses on family, not business matters (Lynn 1971: 279), and its Boston setting is shaped by social standing and cultural forms, not industrial economics. *The Rise of Silas Lapham* uses private homes to characterize the cultural standing of two cohesive families, whose children even-tually join in marriage. It climaxes in the private debacle of a family dinner party and the tragic burning of the Laphams' new home; it tracks Silas's moral "rise" within that family context as he puts personal integrity before economic temptations. *The Rise of Silas Lapham* allows Silas and Persis Lapham to return to their old country origins, while the old-family mercantile power that still dominates Howells's Boston accom-modates industry when young Tom Corey marries Penelope Lapham and takes up Lapham's paint-manufacturing enterprise. Whereas fictional Philadelphia is thor-oughly privatized and fictional Washington thoroughly politicized – the one too private, the other too public – Howells's Boston integrates the public and private futures of the original "city upon a hill" and adds an industrial dimension.

Published just three years later, however, Henry James's *The Bostonians* (1888) confronts what Martin Green has called "the Problem of Boston": as economic power shifted to New York City, "the idea of culture," on which Boston based its status as the nation's urban center of literature and reform, "grew emptier" (1967: 108). While James's 1883 notebook claims Boston to be "very national, very typical" in its "friendships between women" (quoted in Howe 1956: ix), *The Bostonians* dramatizes the sterility of Boston's private and public realms in isolation from each other. During New England's "heroic age," private "plain living" supported public "moral passion" in "the city of reform"; but this ethos is dying in the post-Civil War "city of culture." The reform movement is maintained only artificially there, in domineering but shy Olive Chancellor's "interior." The limited views from her narrow parlor's "organized privacy" even misrepresent the city's "inexorable . . . poverty" as "very picturesque" and "lovely." Split off from the male cohort of commercial publicists who dominate the city's public business in *The Bostonians*, Boston's remnant of female reformers lack power – both metaphorically and biologically – to engage public realities and generate civic change. As Olive's sister insists, the new reform movement "isn't the city; it's just Olive Chancellor."

At the dramatic center of the novel, Olive Chancellor "battles" in vain with displaced southerner Basil Ransom over a young woman; Olive wants Verena Tarrant as her public voice, but Basil wants Verena as his private wife. The conflict builds when the novel moves to New York, the city that was indeed usurping Boston as the nation's publishing center, having already emerged as the nation's economic center and gateway city. In *The Bostonians*, New York is "a larger world" with "the infinite possibilities of a great city..." both for public engagement and for marital options. There Verena's "local [Boston] reputation" can become "a first-class national glory." There, too, Basil lives cheek by jowl with new urban realities, in a shabby boarding house across from "a row of tenements" overhung by "the fantastic skeleton of the Elevated Railway." He wins Verena's love in New York's Central Park, "sequestered" but not insulated from the "near neighborhood" of commerce. Although the novel brings the battle back to Boston, where Basil tears Verena away from a public speaking engagement Olive has made for her, it is New York that offers larger possibilities for both public and private life.

This New York is much more public than the fictional New York James had created just seven years earlier in *Washington Square* (1881), which anticipates the neighborhood focus that would sustain the family-centered imagery of the cultural city into the twentieth century. The novel's characters are all members of Catherine Sloper's extended family – even including, by marriage, her gold-digging suitor. Her father's "wide-fronted house" on Washington Square expresses his cultural standing; and staying there initially symbolizes her own inability to marry Morris Townsend without paternal blessing, and later her mature refusal to betray her selfhood to him after Dr. Sloper's death. Catherine Sloper is both outwardly constrained and inwardly strengthened by family privacy, whereas her silly Aunt Penniman's passion for public encounters has an illicit, dangerous quality. Even as a pre-Civil War neighborhood, however, James's fictional Washington Square is remarkable for its "history" and an "established repose" already unusual in the "shrill city." A remnant of the cultural city, it is smaller spatially and socially than Boston in *The Bostonians* (generally acknowledged as James's broadest social canvas) – and lies a world away from Howells's breakthrough New York novel of just a few years later.

In *A Hazard of New Fortunes* (1890), Howells plunges middle-aged Basil and Isabel March into a new economic city. The Marches reprise Howells's own job-related move from Boston – where he felt "at home" with a close circle of literary friends (Cady 1956: 163) – to New York, where he felt "homeless" like everyone else (quoted in O'Connor 1974: n.p.). They are especially fascinated by the elevated railroad, built in 1868 but still unique among American cities. Its mechanical network delineates the city's class-divided neighborhoods, in which the Marches get lost on foot while hunting for an apartment. A journal editor like Howells, Basil tries to keep the urban "spectacle" at a "picturesque" aesthetic distance (Haenni 1999: 494):

"... it shrieks and yells with ugliness here and there; but it never loses its spirits. . . .
[New Yorkers are] as gay as an L road. . . . [The L roads] kill the streets and avenues; but
at least they partially hide them, and . . . triumph over their prostrate forms with a
savage exultation that is intoxicating. . . . Perfectly atrocious, of course, but incompar-
ably picturesque! And the whole city is. . . . gay always." (Haenni 1999: 494)

Isabel demurs: "But frantic. I can't get used to it. They forget death, Basil; they
forget death in New York." Focusing the Marches' ambivalence, the El is Howells's
breakthrough metaphor for the new urban forces shaping American cities. Together
with the streetcar strike that forms the climax of the novel, the elevated railroad
emphasizes three troubling effects of urban industrialization: society's division by
monopolistic capitalism into economic classes; the "violent invasion" of private life
by public technology; and the city's reach along its streetcar lines "into the country,"
foreclosing escape. The city's public upheavals affect the lives of all the novel's
characters. Even Howells's pedestrian observers Basil and Isabel March are caught
up in its machinery – unlike the idly observant *flâneur* that Walter Benjamin
(1973: 36, 54) finds strolling in "protest against . . . industriousness" in Baudelaire's
works.

A Hazard of New Fortunes is the first novel to find an adequate structure for the new
urban world dominated by industrial economics – in the mechanical El and public
strike that shape its New York setting and plot, and in its lack of any leading
character. In almost schematic contrast to *The Rise of Silas Lapham* published just
five years earlier, Howells's *A Hazard of New Fortunes* replaces private family homes
with flats that "abolish . . . the family consciousness" and a commercial publishing
"house" that delineates the divergent cast of characters; climaxes in class conflicts that
erupt at an all-male business dinner, then a violent streetcar strike; and tears a tycoon's
family apart and leaves the empty-nest Marches adrift with no possibility of rural
escape. Most importantly, in shifting his focus from Boston to New York, Howells
stops presenting cities as cultural expressions of human capacities, as "homes" to be
known and shaped from within, and confronts The City as an external force shaping
human character, to be studied carefully at arm's length by "homeless" newcomers.
Although earlier US novels explored an impressive range of new urban developments,
A Hazard of New Fortunes is the first to leave the cultural city-town behind and present
an economically constructed city – as its subject, as well as its setting.

For here, with the publication of *A Hazard of New Fortunes* midway between the
Civil War and World War I, occurred a "paradigm shift" in the full sense established
by Peter Berger and Thomas Luckmann (1966). The leap from the cultural morals of
Rise to the economic risks of *Hazard* was not easy for Howells to make. A painful part
of his "conversion" to Christian socialism (Woodress 1993: 19), it meant relinquishing an expressive, family-based civic life to confront national economic inequities as
limits on urban life. As a paradigm shift, moreover, this was not just a personal affair.
Howells's recognition of the new economic city as a subject for literature reflected the
nation's previous quarter-century of major historical changes. It built upon new

elements in other authors' fictional cities. And it set the terms for the dominant thread in US urban literature for the next quarter-century and beyond.

Big, nationally connected, industrial cities replaced the pre-Civil War's mercantile cities serving rural communities. American cities were joined not only by railroads, but in 1883 by railroad standard time; and street railroads linked them to "streetcar suburbs" (Warner 1962). With capitalist production needing urban concentrations of material, labor, and financial resources, nine-tenths of US manufacturing was done in cities by 1900 (Trachtenberg 1982: 114). Manufactured goods replaced home production in daily urban life – first spinning and weaving, then food processing. Wholesale enterprises developed retail arms, and commercial centers became shopping spectacles, with the family's primary homemaker now its primary consumer. The privacy of city homes was breached by utility networks for gas and sewage, later for electricity and telephones; and many downtown residents crowded into apartment buildings and tenements. Widening socio-economic divisions were reinforced by increasing ethnic differentiation, with half of a major city's residents likely to be immigrants or their children by 1900. Total urban populations grew overwhelming, too: from nearly 20 percent of Americans living in cities in 1860 to over 45 percent by 1910; from nine cities with populations over 100,000 in 1860 to fifty-five by 1910 (McKelvey 1973: 104, 37, 73). By the turn of the century, Americans were debating whether The City was the nation's "shame" or its "hope," in the terms set by Lincoln Steffens (1904) and Frederic Howe (1906).

Besides external changes in urban places, the paradigm shift reflects changes in turn-of-the-century authors' perspectives. James's and Howells's mobility and increasing authorial distance from their fiction's cities typify an ascendant, new perspective. Young Stephen Crane, for instance, adopted a journalist's objectifying stance after moving from upstate New York to work for the metropolitan *Herald* and *Tribune*. He also took New York City's heterogeneity and poverty as fictional subjects for his first novel, *Maggie, A Girl of the Streets* (1893). In keeping with emergent economic-city patterns, *Maggie* focuses on the gap between rich and poor (although Crane's Rum Alley still echoes cultural-city patterns by presenting Maggie Johnson's descent into prostitution as the private failure of her abusive parents more than the public failure of the urban garment industry).

Increasing numbers of professional journalists created fictional exposés of poverty along lines made famous in Jacob Riis's nonfiction *How the Other Half Lives* (1890). Emphasizing the contrasts central to economic-city novels, Riis's title translates a Rousseau epigram introduced in an 1888 novel by Alice Wellington Rollins. Her *Uncle Tom's Tenement* re-creates key characters from Harriet Beecher Stowe's *Uncle Tom's Cabin* (1852) to contrast degrading Cherry Street tenement life with Madison Avenue's ignorant ease. This and other tenement tales, Bowery tales, and slum novels like Ernest Poole's *The Voice of the Street* (1906) became quite popular. Because they usually leaven their realism with picturesque sentimentality, Sabine Haenni (1999: 494) argues that they present fictional slums "as a public, familiarized, and detoxified pleasure zone" for readers seeking low-life excitement.

Figure 15.1   Jewish immigrants on Hester Street in New York City
Hester Street, on the Lower East Side of Manhattan, was a central location for new Jewish immigrants, with its cramped tenements, small businesses, and street marketplace. This 1899 photograph shows the heart of the Jewish ghetto. Although most immigrants came from rural backgrounds, they tended to settle in large cities for a number of reasons. First, that is where they disembarked and where, once the ethnic group had established itself, they found others from their original culture. Second, as urban industries made cities less appealing living environments, native-born Americans fled to the suburbs; but immigrants could not afford to commute, and so had to live near their workplaces. Third, fearing unemployment, immigrants wanted to live in cities where, if they were laid off, they could find other work. As the well-to-do left the cities, their former residences were converted by landlords into multi-family structures, with five or more households crammed into the space.

Meanwhile, New York immigrants and journalists focused on ethnic neighborhoods for "local color" sketches of the sort *A Hazard of New Fortunes* had legitimized. Best known was the Jewish *Daily Forward*'s editor, Abraham Cahan from the Lithuanian pale. Howells helped make Cahan's first English-language novel, *Yekl* (1896), a success; *The Imported Bridegroom* (1898), a collection of Cahan's New York periodical sketches and stories, soon followed. His tales emphasize contrasts between the Jewish immigrant dream of a Promised City (like the Pilgrims' "city upon a hill") and the clashing crowds of ethnic ghettos – a contrast critic Martha Banta (1995: 37) epitomizes as the "pastoral" harbor view versus the "contested" street. Originally titled *Yankele the Yankee, not Yankele the Jew* (Chametzky 1977: 67–8), however, *Yekl* still belongs to the cultural more than the economic city. It focuses on its title character's efforts to be culturally assimilated – into Jacob – even at some economic cost. Yekl replaces his own sober greenhorn suit with loud city slicker clothes, his Yiddish with American slang; and he goes into debt to divorce his old-world wife, Gitl, for a dancehall floozie.

Mobile journalists' objectifying stances, dramatic contrasts between wealth and poverty, and local color details of urban heterogeneity cultivated the ground for fiction's economic city. Even as cultural-city imagery remained available for fictional cities centered in residential life and shaped by private choices, the economic city became the paradigm for showing the impact of national systems on local, even private urban affairs. Fiction's economic city confronts individuals as a powerful phenomenon outside human control. Its public economic forces threaten private choices and shape political, aesthetic, and social institutions. Primarily a "streetcar city" (Weber and Lloyd 1975: *passim*), its anti-natural environment is a belated expression of Romantic anti-urbanism. Its physical spaces are determined by economic systems, especially the mechanical networks of factories, rail transportation, and utilities. Its society is articulated by economic classes and segregated residential patterns, which fragment community and family alike. Its heterogeneous population shares little beyond a belief in economic individualism, leaving each person

---

previously occupied by a single family. New tenements were also built, creating an unimaginable density and eliminating yards, trees, and sunlight. On the Lower East Side in 1890, the population density was an astonishing 334,000 people per square mile. Rents were exorbitant, with landlords making profits of 15–30 percent while their properties degenerated beyond repair. By 1894 half the population of New York City lived in 39,000 "dumb-bell" tenements, most of them without bathtubs, toilets, or running water. The result was an unsanitary slum, rife with disease and crime.

Inhabitants were also vulnerable to nativist stereotyping and hostility, both from Anglo-Americans and from the descendants of former immigrants. Because Italians, Greeks, Jews, and Slavs were darker-skinned than earlier immigrants, racism and nativism were conflated, with the new immigrants being seen as inferior on the racialist spectrum that placed Anglo and Nordic Americans on top and African Americans on the bottom. Eventually, fears of being overwhelmed by non-Anglo peoples – what was termed "race suicide" or the "annihilation of native American stock" – would lead to the immigration restriction statutes of the 1920s. (Photograph © Museum of the City of New York, Print Archives.)

dangerously isolated. And the city itself is often the subject of economic-city fiction. Edward Bellamy, author of *Looking Backward* (1888), was prescient when he told Howells in 1889, "You are writing of what everybody is thinking and all the rest will have to follow your example or lose their readers."

Specifically, a flood of Chicago novels did "follow [Howells's] example." They brought all the elements of the economic city into cohesive focus for two decades, starting when the 1893 Columbian Exposition shone a national spotlight on Chicago (Bremer 1992: 60ff.). Over twenty special issues of national magazines, besides innumerable news stories and periodical articles, were devoted to the temporary "White City" of the World's Fair and the factory-smoked "Black City" of Chicago (Bourget 1893: 135). The nation gaped at illustrations of the fair's 686-acre display of white Beaux Arts buildings, its Midway Plaisance starring Little Egypt and the first Ferris wheel, its elaborate congresses and meetings, its huge crowds. The nation also gasped at Chicago itself as the "first," "most," or "greatest" example of the new American city, the nation's "inevitable" future (Fuller 1968).

In fact, Chicago did exemplify the concentration and diversification of urban populations, the consolidation and expansion of urban spaces, and the shift to industrial capitalism in urban institutions. Its population had grown from 300,000 in 1870 to a million in 1890; with people then "pouring in at the rate of 50,000 a year," as Theodore Dreiser's *Sister Carrie* (1900) correctly noted, it would double to two million by 1910, when Chicago became the fourth largest city in the world. By 1890, first- and second-generation immigrants comprised three-quarters of Chicago's population, compared to half of New York's. As the nation's "railroad capital," Chicago had the highest concentration of interurban trunk lines and boasted far-flung streetcar tracks and an elevated downtown "loop," which encircled the nation's first skyscrapers. City blocks razed by the 1871 fire provided large acreage for manufacturing plants, warehouses, department stores, and centralized stock and commodity exchanges. Speculators like Philip Armour, George Pullman, and Samuel Insull controlled Chicago's major factories and transit and utility systems, bringing finance and industry into obvious combination and becoming prime targets for working-class protests like the 1886 Haymarket Affair. And Chicago's violent 1894 Pullman Strike went national, just after the industrial "black city" plunged into the 1893–4 depression and the city's mayor was assassinated – in dramatic contrast to the civic building in 1891–3 of a symphony hall, a university, museums, libraries, and the "white city" fairgrounds.

Even Henry Blake Fuller, a native Chicagoan who otherwise boosted the White City as the outgrowth of Chicago enterprise, found the White/Black City dichotomy irresistible. His 1895 novel about Chicago society, *With the Procession*, "met half-way the universal expectation that the spirit of the White City was but just transferred to the body of the great Black City. . . . In fact, [it] sprawled and coiled . . . like a hideous monster – a piteous, floundering monster, too." Moreover, Fuller's first Chicago novel, *The Cliff-Dwellers* (1893), was narrated from the outsider perspective of a newcomer and made a skyscraper its microcosm for the city. Economic structure determines this

Chicago. All the novel's characters – from waitress to salesman to bank clerk to tycoon to society dame – are linked through the economic enterprise of the Clifton Building – like Howells's commercial "house" – with no other shared interest except in the city's egotistic spirit of "I will." The Clifton is a metaphor for both socio-economic diversity and capitalistic dominance. It is part of an unprecedented cityscape, which the novel's first two pages elaborate in a parody of contemporary scientific reports on Mesa Verde's cliff dwellings: carved by a "seething flood" of commerce that has "devastated" the land to a depth of sixteen "stories," Chicago's skyscraper "cañons" have been worn down, rather than built up, into overpowering "perpendicular precipices." Even the novel's "oldest and most sedate" Chicagoan asserts the city's superhuman power to realize its destiny as the nation's "ultimate metropolis."

That Fuller was the Chicago novel's "pioneer" was acknowledged by Theodore Dreiser (1928: viii), whose *Sister Carrie* is the most famous of some thirty economic Chicago novels written by and about newcomers to the city between 1893 and 1914. Their numbers testify to the "many and growing commercial opportunities" that helped to make Chicago "a giant magnet" for the likes of Carrie Meeber and her author, as well as the interpretive power of the economic-city paradigm for new-comers' urban experiences. These novels regularly use the literary devices introduced by *The Cliff-Dwellers* to characterize Chicago as the nation's premier economic city: elaborate metaphors and documentation, anti-natural settings, alienated characters, and economic plots that critique individualism.

The first pages of Dreiser's *Sister Carrie* typify the metaphors and documentary reportage that economic Chicago novels employ to pit the individual against the strange new phenomenon of the city. As Carrie Meeber travels alone by railroad toward Chicago, Dreiser emphasizes her vulnerability, contrasting her "small . . . cheap . . . small . . . scrap" of personal resources to "the great city" ahead. Described metaphorically as a deceptive, "superhuman seducer," Chicago is personified by Carrie's first human seducer, Charles Drouet, whose socio-economic role as a com-mercial "drummer" (a traveling salesman) the narrative carefully explains. Then, making an explicit break "before following" Carrie, to "look at the sphere in which her future was to lie," several pages rhapsodize about Chicago's "magnetic" powers of attraction and document its physical arrangements. This new economic city confronts the lone newcomer as a powerful antagonist from the start – in clear contrast to the cultural city that emerges as an expression of communal character.

Emphasizing the city's anti-natural environment with exclamatory metaphors, Chicago economic novels regularly begin, like both *Sister Carrie* and *The Cliff-Dwellers*, with a newcomer's entry into the city by railroad. A railroad approach is the "best" way to see the city as "a stupendous piece of blasphemy against nature," *The Gospel of Freedom* (1898) by Robert Herrick declares. It plunges newcomers into "a modern inferno" when transcontinental rails meet skyscrapers in Herrick's *The Web of Life* (1900). Not only artificial, but ungoverned by any cohering unity, the vaunting downtown becomes "a burnt-out volcano" in Hamlin Garland's *Rose of Dutcher's Coolly* (1895), monoliths "without sign of life" in *The Pit* (1903) by Frank Norris. And

The Jungle (1906) by Upton Sinclair links mechanical and organic images of destruction when the railroad eventually leads into the stockyards' great "machine," where Chicago turns upon itself like a cancer, a "great sore of a city."

Also as in *Sister Carrie* and *The Cliff-Dwellers*, the protagonists of economic Chicago novels are regularly on their own, and the human population is rent by competitive divisions – in "the vast web of petty greed and blind efforts" from which *The Web of Life* takes its title. One person's success is inevitably offset by the failure of others, as Carrie Meeber's rise is contrasted step by step (from factory girl to Broadway star) to the fall of her second lover, George Hurstwood (from successful restaurateur to Bowery bum). The separation of families by conflicting economic interests is thoroughly anatomized in *The Gospel of Freedom* and figures prominently in *The Pit* and *The Jungle*. *The Pit* establishes Chicago as a city of divisions in its opening scene of "millionaires" parading into an overheated theater lobby under the gaze of "a crowd of miserables shivering" outside. Chicago is an economic "battle-field" with poverty on "that side of the city" and wealth on "this" in *Rose of Dutcher's Coolly*.

Starting with *The Cliff-Dwellers*, the plots of many economic Chicago novels detail financial and industrial systems, showing them to be fueled paradoxically by a rampant individualism that is inadequate to control them. The city's political–economic machinery destroys even tycoons who appear in control – first Will Payne's fictionalization of Samuel Insull as *The Money Captain* (1898), later streetcar magnates in Herrick's *Memoirs of an American Citizen* (1905) and Dreiser's *The Titan* (1914). *The Pit* raises to epic pitch a financier's "Napoleonic" attempt to leash the unnatural "whirlpool" of grain futures and his destruction in its "undertow." The "machine" is still more destructive of the poor, even the one family that sticks together in economic Chicago novels, in *The Jungle*. Eager to become "a part of" the slaughterhouse that efficiently turns hogs and cattle into canned meat and sausage, Sinclair's exemplary immigrant laborer, Jurgis Rudkus, recognizes his oppression only after his wife is raped and dies with his son – marched like animals to the slaughter – and he himself is discarded like the machine's other "worn-out parts." Yet readers have found discordant Jurgis's loud affirmation of proletarian power, in the "voice of the wild beast" that choruses "CHICAGO WILL BE OURS" at the end of *The Jungle*. It exemplifies what critic Amy Kaplan (1988: 160) calls "the desire to posit an alternative reality" – in this case, any possibility of communal control over the hugely alienating, anti-natural, enslaving powers of the economic city. As Fuller declared in an 1897 essay, "the abuse of private initiative" has "reached its most monumental dimensions" in Chicago's "astounding and repelling region of 'sky-scrapers.'" At best the economic Chicago novels reflect "exhilaration" along with "moral shock" (Szuberla 1971: 152) in the face of Chicago's "portentous" power (Garland 1899). At worst, they despair of any escape from the destructive new urban phenomena their Chicago epitomizes.

Their view was in turn "portentous" for US literature. Even expatriates from the cultural city's hegemonic families, like ex-Bostonian Henry James and ex-New Yorker Edith Wharton, now saw New York in this new way. James's description of the

New York harbor as a powerful "machine-room" crossed by ferries like "steam-shuttles" and bridges like "horizontal...pistons" in *The American Scene* (1907) is not just two decades but a paradigm away from the quietude of Washington Square. Similarly, Wharton bows to a newly mechanized view of urban settings by opening *The House of Mirth* (1905) at Grand Central Station, where Lily Bart's missed train prefigures her repeated failures to catch the economic main chance in the city's matrimonial sweepstakes. Although the novel emphasizes social occasions in detailed home interiors, in keeping with the cultural-city paradigm, Lily is a commodity on these private stages no less than Dreiser's Sister Carrie on Broadway. Lily is "just a screw or cog in the great machine," her economic fall contrasted to the rise of a Jewish outsider, a nouveau-riche Wall Street tipster. "The power of money" undergirds all the novel's transactions, including the social "influence" of Old New York's lingering representatives, Lily's aunt and her friend Lawrence Selden. Only less bluntly than Wharton's later novel *The Custom of the Country* (1913), *The House of Mirth* demonstrates "the power of the marketplace in its ability to assimilate everything else into its domain," as critic Wai-Chee Dimock (1985: 783) has argued. The economic-city paradigm ruled.

However, the organic, communal continuities that economic-city novels denied still remained part of the urban and literary scene. Even in Chicago, family-centered neighborhoods, prairie surroundings and forest preserves, City Beautiful planning and the Columbian years' civic institution-building all helped to characterize an alternative to the economic city in fiction. Novels with Chicago settings that carried on the cultural-city tradition, written by authors who grew up there – mostly women – were equal in quality but less lasting in renown than the economic Chicago novels written mostly by men whose work brought them to Chicago as adults. *The Song of the Lark* (1915) by Chicago visitor Willa Cather suggests key elements in the alternative, cultural-city vision, even though its heroine Thea Kronberg, like Dreiser's Sister Carrie, arrives by railroad as a newcomer, uses Chicago's resources to begin a stage career, then moves on to national fame in New York. But Thea, unlike Carrie, never breaks her ties to family and friends, sees Chicago as similarly bound by social ties, and probes beneath material surfaces to find urban–rural continuities – first in the pastoral painting and music in Chicago's Art Institute and Auditorium Theater, then in urban cliff dwellings in the desert Southwest. These continuities feed her own art. Thea's – and Cather's – vision of the city is culturally expressive, not economically shaped.

Unlike *The Song of the Lark*, however, most depictions of Chicago as a cultural city were profoundly residential. Even the World's Fair took on a lived-in flavor in their works: "We Chicagoans aren't Fair visitors. We are Fair livers," declares a character in Clara Burnham's *Sweet Clover: A Romance of the White City* (1894). So Chicago native Henry Blake Fuller deserted *The Cliff-Dwellers'* economic view of the "black city" to embrace a residential view of Chicago in his second novel, *With the Procession* (1895). No portent for the nation, Chicago "is simply there" in residential novels – as their leader Edith Wyatt (1914) also said of Frank Norris's hometown San Francisco in

Vandover and the Brute, in contrast to *The Pit*'s economic Chicago, which she considered "unrealized."

Wyatt's own *True Love* (1903), the novel that led Howells to declare a "Chicago School of Fiction" in 1903, exemplifies this residential version of turn-of-the-century Chicago as a cultural city. Its opening scene establishes Chicago's natural, historical, and residential ground as a regional base of social action, infused by the continuities of natural generation and human association. Guiding young Emily Marsh and her country cousin Inez past the site of Fort Dearborn and up residential streets with trimmed lawns, Wyatt forgoes extended exclamations about "the sights of Chicago" to introduce urban ethics as the subject of cousinly conversation. The novel's primary concern with democratic ethics is worked out through family groups in both the city and the country. The democratically inclusive Chicago Marshes are linked to the city's natural setting by name, to its rural environs by downstate relatives, to its past by a deceased grandfather's Civil War comrade, and to its future by Emily and her three siblings. The ups and downs of several romances link them in turn to their elitist city friends the Hubbards, elitist Inez Marsh's country family, and their democratic, small-town friends the Coltons. Social collectivities and regional continuities, not class conflicts and economic machinery, define *True Love*'s Chicago.

Chicago is part of a historically, naturally continuous life experience in residential fictions like *True Love*. So *Sweet Clover* recognizes the "pioneer" past as part of the "cosmopolitan" present; and *With the Procession* underscores the growth of "the city from an Indian village to a metropolis." The characters of residential narratives move easily between Chicago and the surrounding countryside. Not radically different from the country, the city simply extends social possibilities that sparsely settled areas constrain. So the heroine of Elia Peattie's suffrage novel, *The Precipice* (1914), brings the "Silvertree method" of "neighborly" dialogue from her rural childhood into her Chicago social work. Nature itself interpenetrates the city in its many parks and its weather's seasonal extremes. In *The Song of the Lark*, Thea Kronberg realizes "the city itself" not in her railroad arrival, but later in the streets' "congestion of life" during a "furious gale."

In residential fictions, city-dwellers are intimately connected with one another, usually in family networks – like the "communal protagonist" and social matrices that Rachel Blau DuPlessis (1985: 163) and Christine Sizemore (1989: 11) find characteristic of women's literature. Perhaps this is as much a matter of lifelong residency as gender, however. Native Chicagoan Henry Blake Fuller prefigures Wyatt's collective protagonist and interlocking families, even using *With the Procession*'s three central families to chart his novel's structure in his personal copy. The pattern goes beyond biological families. When social worker Beth Tully strikes out on her own in Clara Laughlin's *"Just Folks"* (1910), the entire working-class neighborhood she serves becomes her extended family. *The Precipice* (1914) pointedly examines such urban family substitutes. Rejecting the "commonplace . . . home" as "stultifying" like "walled cities," Peattie's "maternal" social worker Kate Barrington serves the "civic family" that makes Chicago "a great home" – those last two phrases quoted in the novel from Hull-House founder Jane Addams. When Kate is called to Washington DC to head a new children's bureau and be a "mother . . . to thousands" and "Sister to the World" (as Peattie also called Addams, in a 1910 review), Kate's more difficult victory is to claim her right to "the joy of woman" as a wife, too. In Alice Gerstenberg's *Unquenched Fire* (1912), would-be actress Gerstenberg's fictional alter ego fails to resolve tensions between the city's familial bonds and her individual ambitions, finding she has "more to regret than she had realized" when she rejects the one for the other. Residential Chicago fictions enact urban interdependence as a complex reality as well as a profound ethic.

Above all, these residential novels explore social ethics in the city. *True Love* centers on choices between democratic inclusiveness and elitist snobbery, *The Precipice* on choices between the private and public forms of family, and *"Just Folks"* on choices between parochialism and neighborliness. Their social ethics are most sorely tested when they bring ethnically and economically diverse characters together. Wyatt's urban story cycle *Every One His Own Way* (1901), for example, includes WASPs and Jews, Irish and Scandinavian immigrants in celebrating cultural differences, folk wisdom, and "large and various . . . toleran[ce]"; but it trips over ethnic stereotypes, as do also the fictional sketches of Chicago's local color humorists Finley Peter Dunne (1898) and George Ade (1893–1900). Moreover, economically diverse characters manage to sustain neighborly mutuality only in *"Just Folks."* While middle-class "ladies" join with "working girls" to create a "homelike" club for factory workers in Clara Laughlin's *The Penny Philanthropist* (1912), both lack the power to "let them *earn* enough!" The residential novels realize interdependence as a force for urban improvement, but do not directly challenge the structures undergirding poverty.

Whereas the economic Chicago novels treat the city as a critical "subject" – and therefore meet Blanche M. Gelfant's criteria for "city novels" (1954: 2–3; cf. Nevius 1962: 88) – the residential Chicago novels are less *about* than *of* the city. They articulate Chicago as insiders participate in it, with more flexibility than the economic-city paradigm offers. Except for Cather, their authors were raised in Chicago from childhood, remained there as adults, and died there. Except for Fuller, they were women, encouraged by Victorian gender roles to stay within the family circle. Except for Peattie, they were middle-class. They were familiar with daily family life and stable neighborhoods, with the evolving nuances of civic issues and projects, and with the collaborative enterprises of civic clubs, Little Theater, and Hull-House – all of which they reported as journalists. The economic novelists were also white and, except for Dreiser, from the middle class. But they were all men and economically mobile professionals, as Victorian gender roles encouraged men to be. Except for Fuller, they came to Chicago only as adults – Norris spending only two months, Sinclair only six weeks there. They encountered Chicago as a *fait accompli*, a phenomenon; they were "outsiders who simply managed to capture [its national] significance," as critic Kenny Williams has noted (1980: 443).

Although shadowed by the economic-city novel's ascendancy, residential novels more closely reflected the urban experience of most American city-dwellers until population mobility exploded after World War I. As it had dominated America's fictional cities for so long before Howells and Columbian Chicago, the cultural image of the city remained a vital fictional pattern – particularly for cities relatively free of industry and distant from the nation's economic centers. San Francisco is a good example. The Gold Rush established its reputation for rough culture and exoticism, as in Mark Twain's *Roughing It* (1872). Tapping that frontier imagery, Bret Harte's 1890s stories cast San Francisco back to "mid-century" (Scharnhorst 1995: 29) and native Gertrude Atherton's turn-of-the-century novels concern the city's "wayward formative years" back to 1860 (McClure 1995: 82). Although "written for people living elsewhere" – whether "by writers who came from elsewhere" (Fine and Skenazy 1995: 8) or by San Francisco-raised Norris, Atherton and Jack London – literature's San Francisco follows the residential–cultural pattern in its inhabitants' cultural expressiveness and its vast frontier reaches. For example, Frank Norris's apprenticeship novel *Blix* (1899) portrays two young lovers who reject the conventions of the city's wealthy to explore Chinatown, frequent a Mexican restaurant, and visit an oceanside lifeboat station – their "rambles" always starting from the heroine's family home and invoking its panoramic views of the "sweep of San Francisco bay." Norris assumed a residential attitude toward the Western city even in his raw naturalistic novels. Dreiser (1928: ix–x) called *McTeague: A Story of San Francisco* (1899) "indigenous," and Wyatt (1914: n.p.) considered *Vandover and the Brute* (1914) "far better" than *The Pit* "in its evocation of a city atmosphere."

In Norris's novels, Gertrude Atherton's *The Californians* (1898), and Jack London's *Martin Eden* (1909), San Francisco expresses its inhabitants' choices – specifically, its women's choices of morality and its men's choices of women in *The Californians*, *Martin Eden*, and *Vandover and the Brute*. Atherton's hero vacillates between a Latina woman of the "spirit" and a reckless Anglo woman of the "senses," themselves friends and each described as the region's personification. London and Norris use a Manichean shorthand in tracing their title characters' changing experience of the city as they turn from women who represent San Francisco's "better" or "best" people to the "beastly" life of "brute" women in its vice districts. Norris, moreover, underlines the change by making a metaphoric shift into the economic city's machine imagery, thereby suggesting that gross immorality negates the cultural city's choices; Vandover comes to experience the city as "some enormous engine, resistless, relentless, an engine that sped . . . no one knew whither." Similarly, when Norris's McTeague sinks into lethargy and his wife into miserliness, he assaults her with fists as "swift as the leap of a piston" and leaves her to die "like a piece of clockwork running down."

Like Chicago's residential novels, these fictional San Franciscos root choices not only in social morality, but also in the natural beauty and historical bounty of the region. Greed is fed by Gold Rush promises in *McTeague*; the frontier's sudden wealth and fame are evoked by Old San Francisco family names in *The Californians* and *Vandover and the Brute*. Simultaneously, the panoramic descriptions of the city's hills and the foothills beyond, of its Golden Gate and the wide Pacific, reinforce the sense of many choices – at least for men. While Atherton's recurrent heroine Helena

Belmont (Leider 1991: 167–8) dramatizes elite society's constraints upon women, her heroes – like Norris's and London's – encounter no serious limitations in the city. Fictional San Francisco's critical problem is not poverty but vice, represented also by its easy escapes to the gold fields or sea. Its geographic distance from the nation's financial capitals protects the entire region's openness.

Culturally if not geographically, fiction's Southern cities were also a world away from Chicago and New York. Rooted in the urban industrial North's victory over the agricultural South, the nation's urban consciousness ignored Southern cities. Indeed, until World War I most of the South's urban growth occurred in cities of under 100,000 inhabitants, which lagged well behind the North in manufacturing. In fiction, Southern cities are still part and parcel of their regional surroundings. Rural or small-town inhabitants go there for special occasions, and urban residents have easy access to the country. Characterized by the cultural city's continuities, fiction's Southern cities both relax and clarify social mores also common to country life. Kate Chopin's novel *The Awakening* (1899) about wealthy New Orleans Creoles, for instance, opens at their summer gulfside resort. Edna Pontellier "awakens" to her "sensuous" powers there, but finds more room to explore them when she returns to the city's more diverse social cohorts.

Even within the cultural-city pattern, however, *The Awakening* and other Southern novels focus on a primary concern running through all post-Civil War fictions set in cities: the relationship of private to public life. Perhaps this is why New Orleans is Southern fiction's most frequent urban setting – because its French founding and exotic Creole roots in Parisian and African cultures buttressed its reputation for offering unusual public license for "clandestine activities and sinful pursuits" (Taylor 1997: 76) – not unlike fictional San Francisco. English-born Lafcadio Hearn's "Fantastics" sketches in the New Orleans *Picayune* (1877–87) paint local color scenes of decadence and racial mixing, assuming a *flâneur*'s stance that "call[s] into question the American work ethic" (Roskelly 1992: 24). Native New Orleanean George Washington Cable explores as troubling moral choices the similar racial ambiguities embedded in the French Quarter – rather tamely in *Old Creole Days* (1879), with pointed social criticism in *The Grandissimes* (1880), then with the increasing nostalgia of distance in *Madame Delphine* (1881), *Doctor Sevier* (1884), and *The Cavalier* (1901). Challenging Cable's critical view of their native city, Grace King still constructs ambiguous spaces in *Balcony Stories* (1893) – between the multicultural vitality of the streets and the house-bound privacy of upper-class Creole women. From the other side of the color line, New Orleans-bred Alice Dunbar-Nelson also pursues a contrast between public and private worlds, with a clear moral preference for the private refuge of a convent, in "Sister Josepha" (1899). And *The Awakening* discovers the public limits on Edna Pontellier's private desire for freedom. As a woman she lacks "the easy [public] anonymity and marginality" to indulge the "irresponsibility and openness to erotic encounter" she shares with Baudelaire's classic *flâneur* – for which reason Janet Wolff argues that the female equivalent to the *flâneur*, the "*flâneuse*," is a "non-existent role" (Wolff 1985: 41; cf. Taylor 1997: 83). Edna Pontellier can neither ignore the social stigma that would hurt a sexually active woman's children nor accept social isolation in disciplined devotion to art; she can free herself only by drowning in the Gulf.

In African American novels written during the turn-of-the-century period of increasing black migration, public anonymity is often possible for urban women and men alike. In Pauline E. Hopkins's *Contending Forces* (1900), Boston provides anonymity for Bermuda-born Jesse Monfort, escaped from Southern enslavement, while New Orleans provides anonymity for his brother-in-law's beloved, Sappho Clark, escaping from her past as a rape victim. In Paul Laurence Dunbar's *The Sport of the Gods* (1902), New York offers anonymity to the family of a falsely imprisoned black man. And in James Weldon Johnson's *The Autobiography of an Ex-Coloured Man* (1912), the vast anonymity of New York even allows the nameless hero to pass as white. Importantly, such anonymity offers freedom, the traditional keynote of African American urban imagery ever since *Narrative of the Life of Frederick Douglass* (1845) and Harriet Jacobs's *Incidents in the Life of a Slave Girl* (1861). For African Americans, plantation slave history contradicted Euro-American pastoralism and the corresponding "anti-urbanism" that Morton and Lucia White (1962: 15 and *passim*) asserted as the primary tradition in American literature. While an anti-urban bias does indeed pervade the economic city in fiction after 1890, African American fiction more often belongs to the much longer tradition of the cultural city. Specifically, African American autobiographies and novels construct a world in which cities – especially but not only Northern cities – represent the promised land of freedom.

African American fictions also dramatize the limits of urban freedom in two ways that point toward post-World War I variations on the cultural- and economic-city paradigms. On the one hand, they often embrace community in preference to anonymous freedom, thereby looking forward to the cultural-city neighborhood of Harlem Renaissance literature. *Contending Forces*, for example, advances family union and reunion over anonymity. In Hopkins's Boston, Ma Smith's boarding house is a familial "nest" and "refuge" as well as a business, providing the Smith family and their boarders with social interaction, musical culture, and nursing care; churches offer worship, political forums, and social entertainments; and the "free" library and Harvard share learning resources. In New Orleans, a college campus and a convent orphanage provide home communities for newcomers; and the orphanage reunites Will Smith with his beloved Sappho, despite her fearful desire to "lose myself in that city." Firmly centered in such communal institutions, *Contending Forces* depicts a "secularized city on a hill," as critic Charles Scruggs (1993: 28, 31) claims.

On the other hand, in exposing the moral emptiness of freedom in urban isolation, African American fictions anticipate the economic city's fictional explosion into a post-World War I megalopolis, stretching from coast to coast in Dos Passos's *Manhattan Transfer* (1925) and Nathanael West's *The Day of the Locust* (1939). Without social supports, New York's freedoms complete the family disintegration and loss of moral compass begun in the post-Civil War plantation South in Dunbar's *The Sport of the Gods*, for example. When Berry Hamilton is falsely accused and imprisoned for a plantation theft, his wife and children seek anonymity in New York, where the "metropolis" snares his son in alcoholism, his daughter in promiscuity, and his wife in bigamy and abuse. Although little concerned with socio-economic classes, anti-natural environments, or industrial machinery, *The Sport of the Gods* echoes the structure and imagery of *Sister Carrie*'s famous description of Chicago to present New York as ambiguous, intoxicating, deceptive:

> To the provincial coming to New York for the first time, ignorant and unknown, the city presents a notable mingling of the qualities of cheeriness and gloom. If he have any eye at all for the beautiful, he cannot help experiencing a thrill as he . . . catches the first sight of the spires and buildings of New York. . . . Later, the lights in the busy streets will bewilder and entice him. . . . The subtle, insidious wine of New York will begin to intoxicate him.

Ten years later, James Weldon Johnson elaborates nearly the same imagery as his "ex-colored man" steams into New York harbor:

> New York City is the most fatally fascinating thing in America. She sits like a great witch at the gate of the country, showing her alluring white face and hiding her crooked hands and feet under the folds of her wide garments – constantly enticing thousands [of] victims of her caprice. Some she at once crushes. . . . a few she [rides] high on the bubbles of fortune [until they] fall.
> . . . To some natures this stimulant of life in a great city becomes a thing as binding and necessary as opium is to one addicted to the habit.

When the ex-colored man deserts his ethnic dreams of concert ragtime, in order to "pass" in New York's white society, Johnson exposes the emptiness of a freedom with no communal context. *The Autobiography of an Ex-Coloured Man* carries further than any other pre-World War I novel the spiritual bankruptcy invited by urban freedom and wealth.

Even as its elliptical style points toward post-World War I modernism, Johnson's ironic counterpoint to the city as a promised land finds a close corollary in Jewish American social realism, in the novel Abraham Cahan began in 1912 (Marovitz 1996: 135), *The Rise of David Levinsky* (1917). Each man led a major institution in his New York ethnic community – Johnson as the NAACP's first African American executive director, Cahan as the founding editor of the *Jewish Daily Forward*. Each novel plumbs the depths of urban isolation and prepares the ground for a flowering of communal ethnic literature after World War I (Bremer 1992: 165ff.). Each seeks to enlighten the ignorant about an entire minority group's history by presenting an individual life as illustrative. The leading character of each disavows a childhood ethnic "dream" to play the "games" of success on the majority's economic terms: Johnson's ex-colored man leaving music for gambling, Cahan's David Levinsky leaving education for business. And each is enchanted by, then addicted to, New York City. As the "fatally fascinating" city "entices" the ex-colored man, the same "new world" harbor awes David Levinsky like "a new born babe." As that "enchanted spot" "intoxicates" the ex-colored man, who catches money's "fever," so "enchanted" New York and its "magic" money lure David Levinsky into "intoxication," then "moth-like... to the flame." In opposition to the empty successes of their anti-heroes, moreover, these fictions identify cultural-city sources for the urban visions of future Harlem and Lower East Side literary generations: the musical possibilities of jazz and blues that Langston Hughes and Ralph Ellison later realize, and the ritual voices of the talmudic family that Anzia Yezierska and Henry Roth later weave. Johnson's and Cahan's achievements thus leave a promising legacy for post-World War I urban literature.

Centering chronologically on the fictional shift from Howells's 1885 Boston "home" to his 1890 New York "hazard," the period between the Civil War and World War I illustrates the variety of fictional cities in US literature. Pre-1890 images of Philadelphia, Boston, and Old New York, Chicago women's residential literature, and regional and ethnic urban imagery carry the cultural-city tradition of John Winthrop's "city upon a hill" (1630) forward into the twentieth century: to fictional cities like Jessie Fauset's "cosmopolitan... small town" Harlem in *Plum Bun* (1929), Saul Bellow's neighborhood Chicago in *The Adventures of Augie March* (1953), Maxine Hong King-ston's legend-laced Sacramento Chinatown in *The Woman Warrior* (1976), and on. The 1890s discovery of Chicago as a national economic city lays the ground for F. Scott Fitzgerald's New York wasteland in *The Great Gatsby* (1925), the Chicago protests of Richard Wright's *Native Son* (1940), the New York factories and freak shows of Kevin Baker's *Dreamland* (1999), and much more. Fictional cities from Davis's *Waiting for the Verdict* (1867) through Dreiser's *Sister Carrie* (1900) and Wyatt's *True Love* (1903), to Johnson's *Autobiography of an Ex-Coloured Man* (1912) illustrate the interactions of paradigmatic traditions and symbolic breakthroughs, of historical changes and geo-graphical differences, of residential and newcomer perspectives, of gender- and ethnic-differentiated experiences. No one of these factors explains the variety of our urban imagery; all interact in each literary act. So we need the full range of our fictional cities to interpret the complexities of urban experience and to inspire future cities.

Primary Texts

Adams, Henry. *Democracy*. 1880.

Atherton, Gertrude. *The Californians*. 1898.

Bellamy, Edward. *Looking Backward: 2000–1887*. 1888.

Bellamy, Edward. Letter to William Dean Howells, Oct. 17, 1889.

Burnham, Clara. *Sweet Clover: A Romance of the White City*. 1894.

Cable, George Washington. *Old Creole Days*. 1879.

Cable, George Washington. *The Grandissimes: A Story of Creole Life*. 1880.

Cable, George Washington. *Madame Delphine*. 1881.

Cable, George Washington. *Doctor Sevier*. 1885.

Cable, George Washington. *The Cavalier*. 1901.

Cahan, Abraham. *Yekl: A Tale of the New York Ghetto*. 1896.

Cahan, Abraham. *The Imported Bridegroom, and Other Stories of the New York Ghetto*. 1898.

Cahan, Abraham. *The Rise of David Levinsky*. 1917.

Cather, Willa. *The Song of the Lark*. 1915.

Chopin, Kate. *The Awakening*. 1899.

Cooper, James Fenimore. *The Pioneers*. 1823.

Crane, Stephen. *Maggie, A Girl of the Streets: A Story of New York*. 1893.

Davis, Rebecca Harding. *Life in the Iron Mills; or, The Korl Woman*. 1861.

Davis, Rebecca Harding. *Waiting for the Verdict*. 1867.

Davis, Rebecca Harding. "Boston in the Sixties." 1904.

De Forest, John W. *Honest John Vane*. 1875.

Dos Passos, John. *Manhattan Transfer*. 1925.

Douglass, Frederick. *Narrative of the Life of Frederick Douglass, an American Slave*. 1845.

Dreiser, Theodore. *Sister Carrie*. 1900.

Dreiser, Theodore. *The Titan*. 1914.

Dunbar, Paul Laurence. *The Sport of the Gods*. 1902.

Dunbar-Nelson, Alice. "Sister Josepha." 1899.

Dunne, Finley Peter. *Mr. Dooley in Peace and War*. 1898.

Fauset, Jessie Redmon. *Plum Bun*. 1929.

Fitzgerald, F. Scott. *The Great Gatsby*. 1925.

Fuller, Henry Blake. *The Cliff-Dwellers*. 1893.

Fuller, Henry Blake. *With the Procession*. 1895.

Garland, Hamlin. *Rose of Dutcher's Coolly*. 1895.

Gerstenberg, Alice. *Unquenched Fire: A Novel*. 1912.

Hawthorne, Nathaniel. "My Kinsman, Major Molineux." 1832.

Hawthorne, Nathaniel. *The Blithedale Romance*. 1852.

Hawthorne, Nathaniel. *The Marble Faun; or, The Romance of Monte Beni*. 1860.

Herne, Lafcadio. *Fantastics and Other Fancies*. 1877–87.

Herrick, Robert. *The Gospel of Freedom*. 1898.

Herrick, Robert. *The Web of Life*. 1900.

Herrick, Robert. *The Memoirs of an American Citizen*. 1905.

Hopkins, Pauline E. *Contending Forces: A Romance Illustrative of Negro Life North and South*. 1900.

Howe, Frederic C. *The City: The Hope of Democracy*. 1906.

Howells, William Dean. *The Rise of Silas Lapham*. 1885.

Howells, William Dean. *A Hazard of New Fortunes*. 1890.

Howells, William Dean. "Certain of the Chicago School of Fiction." 1903.

Jacobs, Harriet. *Incidents in the Life of a Slave Girl*. 1861.

James, Henry. *Washington Square*. 1881.

James, Henry. *The Bostonians*. 1886.

James, Henry. *The American Scene*. 1907.

Johnson, James Weldon. *The Autobiography of an Ex-Coloured Man*. 1912.

King, Grace. *Balcony Stories*. 1893.

Laughlin, Clara. "Just Folks." 1910.

Laughlin, Clara. *The Penny Philanthropist*. 1912.

London, Jack. *Martin Eden*. 1909.

Melville, Herman. *Redburn: His First Voyage*. 1849.

Melville, Herman. "Bartleby the Scrivener: A Story of Wall Street." 1853.

Melville, Herman. *Pierre; or, The Ambiguities*. 1852.

Norris, Frank. *Blix*. 1899.

Norris, Frank. *McTeague: A Story of San Francisco*. 1899.

Norris, Frank. *The Pit*. 1903.

Norris, Frank. *Vandover and the Brute*. 1914.

Payne, Will. *The Money Captain*. 1898.

Peattie, Elia. *The Precipice: A Novel*. 1914.

Poe, Edgar Allan. "The Man of the Crowd." 1840.

Poole, Ernest. *The Voice of the Street*. 1906.

Riis, Jacob. *How the Other Half Lives*. 1890.

Rollins, Alice Wellington. *Uncle Tom's Tenement*. 1888.

Sinclair, Upton. *The Jungle*. 1906.

Steffens, Lincoln. *The Shame of the Cities*. 1904.

Stowe, Harriet Beecher. *Uncle Tom's Cabin; or, Life among the Lowly*. 1852.

Twain, Mark. *Roughing It*. 1872.

Twain, Mark, and Warner, Charles Dudley. *The Gilded Age: A Tale of To-Day*. 1873.

West, Nathanael. *The Day of the Locust*. 1939.

Wharton, Edith. *The House of Mirth*. 1905.

Wharton, Edith. *The Custom of the Country*. 1913.

Wright, Richard. *Native Son*. 1940.

Wyatt, Edith. *Every One His Own Way*. 1901.

Wyatt, Edith. *True Love: A Comedy of the Affections*. 1903.

References and Further Reading

Ade, George (1941). *Stories of the Streets and of the Town: From the Chicago Record, 1893–1900*, ed. Franklin J. Meine. Chicago: Caxton Club. (First publ. 1893–1900.)

Baker, Kevin (1999). *Dreamland*. New York: HarperCollins.

Banta, Martha (1995). "The Three New Yorks: Topographical Narratives and Cultural Texts." *American Literary History* 7: 1, 28–54.

Bellow, Saul (1953). *The Adventures of Augie March: A Novel*. New York: Viking.

Benjamin, Walter (1973). *Charles Baudelaire: A Lyric Poet in the Era of High Capitalism*, trans. Harry Zohn. London: Verso.

Berger, Peter, and Luckmann, Thomas (1966). *The Social Construction of Reality: A Treatise in the Sociology of Knowledge*. Garden City, NY: Doubleday.

Bourget, Paul (1893). "A Farewell to the White City." *Cosmopolitan* 16 (Dec.), 173–86.

Bremer, Sidney H. (1992). *Urban Intersections: Meetings of Life and Literature in United States Cities*. Urbana: University of Illinois Press.

Bryan, Violet Harrington (1993). *The Myth of New Orleans in Literature: Dialogues of Race and Gender*. Knoxville: University of Tennessee Press.

Cady, Edwin H. (1956). *The Road to Realism: The Early Years 1837–1885 of William Dean Howells*. Syracuse, NY: Syracuse University Press.

Chametzky, Jules (1977). *From the Ghetto: The Fiction of Abraham Cahan*. Amherst: University of Massachusetts Press.

Dimock, Wai-Chee (1985). "Debasing Exchange: Edith Wharton's *The House of Mirth*," *PMLA* 100, 783–92.

DuPlessis, Rachel Blau (1985). *Writing beyond the Ending: Narrative Strategies of Twentieth-Century Women Writers*. Bloomington: Indiana University Press.

Fine, David, and Skenazy, Paul, eds. (1995). "Introduction: San Francisco." In David Fine and Paul Skenazy (eds.), *San Francisco in Fiction: Essays in a Regional Literature*, 3–20. Albuquerque: University of New Mexico Press.

Fuller, Henry Blake (1897). "The Upward Movement in Chicago." *Atlantic Monthly* 80 (Oct.), 534–47.

Fuller, Henry Blake (1968). *The Cliff-Dwellers*. Ridgewood, NJ: Gregg.

Garland, Hamlin (1899). *Rose of Dutcher's Coolly*. New York: Macmillan.

Gelfant, Blanche M. (1954). *The American City Novel*. Norman: Oklahoma University Press.

Green, Martin (1967). *The Problem of Boston*. New York: Norton.

Haenni, Sabine (1999). "Visual and Theatrical Culture, Tenement Fiction, and the Immigrant Subject in Abraham Cahan's *Yekl*." *American Literature* 71, 493–527.

Harte, Bret (1894). *The Best of Bret Harte*, ed. Wilhelmina Harper and Aimée M. Peters. Boston: Houghton Mifflin.

Hawthorne, Nathaniel (1860). *The Marble Faun; or, The Romance of Monte Beni*. Boston: Ticknor & Fields.

Hawthorne, Nathaniel (1965). *The Blithedale Romance*. Columbus: Ohio State University Press.

Hawthorne, Nathaniel (1974). "My Kinsman, Major Molineux." In *The Snow Image, and Uncollected Tales*, ed. William Charvat et al., 208–31. Columbus: Ohio State University Press.

Herne, Lafcadio (1914). *Fantastics and Other Fancies*, ed. Charles Woodward Hutson. Boston: Houghton Mifflin.

Howe, Irving (1956). "Introduction." In Henry James, *The Bostonians*, v–xxviii. New York: Random House.

Howells, William Dean (1903). "Certain of the Chicago School of Fiction." *North American Review* 176, 734–46.

Kaplan, Amy (1988). *The Social Construction of American Realism*. Chicago: University of Chicago Press.

Kazin, Alfred (1991). "The New York Writer and his Landscapes." In Mary Ann Caws (ed.), *City Images: Perspectives from Literature, Philosophy, and Film*, 129–42. New York: Gordon & Breach.

Kingston, Maxine Hong (1976). *The Woman Warrior: Memoirs of a Girlhood among Ghosts*. New York: Knopf.

Leider, Emily Wortis (1991). *California's Daughter: Gertrude Atherton and her Times*. Stanford, Calif.: Stanford University Press.

Lynn, Kenneth S. (1971). *William Dean Howells: An American Life*. New York: Harcourt Brace Jovanovich.

McClure, Charlotte S. (1995). "Gertrude Atherton and her San Francisco: A Wayward Writer and a Wayward City in a Wayward Paradise." In David Fine and Paul Skenazy (eds.), *San Francisco in Fiction: Essays in a Regional Literature*, 73–95. Albuquerque: University of New Mexico Press.

McKelvey, Blake (1973). *American Urbanization.* Glenview, Ill.: Scott Foresman.

Marovitz, Sanford E. (1996). *Abraham Cahan.* New York: Twayne.

Nevius, Blake (1962). *Robert Herrick: The Development of a Novelist.* Berkeley: University of California Press.

O'Connor, Leo (1974). "Howells' New York." Paper presented at MLA Convention, New York, Dec.

Peattie, Elia W. (1910). Review of *Twenty Years at Hull-House* by Jane Addams. *Chicago Tribune,* Nov. 26, 9.

Phillips, E. Barbara, and LeGates, Richard T. (1981). *City Lights: An Introduction to Urban Studies.* New York: Oxford University Press.

Roskelly, Hephzibah (1992). "Cultural Translator: Lafcadio Hearn." In Richard S. Kennedy (ed.), *Literary New Orleans: Essays and Meditations,* 16–28. Baton Rouge: Louisiana State University Press.

Scharnhorst, Gary (1995). "Mark Twain, Bret Harte, and the Literary Construction of San Francisco." In David Fine and Paul Skenazy (eds.), *San Francisco in Fiction: Essays in a Regional Literature,* 21–34. Albuquerque: University of New Mexico Press.

Scruggs, Charles (1993). *Sweet Home: Invisible Cities in the Afro-American Novel.* Baltimore: Johns Hopkins University Press.

Sizemore, Christine Wick (1989). *A Female Vision of the City: London in the Novels of Five British Women.* Knoxville: University of Tennessee Press.

Szuberla, Guy (1971). "Urban Vistas and the Pastoral Garden: Studies in the Literature and Architecture of Chicago (1893–1909)." Ph.D. diss., University of Minnesota.

Taylor, Helen (1997). "Walking through New Orleans: Kate Chopin and the Female Flâneur." *Symbiosis: A Journal of Anglo-American Literary Relations* 1 (April), 69–85.

Trachtenberg, Alan (1982). *The Incorporation of America: Culture and Society in the Gilded Age.* New York: Hill & Wang.

Warner, Sam Bass, Jr. (1962). *Streetcar Suburbs: The Process of Growth in Boston, 1870–1900.* Cambridge, Mass.: Harvard University Press.

Weber, Michael P., and Lloyd, Anne (1975). *The American City.* St. Paul, Minn.: West.

White, Morton, and White, Lucia (1962). *The Intellectual versus the City.* Cambridge, Mass.: Harvard University Press.

Williams, Kenny (1980). *Prairie Voices.* Nashville: Townsend.

Winthrop, John (1929–47). "A Modell of Christian Charity" (first publ. 1630). In Allen B. Forbes (ed.), *Winthrop Papers,* vol. 2, 293–5. Boston: Massachusetts Historical Society.

Wolff, Janet (1985). "The Invisible *Flâneuse:* Women and the Literature of Modernity." *Theory, Culture and Society* 2, 37–46.

Woodress, James (1993). "Howells in the Nineties: Social Critic for All Seasons." *American Literary Realism, 1870–1910* 25: 3, 18–25.

Wyatt, Edith (1914). Review of *Vandover and the Brute* (newsclipping). In Scrapbooks, Wyatt Papers, Newberry Library, Chicago.

16
Mapping the Culture of Abundance: Literary Narratives and Consumer Culture
Sarah Way Sherman

Between the end of the Civil War and the First World War the United States saw the rise of mass media, the proliferation of consumer goods, and the burgeoning of department stores: a major cultural transformation heralding a new culture of abundance. Unlike the old Puritan culture of scarcity – dedicated to discipline, production, and the accumulation of capital – this new culture celebrated display, performance, and the consumption of commodities. With it, according to historian Warren Susman, emerged a new form of American identity. Instead of "character," there appeared "personality," based not on an internal and essential self answerable to God, but on a performance responsive to context, a mastery of cultural signs and social appearances (1984: xx, xxii). At the same time, the intensification of industrialization, the shift of rural populations to urban centers, and the flood of ethnically diverse immigrants into cities like New York, Boston, and Chicago precipitated a national sense of disorientation. This disorientation, Andrew Heinz argues, ultimately threatened "belief in the unitary and solid nature of personal and national identity" (2003: 228). Its more immediate effect was a crisis of representation, what Thomas Richards calls "a chaos of signs" (1990: 3). Social life was outstripping its traditional categories. Moreover, those categories, once seen as natural, were now increasingly perceived as human constructions – a process also related to the corrosive, iconoclastic effects of modernization. As the need for some new kind of ordering became acute, material goods and literary narratives both rose to the task.

According to historians such as Richards and Robert Rydell, the commodity exposition or world's fair played a crucial role in this reordering. Structuring goods into new categories and hierarchies of meaning, the displays at London's 1851 Crystal Palace or Chicago's 1893 Columbia Exposition gave commodities cultural form and signifying power, and thereby provided the tools necessary to map a cultural territory in the throes of massive transformation. The analogy comparing map and territory to goods and culture comes from Mary Douglas and Baron Isherwood's *The World of Goods: Towards an Anthropology of Consumption* (1979), which demonstrates how, over and above their use-value, goods function as signifying systems through which cultures makes their structures visible. Goods model their cultural context. Just as this period's exhibitions and displays organized new commodities into sign systems representing the emergent social scene, so advertising, advice books, magazines, and literary narratives also came into play. And they too used goods – images of clothing, houses, and material possessions – to make the new cultural landscape visible.

However, as representations, both narratives and goods present problems. First, while the analogy of map to territory suggests that representations simply mirror the social territory, in practice representations often intervene in the phenomena they signify. For example, Victorian domestic fictions shaped readers' gender roles as much as they described them. Second, representations reflect the social groups controlling them. As Thomas Richards explains, England's Crystal Palace exhibition displayed an emergent middle class speaking to itself about itself. One could say the same for most literary narratives of the time. For example, as I shall show later, popular novels such as Louisa May Alcott's *Little Women* (1868–9) and Horatio Alger's *Ragged Dick* (1868) were more concerned with reassuring middle-class readers about an increasingly ambiguous world than surveying that world accurately. However, as Amy Kaplan argues in *The Social Construction of American Realism*, and as I will also argue below, realist fictions by William Dean Howells, Edith Wharton, and Theodore Dreiser mapped a social territory that was neither static nor stable, but contested and changing.

In *Confidence Men and Painted Women*, historian Karen Halttunen shows how difficult it was to negotiate this territory. The new urbanization and social mobility resulted for many people in a "world of strangers" (1982: 33–55). Judgments about character were now necessarily based less on continuous knowledge and more on instantaneous impressions – hence the threat represented by the "confidence men" and "painted women" of Halttunen's title. Earlier in the century, even before immigration surged, the French observer Alexis de Tocqueville commented in his *Democracy in America* (1835, 1840) that identity in the United States seemed less secure than in Europe where status, conferred more through birth and inheritance, seemed more fixed and "natural." Because class identity *could* change in America, for better or for worse, it seemed more constructed, more in need of material props. In the flux of midcentury America, where appearances were increasingly difficult to read, this insecurity was heightened, and a generation turned to advice books and moralist narratives for guidance. Without acknowledging the inherent contradiction between authenticity and theatricality, their authors advised readers to mount a sincere performance of self. To be recognized, virtue must be skillfully displayed. Even honest men and women needed the con-man's art.

Halttunen thus finds that anxiety over the relationship between surface appearances and internal realities was a widespread response to the crisis of representation. She links this anxiety to earlier Protestant debates over true grace and hypocrisy – debates which, given their continuing influence, are worth reviewing along with their new applications. The orthodox Calvinist Protestant view was that salvation was received only through God's grace. However, because such grace would inevitably result in good works, it was extremely difficult to separate the hypocrite's good works, motivated by sinful self-interest, from the saint's. Scrupulous psychological examination was required. It was equally difficult to separate a true conversion from a false one, the latter resulting, not from grace, but from self-aggrandizement, madness, or even satanic influence. In this case, the doctrines that God no longer communicated through direct revelation and that true virtue never contradicted Scripture protected the church from dangerous pathologies and ensured moral order. Finally, although Puritanism urged believers to accumulate capital and goods, they were to use those material fruits of grace only for God's glory, not for their own self-aggrandizement or sensuous gratification. The result, as Max Weber famously argued, was a distinctive worldly asceticism, a Protestant ethic contributing to the rise of capitalism.

Orthodox Calvinist Protestantism can thus be described as holding in tension two aspects of the self: its internal, moral depths, in unmediated relationship to God; and its external, moral appearance, in mediated relationship to society. These two poles, rigorously aligned and yet rigorously separate, can also be seen as shaping the two major heresies against which orthodox Puritanism struggled. On the one hand, the heretical Arminian view was that good works *could* result in salvation. Here the process was one of cultivation or refinement, a "Christian nurture" through which one "developed" moral awareness and slowly grew toward grace through the disciplined imitation of moral models. On the other hand, the equally heretical Antinomian view held that the saved *could* receive direct, individual revelation from God, a revelation that need not be consistent with received doctrine or even Scripture. Rather than the rational self-mastery prescribed by the Arminian, the Antinomian grounded salvation in internal religious experience and individual expression. Cultural historians such as Warren Susman, Colin Campbell, and Jackson Lears see these two poles of Protestantism, no longer constrained by orthodoxy, as founding the two concepts of selfhood competing in this period. The rationalist, Arminian strand formed the basis of nineteenth-century "character," and the pietist, individualist strand contributed to the development of "personality," the latter intimately linked, Campbell argues, to the spirit of "Romantic Bohemianism" (1987: 201). And it was "personality," all agree, that ultimately dominated the new culture of abundance.

However, historians of the period tend to overlook what I believe is another important strand in this conversation on consumerism and the construction of identity: Roman Catholicism. Disavowed as idolatrous by all Protestants – orthodox, Arminian, and Antinomian – nevertheless the Catholic doctrine of sacramentalism was an important "other" against which Protestantism measured itself. In Catholicism, salvation was won through the mediation of the church: the priest's absolution of the sinner and the extension of grace through the sacraments. This last is especially important for the discussion of materialism, since the Catholic Eucharist was seen by Protestants as the paradigmatic example of materialistic practice. Catholics believed that the ritual of the mass transformed the original substance of the bread and wine into the miraculous body and blood of Christ. Those sacred objects could then confer

Christ's divine grace on their recipients. Vehemently disagreeing, Protestants argued that the bread and wine were only a remembrance of Christ. They were only signifiers of his grace; they could not confer it. To believe that salvation could come from a material object, however symbolic, was idolatrous. For Protestants there was an unbridgeable gap between a symbol and its referent. Surface and depth might be perfectly aligned, but they could never be confused.

Hence the effect of Protestantism on the older Catholic world, as scholars like Jean-Christophe Agnew and Jackson Lears explain, was a disenchantment, a draining of magical powers, not only from the sacred bread and wine of the mass, but from all such sacralized objects. Material surface and spiritual depth, which interpenetrated in Catholic sacramentalism, were separated by Protestant iconoclasm. Just as Protestants denounced Catholic sacramentalism, with its idolatrous rituals and theatricality, so they denounced consumer materialism: a link between theology and consumption acknowledged in Karl Marx's famous term "commodity fetishism" and explored more recently in David Hawkes's study of seventeenth-century English Protestants and the early modern marketplace. Finally, it is important to point out that Catholics also rejected commodity fetishism on the grounds of its idolatry; however, for them the idolatry lay in ascribing to secular, profane objects a miraculous, transformative power reserved for the consecrated host.

Roman Catholic sacramentalism thus provided a model of materialism which could be applied by nineteenth-century Protestant moralists to what they saw as an equally materialistic misuse of goods. At least one recent historian, Jay Mechling, has defined materialism in a similar way. Drawing on Douglas and Isherwood's description of goods as a signifying system, Mechling sees materialism as the consumer's failure to distinguish the material map from the social territory, and he compares the materialist's thinking to the schizophrenic's. When confronted with a literary metaphor, the schizophrenic is unable to distinguish its symbolic from its literal meaning. The poetic gap between signifier and signified disappears. In the same way, Mechling argues, the materialist consumer, whose "personality" depends on performance and socially constructed signs, confuses the material symbols of identity for identity itself. The result is an addictive dependence on commodities that appear not just to represent the self, but to confer it. Mechling sees the rise of American materialism in the so-called Gilded Age as a response to the period's crisis of representation: a pathological belief in the power of commodities to stabilize identity. While Mechling's language is psychological, not theological, nineteenth-century critics of consumer culture would have readily recognized his critique. As they saw it, consumer materialism threatened to become the idolatrous faith of a new culture of abundance.

Turning to literary narratives, we can see these issues clearly in Henry David Thoreau's *Walden* (1854), which attacks the emergent consumer culture from a radically individualistic, and Antinomian, position. Ridiculing his neighbors' dependence on commodity display, Thoreau argues that their hunger for status symbols condemns them to a lifetime of debt and "quiet desperation." His solution is to reject the symbolic use of goods altogether. The function of clothing should be solely to preserve the body's vital heat. Unlike the moralists studied by Karen Halttunen, Thoreau advises readers to "beware all enterprises that require new clothes." Crisis of representation be damned. His contemporaries, he writes, worship Fashion, not the Graces or the Parcae. They put their faith in a commodity system run by faceless others. When Thoreau asks the local seamstress to make a pair of pants to his own design, she says, "They do not make them so now." He replies, in just as oracular a tone, "It is true, they did not make them so recently, but they do now." Thoreau's reappropriation of a reified fashion's ordering power is a true Antinomian approach to the problem of identity: a confident assertion that he can stand outside the socially constructed territory. His pants map a world of his own. And yet, as we shall see in the fiction of his neighbor and student Louisa May Alcott, Thoreau's admonitions have an unforeseen consequence: the validation of consumption as self-expression through goods of one's "free choice."

Horatio Alger's *Ragged Dick; or, Street Life in New York with the Boot Blacks* (1868), a story for boys written by a former Unitarian minister, provides a solution to the crisis of representation radically different from Thoreau's. Here the approach is Arminian, not Antinomian. The main character, Ragged Dick, is a fourteen-year-old, homeless orphan living hand-to-mouth blacking shoes in New York. He sleeps in a packing box, and spends his hard-earned money on steaks, cigars, and P. T. Barnum. Despite hard times, Dick refuses to steal because it feels "mean." Without a family or education, he is nevertheless compassionate and wise to the ways of the street. Rooted in the moment and independent of the world's opinion, Dick is one of nature's noblemen, leading a life rich in what Thoreau calls "savage luxury." However, it turns out that Dick is hungry to acquire the very material signs Thoreau advises he discard. But first Dick has to be made aware of their value. This awakening occurs through the intervention of Mr. Whitney, a self-made businessman. Liking Dick's honest looks, Whitney hires him to guide his nephew around New York, and decides to clean the ragged boy up to make a more presentable companion. The result of Dick's "make-over" is a paradigmatic American moment, one still reproduced in an apparently endless succession of advertisements, magazine features, television shows, and films. Dressed in a new suit of clothes, with his face and hands scrubbed, Dick "now looked quite handsome, and might readily have been taken for a young gentleman, except that his hands were red and grimy." Led before a mirror, a startled Dick exclaims, "It reminds me of Cinderella...when she was changed into a fairy princess."

Dick's astonishment suggests clothing's transformative powers. And yet the process here is complex. Dick might have been "taken for" a gentleman, but he is not one in reality. To believe that this new costume has conferred an unearned identity on him would be materialist idolatry. To use his new appearance to fool others into believing he is a gentleman would be a con-game. Instead, Dick takes his new appearance, not as reality, but as the promise of a future reality, and he sets about acquiring the internal qualities his external appearance symbolizes. With "respectability" as his goal, he saves his money, learns how to read, acquires a boarding-house domesticity, and attends a church service. He becomes an exemplary Protestant capitalist: frugal, self-disciplined, and goal-oriented. His new clothes are the symbolic map to a territory he aspires to enter. Dick's Cinderella transformation thus awakens him to the American promise of social mobility and self-transformation, inaugurating a new psychic state of work and struggle, a restlessness whose pervasiveness in American life de Tocqueville found unique. De Tocqueville's description of Americans' endless striving – their ambitious pursuit of an ever-receding horizon – prophesies Alger's conclusion. Dick finally achieves his goal of a white-collar clerical position, but rather than rest there, the novel closes with his being given yet another suit of clothes, signs of an even more ambitious identity to which he can now aspire. Alger's ladder of success stretches upward, with no end in sight.

Ragged Dick negotiates the issues raised by social mobility and misrepresentation through its implication that Dick's transformation is not a change in his essential character, which was good to begin with, but a *refinement* of that character. This idea of refinement eased anxieties about the process of social mobility, in which old identities seemed exchanged for new. Mapping the narrow path between commodity fetishism and deceptive misrepresentation, stories like *Ragged Dick* moralized self-refashioning as the foundation of American meritocracy. Although America still had social classes, the difference between American democracy and European aristocracy was that America theoretically allowed those with the potential for refinement, like the lovely Cinderella, to rise. It also allowed those without such potential, like Cinderella's ugly stepsisters, to drop like stones. This vision of meritocracy and democratic social mobility was, of course, contradicted by at least one element of American life: institutionalized racism. Few "respectable gentlemen" of the time would see potential success in the face of an African American bootblack – a problem to which I will return later.

Its first part published in the same year as *Ragged Dick*, Louisa May Alcott's *Little Women* offered yet another solution to the era's crisis of representation. A student of Thoreau and daughter of Bronson and Abby Alcott (Transcendentalists and Romantic Bohemians of unquestioned credentials), Alcott has a more Arminian sense of moral development than her iconoclastic teacher, but maintains his Antinomian stress on individual authenticity. Hence *Little Women*'s characters realize their potential less by imitating external models, as we see in *Ragged Dick*, and more by expressing their personal "styles," a difference revealed by comparing Alcott's version of the Cinderella makeover to Alger's. In this case, the young person transformed is Meg March, the pretty oldest daughter of the shabby but genteel March family, modeled on the Alcotts themselves.

Although attached to her three sisters and idealistic parents, Meg longs for the luxurious clothing that signifies the supposed happiness of her *nouveau riche* friends. Visiting one such family, Meg succumbs to her consumer desires and lets the Moffats make her over "like Cinderella" in the latest "French style." Confronted with the mirror reflection of her refashioned self, Meg is astonished. She doesn't, her friend Sallie Moffat remarks, "look a bit like herself." Her new dress, low-cut and tightly fitted, immediately attracts the gaze of those fashionable people to whom she was formerly invisible. She assumes a new name, "Daisy," and romps and flirts "outrageously." However, when Meg returns home she finds herself ashamed. After confessing to her mother, she reassumes her old identity, the one reflected in her family's kindly faces. Here the family is the only reliable mirror of self, a function once played by the Puritan community of saints. Authentic identity must be nurtured from the inside, developed through the family's emotional bonds, before it can be displayed on the outside. When Meg later marries John Brooke, a relatively poor young clerk, it is for love, not money. Her wedding dress is chastely elegant, and her going away outfit is a dove-colored suit in the "Quaker" style. Representing the "real Meg," their style is not gilding, but a polished surface integral with the depths beneath.

And yet, it is significant that this style is described so carefully. Like Thoreau, Alcott castigates fashion; but, unlike *Walden*'s author, she approves the symbolic use of goods when that use is "sincere." Just as the Puritan saints performed good works expressive of their true love of God, domestic women like Meg March display consumer goods expressive of their moral natures. This "pious consumption," as historian Colleen McDannell shows, moralized the middle-class accumulation of goods just as Calvinist worldly asceticism moralized the accumulation of capital. Both housewife and capitalist were stewards of material wealth: acquiring and displaying it, not for the sake of self-aggrandizement, but for the sake of making the kingdom of God, and their own participation in it, visible. Moreover, the female consumer's respectability was signified by the refinement of her taste. Meg, for example, ultimately recoils from Belle Moffat's fashionable but immodest dress. Much like Ragged Dick's honesty, her taste expresses her innate moral superiority. As sociologist Pierre Bourdieu argues, taste, seemingly natural, is an important weapon in the battle to construct and defend class boundaries. Hence the narrator's comment that the Moffats are made of very "ordinary" materials, despite their "gilding." Moreover, according to Alcott, no matter how one tries to disguise it, one's inner nature will eventually shape or even subvert one's outer appearance – just as a hypocrite's true motivation will eventually taint his or her effort at good works. In this vision of what sociologist Arjun Appadurai calls the "social life of things," influence always moves from subject to goods, depth to surface, never the other way.

Finally, despite their doctrinal differences, both Alger and Alcott offer a profoundly Protestant view of the relationship between material representation and moral reality, map and territory. Both resolve the crisis of representation by advocating that middle-class citizens display their worthiness through a "sincere" consumer style: one whose simplicity and self-restraint parallel the "plain speech" style of Protestantism itself. As this style became widely recognized as the display of respectable Protestant identity, it became the signifier of an elite group intent on defining and defending its boundaries. However, Halttunen argues that once those boundaries stabilized, an emergent American middle class began to acknowledge the contradiction in its demand for sincere performance and to accept the necessity of theatricality in social life. After the Civil War, the Protestant plain style was increasing perceived, not as the natural expression of moral people, but as the socially constructed mark of a dominant group. This new understanding of taste and its role in defining class boundaries can be seen in William Dean Howells's *The Rise of Silas Lapham* (1885), a novel that struggles to maintain its faith in democratic meritocracy despite its recognition of class prejudice.

Howells's novel has a double plot. The first adapts the Horatio Alger tale to the story of Silas Lapham, an old-fashioned Protestant and self-made man who has climbed the ladder of success. However, once at its height, he is corrupted by pride and rescues his moral character only through a painful choice that results in the loss of his fortune. The second is a romantic comedy with the traditional comic ending: marriage between members of opposing families. The tension here is between the "new money" Laphams and "old money" Coreys, families whose differences represent the conflict between the ideal of social mobility and the reality of cultural elitism.

To begin with the Laphams, the family's success in paint manufacturing takes them from their Vermont farmstead to Boston. Adrift in the urban world of strangers, they have no church, no friends: only their business, their family, and a house of store-bought furniture. That house, though large and expensive, is in a nondescript, unfashionable neighborhood. If its garish furniture displays any identity, it is that of the store that sold it. Through a social accident at a summer resort, the Laphams make the acquaintance of the Coreys, an "old" Boston family that lives across town, on Beacon Hill. Their house is in the most refined, neo-classical style: chaste and restrained, like Meg March's wedding dress. The dining room displays inherited antiques with the patina of age and old money. Bromfield Corey, head of the family, is an amateur painter who affects a European, aristocratic leisure which is slowly draining his family's resources. Despite the evident differences in background, the Coreys' son, Tom, is drawn to the Laphams: to the father because Tom wants a more entrepreneurial job than his highbrow connections can offer him, and to the daughter because he has fallen in love. The courtship of Tom Corey and Penelope Lapham represents Howells's hope for a democratic meritocracy which can transcend class barriers. Although elegant in dress and manners, Tom has the face of his merchant grandfather, the hard-working Puritan originator of the family's wealth, while Penelope is an unusually intelligent, self-taught cultural critic schooled by her voracious reading. Her ironic observations charm her would-be lover, hitherto burdened by his family's social rigidity.

Although the Corey parents grudgingly consent to Tom's employment in the Lapham business, when Tom asks them to socialize with the Lapham family, they balk. Anticipating their objections, Tom admits that Silas is not *entirely* grammatical in his conversation, and apt to boast of his wealth, but he argues that the Laphams "are all people of good sense and – right ideas." To which Bromfield replies firmly, "Oh, that won't do. If society took in all the people of right ideas and good sense, it would expand beyond the calling capacity of its most active members." Their elite circle might be originally based on "good sense and right ideas," but "the airy, graceful, winning superstructure which we all know demands different qualities." His concluding judgment is simple: Silas Lapham "isn't to my taste, though he might be ever so much to my conscience." This distinction between taste and conscience marks the novel's uncoupling of surface appearance from moral depths. Taste here is a matter of aesthetic preference and cultural practice: a product of "refinement," but with no moral referent.

After various complications, Tom and Penelope are finally wed. Silas eventually earns the Coreys' respect through his refusal to compromise his honor to save his fortune. However, if Silas is acceptable to the Corey conscience, he is still not to the Corey taste. Tom's parents shudder at the vision of their son's wedding in the Laphams' garish parlor, overseen by its sculpture of Lincoln freeing the slaves, a decoration their conscience may approve, but their taste rejects. Finally, taste rules private association: the exclusive club, the special dancing class, the debutante ball. As the narrator comments, "in novels" the upper-class family would come to love their new daughter-in-law, and all would be well. But in this case, "the differences remained uneffaced, if not uneffaceable, between the Coreys and Tom Corey's wife." As the narrator further explains, "our manners and customs go for more in life than our qualities. The price that we pay for civilization is the fine yet impassable differentiation of these." Walter Benjamin once wrote that the monuments of civilization are also documents of barbarism. Howells does not go that far, but he suggests that the price of civilization is discrimination based, not on moral depths, but on surface appearances. And yet the Coreys' class loyalty also has a price. Tom's marriage "was the end of their son and brother for them; they felt that; and they were not mean or unamiable people."

While Amy Kaplan argues that Howells's realism tries to find a common ground for members of differing classes, this common ground does not extend to that on which domestic lives are built. Indeed, his narrator admits helplessly that discrimination is nearly ineradicable in the private sphere, a sphere we would now argue is both interdependent and complicit with the public one. As Sarah Orne Jewett wrote in *The Country of the Pointed Firs* (1896), "clannishness is an instinct of the heart." In that story, an elite summer visitor and her working-class hosts appear to overcome the class barriers that divide them. And yet, Jewett's phrase seems chilling in light of the 1896 legalization of racial segregation in *Plessy* vs. *Ferguson*, and especially so in light of the Ku Klux Klan's violent defense of racial boundaries. Read in this context, Howells's depiction of social segregation shows a subtle racializing of the Coreys' objections to Penelope Lapham. Dark-complexioned, Penelope is even described by Mrs. Corey as that "black little thing." The Coreys would prefer Penelope's less intelligent and fairer-skinned sister; at least her beauty would compensate for her class. To his credit, Tom, Howells's hope for a democratic future, chooses moral depth over spectacular surface.

This racializing of class differences can be seen in another important realist text of the period, Edith Wharton's *The House of Mirth* (1905). As it opens, a genteel Lawrence Selden is refreshed by the "spectacle" of the beautiful socialite Lily Bart issuing from Grand Central Station in New York. Gallantly escorting her "past sallow-faced girls in preposterous hats, and flat-chested women struggling with paper bundles and palm-leaf fans," he reflects, "Was it possible that she belonged to the same race? The dinginess, the crudity of this average section of womanhood made him feel how highly specialized she was." While Lily seems the most elegant of Cinderellas, Selden wonders whether it is only her elegant surface that differentiates her, "as though a fine glaze of beauty and fastidiousness had been applied to vulgar clay." However, "the analogy left him unsatisfied, for a coarse texture will not take a high finish; and was it not possible that the material was fine, but that circumstance had fashioned it into a futile shape?" Perhaps Lily's exquisite appearance is not gilding, but the polished surface of a fine internal nature; and yet Selden further reflects that, if this is so, the fine material has been shaped in the futile shape: an ornament for sale to the wealthiest buyer. To use a term from sociologist Thorstein Veblen, Wharton's contemporary, Lily is a symbol of "conspicuous leisure," designed to signify the status of her ultimate possessor.

Indeed, Lily has been raised for the marriage market, and her apparent racial superiority raises the question of how much that difference is essential and how much constructed, a question that Selden never resolves, despite his "confused sense that she must have cost a great deal to make, that a great many dull and ugly people must, in some mysterious way, have been sacrificed to produce her." Insofar as Lily *is* a commodity, her production is carefully hidden. Her exquisite beauty blooms in a hothouse sustained by workers whose labor drains the blood from their faces. Of course, Lily's performance of beauty and leisure is also labor, a contradiction also concealed in the social theater. And she herself is haunted by a fear of falling into "dinginess": into the mass of devalued people on which she is "pedestalled." That dependency and fear are illuminated by Mary Douglas and Baron Isherwood's assertion that commodities achieve their meaning and value only through systems of interrelationship. The sallow-faced crowd in the novel's opening scene is thus more than a random backdrop: rather, its contrast with Lily renders the spectacle of her beauty meaningful. Posed against those dingy women, Lily appears pristine and pure. Against their labor, she appears leisured and free. Against their degradation, she appears of a different and superior race.

In *Imperial Leather*, cultural critic Anne McClintock examines how such oppositions create meaning in the consumer's political unconscious. Ultimately, she argues that the value of the commodity itself, formerly a "trivial thing," derived from its opposition to the labor that produced it. While commodities were glorified and overvalued, labor was rendered invisible and undervalued. As Karl Marx explained, the commodity fetish appeared to be the product of miraculous birth: emerging full-grown from the mind of the marketplace. Supposedly dark and dirty, labor, like sex, was racialized in the Victorian imagination and placed in opposition to the civilized cleanliness of white, middle-class Victorian culture. Thus historian Lori Merish writes that the refined taste and liberal subjectivity of emergent middle-class women were constructed against the degraded existence and enslaved bodies of dark-skinned women whose labor went unrecognized and whose access to the commodity symbols of respectability was denied. No wonder Lily fears falling into dinginess.

At least, one might argue, white working-class women could attempt Cinderella's miracle: transforming their identities by washing the signs of labor from their faces and donning the costumes of respectability. However, customs and manners can be learned only with difficulty; and, as Lily Bart knows, tasteful clothing costs money. Further, those aspiring to enter the dominant Protestant middle and upper classes face a difficult choice, as Penelope Lapham learns. You can imitate the style of the elite, or keep your original style and take your chances, knowing the risk of rejection is high. As Bromfield Corey admits, the elite rarely accept someone different from themselves, and then only when the nonconformist brings some exotic, "piquant" flavor to the social scene. In his autobiography *Up from Slavery* (1901), the ever-pragmatic Booker T. Washington advises young Native Americans at Hampton Institute to cut their Indian braids: "No white American ever thinks that any other race is wholly civilized until he wears the white man's clothes, eats the white man's food, speaks the white man's language, and professes the white man's religion." And yet, as African Americans like Washington were all too aware, skin color cannot be changed like clothing. Although a middle ground existed where those of mixed race might "pass" as white, if they were willing to suppress their history, the rigid boundaries of caste prevented those with darker skins from taking advantage of America's more permeable boundaries of class. Nevertheless, narratives of the period show how ambitious African Americans attempted to follow the trajectory traced by Horatio Alger.

One such narrative, Charles Chesnutt's "The Wife of His Youth" (1899), skillfully maps these subtle intersections of racism and meritocracy. Chesnutt's plot centers on an exclusive social club for aspiring African Americans nicknamed, by critical outsiders, "the Blue Vein Club," a reference to its supposed requirement that members have skin so light their veins appear blue. However, the Blue Veins declare "that character and culture were the only things considered; and that if most of their members were light-colored, it was because such persons, as a rule, had had better opportunities to qualify themselves for membership." That is, the Blue Veins are not racist, but elitist. While the foundation of their group is character, the "airy superstructure" of culture is also required. Their membership may reflect a racist bias, but it is not *their* bias; rather, it is that of a dominant white society that withholds opportunity from all but the most light-skinned among them. As the club's leader explains, "We people of mixed blood are ground between the upper and the nether millstone. Our fate lies between absorption by the white race and extinction in the black. The one doesn't want us yet, but may take us in time. The other would welcome us, but it would be for us a backward step."

This leader, the story's Algeresque hero, is Mr. Ryder, a man of mixed race who started life as Sam Fuller, an indentured servant married to Eliza Jane, an older slave on the plantation. Having overheard their master planning to sell Sam down the river, Eliza Jane warned her husband, who consequently made his escape, while she was punished by being sold down the river herself. After emancipation, Sam briefly searched for his lost wife, although their marriage was not legally binding. Not finding her, he took the name of Mr. Ryder, acquired a gentleman's tastes, and worked his way as far up the ladder of success as white society would allow. When the story opens Mr. Ryder, disturbed that he has "been forced to meet in a social way persons whose complexions and callings in life were hardly up to the standard which he considered proper," is planning a ball at the Blue Vein Club that "would serve by its exclusiveness to counteract leveling tendencies." His own aspirations he expects to further through marriage to a Mrs. Dixon, a relatively wealthy widow whose skin is even lighter than his own, and whose very name signifies the color line he hopes eventually to cross.

However, shortly before the ball, his repressed past returns. Eliza Jane has been searching for her lost husband all these years, and now she appears on Mr. Ryder's doorstep just as he is musing on a toast proper to his future fiancée. As he debates various passages from Tennyson's "A Dream of Fair Women," this vision from his former plantation life appears: "A little woman, not five feet tall ... very black – so black that her toothless gums ... were not red, but blue." In contrast to Tennyson's lovely Guinevere, dressed in "a gown of grass-green silk ... buckled with golden clasps," this visitor wears "a blue calico gown of ancient cut, a little red shawl fastened around her shoulders with an old-fashioned brooch, and a large bonnet profusely ornamented with faded red and yellow artificial flowers." Apparently not recognizing her former husband, Eliza Jane appeals to Mr. Ryder for information on his where-abouts and displays an ancient daguerreotype of the man she knew. Unlike Ragged Dick gazing at the image of the person he will become, Mr. Ryder gazes at the image of the person he once was. Choosing not to claim that identity, he promises "to give the matter some attention, and if I find out anything I will let you know." After she leaves, "he went up stairs to his bedroom, and stood for a long time before the mirror of his dressing-case, gazing thoughtfully at the reflection of his own face."

What he sees there is withheld from readers until the Blue Vein Club ball. When the time comes for the traditional toast "to the ladies," Mr. Ryder sets aside his Tennyson and tells, without divulging his own involvement, the story of Eliza Jane's faithful quest for her lost husband. As he does so his voice lapses back into the soft dialect of his own plantation days. At the story's close, he brings it near his own, that of a man who left his former wife behind "in his upward struggle." What, he asks his audience, should this man do? "I will presume that he is one who loved honor, and tried to deal justly with all men." Given that his former marriage was not legally binding, should he acknowledge the woman seeking him as his wife? Mrs. Dixon is the first of the unanimous group to answer, "He should acknowledge her." With that Mr. Ryder opens the closed door of an adjoining room, and returns, "leading by the hand the visitor of the afternoon, who stood startled and trembling at the sudden plunge into this scene of brilliant gayety. She was neatly dressed in gray, and wore the white cap of an elderly woman." Mr. Ryder then explains, "Ladies and gentleman, this is the woman, and I am the man whose story I have told you. Permit me to introduce the wife of my youth."

The ambiguity of this ending has troubled many readers. Take the opposition of Eliza Jane with Guinevere. While Eliza Jane's surface appearance seems to contrast negatively with Guinevere's, those values are reversed when their moral depths are considered. Now Eliza Jane's fidelity contrasts favorably with Guinevere's adultery. Chesnutt has designed a situation in which taste conflicts with conscience. And yet it should be noted that the taste for Guinevere over Eliza Jane is at least partially the product of white culture, the culture whose approval the Blue Veins desire. To accept Eliza Jane into their charmed circle would be to affirm the group's moral values, but lower its class boundaries, thereby forfeiting its eventual "absorption" into white society. One could argue that by acknowledging "the wife of his youth," Mr. Ryder is choosing moral depth over spectacular surface. Such a reading would see him as acknowledging his own "dark" past, thereby overcoming the racist and elitist ideals that have hitherto shaped his aspirations and affirming his solidarity with all African Americans, whatever their complexions and callings.

However, Mr. Ryder's solution to his dilemma may be more problematic. Not only is his introduction of Eliza Jane a model of genteel refinement (his soft dialect has now disappeared), but he has given the wife of his youth a makeover. Although he cannot lighten her skin, he has whitened her taste. She appears in "decent" gray with a white cap: all the vivid color and assertiveness have been drained from her appearance. The contrast of this Protestant plain style with her original clothing deserves a closer look. As Lori Merish explains, "dress was a site of struggle for masters and slaves" (2000: 238). Plantation owners asserted dominance over slaves' bodies by prescribing their dress, often requiring that slaves wear only the cheapest, roughest materials, devoid of color and ornament. In response, slaves resisted "by dressing in colorful and fancy clothing, decorated with buttons and other finery, for church on Sundays and on holidays" (p. 237). Some of these costumes were the discarded garments of white mistresses; others were earned by slaves through extra paid labor. Such "fancy dress" was a powerful expression of individual identity and self-possession, its vivid color and ornamentation a defiant rejection of white control. Given this history, what does Eliza Jane think of her makeover? All we know of Eliza Jane's response must be inferred from her startled expression as she is presented to the gaze of the Blue Veins. Just as Chesnutt refuses to describe what Mr. Ryder thinks as he contemplates his face in the mirror, he does not say what Eliza Jane feels when she sees her reflection in its new clothes. Did she, like Ragged Dick, see the promise of a brighter future, or did she, like Meg March, see the obliteration of a valued past?

Finally, despite his effort to finesse it, Mr. Ryder has not resolved the underlying conflict between conscience and white-defined taste. Eliza Jane's story, told deliberately *before* she is introduced, gives her the piquant flavor Bromfield Corey said could ease the acceptance of those otherwise unqualified for elite society. But, like Lily Bart, the Blue Veins still fear extinction in the "dinginess" beneath them. It would take the powerful analysis of W. E. B. Du Bois to assert that the African American community produced its own culture with its own systems of meaning and distinctive styles of self-expression; moreover, that this culture's music, spirituality, and humor were valuable contributions to a hybrid American civilization. This culture the Blue

Veins reject for the sake of middle-class respectability; hence Mr. Ryder's substitution of "decent" clothing for Eliza Jane's resistant fancy dress.

This substitution highlights another important issue. As we have seen, the idea that inner identity could influence outer appearance was acceptable to Protestant moralists; however, the notion that influence could move in the other direction, from surface to depth, was dangerous and disturbing. It suggested that core identity was at the mercy of social context: malleable and without innate stability. Clothes might really make the man. However, key practices during the period reflect exactly this materialistic assumption, as we see in narratives, like "The Wife of His Youth," that describe cultural assimilation, whether voluntary or forced. A powerful description of the role materialism played in such assimilation appears in the autobiographical sketches of Zitkala Ša, published in the *Atlantic Monthly* in 1900. Zitkala Ša's narrative opens with an idyllic childhood safe with her mother and her tribe, the Lakota Sioux. Tempted by some white missionaries' promise that they will take her to the "land of red apples," the young girl pleads with her mother to let her go. Although fearful, her mother agrees. However, as Laura Wexler writes, the missionaries' sentimentalism is inextricably linked with imperialistic domination. Once at the school Zitkala Ša finds, not red apples, but a fall from native grace.

On her first day, still wearing her soft moccasins, the young Sioux is lined up with other new arrivals and marched into the school dining room. She feels "like sinking to the floor" because her blanket, a tribal sign of female modesty, "has been stripped from [her] shoulders." Scrutinizing the older Indian girls, she notes their tightly fitted clothes, hard shoes, and short hair: "Our mothers had taught us that only unskilled warriors who were captured had their hair shingled by the enemy. Among our people, short hair was worn by mourners, and shingled hair by cowards!" Attempting to evade her own transformation, Zitkala Ša hides, and once captured, fights fiercely: "In spite of myself, I was carried downstairs and tied fast in a chair." Resisting even then, "I cried aloud, shaking my head all the while until I felt the cold blades of the scissors against my neck, and heard them gnaw off one of my thick braids. Then I lost my spirit." The missionary school's makeover of Zitkala Ša's appearance is not a symbol of its assault on her Indian identity; it *is* that assault. The missionaries believe, not that her Sioux identity will impress itself on her American clothing, but the opposite: that the American surface will force the inner Sioux to conform. Their signs of victory are her signs of defeat. To Zitkala Ša, her shingled hair signifies, not respectability, but loss. Although these two significations, American and Sioux, may come of different cultures, in this moment of contact they ironically agree: her Indian spirit *has* been defeated by this civilized costume, which, like a blanket impregnated with smallpox, is animated with the contagious spirit of America.

Contrary to nineteenth-century Protestant critiques, Zitkala Ša's narrative demonstrates the effectiveness of the missionaries' materialist practice. By forcibly changing her appearance, they change her internal perception of self. By the turn of the century realist writers like Wharton and Theodore Dreiser had also begun to explore materialism as a socially ubiquitous, if morally disavowed, practice. Dreiser's *Sister Carrie* (1900), for example, reveals a radically new approach to the relationship of materialism and identity. While Zitkala Ša describes materialism's dystopian effects, Dreiser focuses on its utopian promises. In his epic novel, materialism represents the magical promise of consumer goods to confer happiness and power, to create new identities and new access to realms of entitlement: the faith of a new consumer culture.

The novel opens with young Carrie, the epitome of the modern "personality," traveling from her Wisconsin home to Chicago. She is leaving her small, traditional community behind for the urban "world of strangers." Unlike Ragged Dick, Carrie can neither live in a box nor find an honest way to earn a living. Her brief employment at a shoe factory is dirty, exhausting, and demeaning. While she finds a home with her sister, this family is not the "haven in a heartless world" we see in *Little Women*. Her brother-in-law appropriates her scanty earnings without leaving her enough for a winter coat. When Carrie falls sick, she loses her job. In this state, dingy and hungry, she encounters Charles Drouet, a traveling salesman who feeds her a good breakfast, gives her some money, and buys her a stylish new jacket. Soon she is his mistress, living in a well-furnished apartment and "altogether so turned about in all of her earthly relationships that she might well have been a new and different individual" (Dreiser 1981: 89).

Carrie is keenly aware of the contradiction between her respectable appearance and her disreputable situation: "She looked into her glass and saw a prettier Carrie there than she had seen before; she looked into her mind, a mirror prepared of her own and the world's opinions, and saw a worse. Between these two images she wavered, hesitating which to believe" (Dreiser 1981: 89). The internal voice of conscience admonishes, "Remember how men look upon what you have done." Trying to drown it out, Carrie hums, "I have nice clothes. . . . They make me look so nice. I am safe. The world is not so bad now." However, this conscience with which she argues "was only an average little conscience, a thing which represented the world, her past environment, habit, convention, in a confused, reflected way. With it, the voice of the people was truly the voice of God" (p. 89). In Dreiser's version of the Cinderella-before-the-mirror scene, *both* material surface *and* moral depth are social constructions. Carrie's internal conscience is no more essential or authoritative than her external appearance. Given a choice, she opts for the more powerful force: her pretty new clothes.

Just as Dreiser deconstructs the opposition between surface and depth, so he deconstructs the Protestant opposition between authenticity and theatricality. If social roles are themselves performances, then theater can liberate us from the restrictions of everyday life. On stage we can speak words and express emotions that our "real" roles would never allow. Theater provides access to aspects of the self that would otherwise remain forever hidden. The costumes, the sets, the make-up, all "breathe of the other half of life in which we have no part, of doors that are closed, and mysteries which may never be revealed. Through these we may be admitted – through these get a glimpse of the joys and sorrows which we may never be permitted to feel on our own behalf"

(Dreiser 1981: 176–7). While Chicago's great mansions seem distant and closed to Carrie, its theaters welcome her. She sees "the beauty of the dresses upon the stage – the atmosphere of carriages, flowers, refinement. Here was no illusion" (p. 177). If all versions of reality are fictive, then the most frankly artificial is ironically the most sincere. In theater there is "no illusion." Dreiser and Oscar Wilde are not that far apart.

Dreiser's respect for imagination also shapes his approach to materialism. Carrie's imitative facility allows her to master a diversity of roles as she progresses from rural waif to urban actress. A keen observer, she soon polishes her taste and refines her manners. Studying the "magical order and sequence of dress," she sees an "ineffable charm" in material display, "a halo about nice clothes, showy manners, sparkling rings" (Dreiser 1981: 23, 105). These goods, speaking "tenderly and Jesuitically for themselves," literally appeal to Carrie. From the soft leather shoes at Pardridge's Department Store, she hears, "Ah, such little feet . . . how effectively I cover them up; what a pity they should ever want my aid" (p. 98). Strange that a young woman who once assembled shoes in a factory should experience such goods as enchanted, animated, and ready to use their magic on her behalf. This, of course, was the question that Marx explored in his discussion of the commodity fetish: where do Carrie's shoes get their power?

As a materialistic practice, commodity fetishism seemed, to Protestants at least, closely related to the equally mysterious transubstantiation of the sacraments. In Catholic doctrine, the sacraments received their transformative power through the consecration of the mass. Thus one answer to the question of commodity fetishism was similar to the Enlightenment debunking of Catholicism itself: it's all a humbug, a plot designed to brainwash the believer into dependence on the priesthood (read manufacturers and marketers) for the salvation (read happiness) they desperately pursue. However, in Dreiser's novel the Wizard of Oz is well hidden behind his curtain. The halo that appears about the goods Carrie desires appears to be the emanation of her own imagination. Ludwig Feuerbach, the nineteenth-century theologian whose work influenced Marx's discussion of commodity fetishism, argued that the gods were invented by human beings out of their unconscious need for a force greater than themselves. Carries invests those shoes with her own dreams of transformative power.

The power of goods thus comes not only from the capitalist apparatus of marketing and display, designed to stabilize the meaning of commodities, but also from the collective beliefs and political unconscious of consumers themselves. Just as Roman Catholics have to bring their faith to the communion table, so consumers have to bring their dreams to the department store. However, consumers' dreams are far more diverse and unstable than the doctrines of Catholic orthodoxy. As Jackson Lears and William Leach point out, the marketplace retains an anarchic quality, a liberating potential for self-fashioning that goes back to the anti-authoritarian practices of the carnivalesque. While a department store display might attempt "Jesuitically" to seduce the shopper's imagination, the transaction cannot be completed without the

Figure 16.1   The noonday shopping crowd on State Street in Chicago

One of the most important phenomena of the late nineteenth and early twentieth centuries was the rise of mass consumption. Linked with the emergence of the cities, the growth of industry, and the transportation and communication revolutions, mass consumption was fueled by mass advertising, which spread a distinctly middle-class culture throughout American life. Goods were advertised in various ways: in mail-order catalogues from such establishments as Montgomery Ward and Sears Roebuck; through displays in department-store windows to entice passersby inside; and in nationally circulated magazines like the *Ladies Home Journal* and newspaper chains like those of the Hearst Syndicate (the circulation of daily newspapers increased by 900 percent between 1870 and 1910). White-collar purchasing power grew by over 30 percent between 1890 and 1910, leading to more disposable income and more leisure time. Advertisements for new labor-saving devices, furniture sets, ready-made garments, and processed food pervaded the public psyche. Urban leisure led to the building of public parks, amusement parks, skating rinks, dance halls, theaters, movie palaces, and sports stadiums. Indoor electric lighting increased novel-reading, music-playing, and sales of books and sheet music. Women increasingly began leaving the domestic sphere to become clerks in department stores and to participate in the new world of fashion.

One of the results of the rise of mass society was a subtle shift in the perception of the self, which was no longer assessed so much in terms of who a person was (character) or what they produced (work), but instead in terms of how they were seen by others (appearance) and how others judged them (personality). The culture of consumption also constructed anticipatory psyches, with the focus more on what one might hope to have in the future than on what one currently had in the present. In this 1907 photograph, a bustling noonday crowd on Chicago's State Street promenades past large department stores, window-shopping. Note the presence of both horse-drawn vehicles and gas-powered automobiles. (Photograph by permission of Picture History.)

shopper's consent. To apply Louis Althusser's analysis of ideological belief, the commodity might "hail" the consumer, but the consumer must hear its appeal and consent to the system of meanings it represents. For Carrie, commodity display and consumer unconscious are in perfect alignment; her consent is wholehearted.

And what does she receive in return? If we accept that identity is even partially socially constructed, then intervention in appearance is an intervention into social interpretation, with real-life consequences. When the consumer's goal is a change in status and affiliation, then new clothes might even be required. Carrie does, in fact, see herself transformed by the goods she buys. As she refines her manners and her dress, her worldly fortunes improve. Her pretty jacket and soft leather shoes do keep her safe from cold winds and hard labor. At the same time, these material possessions do not satisfy her. If Carrie climbs high up the ladder of success in one sense, in another sense she stays right where she is. As Philip Fisher writes, her psychological progress is like a Ferris wheel: a continuous movement that never goes anywhere. The novel's recurring image is of Carrie in her rocking chair, dreaming of things to come: "Every hour the kaleidoscope of human affairs threw a new luster upon something and therewith it became for her the desired – the all. Another shift of the box and lo, some other had become the beautiful, the perfect." By the novel's end, even though she has acquired many of those enchanted objects, she is still "the old, mournful Carrie – the desireful Carrie, – unsatisfied" (Dreiser 1981: 145).

As Carrie discovers, if the consumer's goal is something as intangible as happiness, purchase often results in disappointment. While the consumer's will to believe may have a temporary placebo effect, the enchantment soon drains from goods once they are acquired. This, Colin Campbell writes, is one of the key problems underlying consumer culture: the insatiability of consumer desire. Acquisition may be motivated by the consumer's imaginative displacement of utopian desires onto goods; however, no real object can ever live up to those expectations. In the culture of abundance, it is consumption, not religion, which is the opiate of the people. Shopping can become pathological addiction, in which the serial acquisition of goods temporarily dulls the original dis-ease without addressing its source – hence the various critiques of materialism. Roman Catholics offered the sacraments, but denounced any material source of grace outside the Mother Church. Puritans believed that true grace could only come from God; no material object, however consecrated, could convey it. Writers like Thoreau, Alcott, and Alger advised their readers to ground their happiness in the invisible qualities for which goods are only a sign: individual freedom, family love, social mastery. Marxist critics acknowledged the utopian wishes displaced onto the symbols of luxury and leisure, but they too saw goods failing to deliver, since their acquisition left untouched the oppressive conditions consumers longed to escape. The cycle of dream, purchase, and disillusion supported a capitalist economy dependent on insatiable desire to renew demand, and to renew it endlessly. Only social change could bring about the transformation goods merely symbolized. However, contemporary theorists such as Campbell and Grant McCracken argue that no matter how diligently consumers strive to make their ideals real, the conflict between the ideal and the real is finally intractable; reality alone will never satisfy.

This more pessimistic vision seems to be Dreiser's as well. In his final passages, his character Ames explains to Carrie, "When I was quite young I felt as if I were ill-used because other boys were dressed better than I was, were more sprightly with the girls than I, and I grieved and grieved, but now I'm over that. I have found everyone is more or less dissatisfied. No one has exactly what his heart wishes." When Carrie wistfully asks, "Not anybody?" he replies simply, "No" (Dreiser 1981: 482–3). And yet, Ames also tells Carrie that her happiness is wholly within herself, if only she would believe it. He refers not to some innate conscience or bedrock identity, but to her expressive power. Her only fulfillment will come through using her gift for acting, not to "play a role," but to represent the longing that drives her. Longing is the inescapable human condition, and Carrie's only true happiness will come from expressing that longing on behalf of those unable to express it for themselves.

Although Dreiser rejected orthodoxy and wrote novels that scandalized the church, he was raised as a Roman Catholic, and his work reveals a sympathy toward materialistic belief that may stem from that early religious training. Treating his characters' idolatrous faith with great sensitivity, he acknowledges that the commodity fetish is a fiction, but respects the imaginative power and emotional needs invested in it. Perhaps more than writers raised within the Protestant tradition, he understands the dynamics of the new culture of abundance, with its enchanted objects and manufactured miracles. To quote F. Scott Fitzgerald, another American writer raised as a Roman Catholic, the spectacle of consumer culture is a vast World's Fair, emanating a "vulgar and meretricious beauty," a promise of "something ineffably gorgeous somewhere that [has] nothing to do with God." That this promise should fail, Fitzgerald writes, reflects less on our dreams than on reality's inability to live up to them.

Finally, the literary narratives of this period show how people use consumer goods, not only to orient themselves in this world, but also to embody their hopes for a better one. Who we wish we were, or fear to become, is part of who we are. Writers like Dreiser, Zitkala Ša, Wharton, and Chestnutt question the authenticity extolled by Protestant moralists by demonstrating that human depth and material surface cannot be easily disentangled. In their work, power and contestation shape imagined identities, along with the boundaries between them. And those identities are not fixed and stable, essential and internal, but shifting and contextual, a matter of performing as much as being. Confirming de Tocqueville's observation of our restlessness, these writers reveal a disturbing emptiness on the other side of the American dream: the defeated spirit of Zitkala Ša, the lonely fear of Lily Bart, the startled disorientation of Eliza Jane, the unsatisfied longing of Carrie Meeber. Anticipating modernist and even postmodernist texts, their narratives paradoxically map, not stability, but mutability, at times an essential formlessness: an elusive territory unmarked by material signs.

PRIMARY TEXTS

Alcott, Louisa May. *Little Women*. 1868–9.

Alger, Horatio. *Ragged Dick; or, Street Life in New York with the Boot Blacks*. 1868.

Channing, William Ellery. "Likeness to God." 1828.

Chesnutt, Charles W. *The Wife of His Youth and Other Stories of the Color Line*. 1899.

Dreiser, Theodore. *Sister Carrie*. 1900.

Du Bois, W. E. B. (William Edward Burghardt). *The Souls of Black Folk*. 1903.

Fitzgerald, F. Scott. "Absolution." 1924.

Fitzgerald, F. Scott. *The Great Gatsby*. 1925.

Franklin, Benjamin. *The Autobiography of Benjamin Franklin*. 1771–90; 1868.

Howells, William Dean. *The Rise of Silas Lapham*. 1885.

Jewett, Sarah Orne. *The Country of the Pointed Firs*. 1896.

Thoreau, Henry David. *Walden*. 1854.

Washington, Booker T. *Up from Slavery*. 1901.

Wharton, Edith. *The House of Mirth*. 1905.

Zitkala Ša. "Impressions of an Indian Childhood." 1900.

Zitkala Ša. "The School Days of an Indian Girl." 1900.

REFERENCES AND FURTHER READING

Abelson, Elaine S. (1989). *When Ladies Go A-Thieving: Middle-Class Shoplifters in the Victorian Department Store*. New York: Oxford University Press.

Agnew, Jean-Christophe (1986). *Worlds Apart: The Market and the Theater in Anglo-American Thought, 1550–1750*. Cambridge, UK: Cambridge University Press.

Althusser, Louis (1971). *Lenin and Philosophy and Other Essays*, trans. Ben Brewster. London: New Left Books.

Appadurai, Arjun, ed. (1988). *The Social Life of Things: Commmodities in Cultural Perspective*. Cambridge, UK: Cambridge University Press. (First publ. 1986.)

Baudrillard, Jean (1998). *The Consumer Society: Myths and Structures*. London and Thousand Oaks, Calif.: Sage. (First publ. 1970.)

Benedict, Burton (1993). *The Anthropology of World's Fairs*. Berkeley: University of California Press.

Benjamin, Walter (1968). "Theses on the Philosophy of History." In *Illuminations: Essays and Reflections*, ed. Hannah Arendt, trans. Harry Zohn. New York: Schocken. (First publ. 1950.)

Benjamin, Walter (1978). "Paris, Capital of the Nineteenth Century." In *Reflections: Essays, Aphorisms, Autobiographical Writing*, ed. Peter Demetz, trans. Edmund Jephcott. New York and London: Harcourt Brace Jovanovich. (First publ. 1955.)

Blumin, Stuart (1989). *The Emergence of the Middle Class: Social Experience in the American City, 1760–1900*. Cambridge, UK and New York: Cambridge University Press.

Bocock, Robert (1993). *Consumption*. London and New York: Routledge.

Bourdieu, Pierre (1984). *Distinction: A Social Critique of the Judgement of Taste*, trans. Richard Nice. Cambridge, Mass.: Harvard University Press.

Bowlby, Rachel (1985). *Just Looking: Consumer Culture in Dreiser, Gissing, and Zola*. New York: Methuen.

Bronner, Simon, ed. (1989). *Consuming Visions: Accumulation and Display of Goods in America, 1880–1920*. New York: Norton.

Brown, Bill (2004). *A Sense of Things: The Object Matter of American Literature*. Chicago: University of Chicago Press.

Bushman, Richard L. (1992). *The Refinement of America: Persons, Houses, Cities*. New York: Knopf.

Campbell, Colin (1987). *The Romantic Ethic and the Spirit of Modern Consumerism*. Oxford, UK and Cambridge, Mass.: Blackwell.

Douglas, Mary (1966). *Purity and Danger: An Analysis of Concepts of Pollution and Taboo*. London: Routledge & Kegan Paul.

Douglas, Mary, and Isherwood, Baron (1979). *The World of Goods: Towards an Anthropology of Consumption*. New York: Basic Books. Repr. with new intro. London: Routledge, 1996.

Dreiser, Theodore (1981). *Sister Carrie*. The Pennsylvania Edition, historical eds. John C. Berkey and Alice M. Winters, textual ed. James L. W. West IV, gen. ed. Neda M. Westlake. Philadelphia: University of Pennsylvania Press.

Enstad, Nan (1999). *Ladies of Labor, Girls of Adventure: Working Women, Popular Culture, and Labor Politics at the Turn of the Twentieth Century*. New York: Columbia University Press.

Ewen, Stuart (1976). *Captains of Consciousness: Advertising and the Social Roots of the Consumer Culture*. New York: McGraw-Hill.

Featherstone, Mike (1991). *Consumer Culture and Postmodernism*. London and Thousand Oaks, Calif.: Sage.

Feuerbach, Ludwig (1957). *The Essence of Christianity*, trans. George Eliot, intr. Karl Barth, foreword by H. Richard Niebuhr. New York: Harper. (First publ. 1841.)

Fisher, Philip (1987). "The Life History of Objects: The Naturalist Novel and the City." In *Hard Facts: Setting and Form in the American Novel*, 128–78. New York and Oxford: Oxford University Press.

Fox, Richard Wrightman, and Lears, T. J. Jackson, eds. (1983). *The Culture of Consumption: Critical Essays in American History, 1880–1980*. New York: Pantheon.

Garvey, Ellen Gruber (1996). *Magazines and the Gendering of Consumer Culture, 1880s to 1910s*. New York: Oxford University Press.

Griffin, Susan M. (2004). *Anti-Catholicism and Nineteenth-Century Fiction*. Cambridge, UK and New York: Cambridge University Press.

Halttunen, Karen (1982). *Confidence Men and Painted Women: A Study of Middle-Class Culture in America, 1820–1870*. New Haven and London: Yale University Press.

Hawkes, David (2001). *Idols of the Marketplace: Idolatry and Commodity Fetishism in English Literature 1580–1680*. New York: Palgrave Macmillan.

Heinz, Andrew R. (1990). *Adapting to Abundance: Jewish Immigrants, Mass Consumption, and the Search for American Identity*. New York: Columbia University Press.

Heinz, Andrew R. (2003). "*Schizophrenia Americana*: Aliens, Alienists and the 'Personality Shift' of Twentieth-Century Culture." *American Quarterly* 55: 2, 227–56.

Horowitz, Daniel (1985). *The Morality of Spending: Attitudes toward the Consumer Society in America, 1875–1940*. Baltimore: Johns Hopkins University Press.

Kaplan, Amy (1988). *The Social Construction of American Realism*. Chicago and London: University of Chicago Press.

Kasser, Tim, and Kanner, Allen D., eds. (2004). *Psychology and Consumer Culture: The Struggle for a Good Life in a Materialistic World*. Washington DC: American Psychological Association.

Leach, William (1993). *Land of Desire: Merchants, Power, and the Rise of a New American Culture*. New York: Vintage.

Lears, Jackson (1994). *Fables of Abundance: A Cultural History of Advertising in America*. New York: Basic Books.

McClintock, Anne (1995). *Imperial Leather: Race, Gender and Sexuality in the Colonial Contest*. New York and London: Routledge.

McCracken, Grant (1988). "The Evocative Power of Things: Consumer Goods and the Preservation of Hopes and Ideals." In *Culture and Consumption: New Approaches to the Symbolic Character of Consumer Goods and Activities*, 104–17. Bloomington: University of Indiana Press.

McDannell, Colleen (1986). *The Christian Home in Victorian America, 1840–1900*. Bloomington and Indianapolis: Indiana University Press.

Marx, Karl (1967). *Capital: A Critique of Political Economy*, vol. 1, ed. Frederick Engels, trans. Samuel Moore and Edward Aveling. New York: International Publishers. (First publ. 1867.)

Mechling, Jay (1989). "The Collecting Self and American Youth Movements." In Simon Bronner (ed.), *Consuming Visions: Accumulation and Display of Goods in America, 1880–1920*, 255–85. New York and London: Norton.

Merish, Lori (2000). *Sentimental Materialism: Gender, Commodity Culture, and Nineteenth-Century American Literature*. Durham, NC and London: Duke University Press.

Michaels, Walter Benn (1987). *The Gold Standard and the Logic of Naturalism: American Literature at the Turn of the Century*. Berkeley: University of California Press.

Miller, Daniel, ed. (1995). *Acknowledging Consumption: A Review of New Studies*. London and New York: Routledge.

Montgomery, Maureen E. (1998). *Displaying Women: Spectacles of Leisure in Edith Wharton's New York*. New York: Routledge.

Patten, Simon N. (1907). *The New Basis of Civilization*. New York: Macmillan.

Potter, David M. (1954). *People of Plenty: Economic Abundance and the American Character*. Chicago: University of Chicago Press.

Richards, Thomas (1990). *The Commodity Culture of Victorian England: Advertising and Spectacle, 1851–1914*. Stanford, Calif.: Stanford University Press.

Rydell, Robert W. (1984). *All the World's a Fair: Visions of Empire at American International Expositions, 1876–1916*. Chicago: University of Chicago Press.

Scanlon, Jennifer (1995). *Inarticulate Longings:* The Ladies' Home Journal, *Gender, and the Promises of Consumer Culture*. London and New York: Routledge.

Scanlon, Jennifer, ed. (2000). *The Gender and Consumer Culture Reader*. New York and London: New York University Press.

Sherman, Sarah Way (2001). "Sacramental Shopping: *Little Women* and Consumer Culture." *Prospects: An Annual of American Cultural Studies* 26, 183–237.

Susman, Warren (1984). *Culture as History: The Transformation of American Society in the Twentieth Century*. New York: Pantheon.

Tocqueville, Alexis de (1945). *Democracy in America*, vol. 2, trans. Henry Reeve, rev. Francis Bowen. New York: Vintage. (First publ. 1840.)

Trachtenberg, Alan (1982). *The Incorporation of America: Culture and Society in the Gilded Age*. New York: Hill & Wang.

Veblen, Thorstein (1994). *The Theory of the Leisure Class*. New York: Penguin. (First publ. 1899.)

Weber, Max (1958). *The Protestant Ethic and the Spirit of Capitalism*, trans. Talcott Parsons. New York: Scribner. (First publ. 1904.)

Wexler, Laura (1993). "Tender Violence: Literary Eavesdropping, Domestic Fiction, and Educational Reform." In Shirley Samuels (ed.), *The Culture of Sentiment: Race, Gender, and Sentimentality in Nineteenth Century America*, 12–32. New York: Oxford University Press.

White, Shane, and White, Graham J. (1998). *Stylin': African American Expressive Culture from Its Beginnings to the Zoot Suit*. Ithaca, NY: Cornell University Press.

Wicke, Jennifer (1988). *Advertising Fictions: Literature, Advertisement, and Social Reading*. New York: Columbia University Press.

Williams, Rosalind H. (1982). *Dream Worlds: Mass Consumption in Late Nineteenth-Century France*. Berkeley: University of California Press.

Wilson, Elizabeth (1985). *Adorned in Dreams: Fashion and Modernity*. Berkeley: University of California Press.

17

Secrets of the Master's Deed Box: Narrative and Class

Christopher P. Wilson

I

Because the industrial barons of the Gilded Age were frequently so unabashed about exhibiting their wealth and leisure – in the mansions of Fifth Avenue, the *tableaux vivants* of Newport, the gossip of the society page – we might do well to remember that even those venues sometimes witnessed a different kind of class display. In fact, Stephen Crane witnessed one such rival event in 1892, while working as a stringer for the *New York Herald Tribune* in Asbury Park, New Jersey. There – as recounted in a squib entitled "Parades and Entertainments" – Crane watched a parade of the local Junior Order of United American Mechanics, marching on a boardwalk normally reserved, he wrote, for "lace parasols," "summer gowns," and "tennis trousers." From a slightly bemused and unstable vantage point, Crane's voice wavered between the miffed cadences of the society page itself and a satiric bite worthy of Thorstein Veblen's *Theory of the Leisure Class* (1899). He began by describing the "most awkward, ungainly, and uncarved procession" that his home resort city had ever seen – but then quickly reversed himself into a rhetoric that echoed the producer ethos of the artisans themselves. After all, Crane suddenly intoned, Asbury Park society "creates nothing. It does not make; it merely amuses." "The bona fide Asbury Parker," the article went on to say, "is a man to whom a dollar, when held close to his eye, often shuts out any impression he may have had that other people possess rights." With this anger focusing his own mind's eye, the "men, bronzed, slope-shouldered, uncouth and begrimed with dust" Crane now called "dignified" and colored with "sun-beaten honesty." And then, just as oddly, he resumed a Cheshire-Cat smile, stringing in insipid announcements of future piano recitals and summer visitors. In the end, Asbury Park can only seem haunted by the discrepancy Crane's report has re-created: leisure generates only an indifference born, we think, of class privilege.

That depends, of course, on what we mean by "class" to begin with. In general, class is produced, as Max Weber famously formulated it, by the unequal distribution of life-chances, power, or prestige. Yet different definitions of the term might provoke different readings of Crane's sketch. A strong empiricist leaning in American social thought, first of all, asks us to think of class as a "thing in itself" – as a coherent, statistically measurable segment or stratum of the social whole. By contrast, as E. P. Thompson reminded us, the Marxist tradition counters that classes are not discrete structures, but aggregates produced only in *relation* to each other, through human conflict starting in the workplace – as Crane would have it, between mechanics and the partially hidden masters with an eye only for dollars. Analysts also commonly describe class as having both an objective and a subjective dimension, of both of which literature necessarily partakes. And on top of all that, fictional representations are also shaped, as Michael Denning has argued, by prevailing social *rhetorics* – the vocabularies of common usage and the genres writers deploy – as well as by cultural *formations* of class, by the reading practices and institutions that, for instance, shape audiences and provide venues for reading itself. What is intriguing about Crane's sketch is that it seems to traffic in these and many other dimensions of class – to devote, that is, uneven attention to the uses of leisure, to the cultural work of display, to gender, and even to rights.

These various dimensions of class difference, however, have not always been highlighted in American literary criticism. Especially during the Cold War, American critics preferred to minimize the place of social class in their national idiom, especially in contrast to European traditions. At the moment American literature found a new home in the university following World War II, class – formerly a vital topic in the proletarian 1930s – found itself by the wayside. Instead, midcentury critics preferred to demarcate the American difference by citing Alexis de Tocqueville's famous distinction between aristocratic and democratic societies. Similarly, Henry James's famous litany of the "absent things in American life," from his study of *Hawthorne* (1879), was often made to lead with the phenomenon of class. An ostensibly egalitarian American aesthetics, supposedly built around the genre of romance, was contrasted to the class-bound conventionality of the British novel of manners. As Richard Chase wrote in *The American Novel and its Tradition*, American social manners had been so leveled that in our literature it simply did "not matter much what class people came from" (1957: 13). Although this contrast was more seminal to antebellum writers, even postbellum novelists, Chase said, were more interested in personalities who transcended "the amenities and discipline of social intercourse" (p. 159). The American penchant for geographic and social mobility was often taken to be a solvent upon European-style class systems. To Lionel Trilling, for instance, the frequent availability of new money made for "a constant shifting of classes, a frequent change in the personnel of the dominant class" (1954: 203–4). Thus, his book of essays *The Liberal Tradition*, first published in 1950, rejected Vernon L. Parrington's "informing idea of the economic and social determination of thought" (p. 1). It was an outmoded idea which, Trilling said, was often tantamount to saying "most writers incline to stick to their own class" (p. 2). Rather famously, Trilling also quarreled with the partisan critical indulgence that had been granted writers of working-class affiliations like Theodore Dreiser or John Steinbeck. There was little reason, Trilling wrote – here his distaste was palpable – to attribute moral acumen to the "odors of the shop" (p. 11). Of the famous argument between F. Scott Fitzgerald and Ernest Hemingway over how the rich were different from you and me, Trilling said – contrary to the customary interpretation – that Fitzgerald had gotten the better of the contest (p. 208).

Looking back, these classic critical generalizations about American fiction seem about as brittle as their construction of the British tradition. And perhaps because class was declared so untouchable in American romance, it retained an underground presence in American criticism on the subsequent realist and naturalist traditions. Particularly as the 1960s unfolded, many critics explicitly connected the late Victorian realism war, stimulated by William Dean Howells's advocacy, to an emergent liberal ferment concerned with social division and poverty. Much of this essentially mimetic literary-historical criticism, which recuperated the earlier work of Parrington, Alfred Kazin, and others, connected the evolution from realism to naturalism in the late nineteenth century to a heightened awareness of class. This scholarship itself drew upon the critical writings of writers like Frank Norris, Willa Cather, Hamlin Garland, and Jack London, who had argued in favor of forsaking the "broken teacup" dramas of Victorian parlors for places like the factory, the Bowery, or the stockyards.

And yet, a mere cataloguing of such class *descriptions* in turn-of-the-century fiction would be endless. More to the point, it might well distract us from the different ways in which our criticism now takes up the topic of social class. Indeed, partly in reaction to midcentury critical paradigms – and, as we shall see, the claims to an ideal American classlessness they sometimes inherited – there has recently been a critical movement away from what theorists term *reflective* models of class description. Instead, investigations have focused on the fundamental ways social divisions were inscribed into the vocabularies, popular idioms, and even the forms of turn-of-the-century fiction itself. That is, class is seen as written *into* semantic fields, into the constructive, classificatory, and aesthetic choices writers made. In general, these studies of class inscription have followed three routes: the tracing of the *vocabularies* or discourses of class; the delineation of fiction's cognitive and *boundary-setting* functions; and explorations of class's *differential* status in relation to gender, ethnicity, and race. While these do not exhaust current approaches to class, they begin to delineate the lines and shadows of this often least visible of topics. Thanks to a body of new scholarship, social class, its disciplines, its "amenities" – and, yes, even its odors – now seem, contrary to Richard Chase's assertion, to matter quite fundamentally.

II

Read as a simple reflection of social realities, Crane's Asbury Park sketch anticipates many features of the urban excursions that would result in *Maggie, A Girl of the Streets*

(1893) and its companion pieces. Crane describes social divisions as reflected in physical features, literally embodied in abstracted "men" with shoulders sloped by poverty and crime, and sharply juxtaposed against more genteel pedestrians blinded by their eye for money. Distinctively, Crane converts social power into the priorities of syntax and vision, as different characters are empowered to judge or look away while others become "outa sight," or merely social adverbs.

And yet, distinctive as his personal vision was, Crane also used vocabularies of class division that were actually quite common in his day. For instance, he depicted late-Victorian class structure as increasingly polarized, a two-tier society separating the educated, genteel upper stratum of luxury from the world of misery and poverty. Like other writers, he often viewed immigrants and the laboring poor with a complex mixture of patronizing sympathy, affection for their rough amusements – and something like awe at what he cast as their bestiality and violence. Indeed, "Parades and Entertainments" encapsulates, along with its theme of social polarization, quite a few of the dominant American class vocabularies of this period: the tendency to see class through consumption, leisure, and cultivation rather than through labor as such; the feeling that class warfare marked itself on physical bodies; the notion that class division was a particular anathema to American ideals of nationhood; and the presentation of class divides through the medium of middle spectator, transfixed by class difference and also potentially imprisoned in his watching. While a traditional approach might leave us to choose between reproaching Crane's supposed false consciousness and, on the other hand, praising his uncanny ability as a realist to transcend social divisions, recent interpretations have stressed the complex plurality of class vocabularies his fiction put in play.

In addition, this attention to the fluidity of such vocabularies allows us to move beyond thinking that writers simply affixed labels to unproblematic realities. It might seem, for example, that the rhetoric of class polarization was an inevitable response to new industrial fortunes that accompanied the precipitous declines in farm employment and small-scale industries after the Civil War. Yet in fact this rhetoric may actually have disguised a more complex shuffling of classes: for instance, the less visible rise in clerical and office work, in university-trained professions, and in middle management (to some, the rise of a professional–managerial class). Similarly, turn-of-the-century public commentary often directed its eye (and its ire) at what it called "The New Woman," who had ostensibly left domestic life for the modern office. In fact, women did enter the professions at triple the rate of men in the three decades between 1890 and 1920; and by the latter year, 90 percent of all women in the industrial workforce were indeed unmarried (Ryan 1975: 197, 207, 232). Such trends periodically provoked hysteria about "race suicide" among native-born elites. But an overwhelming percentage of the women who were employed were actually domestics, while immigrant daughters still often contributed their wages to the family economy. As déclassé socialite Lily Bart discovers at the end of Edith Wharton's *The House of Mirth* (1905), some rather old forms of female employment allowed other women to be new. Semantic labels thus coped imperfectly with complex conditions.

Meanwhile, if you go looking for other late Victorian class vocabularies, the enterprise can quickly become quite a catholic business. Gilded Age Americans, for instance, commonly used "working classes" in the plural; in *Democratic Vistas* (1867–8), even the egalitarian Walt Whitman had staked his vision not in the proletariat, but in "the middle and working strata," or what he called "middling property owners." Across literary expression, new terms emerged both from formal discourse and from more intuitive, colloquial idioms. Necessarily, then, vocabularies of class became a palimpsest of often competing meanings. The term "worker" could be laid over polemical republican usages like "wage slave," modified by migrating terms like the French *employé*, reformed by new populist coinages like "the little people." Literary works might well be defined by their inviting this kind of poetic plasticity. In Louisa May Alcott's *Work* (1873), for example, the term "service" might seem to designate the degraded status of maid or servant – as in her semi-autobiographical "How I Went Out To Service" (1874). But Alcott actually parlayed "service" against the honor of military duty, used it to invoke an ideal threatened by slave-like servitude, and ennobled its association by allusion to Protestant good works and the invisible labors of womanhood. Indeed, these poetic extrapolations upon keywords of class often made authors seem to change terms in mid-stride. Even a quick look back at "Parades and Entertainments" unsettles its apparent two-tier class structure. Although Crane would seem, momentarily, to honor the artisan republicanism among the working classes in this era, he actually calls his mechanics "middle class."

To make matters even more complicated, the word "class" did not itself carry a fixed meaning. In particular, use of the term did not necessarily denote rival social or political interests. As Martin Burke explains, since the 1820s an expansive definition of laboring classes had actually militated against the threat of competing class interests. In elite discussion, capitalists were often said to be really laborers, and vice versa. It was thus assumed, much as in Lionel Trilling's argument, that classes were constantly being reshuffled by the healthy competition of the market. Even as late as the Gilded Age, many elite Americans treated the mere mention of the term "class" as an intrinsically foreign intrusion. In perhaps the most notoriously exceptionalist plank of this formulation, American prosperity, it was said, obviated the need or reality of classes in the old world sense; rather, the domestic (US) bonds of sympathy or patronage were silent partners in legitimating a seemingly natural class hierarchy. In a popular work surely playing on this assumption, Horatio Alger's *Ragged Dick* (1868) transposes the street-smarts and boyish pluck of his hero to adult market savvy. Dick forms affectionate bonds with his mates to get ahead, and to lift them up – and yet also ends by rediscovering his natural American gentle-manliness (that is, confirming the Anglo-genteel denial of class division itself). In this ameliorist vision of the liberal society, workers and owners were seen as necessary to each other, and any imputation of disharmony of interests was seen as a misunder-standing of American conditions – a red flag over which, for one, Howells famously vacillated in the Haymarket controversy. But even the open declaration of the existence of social classes, such as one sees in the dime novels Denning has rediscovered, did not necessarily mean, to others, that class separation was *socially* decisive. As Burke points out, in William Graham Sumner's famous "What Social Classes Owe to Each Other" (1883) the distinction the Yale professor posited was that the old-world *political* divisions of class did not exist in the United States; for example, the country had, he reasoned, no aristocracy in the old sense. Socio-economic divisions did exist, but they were merely natural and not, Sumner said, based at all on the division of labor. In one deft move, Marx and "La Marseillaise" could be left on the other side of the Atlantic.

III

Class also involves boundary-setting activities, and here fiction's role can be instrumental. In addition to modeling ways to talk about social ranks, novels and short stories assign value to particular citizens, designate rules of group membership and interclass social intercourse, and assess life-chances. They can even cordon off threats to class leadership in times of flux or vulnerability. In these ways, fiction often works to designate, in Raymond Williams's ambiguous phrase, a knowable community (1973: 165). In turn-of-the-century fiction, class in this more relational sense was often delineated in narrative form itself: in the divisions within social settings, in plots between rival families, or in the intersections of upstairs and downstairs. Fiction produced a fund of social knowledge, often presented through spatial arrangements that displayed the meaning of contact, proper and improper, between classes; the imagination thus helped to anticipate such boundary-setting, and even at times to structure it. Even the imaginary crossing of a class line therefore could, paradoxically, also mark its location; even an acknowledgement of the permeability of class boundaries could conceal a desire to shore them up. This cultural work was frequently defensive, and sometimes connected to the precise etiquette embodied in the novel of manners. In an era when working-class readers often preferred sensational story papers, mass magazines, or the extravaganza of the Sunday editions, the more traditional conventions of the Eurocentric novel – the exhibition of moral balance, mannerly precision, or discrimination about character – could themselves encode class-delimited values for genteel readers.

As noted above, such boundary-setting has often seemed the antithesis of the US national idiom. Rather, the putatively open, fluid or boundless plots of American fiction – stories of the frontier, of rural escape, of immigrant success – have often been taken as a signature of American classlessness, either as a given reality or as a utopian ideal. Indeed, David Seguin and Catherine Jurca have shown how much of early twentieth-century fiction would rhetorically reconstruct bourgeois identities themselves around a release from the boundaries that class entails – by offering an evening on the town, a suburban retreat, a vacation home. Popular fiction often equated the middle class with a social average when it was anything but, thus conveying an image of an easily-ascended social ladder. And it is true that, in the Gilded Age, longings for a lost world in common, for republican neighborliness or rural sociability, particularly in the era's local color fiction, often surfaced as a historical counterpoint to the hardening divisions of industrial society. Country people, presented as a knowable national "folk," often offered an implicit repudiation of urban class snobbery.

Nevertheless, it is probably more accurate to say that even this nostalgia could carry a critical edge, as if to signal that class lines had never really been eradicated in the republican experiment. Take, for instance, the following autobiographical reflection (1906) by Samuel Clemens, whose democratic assaults upon aristocratic blood lines, "First Families of Virginia," and chivalric pretensions have endeared him to generations of readers. The memory follows a meditation on his own mother, and the tension between her "large heart" for the downtrodden, and yet the aristocratic pride that underwrote her acceptance of slavery:

> In the small town of Hannibal, Missouri, when I was a boy everybody was poor but didn't know it; and everybody was comfortable and did know it. And there were grades of society – people of good family, people of unclassified family, people of no family. Everybody knew everybody and was affable to everybody and nobody put on any visible airs; yet the class lines were quite clearly drawn and the familiar social life of each class was restricted to that class. It was a little democracy which was full of liberty, equality and Fourth of July, and sincerely so, too; yet you perceived that the aristocratic taint was there. It was there and nobody found fault with the fact or ever stopped to reflect that its presence was an inconsistency.

Quite pointedly here, Clemens invokes a knowable community in a double sense, voicing praise for social familiarity and dismay over his village's secret pride about titles and rankings. Clemens also portrays the restrictive class instinct as a residual taint of European society. And we also see, alongside his satirizing of hierarchical pride, an equally familiar claim that village social life could create a democracy in miniature, indifferent to the titles it cherished in private. Here Clemens's sentimental nostalgia edges close to the paternalism of plantation fiction, where familial values were said to have trumped the master–slave relation. And yet, as if pulling back from the edge, Clemens ends by placing Hannibal's open public sociality under the sign of blindness. In the end, this memory was an extension of Clemens's belief that the experience of slavery had been degrading to the slave and to the plantation master and mistress. To Clemens, slavery's legacy could become an inbred instinct, a form of denial: race and class superiority work together to set a boundary, limit social knowledge, commit acts of cruelty – large hearts notwithstanding.

This tension between the desire for more a democratic society and yet a fatalism about persisting class boundaries could be found in many late Victorian literary forms. It was present even in novels focused on seemingly internal matters of elite self-definition. Among New England Brahmins after the Civil War, for instance, one could find a particularly complex intraclass dispute about the next generation's life-chances, vocations, and political sensibilities. Debates over the proper professions for a gentleman, over political independence or Mugwumpery, or over the civil service often expressed this anxiety. In Howells's *The Rise of Silas Lapham* (1885), the males of the Corey dinner party adjourn to ponder the marvel of young men sacrificed for the Union, and to wonder whether any new causes would suit the same spirit of service and democratic sacrifice. Howells's *A Modern Instance* (1882), or the lesser-known retort by Robert Grant called *An Average Man* (1884), set the moral dryrot and vocational indecision of Gilded Age young men against a darkening backdrop of backroom political compromise and waning Republican reform – as did, in ways both more oblique and more vicious, Henry Adams's *Democracy* (1880). Here Adams's surrogate heroine, Mrs. Madeleine Lee, "plunged into philanthropy, visited prisons, inspected hospitals." But plagued by her wavering sense of duty, she heads instead to Washington DC. And there, of course, she is repulsed even further, having found a democracy so altered that it has "'has shaken [her] nerves to pieces.'"

Perhaps the most famous way these elite tensions around class membership, social duty, and democratic value were articulated was through fictional conflict between old and new money – that is, through a struggle between landed, aristocratic, or mercantile sources of wealth and that of the new industrial parvenus. The conflict takes center stage in Henry Blake Fuller's *The Cliff-Dwellers* (1893), Henry James's *The American* (1877), Frank Norris's *The Pit* (1903), and María Amparo Ruiz de Burton's *The Squatter and the Don* (1884) – as well as repeatedly in Howells's fiction. Indeed, Howells's presentation of the Corey and Lapham families set a particularly influential template by displaying class through the social geography of Boston. Silas Lapham's movement into "new land" is a momentary disruption of elite boundaries, of lives formerly spent in different neighborhoods, reading different newspapers, summering in different vacation spots. ("What in the world," Mrs. Corey asks, "can a cottage at Nantasket be like?") Tom Corey even inherits a nose that is itself said to be a bodily reminder of his ancestor, "the old India merchant, who had followed the trade from Salem to Boston when the larger city drew it away from the smaller." Here "roots" are literally turned into routes of mercantilism; if Tom is initially said to be a little dull for a profession, he eventually returns to his routes. (In the end he seems, as Christopher Lasch once wrote, emblematic of a ruling class that had rehabilitated itself by a rapprochement with the new fortunes.) Even the book's ultimate tragic turn has seemed, to many readers, only to ratify a certain rightness of everyone's original station. As Elsa Nettels has shown, Howells's own narrative diction may betray his real class affiliation, though his heart is elsewhere. Sometimes using a vernacular that expresses, as with his friend Clemens, a nostalgic, utopian appeal to national common sense, Howells often reverts to a more elite, aloof diction – a voice that, for instance, sounds pleased when Lapham is ultimately deemed a "gentleman" by his Brahmin counterparts. Thus if the Brahmin elite seems to be rising again through the young Tom Corey, moving overseas once more, the Laphams' return to modest means – again, geographically out of Boston – seems only to confirm the sentiments that Silas' wife, Persis, had expressed from the beginning: "I'm satisfied where we be, Si," Persis had said.

It probably should not surprise us that the late Victorian novel's explorations of class often seem contradictory and defensive. In a period of industrial warfare, new immigration, and the threatening of class distinctions by consumerism, securing the knowables of class often meant drawing thresholds that outsiders would find difficult to cross. As Amy Kaplan has argued, even desires for democratic affiliation could simultaneously express a rising class need for security, a push–pull dynamic exhibited in these novels' often unfinished form. To Kaplan as to others, class ambivalence was exemplified by the accenting of the Howellsian keyword of the "common." That is, while writers like Howells, Wharton, or Theodore Dreiser often embraced the common people – and tried to "focus on class difference to forge the bonds of a public world that subsumes those differences" (Kaplan 1988: 12) – they just as often consigned the lower and immigrant orders to a realm beyond the line of assimilation or knowability. Again, Howells's turn upon Clemens's nostalgia for village sociability is telling. Whatever Silas Lapham's abiding duty to his former neighbors, the Millon family, the new odors of class they have acquired – of divorce, alcoholism, and reckless sailors' haunts – mean they will not ultimately be incorporated into his world, any more than they fit the formal equilibrium of Howells's novel. Similarly, if the conversation in the novel opens its back door to the specter of political anarchism – the hundreds of strikes in Massachusetts alone, at the time – that world appears, at best, only a psychological spectre, a shadow on bourgeois success or failure. We see Lapham himself, standing in the ashes of his own house, mistaken by a beat cop for the tramp previously dissected in the Coreys' dinner-party chatter about class rebellion. But even this uneasy reminder is now less an encompassing of others' fates than an internal synopsis of Silas's own.

Nevertheless, at a lower layer, novels of old and new fortunes, new land and familiar routes, might also be said to debate whether class boundaries – legitimate, natural, or even desirable – ultimately secure anyone's fate. We are never sure whether Silas desires his new house to secure a future for his daughters, or to use consumption to paint over his own social crimes. Ultimately, what the novel seems most uneasy about is the insulation a dominant class experiences, whatever the source of its fortunes, from the injuries those fortunes can inflict. What the novel laments as the "curse of prosperity," a malaise akin to Veblen's pecuniary emulation, seems as threatening to bourgeois happiness as lower-class revolution. In Howells's world as in Crane's, visible markers of cultural distinction – parasols or piano lessons, sun-beaten faces or the older pleasure of making something – hardly seem to solve the riddles of industrial society's pain. And in the volatile market itself, where Lapham is both player and eventual victim, all sorts of class relations are put at a disabling distance: workers, customers, even the competitors Lapham squeezed to get to Beacon Street in the first place. Lapham in fact says that he prefers a world where you don't know people "through and through." His former partner Milton K. Rogers, who otherwise would belong to Silas's own class, is perhaps the most unknowable character in the book.

IV

So far, I may have made it seem as if we might isolate the category of class from other social parameters such as race, gender, or ethnicity. But we need to guard against using class as an independent structural category or relation. As Wai Chee Dimock has argued, doing so can easily cause us to use class as an abstract figure for economic fragmentation or blindness, in contrast to the ostensibly whole and disinterested observer common to Romantic criticism. The fact is that the meanings of turn-of-the-century class were inevitably *differential* – shaded by, dependent upon, or in conflict with these other fundamental categories of identity. Even in everyday discourse, class and race, gender, or ethnicity were made semantically coterminous – that is, bound together, or made to qualify each other, or sometimes made preposterously synonymous. This uneven alignment could surface in representations of "true" domesticity, in turn-of-the-century ideas of "good breeding," or in mystic invocations of racial and ethnic memory. The range of the imaginative permutations that could be reconstructed, in American fiction, between class and its close relations was considerable. It is thus no coincidence that – right at the moment when *PMLA* has devoted its millennial issue to representations of class – recent critical emphasis has often fallen on what are termed the "non-aligned," "uneven," and even shape-shifting relations of class to other social variables. As Cora Kaplan has put it, we tend to think of class consciousness, past and present, "more polymorphously and perversely" (2000: 13).

Take, once again, the portraiture of class polarization with which American naturalism is so often associated. Supposedly taking the exploration of experience one step beyond their forefather Howells, the naturalists often defined their art – what they sometimes termed a synthesis of realism and romance – as the imaginative power to see and travel across class boundaries. In what he called "A Plea for Romantic Fiction" (1901), for example, Frank Norris spoke of leaving behind what he disparagingly called the "[p]robable people" of the bourgeois novel:

> So you think Romance would stop in the front parlor and discuss medicated flannels and mineral waters with the ladies? Not for more than five minutes. She would be off up-stairs with you, prying, peeping, peering into the closets of the bedroom, into the nursery, into the sitting-room; yes, and into that little iron box screwed to the lower shelf of the closet in the library; and into those compartments and pigeon-holes of the "secretaire" in the study. She would find a heartache (may-be) between the pillows of the mistress's bed, and a memory carefully secreted in the master's deed-box.

Rather arrestingly, the naturalist aesthetic is linked here to an intrusive, even criminal transgression of the bourgeois deed-box, a symbol of private power, class entitlement, and social authority. At the same time, opening that deed-box is linked to discovering unseen secrets or crimes of the master class itself. Nor was this the only locale for such investigation. Norris goes on to claim that this new American fiction should be equally at home among the "rags and wretchedness" of "the East Side of New York."

Naturalism did seem to expand social investigation over the lines Howells, for one, had customarily drawn. Yet however expansive or clear-cut the class thinking we imagine here, Norris also markedly restricts the canon of his supposedly class-aware fiction. That he so uncharacteristically chooses a female ethos for his fairy spirit of Romance is especially revealing, since he seems at pains to sequester his claim from women writers who had already scouted the territory. Indeed, Norris manages to invoke the aura of sentimental thriller only by claiming to supersede it: one thinks, for instance, of Alcott's *Behind a Mask* (1867), with its devious upending of sentimental notions of the ambiguously classed governess. Thanks to Michael Denning, Cathy and Arnold Davidson, and others, we now also recognize Theodore Dreiser's reworking of working-girl novels like Laura Jean Libbey's *Only a Mechanic's Daughter: A Charming Story of Love and Passion* (1892) as well as the romances Sister Carrie discusses with her engineer mentor Bob Ames. Standard accounts of naturalism now no longer overlook a series of mid-Victorian explorations of industrial class divisions in Elizabeth Stuart Phelps's *The Silent Partner* (1871) or Rebecca Harding Davis's *Life in the Iron Mills* (1861). In these lights, the naturalists' arrogation of the power to write up poverty or class pathologies looks tantamount to merely reinscribing the class and gender privileges they claimed to transcend.

Yet as Eric Schocket and Mark Pittenger have each suggested, urban exposé of the "underclass" commonly took the form of cross-dressing in more ways than this one. What is equally striking is how this myth of the observer's class transcendence was built upon his power to offer differential social judgments. Rather than sweeping away the class taint of the bourgeois parlor, the literature of exposé often seems only to reset a series of differential social cues – through melodramatizing social polarization as a class abyss, or the identification of servants with criminality (here, in Norris's polemic, with petty theft), or the equation of the lower orders with primitive or brutish existence (for example, a jungle). As June Howard has suggested, American naturalism also often casts bourgeois downward class mobility as equivalent to crossing a boundary of individual male brutalization – a syntax, again, whereby the social boundary shape-shifted into a psychological lexicon constituted by invidious discourses of race and gender. To use Jack London's boundary term, explorations "South of the Slot" often seem to celebrate "primitive" working-class vitality. But more often, the racialized brutes of American naturalism are a projection of a privileged class's own fears of proletarianization and decadence. In Howard's telling phrase, naturalism may invoke only a bourgeois "slumming in determinism" (1985: 104): middle-class readers' entertainment of working-class unfreedom driven mainly by their need to control it. Thus, even when the naturalists attempted to cast lower-class, female protagonists with sentimental human longings, or a pragmatic malleability worthy of a Horatio Alger hero – protagonists like Crane's Maggie, or Dreiser's Carrie Meeber, or David Graham Phillips's Susan Lenox (1917) – such figures were often overwhelmed by a realm of masculine desire, built largely out of bourgeois fears.

Naturalism, of course, did not invent this melodramatic warfare of class, race, and gender. As Davis's *Life in the Iron Mills* brilliantly shows, Gilded Age elites frequently justified their social station as natural by invidiously transposing the discourse of savagery to workers. Conversely, fears of wage slavery or "white slavery" implicitly drew upon racial discourses and phobias. Even appeals to class solidarity could disguise a covert appeal to racial difference and manliness. As Eric Lott reminds us, the artisan republicanism Crane witnessed in his mechanics' parade often rhetorically embraced clerks or shopkeepers only by using a shared whiteness (those sun-beaten faces) as the grounds of its masculine populist sensibility. In fiction following the tracks of the slum observer, the Middle Eastern tourist, or the regional vacationer, class was never far removed from its ethnic and racial familiars. In the presumption that lower and foreign orders were intrinsically more bound to their bodies, class was repeatedly made synonymous with such differences.

In a time of deepening segregation, revived imperial adventurism, and growing immigration restriction, such conflations should not be surprising. As the twentieth century began, dominant definitions of ethnic or national origin often seemed to trump outsiders' class mobility, which had – say, in an Alger tale three decades earlier – seemed a trump card itself. Indeed, this is why, to some interpreters today, it is imperative not only to avoid treating class as a discrete category – much less a monochromatic reference to economic status or the division of labor – but to challenge any assumed priority we give it historically. The objection has theoretical grounds as well. As the cultural studies turn from classical Marxism further modifies the meanings of class determination, as multiculturalism stresses cultural difference or hybridity, as the legibility of traditional status distinctions seems blurred by consumerism or transnational migrations, the idea that class was a deep, decisive, or even fully decipherable ground in this era has, in not a few quarters, been called into question. Particularly in light of the color line, class itself can, in these decades, often be made to seem something more like a juncture or relay rather than any irreducible base of social identity.

On the other hand, the common critical refrain that says class, race, or gender are "mutually constitutive" hardly answers all our questions. In texts like Abraham Cahan's *Yekl* (1896), Paul Lawrence Dunbar's *Sport of the Gods* (1902), or Sui Sin Far's (Edith Maud Eaton's) *Mrs. Spring Fragrance* (1912), the category of class is represented through a shape-shifting filtering and contesting of mainstream gender and racial norms. Again, class was differential in that it was always measured against and within racial, ethnic, or gender designation. Writers calibrated class's differential meaning in discussions of the bachelorhood created by chains of immigration, of the place of the domestic realm in shoring up ethnic identity, of the threat of mass entertainment to cultural habits of domestic and foreign migrants. Thus it is hardly the case that class could simply be eclipsed, say, by race or other social designations. Moreover, in imaginative writing, class could be imaginatively transposed to provide momentary ideological leverage or social elusiveness. In essence, class was subject to what sociologists call code-switching. That is, these writers could resort to a tricksterism about class; they could use masks of gentility and even (in Sui Sin Far's case) national origin to "pass" and gain audiences; they could, like African American slave narrators before them, polish their standard English to secure safer passage in an often-threatening world.

It is not that these writers or their works avoided the invidious linking of race, gender, and class that mainstream culture often imposed upon them – quite the contrary. As so famously in anti-semitism, the survival skills and class mobility of migrants and diasporic peoples were often mistaken for the selfsame "racial" characteristics these authors tried to subvert. The white narrator of Charles Chesnutt's *The Conjure Woman* (1899) sees Uncle Julius's ability to secure property, protect his family, and promote his relatives only as signs of his "predial" African blood. Nevertheless, writers on the margin also imagined ways in which the privileges of social class could become an ideological front on which to construct potentially different, protean social possibilities. The title character of Far's *Mrs. Spring Fragrance*, for instance, overtly sustains her merchant husband's social relations with upper-class whites – profiting, that is, from the class-based loophole in Chinese Exclusion acts – and exerts indirect influence over him in the white-bourgeois way. But in the tale called "The Inferior Woman," she just as deftly challenges the same bourgeois domesticity that cements her own privilege. In this story, Mrs. Spring Fragrance presses the romantic case of an immigrant working girl disparaged by her lover's mother – a woman who, in rising up to elite ranks, has forgotten her own Irish roots. The mother now looks down her nose at a younger woman who would have been praised for upward mobility had she been a (white) man. Referring self-reflexively to her own trickster-like slipperiness around class and race, Sui Sin Far designates this working girl as a "Bohemian," a term (as Willa Cather would see) for both an ethnic outsider and a spirit who flouts class conventions. Artistic bohemianism – life lived beyond any one country's ways or boundaries – provides momentary cover for evading racial difference and exclusion.

On the other hand, class can return the minute it seems banished. Sui Sin Far's case may not be so subversive as it seems. As it happens in her tale, at the precise moment modern American suffragism was anchoring its case in a covert appeal to middle-class white domesticity, her Bohemian heroine mocks the modern suffragettes' cause – but not only because of its covert class-based racism: rather, what she really can't abide is their disdain for the boys of the business class who have helped her rise up.

V

In fiction as in everyday life, turn-of-the-century understandings of class were thus reconstructed through both residual and emergent vocabularies, delineated in social boundaries, and transmitted through other modalities of social difference. In all, then, the imaginative or literary construction of class can indeed provide some secrets of the master's deed-box, as well as show how the authority of dominant classes could be contested. The finale of Sui Sin Far's story, however, also identifies some limits to the three essentially semantic approaches to class I have outlined. Deeds, after all, are more than words. If we reduce class to merely its ideological construction in language, or in fictive imaginings, it may end up looking more malleable than it really was in any given historical moment. Linking class to our own notions of linguistic fluidity and disguise, we might return to using "class" as a synonym for virtually *any* kind of status or occupational distinction. The resulting portrait of turn-of-the-century life might not look so very different from that of Richard Chase or Lionel Trilling. In a related vein, if we relegate class to a secondary variable subsumed by its coterminous categories of difference, we risk diminishing the material force of social division even among social newcomers and outsiders themselves.

It is a truism, of course, that class exists in a set of social rhetorics *and* as lived experience. It thus hinges on more than just ideological consciousness, class aware-ness, or its imaginative construction in works of literature. Rather, the meaning of class also pivots on matters of structural placement and material grounding, matters that quite often contest the ideological labeling or accent that a literary text, which we often read in isolation, assigns. The larger issue, therefore, is not only about how much weight to assign to any one particular category of identity, but how much we assign to the semantic field itself. In "The Inferior Woman," class can seem a slippery, intermediating element, yet in complex processes with quite material consequences: processes of negotiating social acceptance, controlling how one is read, or carving out a political affiliation. A transgressor herself, Sui Sin Far knew well that the meaning of class extended well beyond its ideological coding or even code-switching: to her social placements in relation to ethnic whites; to privileges and duties embedded in the domestic labor and service she herself performed; to matters of differential citizenship and, conversely, the legal or illegal exclusion she defied. These conditions explain why, in fact, there has been a persisting scholarly interest in the social processes of class construction that not only precede literary representation but accompany it. Scholars continue to explore the class formations and alliances of literary professionalism and reading communities, the logistical mechanics of under-world exploration, the traversing of class difference in local color or travel writing. These journeys into the powers in and beyond writing help us understand the cultural work not only in exhibiting social "others" but in gathering up and displaying the cultural capital of the observer.

Other explorations await us. We need an understanding of professionalism, or even the professional–managerial class, that is expansive enough to include how women or new immigrants moved into white-collar work and redefined what professions were. We need to refine our sense of how imperial adventurism not only rehabilitated elite masculinity and the color line, but affected domestic US class boundaries and membership. We should continue to explore how debates over "Americanization," mass culture, or standards of "whiteness" enshrined in custom and law played out against class divisions that industrial culture had opened up. We need to understand the relays and code-switching that allowed figures like Abraham Cahan, or Mary Antin, or Booker T. Washington not only to shore up their own vision of racial or ethnic progress, but to strategically traverse boundaries of class, befriend but not transgress the authority of those to whom education or patronage had always been accented by social rank. We need to see how an emergent transnational consciousness modified, as in the case of writers like Sui Sin Far or Finley Peter Dunne or Pauline Hopkins, not only their sense of color or national affiliation, but their eye for lost cultural capital(s) of class standing, whether in China or Ireland or Africa. On these and other fronts, by exploring its public acts and its secrets, class and its mechanics can continue to be rewritten.

PRIMARY TEXTS

Adams, Henry. *Democracy*. 1880.

Alcott, Louisa May. *Behind a Mask*. 1867.

Alcott, Louisa May. *Work: A Story of Experience*. 1873.

Alcott, Louisa May. "How I Went Out to Service." 1874.

Alger, Horatio. *Ragged Dick; or, Street Life in New York with the Boot Blacks*. 1868.

Cahan, Abraham. *Yekl: A Tale of the New York Ghetto*. 1896.

Chesnutt, Charles W. *The Conjure Woman*. 1899.

Clemens, Samuel L. *The Autobiography of Mark Twain*. 1906.

Crane, Stephen. *Maggie, A Girl of the Streets (A Story of New York)*. 1893.

Crane, Stephen. "Parades and Entertainments." 1892.

Davis, Rebecca Harding. *Life in the Iron Mills; or, The Korl Woman*. 1861.

Dreiser, Theodore. *Sister Carrie*. 1900.

Dunbar, Paul Lawrence. *Sport of the Gods*. 1902.

Fuller, Henry Blake. *The Cliff-Dwellers*. 1893.

Grant, Robert. *An Average Man*. 1884.

Howells, William Dean. *A Modern Instance*. 1882.

Howells, William Dean. *The Rise of Silas Lapham*. 1885.

James, Henry. *The American*. 1877.

James, Henry. *Hawthorne*. 1879.

Libbey, Laura Jean. *Only a Mechanic's Daughter: A Charming Story of Love and Passion*. 1892.

London, Jack. "South of the Slot." 1909.

Norris, Frank. "A Plea for Romantic Fiction." 1901.

Norris, Frank. *The Pit*. 1903.

Phelps, Elizabeth Stuart. *The Silent Partner*. 1871.

Phillips, David Graham. *Susan Lenox, Her Fall and Rise*. 1917.

Ruiz de Burton, María Amparo. *The Squatter and the Don*. 1885.

Sui Sin Far [Edith Maud Eaton]. *Mrs. Spring Fragrance and Other Stories*. 1912.

Sumner, William Graham. "What Social Classes Owe to Each Other." 1883.

Veblen, Thorstein. *Theory of the Leisure Class*. 1899.

Wharton, Edith. *The House of Mirth*. 1905.

Whitman, Walt. *Democratic Vistas*. 1867–8.

REFERENCES AND FURTHER READING

Burke, Martin J. (1995). *The Conundrum of Class: Public Discourse on the Social Order in America*. Chicago: University of Chicago Press.

Chase, Richard (1957). *The American Novel and its Tradition*. Garden City, NY: Doubleday.

Davidson, Cathy, and Davidson, Arnold (1977). "Carrie's Sisters: The Popular Prototypes for Dreiser's Heroine." *Modern Fiction Studies* 19, 395–407.

Denning, Michael (1987). *Mechanic Accents: Dime Novels and Working-Class Culture in America*. New York: Verso.

Dimock, Wai Chee, and Gilmore, Michael T. (1994). "Class, Gender, and a History of Metonymy." In Wai Chee Dimock and Michael T. Gilmore (eds.), *Rethinking Class: Literary Studies and Social Formations*, 57–104. New York: Columbia University Press.

Dimock, Wai Chee, and Gilmore, Michael T., eds. (1994). *Rethinking Class: Literary Studies and Social Formations*. New York: Columbia University Press.

Howard, June (1985). *Form and History in American Naturalism*. Chapel Hill: University of North Carolina Press.

Jurca, Catherine (2001). *White Diaspora*. Princeton: Princeton University Press.

Kaplan, Amy (1988). *The Social Construction of American Realism*. Chicago: University of Chicago Press.

Kaplan, Cora, ed. (2000). "Millennial Class." Special issue of *PMLA* on "Rereading Class," 115: 1, 9–19.

Lasch, Christopher (1972). "The Moral and Intellectual Rehabilitation of the Ruling Class." In *The World of Nations*, 80–99. New York: Vintage.

Lott, Eric (1993). "White Kids and No Kids at All: Languages of Race in Antebellum U.S. Working-Class Culture." In Dimock and Gilmore (eds.), *Rethinking Class: Literary Studies and Social Formations*, 175–211. New York: Columbia University Press.

Nettels, Elsa (1988). *Language, Race, and Social Class in Howells's America*. Lexington: University of Kentucky Press.

Pittenger, Mark (1997). "A World of Difference: Constructing the 'Underclass' in Progressive America." *American Quarterly* 49, 26–65.

Ryan, Mary Press (1975). *Womanhood in America: From Colonial Times to the Present*. New York: Franklin Watts.

Schocket, Eric (1998). "Undercover Explorations of the 'Other Half,' or the Writer as Class Transvestite." *Representations* 64, 109–37.

Seguin, Robert (2001). *Around Quitting Time: Work and Middle-Class Fantasy in American Fiction*. Durham, NC: Duke University Press.

Thompson, E. P. (1963). *The Making of the English Working Class*. New York: Pantheon.

Trilling, Lionel (1954). *The Liberal Imagination*. Garden City, NY: Anchor. (First publ. 1950.)

Williams, Raymond (1973). *The Country and the City*. New York: Oxford University Press.

Wilson, Christopher Press (1992). *White Collar Fictions: Class and Social Representation in American Literature, 1885–1925*. Athens, Ga.: University of Georgia Press.

18

Ethnic Realism

Robert M. Dowling

" 'Tis diff'rent now. I don't know why 'tis diff'rent but 'tis diff'rent." (Martin Dooley, publican)

In 1911, *Encyclopedia Britannica* released all twenty-four volumes of its celebrated eleventh edition. *Britannica*'s publishers advertised their new reference books as the most comprehensive compendium of human knowledge the world had ever known, and some epistemologists still regard the eleventh edition as the most significant encyclopedic achievement since Diderot. Not surprisingly, *Britannica*'s article on "Migration" focuses on the United States and its complex relationship between the "native" Anglo-German majority and the new mass of immigrants from eastern and southern Europe. The author reports that in 1910 over 20 percent of the American labor force was foreign-born, almost 40 percent if you count the second generation. Economically speaking, he finds these numbers encouraging, since before the Civil War, "an adult slave used to be valued at from $800 to $1000, so that every adult immigrant may be looked upon as worth that sum to the country" (Mayo-Smith and Ingraham 1911: 431). But he discards this and other careless approximations after taking into account the "more numerously represented" immigrants who came from the "criminal, defective and dependent classes," not to mention that "element which has made itself obnoxious to the local sentiment," namely east European Jews. With the consummate self-assurance of the Victorian classes, however, "Migration" offers this sanguine proclamation about the United States and its noble experiment: "Doubtless immigration in the last fifty years of the nineteenth century had a modifying effect on American life; but on the whole the power of a modern civilized community working through individual freedom to assimilate elements not differing from it too radically has been displayed to a remarkable degree" (p. 431).

Most educated Anglo-Americans by the 1910s shared the "progressive" political view that their collective history would consolidate the visibly chaotic "nation of nations" into one acceptable, respectable norm. As the imagist poet Amy Lowell wrote in a 1917 critique of Carl Sandburg's distinctive new verse from the Scandinavian Midwest, "some day, America will be a nation; some day, we shall have a national character. Now, our population is a crazy quilt of racial samples. But how strong is that Anglo-Saxon ground-work which holds them all firmly together to its shape, if no longer to its colour!" (Lowell 1917: 202). Nevertheless, the "modifying effect" of immigration appeared to intensify rather than subside by the First World War, as the millions of "criminal, defective and dependent" immigrants seemed ill-equipped and unwilling to consent to the procedure of assimilation. Soon after Lowell published her remark, the cantankerous Baltimore journalist H. L. Mencken, whom *The New York Times* called the "most powerful private citizen in America," announced a disturbing trend:

> The truth is that the majority of non-Anglo-Saxon immigrants since the Revolution, like the majority of Anglo-Saxon immigrants before the Revolution, have been, not the superior men of their native lands, but the botched and unfit: Irishmen starving to death in Ireland, Germans unable to weather the *Sturm und Drang* of the post-Napoleonic reorganization, Italians weed-grown on exhausted soil, Scandinavians run all to bone and no brain, Jews too incompetent to swindle even the barbarous peasants of Russia, Poland and Rumania ... the average newcomer is, and always has been simply a poor fish. (Mencken 1982: 14–15)

Immigrants to the United States desired social mobility and removal from the hostile social landscape of the old world; what they offered native-born Americans in return was poverty-stricken ghettos, low-class "peonage," unbridled alcohol consumption, and political dissension on the one hand – traits that spawned rabid immigration restriction leagues run by men like Thomas Bailey Aldrich, Francis A. Walker, Edward A. Ross, and Henry Cabot Lodge – and a bottomless labor force, a sense of cultural mobility, and relief from the doldrums of parochial stagnation on the other. These latter traits attracted, along with developers and industrialists, social scientists like Robert E. Park, Franz Boas, and Charles Lummis, journalists like Lincoln Steffens and Hutchins Hapgood, and leading literary figures like Hamlin Garland, Hjalmar Hjorth Boyesen (himself a Norse immigrant), and the "Dean of American letters" William Dean Howells. Most importantly, ethnic communities themselves became sufficiently cohesive to establish political advocacy groups, labor organizations, social clubs, educational programs, foreign-language newspapers, and only then an intellectual class that might speak to mainstream outsiders, intra-ethnically to insiders, and inter-ethnically as well.

This volume transports us to the nadir of ethnic relations in US history, a period which lasted at least through the 1920s, when ethnic contention in the form of anti-immigration legislation and institutionalized segregation heightened the call for intra-ethnic solidarity. Additionally, a series of transformative historical forces placed new immigrants and other ethnic Americans at the center of national controversy: the

United States changed from a producer economy to a consumer economy; the closing of the frontier opened the door to colonial expansion in Puerto Rico, Cuba, and the Philippines; racially diverse slums turned into ethnically cohesive ghettos; and previous emphases on local communities yielded to, as Carrie Tirado Bramen has recently argued, a nationalization of urban aesthetics (2002: 446). Whether we subscribe to the current "postethnic" school of ethnic American studies, in which the nation self-corrects toward inclusion, or the "borders" school, which foregrounds seclusion, exclusion, and colonization (see Singh and Schmidt 2000: 6–7), authors who proffered the theme of ethnic identity in the decades between Reconstruction and the First World War starkly contrasted with the mainline of American cultural production – that is, "genteel," "Puritan," "Victorian," "white," or, as the exiled Cuban journalist Jose Martí called it in 1891, "Anglo-Saxon" America (as opposed to *"Nuestra America,"* which includes both American hemispheres and their civilizations' cultural and historical cross-currents). There are subtle distinctions between these terms, of course, but with prodigious overlap.

Ethnic American authors at the turn of the twentieth century, including, though not exclusively, new immigrants from Europe, Asia, and Latin America, African Americans, and Native Americans, all grappled with geographic dislocation and the symptoms of being "other" in a foreign land. Whether it's the trials of Lower East Side tenement life in Abraham Cahan's tales of the Jewish ghetto, Sui Sin Far's "Oriental" women laying down their fans in Chinatowns across the North American continent, Finley Peter Dunne and his Irishman Dooley's working-class pub on Chicago's South Side, or narratives of intracontinental migration like those of Paul Laurence Dunbar's and James Weldon Johnson's dislocated Southern black migrants in Manhattan's "black Bohemia" of the 1890s, the struggles of biracial characters caught between a white North and a black South in the mulatto fictionist Charles W. Chesnutt's tales of conjugation and conjuring, Zitkala Ša's Quaker-run school houses for Sioux children on the Midwestern plains, or the blue-tiled fountains of the Mexican peninsula in María Cristina Mena's proto-magical realism, each "ethnic realist" broke through rigidly defined barriers of national cultural life through artistic ambition, social urgency, and their distinctly ethnic deviations off realist themes. Moreover, ethnic authors for better or worse allied themselves with mainstream sponsors in their strivings to become what W. E. B. Du Bois considered the final triumph of black folk in particular: "co-worker[s] in the kingdom of culture" (1986a: 365). In the end, however, it becomes apparent that literary production could not, as ethnic writers and their mainstream advocates might have hoped, alleviate the increasingly violent social contention of the times without the alliance of culture with politics. That was the way of their modernist successors. The following section will set down the changing face of American immigration at the turn of the twentieth century, the subsequent backlash of progressive moral reform, and the pluralistic tenets of the realist movement in the context of ethnic authorship.

II

The first wave of nineteenth-century immigration consisted of over a million Irish exiles escaping the horrors of a potato blight that decimated Ireland's population after 1845. A million or so Germans, or "Forty-Niners," also arrived during this period, many of them having chosen emigration over the violent backlash enacted by central European monarchies after the failed worker revolutions of 1848. A second stage of this first wave, often called the "Teutonic" stage, included mostly English, Scandinavians, north Germans, and Czechs, along with tens of thousands of Japanese, Chinese, Mexicans, and French, though their numbers were significantly lower. A large group of first-wave immigrants circumvented urban centers entirely and either signed on with railroad labor crews or reinvented their old world agricultural lives by forming "compact, stolid, hard-working" farm communities on the Western plains (Spiller et al. 1953: 642). American industrialists and law-makers largely welcomed this first wave, as it supplied workers enough to build a national infrastructure and bodies enough to populate the Western frontier. Conversely, the second wave or "new" immigration transplanted less familiar old world traits to the new world, this time from southern and eastern Europe. As the Irish American author Finley Peter Dunne suggests through his popular character Mr. Dooley, this befuddling new trend defied characterization: " 'Tis diff'rent now," he says, "I don't know why 'tis diff'rent but 'tis diff'rent" (Dunne 2002: 634). They came in alarming numbers – two million east European Jews, five million Italians, and millions more from Austria-Hungary, Ukraine, Poland, Greece, Syria, and other Mediterranean and Slavic jumping-off points. Beginning around 1882, the year the Russian government initiated a series of vicious pogroms against Jewish settlements and the US government simultaneously passed the Chinese Exclusion Act, and ending abruptly in the 1920s, the second wave totaled over twenty million – more than a million a year for over two decades. By 1890 a third of both Boston and New York was foreign-born, and New York alone housed as many Germans as Hamburg, double the number of Irish in Dublin, and two and a half times the number of Jews in Warsaw (Martin 1967: 5): figures that lent new meaning to Walt Whitman's earlier rhapsody of the United States as the "nation of nations."

Only a part of these immigrants were actually from Hamburg, Dublin, or Warsaw, however. Most arrived from rural villages and *shtetl*s, from societies that considered cities morally corrupt and impossibly complex. The future of the United States was no longer one of Manifest Destiny across the continent, but of furthering the twin processes of industrialization and urbanization. As a result, few opportunities remained for the thousands of daily new arrivals to sign on with railroad or land companies and settle the Western plains, as the free land distributed among earlier groups had been inhabited by the 1880s and 1890s (though Western settlement was no holiday, and first-wave immigrants often met with hostile nativist sentiment and environmental disorientation). They schlepped off to the nearest news agent instead and combed the pages of foreign-language presses for lodging and work. They also sought guidance and self-reflection, as Spanish-speaking immigrants from South America might have from the Puerto Rican political exile Pachín Marín's sketch "New York from Within: One Aspect of Its Bohemian Life." This short, passionate piece, which appeared in the separatist newspaper *La Gaceta del Pueblo* in 1892, empathetically, if with a strong dose of irony, addresses a greenhorn Hispanic audience in terms that transcend both its age and Marín's ethnic heritage: "Don't just stand there in perplexed contemplation.... Time is urgent. Walk hurriedly, as if you had the most important business at hand. One must find a friend, a friend or countryman, at all cost. Where? How? Don't you know how?" (1997: 109).

"Outsider" moral reformers throughout this period proliferated horrifying and often tantalizing images of ethnic ghettos in popular sociological treatises like Charles Loring Brace's *The Dangerous Classes of New York* (1872), Helen Campbell's *The Problem of the Poor* (1882), and Jacob Riis's widely read *How the Other Half Lives* (1890). Brace, Campbell, Riis (an assimilated Danish immigrant), and other progressives attempted to improve the conditions of the working poor and at the same time firmly establish ethnic identity as "otherness" in the mainstream American mind. Their conclusions neither flattered their subjects – mainly Irish, east European Jews, Chinese, and African Americans – nor calmed native-born Anglo-Saxons. The rhetoric of reform affirmed the pre-existing view that newly investigated ethnic groups, as their titles imply, were "dangerous," "problematic," and "other," and thus threatened the nation's democratic institutions and economic prosperity from within.

Conversely, a group of liberal-minded idealists, including Hutchins Hapgood, Lincoln Steffens, and William Dean Howells emerged from genteel circles to defend, with varying degrees of sincerity, the cultural legitimacy of the disenfranchised "other." Hapgood, one of the most strident radical voices of the era, regarded this "modern" perspective as a kind of philosophical anarchism: "it means a willingness to receive hospitably whatever dawning forces there may be in the submerged; a refusal to deny their possible validity in a more complex society.... It is deeply sympathetic with the psychology of the underdog" (1939: 277). The muckraking journalist Lincoln Steffens familiarized himself with Manhattan's Jewish Lower East Side so well, in fact, that the British playwright Israel Zangwill chose Steffens as his insider informant in that district (Steffens 1931: 244). Zangwill then returned to London and wrote the now mythic drama of ethnic America, *The Melting Pot* (1908). In other words, perhaps the most resonant immigrant text of the period, whose title entered the American vernacular with terrific force, is a third-hand account from a Gentile source. At the same time, well-known Anglo-Saxon novelists such as Henry Harland, Edward W. Townsend, and Ernest Poole wrote representational fiction about immigrant groups with remarkable success. Poole wrote on the Italians and the Irish to such acclaim that he won the first Pulitzer Prize in 1918.

In his treatise on postbellum American fiction, *Crumbling Idols* (1894), Hamlin Garland railed against the effects of Anglo-Saxon cultural "provincialism," asserting that British cultural influence on the United States was a traditionalist farce perpetuated in the universities, one which precluded the realization of a distinguishable American literary art form. "Provincialism," as Garland defined it, was the "dependence upon a mother country for models of art production," and as such "the history of American literature is the history of provincialism slowly becoming less all-pervasive" (Garland 1894: 7). Of course, this argument had begun much earlier with the Young America movement of the antebellum period, which supported the efforts of Emerson, Hawthorne, Melville, and Whitman to compete with European literary craftsmanship; but in the interest of a "total" view of the American landscape, the realist call for indigenous writing demanded a far broader socio-cultural range. Ethnic realists could ill afford to fool with romantic rhapsodies involving talking birds, transparent eyeballs, witch-meetings, obscure preferences, and bodies electric. Nor were they encouraged to.

One result of avoiding antebellum-style Romanticism was the legitimization of ethnic authorship. Garland professes that in the post-Civil War era "there is the mixture of races; the coming in of the German, the Scandinavian; the marked yet subtle changes in their character . . . the deepening of social contrasts. In short, there is the great heterogeneous, shifting, brave populations, a land teeming with unrecorded and infinite drama" (1894: 15). American literature relied heavily upon this "mixture of races" and its "great heterogeneous, shifting, brave populations." Shifts in ethnic character were "marked yet subtle," neither ethnocentric nor deracinating, changes that literary realists wished to be documented in the new, potentially multicultural literary form. Garland, in his call for an "indigenous literature," argued that "we have had the figures, the dates, the bare history, the dime novel statement of pioneer life, but how few real novels! How few accurate studies of speech and life! There it lies, ready to be put into the novel and the drama, and upon the canvas; and it must be done by those born into it" (p. 16).

The realist movement, then, with its ostensible tenet of all-inclusive representation, enabled traditionally underrepresented groups to demand visibility and participation in the new literary marketplace. Outsiders like Poole, Hapgood, Steffens, and even Zangwill were adept at presenting fairly close representations of ethnic insider worlds, but they could not render faithful ones. The Southern black essayist and activist Anna Julia Cooper, for example, wrote as an insider in 1892 that "the 'other side' has not been represented by one who 'lives there.' And not many can more sensibly realize and more accurately tell the weight and fret of the 'long dull pain' than the open-eyed but hitherto voiceless Black Woman of America" (Cooper 1988: 592). In kind, the Mexican American author María Cristina Mena, whom the *Household Magazine* called the "foremost interpreter of Mexican life," defended the use of cultural detail in her story "John of God, the Water-Carrier" (1913) for *Century* magazine, a conventional organ by all accounts, by submitting to her editor that "American readers, with their intense interest in Mexico, are ripe for a true picture of a people so near to them, so intrinsically picturesque, so misrepresented in current fiction, and so well worthy of being known and loved, in all their ignorance" (quoted in Doherty 1997: xxii). Mena implies that Mexicans are an "ignorant" people, and thus that she, as an educated native Mexican, can draw out their more "picturesque" qualities for an Anglo-Saxon audience. Amy Doherty has argued, however, that because Mena is referring to a pilgrimage to Guadalupe, the scene is more subversive against American interests in Mexico than it may appear, since the protagonist Juan de Dios's "faith in the Virgin of Guadalupe provides strength against U.S. capitalism" (1997: xxiii). Mena's characters often speak in direct translation as well, a technique that accentuates what she calls the "perfume" of her characters' Mexicanness, a scent apprehended only by, as Garland phrased it, "those born into it." In her story "The Birth of the God of War" (1914), Mena's narrator explains that when she tells the *cuentos* (stories) of *mamagrande* (grandmother), "I render the construction literally because it seems to carry more of the perfume that came with these phrases as I heard them by the blue-tiled fountain" (Mena 1997: 65).

Ethnic Americans often enter and subvert mainstream society by means of, not in spite of, ethnic difference in this way, and this trend of pluralistic participation carries over into the publishing world. Robert Park first articulated this ethnicity paradox in the 1910s, and the idea was later developed by Barbara Ballis Lal in the late 1980s (the term "ethnicity paradox" is hers). W. E. B. Du Bois alluded to the paradoxical nature of ethnic identity in *The Souls of Black Folk* (1903) by remarking that the post-Reconstruction American negro "began to have a feeling that, to attain his place in the world, he must be himself, and not another" (Du Bois 1986a: 368). The Anglo-Chinese author Sui Sin Far contemplated the paradox of ethnic authorship in more ironic terms. In her multifaceted autobiographical sketch "Leaves from the Mental Portfolio of an Eurasian" (1909), she wittily recounts a trip to California where she encountered, along with a couple of "broadminded" literary editors "whose interest in me is sincere and intelligent, not affected and vulgar," some

> funny people who advise me to "trade" upon my nationality. They tell me that if I wish to succeed in literature in America I should dress in Chinese costume, carry a fan in my hand, wear a pair of scarlet beaded slippers, live in New York, and come of high birth. Instead of making myself familiar with the Chinese Americans around me, I should discourse on my spirit acquaintance with Chinese ancestors and quote in between the "Good mornings" and "How d'ye dos" of editors. "*Confucius, Confucius, how great is Confucius, Before Confucius, there never was Confucius. After Confucius, there never came Confucius,*" etc., etc., etc., or something like that, both illuminating and obscuring, don't you know. They forget, or perhaps they are not aware that the old Chinese sage taught "The way of sincerity is the way of heaven." (1995b: 230)

Sui Sin Far's sister, the romance novelist Lillie Winifred Eaton, seems not to have shared her sibling's ironic stance toward romantic racialism, as she bizarrely advertised herself as a Japanese noblewoman from Nagasaki named Onoto Watanna. But perhaps this is not so bizarre. Sui Sin Far makes clear that "Americans, having for many years manifested a much higher regard for the Japanese than for the Chinese, several half Chinese young men and women, thinking to advance themselves, both in a social and business sense, pass as Japanese." She theorized that Americans, then, are to blame for such travesties (1995b: 228).

Ethnic writers frequently chose foreign-sounding bylines over "normative" given names to underscore ethnic or racial distinctiveness. In spite of pervasive Sinophobia throughout North America during the 1880s and 1890s, Sui Sin Far, who was an English-bred Canadian named Edith Maud Eaton at birth, published both journalistic and fictional accounts of Chinatown districts in Los Angeles, San Francisco, New York, Montreal, and elsewhere under the pseudonym Sui Sin Far, with the idea of highlighting her "Oriental" roots (her mother was from Shanghai) in order to contest anti-Chinese sentiment from within, while at the same time inducing mainstream periodicals like the *Independent*, *Good Housekeeping*, and *New England Magazine* to publish her work. The second-generation Irish American author Finley Peter Dunne answered to the nickname "Mr. Dooley," the title character of his satiric pieces of dialect commentary, which were assiduously written in a heavy Irish brogue. The half-Sioux realist Gertrude Simmons Bonnin adopted the pen name Zitkala Ša ("Red Bird") in her teens, in "an attempt to assert her own independence and affirm her Indian identity" (Andrews 1992: 413), and she employed it years later as a byline for autobiographical narratives in the *Atlantic Monthly* and short stories in *Harper's* and *Everybody's Magazine*. The Swedish American poet Carl Sandburg introduced himself as "Charles" while a schoolboy, a name he retained until 1908 after marrying the Milwaukee socialist Lilian Paula Steichen. Steichen persuaded her husband to revert back to his given name, Carl, for political reasons, as "Carl" implied foreignness and thus the proletariat. Even the Anglo-Saxon novelist Henry Harland went so far as to publish a series of novels in the 1880s under the Jewish-sounding pseudonym "Sydney Luska," as if he were writing from the merchant class of German Jews. For years Harland dissembled his true identity among Gentiles and Jews alike (Ferraro 1991: 384).

Lincoln Steffens's autobiography provides a rare sociology of the reception for ethnic material; he explains that immigrants lived in a "a queer mixture of comedy, tragedy, orthodoxy, and revelation," and he emphasizes that the mixture "interested our Christian readers" (Steffens 1931: 243). Their stories drew a mainstream audience because the immigrant experience triggered "heart-breaking comedies of the tragic conflict between the old and the new, the very old and the very new; in many matters, all at once: religion, class, clothes, manners, customs, language, culture" (p. 244). As a result, nearly all ethnic realists toggled between fictional narrative, autobiography, and sociology in their fiction. This auto-ethnographic mode humanized the ethnic "other" and belied mainstream type-castes by including straightforward documentary prose to elucidate the realities of ethnic life. I have chosen several texts from which to draw out the "queer mixture" of ethno-racial identity and the migration experience – Finley Peter Dunne's "Immigration" (1902), Abraham Cahan's *Yekl: A Tale of the New York Ghetto* (1896), Paul Laurence Dunbar's *The Sport of the Gods* (1902), Charles Chesnutt's "The Future American" (1900), and Sui Sin Far's autobiographical sketch "Leaves from the Mental Portfolio of an Eurasian" (1909) and two stories from her

collection *Mrs. Spring Fragrance* (1912): Dunne for his reportage of first-wave encounters with the second wave, Cahan for the second-wave perspective, Dunbar for the
early stages of Southern black migration to Northern cities, and Chesnutt and Sui Sin
Far together for their deliberations over their respective biracial balancing acts.

III

Moral reform writers regularly accused Irish Catholics in the late nineteenth century
of agitating a brand of political fanaticism bent on disrupting the already tenuous
American democratic process. Not only were they an apparent threat to the cities, but
the slums began hemorrhaging Irish families into the countryside as well. Helen
Campbell professed in her waterfront exposé *The Problem of the Poor* (1882) that Irish
immigrants "form a larger portion" of her titular problem, whereas "German or
French paupers [are] almost an anomaly." She upholds the prevailing Protestant
American view that Irish Catholics as a group, once in the United States, abandoned
any redeeming qualities they might have had in the old world:

> They are a class apart, retaining all the most brutal characteristics of the Irish peasant at
> home, but without the redeeming lightheartedness, the tender impulses and strong
> affections of that most perplexing people. Sullen, malicious, conscienceless, with no
> capacity for enjoyment save in drink and the lowest forms of debauchery, they are filling
> our prisons and reformatories, marching in an ever-increasing army through the quiet
> country, and making a reign of terror wherever their footsteps are heard. (Campbell
> 1882: 215)

The pioneering Irish American realist Finley Peter Dunne responded to Campbell's
variety of righteous Anglo-Protestant ire by turning old-world "lightheartedness"
against nativist vitriol. Dunne's immensely popular "Mr. Dooley" columns appeared
for over a decade in the *Chicago Evening Post*, and numerous collections followed. The
first Irish dialect character to transcend the mockery of early American stage Irish,
Dunne's fictional bar-room philosopher Mr. Dooley talked, as Dunne characterized
Dooley's dialogue in an 1899 interview with *Bookman* magazine, "as an Irishman
would talk who has lived thirty or forty years in America, and whose natural
pronunciation had been more or less affected by the slang of the streets" (quoted in
Fanning 1987: xix). Dunne was a master of dialect writing, and through dialect he
captured the absurdity of, among many other issues, anti-immigrant sentiment by
Irish Americans who were themselves born of immigrant families, as he was in 1867,
but wished to distance themselves from marginalizing racial and political affiliations.

    In Dunne's sketch "Immigration" (1902), Martin Dooley sits, as always, behind the
bar of his pub in the predominantly Irish Bridgeport section of Chicago's South Side.
Across the bar is a plainspoken regular, the millworker Malachi Hennessey. The
subject of the afternoon, as the title implies, is immigration. Dooley recounts his

first few months stateside when nativist factions in Chicago violently attacked him at
a St. Patrick's Day parade, burned down Irish Catholic churches, and treated him
unfairly at his first menial job. Early arrivals, Protestant, Catholic, or otherwise,
addressed him with the air of "pilgrim fathers," each on the dubious authority that
their "grandfathers had bate me to th' dock" (Dunne 2002: 634). Immigrants who
successfully triumphed over the environmental forces faced by new immigrants often
chose to dissent from their ancestral roots to avoid associations with urban unpleas-
antness, a theme one also finds in the works of Sui Sin Far, Abraham Cahan, and
Sidney Nyburg, among others.

Dooley's first job was in street excavation, and he recalls that "th' pilgrim father
who bossed th' job was a fine ol' puritan be th' name iv Doherty, who come over in th'
Mayflower about th' time iv the potato rot in Wexford" (Dunne 2002: 634). Dooley
admits that nativist abuses subsided soon after his arrival, partly because "before I was
here a month, I felt enough like a native born to burn a witch" and partly because the
anti-immigrant mobs found their assaults "too much like wurruck" (p. 634). Dooley
continues in the satiric vein to note that many immigrants after living in the United
States for more than a month claim the moral high ground of American families
whose bloodlines go back to the Puritans, themselves an immigrant group. To drive
the point home, he recounts a conversation with his friend Shaughnessy the previous
day. Shaughnessy, like many first-wave immigrants, ironically echoes nativist rhetoric
like Campbell's, regarding the second wave as "dangerous," "arnychists," "th' off-
scourin's iv Europe." True to form, the philosopher Dooley apprehends a mordant
comedy in the situation:

> " 'Tis time we done something to make th' immigration laws sthronger," says he
> [Shaughnessy]. "Thrue f'r ye, Miles Standish," says I; "but what wud ye do? . . . if
> immigrants is as dangerous to this country as ye an' I an' other pilgrim fathers believe
> they are, they'se enough iv' thim sneaked in already to make us aborigines about as
> infloointial as the prohibition vote in th' Twenty-ninth Ward." (p. 634)

Dooley compares the "arnychist" tendencies of the east Europeans — "There's
warrants out f'r all names endin' in 'inski" (Dunne 2002: 635) — with violent Irish
responses to British aristocracy, making Irish Americans hypocrites if they discriminate against east Europeans for their political views: "if we'd begun a few years ago
shuttin' out folks that wudden't mind handin' a bomb to a king, they wudden't be
enough people in Mattsachoosetts to make a quorum f'r th' Anti-Impeeryal S'ciety,"
"An' so," he says, "th' meetin' iv th' Plymouth Rock Assocyation come to an end"
(p. 635). Dunne achieves ethnic realism's singular unaffectedness in that he rises above
both degrading stereotypes and romantic idealization and depicts the Irish point of
view with a sobriety few outsiders wished to pursue — "no one but an Irish-American,"
William Dean Howells wrote, "could have invented such an Irish-American [as
Dooley], or have invested his sayings with such racial and personal richness" (quoted
in Fanning 1987: xxii).

Like Dunne with the Irish, the Jewish American author, labor leader, and editor of the *Jewish Daily Forward* Abraham Cahan freed his Jewish characters from the roles assigned them by Gentile and other immigrant caricaturists of the period. Lincoln Steffens hired Cahan, already a minor celebrity, in 1897 as a reporter for the New York *Daily Commercial Advertiser*. Cahan found himself alone in a crowd of privileged Gentiles, most of them hand-picked Harvard University graduates. By this time in his early forties, Cahan had already spent the previous twenty years or so covering the Jewish Lower East Side as a reporter and editor for the Yiddish papers. The sketches that Cahan produced for the *Commercial Advertiser* were more informative than literary, but his fiction moved beyond the sociology of his journalistic sketches as, along with the trials of ghetto life, it embraced a more inclusive range of aspects of the human experience. Hutchins Hapgood emphasized the importance of distinguishing Cahan's literary prowess from his social commentary in his book-length study of Jewish New York, *The Spirit of the Ghetto* (1902):

> If [Abraham] Cahan's work were merely the transcribing in fiction form of a great number of suggestive and curious "points" about the life of the poor Russian Jew in New York, it would not of course have any great interest to even the cultivated Anglo-Saxon reader, who, tho he might find the stories curious and amusing for a time, would recognize nothing in them sufficiently familiar to be of deep importance to him. If, in other words, the stories had lacked the universal element always present in true literature they would have been of very little value to anyone except the student of queer corners. (Hapgood 1967: 237)

Hapgood suggests that Cahan's stories inform the reader about the inherent truths of the Jewish quarter, while at the same time rendering those truths "sympathetic by the touch of common human nature" (1967: 237).

When Cahan first introduces his character Jake in the short novel *Yekl* (1896), later made into the film *Hester Street* (1974), Jake is relating a professional boxing match to a group of fellow sweatshop workers. The conspicuously working-class anecdote is secondary to Jake's desire to show off his knowledge of the American vernacular. Cahan invites the audience here, along with Jake's colleagues, to register the absurdity of Jake's attempt at pure assimilation:

> "Why, don't you know? Jimmie Corbett *leaked* him, and Jimmie *leaked* Cholly Meet-chel, too. *You can betch you' bootsh!* Johnny could not leak Chollie, *becaush* he is big *bluffer*, Chollie is," he pursued, his clean-shaven florid face beaming with enthusiasm for his subject, and with pride in the diminutive proper nouns he flaunted. "But Jimmie *punished* him. *oh, didn't he knock him out off shight!* He came near making a meat ball of him." (Cahan 1970: 2)

Jake *should* take pride in his language exercises, but his attempts serve more to draw attention to his Yiddish linguistic roots than his potential Americanization.

The impact of Cahan's commentary makes the dramatic irony of the situation more unnerving than funny, though Jake's dialogue would have met with big laughs on the popular stage.

Jake strikes up a relationship with Mamie, an "Americanized" young woman whose flamboyant dress and manners, along with her outspoken contempt for "greenhorns," persuades him to reject his Semitic heritage. Nevertheless, he honors his commitment to send for his wife Gitl and son Yossele. Upon their meeting at Ellis Island, however, Jake's heart sinks "at the sight of his wife's uncouth and un-American appearance." Gitl is equally disappointed, and "she felt like crying to the image [of three years before] to come back to her and let her be *his* wife" (Cahan 1970: 36). Gitl initially revolts from the unorthodox lifestyle of American Jews, but she recognizes over time that for her and Yossele to survive in the new world they must shed socially limiting traditions, while at the same time maintaining some old-world values that are critical for survival in a foreign land. In the end she divorces Jake, who has indiscriminately Americanized himself into self-destruction, and decides to marry a more cautious immigrant, Mr. Bernstein, who has both conviction in his Semitic teachings and the ability to adapt himself to the requirements of his new environment. We are told that Gitl and her new husband, profiting from a divorce that would have been unthinkable had they remained in Russia, will open a grocery store. They, not the fully assimilated Jake, will realize their American dream. By the end of the novel, "the rustic 'greenhornlike' expression was completely gone from her face and manner, and . . . there was noticeable about her a suggestion of that peculiar air of self-confidence with which a few months life in America is sure to stamp the looks and bearing of every immigrant" (p. 83).

Cahan's self-professed influences – Tolstoy, Turgenev, Dostoevsky, and Henry James – were the same authors whose art helped drive the realist movement forward in the United States. Much of American realism was Russian-born, like so many of Cahan's subjects in the ghetto, and this fact was not lost on the Dean of American letters. William Dean Howells praised Cahan in a New York *World* review, side by side with Stephen Crane, as "a new star of realism" (quoted in Richards 1970: vii) and significantly remarked in the 31 December 1898 issue of *Literature* that "it will be interesting to see whether Mr. Cahan will pass beyond his present environment out into the larger American world, or will master our life as he mastered our language. But of a Jew, who is also Russian, what artistic triumph may not we expect?" (quoted in Richards 1970: vii). Cahan's career, as it turns out, was not destined for the "artistic triumph" Howells imagined, that of passing from his "present environment out into the larger American world." Indeed, there is no indication he ever planned to do so. Cahan understood, perhaps earlier than the rest, that what W. E. B. Du Bois called the "kingdom of culture" (1986a: 365) was insufficient to combat the period's racial and ethnic injustices, nor was the country at large ready for substantial modification.

Anglo-Saxon bohemians from privileged backgrounds actively sought cross-cultural experiences in Irish, Jewish, and Italian enclaves, but for the most part circumvented cross-racial contact. Carrie Tirado Bramen makes it clear that if

Figure 18.1   "Yearning to be free"

This photograph by Edwin Levick, taken on December 10, 1906, shows hundreds of European immigrants packed into steerage aboard the SS *Patricia* on their way to America. The period from 1905 to 1914 was the zenith of US immigration: in these years 10,121,940 people officially arrived, nearly three-quarters of them from southern and eastern Europe. Before 1882, modernization in western and northern Europe had led to an excess rural population that was available for emigration, but toward the end of the century this process had spread both south and east, and it was from the latter areas that most of the immigrants of these years came. In addition, specific events caused people to leave Europe: just as the potato blight and famine in Ireland had led to the huge Irish emigration in the mid-1840s, so the increasingly intense and frequent pogroms in Poland and Russia after 1881 led to the large-scale emigration of Jews, and the severe cholera epidemic in southern Italy compelled survivors to seek escape. Emigration was global, with almost a third of European emigrants going to places other than the United States, including South America, Australia, Canada, and Mexico. Immigration to the United States waxed and waned partly in response to specific developments there, particularly the boom and bust cycles of the US economy. And many emigrants simply went wherever the ship they embarked on took them.

All immigrants, as historian Oscar Handlin has shown, went through five disorienting stages in their journey. First was the challenging travel on foot from the local village to a large port of embarkation; then the difficulty of dealing with urban hucksters who often robbed or cheated them of their fare; then the crossing in the cramped quarters of steerage on a ship; then the debarkation in a strange new city like New York where they knew neither the customs nor the language; and finally the difficult business of finding employment and a place to live. Many gave up somewhere along the way; others returned to their homelands after disappointing experiences in the new world. (Photograph by permission of Picture History.)

immigrants like Gitl and Mr. Dooley were "colorful" at the turn of the twentieth century, African Americans were just "colored" (Bramen 2002: 470). Bramen correctly cites white supremacy for this exclusion, but we must also take into account the minuscule black population in the North at that time, an admittedly banal demographic fact that in part explains why canonical realists – Stephen Crane, Henry James, Edith Wharton – almost never included black characters in their urban fiction. The centers of African American life in New York, for example, were located in the black sections of the Tenderloin and San Juan Hill, areas which combined took up no more than fifteen blocks. Aside from a few thrill-seeking reporters, the only literary investigators who explored those areas were black migrants themselves.

Paul Laurence Dunbar's naturalistic novel *The Sport of the Gods* (1902) derived from Dunbar's Manhattan years in the late 1890s, when he co-wrote and produced a number of lucrative Broadway musicals and vaudeville shows. Set in the Tenderloin, located just southwest of the Broadway theater district, the novel's New York chapters explore the gambling, drinking, and ragtime music offered in what James Weldon Johnson later coined the "black Bohemia" of the 1890s (1990: 82; 1991: 73). The novel has as much to say about migration as about race, if not more – the Southern black population in New York might as well have been from the west coast of Ireland or a hilltop village in western Russia. For one thing, they too saw the city in the typological framework of a "Promised Land" (see Sollors 1986: ch. 2, on "typology"). The city itself is a fiction in this novel, and thus Dunbar unveils an illusion within an illusion that renders Southern blacks helpless in the face of painful dislocation. As such, the novel's protagonist, the guileless country boy Joe Hamilton, evolves from well-meaning son and brother to gambling addict, violent drunk, and murderer. One character sums up the consequences of Southern black migration this way: "Oh, is there no way to keep these people from rushing away from the small villages and country districts of the South up to the cities, where they cannot battle with the terrible force of a strange and unusual environment?" (160)

New Yorkers, both black and white, regarded the handful of Southern black migrants in their city as "rovers," "wanderers," "vagrants," "a hoodlum element," "criminals in search of a sporting life" (Osofsky 1968: 21). Dunbar shows in *The Sport of the Gods* that this discrimination is largely the result of the Southerners' tendency to convert themselves in a matter of months, like Dunne's "pilgrim fathers" and Cahan's Jake, into caricatures of urbanity, rejecting the positive moral foundation of the rural South – the family, the church, the local community – for the attitudes and ways of the fashionable New York sporting set. He classifies these migrants into two categories: the wise and the foolish. The wise will recognize their love for the great metropolis, but eventually escape: "he will go away, any place – yes, he will even go over to New Jersey." The fools, of course, remain:

They will stay and stay on until the town becomes all in all to him; until the very streets are his chums and certain buildings and corners his best friends. Then he is hopeless, and to live elsewhere would be death. The Bowery will be his romance, Broadway his lyric, and the park his pastoral, the river and the glory of it all his epic, and he will look down pityingly on the rest of humanity. (Dunbar 1999: 47)

By identifying New York's most famous offerings with traditional literary genres – the romance, the lyric, the pastoral, and the epic – Dunbar demonstrates how popular conceptions of New York belie its corruption, as fiction belies the reality it represents, and he illustrates its false representation in the Southern black consciousness: "They had heard of New York as a place vague and far away, a city that, like heaven, to them had existed by faith alone. All the days of their lives they had heard of it, and it seemed to them the centre of all the glory, all the wealth, and all the freedom of the world. New York. It had an alluring sound" (Dunbar 1999: 43–4). The city tantalizes rural migrants and crushes their moral will – just as it does in *Social Strugglers* (1893), the migration novel in which the Norse American realist and critic Hjalmar Hjorth Boyesen considers these same themes from the Scandinavian Midwestern perspective.

Dunbar's post-Reconstruction South is ironically superior to the Northern city, regardless of the injustices dealt to postbellum African Americans at the hands of Jim Crow. "[T]he South has its faults – no one condones them – and its disadvantages," he writes, "but . . . even what [migrants] suffered from there was better than what awaited them in the great alleys of New York" (Dunbar 1999: 122–3). The Great Migration of Southern blacks to the North was less than two decades away, and Dunbar concludes that Southern blacks should beware of "the pernicious influence of the city on untrained Negroes" (p. 122). Dunbar never lived to see the Great Migration or the New Negro Renaissance of the 1920s, dying young in 1906, but no doubt he would have read those events as fictions within fictions, just as doomed, in the short run at least, as his own, less romanticized black Bohemia downtown.

Dunbar's novel at last offered the white imagination an insider's view of black migrant life – as one reviewer importantly asked, "Do we ever think of how such people live? It is a . . . whole stratum of society of which all of us are densely ignorant and of whose very existence most of us are wholly unaware" (quoted in Osofsky 1968: 41). Similarly, William Dean Howells applauded the mulatto Charles Chesnutt's fiction for expanding the context of American race writing: "We had known the nethermost world of the grotesque and the comical negro and the terrible and tragic negro through the white observer on the outside, and black character in its lyrical moods from such an inside witness as Mr. Paul Dunbar; but it had remained for Mr. Chesnutt to acquaint us with those regions where the paler shades dwell as hopelessly, with relation to ourselves, as the blackest negro" (Howells 1900: 701). Anne Fleischmann has convincingly argued that prominent scholars focus unwisely on Chesnutt's blackness, making them complicit with the US Supreme Court's *Plessy* v. *Ferguson* verdict (1896), which legitimized Jim Crow segregation laws, since "mulatto" was a category *Plessy* officially expunged (2000: 245–6). But Howells made a similar argument over a century ago. Along with Chesnutt's contributions to "good art," it was the author's identity as a mulatto, rather than a black like Dunbar, that lent added significance to his contributions to American realism.

Chesnutt straddled the color line in complicated ways, and if Howells saw Chesnutt as a mixed-race author dwelling as hopelessly as the blackest negro, Du Bois gazed at Chesnutt from the opposite side of the line: "Chesnutt was of that group of white folk who because of a more or less remote Negro ancestor identified himself voluntarily with the darker group, studied them, expressed them, defended them, and yet never forgot the absurdity of this artificial position and always refused to admit its logic or its ethical sanction" (Du Bois 1986b: 1234). The ambiguity of this cross-racial discourse caused psychological identity crises among products of assimilation and miscegenation like Chesnutt and other marginal figures. "I am neither fish, flesh, nor fowl," he lamented in 1881, "neither 'nigger,' white, nor 'buckrah.' Too 'stuck-up' for the colored folks, and, of course, not recognized by the whites" (Chesnutt 1993: 157). Rather than climbing the racial ladder toward whiteness and away from blackness through miscegenation, Chesnutt felt that *all* shades should merge into one. His notorious essay "The Future American" (1900) makes the controversial assertion (even by contemporary standards) that for race no longer to exist as a destructive category, the black, white, and indigenous American races must and most likely will cross-pollinate into one American racial amalgamation. The essay appeared in three installments with titles meant to provoke a discourse: "What the Race is Likely to Become in the Process of Time," "A Stream of Dark Blood in the Veins of Southern Whites," and "A Complete Race-Amalgamation Likely to Occur." In the last of these, Chesnutt arrives at the conclusion that "there can manifestly be no such thing as a peaceful and progressive civilization in a nation divided by two warring races, and homogeneity of type, at least in externals, is a necessary condition of harmonious progress" (Chesnutt 2002a: 862).

Sui Sin Far concurred with Chesnutt's notion of peace and progress through miscegenation, specifically in the context of her personal experience, caught between competing national and racial identities: "I have no nationality and am not anxious to claim any. Individuality is more than nationality. 'You are you and I am I,' says Confucius. I give my right hand to the Occidentals and my left to the Orientals, hoping that between them they will not utterly destroy the insignificant 'connecting link'" (1995b: 230). One of Sui Sin Far's editors, Charles Lummis, himself an ethnographer, praised the humanizing quality of her work, professing that "to others, the alien Celestial is at best mere 'literary material'; in [Sui Sin Far's] stories he (or she) is a human being" (quoted in Tonkovich 2000: 99). Though she avoided marriage, most likely fearing the stigma attached to a mixed-race woman marrying either a Chinese or an Anglo-Saxon, she bolstered Chesnutt's radical deracination, but this time on a global scale: "Fundamentally, I muse, all people are the same. My mother's race [Chinese] is as prejudiced as my father's [Anglo-Saxon]. Only when the whole world becomes as one family will human beings be able to see clearly and hear distinctly. I believe that some day a great part of the world will become Eurasian"

(1995b: 223–4). Two of her stories "Her Chinese Husband" and "The Story of One White Woman Who Married a Chinese," which originally appeared in the *Independent* in 1910 and were later published in her collection of short stories *Mrs. Spring Fragrance* (1912), show the complexity of amalgamation and deal with the issue of "passing" and miscegenation in unorthodox ways. Her white character, Minnie, divorces her first, white husband, who performed a cruel sexist leverage in the partnership, and soon after marries a kind, respectful Chinese man. She bears a son, and though her husband, Liu Kanghi, looks upon their child as a "future American" – "he will fear none and, after him, the name of half-breed will no longer be one of contempt" (1995a: 82) – Minnie is less hopeful of her son's future: "if there is no kindliness nor understanding between [the races], what will my boy's fate be?" (1995c: 77). Sui Sin Far further alludes to the complexities of race amalgamation and conflict by making her nurse in the pregnancy a "mulatto Jewess" and concluding her story with Liu Kanghi's assassination by a group of racist Chinese Americans.

Sui Sin Far, who could "pass" with impunity, identified more with black servants she met in the Caribbean than with the Anglo-Saxon blood on her father's side. "I too am of the 'brown people' of the earth" (1995b: 225). Her interracial identity was further complicated in California, for in that state "it is not difficult . . . for a half-Chinese, half white girl to pass as one of Spanish or Mexican origin" (p. 227). Nevertheless, Sui Sin Far openly identified herself as Chinese in uncomfortable Anglo-Saxon settings, as her ethnic pride endowed her (and by association her peers) with personal strength in a hostile social atmosphere. At the dinner table of one of her employers, where no one was conscious of her mixed-race identity, a conversation took place in which they summed up the Sinophobic attitude of the times: "[Chinese] faces seem so utterly devoid of expression"; "A Chinaman is . . . more repulsive than a nigger"; "They always give me a creepy feeling"; "I wouldn't have one in my house." The question naturally came up – "what makes Miss Far so quiet?" – to which she replied, "the Chinese people may have no souls, no expression on their faces, be altogether beyond the pale of civilization, but whatever they are, I want you to understand that I am – I am a Chinese" (pp. 224–5).

New immigrants, African Americans, and Native tribes could hardly rely on artistic achievement, the realist movement, and the sponsorship of people like Steffens, Hapgood, and Howells in their effort to gain democratic participation and empathy from the larger "Anglo-Saxon" America. Literature alone could never ac-complish the egalitarian policies these authors and their advocates championed. Co-working in the "kingdom of culture," as W. E. B. Du Bois discovered some time after the publication of *The Souls of Black Folk*, meant co-working in the kingdom of the Anglo-Saxon marketplace as well. And by 1914, nearly all ethnic realists became political activists in the fiefdoms of public policy instead. As Werner Sollors has shown, when we compare James Weldon Johnson's *The Autobiography of an Ex-Coloured Man* (1912) and Abraham Cahan's second novel *The Rise of David Levinsky* (1917) to their authors' actual biographies, *Along This Way: The Autobiography of James Weldon Johnson* (1933) and *The Education of Abraham Cahan* (1926), we find that both authors' fictions portray the "external rise [of their narrators] as an internal fall" (Sollors 1986: 171). By contrast, rather than passing, as their fictional narrators do, into an assimilated "American world," in actual life Cahan and Johnson emphasized their ethno-racial status in the interest of political activism. Cahan upheld his role as a socialist leader and editor of the *Jewish Daily Forward*, the mainstay of the Yiddish-language press, and stood by his work as a proponent of immigrant communities and the labor movement to his death in 1951. Johnson became the national organizer of the National Association for the Advancement of Colored People (NAACP) in 1916, and within four years expanded the association from one that employed three full-time staff members and a membership of under 9,000 to one that boasted 44,000 members and 165 branches nationwide. Four years later, he became the first African American to head the NAACP.

Indeed, the historical record reveals that along with Cahan and Johnson, few early ethnic writers who survived into the 1920s chose assimilation over ethnic cohesion, regardless of their potential to "pass" into the American mainstream, and most abandoned fiction writing altogether. Sui Sin Far, who could easily pass as white, chose instead to defend the human rights of North American Asians in a series of sociological feature stories in prominent American and Canadian newspapers. "The Chinese in America," one Chinese reporter wrote, "owe an everlasting debt of gratitude to Sui Sin Far for the bold stand she has taken in their defense" (quoted in Sui Sin Far 1995b: 223). Charles Chesnutt, who could have just as easily "passed," regularly addressed local and national audiences on the future of African Americans. He was an active member of George Washington Cable's Open-Letter Club for aiding the South in the post-Reconstruction era, and he sat on the General Committee of the NAACP and Washington's Committee of Twelve for the Advancement of the Interests of the Negro Race. In 1928 the NAACP awarded Chesnutt the esteemed Spingarn Medal for his significant literary and political achievements. Zitkala Ša accepted a commission by the Indian Rights Association to scrutinize the federal government's policies toward the Oklahoma tribes, and she subsequently co-authored *Oklahoma's Poor Rich Indians* in 1924, the year Native Americans received American citizenship. Two years later, she founded the National Council of American Indians, and served as president of that political lobbying group until her death in 1938.

Ethnic American literature achieved formation, not fruition, at the turn of the twentieth century. Immigrants in particular only fully impacted American cultural production when they turned to the earliest venues of the mass media — vaudeville, music, silent film, and radio — as current scholarship by Marc Dolan will soon show. The golden age of ethnic "insider" writing took place in the 1920s, 1930s, and early 1940s. In these years between the world wars, the Norse American novelist Ole Edvart Rölvaag; the Korean American novelist Younghill Kang; Jewish American authors Anzia Yezierska, Mike Gold, and Henry Roth; contributors to Harlem's New Negro Renaissance, Langston Hughes, Jean Toomer, Claude McKay, and Zora Neale Hurston; and later Italian American novelists John Fante, Mari Tomasi, and Pietro DiDonato — all rose up and employed ethnic difference, in part, as a political tool to defend their groups' legitimate place in a democratic society. Rölvaag's *Giants in the Earth* (1927), Roth's *Call It Sleep* (1934), Hurston's *Their Eyes Were Watching God* (1937), and DiDonato's *Christ in Concrete* (1939) rightfully emerged as classics of American literature in the last two decades of the twentieth century, but their inclusion expands the canon of modernism, in truth, more than that of realism. Ultimately, what ethnic realists took away from their experiences in the Anglo literary marketplace, and passed on to the brimming new generation of modernists, was that being "themselves and not another" was invaluable for achieving their rightful legitimacy in "Anglo-Saxon" America.

PRIMARY TEXTS

Boyesen, Hjalmar Hjorth. *Social Strugglers*. 1893.

Cahan, Abraham. *Yekl: A Tale of the New York Ghetto*. 1896.

Cahan, Abraham. *The Imported Bridegroom and Other Stories of New York*. 1898.

Chesnutt, Charles W. "The Future American." 1900.

Chesnutt, Charles W. "Post-Bellum – Pre-Harlem." 1931.

Cooper, Anna Julia. *A Voice from the South: By a Black Woman of the South*. 1892.

Du Bois, W. E. B. *The Souls of Black Folk*. 1903.

Du Bois, W. E. B. "Chesnutt." 1933.

Dunbar, Paul Laurence. *The Sport of the Gods*. 1902.

Dunne, Finley Peter. "Immigration." 1902.

Garland, Hamlin. *Crumbling Idols: Twelve Essays on Art Dealing Chiefly with Literature, Painting and the Drama*. 1894.

Hapgood, Hutchins. *The Spirit of the Ghetto*. 1902.

Howells, William Dean. "New York Low Life in Fiction." 1896.

Howells, William Dean. "Mr. Charles W. Chesnutt's Stories." 1900.

Johnson, James Weldon. *The Autobiography of an Ex-Colored Man*. 1912.

Johnson, James Weldon. *Black Manhattan*. 1930.

Johnson, James Weldon. *Along This Way: The Autobiography of James Weldon Johnson*. 1933.

Mena, María Christina. "John of God, the Water-Carrier." 1913.

Mena, María Christina. "The Birth of the God of War." 1914.

Sui Sin Far. "Leaves from the Mental Portfolio of an Eurasian." 1909.

Sui Sin Far. "Her Chinese Husband." 1910.

Sui Sin Far. "The Story of One White Woman Who Married a Chinese." 1910.

Sui Sin Far. *Mrs. Spring Fragrance and Other Stories*. 1912.

REFERENCES AND FURTHER READING

Andrews, William L. (1992). "Zitkala Sa (Gertrude Bonnin)." In William L. Andrews (ed.), *Classic American Autobiographies*, 413–14. New York: Mentor.

Bramen, Carrie Tirado (2002). "The Urban Picturesque and the Spectacle of Americanization." *American Quarterly* 52: 3 (Sept.), 444–77.

Cahan, Abraham (1970). *Yekl and the Imported Bridegroom and Other Stories of Yiddish New York*, intr. Bernard G. Richards. New York: Dover.

Campbell, Helen (1882). *The Problem of the Poor: A Record of Quiet Work in Unquiet Places*. New York: Fords, Howard, & Hulbert.

Chesnutt, Charles W. (1993). *The Journals of Charles W. Chesnutt*, ed. Richard H. Brodhead. Durham, NC: Duke University Press.

Chesnutt, Charles W. (2002a). "The Future American." In *Chesnutt: Stories, Novels, and Essays*, ed. Werner Sollors, 845–63. New York: Library of America.

Cooper, Anna Julia (1988). *A Voice from the South: By a Black Woman of the South*, ed. Mary Helen Washington. Oxford and New York: Oxford University Press. (Schomburg Library of Nineteenth-Century Black Women Writers, gen. ed. Henry Louis Gates.)

Doherty, Amy, ed. (1997). "Introduction." In *The Collected Stories of Maria Christina Mena*, vii–l. Houston: Arte Publico (Recovering the US Hispanic Literary Heritage Series).

Du Bois, W. E. B. (1986a). *The Souls of Black Folk*. In *Du Bois: Writings*, ed. Nathan Huggins, 357–547. New York: Library of America.

Du Bois, W. E. B. (1986b). "Chesnutt." In *Du Bois: Writings*, ed. Nathan Huggins, 1234–5. New York: Library of America.

Dunbar, Paul Laurence (1999). *The Sport of the Gods*, intr. William L. Andrews. New York: Signet Classics.

Dunne, Finley Peter (2002). "Immigration." In Paul Lauter (gen. ed.), *The Heath Anthology of American Literature*, 4th edn., vol. 2, 633–6. New York: Houghton Mifflin.

Fanning, Charles (1987). "Introduction." In *Mr. Dooley and the Chicago Irish: The Autobiography of a Nineteenth-Century Ethnic Group*, xiii–xxvii. Washington DC: Catholic University of America Press. (First publ. 1976.)

Ferraro, Thomas J. (1991). "Ethnicity and the Marketplace." In Emory Elliot (gen. ed.), *The Columbia History of the American Novel*, 380–406. New York: Columbia University Press.

Fleischmann, Anne (2000). "Neither Fish, Flesh, Nor Fowl: Race and Region in the Writings of Charles W. Chesnutt." In Amritjit Singh and Peter Schmidt (eds.), *Postcolonial Theory and the United States: Race, Ethnicity, and Literature*, 244–57. Jackson: University of Mississippi Press.

Garland, Hamlin (1894). *Crumbling Idols: Twelve Essays on Art Dealing Chiefly with Literature, Painting and the Drama*. Chicago: Stone & Kimball.

Hapgood, Hutchins (1967). *The Spirit of the Ghetto*, ed. Moses Rischin. Cambridge, Mass.: Belknap/Harvard University Press.

Hapgood, Hutchins (1972). *A Victorian in the Modern World*, ed. and intr. Robert Allen Skotheim. Seattle: University of Washington Press. (First publ. 1939.)

Howells, William Dean (1900). "Mr. Charles W. Chesnutt's Stories." *Atlantic Monthly* (May), 699–701.

Johnson, James Weldon (1990). *The Autobiography of an Ex-Colored Man*, intr. William L. Andrews. New York: Penguin.

Johnson, James Weldon (1991). *Black Manhattan*. New York: Da Capo.

Lal, Barbara Ballis (1990). *The Romance of Culture in an Urban Civilization: Robert E. Park on Race and Ethnic Relations in the Cities*. New York: Routledge.

Lowell, Amy (1917). *Tendencies in Modern American Poetry*. New York: Macmillan.

Mayo-Smith, Richmond, and Ingraham, Thomas Allan (1911). "Migration." *Encyclopedia Britannica*, 11th edn., vol. 18, 431–3. London: Britannica.

Marín, Pachín (1997). "New York from Within: One Aspect of its Bohemian Life." In Harold Augenbraum and Margarite Fernández Olmos (eds.), *The Latino Reader: An American Literary Tradition from 1542 to the Present*, 108–11. New York: Houghton Mifflin.

Martin, Jay (1967). *Harvests of Change: American Literature, 1865–1914*. Englewood Cliffs, NJ: Prentice-Hall.

Mena, María Christina (1997). "The Birth of the God of War." In *The Collected Stories of Maria Christina Mena*, ed. Amy Doherty, 63–9. Houston: Arte Publico (Recovering the US Hispanic Literary Heritage Series).

Mencken, H. L. (1982). "On Being an American." In Huntington Cairns (ed.), *The American Scene: A Reader*, 6–38. New York: Vintage.

Mencken, H. L. (1987). "The Negro as Author." In William H. Nolte (ed.), *H. L. Mencken's Smart Set Criticism*, 320–2. Washington DC: Regnery.

Osofsky, Gilbert (1968). *Harlem: The Making of a Ghetto, Negro New York, 1890–1930*. New York: Harper Torchbooks. (First publ. 1963.)

Richards, Bernard G. (1970). "Introduction: Abraham Cahan Cast in a New Role." In *Yekl and the Imported Bridegroom and Other Stories of the New York Ghetto*, iii–viii. New York: Dover.

Singh, Amritjit, and Schmidt, Peter, eds. (2000). *Postcolonial Theory and the United States: Race, Ethnicity, and Literature*. Jackson: University of Mississippi Press.

Sollors, Werner (1986). *Beyond Ethnicity: Consent and Descent in American Culture*. New York: Oxford University Press.

Sollors, Werner (1997). *Neither Black Nor White But Both: Thematic Explorations of Interracial Literature*. New York: Oxford University Press.

Sollors, Werner, ed. (1996). *Theories of Ethnicity: A Classical Reader*. New York: New York University Press.

Spiller, Robert E.; Thorp, Willard; et al., eds. (1953). *Literary History of the United States*, 4th rev. edn., vol. 1. New York: Macmillan. (First publ. 1946.)

Steffens, Lincoln (1931). *The Autobiography of Lincoln Steffens*. New York: Harcourt, Brace, & Co.

Sui Sin Far (1995a). "Her Chinese Husband." In *Mrs. Spring Fragrance and Other Stories*, ed. Amy Ling and Annette White-Parks, 78–83. Urbana and Chicago: University of Illinois Press.

Sui Sin Far (1995b). "Leaves from the Mental Portfolio of an Eurasian." In *Mrs. Spring Fragrance and Other Stories*, ed. Amy Ling and Annette White-Parks, 218–30. Urbana and Chicago: University of Illinois Press.

Sui Sin Far (1995c). "The Story of One White Woman Who Married a Chinese." In *Mrs. Spring Fragrance and Other Stories*, ed. Amy Ling and Annette White-Parks, 66–77. Urbana and Chicago: University of Illinois Press.

Tonkovich, Nicole (2000). "Edith Maud Eaton (Sui Sin Far)." In *Dictionary of Literary Biography: American Women Prose Writers, 1870–1920*, vol. 221, 91–102. Detroit: Gale Group.

19
Darwin, Science, and Narrative
Bert Bender

Responding to developments in early nineteenth-century science, particularly Jean Baptiste Lamarck's theory of evolution and Charles Lyell's *Principles of Geology* (1830–3), writers such as Emerson, Thoreau, and Melville questioned traditional conceptions of the Creation and embraced versions of natural theology or transcendental evolution. But "the greatest of all scientific revolutions" began in 1859, with the publication of Charles Darwin's *On the Origin of Species* (Mayr 1982: 501). That cataclysmic event soon produced great aftershocks in Lyell's *The Antiquity of Man* (1863), Thomas Henry Huxley's *Man's Place in Nature* (1863), and, most profoundly, Darwin's *The Descent of Man, and Selection in Relation to Sex* (1871) and *The Expression of the Emotions in Man and Animals* (1872). As Sigmund Freud would put it some years later, Darwin had dealt a great "*biological* blow to human narcissism," compelling humankind to contemplate its place within the community of common descent (1953–74: vol. 17, 141). The biological blow was first felt as a wound to the spirit, when the *Origin of Species* sparked the heated debate over whether we are apes or angels. But by around 1870 that debate had cooled, and the "overarching . . . supernatural presence" once envisioned by the American Transcendentalists was simply "gone" (Cummings 1988: 41).

In 1865 the *Atlantic Monthly* began to call itself "A Magazine of Literature, Science, Art, and Politics," acknowledging the scientific revolution that was already beginning to shape literary realism. Soon all the leading magazines would be giving new emphasis to science: *Galaxy*, for example, justified its new department, "Scientific Miscellany" (in 1871), by noting that "science has given us a new reading of nature, has opened the higher questions of life and human relations, has furnished a new method to the mind, and is fast becoming a new power in literature" (Jan. 1871). The scientific "new reading of nature" and new way of viewing "human relations" supported the possibility of valid social sciences and encouraged novelists to examine human nature and society in the same vein. Indeed, because Darwin's theory of evolution is itself a narrative of struggle and change encompassing all life, it is not surprising that novelists would have found that *The Descent of Man* contained "a rich mine of facts," as the *Galaxy* wrote in March 1871.

In another cultural landmark, the *Popular Science Monthly* began its long career in May 1872 with a lead article by Herbert Spencer, chapter one of the serialized version of *The Study of Sociology*. In the first installment Spencer argued the need for sociology and its validity as science. In successive installments he asserted the biological foundations of sociology and emphasized the evolutionary causes of what he called "the comparative psychology of the sexes." In 1883 *Popular Science* published the index to its first twenty volumes and expressed its pleasure at having helped to develop "the conception of evolution as a universal process throughout all nature, to be discerned alike in the unfolding order of plant and animal life, and in the growth and progress of human society." Indeed, "the greatest value" of these many articles had been "chiefly" in showing how evolutionary theory bears "upon human life and social development." But while intellectuals were generally agreed that evolution shaped human life and social development, it is worth emphasizing that they sharply disagreed on many other points. For example, in "Great Men, Great Thoughts, and the Environment," William James attacked Spencer's "'philosophy' of social and intellectual progress" and argued what he thought was a more truly Darwinian analysis of the mind. Affirming the roles of natural selection and sexual selection, James emphasized "the excessively unstable human brain" and began to explore the "lower strata" of the human mind, "its least evolved functions from the region of intelligence which man possesses in common with the brutes" (James 1880: 456).

As for the young American realists of the 1870s, Darwin's anthropological and psychological themes in *The Descent of Man* and *The Expression of the Emotions* left them in no mood to minister to the wounded spirit or defend the principle of Design. Instead, assuming a universe of endless struggle and change, they assented to the new anthropological critique of religion as primitive superstition and began their studies of how evolution *works*, both in the larger sweep of time and in the immediate drama of courtship behavior or other scenes in the human struggle for existence. Howells, for example, saw at once that the new evolutionary theory could clarify one's understanding of American life. He worked from the anthropological assumption that human evolution had progressed from a state of savagery, through barbarism, to civilization; and, more important, he built on Darwin's tentative speculations on the "obscure . . . problem of the advance of civilization." In Darwin's view it seemed not only that "the wonderful progress of the United States, as well as the character of the people" had resulted from natural selection, but also that civilization had progressed from ancient Greece through Rome to what was now a "'great stream of Anglo-Saxon emigration to the west.'" In theory, Darwin wrote, "a nation which produced the greatest number of highly intellectual, energetic, brave, patriotic, and benevolent men would generally prevail over less favoured nations" (Darwin 1981: vol. 1, 179–80). Working with these ideas, Howells constructed an idealized view of American life, a "genteel society" presided over by males whose intellectual strength and restrained sexual passion were the key measures of their evolutionary progress.

Superior to both the so-called "savages" and what Howells considered the barbarism of the slave-owning Southern patriarchs, these gentlemen also made Howells's point — at a time when American women were campaigning for the right to vote and for access to higher education — that the new American male had evolved beyond sexual brutality.

Of course, Howells's interpretation of America's evolutionary reality was only one of many possible interpretations. Indeed, by the turn of the century many anti-Darwinian theories of evolution had emerged, producing what historians of science know as an "eclipse of Darwinism" that lasted until the 1940s. Moreover, the Darwinian revolution sparked a great social debate over supposed evolutionary hierarchies within American culture, wherein writers could construct evolutionary narratives that favored their own points of view. Most importantly, these points of view reflected the struggle over women's rights and the social status of African Americans.

It is certainly true that some in the scientific community were arguing versions of evolutionary theory that sought to restrict the freedom of women and African Americans — in what we know today as Victorian sexual science and racial science. By this atrocious reasoning both groups were described as "outcasts from evolution," women because the energy necessarily devoted to their evolutionary roles as mothers left them in a childlike mental state, and blacks because they had simply failed to evolve, mentally and beyond sexual promiscuity. As Stephen Jay Gould showed in *The Mismeasure of Man*, much of this misguided racial and sexual science relied on craniology. However, far too little is known about the ways in which both women and African Americans were also *liberated* by Darwinian thought. For they quickly realized that evolutionary theory empowered them to argue on a scientific basis against racial or sexual science, rather than against religious or cultural dogma.

This little-known response to Darwin is evident in Frederick LeRoy Sargent's poem of 1898, "Lincoln and Darwin," in which both men (born on the same day, February 12, 1809) are celebrated as "emancipators" who taught "what freedom means at last to freeborn men" (*Outlook*, Feb. 5, 1898); and in the remark made in 1919 by Rudolph Fisher (the biologist, MD, and novelist of the Harlem Renaissance) that "evolution" was the "savior" of science (McCluskey 1987: xiv). Charlotte Perkins Gilman quoted Darwin in arguing that sexual difference, itself, is not absolute or original in nature, but merely an adaptation. And Kate Chopin found in Darwin's theory of sexual selection a powerful basis for exploring the human female's natural sexual desire. Similarly, African Americans such as Charles Waddell Chesnutt and others before and throughout the Harlem Renaissance, found that Darwin's theory of race offered a powerfully liberating basis for combating "scientific" Anglo-Saxonism (as in Thomas Dixon Jr.'s widely read *The Leopard's Spots: A Romance of the White Man's Burden* [1902], and other novels), and for breaking down the racial barriers of American culture. As Darwin explained in *The Descent of Man*, racial difference is not fixed in nature (or in some supposed biblical sense), but is highly fluid and largely dependent on sexual selection. Extending this kind of evolutionary analysis in opposition to racist theories claiming that racial mixture resulted in sterility (as reflected in the terms "mule" and "mulatto"), W. E. B. Du Bois showed in *The Health and Physique of the Negro American* (1906) that African Americans of all tints of skin color were perfectly fit. Du Bois also based his argument for encouraging "the talented tenth" on Darwinian theory, claiming that solutions to African American social problems "must be slowly and painfully evolved." He defined "slavery [as nothing but] the legalized survival of the unfit and the nullification of the work of natural internal leadership" and wrote that "Negro leadership" had always sought to "make way for natural selection and the survival of the fittest" (Du Bois 1986: 852, 842–3).

It is also important to realize that, just as there was no single, widely accepted version of Darwinism, either among biologists or novelists, so are often different narrative interpretations of evolution within a particular writer's career. Many writers who were attuned to evolutionary thought during their lifetimes modified their views as they extended their careers, often in ways that closely paralleled developments in scientific theory. At around the turn of the century, for example, two important developments in evolutionary theory were clearly reflected in the fiction of those years. First, the famous experiments by August Weismann (denying Lamarckian heredity) and the subsequent rediscovery of Mendelian genetics emphasized the role of heredity: this gave us characters such as Frank Norris's McTeague, who was chained to his hereditary past; caused Gertrude Stein to agonize over "the dreary business [of] living down the tempers we are born with" when she wrote her first version of *The Making of Americans* in 1903 (Stein 1971); and, a decade later, troubled the young F. Scott Fitzgerald when he was exposed to Princeton University's rather intense interest in eugenics. Second, the theory of sexual selection led inevitably to the new field of sexology and to modern psychology, causing Havelock Ellis to regard "sex as the central problem of life" (Ellis 1936: vol. 1, xxx). This increased emphasis on the role of sex is evident in Harold Frederic's remark in 1885 that sex "is the mainspring of human activity" (Haines 1945: 138); in the dramatically liberated sexuality of Kate Chopin's Edna Pontellier in *The Awakening* (1899); and in the increasingly unruly sexuality of Howells's males, as in his stallion-like character Dylks in *The Leatherwood God* (1916).

Broadly speaking, then, anyone seeking to comprehend the role of scientific thought in American fiction between 1865 and 1914 should first recognize the complex and often contradictory developments in science over those years, when every discipline from anthropology to psychology and political science was compelled to establish new foundations in evolutionary theory *of some kind*. It is worth recalling, for example, that even the co-discoverer of natural selection, Alfred Russel Wallace, did not accept either Darwin's theory of sexual selection or his assertion that the human mind had evolved through natural and sexual selection.

Despite the complex developments in evolutionary thought during this period, however, a number of general points can serve as guides to the American fiction of those years. First, throughout the period, and well beyond the Scopes Trial of 1925, novelists who wanted to be taken seriously and to be regarded as "realists" knew that their individual narratives had to be set within an overarching evolutionary narrative of some kind. This general truth is evident in a number of ways. First, for example, beginning in the 1870s one finds many fictional doctors whose authority as scientific interpreters of life contrasts sharply with doctors in earlier fiction. Whereas Hawthorne's melodramatic portrait of Dr. Rappaccini underscored the egotism and evil in his attempts to improve creation, Henry James and Kate Chopin, for example, gave us doctors who voice the scientific views that underlie their narratives, for example Dr. Prance in *The Bostonians* (1886) and Dr. Mandelet in *The Awakening* (1899). Related to this new confidence in the doctor's ability to interpret life from the scientific point of view is a general relocation of evil, not in a character's egotism or intellectual pride, but in his animalistic nature or the taint of his being uncivilized or of a low or retarded evolutionary status — as in Howells's Bartley Hubbard or, later and more darkly, in Frank Norris's Vandover. It is also generally true that narratives of these years acknowledge the struggle for existence in an entangled world (echoing Darwin's famous image from the *Origin of Species*), and the anthropologists' views on primitive culture, including the idea that civilization originated in the capture of brides and the principle that religion is a form of primitive superstition.

During the first decades of the Darwinian revolution, writers tended to affirm the idea of civilization and evolutionary progress and to emphasize the evolutionary virtues of strength and beauty. A fictional hero's strength of mind might well take precedence over his physical strength, but weak and especially weak-minded or effeminate males are frequently cast as another recognizable type during these years: the romantic idealist, as in Howells's Ben Halleck in *A Modern Instance* (1882) or James's Ralph Touchett in *The Portrait of a Lady* (1881). Similarly, during these years the fictional heroine's evolutionary success often depends largely on her beauty, as is reflected in the number of characters named Belle or Isabelle. Moreover, in reference to the evolutionary values of strength and beauty, as these come into play in novels of courtship and marriage, the literature of this period constitutes a profound questioning of idealized love. A final example of the evolutionary reality as reflected in fiction is that many narratives from the 1870s well into the twentieth century feature plots that rely on the principle of chance or accident. Such chance events might be interpreted either in optimistic and teleological ways, as in Howells's *A Chance Acquaintance* (1873) and *The World of Chance* (1893); or pessimistically, as in *The Great Gatsby* (1925), when "a small gust of wind" creates an "accidental" current in the water of Gatsby's swimming pool, his floating body "its accidental burden."

Beyond these general contours of evolutionary thought, novelists implicitly agreed that the most compelling subjects for fictional exploration were those associated with the first principle of evolution, the reproductive force. As Darwin wrote, there is "one general law leading to the advancement of all organic beings — namely, multiply, vary, let the strongest live and the weakest die" (Darwin 1966: 208). Thus, realizing that for the human being there can be no biological or social evolution without sexual reproduction, that sex creates the essential bond in human society, and that civilization had originated in the capture of wives in primitive marriage, early realists such as William Dean Howells and Henry James saw at once that Darwin's theory of sexual selection was the crucial element in novels of courtship and marriage. Successive generations of novelists extended the realists' exploration, paralleling in literature the continuity that clearly exists in the scientific study of human sexuality: from *The Descent of Man* to Havelock Ellis's *Sexual Selection in Man* (1905) and Freud's *Three Essays on the Theory of Sexuality* (1905). As Frank Sulloway concluded in *Freud, Biologist of the Mind*, "Freud's theory of mind is the embodiment of a scientific age imbued with the rising tide of Darwinism" (Sulloway 1979: 497). This continuity is clearly evident in American fiction between 1865 and 1914, a period that ends with the first impulses of literary Freudianism and what goes by the name of modernity.

Darwin's Theories of Sexual Selection, the Mind, and the Emotions

Darwin developed his theory of sexual selection in order to account for the dramatic differences between the sexes that had sometimes caused naturalists to regard them as different species – the well-known differences in size, strength, and structure, such as the peacock's ornamentation and the stag's antlers. He realized that the "sexual struggle" is an essential part of the general struggle for existence and that "the season of love is that of battle." Accordingly, he theorized that certain adaptive structures among males, such as antlers or spurs, enabled them to contend with other males in "the law of battle" for possession of the female; and that "special organs of prehension" such as the large claws of many male insects or oceanic crustaceans enabled them to capture and hold the female. Also, the male's struggle with other males reflects his need to attract the female by means of his colorful plumage, as in the peacock; or his skills in vocal or instrumental music and dance, as in birdsong and what Darwin called "love-antics." Moreover, the male's need to attract a mate, by displaying either his strength in battle or his ornamental beauty, underscores the extremely important role of the female in sexual selection: her power to select the most promising male. "It is to be especially observed," he wrote, "that the males display their attractions with elaborate care in the presence of the females," and that females prefer "the more attractive but at the same time the more vigorous and victorious males" (Darwin 1981: vol. 2, 399–400).

Anticipating the resistance his theory soon aroused in many quarters, Darwin granted that it was "an astonishing fact" that females of various species "should be endowed with sufficient taste" to select in this way; indeed, he knew "of no fact in natural history more wonderful" than the female pheasant's power to discriminate among the exquisite shadings and patterns of the male's wing-feathers. Thus, referring especially to the male's "courage" and "pugnacity," and the female's sensitivity to the strength and beauty of males, Darwin concluded not only that "the two sexes of man . . . differ in body and mind," but that "the differences in external appearance between the races of man" are also largely determined by the workings of sexual selection. Moreover, he asserted that "the principle of sexual selection" leads "to the remarkable conclusion that the cerebral system not only regulates most of the existing functions of the body, but has indirectly influenced the progressive development of various bodily structures and of certain mental qualities" (Darwin 1981: vol. 2, 400, 384, 402).

In exploring the connection between sex and the mind, Darwin was the first to demonstrate the truth of his earlier prediction in the *Origin of Species*, that "psychology will be securely based on [a] new foundation . . . that of the necessary acquirement of each mental power and capacity by gradation" (Darwin 1966: 488). His theory of sex and the mind laid the foundations for Havelock Ellis's *Studies in the Psychology of Sex* (1936) and Freud's writings on the oedipus complex, hysteria, and repression. But beyond *The Descent of Man*'s analysis of sex and mind, Darwin's subsequent volume, *The Expression of the Emotions in Man and Animals* (1872), began to shape modern psychology and the psychological novel in very important ways. In his new psychology, William James, for example, cited *The Expression of the Emotions* more than any other Darwinian text, building on Darwin's analysis of the "innate or instinctive" expressions "which we involuntarily and unconsciously perform" (Darwin 1965: 15, 195). And it is hard to imagine that any novelist who wanted to dramatize the subtleties of human behavior would have ignored Darwin's analyses of the ways in which humans express and attempt to conceal their emotions – and his general point that "the language of the emotions" reveals one's "thoughts and intentions . . . more truly than do words, which may be falsified" (p. 364).

Novelists were especially interested in particular ideas or observations by Darwin, some of which soon became stock narrative devices. First, regarding sexual difference, in general, we will see many males whose sexual passion or eagerness reflects Darwin's description of males as "active seekers"; that is, as being more active and passionate in courtship than females. While this and other of Darwin's observations about human behavior were treated comically in the 1870s, as reflected in the proliferation of demeaning cartoons of Darwin and apes, writers soon began to take them much more seriously. Also in reference to males, writers quickly began to suggest their characters' sexual motives by noting what Darwin called their "secondary sexual characters" – especially their moustaches and beards as sexual ornaments, and their powerful hands as the "prehensile organs" enabling them to grasp the female. This way of depicting the male is evident in James's portrait of Lord Warburton, for example, in *The Portrait of a Lady*. Warburton (whose name suggests his nature as a "pugnacious male" in the necessary "law of battle" among males, in Darwin's terms) is "a favourable specimen" who sports not only "spurred" boots (like any good cock) but "the rich adornment of a chestnut beard"; and he immediately declares his intention to "lay hands on [a pretty woman] as soon as possible."

According to Spencer's "comparative psychology of the sexes," women's minds suited their roles as mothers and were not adapted for intellectual effort. Rather, because of her highly imaginative and emotional nature, the Spencerian woman tends to admire authority and desires to please the male. Of course this idea was hotly contested in novels by men and women. Beyond this, as the female is less animated than the male in Darwinian courtship, her essential traits in fiction are mainly her beauty and her aesthetic sense for selecting the superior male. But, regarding the process of selection, it is important to realize that novelists also followed Darwin's point that in primitive times the human female lost much of her power to select when women were captured as wives and held in bondage; and therefore that among civilized humans, the power to select is shared, somewhat, and is guided by considerations of wealth and social position.

All these issues of sexual difference find their place within the essential evolutionary narrative: courtship and marriage. And as novelists traced this narrative from their own points of view, they recreated innumerable scenes of courtship behavior that featured men or women either attempting to attract each other or being attracted by the other. Exploring the mechanisms of biological beauty, novelists were especially interested in the musical appeal of the female voice, as in James's Verena Tarrant in *The Bostonians* or Fitzgerald's Daisy Buchanan in *The Great Gatsby*. And in their re-creations of the age-old drama of men pursuing women, novelists insinuated the Darwinian elements of men engaged in "the law of battle" and of women consciously and unconsciously evaluating and selecting men.

Clearly, all these narratives of courtship and sexual selection reflect the novelists' ways of exploring the psychological materials implicit in Darwin's theory of sex and the cerebral system, and it is too little known that these explorations of instinctive or unconscious behavior occurred before Freud is mistakenly thought to have discovered the unconscious. For example, during the time when Freud himself was studying Darwin, Howells examined the unconscious sexual motives in the priest Don Ippolito, in *A Foregone Conclusion* (1874) and, more famously, deepened his analysis of Bartley Hubbard in *A Modern Instance* by entering what he called "the fastnesses of his nature which psychology has not yet explored." Finding in those dark recesses that the male regards the female as his "prey," Howells also dramatized his hero's unconscious behavior in other ways, particularly in a daring scene of music and dance at a logging camp in Maine. Moreover, from the 1880s throughout the period novelists intensified their efforts to dramatize the psychological conflicts of characters who either unconsciously expressed or attempted to conceal their emotions, as Darwin had theorized and illustrated these phenomena in *The Expression of the Emotions*. Acting out such conflicts, innumerable characters reveal their motives or their true inner states by blushing or starting, or, like Henry Fleming in the *Red Badge of Courage* (1895), by expressing his fear or his "war ardor." Similarly, novelists dramatize their characters' efforts to gain an advantage over their opponents by concealing their emotions or by reading those of their adversaries. In *The Market-Place* (1899), for example, Harold Frederic analyzes his hero's "nerve force" as he controls his "facial muscles" when wielding his brutal power both in courtship and his dealings in the financial world.

Civilization and Courtship in the 1870s

While Howells was plotting progress through evolutionary "love" and what only appeared to be the element of chance as his heroines selected gentle males, as in *A Chance Acquaintance*, Henry James was construing the evolutionary plot in quite different ways. In "The Madonna of the Future" (1873) he satirized a painter's attempt to preserve the image of ideal womanhood, revealing that this "madonna" has a lover, a rather greasy Italian who produces human-like figurines of coupling "cats and monkeys." In his more ambitious "Daisy Miller: A Study" (1878), James explored the idea of the environment's role in shaping human character. In this "study," not so much of the title character as of the hero Winterbourne, James portrays a man who has lived so long in Geneva, "the little metropolis of Calvinism," that he "had become dishabituated to the American tone" and had "lost his instinct in this matter" of judging the nature of young American women such as Daisy. James writes that Winterbourne's "reason could not help him." Whether simply because he is over-civilized, or because his Calvinist sense of evil causes him to misinterpret Daisy's forward ways, Winterbourne becomes "vexed with himself that, by instinct, he should not appreciate [Daisy] justly"; "vexed," James emphasizes, "at his want of instinctive certitude." Often "afraid – literally afraid" of women, Winterbourne has lost the necessary instinct for survival in the struggle for reproductive success. Although we see Winterbourne "smiling and curling his moustache" (a sexual ornament in the human male), when he follows Daisy to Rome the news that Daisy "was now surrounded by half-a-dozen wonderful moustaches checked [his] impulse to go straightway to see her." Winterbourne not only shrinks from Darwin's obligatory "law of battle" among males for possession of the female, he squirms in seeing one of his Italian competitors entertaining Daisy with his splendid singing and damnable "good looks." And he further reveals his instinctive failure in the courtship drama by telling Daisy, "I don't dance." By contrast, although Daisy's little brother has already lost a few teeth because of the "climate" in "this old Europe," his phallic instinct is intact. He "poked his alpenstock, lance fashion" into nearly everything, including "the trains of the ladies' dresses," and at one point got "astride" of it. In this way, James develops an "international theme" that is frequently misunderstood because critics have not detected the underlying evolutionary logic that links it with his brother William's explorations of the American reality at this time, as in "Great Men, Great Thoughts, and the Environment" (1880).

"The Woman Business" in the 1880s

By the 1880s Henry James had shifted his focus from males who failed to meet the challenges of natural and sexual selection to what he called "the woman business." In his two novels of 1881, for example, *Washington Square* and *The Portrait of a Lady*, he constructed plots that denied what many others were celebrating as the female's power to shape the evolutionary future by exerting her power to select. In doing so he aligned himself with anthropological thought on the origin of marriage in the capture of brides and with Darwin's belief that in those primitive times the human female had lost much of her power to select. Although Catherine Sloper, the heroine in *Washington Square*, typifies the Darwinian female when she is immediately struck by her lover's "beauty," her powerful father intervenes and claims for himself the right to select her mate. Dr. Sloper's ability to prevail in this contest derives not only from the strength of mind wielded by many men of science in the fiction of these years, but by Catherine's supposed evolutionary desire to please the powerful male. Although James is somewhat sympathetic with Catherine's plight, especially when she resigns herself to her life as a spinster, he criticizes her weakness of mind in the process of selection. By contrast, the one woman in the novel who does win James's approval is a Mrs. Almond, who had married not for love but money and whose children ("the little Almonds") demonstrate her reproductive success by dispersing themselves, like so many seeds.

James's portrait of Isabel Archer is also based on principles that resemble those in Spencer's "comparative psychology of the sexes." Isabel's "imagination was by habit ridiculously active," to the point that "if the door were not opened to it, it jumped out of the window." According to his plan for the novel (in his *Notebooks*), he would take a "poor girl, who had dreamed of freedom and nobleness" and then make her aware that "in reality [she had been] ground in the very mill of the conventional" (James 1947: 15). Thus Isabel begins by imagining that she need not marry and then demonstrates that, like Catherine Sloper, her "ridiculous" imagination gives her no sound basis for selecting a husband. She asks, "What does one marry for?" and admits that she "can't judge" between one suitor's estate and another's. Thus, because Isabel's "mind contained no class which offered a natural place to Mr. Osmond – he was a specimen apart," she unsuspectingly entered the "steel trap" of marriage to the self-interested Osmond, and their single child died. Then, sealing her fate, Isabel exhibits a final trait of the Spencerian female whose "admiration for power" makes her "religiously excitable" and susceptible to "transcendent force." When Osmond refuses Isabel's talk of divorce, his words "represented [to her] something transcendent and absolute, like the sign of the cross."

Although James's demeaning portrait of Isabel Archer is an important landmark in American fiction, more important and far graver issues involving Victorian sexual science were contested in a series of novels about women doctors during the 1880s. In these novels by both men and women, the question was whether women should have access to higher education (much less the vote) and, relatedly, whether women are *fit*, from the evolutionary point of view, to be doctors. Dr. E. H. Clarke had argued in *Sex in Education; or, A Fair Chance for the Girls* (1873) that it was unfair and unnatural to subject girls to the rigors of higher education at the time when their ovaries were developing. Because their energies were necessarily devoted primarily to their reproductive functions, resulting in their brains being smaller and more delicate, they would suffer psychological stress and damage to their reproductive health. In short, higher education for women posed a dire threat to the nation's very survival. Of course, women didn't take this lying down and immediately declared that they knew better and would "give him theory for theory," as Elizabeth Stuart Phelps put it (Howe 1972: 129).

The fictional debate over this question began with Howells's *Doctor Breen's Practice* (1881), wherein the heroine, Grace Breen, has already completed her medical training but demonstrates that it had been a mistake. Grace is "too nervous"; both she and her mother declare her unfit for such work, and, to make things worse, her single patient, a woman friend, abandons her in order to be treated by "a *man* doctor!" In the end Grace wins Howells's approval by giving up her practice, marrying, and taking care of the children of employees at her husband's business. To Howells's great credit, however, he published Elizabeth Stuart Phelps's competing novel, *Doctor Zay* (1882), this even after she had complained to him that his Grace Breen was not "a fair example of professional women." In complete contrast to Dr. Breen, Dr. Zay is a strong and competent "woman of science" whose main problem in life is how to fend off the advances of Waldo Yorke, the hero. A romantic idealist, Yorke becomes Dr. Zay's patient, and along the way she tells him, "You are not in love . . . you are only nervous." In the end, however, she not only brings him back to health but causes him to subdue his overheated passion; at that point, he becomes a new or rehabilitated man, suitable for her (a "new woman") to accept as a husband on the understanding that she will retain her medical practice. As an essential part of his rehabilitation, in Phelps's clever strategy, Dr. Zay instructs Yorke in "the natural history of doctresses," partly by giving Yorke a copy of Darwin's *latest* book, *The Power of Movement in Plants* (1880). This, along with Phelps's profuse use of plant imagery in describing the subtle movements of Dr. Zay, suggests that *The Descent of Man* is not the last word in evolution and that the "new woman" is not only fit for the mental work of science, but aspires, plant-like, to a higher light.

Sarah Orne Jewett presented yet another view of the female doctor in *A Country Doctor* (1884), wherein she portrays the heroine Nan Prince as belonging to a "class of women who are the result of natural progression and variation." But, unlike Dr. Zay, Dr. Prince decides in the end to continue in her medical practice and *not* marry. Finally, in this series of novels about women doctors, Henry James gave us Dr. Mary J. Prance (no doubt a reference to Jewett's Dr. Prince) in *The Bostonians* (1886). Dr. Prance, a minor character in the novel, is certainly an accomplished woman of science. But, according to his witty and wicked design, James suggests that the price of Dr. Prance's medical training is just as Dr. Clarke and Howells would have predicted, for this "dry little woman" "looked like a boy." Moreover, James uses Dr. Prance to voice his criticism of the women's movement, in part by showing her sympathy with the hero, Basil Ransom, who threatens "the little knot of reformers" by courting their heroine, Verena Tarrant. Dr. Prance leaves the lecture hall before Verena completes her feminist talk, thus dramatizing her impatience with the feminists' idealism, as encapsulated in Miss Birdseye's faith in "the elevation of the species by the reading of Emerson." Also, with her scientific and "ironical view" of "courtship," Dr. Prance realizes that, according to the theory of sexual selection, Verena's musical oratory serves mainly to attract the male. Thus, this story ends in Ransom's disruption of the feminist movement when he "wrenche[s]" Verena away to marriage by "muscular force," a re-enactment of the origin of civilization in the capture of brides.

The 1890s: Environment, Heredity, Sexual Selection, and Evolutionary Psychology

By the early 1890s the gravity of evolutionary thought had intensified, and novelists began to address a greater range of evolutionary problems. In Hamlin Garland's *Rose of Dutcher's Coolly* (1895) and Stephen Crane's *Maggie, A Girl of the Streets* (1893), for example, the workings of sexual selection are clearly evident in the lives of Rose and Maggie, but the authors also emphasize the role of environment in shaping these lives. The intensifying interest in evolutionary thought between the 1870s and 1890s is also evident in the career of Mark Twain, who began reading science (*The Descent of Man*, for example) in the 1870s, but in those early years was "ambivalent about science" or comically distanced from it (Cummings 1988: 15). In *The Tragedy of Pudd'nhead Wilson* (1894), however, and *What Is Man?* (1898–1906) he became far more serious about the roles of heredity and environment in shaping life. He made the study of fingerprints pioneered by Sir Francis Galton (Darwin's cousin) a key element of his plot in *Pudd'nhead Wilson*, and his anger with the human being's pride in being different from the other animals accounts for much of the bitterness in his late work.

By 1894, when Frank Norris began work on *Vandover and the Brute* (posthumously published in 1914) and *McTeague* (1899), he had already studied evolutionary biology under Joseph Le Conte at the University of California. He would always subscribe to Le Conte's belief in a kind of transcendent evolution from mere sexual reproduction to altruistic love, but, studying now at Harvard, he drew also on Max Nordau's work on degeneration and similar studies to emphasize the human's animality in Vandover and McTeague. Working also with the theory of sexual selection in the lives of these characters, he suggested that neither had evolved a capacity for "love." Moreover, in portraits of minor characters in these novels Norris dramatized his belief in the anti-semitic and racist views of theorists such as Le Conte (a Southerner who maintained that racial mixture produced "inferior" types). In *McTeague*, for example, the child born to the "Polish Jew" Zerkow and the Mexican woman Maria Macapa is a short-lived "strange hybrid little being," and because Norris views the parents as almost subhuman, they can neither love the child nor even be moved by its death.

In Kate Chopin's presentation of African Americans there is also a disturbing reflection of the misguided racial science of that time, but her interest in Darwinian theory bears on the question of the female's role in sexual selection. Although she revered Darwin and even captured his image in her portrait of Dr. Mandelet in

The Awakening, she questioned his views on the mothering instinct and on the female's sexual desire. In several stories, such as "The Story of an Hour" (1894), and *The Awakening*, she drew deeply on Darwin's chapter on "choice exerted by the female" among birds. Thus Edna Pontellier doubts whether a civilized woman would "select" according to wealth and social position, as Darwin had theorized. Instead, Edna feels sexual antipathy for her husband and selects two lovers, one to satisfy her sexual needs and another because she is attracted to his physical beauty. Although she is a loving mother, she cannot be fulfilled in that way alone, and she hears from Dr. Mandelet that the illusion of sexual love is a "provision of Nature; a decoy to secure mothers for the race." In a key scene that clearly echoes Darwin's language in analyzing the sexual origins of music, Edna responds to a performance of Frederick Chopin's music by awakening to her sexual nature; and when she moves from her husband's home into her own "pigeon house," Edna re-enacts a scene from Darwin's discussion of female choice, in which a female pigeon violently refuses to mate with males chosen for her by a breeder. *The Awakening* is only one of many novels during these years to explore the darkness and violence of sexual "love."

In two other landmarks of scientific narrative in the late 1890s, *The Damnation of Theron Ware* (1896) and *The Market-Place* (1899), Harold Frederic developed his point that sex is "the mainspring of human activity." In *Theron Ware*, Frederic introduces his bewildered hero to the astonishing complexities of Darwinian sex when Theron visits Dr. Ledsmar's greenhouse laboratory. In this setting (recalling Frederic's own interest in horticulture), Theron hears Ledsmar talk of his own Darwinian studies of "hermaphroditism" in the evolution of plants. Unable to appreciate Ledsmar's "great fuss" over "orchids," Theron is also blind to the sexual motives that lead to his own ruin. Frederic exposes Theron to the sexual power of music in an unforgettable scene with his lover, Celia, and to Darwin's "law of battle" when Theron is faced down by a man who appears to be courting his wife. In the end Frederic suggests that Theron is "damned" not in a theological but in the evolutionary sense – because he is a weak man, intellectually, and because he is a complete failure in "the work of selection." In Frederic's second and still vastly unappreciated masterpiece, his (anti-)hero succeeds in both the marketplace and sexual selection by sheer brute force, much of which derives from his power to conceal his emotions in his financial and sexual dealings. Here Frederic's related main interests are in exploring the female's attraction to the hero's "frank barbarism of power," thus developing Spencer's earlier point in his "comparative psychology of the sexes"; and in exploring the ways in which Darwin's study of the expression and concealment of the emotions figures into the general conflict of the struggle for existence. To these ends, then, Frederic's heroine confesses her desire to experience "the grand emotions with the big, dark brute" whose "masterful character" is capable of reducing her "brain to sort of porridge." Frederic also emphasizes his hero's power to control his fear, comparing him with General Grant and writing that "all really brave men have those inner convictions of weakness, even while they are behaving like lions." Scholars have been slow to detect Frederic's and his friend Stephen Crane's interest in Darwinian psychology, as in *The Red Badge of Courage*

(1895), but these novelists too were exploring the same field that William James had worked for the two decades preceding *The Principles of Psychology* (1890).

1900–1914: Evolution and Modernity

The role of evolutionary theory in American fiction from the turn of the century to the Great War is so profound that several volumes will be required to do it justice. The main currents of scientific thought that most interested novelists of these years were those involving, first, the evolution of race; second, the development – from the foundation provided by Darwin's theories of sexual selection and the expression of emotions – of sexology and modern psychology (especially in the writings of Havelock Ellis and Sigmund Freud); third, the rediscovery and application of Mendelian genetics; fourth, the various "anti-Darwinian evolution theories" that emerged during this part of the eclipse of Darwinism (especially Bergson's *Creative Evolution*); and fifth, the awakening of what we know today as our ecological sensibility.

Taking up Darwin's conclusion that racial differences are not fixed and are largely the product of sexual selection, Havelock Ellis declared in 1897 that "sex [is] the central problem of life" and that "with the racial questions that rest on it," it "stands before the coming generations as the chief problem for solution." With his more acute sense of the American reality, W. E. B. Du Bois wrote in 1903 that "the problem of the Twentieth Century is the problem of the color-line" (Du Bois 1986: 359). An important part of Du Bois' interest in the "color-line" derived not only from the idea that blacks are of a lower evolutionary order, but from the hysteria about racial mixture that had intensified after Reconstruction in white supremacist racial science. Thus in *The Health and Physique of the Negro American* Du Bois refuted the claims of scientists and writers such as Le Conte and Norris or Thomas Dixon, Jr. that people with any degree of racial mixture (such as the mulatto) were doomed to suffer biological infirmity like that of the sterile mule. Pursuing these questions from his own point of view, Charles W. Chesnutt argued that laws against race mixture violated the *natural* laws of natural and sexual selection, wherein any individual is free to attract a mate based on his or her own merit and beauty, thereby marrying "up" in the social hierarchy. In this way, he believed, Southern law and custom merely served to impede the inevitable *evolutionary* solution to the race problem, complete race-amalgamation. In his novel *The House Behind the Cedars* (1900), especially, Chesnutt dramatizes this theory of racial evolution through sexual selection, wherein two very light-skinned and emphatically healthy blacks pass for white. Yet while they improve their condition until their "tainted" heritage is revealed, they also express Chesnutt's own prejudicial sense – against their mother – that darker-skinned blacks represent a simpler but more lowly state. A quarter-century later, following Gertrude Stein's exploration of race mixture in "Melanctha" (1909), novelists of the Harlem Renaissance would debate similar questions about skin color and racial evolution, now complicated by Freudianism and "black primitivism."

Aside from its relationship with questions of race, the theory of sexual selection continued to be a crucial element in novels by a wide range of writers during these years. Signaling her great admiration for Darwin, Edith Wharton, for example, published *The Descent of Man and Other Stories* (1904) and in many later stories and novels explored Darwinian materials with increasing depth and sophistication, often constructing plots based on the drama of mate selection, as in "The Choice," *The Custom of the Country* (1913), and *The Reef* (1912). In the last of these she also drew on her close reading in the most recent developments in Darwinism, such as R. H. Lock's *Recent Progress in the Study of Variety, Heredity, and Evolution* (1907), and at the same time produced a psychological *tour de force* that drew heavily on Darwin's *Expression of the Emotions*. Similarly, Theodore Dreiser drew heavily on the theory of sexual selection in describing Carrie's series of relationships in *Sister Carrie* (1900), and in his "trilogy of desire," concerning the financier Frank Cowperwood, he explored the psychobiology of the polygamous male.

The new emphasis on heredity following the development of Mendelian genetics is evident in many novels of these years, but especially in Gertrude Stein's *The Making of Americans* (completed 1911, published 1925) and *Three Lives* (1909), in which Stein's impressive background in science is evident. A number of her characters express the anxiety many felt during these years in being bound genetically to the disagreeable attributes of their parents. As Julia Dehning struggles "to live down her mother in her," Melanctha cannot survive the way she is "made," the dominant hereditary strain coming from her "big black virile" father. Thus the problem of heredity, like the innate violence of what Darwin called the "sexual struggle," became another of the obstacles which a great many theorists sought to overcome during the eclipse of Darwinism. As Norris, relying on Le Conte, had projected a transcendent evolution through a mystical, altruistic love in *The Octopus* (1901), Willa Cather found another theoretical way to overcome what she thought were the disagreeable elements of sexual selection. Several of her early stories are attempts to revise Chopin's views on sexual passion, but before publishing her first great novel in 1913 (*O Pioneers!*), she had read Henri Bergson's *Creative Evolution*. Immediately, like many others at this time, Cather embraced this liberating theory of evolution largely because the *élan vital* not only overpowers Darwin's theory of natural selection but virtually erases the theory of sexual selection. Moreover, as Cather extended her Bergsonian vision in *The Song of the Lark* (1915), she produced a heroine who freed herself from the power of both sex and heredity: "she entered into the inheritance that she herself had laid up."

Of the many writers who dealt with scientific questions that arose between 1865 and 1914, none is more impressive in his study and fictional interpretation of the key problems than Jack London. The extent of his interest in science is evident in his remarkable library, especially in works that focus on what he called "the sex problem," from *The Descent of Man* to the early major works of Sigmund Freud. It is to London's great credit that during those years of the eclipse of Darwinism he maintained his grasp on the essential features of Darwin's theories of natural selection, sexual selection, and the expression of the emotions — and did so after close reading of

Spencer, Le Conte, Kropotkin (whose *Mutual Aid* would sway a number of leftist writers up through the 1930s), and many others. He was quick to question Bergson's scientific legitimacy, calling him "a charlatan" at the time when Bergson was generally revered. And London realized that Freudian psychology had emerged from Darwin's theory of sex and the mind.

In a number of early novels London focused on the theory of sexual selection, failing, in *The Sea-Wolf* (1904), to convince even himself that the female's selection against the brutal Wolf Larsen and for a man with the moral sense could lead to evolutionary progress (as many others maintained at that time). By the time he wrote *Martin Eden* (1909) he could build on more recent work in the psychology of sex by Havelock Ellis and others, dramatizing for example Ellis's conclusion about the sexual touch and the idea that "the skin" is a "primeval" source of knowledge about "the archaeological field of psychology" (Ellis 1936: 1:3:4); at the same time he expressed through his hero the kind of disillusionment about sexual selection and "love" that had troubled other writers such as Kate Chopin. In *The Valley of the Moon* (1913) he presented the first, and to this day one of the most comprehensive, fictional studies of ecology, motivated largely by his concern for the world's growing population and the "veritable rape of the land" in the United States. Realizing that he needed to imagine a fertile marriage (there is no evolution without reproduction), he shows how his hero and heroine must first solve aspects of "the sex problem" in their own lives before they could establish a viable way of life in small-scale farming. Thus London dramatized solutions to the two most pressing psychological issues of his time: female hysteria (as that subject dominated modern psychology at that time in work by Ellis, Freud, and others), and the male's sexual violence. Then, drawing again on his reading in Ellis, he shows that the heroine must not only select a strong yet sensitive husband, but retain him in a healthy marriage (by whetting and satisfying the male's potentially polygamous sexual appetite). Finally, in 1914, London completed work on his vastly undervalued and misunderstood novel *The Little Lady of the Big House* (1916), the first and still one of the most impressive Freudian novels in American literature. In this novel, set on a ranch very like his own, he built on his career-long study of Darwin; his own considerable knowledge of selective breeding, as sharpened by his study of Mendel and his friendship with Luther Burbank; his fascination with the new sexology and what Ellis had written of the sexual impulse in frogs and human beings, for example; the still daring and disturbing subject of the female's polyandrous sexual desire; and the self-analytical insights that he had developed from reading Freud.

Of course, the Great War was at this time dealing yet another blow to the modern mind and spirit, resulting in visions of the Wasteland. But American culture could not rid itself of the questions late nineteenth-century science had posed about human nature, as evidenced in the Scopes trial of 1925. In subsequent work by writers seldom thought to have been interested in science, novelists continued to explore the evolution of race, the problems of heredity and eugenics, the implications of the bisexual human embryo, and the Freudian mind. And as the eclipse of Darwinism drew to a close in the 1940s, writers such as Ernest Hemingway gave us further explorations of natural history and human nature, while John Steinbeck and Aldo Leopold gave us more specifically biological studies of human nature and ecology that have taken on renewed interest in our own time.

Primary Texts

Cather, Willa. *O Pioneers!* 1913.

Cather, Willa. *The Song of the Lark.* 1915.

Chesnutt, Charles W. *The House Behind the Cedars.* 1900.

Chopin, Kate. "The Story of an Hour." 1894.

Chopin, Kate. *The Awakening.* 1899.

Crane, Stephen. *Maggie, A Girl of the Streets (A Story of New York).* 1893.

Crane, Stephen. *The Red Badge of Courage; an Episode of the American Civil War.* 1895.

Dixon, Thomas, Jr. *The Leopard's Spots: A Romance of the White Man's Burden.* 1902.

Dreiser, Theodore. *Sister Carrie.* 1900.

Du Bois, W. E. B. *The Souls of Black Folk.* 1903.

Du Bois, W. E. B. *The Health and Physique of the Negro American.* 1906.

Fitzgerald, F. Scott. *The Great Gatsby.* 1925.

Frederic, Harold. *The Damnation of Theron Ware.* 1896.

Frederic, Harold. *The Market-Place.* 1899.

Garland, Hamlin. *Rose of Dutcher's Coolly.* 1895.

Howells, William Dean. *A Chance Acquaintance.* 1873.

Howells, William Dean. *A Foregone Conclusion.* 1875.

Howells, William Dean. *Doctor Breen's Practice.* 1881.

Howells, William Dean. *A Modern Instance.* 1882.

Howells, William Dean. *The World of Chance.* 1893.

Howells, William Dean. *The Leatherwood God.* 1916.

James, Henry. "The Madonna of the Future." 1873.

James, Henry. "Daisy Miller: A Study." 1878.

James, Henry. *The Portrait of a Lady.* 1881.

James, Henry. *Washington Square.* 1881.

James, Henry. *The Bostonians.* 1886.

Jewett, Sarah Orne. *A Country Doctor.* 1884.

London, Jack. *The Sea-Wolf.* 1904.

London, Jack. *Martin Eden.* 1909.

London, Jack. *The Valley of the Moon.* 1913.

London, Jack. *The Little Lady of the Big House.* 1916.

Norris, Frank. *McTeague: A Story of San Francisco.* 1899.

Norris, Frank. *The Octopus.* 1901.

Norris, Frank. *Vandover and the Brute.* 1914.

Phelps, Elizabeth Stuart. *Doctor Zay.* 1882.

Stein, Gertrude. *Three Lives.* 1909.

Stein, Gertrude. *The Making of Americans.* 1925.

Twain, Mark. *The Tragedy of Pudd'nhead Wilson.* 1894.

Twain, Mark. *What Is Man?* 1898–1906.

Wharton, Edith. *The Descent of Man and Other Stories.* 1904.

Wharton, Edith. *The Reef.* 1912.

Wharton, Edith. *The Custom of the Country.* 1913.

References and Further Reading

Bannister, Robert C. (1979). *Social Darwinism: Science and Myth in Anglo-American Social Thought.* Philadelphia: Temple University Press.

Beer, Gillian (1983). *Darwin's Plots: Evolutionary Narrative in Darwin, George Eliot and Nineteenth-Century Fiction.* London: Routledge & Kegan Paul.

Bender, Bert (1996). *The Descent of Love: Darwin and the Theory of Sexual Selection in American Fiction, 1871–1926.* Philadelphia: University of Pennsylvania Press.

Bender, Bert (2004). *Evolution and "the Sex Problem": American Narratives during the Eclipse of Darwinism.* Kent, Ohio: Kent State University Press.

Bergson, Henri (1911). *Creative Evolution.* New York: Holt.

Bowler, Peter J. (1983). *The Eclipse of Darwinism: Anti-Darwinian Evolution Theories in the Decades around 1900*. Baltimore: Johns Hopkins University Press.

Cummings, Sherwood (1988). *Mark Twain and Science: Adventures of a Mind*. Baton Rouge: Louisiana State University Press.

Darwin, Charles (1896). *The Power of Movement in Plants*. New York: Appleton. (First publ. 1889.)

Darwin, Charles (1965). *The Expression of the Emotions in Man and Animals*. Chicago: University of Chicago Press. (First publ. 1872.)

Darwin, Charles (1966). *On the Origin of Species by Means of Natural Selection, Or the Preservation of Favoured Races in the Struggle for Life*. A facsimile of the first edition. Cambridge, Mass.: Harvard University Press. (First publ. 1859.)

Darwin, Charles (1981). *The Descent of Man, and Selection in Relation to Sex*, 2 vols. in 1. Princeton: Princeton University Press. (First publ. 1871.)

Du Bois, W. E. B. (1986). *W. E. B. Du Bois: Writings*. New York: Library of America.

Du Bois, W. E. Burghardt, ed. (1968). *The Health and Physique of the Negro American*. Atlanta University Publications No. 11. New York: Octagon. (First publ. 1906.)

Ellis, Havelock (1936). *Studies in the Psychology of Sex*, 2 vols. New York: Random House.

Freud, Sigmund (1953–74). *The Standard Edition of the Complete Psychological Works of Sigmund Freud*, ed. James Strachey, 24 vols. London: Hogarth/Institute of Psycho-Analysis.

Gould, Stephen J. (1981). *The Mismeasure of Man*. New York: Norton.

Haines, Paul (1945). "Harold Frederic." Ph.D. diss., New York University.

Haller, John S., Jr. (1971). *Outcasts from Evolution: Scientific Attitudes of Racial Inferiority, 1859–1900*. Urbana: University of Illinois Press.

Hofstadter, Richard (1955). *Social Darwinism in American Thought*, rev. edn. Boston: Beacon.

Howe, Julia Ward, ed. (1972). *Sex in Education: A Reply to Dr. E. H. Clarke's "Sex in Education."* New York: Arno.

Huxley, Thomas H. (1871). *Evidence as to Man's Place in Nature*. New York: Appleton.

James, Henry (1947). *The Notebooks of Henry James*, ed. F. O. Matthiesen. New York: Oxford University Press.

James, William (1880). "Great Men, Great Thoughts, and the Environment." *Atlantic Monthly* 46, 441–59.

James, William (1981). *The Principles of Psychology*. Cambridge, Mass.: Harvard University Press. (first publ. 1890.)

Jones, Arthur E., Jr. (1950). *Darwinism and its Relation to Realism and Naturalism in American Fiction, 1860 to 1900*. Madison, NJ: Drew University Press.

Kropotkin, P. (1910). *Mutual Aid: A Factor of Evolution*. London: William Heinemann.

Le Conte, Joseph (1896). *Evolution: Its Nature, its Evidences, and its Relation to Religious Thought*. New York: Appleton.

Lock, Robert Heath (1911). *Recent Progress in the Study of Variation, Heredity, and Evolution*. London: John Murray.

Lyell, Charles (1830–3). *Principles of Geology, Being an Attempt to Explain the Former Changes of the Earth's Surface by Reference to Causes now in Operation*. London: J. Murray.

Lyell, Charles (1863). *The Geological Evidences of the Antiquity of Man, with Remarks on Theories of the Origin of Species by Variation*. London: J. Murray.

McCluskey, John, Jr. (1987). *The City of Refuge: The Collected Stories of Rudolph Fisher*. Columbia: University of Missouri Press.

Mayr, Ernst (1982). *The Growth of Biological Thought: Diversity, Evolution and Inheritance*. Cambridge, Mass.: Harvard University Press.

Russett, Cynthia Eagle (1989). *Sexual Science: The Victorian Construction of Womanhood*. Cambridge, Mass.: Harvard University Press.

Spencer, Herbert (1896). *The Study of Sociology*. New York: Appleton.

Sulloway, Frank (1979). *Freud, Biologist of the Mind: Beyond the Psychoanalytical Legend*. New York: Basic Books.

20

Writing in the "Vulgar Tongue": Law and American Narrative

William E. Moddelmog

If it seems that we live in the age of hyper-publicized legal dramas – celebrity murder trials, presidential impeachments, contested national elections, and other inducements to the contemporary feeding frenzy known as the "media circus" – it may be oddly comforting to know that the American tradition of sensationalizing legal conflict goes back well over a hundred years. One of the most highly publicized American trials of the nineteenth century involved a "superstar" in his own right – the preacher Henry Ward Beecher – and the claim that he had committed adultery with Elizabeth Tilton, the wife of a good friend. Tame as this may seem to us today, the legal dispute between Theodore Tilton and Beecher, as one scholar notes, mesmerized the nation for a year beginning in July 1874:

> Huge crowds surged around the courthouse, often waiting all night for a chance to get a ticket for one of the limited spectator seats inside the courtroom . . . . Scalpers sold the free tickets for as much as five dollars each. Immense bouquets of flowers were delivered to Beecher and to Tilton where they sat with counsel, until the courtroom reeked of hothouse plants and the competition by each party's supporters to produce ever more magnificent and showy bouquets thoroughly upstaged the ongoing interrogation of witnesses on the stand . . . . Trial transcripts, printed daily in several New York newspapers, were also sold to the public in booklet form as the trial continued. (Korobkin 1998: 58)

Ultimately, the trial came to nothing: the jury failed to reach a verdict and the claim against Beecher was dismissed. But the intensity of public interest in the scandal reveals much about the place of law in American life in the late nineteenth century, and about narratives that Americans found compelling in the postbellum era.

One explanation for the intensity of interest in the trial, in addition to its salacious subject matter, is that its legal issues also reflected broader cultural conflicts. The meaning and permanence of marriage was, in the 1870s, a subject of great controversy in the country. Many advocates of women's rights claimed that strict divorce laws made women slaves to their husbands. Some states were liberalizing those laws in efforts to attract new residents, while others rigidly adhered to standards that allowed divorce only for adultery or extreme cruelty. Moreover, marriage had traditionally been viewed as a covenant rather than a contract, a promise sanctioned by God rather than a contingent arrangement alterable at will by the parties themselves. This issue also implicated the nation's view of itself as bound together by a sacred compact – a national self-image that had been tested severely by the Civil War. Finally, the trial itself allowed its audience to witness this play of cultural anxieties and conflicts while reducing the complexity of the issues to a simple factual question: Did Beecher and Elizabeth Tilton have sex?

One of the principal functions of the law in American life has been to translate deeply troubling and seemingly irresolvable cultural conflicts into clearly answerable legal questions, thereby managing the underlying tensions by masking them. Presenting themselves in the language of objectivity and neutrality – "facts," "evidence," "reason" – legal pronouncements have historically carried an authority in the United States that allows for the settlement (if only temporarily) of disputes that otherwise might tear the nation apart. To perform this function, however, the law must be viewed as occupying a privileged position within the larger culture; it must be thought immune from partisan interests, class affiliations, and personal prejudices.

While the rapidity of social and cultural change in the late nineteenth century made the law's ability to mediate between clashing interests more important than ever, Americans in the postbellum era increasingly expected the law to conform to the public will – to adapt to changing social, economic, and cultural conditions. In fact, the jury in the Beecher–Tilton case exemplified this trend when it failed to reach a verdict. Although strong evidence existed of an adulterous relationship between Beecher and Elizabeth Tilton, the jury had refused to find Beecher liable. Its unwillingness to hold him accountable for conduct tied to personal feelings and sexual acts may indicate a greater respect for individual autonomy and privacy than for a conception of marriage as a sacred and inviolable covenant. If so, the jury anticipated the general thrust of public opinion over the next century, as divorce laws were relaxed throughout the country and the tort of "criminal conversation" (adultery) became virtually unknown.

But can the law help to resolve cultural tensions if, by responding to the public will, it is buffeted by the very forces that create those tensions in the first place? Many scholars have begun to highlight this problem by focusing on the law's relation to disciplines that have traditionally been viewed as cultural barometers, such as literature. Scholars in what has become known as the "law and literature" movement argue that the law responds not just to overt manifestations of the public will – specific, articulable beliefs measurable by surveys and opinion polls – but also to its less visible elements: feelings, popular images, indefinable senses of justice and morality that may vary depending on the context. And it is at this level that law and narrative are related. Every legal case or judicial opinion involves the telling of a story; the operation of the law always takes place in the context of a particular set of facts that must be related in a manner that makes sense to the listener or reader – in other words, by means of a narrative. And just as the shape and content of narratives told within American culture can affect the legal consequences that spring from them, so the kinds of narratives that legal institutions recognize can affect the public's sense of what constitutes a good story. This means that narratives are written not only by authors of literary works, but by journalists, politicians, judges, and lawyers, as well as by the audiences that embrace or discard the stories that they tell.

Moreover, both law and narrative are constituted by language. The law employs language in a unique and highly specialized way, implicitly discrediting language that fails to conform to its professional standards (for instance, language that is too "emotional" or that raises issues determined to be outside the scope of legal authority). Claims must be made in forms that have been recognized by legal institutions, thus limiting the kinds of "stories" that can be told. One way to look at these forms is to consider them a kind of "discourse." Discourse is language charged with ideological content, and can be viewed, as Michel Foucault has argued, as "strategic games of action and reaction, question and answer, domination and evasion, as well as struggle" (Foucault 2000: 2). The term implies that our relation to knowledge, and even to ourselves, is mediated; that we can speak, think, and ask or answer questions only in units of meaning developed on a social rather than individual scale. Foucault considers the law to be one of the institutions that define these units of meaning:

> Judicial practices, the manner in which wrongs and responsibilities are settled between men, the mode by which, in the history of the West, society conceived and defined the way men could be judged in terms of wrongs committed, the way in which compensation for some actions and punishment for others were imposed on specific individuals – all these rules or, if you will, all these practices that were indeed governed by rules but also constantly modified through the course of history, seem to me to be one of the forms by which our society defined types of subjectivity, forms of knowledge, and, consequently, relations between man and truth. (Foucault 2000: 4)

Legal discourse creates, or at a minimum endorses, particular forms of knowledge, and in so doing endows some social groups with power while denying it to others. Speaking or writing in a legal context requires that one adhere to legal conventions, or risk going unheard.

But why does legal discourse matter to those of us who never enter a courtroom? Foucault's notion that the law defines "types of subjectivity" suggests that legal ways of thinking and speaking are not self-contained, but rather interact with the culture at large. The California Supreme Court's description of its own approach to interpreting statutory law indicates a similar perspective:

To seek the meaning of a statute is not simply to look up dictionary definitions and then stitch together the results. Rather, it is to discern the sense of the statute, and therefore its words, *in the legal and broader culture*. Obviously, a statute has no meaning apart from its words. Similarly, its words have no meaning apart from the world in which they are spoken. (*Hodges v. Superior Court* 1999: 114; emphasis in original)

The justices joining the opinion in *Hodges* clearly believe that the law is shaped by the larger culture, and must therefore be interpreted in a cultural context – a position that I take as one of my premises in this essay. And one can also argue the converse: that the larger culture is shaped by the law. Alexis de Tocqueville's comments about the legal nature of American culture in the antebellum era suggest that legal discourse has infused the lives of Americans to a degree not seen in other countries:

Scarcely any question arises in the United States which does not become, sooner or later, a subject of judicial debate; hence all parties are obliged to borrow the ideas, and even the language, usual in judicial proceedings in their daily controversies. As most public men are, or have been, legal practitioners, they introduce the customs and technicalities of their profession into the affairs of the country. The jury extends this habitude to all classes. The language of the law thus becomes, in some measure, a vulgar tongue; the spirit of the law, which is produced in the schools and courts of justice, gradually penetrates beyond their walls into the bosom of society, where it descends to the lowest classes, so that the whole people contracts the habits and the tastes of the magistrate. (Tocqueville 2000: 323–4)

Tocqueville's comments strike me as true, and even more so after the Civil War than in the 1830s when they were written. The authors of literary works in the postbellum era frequently addressed matters of public interest by employing legal perspectives – in many cases addressing specific legal and constitutional issues – and thus by using legal discourse to help frame their stories. While few Americans in the nineteenth century would have consciously adopted a view of law as narrative, the belief that the law should embody the public will implicitly tied it to the kinds of narratives that both shaped and reflected that will. At the same time, however, the ideal that the law should be above the fray – immune to the partisan interests of powerful groups and the shifting whims and impulses of the masses – remained a strong part of the law's image in the public mind. Thus, the law was expected to change, but to remain true to foundational principles that have always been difficult to define – concepts like justice, equality, rights, and neutrality. Legal discourse was, and is, a battleground – a field of conflict in which language and narratives emerge as authoritative only to be replaced by new versions, or by old models resurrected. I contend that this was especially true in late nineteenth-century America, and that many authors of fiction sought to enter the battle armed with their ability to influence the public will through narrative.

Law in the Postbellum Era

Public life in the antebellum United States had been dominated by lawyers and jurists whose rhetorical skills endowed them with a certain aura of majesty. John Marshall, Daniel Webster, John Quincy Adams, Joseph Story – these are just a few of the legal figures whose writings and oratory turned them into larger-than-life personifications of the law itself, and of the Constitution that served as the fount of all legal authority. As the nation moved toward civil war, however, that aura was considerably tarnished. The power to construct a sense of national unity out of words failed men such as Webster, Roger Taney (Chief Justice of the US Supreme Court and author of the *Dred Scott* decision), and the backwoods lawyer Abraham Lincoln, each of whom proved more adept at inflaming the impending crisis than resolving it.

But while the Civil War tarnished the image of the law in the nation's public consciousness, it by no means eliminated the country's historic tendency to search for legal solutions to its most intractable political and cultural conflicts. Instead, Americans rewrote the law, engaging in acts of authorship akin to those that had produced the Declaration of Independence and Constitution in the previous century. If the law had failed to ensure equality and bind the nation together sufficiently to avoid war, then surely legal texts could be created that would accomplish these goals. This attitude led to the creation of the Thirteenth, Fourteenth, and Fifteenth Amendments to the Constitution (collectively known as the Civil War amendments) abolishing slavery and granting African Americans equal protection and voting rights, as well as to similar federal legislation. It also lent momentum to the movement for the codification of state law. By adopting their own legal codes, states saw themselves as "democratizing" the law by making it accessible to non-lawyers and decreasing its reliance upon a common law corrupted by British class hierarchies (decades earlier, Thomas Jefferson had argued fervently for the United States to reject the common law, to no avail). Finally, the postbellum era saw a proliferation of writing *about* the law: the professionalization of legal practice and the new emphasis on attending law school led to the creation of numerous law reviews and other forms of legal commentary, and the sensationalist journalism of the time found ample fodder in lurid criminal cases and private legal suits between the famous or wealthy (as the Beecher–Tilton scandal indicates). Consequently, the law began to seem less like a set of eternal precepts laid down by an inspired generation of founding fathers and centuries of legal precedent, and more like a contingent and ever-evolving instrument for implementing current policy determinations – a view espoused by the towering legal figure of the period, Oliver Wendell Holmes, Jr. At the same time, however, the American public continued to idealize the law as a realm of neutrality, objectivity, and truth, even when (or especially when) it failed to live up to those ideals.

Although recent scholarship largely agrees that fiction writers participated significantly in this explosion of discourse about the law, scholars have characterized that participation in different ways. Robert Ferguson maintains that the historically close relation between law and literature in the United States ended in the mid-nineteenth century with the demise or discrediting of figures such as Webster, whose authority had arisen from their status as both lawyers and men of letters. After this change, Ferguson argues, literary works tended to speak about the law from a critical vantage point removed from legal conventions and norms. William E. Moddelmog, however, contends that writers in the postbellum era continued to produce works that were in a sense "legal" by employing language and narratives drawn from legal texts and offering revisionary versions of legal standards. Brook Thomas takes a similar approach in focusing his discussion of late nineteenth-century works on the issue of contract, which he claims was a concept central to both literary and legal figures at the time. According to Thomas, these two groups sought to envision a social order grounded in individual acts of promising as a way of promoting egalitarian ideals and discrediting hierarchies based on status. Nonetheless, Thomas also notes that writers were generally forced to acknowledge the "promise of contract" as an unfulfilled one.

Other scholars have focused their attention on literary and legal attempts to grapple with specific legal issues. Nan Goodman, for instance, looks at changes in tort law in the late nineteenth century and the invention of negligence as a standard of liability for accidents. Goodman claims that changes in the legal concept of negligence precipitated new cultural understandings of individual agency and responsibility for risk that were reflected in works by authors such as Mark Twain, Charles Chesnutt, and Stephen Crane. Eric J. Sundquist, Gregg D. Crane, and Jon Christian Suggs assert the importance of race-related legal standards to the production of literary works during the period. And Laura Hanft Korobkin concentrates on the effects that sentimental modes of narrative had on stories of adultery that appeared in courts, in the press, and in literary works.

Rather than seek to describe all of the approaches to law and narrative during this era that scholars have taken, or to account for each of the authors whose works have been linked to the law, the remainder of this essay will focus on three broad cultural issues that also appear as major legal issues in the late nineteenth century, and on specific authors who raise those issues explicitly. I will first discuss literary responses to changes in popular conceptions of the law after the Civil War. I will then examine narratives relating to civil rights for racial and ethnic minorities, and finally those dealing with the status of women in American law and culture.

Law, Narrative, and Power

In "The Fall of Richmond," a poem about the final days of the Civil War, Herman Melville deflates the triumphal rhetoric that pervaded the North at the time, stating "God is in Heaven, and Grant in the Town / And Right through might is Law" (Melville 1976: 99). Melville's ironic implication is that, rather than a victory for the forces of good over evil, or law over anarchy, the North's triumph in the war was a matter of simple force. Throughout his writing career, Melville consistently described social and political issues in Hobbesian or even Machiavellian terms – that is, as fields of combat in which claims of right serve only as smokescreens for self-interest and the desire for power. This is as true of his early criticisms of missionary activity in the novels *Typee* and *Omoo* as it is of his celebrated works of the 1850s, such as *Moby-Dick*, "Benito Cereno," and *The Confidence Man*. Yet it is perhaps most evident in the last work of fiction he produced (and left unfinished at his death in 1891), *Billy Budd, Sailor (An Inside Narrative)*.

Much has been written about *Billy Budd* and the law, and there is by no means a consensus of opinion on its legal implications. Yet virtually all who have commented on its legal dimensions agree that it presents a stark view of law as a field of power, intimidation, and social control. Whether Melville accepts this as a necessary byproduct of social life or rails against it as an affront to the sanctity of the individual is a subject of scholarly dispute. Billy's execution by Captain Vere for the murder of John Claggart – a man presented in biblical terms as Satan-like – after a trial that Vere controls and in which a guilty verdict seems predetermined registers Melville's skepticism about the law's claims to neutrality in the search for justice. Nonetheless, it is possible to argue that the work reflects a belief, famously articulated by Holmes in his seminal work *The Common Law* (1881), that the state is justified in suppressing individual life and liberty when faced with a threat to its own perception of the public good. My own view is that the chilling depiction of Billy's execution – described as an example of the "forms, measured forms" that intimidate the multitude into obedience to the state – render the work a final protest against the officially sanctioned tyrannies of American social life that deprive individuals of their deepest sources of meaning. Billy's inner life remains a mystery to the reader throughout *Billy Budd*, and Captain Vere goes to his grave calling out his name in apparent recognition of having destroyed, in the name of law and order, his sense of purpose and his access to spiritual understanding. Literary and religious modes of knowing prove no match for the rational, detached, but ultimately biased narratives of the law, and Melville's text serves as a final protest against the triumph of legal discourse in American culture.

A more ambivalent view of shifting legal and literary relations appears in the fiction of William Dean Howells, one of the foremost promoters and practitioners of American literary realism. Much of Howells's writing explores ethical and moral dilemmas from several distinct cultural vantage points, including that of the law. In *A Modern Instance* (1882), his most explicit depiction of the law's prevalence in American life, Bartley Hubbard – a young journalist interested in becoming a lawyer – marries the daughter of the aging but nonetheless imposing rural lawyer, Squire Gaylord. Bartley's form of journalism is unprincipled and misleading, but Howells takes pains to show that Bartley is nonetheless adept at creating narratives that resonate in the public consciousness. Bartley eventually abandons both his wife, Marcia, and his legal aspirations, but publishes a public notice of divorce that demonstrates the legal nature of his form of storytelling. Although Squire Gaylord successfully represents Marcia in the divorce proceeding, his melodramatic collapse in the courtroom and Bartley's escape to the frontier indicate a shift in the foundations of legal authority in the nation. Gaylord's authority, springing from his embodiment of stable and enduring moral precepts defined without reference to current social or political standards, has given way to Bartley's authority as a creator of public stories that, by shaping the public will, inevitably shape the law as well. Although Howells implicitly condemns the ascension to power of America's Bartley Hubbards, he nonetheless grudgingly accepts the primacy of narratives in the postbellum social order, suggesting that in an age in which traditional forms of moral authority no longer inspire assent, it is storytellers (including more principled ones, like realists) who may finally determine the content of the nation's codes and the character of its judgments.

Narratives of Civil Rights

For many anti-slavery writers before the Civil War – particularly those writing after the Compromise of 1850 – the relationship of their own literary works to the law was clear and unambiguous: they sought to create works that would marshal religious, moral, and literary modes of expression against the corrupt legal discourse of the Constitution, the Compromise, and the judiciary that upheld them. While some abolitionists, such as Frederick Douglass, maintained a more nuanced view of the law that held open the possibility of an anti-slavery constitutionalism, writers like Harriet Beecher Stowe and Henry David Thoreau presented their works as occupying a moral and spiritual plane wholly distinct from the sphere of politics and law. In the wake of the Civil War amendments, however, this rarefied literary space was less accessible to the proponents of civil rights for African Americans, Native Americans, women, and other oppressed groups. The abolition of slavery and the granting of civil rights to African Americans had transformed the law from an obstacle to equality into a tool for achieving it. To be sure, the limitations of the law became painfully obvious as Reconstruction progressed, disintegrated, and finally collapsed, but the texts of the law could nonetheless serve as foundations for literary works addressing legal issues. Rather than critiquing the law for its failure to serve the interests of social justice, writers in the postbellum era frequently critiqued legal and social institutions for failing to give full effect to the law.

Among the authors who wrote about the status of African Americans after the Civil War, Mark Twain and Charles Chesnutt stand out for their sustained attention to both the promise and the disappointment of the war's legal legacy. Twain – who briefly fought for the Confederacy before abandoning the war effort and heading West – returned obsessively in his fiction to the themes of slavery, civil rights, and the significance of race in American life. The ending of *Adventures of Huckleberry Finn* (1884), for instance, turns on the legal status of the slave, Jim, whom Huck has helped to escape. Unbeknown to either character, Jim has already been legally emancipated and thus endures for nothing a rather degrading and dangerous game concocted by Tom Sawyer to free him – a development that may be read as a criticism of the return to government-sponsored racial oppression in the South following Reconstruction (the process of "freeing" Jim ends up enslaving him in new ways). Legal decisions such as that delivered by the US Supreme Court in the *Civil Rights Cases* (1883) had rendered impotent much of the federal civil rights legislation passed during Reconstruction, and Northern weariness at policing white racism in the South essentially turned the Civil War amendments into dead letters through lack of enforcement. Twain's bleak assessment of Southern race relations in *Huckleberry Finn* invokes the ideals that lay behind postbellum civil rights reforms while condemning American society for failing to remain true to their spirit.

This is even more true of Twain's cynical masterpiece of racial passing, *Pudd'nhead Wilson* (1894), and its oddly conjoined story, "Those Extraordinary Twins." Published during the formative era of Jim Crow – the system of "separate but equal" facilities for blacks and whites in the South that was upheld by the US Supreme Court in *Plessy v. Ferguson* (1896) – *Pudd'nhead Wilson* relates the story of a black child and a white one switched at birth in antebellum Missouri, with the black one light enough to "pass" as white. The true identities of the two are not uncovered until years later, when the novel's lawyer, David Wilson, exposes Tom Driscoll – the "black" man passing for "white" – as both a murderer and as legally black by referring to fingerprints he took when they were infants (fingerprinting was still virtually unknown when the novel was written). The discovery of Tom's black heritage consigns him to slavery instead of to the gallows, while Chambers – the "white" man assumed to be "black" – is freed, only to become a social outcast in the white community by virtue of his African American dialect and mannerisms. The story mocks prevalent legal definitions of race based on the percentage of white or black "blood" in an individual's background – definitions that served as the foundation for Jim Crow. Moreover, Twain skewers the law's claim to effect neutral and evenhanded justice by suggesting that it ultimately worships at the altar of property rights, as Tom's "value" as a slave is given greater significance than the need to punish his crime. Yet Wilson, the lawyer, serves as the closest thing to the voice of reason in Dawson's Landing, Missouri – a town otherwise composed of ignorant yokels and degenerate Southern aristocrats. After listening to an incessantly barking dog, Wilson jokes that he wishes he owned half that dog, so that he could kill his half. The literalist townspeople don't understand irony, and label Wilson a "pudd'nhead." But the joke's implications reverberate through the work, as Twain shows that "dividing" racial identity into black and white blood (the latter imagined as property) is just as nonsensical as physically dividing a dog on the basis of ownership.

Furthermore, the story that Twain extracted from an earlier draft of *Pudd'nhead Wilson* – "Those Extraordinary Twins" – rehearses that theme again. It involves a pair of Siamese twins from Italy (Twain "separates" the twins in *Pudd'nhead Wilson*) who settle in Dawson's Landing and eventually run for local office. After one twin beats the other in the election, a court rules that only the winner can sit on the board of aldermen – an absurd ruling that presumes the twins are separate physical entities. The townspeople resolve the political impasse with the equally absurd act of hanging one twin. The similar themes of the two works and the fact that the "extraction" of "Twins" from *Pudd'nhead Wilson* was incomplete (portions of *Pudd'nhead Wilson* continue to depict the twins as conjoined) suggest that "Twins" is also, to some extent, about race. The hanging of one twin may be Twain's comment on the absurdity and barbarity of lynching African American men – a growing epidemic in the South in the 1890s. Twain seems to implicate the law in this practice, as judges refused to provide adequate legal remedies for the degradation inflicted by Jim Crow and for the disfranchisement of black voters in the South through poll taxes and similar means. With African Americans claiming a right to an equal political voice, and with the law unwilling to offer workable solutions to the South's racialized politics, Southern whites "solved" the problem through violence.

Twain's works satirize these developments, but offer no overt answers. Yet the conflicted representations of the law contained in these works, along with the intertextual relation of the two stories, can be seen as a kind of narrative solution. If Twain's problem with the law is that it divides the world, humankind, and even individuals into neat but ultimately arbitrary categories (such as race), then the very messiness of his literary texts serves as a kind of corrective to the law. That messiness also suggests that Twain did not conceive of his fiction as separate from, and morally superior to, the legal discourse of race, but as intimately bound up with – even in conversation with – legal texts and standards.

The same can be said of Charles Chesnutt's fiction. Chesnutt – an African American writer who was trained as a lawyer and earned his living as a legal stenographer – constructed many of his plots around legal conceptions of race, seeking through narrative to expose those conceptions as fundamentally flawed. His seminal collections of short stories, *The Conjure Woman* (1899) and *The Wife of His Youth and Other Stories of the Color Line* (1899), address the legacy of slavery in the postbellum United States and the ways in which the law perpetuates that legacy, especially through seemingly race-neutral concepts like property rights. In the story "Po' Sandy," for instance, a slave named Sandy is transformed into a tree by a conjure woman (a practitioner of a form of African American folk magic known as "conjure") so that he will not be sent to work on other plantations, separating him from his wife. The tree is eventually cut down and sawed into boards for a new schoolhouse. Years later, after emancipation, John – a white Northerner who purchases the old plantation – decides to use the wood from the now abandoned schoolhouse (considered to be haunted) to build a new kitchen. After hearing the story of Sandy from Uncle Julius – a former slave and the primary storyteller of the tales contained in *The Conjure Woman* – John's wife, Annie, decides instead to let Uncle Julius use the schoolhouse for religious meetings. The story subtly demonstrates how postbellum assertions of property rights help to maintain antebellum forms of racial oppression: John "owns" the wood from the schoolhouse (and by extension his entire plantation) only to the extent that he ignores the slave labor that went into creating its value. Much of Chesnutt's short fiction accuses the law of promoting seemingly benign concepts – such as property rights – to continue master–slave relations between whites and blacks. This point lies behind many of the stories in *The Wife of His Youth* as well, including "Uncle Wellington's Wives" and "The Web of Circumstance," each of which makes it clear that the specter of slavery continues to "haunt" the law and the nation decades after Appomattox.

Chesnutt's novels invoke the law even more explicitly than his short works. His first published novel, *The House Behind the Cedars* (1900), depicts the lives of John and Rena Walden, who are of mixed racial heritage and who move from North Carolina to South Carolina in an attempt to pass as white. John does so successfully, but his sister's secret is ultimately revealed, leading to her death. Although the plot follows many of the sentimental conventions of the "tragic mulatta" story that was emerging as a popular genre in the late nineteenth century, it departs from those conventions by using legal conceptions of race to ground its narrative. Although under North Carolina law John and Rena are black by virtue of their "blood," South Carolina law accepted reputation as one element that defined racial identity. Thus, by being accepted into the community as white people, John and Rena are able, at least in theory, to "make" themselves legally white. South Carolina only made explicit what all states were forced to do; because genealogies were always murky, reputation rather than "blood" served as the true (but usually unacknowledged) determinant of race in the courtroom. Thus, Chesnutt's use of South Carolina law turns the novel into an affirmation of the social rather than biological nature of race. Moreover, by using the law's practices (its reliance on reputation) to cast doubt on its doctrines (race is biological), the novel positions itself within, rather than outside, legal discourse. Chesnutt's insightful depiction of the Wilmington race riots of 1898 in *The Marrow of Tradition* (1901) and his novel of a failed Southern reformer, *The Colonel's Dream* (1905), continued to evoke legal principles in the process of undermining the authority of Jim Crow, racial lynching, disfranchisement, and the South's convict-lease system (portrayed in *The Colonel's Dream* as simply a new version of slavery).

In addition to Chesnutt's fiction, the law appears as a prominent theme in the works of many other African American authors of the late nineteenth and early twentieth centuries. This was a time in which Booker T. Washington emerged as the most prominent black leader in the country, and his message – grounded in an odd combination of self-help and black capitulation to racism – emphasized that African American reliance on legal rights was misplaced. Washington counseled blacks to eschew voting, politics, lawsuits, and other forms of protest against white dominance in the South, and to focus instead on private industry. His main rival turned out to be W. E. B. Du Bois, whose activist message appealed much more to black intellectuals and writers of the era. The public debate between the two was largely over the law – Du Bois wanted to use it as a sword to effect social change (he would later become a founding member of the NAACP), Washington only as a shield to protect blacks in the pursuit of their own livelihoods. This conflict over the proper approach to the law is evident in Sutton Griggs' *Imperium in Imperio* (1899), which places two friends at odds over a plan to foment a black rebellion against the United States and establish an independent black nation, and in Pauline Hopkins's *Contending Forces: A Romance Illustrative of Negro Life North and South* (1900), in which a character modeled on Du Bois discredits the ideas of a more Washingtonian figure and employs the law to right a wrong done to his family in the antebellum era.

Other writers used strategies similar to those employed by African American authors to challenge injustices done to Mexican American and Native American populations. In *The Squatter and the Don* (1885), María Amparo Ruiz de Burton delves into the plight of Mexican American families in California whose land was taken from them after the Mexican War. Although the property rights of these Californios were to be respected under the Treaty of Guadalupe Hidalgo, which also granted them full citizenship, in practice courts found ways to discredit their title and deprive them of the majority of their land. By documenting this dispossession, Ruiz de Burton highlights the disjunction between the law's ideals and its actual practices. The same can be said of Helen Hunt Jackson's novel *Ramona* (1884), which chronicles the injustices perpetrated against California's Mission Indians by means similar to those that dispossessed Mexican Americans. Originally titled "In the Name of the Law," Jackson's novel serves as a fictionalized version of the issues she discussed in her nonfiction work *A Century of Dishonor* (1880), which exposed US–Indian relations as a series of broken promises and treaty violations on the part of the federal government. Once again, the emphasis is not simply on the immorality of such actions, but on their *illegality*, and Jackson's novel should be read as a kind of legal argument in narrative form.

Narratives of Women's Rights

Although scholars tend to associate the birth of the women's movement in the United States with the Seneca Falls Convention of 1848, prior to the Civil War the movement for women's rights had largely taken a back seat to the abolitionist movement. After the war, however, women activists began to gain more national recognition, successfully promoting causes such as Married Women's Property Acts (granting married women the right to hold property and make contracts), liberalized divorce laws, and state voting rights (women could not vote in federal elections until 1920). Although novels focusing on women tended to avoid invoking the women's rights movement explicitly, beneath the surface of many of these stories lie attempts to combat or rewrite the legal narratives that established the second-class citizenship of women.

One novel that did address the women's rights movement overtly – in a largely hostile way – was Henry James's *The Bostonians* (1886). Its hostility, however is tempered by James's sympathetic view of feminists' dissatisfaction with the institution of marriage. The novel's heroine, Verena Tarrant, is the subject of a battle for control between Olive Chancellor – the representative of the women's movement – and Basil Ransom – a dashing former Confederate officer who wishes to marry Verena. Although James strongly implies that marriage to Basil will destroy any independent identity that Verena possesses, he presents Verena's alternative – participation with Olive in the movement – as an equally bad option. Olive seeks to control Verena as much as Basil does, and James hints subtly that her desire for power has a sexual element as well. Brook Thomas connects the novel to the issue of privacy rights, noting that although marriage was supposed to be a private relation, many nineteenth-century feminists argued that wives were essentially expected to perform in a socially constructed role and thus occupied a public space within marriage. But since Verena will lack a private self in the women's movement as well (she is highly valued as a public speaker), James suggests that women's opportunities for true privacy and self-definition are extremely limited. Although this position seems to embody a moral critique of legal discourse, Thomas argues that James places faith in the logic of contract, which posits the possibility of an equal partnership between two individuals as separate, autonomous entities. Thus, *The Bostonians* can be read as a work that invokes ideals central to the law and uses them to attack as unjust the legal and personal consequences to women of marriage.

More closely aligned with the philosophy of the women's movement is Kate Chopin's *The Awakening* (1899). Chopin's heroine, Edna Pontellier, struggles with the stifling duties imposed on her as a wife and mother. She eventually moves into a house of her own and takes a lover, but, failing to find fulfillment, commits suicide. Unlike *The Bostonians*, the novel does not address the women's movement explicitly, focusing instead on Edna's inner life. But the terms that Edna uses to assess her position are nonetheless drawn from the legal discourse of individual rights that was frequently invoked by the movement. Edna continually takes stock of her own rights, and pits them against the demands placed upon her by her husband and children. In fact, Wai Chee Dimock, sounding much like Tocqueville, reads the work as "a tribute to the primacy of jurisprudence in American life: a tribute to its adversarial language, its tendency to saturate other domains of discourse, not the least of which being the discourse of subjectivity" (Dimock 1996: 209). Edna's private thoughts are determined to a significant extent by a conception of herself as a rights-holder, and the unitary, autonomous self implied in that concept. With that in mind, Edna's death might be interpreted in different ways. Dimock maintains that Chopin criticizes, at least in part, Edna's reliance on this jurisprudential conception of self. I believe, however, that Edna's death reflects Chopin's critique of a society that refuses to recognize women's rights, and that suicide is paradoxically the only means available to Edna for asserting her independence and autonomy.

Like Chopin's Edna, Edith Wharton's female characters are often victims of patriarchal social and legal standards. Unlike Chopin, however, Wharton's fiction does not endorse a rights-based model of the self. Wharton values acts of renunciation rather than expressions of entitlement, presenting her female characters as most admirable when they give up their "rights" for the sake of others. This is true of

Lily Bart in *The House of Mirth* (1905), who possesses evidence admissible in a divorce trial that her nemesis, Bertha Dorset, has been unfaithful to her husband. Lily's reputation has been unjustly impugned by Bertha and, as a result, Lily has been ostracized by the only social element in which she can survive. Yet Lily refuses to assert her "rights" by threatening Bertha with exposure (in part because it would also expose the object of her love, Lawrence Selden). Wharton's language with respect to Lily's predicament is unambiguously legal – she has been "tried" and "convicted" in the "court" of public opinion, yet nonetheless refuses to speak up in her own defense. Although Lily's silence is problematic and leads implicitly to her demise, Wharton nevertheless suggests that making public the sordid evidence of the affair would result in a form of spiritual, if not physical, death.

A similar predicament exists for Ellen Olenska in Wharton's *The Age of Innocence* (1920). Ellen forgoes her right to obtain a divorce from her unfaithful husband, thus sparing the feelings and beliefs of the aristocratic New Yorkers who offer her refuge. In renouncing her own personal happiness, including a relationship with her love, Newland Archer, she gains a measure of spiritual comfort that, for Wharton, becomes possible only by rejecting a self-centered, rights-based model of identity. The female character in Wharton's *œuvre* who most forcefully asserts her individual rights – Undine Spragg in *The Custom of the Country* (1913) – is also presented as the most morally reprehensible. Thus, while Wharton attacks the forms of oppression that stem from a patriarchal social and legal system, she refuses to embrace the version of female selfhood implicit in the legal reforms promoted by the women's rights movement. Unlike Chopin and many of the other authors discussed above who draw upon the law to address matters of social injustice, Wharton attempts to position her fiction outside dominant modes of legal discourse.

In this respect, Wharton anticipates the views of a later generation of literary modernists, who by and large (and with notable exceptions, such as William Faulkner) turned away from the law and other public discourses in the construction of their narratives. If writers in the late nineteenth century began to feel a need to speak directly to, and in the language of, the law, writers who emerged after World War I tended to view the public sphere as a corrupting influence on literature, and to attempt to purge that influence from their work. As Tocqueville would undoubtedly have noted, however, legal discourse has been too deeply ingrained in the language and collective psyche of Americans to be eliminated completely from literary narratives. For all that Americans today lament the debasement of legal ideals in the name of spectacle and titillation, sensationalized depictions of legal conflict simply evidence the ongoing dialogue between the law's texts and the public's anxieties, desires, and beliefs. In fact, to hope that literary works might remove themselves from that dialogue would not only be wishful thinking; it would also be to ask for an impoverishment of literature's power to address one of the deepest and most pervasive elements of American cultural life.

PRIMARY TEXTS

Chesnutt, Charles W. *The Conjure Woman*. 1899.

Chesnutt, Charles W. *The Wife of His Youth and Other Stories of the Color Line*. 1899.

Chesnutt, Charles W. *The House behind the Cedars*. 1900.

Chesnutt, Charles W. *The Marrow of Tradition*. 1901.

Chesnutt, Charles W. *The Colonel's Dream*. 1905.

Chopin, Kate. *The Awakening*. 1899.

Griggs, Sutton. *Imperium in Imperio*. 1899.

Holmes, Oliver Wendell, Jr. *The Common Law*. 1881.

Hopkins, Pauline E. *Contending Forces: A Romance Illustrative of Negro Life North and South*. 1900.

Howells, William Dean. *A Modern Instance*. 1882.

Jackson, Helen Hunt. *A Century of Dishonor: A Sketch of the United States Government's Dealings with Some of the Indian Tribes*. 1880.

Jackson, Helen Hunt. *Ramona*. 1884.

James, Henry. *The Bostonians*. 1886.

Melville, Herman. *Billy Budd* (unfinished 1891).

Ruiz de Burton, María Amparo. *The Squatter and the Don*. 1885.

Tocqueville, Alexis de. *Democracy in America*. 1835, 1840.

Twain, Mark. "Those Extraordinary Twins." 1894.

Twain, Mark. *The Tragedy of Pudd'nhead Wilson*. 1894.

Wharton, Edith. *The House of Mirth*. 1905.

Wharton, Edith. *The Custom of the Country*. 1913.

Wharton, Edith. *The Age of Innocence*. 1920.

REFERENCES AND FURTHER READING

Brooks, Peter, and Gewirtz, Paul, eds. (1996). *Law's Stories: Narrative and Rhetoric in the Law*. New Haven, Conn.: Yale University Press.

Carton, Evan (1982). "Pudd'nhead Wilson and the Fiction of Law and Custom." In Eric J. Sundquist (ed.), *American Literary Realism*, 82–94. Baltimore: Johns Hopkins University Press.

Castronovo, Russ (2001). *Necro Citizenship: Death, Eroticism, and the Public Sphere in the Nineteenth-Century United States*. Durham, NC: Duke University Press.

Civil Rights Cases (1883). 109 U.S. 3.

Cover, Robert M. (1992). *Narrative, Violence, and the Law: The Essays of Robert Cover*, ed. Martha Minow, Michael Ryan, and Austin Sarat. Ann Arbor: University of Michigan Press.

Crane, Gregg D. (2002). *Race, Citizenship, and Law in American Literature*. Cambridge, UK: Cambridge University Press.

Dimock, Wai Chee (1996). *Residues of Justice: Literature, Law, Philosophy*. Berkeley: University of California Press.

Ferguson, Robert A. (1984). *Law and Letters in American Culture*. Cambridge, Mass.: Harvard University Press.

Fish, Stanley (1989). *Doing What Comes Naturally: Change, Rhetoric, and the Practice of Theory in Literary and Legal Studies*. Durham, NC: Duke University Press.

Foucault, Michel (2000). "Truth and Juridical Forms." In *Essential Works of Michel Foucault, 1954–1984*, ed. James D. Faubion, trans. Robert Hurley, vol. 3, 1–89. New York: New Press.

Fox, Richard Wightman (1999). *Trials of Intimacy: Love and Loss in the Beecher–Tilton Scandal*. Chicago: University of Chicago Press.

Goodman, Nan (1998). *Shifting the Blame: Literature, Law, and the Theory of Accidents in Nineteenth-Century America*. Princeton: Princeton University Press.

Hodges v. Superior Court (1999). 21 Cal. 4th 109.

Horwitz, Morton J. (1992). *The Transformation of American Law, 1870–1960: The Crisis of Legal Orthodoxy*. New York: Oxford University Press.

Korobkin, Laura Hanft (1998). *Criminal Conversations: Sentimentality and Nineteenth-Century Legal Stories of Adultery*. New York: Columbia University Press.

Melville, Herman (1976). *Poems of Herman Melville*. Albany, NY: New College and University Press.

Miller, Perry (1965). "Book Two: The Legal Mentality." In *The Life of the Mind in America: From the Revolution to the Civil War*. New York: Harcourt, Brace.

Moddelmog, William E. (2000). *Reconstituting Authority: American Fiction in the Province of the Law, 1880–1920*. Iowa City: University of Iowa Press.

Plessy v. *Ferguson* (1896), 163 U.S. 537.

Posner, Richard A. (1988). *Law and Literature: A Misunderstood Relation*. Cambridge, Mass.: Harvard University Press.

Suggs, Jon Christian (2000). *Whispered Consolations: Law and Narrative in African American Life*. Ann Arbor: University of Michigan Press.

Sundquist, Eric J. (1993). *To Wake the Nations: Race in the Making of American Literature*. Cambridge, Mass.: Belknap/Harvard University Press.

Thomas, Brook (1997). *American Literary Realism and the Failed Promise of Contract*. Berkeley: University of California Press.

Thomas, Brook (1987). *Cross-Examinations of Law and Literature: Cooper, Hawthorne, Stowe, and Melville*. Cambridge, UK: Cambridge University Press.

Tocqueville, Alexis de (2000). *Democracy in America*. New York: Bantam.

Weisberg, Richard (1984). *The Failure of the Word: The Protagonist as Lawyer in Modern Fiction*. New Haven, Conn.: Yale University Press.

Weisberg, Richard (1992). *Poethics, and Other Strategies of Law and Literature*. New York: Columbia University Press.

White, James Boyd (1984). *When Words Lose Their Meaning: Constitutions and Reconstitutions of Language, Character, and Community*. Chicago: University of Chicago Press.

21

Planning Utopia

Thomas Peyser

Hail, hail, the light of the morning, hail consecrated plan! (*Hymn of the Nationalist*)

That the student of American fiction between the Civil War and World War I must attend to the question of utopia is due almost entirely to one book published in 1888: Edward Bellamy's celebration of socialism, *Looking Backward: 2000–1887*. Dozens and dozens of utopian novels were dashed off in the 1890s (mostly in direct response to, and often in refutation of, Bellamy's bestseller), but only two other utopias from the period come in for much discussion any more: William Dean Howells's *A Traveller from Altruria* (1894) and Charlotte Perkins Gilman's *Herland* (1915). Neither of these works, however, had anything like the impact of the book that made Bellamy's reputation. Had it not been written by Howells, *A Traveller from Altruria* would almost certainly have sunk into complete obscurity long ago, and *Herland* was not published in book form until the 1970s, on the heels of renewed interest in Gilman's sensational short story, "The Yellow Wall-paper" (1892). *Looking Backward*, by contrast, was widely consumed and discussed both in the United States and abroad – many Bolsheviks, for example, were familiar with it, including Lenin's wife, who gave it a mixed review – and the common feeling that among American novels it can be ranked only with *Uncle Tom's Cabin* on the score of its influence on public debate is probably just. Bellamy's work even inspired a short-lived but moderately noisy political movement with which both Howells and Gilman affiliated themselves. Although the "Bellamy Clubs" that sprang up in the United States in an effort to realize the society Bellamy had imagined did not survive the Progressive era, *Looking Backward* left enough of a mark on the generations that came of age following its publication for both historian Charles Beard and philosopher John Dewey to proclaim in the early 1930s, in a complimentary vein, that it and Marx's *Das Kapital* were the most influential books published in the preceding half-century.

The vogue for utopian writings may have depended on the appearance of a single book, but it hardly seems an accident that utopias should have received so enthusiastic a reception at just this time. As in other countries, the nineteenth century was a time of dramatic transformation in the United States, and the advent of industrialization, along with the concomitant growth in urban centers, increasingly peopled by immigrants from Europe, had left many confused and unsettled about the future. Moreover, the fabulous fortunes generated by economic growth pushed the question of inequality to the forefront of debate about the relationship between capital and labor, for while the poor were not getting poorer, the rich were getting richer. To many sensitive observers, therefore, it appeared that the nineteenth century had been a disaster for the workers of the world, an impression furthered by the strikes and demonstrations, some of them bloody, that punctuated the news of the day with what seemed alarming regularity, even if these took place against the backdrop of something far less likely to produce headlines: the gradual but steady economic amelioration capitalism had made possible. It is not, therefore, difficult to imagine why a large middle-class audience should have been waiting for a vision such as that offered by Bellamy to appear. Fearful that the already fast pace of historical change might accelerate still further (to adopt a metaphor favored by Henry Adams), possibly in a violently revolutionary direction, such readers were apparently hungry for a vision of the future from which economic inequality and the hubbub of an ethnically and culturally diverse populace had been banished, superseded by a uniform affluence and a prim gentility that even a cultivated Bostonian could regard without a shudder. The directness of Bellamy's appeal to his readers can be gauged by the fact that he makes someone very like them the hero of his novel: one Julian West, who, having been mesmerized in 1887, wakes to find himself in Boston in the year 2000, a bloodless revolution having transformed the nation while he was slumbering.

The name of the genre to which *Looking Backward* belongs comes from Thomas More's *Utopia* (1516), whose title is a Greek pun meaning either "noplace" or "happy place." More's text, like many similar works that preceded and followed it, is full of ambiguities and ironies, and the fabulous realm it describes is not to be taken as a straightforward model for political reform, but rather as a site from which all manner of barbs and skeptical questions can be launched toward the prevailing customs of Europe. By contrast, Bellamy claimed that his utopia was "intended, in all seriousness, as a forecast, in accordance with the principles of evolution, of the next stage in the industrial and social development of humanity, especially in this country." As such, he put his imaginative labors entirely in the service of an economic and political system that was to rise to ascendancy in the coming century, but which, for prudential reasons, he refrained from naming explicitly anywhere in his novel: socialism. Surmising, perhaps correctly, that the middle-class Americans to whom he wished to appeal associated socialism with sexual licentiousness – the "free love" advocated by some socialists of the time – and with immigrants, whom they feared as unassimilable and reprehensibly unruly additions to the nation, Bellamy explained in a letter to an associate that the word "socialism" had to be kept out of his book if the thing itself were ever to get a purchase on the American mind.

The assiduousness with which Bellamy refrained from applying the readily available label to his proposed system was matched by the thoroughgoingness of his application of socialist principles. Everywhere in *Looking Backward*, the individual is conceived as owing his very being to the society and its governmental institutions, in stark contrast to the constitutional principles according to which government is merely an instrument contrived by individuals who agree to put themselves under it so that it may carry out particular and carefully delineated functions deemed essential for the maintenance of order. Giving voice to Bellamy's disdain for a system that makes paramount so paltry a thing as the liberty of the individual, Julian West's guide to the world of 2000, Dr. Leete, explains that the purpose of those who overthrew the old order

> was to realize the idea of the nation with a grandeur and a completeness never before conceived, not as an association of men for certain merely political functions affecting their happiness only remotely and superficially, but as a family, a vital union, a common life, a mighty heaven-touching tree whose leaves are its people, fed from its veins, and feeding it in turn.

As is the case with much in the novel, Bellamy uncannily foreshadows the rhetoric and cultural style favored by fascists and other totalitarians in the century following the publication of *Looking Backward*. Glorifying the "common life" that requires that the people see themselves as belonging to the nation, Leete surveys the institutions that by 2000 have made "the native land truly a fatherland."

Chief among these is the "industrial army," the labor force into which all youth are marshaled in an annual celebration replete with badges and military-style parades, and in which they serve until the age of forty-five. Anyone who at first refuses to take up the post assigned by the state "is sentenced to solitary imprisonment on bread and water till he consents." Indeed, one of Bellamy's great youthful disappointments was his failure to gain admission to West Point, and his continued sense that the soldier's relation to the corps he serves is the proper model of the citizen's relation to society is suggested not only by such curious facts as his playing with the toy soldiers that he ranged upon the coverlet of his deathbed, but, more importantly, by the martial trappings of life in his utopia. The totalitarian bent of his thinking is indicated by the care his mouthpiece Dr. Leete takes to claim that absolutely no cranny of the nation has been left out of the plans, noting that "a solution which leaves an unaccounted-for residuum is no solution at all." Those who, because of physical or mental problems, might be deemed unable to work belong to "a sort of invalid corps" to which "even the insane belong . . . and bear its insignia. . . . In their lucid intervals," they "are eager to do what they can."

The century that intervened between Bellamy and ourselves has done little to endear the martial flavor of his utopia to us, and it has been no more kind to the economic system whose delineation takes up a significant portion of the narrative. In general, Bellamy fell prey to the misunderstandings of free markets prevailing among socialists and those (like his readers and himself) who had little or no formal education in economics. The great refrain of *Looking Backward* is that capitalism, because it demands competition among producers who provide similar goods and services to their customers, is tremendously wasteful. Somewhat oddly, Bellamy looked to a prime instance of capitalist competition for a model of the kind of economic cooperation he advocated: the department store, which, at the time, was still a relatively novel phenomenon. (One of Bellamy's followers, Bradford Peck, went so far as to title his own utopian refinement of Bellamy's vision *The World a Department Store* [1900].) Gathering under one roof goods often sold at separate establishments, the department store seemed to Bellamy to foreshadow an economy in which one entity, the state, took control of all production and distribution, thus eliminating any need for the competition that "wasted" resources and pitted one economic agent against another.

What Bellamy wanted, therefore, was a radicalizing of the "vertical integration" that was then taking place in the American corporation, the most often-cited example being Standard Oil, even if the competitive, capitalist motivation for such reorganization had been kicked away. Since in Bellamy's utopia all citizens are equally compensated employees of the same corporation – the state – no one can conceivably compete with anyone else, or even engage in mutually agreed-upon exchange. As Dr. Leete explains,

> buying and selling is considered absolutely inconsistent with the mutual benevolence and disinterestedness which should prevail between citizens and the sense of community of interest which supports our social system. According to our ideas, buying and selling is essentially antisocial in all its tendencies. It is an education in self-seeking at the expense of others, and no society whose citizens are trained in such a school can possibly rise above a very low grade of civilization.

Such anti-competitive thinking suits the functions of an army (one has only to imagine an engagement in which officers on the same side each pursue their own battle plans without conferring with the others), but makes little sense when applied to an economy. To be sure, in Bellamy's time some of the best work showing how free markets function as tools for discovering the most efficient ways of producing and distributing goods was yet to appear, as were the arguments definitively demonstrating that socializing the means of production could not fail of giving rise to chaotic economic disruptions (Ludwig von Mises' *Economic Calculation in the Socialist Commonwealth*, to cite the most important instance of the latter, was not published until 1920). Moreover, of course, Bellamy could know nothing of the century of failure in store for socialist intervention in economic life. In any case, while it is certainly not amiss for a student of American fiction to be aware of the fact that Bellamy's pronouncements are unsound, if one wanted to analyze socialist economic theory in detail there are far better texts to engage than *Looking Backward*, with its simplistic arguments that, however much they satisfied those longing for an equal distribution of property and an end to capitalism, have neither theoretical rigor nor empirical analysis to recommend them.

The cultural or literary historian, however, can profitably turn to Bellamy and to the utopians he inspired to find especially pristine examples of a network of beliefs reinforcing a position that since his time has become so widespread that its ideological character is often missed altogether: namely, the predisposition to believe that order comes from planning, and that a lack of planning will produce disorder, especially in extraordinarily complex phenomena such as cities and economies. One of the great successes of twentieth-century intellectual life was the demonstration of the importance of what is called spontaneous order, the tendency of agents in complex systems (such as economies) to coordinate their activity through discrete actions (such as buying and selling) and thus produce an overarching order whose construction or design was no part of any particular agent's intention. Two books offering useful summaries of work in this area are Robert Wright's *NonZero* (2000) and F. A. Hayek's *The Fatal Conceit* (1988), both of which draw on analogies between economic and biological evolution, the latter being another example of a process that produced complex order, at the level of the organism and ecosystem, without the benefit of conscious design. Working against the grain of such findings, even as some of their theoretical foundations were being laid, Bellamy stands as an early figure of a distinctly modern culture of planning, a culture whose adherents take as a given the idea that, in Hayek's words, "no result of the action of many men can show order or serve a useful purpose unless it is the result of deliberate design" (Hayek 1952: 142). When looking for an event that crystallizes the historical moment to which Bellamy was responding, critics often mention the Haymarket Riot of 1886, with its adumbration of irrepressible, violent conflict between capital and labor. However, if we keep in mind Bellamy's dedication to centralized planning, a better, if less dramatic, candidate might be the authorization, in 1887, of the Interstate Commerce Commission, which was to become the prototype of the governmental regulatory bodies that have played such a prominent role in the United State since the Progressive era.

To say that a predisposition to plan is part and parcel of a cultural configuration is right away to challenge the ideological roots that make planning on a large scale seem merely rational or commonsensical. The discourse that surrounds planning, after all, portrays the necessity of the plan not as a result of this or that cultural or aesthetic preference, but rather as a demand of reason or as the logical outcome of careful scientific inquiry. To quote from the title page of *The Radiant City* (1933), the magnum opus of one of the exemplary voices of planning in the twentieth century, the Swiss architect Le Corbusier: "Plans are the rational and poetic monument set up in the midst of contingencies. Contingencies are the environment: places, peoples, cultures, topographies, climates." Here we see a typical suggestion that the plan, far from reflecting a cultural prejudice, stands outside culture altogether and is in fact above it. Culture, like the landscape and the weather, is a mere "contingency" – it is simply something with which the disinterested reason of the planner must deal. At a moment like this Le Corbusier sounds very much like Bellamy's Dr. Leete, who patiently explains to Julian West that "our system . . . is . . . the logical outcome of the operation of human nature under rational conditions." Unlike all existing societies on earth, which derive their order in part from institutional or cultural traditions whose adherents often do not know either their origin or function, the society of Bellamy's 2000 is based on logic and reason: everyone knows precisely why each institution and custom exists, and can explain how its existence serves to tether the individual to the polity.

What such claims for the disinterested rationality of planning obscure is their foundation on decidedly irrational, culturally ingrained preferences that belong more to the realm of taste than to that of science. If one feels one's heart swell at the spectacle of a military parade, in which the idiosyncrasies of each of the participants are absorbed into the geometric pattern of the whole, and if one finds the apparently uncoordinated activity of individuals in, for example, a crowded bazaar appalling, then one may be disposed to believe that the kind of order produced by planning, which alone can result in the former, is obviously superior to the kind of complex and not immediately apparent order that arises spontaneously in nature and cities, and one will apply laudatory adjectives like "rational" and "logical" to what is planned, while denigrating complexities one cannot immediately fathom as "chaotic" or "inefficient." What one must keep in mind while digesting such appraisals is that, however beneficial regularized patterns of behavior may be to supervising authorities, the preference for planned order to spontaneous order is not founded on empirical evidence that the former produces objectively superior outcomes for people on the ground than does the latter.

In fact, the degree to which Bellamy presents the superiority of his utopia in aesthetic terms is striking. When, early in *Looking Backward*, Julian West surveys the new Boston from a rooftop, we are presented with a vista meant to inspire us with its beauty.

> At my feet lay a great city. Miles of broad streets, shaded by trees and lined with fine buildings, for the most part not in continuous blocks but set in larger inclosures, stretched in every direction. Every quarter contained large open squares filled with trees, among which statues glistened and fountains flashed in the late afternoon sun. Public buildings of a colossal size and an architectural grandeur unparalleled in my day raised their stately piles on every side. Surely I had never seen this city nor one comparable to it before.

What is being "sold" here by Bellamy is the pleasure of coordinated design itself We are to marvel at the spatial rhythms conjured into being by the plan, rather than at the details of particular structures, and thus we are confronted with an array of plurals: "public buildings of a colossal size," "open squares," "broad streets." It is hardly surprising that when West dreams that he has returned to nineteenth-century Boston, he finds himself sickened by the uncoordinated hubbub and "malodorousness" of the town.

To be sure, the sort of architectural arrangements favored by Bellamy promote the supremacy of the collective over the individual; but his preference for the collective results from particular ideological commitments, and not from disinterested reason. Here, as elsewhere in *Looking Backward*, with its emphasis on the delights of a lavish consumerism made possible by the alleged efficiencies of bureaucratically managed production, one is struck by the degree to which Bellamy put himself in line with tendencies that would become marked in the decades following his death, when his preference for the colossal and coordinated in city design would be realized by such representative modernist architects as Mies van der Rohe and Walter Gropius, whose work can be critiqued in ways quite similar to Bellamy's. Describing the work of such designers, architectural historian Manfredo Tafuri postulates that they offered not individual objects for judgment,

> but a process to be lived and used as such. The user, summoned to complete Mies van der Rohe's or Gropius' "open" spaces, was the central element of this process. Since the new forms were...meant to be...proposals for the organization of collective life... architecture summoned the public to participate in its work of design. Thus through architecture the ideology of the public took a great step forward.

There is good reason to emphasize the descriptions of urban design scattered throughout *Looking Backward*, for that is the field in which Bellamy has arguably had the greatest direct influence. Among Bellamy's early admirers was British planner Ebenezer Howard, who, although skeptical of the vast scale of Bellamy's centrally planned economy, was enchanted by its attention to communally designed space. When Howard created his concept of the "garden city" in the 1890s, he was in part attempting to realize Bellamy's notion that open spaces of a particular kind could foster a commitment to social solidarity in his proposed towns' inhabitants. Although Howard's village-like designs were for a time eclipsed by the gargantuan projects fashionable when Le Corbusier was in the ascendant, he has recently been revived as the forerunner of what is now probably the chief orthodoxy of city planning, the so-called New Urbanism, which, true to the vision of Bellamy and Howard, seeks to teach citizens the need to value the communal over the private by doing such things as demoting the automobile and promoting mass transit and pedestrianized zones. In his essay "Planning the American Dream," for example, Todd W. Bressi explains that the New Urbanism is dedicated to one basic principle: "Community planning and design must assert the importance of public over private values" (Bressi 1993). Here again we see that planning, far from being the purely rational enterprise it is often claimed to be, goes hand in hand with the promotion of particular values, debate about the questionable nature of which is often forestalled by sometimes extravagant claims of disinterested objectivity on the part of the planners. Although scientific thinking may stand behind particular methods for achieving the vision of the plan, that vision itself cannot be established by reason alone: goals such as the triumph of the public over the private, of the communal over the individual, derive from cultural or political orientations – just the sort of value-laden, historically contingent tangle of prejudices from which planners claim the plan will allow us to escape.

The broader influence of Bellamy's thought is hard to gauge, since we do not know what would have happened had *Looking Backward* never been published, and since the socialist orientation of his work was common coin in the writings of the period. What we can say – as the remarks of Beard and Dewey quoted above make clear – is that Bellamy was the favored exemplar of socialist thinking for many in the generation that created the New Deal. Indeed, Arthur E. Morgan, the first head of that representative New Deal institution, the Tennessee Valley Authority, was also the first man to write a full-length biography of Bellamy. Reading Morgan's description of his work at the TVA, in fact, sheds light on the degree to which, for Bellamy and those of like mind, planning had become something of a goal in itself, and the necessity of planning a deeply ingrained imperative that colored much of what they did and said. Dismissing everything outside the compass of the plan as "chaos," Morgan writes: "There is no traditional line . . . at which men must stop in their efforts to bring order out of chaos; no limits need be set on our hopes for a more inclusive and masterly synthesis." Explaining that the TVA "is not primarily a dam-building job, a fertilizer job or power-transmission job," Morgan showed that absolute comprehensiveness in the planned transformation of human life was his goal: "the improvement in that total well being, in physical, social, and economic condition, is the total aim" (quoted in Schlesinger 1959: 327).

These words, which could have come from Bellamy's pen, at once exemplify the culture of planning so prominent in the world from Bellamy's time to ours, and expose why such enterprises can never succeed in realizing their goals. We can see why by turning to social theorist Niklas Luhmann's explanation, carried out a very high level of abstraction, of the fact that "no society so far has been able to organize itself." Luhmann writes:

> Planners have to use a description of the system, and will thus introduce a simplified version of the complexity of the system into the system. . . . The system then will stimulate reactions to the fact that it includes its own description, and it will thereby falsify the description. Planners, then, will have to renew their plans. . . . They may try reflexive planning, taking into account reactions to their own activity. But, in fact, they can only write and rewrite the memories of the system, using simplistic devices which they necessarily invalidate by their own activity. (1990: 179, 180)

We need not have recourse to high theory, however, to see the problems besetting any attempt to plan on a vast scale, and neither do we need to focus narrowly on economic matters. An examination of Bellamy's depiction of human motivation in his utopia is enough to show that the institutions he advocates might, if realized, founder on the rocks of human nature itself. Following in the footsteps of Rousseau, Bellamy supposed that the right kind of society might foster the creation of a new kind of human being, one from whom self-seeking or even predatory impulses had been eradicated. What he refuses even to acknowledge, however, is that precisely these impulses, which when abstracted from the whole of human behavior can hardly help but appear in a negative light, might serve a crucially important social function. For example, if we consider the place of honor in *Looking Backward*, to which Dr. Leete devotes considerable attention, we see that Bellamy may be building his entire utopian edifice on a psychological impossibility. In Bellamy's utopia, the profit motive has been removed from the economic system, since all employees of the state – that is to say, all citizens – receive exactly the same salary, which they receive annually, and which is wiped off the slate if not "spent" during the course of the year. Julian West naturally wonders what incentive anyone has to do any work, since everyone's paycheck is guaranteed, and since there is no prospect of individual economic advancement. In particular, West wonders why anyone would choose to pursue occupations that are particularly arduous or hazardous. The response of his host, Dr. Leete, has a peculiarly archaic ring to it:

> If... the unavoidable difficulties and danger of such a necessary pursuit were so great that no inducement of compensating advantages would overcome men's repugnance to it, the administration would only need to... [declare] it "extra hazardous"... to be overrun with volunteers. Our young men are very greedy of honor, and do not let slip such opportunities.

This response is curious for a number of reasons. The idea of honor, after all, is something of a survival from aristocratic societies, and, in its origins at least, is based on quite inflexible ideas about the hierarchical ranking of human beings. Ideas of this stripe seem at odds with the absolutely democratic principles informing Bellamy's 2000. Moreover, the psychological effects of a belief in honor have long been noted for their potentially anti-social tendencies. The very first event narrated in the Western literary tradition is Achilles' bringing his comrades' siege of Troy to a halt because he feels he has been treated dishonorably by Agamemnon. In the ancient world, the potentially disruptive effects of the quest for honor, and its ugly psychological origins, were thought to be offset by the social benefits derived from individuals' lust for recognition, for the recognition that they were in fundamental respects superior to others. Nietzsche perceived a general agreement among the Greeks on this point, arguing that for Aristotle and others "jealousy, hatred, and envy" were "spurs... to activity.... The Greek is envious, and he does not consider this quality a blemish but the gift of a *beneficent* godhead" (1954: 35). Nietzsche postulates that "Those of [man's] abilities which are terrifying and considered inhuman may even be the fertile soil out of which alone all humanity can grow in impulse, deed, and work" (p. 32). The aristocratic desire for honor and recognition, therefore, may be linked to feelings of hatred and jealousy that are at odds with the philosophy prevailing in Bellamy's

2000, for if one of the pillars of the system is greed for honor, the other is – Dr. Leete's words again – "the fact that the solidarity of the race and the brotherhood of man . . . are, to our thinking and feeling, ties as real and as vital as physical fraternity."

Can honor cohabit in the same soul with an intensely felt belief in the solidarity of humanity, or is that ruled out by the psychology with which evolution has endowed us? Is the desire for honor, in other words, a result of regarding others with envy, jealousy, or even hatred? Bellamy's system cannot work unless these questions can be answered affirmatively. If, on the other hand, solidarity and honor are mutually exclusive, and if solidarity rules the day, then no one will feel obliged to work hard or to take risks – the population will quickly decline into poverty. If honor prevails, then competition – original sin in Bellamy's eyes – will reassert itself with a vengeance. Bellamy's crucial assumption about the compatibility of the "brotherhood of man" and the desire for aristocratic recognition, which is never presented in the novel as at all problematic, is representative of the minute and utterly comprehensive knowledge of human psychology that must be in place for a plan to present itself as authoritative. Such bold claims are seldom openly made, but their implicit presence alone can guarantee a plan's validity. Moreover, since there does not yet exist any comprehensive map of human psychology, we are often able to accept as plausible the most questionable ideas about it, especially merely implicit ones.

At one point in *Looking Backward*, Bellamy himself exposes a related problem, when he perhaps unintentionally suggests why a writer in his position is in fact incompetent to make plans for the future. In the course of a Sunday sermon that once more suggests Bellamy's affinities with Rousseau, the most famous preacher of the year 2000 asserts that only after the new society was created could one begin to understand what human beings in fact are: "Now that the conditions of life for the first time ceased to operate as a forcing process to develop the brutal qualities of human nature . . . it was for the first time possible to see what unperverted human nature really was like." According to this statement, Bellamy in 1887 could not have known for what kind of creatures he was planning a society. Indeed, all utopians have to explain why it is that they, mired in a civilization that they themselves describe as perverted and perverting, have managed to avoid the confusion of their contemporaries and see so clearly the truth of the principles that others deny. Very often, the result is a claim that logic itself demands a particular set of social arrangements, and that a straightforward application of a few simple principles will result in a clear picture of what the world will look like after the illogical embroilments of history are over, after, that is, the end of history itself. In fact, the positing of some post-historical condition, and of a knowledge purporting to be derived from it, is something like a generic necessity of utopias, since utopian authors must seek out some Archimedean point outside their society from which to launch a critique of it, even if the existence of such a point does not explain how they have access to it. That is why Bellamy claims that his utopia is both perfect and permanent, incapable of further alteration. In response to Julian West's question about how new laws are made, Dr. Leete explains, "We have no legislation," for "we have nothing to make laws about. The fundamental principles on which our society is founded settle for all time the strifes and misunderstandings which in your day called for legislation." Aware that their plans might be judged merely a symptom of the problems they seek to overcome, utopian writers frequently struggle to extricate themselves from the paradox of laying out blueprints for a post-historical formation that, in principle, they suggest they should not be able to know anything about. Utopian plans ask to be taken not as the statement of a particular human being at a particular historical moment, but as a message from the future or from afar that has somehow penetrated the ideological interference of the present with its pristine clarity intact.

Even writers with much more limited goals and much greater theoretical sophistication than Bellamy's cannot help encountering difficulties when it comes to the knowledge upon which they seek to base their hopes for the future. The problem is most pointedly expressed in one contemporary architectural historian's call for buildings that will "cultivate a resistant, identity-giving culture." The coincidence of the cognate words "culture" and "cultivate" point to a difficulty that will likely frustrate those who attempt to cultivate a culture, namely that a culture cannot *be* cultivated; a culture is what cultivates. If someone is concerned about cultivating a culture, it must be because she feels that a culture is the thing that conditions the thoughts and actions of those who take shape within it, and that the limitations imposed by a culture cannot be transcended. Dr. Leete himself crisply sums up this position when he remarks, "the conditions of human life have changed, and with them the motives of human action." But if that is the case, then the vision of a new culture that comes to the would-be culture cultivator is likely not to be something outside the culture she wishes to replace; it will be rather a product of that culture. If the culture needs to be changed because it distorts human desires, then the desires a proposed future is designed to satisfy will themselves be distorted – and, what is more, if the new culture is somehow brought into being, the old desires may not even exist, for the culture that nurtured those desires will have been destroyed by the utopia designed to satisfy them. The future imagined by utopians will thus tend to be a future with a great future behind it, for utopia always comes too late, always gives shape to the hopes of people who, in altering the structures that condition their thoughts, will have ceased to exist.

Alfred North Whitehead famously declared that the European philosophical tradition consists of nothing but a series of footnotes to the work of Plato. While that remark has the ring of hyperbole, it can be said without exaggeration that the utopias produced in the United States, in the decade and a half after *Looking Backward* appeared, read like a series of addenda to that novel. Even the most original of them, Charlotte Perkins Gilman's *Herland*, bears the unmistakable mark of her early admiration of Bellamy and affiliation with Nationalism, the political movement *Looking Backward* inspired. Turning, then, to Howells and Gilman, we can limit ourselves to an examination of questions that can shed light on problems in the study of literary history generally: the apparently paradoxical attraction of Howells, the great advocate of realism, to the utopian mode; and, in connection with Gilman, the difficulties involved in abstracting the evidently "progressive" elements of literary works from their historical context.

Anyone with even a passing acquaintance with Howells's realist works of the 1880s, culminating with *A Hazard of New Fortunes* (1890), will see at once why the vision presented by Bellamy would have attracted Howells strongly. Howells despaired at the glaring inequality of wealth apparent in the Gilded Age, and, at least in certain respects, sympathized with the demands of workers he felt were being exploited by a heartless, profit-driven capitalist system. When anarchists who almost certainly had nothing directly to do with the bomb-throwing at Haymarket were sentenced to death, Howells was one of the few literary luminaries who publicly denounced this miscarriage of justice, an act that would earn him the ire of Theodore Roosevelt, who, reflecting on McKinley's assassination, fulminated that people like "William Dean Howells, who unite in petitions for the pardon of anarchists, have a heavy share in the burden of responsibility for crimes of this kind" (Roosevelt 1925: vol. 1, 501). Such was his disgust with the uneven distribution of wealth occasioned by the massive economic growth in the United States that in 1888, the year *Looking Backward* was published, Howells wrote to Henry James that "after fifty years of optimistic content with 'civilization' and its ability to come out all right in the end, I now abhor it, and feel that it is coming out all wrong in the end, unless it bases itself anew on a real equality" (Howells 1928: vol. 1, 417). Bellamy, of course, provided a vision of just the sort of social transformation Howells longed for, and when a meeting was held to found the First Nationalist Club in Boston, one of the first political organizations dedicated to the realization of Bellamy's goals, Howells was there.

If there is little mystery in Howells's attraction to Bellamy's ideas, the fact that he was attracted to the utopian mode has seemed to many an odd coda to a career founded on a dedication to realist principles. For Howells, realism was an imperative because, according to his view in the 1880s, what society needed if it were ever to reform itself was an accurate picture of what it in fact was; realism was to burrow down to the truths that were obscured in the hubbub of daily life, suffused, as that life was, with misrepresentations of every stripe, whether they were found in newspapers, sentimental novels, or slanted, ideologically charged portrayals of the social scene. What Howells and those sharing his literary aspirations wanted was a way of writing that could accurately translate the world as it existed into language, a goal that is likely to strike contemporary critics as naïve, since it is predicated upon a use of language that is somehow transparent, and that does not in any significant way distort or color the "hard facts" of the world it seeks to represent. One of the burdens of twentieth-century thinking, indeed, has been that we have no access to those facts except through the medium of inevitably distorting categories given to us by our language and culture.

Although Howells never worked up an elaborate theory of the relation between language and things, and never offered a compelling explanation of his departure, after 1890, from the realist mode that had served him so well, it is possible to offer an explanation for the surprising trajectory of his career. Even though Howells staked his literary ventures on the idea that, given a sufficiently objective stance on the part of the author, words could be used to depict reality in a tolerably unproblematic way, by mid-career he seemed more and more aware of the tendency of words, however deployed, to create the very reality they seem only to describe. In particular, with the increasing dominance of mass media and of the advertising (an enterprise very much on the rise at the time) that accompanied and fueled it, Howells saw an America awash in representations that swamped any reality that might be buried beneath them – if that reality had any ascertainable shape at all. In *Literature and Life* (1902) he predicted that "the supreme artist of the twentieth century" would be not the realist novelist, but rather the "adsmith," and whimsically, if pointedly, prophesied that "there will presently be no room in the world for things; it will be filled up with advertisements of things." Whereas his realist productions were based on the faith that the right words could lead his readers to the state of things themselves, by mid-career he was worried that words could "only breed more words" (Lynn 1971: 9), a remark pointing towards the characteristically twentieth-century idea that the representations offered by language become meaningful because of their relations with each other, and not with the world we may naïvely suppose they present to us in an undistorted manner.

If to the Howells of the 1880s, therefore, a utopian romance might seem an irrelevant distraction from the needed work of accurate representation, by the time *Looking Backward* appeared Howells seemed less interested in the distinction between true and false representations of the world than with the distinction between representations that would lead to human happiness – that is, those that would promote the cause of social and economic equality – and those that would prolong what he regarded as the nightmare of an unjust capitalist order.

Even so, there is a rather tentative quality to Howells's utopian writings, which involve the antipodal country Altruria, a land, as the name suggests, in which self-interest has been replaced by an overriding concern for the well-being of others. His first and still by far most widely known novel in this vein, *A Traveller from Altruria*, depicts a visit of the Altrurian Mr. Homos to a New England summer resort, where he refutes those such as a vacationing economist who defend capitalism in rather harsh, Darwinian terms, and presents the virtues of his homeland. There, as in Bellamy's utopia, the dedication of the individual to the thoroughly regimented society is paramount, even if Howells avoids Bellamy's emphasis on the lavish consumerism enjoyed by Bostonians in 2000; in Altruria, simplicity enjoys an eternal vogue. Altruria itself gets represented directly only in a sequel, *Through the Eye of the Needle* (1907), which tells the tale of an American woman who has traveled to Altruria because of her love for Mr. Homos. In spite of his apparent aim of presenting a perfect society, Howells seemed aware that the regimentation necessary to freeze social arrangements permanently in their allegedly perfect form had a darker side. When, for example, a ship wrecks on the coast of Altruria, and its crew are absorbed into the society, "each of them was fitted with a kind of shirt of mail, worn over his coat, which could easily be electrized by a metallic filament connecting with the communal dynamo, and under these conditions they each did a full day's work." Although Bellamy seems to have had no qualms about the solitary confinement to which he has his utopians condemn all those who refuse to take up the posts allotted them by the state, Howells was more ambivalent about what we would now be likely to describe as the authoritarian and even totalitarian aspects of utopian schemes and the centralized direction of human life that they demand. "All other dreamers of such dreams," Howells wrote to a friend, "have had nothing but pleasure in them; I have had touches of nightmare."

Like Howells, Charlotte Perkins Gilman attached herself to the movement spawned by *Looking Backward*, and her first publication, a satirical poem that garnered her a letter of praise from Howells, appeared in the Bellamyite journal the *Nationalist*. Unlike the utopian writings of Howells and Bellamy, however, Gilman's chief utopian work depicts a society whose realization would face biological, and not just institutional, impediments, for her utopian country, Herland, is inhabited only by women who have the power to reproduce parthenogenetically. They are discovered deep in the jungles of South America, on a plateau accessible only by airplane, by a trio of male adventurers who learn that the women are descendants of European colonizers from the Age of Discovery.

Like the other utopias of the period, *Herland* is collectivist in spirit, and displays the hallmark affinity for regimentation and planning that we have seen in its predecessors. When the men try to escape the temporary confinement imposed on them by the Herlanders, they are confronted by a group of the women, who "evidently relied on numbers, not so much as a drilled force but as a multitude actuated by a common impulse." Thus we see that the communal feeling carefully instilled in the citizens of Bellamy's utopia has become second nature in Herland, and it expresses itself in everything from their mode of governance to their stewardship of the landscape. Gilman's desire for a world where everything comes under the management of a collective plan is suggested by the country's being "a land in a state of perfect cultivation, where even the forests looked as if they were cared for; a land that looked like an enormous park, only it was even more evidently an enormous garden." To be sure, the abiding concern of Gilman here, as in all her major writings, is the status of women, who in Herland have overcome the patriarchal oppression so memorably depicted in what is by far her best-known work, "The Yellow Wall-paper." What reading *Herland* in the context of other utopias of the time makes clear, however, is the striking fact that she found the remedy to this unacceptable situation not in the liberation of the individual, but rather in the absorption of the individual into a new form of strictly regimented collective life.

As we have seen in the case of Bellamy, although utopias often present themselves as offering alternatives to the prevailing culture, it is sometimes difficult, particularly at a historical distance, to extricate what might be truly innovative in a utopian vision from what merely amplifies something already present in the culture the utopia claims to transcend. This is also the case with Gilman, for even what would seem her most fantastic utopian gesture, namely her utopians' ability to reproduce themselves without men, has its roots in theories in vogue in her time that have long since been discarded. Although recent commentators have tended to view the parthenogenesis of the Herlanders as a playful device allowing Gilman to conduct a thought experiment, this aspect of her utopia may have meant something more to Gilman herself.

Gilman first made something of a name for herself in 1898 with the publication of *Women and Economics*, a panoramic, free-wheeling work that bore strong affinities to the then just emerging discourse of sociology in the United States. Unfettered by a need to back up their claims with empirical studies, sociologists and psychologists often engaged in lofty speculation that appealed strongly to Gilman, especially when they addressed the nature of women, which some saw as somehow more basic than the nature of men. For example, G. Stanley Hall, founder of the *American Journal of Psychology* and president of Clark University, told the National Congress of Mothers that women "are themselves by nature in every faculty of their mind and in the very composition of their body more generic; they are nearer the race" (1905: 20). Men, on the other hand, possess "the far more highly specialized and narrowed organism" (p. 27). The prominent sociologist Lester Ward, who was something of a mentor to Gilman, concurred: "from Nature's standpoint the female is the organism and the male only a sometimes useful, sometimes necessary adjunct or incident;" "from the standpoint of nature . . . the female is the principal sex and constitutes the main trunk of development, she alone continuing the race" (Ward 1906: 87). This was an idea "than which," Gilman claimed in *The Man-Made World* (1911), "nothing so important to humanity has been advanced since the Theory of Evolution."

As early as *Women and Economics* Gilman was herself echoing these thoughts, with their now odd-sounding abstraction of the nature of the species as something that can be talked about in isolation from the actual creatures, male and female, that constitute it. As if sketching out a treatment of *Herland*, Gilman wrote that primordial woman "was the deep, steady, main stream of life, and [man] the active variant, helping to widen and change that life, but rather as an adjunct than as an essential. Races there were and are which reproduce themselves without the masculine organism – by hermaphroditism and parthenogenesis." Thus while a contemporary reader might at first suppose that Gilman's parthenogenetic women are a gauge of her playfulness or that they function as a kind of declaration of independence from habits of thought governing patriarchal culture, the intellectual milieu from which Gilman emerged suggests that there was a serious, if only pseudo-scientific, point behind their end-run around normal reproductive procedure: to show that women are the essential members of the human race, and men merely the "adjuncts" or "variants."

This rather eccentric aspect of Gilman's thought reminds us that the foundations for the plans that Bellamy and his fellow utopians hoped would usher in a happy future rested on unproven and sometimes unprovable assumptions about the creatures on whose behalf the plans were formulated. Indeed, in the aftermath of a century in which whole nations were subjected to grand utopian schemes, often brutally imposed, we can see that the cast of mind exemplified by Bellamy cannot be considered merely an oddity of literary history. Although the plans proposed by Bellamy have never been adopted, the itch to place a grid over human life and to master it systematically through centralized, allegedly rational control has been and continues to be a distinctive, and perhaps defining, ingredient in our planning culture.

PRIMARY TEXTS

Bellamy, Edward. *Looking Backward: 2000–1887.* 1888.

Gilman, Charlotte Perkins. "The Yellow Wallpaper." 1892.

Gilman, Charlotte Perkins. *Women and Economics.* 1898.

Gilman, Charlotte Perkins. *The Man-Made World.* 1911.

Gilman, Charlotte Perkins. *Herland.* 1915.

Howells, William Dean. *A Hazard of New Fortunes.* 1890.

Howells, William Dean. *A Traveller from Altruria.* 1894.

Howells, William Dean. *Literature and Life.* 1902.

Howells, William Dean. *Through the Eye of the Needle.* 1907.

Mises, Ludwig von. *Economic Calculation in the Socialist Commonwealth.* 1920.

More, Thomas. *Utopia.* 1516.

Peck, Bradford. *The World a Department Store: A Story of Life under a Cooperative System.* 1900.

REFERENCES AND FURTHER READING

Banta, Martha (1993). *Taylored Lives: Narrative Productions in the Age of Taylor, Veblen, and Ford.* Chicago: University of Chicago Press.

Bressi, Todd W. (1993). "Planning the American Dream." In Peter Katz, *The New Urbanism: Towards an Architecture of Community*, 15–28. New York: McGraw-Hill.

Hall, G. Stanley (1905). "New Ideals of Motherhood Suggested by Child Study." In *The Child in Home, School, and State: Report of the National Conference of Mothers.* N.p.: National Conference of Mothers.

Hayek, Friedrich A. von (1952). *The Counter-Revolution of Science: Studies in the Abuse of Reason.* Glencoe, Ill.: Free Press.

Hayek, Friedrich A. von (1988). *The Fatal Conceit: The Errors of Socialism.* London: Routledge.

Howells, Mildred, ed. (1928). *Life in Letters of William Dean Howells.* Garden City, NY: Doubleday.

Kasson, John F. (1977). "Technology and Utopia." In *Civilizing the Machine: Technology and Repub-lican Values in America, 1777–1900*, 183–234. New York: Viking, 1977.

Le Corbusier [Charles Edouard Jeanneret] (1970). *The Radiant City.* New York: Viking. (First publ. 1933.)

Luhmann, Niklas (1990). *Essays in Self-Reference.* New York: Columbia University Press.

Lynn, Kenneth S. (1971). *William Dean Howells: An American Life.* New York: Harcourt Brace Jovanovich.

Manuel, Frank E., and Manuel, Fritzie P. (1979). *Utopian Thought in the Western World.* Cambridge, Mass.: Harvard University Press.

Nietzsche, Friedrich (1954). *The Portable Nietzsche*, trans. Walter Kaufmann. New York: Viking.

Peyser, Thomas (1998). *Utopia and Cosmopolis: Globalization in the Era of American Literary Realism.* Durham, NC: Duke University Press.

Roosevelt, Theodore, and Lodge, H. C. (1925). *Selections from the Correspondence of Theodore Roosevelt and H. C. Lodge 1884–1918.* New York: Charles Scribner's Sons.

Schlesinger, Arthur M. (1959). *The Age of Roosevelt: The Coming of the New Deal*. Boston: Houghton Mifflin.

Thomas, John L. (1983). *Alternative America: Henry George, Edward Bellamy, Henry Demarest Lloyd and the Adversary Tradition*. Cambridge, Mass.: Harvard University Press.

Ward, Lester F. (1906). *The Psychic Factors of Civilization*, 2nd edn. Boston: Ginn.

Wright, Robert (2000). *NonZero: The Logic of Human Destiny*. New York: Pantheon.

22

American Children's Narrative as Social Criticism, 1865–1914

Gwen Athene Tarbox

Children's literature as a recognized genre developed in concert with the colonization of the Americas and the circulation of revolutionary political and economic theories across Europe and the New World. The transition towards representative democracy, begun in the latter half of the seventeenth century and realized in the aftermath of the Revolutionary War, was predicated upon the existence of an educated populace. As a result, the sanctity of childhood as a site for social instruction gained unprecedented cultural currency in the colonies and led to the establishment of literacy as the primary benchmark of a progressive society. Members of the colonial cultural elite recognized that children's literature could serve as an effective medium for ensuring widespread support for the imperatives of nation-building. In popular colonial and antebellum children's novels, youthful protagonists were shown to prosper, both financially and spiritually, in direct proportion to their willingness to espouse societally sanctioned ideas, including Protestantism, capitalist logic, and the ethos of Manifest Destiny.

The resulting body of narrative work, with its overt didacticism and its insistence on verisimilitude over fantasy, has inspired very little in the way of approval by subsequent generations of reviewers and scholars. In 1871 Bret Harte, writing one of his final literary columns for the *Overland Monthly*, cast a critical lens over children's narrative of the eighteenth and nineteenth centuries and proclaimed it to be "a clumsily adjusted mixture of didactic truth and saccharine rhetoric administered like sulphur and treacle for the moral health of the unhappy infant" (Harte 1871: 199). Most contemporary scholars would concur. Anne Scott MacLeod, a noted children's historian, puts it this way: "No one can make a claim for the literary merit of this fiction: there was none. . . . The characteristically sober tone of all the literature [was] a natural consequence of the authors' view of the purpose of childhood, which was serious in the extreme. Childhood was wholly preparation, entirely a moral training ground for adult life" (1994: 94). Another critic, Gillian Avery, succinctly labels colonial and antebellum children's literature as "virtuous twaddle" (1994: 93).

Nevertheless, beneath the didactic veneer of pre-Civil War children's literature, there existed the indisputable fact that child protagonists were accorded important and highly visible roles as empowered individuals. *A Token for Children* (1642), James Janeway's bestselling chronicle of the hardships of Puritan life, provides an excellent example of a text that uses vocal children in the service of valued cultural practices. While *A Token for Children* echoes the primers and chapbooks of the day by reminding children that "they are not too little to dye; they are not too little to go to hell," it also emphasizes the power children can possess if they choose to uphold the religious tenets of their communities. In each of his accounts, Janeway features protagonists who exert influence over parents and other adult authority figures. Typical of the group is Anne Lane, a child who is "sanctified from the very Womb." Once assured of her own state of grace – at the age of four – Anne is shocked to find that her father is "little acquainted with the power of Religion." As Janeway describes it, she "put him upon a thorow [sic] inquiry into the state of his Soul, and . . . that a Babe and suckling should speak so feelingly about the things of God, and be so greatly concerned not only about her own soul, but about her Father's too, [led to] the occasion of his conversion" (Janeway 1977: 15–17). In another story, an adolescent girl defies the authority of village elders by withholding her deathbed visions of the afterlife, implying that if her family and friends wished to share in sacred knowledge, they must be deserving of God's grace, an assurance that she could not guarantee. The collection also includes an episode in which a young boy is taken into heaven directly after delivering a stirring public sermon, as adults and community leaders are brought to their knees in supplication.

During the late eighteenth and early nineteenth centuries, Janeway's text was followed by hundreds of novels and short stories in which young children admonished adults who failed to uphold the paramount virtues of American cultural life, including self-reliance, industry, and patriotism. What these early fictionalized accounts of American childhood lacked, however, were protagonists who called into question the legitimacy of the status quo, an absence that would be addressed as the Romantic literary tradition that was burgeoning in Europe entered into the American consciousness, principally through the work of Ralph Waldo Emerson. Arguing that children's intrinsic innocence enabled them to experience an unmediated connection with the divine, Emerson viewed children as potential revolutionaries, whose ability to stand apart from adult society and to identify its shortcomings invested them with cultural potency.

In *Nature* (1836), Emerson observed that "the sun illuminates only the eye of the man, but shines into the eye and the heart of the child" (Emerson 1983: 24), a belief that forms the core of the character of Pearl in Nathaniel Hawthorne's *The Scarlet Letter* (1850) and most notably, of Eva St. Clare in Harriet Beecher Stowe's *Uncle Tom's Cabin* (1852), a sentimental novel that reifies the figure of the seer-like child reformer. The numerous scenes in which Eva gradually succumbs to tuberculosis echo passages from *A Token for Children*, insofar as the young girl's scrutiny of her father's soul is designed to effect his conversion, but her disdain for slavery, and especially her assertion that slave-holding forms the basis of her father's transgression, challenged the views held by the majority of Americans during the antebellum era. Consider, for example, this passage, in which Eva empathizes with the plight of her father's slaves:

> "Papa," said Eva, with sudden firmness "I've had things I wanted to say to you, a great while. I want to say them now, before I get weaker. . . . You want me to live so happy, and never to have any pain, – never suffer anything, – not even hear a sad story, when other poor creatures have nothing but pain and sorrow, in their lives; – it seems selfish. I ought to know such things, I ought to feel about them! Such things always sunk into my heart; they went down deep; I've thought and thought about them. Papa, isn't there any way to have all slaves made free?" (Stowe 1996: 401–2)

Through Eva's persistent questioning of the institution of slavery, Stowe manipulates her readers' expectation that child protagonists should serve as defenders of established cultural mores; Eva's ascension into heaven, which follows her scathing indictment of the status quo, is met not with punishment, but with the ultimate reward – God's approbation. Stowe recognized that the figure of the outspoken child represented a powerful weapon in the fight for abolition.

The surprising success of *Uncle Tom's Cabin*, combined with the transatlantic popularity of Charles Dickens's own brand of child-centered activist novels, sparked debate within the literary community regarding the advisability of including political dissent in fiction written specifically for young readers. By 1865 authors of children's literature were compelled to engage in conscious reflection regarding dominant cultural ideas and the power of children's literature to convey those ideas. On the basis of these deliberations, authors came to identify themselves with one of three distinct narrative strains that would characterize children's literature in the aftermath of the Civil War. The majority of texts published during the era can be classified either as *conventional novels*, in which a protagonist takes action in defense of established cultural customs, or as *speculative novels*, in which a protagonist questions the status quo, but ultimately conforms to it. There were, however, a handful of groundbreaking texts – *insurgent novels* – that featured protagonists who openly advocated social change, regardless of the consequences. These narratives were among the most controversial – and the most financially successful – of all children's novels published between 1865 and 1914. In the discussion that follows, I will comment upon the differences between these narrative strains, in order to explain the enduring political and cultural significance of the element of social criticism in American children's narrative.

The conventional novel supports what Anne Scott MacLeod identifies as two key assumptions common to modern views of childhood:

> The first is that children need to be separated to some degree from adult life until they have been educated or ripened in some important way. The second is that adults have something of value to teach children, so that the very concept of childhood in modern

history is closely associated with that of the nurture, training, and conscious education of the child by responsible adults. (1994: 176)

If a protagonist speaks out in a conventional novel, it is typically in order to promote or to restore responsible adult authority, as in Martha Finley's *Elsie Dinsmore* (1867), a novel set in the antebellum South that concerns the troubled parent–child relationship between plantation owner Horace Dinsmore and his eight-year-old daughter, Elsie. Following the example of Eva St. Clare, Elsie attempts to bring religious decorum to bear upon her father's household. However, the similarity between the two novels ends there. Elsie Dinsmore never questions the larger culture in which she lives; she is solely concerned with her family's adherence to appropriate religious standards.

The conflict between father and daughter begins when Mr. Dinsmore breaks the Sabbath by hosting a raucous dinner party at his estate. In an attempt to show off Elsie's "precocious musical talent" to the assembled guests, he crosses the room to pull the bell to summon her. However, his aunt, who resents Elsie's unceasing evangelism, stays his hand, telling him,

> "You had better not send for her...she will not sing. She will tell you she is wiser than her father, and that it would be a sin to obey him in this. Believe me, she will most assuredly defy your authority; so you had better take my advice and let her alone – thus sparing yourself the mortification of exhibiting before your guests your inability to govern your child." (Finley 1896: 237)

Of course, in Finley's estimation, Mr. Dinsmore's inability to govern Elsie is based not upon her bad behavior, but upon his. Elsie's subsequent refusal to play the piano – even under the threat of punishment – represents her desire to restore Mr. Dinsmore's appropriate authority as the *religious leader* of his household. Elsie's reply to her father's assertion that she must obey him and not God, includes an appeal to the highest power: "Jesus says, 'He that loveth father or mother more than me, is not worthy of me'; and I cannot disobey Him, even to please my own dear papa" (Finley 1896: 242). Ultimately, after passing out and hitting her head on the piano, Elsie wins her father's sympathy and begins in earnest her campaign to return Horace Dinsmore to his appropriate role as a Christian parent.

The figure of the pious child who restores purpose to the lives of adult authority figures remains a constant feature of the conventional novel throughout the nineteenth and early twentieth centuries. In Eleanor H. Porter's *Pollyanna* (1913), which appears at the end of the Progressive era, Pollyanna Harrington, an orphaned child, repeatedly suppresses genuine emotions such as rage and sorrow by playing the "glad game," in which she searches for the "silver lining" to be found in the death of her parents and in the cruelty of her guardian, Aunt Polly. Although this attitude ultimately softens the stoicism of her domineering and shrewish aunt, the relativism inherent in Pollyanna's "gladness" underscores the fact that Pollyanna's continual self-improvement often comes at the expense of her personality and her dignity. After she is crippled in an accident, Pollyanna learns that the entire population of her small New England town has agreed to play the "glad game," to which Pollyanna replies that if her injury could inspire her neighbors to adopt a more positive outlook, then that was "something to be glad about" (Porter 1913: 206).

At first glance, Horatio Alger, Jr.'s *Ragged Dick; or, Street Life in New York with the Boot Blacks* (1868), seems out of place alongside such conventional novels as *Elsie Dinsmore* or *Pollyanna*. Unlike Finley and Porter, Alger appears to engage directly with social problems, noting in his preface that *Ragged Dick* was written to enlist the concern of his readers "on behalf of the unfortunate children whose life is described, and of leading them to co-operate with the praiseworthy efforts . . . by the Children's Aid Society and other organizations to ameliorate their condition" (Alger 1990: 1–2). The novel is set in the street shanties of New York City, where young, unsupervised boys compete for the meager wages that can be earned running errands, delivering newspapers, or shining shoes. Every element would seem to be in place for a critique of capitalism, whereby representatives of the ruling class would be brought to task for allowing a system of child labor and homelessness to exist alongside a world of privilege in which middle- and upper-class children were nurtured by responsible adults.

Instead, Alger deflects criticism away from New York City's bankers, merchants, and stockbrokers by devising a fictive reality in which enterprising Protestant orphans such as Richard Hunter merely serve limited time in the streets as apprentices, whereas Irish boys such as Micky Maguire and Jim Travis, who are portrayed as inherently lazy and brutish, deserve their fate as lifelong denizens of the slums. Far from serving as an indictment of the status quo, Alger's novel upholds the ethos of the Protestant work ethic and supports the virulent anti-Irish sentiment of the day, while glossing over the worst aspects of street life – especially regarding the routine financial and sexual exploitation of street children.

During his "rise from rags to riches" Dick is mentored by two businessmen, both of whom adhere to ethical practices and who reward Dick for his honesty and his ambition. Unlike Elsie and Pollyanna, Dick's primary goal is not the reformation of adult authority figures; rather, he imitates his elders in order to transform himself from a street urchin into a capitalist. Early in the text, Dick meets Mr. Whitney, a businessman who is appalled by Dick's "ragged" condition, but who can see – just by casual observation – that Dick is a reliable boy. In order to free up his own time for business meetings, Mr. Whitney sends his nephew Frank out on the town, with Dick as tour guide, so that his young, sheltered relative can learn about the "school of hard knocks." Alger's purpose here is evident; he wishes to argue that Dick's rough-and-tumble upbringing has better prepared him for financial success than has the posh upbringing enjoyed by Frank Whitney. By comparing Dick's street-smarts to Frank's naïveté, Alger romanticizes street life, while advocating the newly popular Darwin-influenced model of capitalism, in which the strongest and sharpest competitors rise to prominence. Dick's quick wit and his ability to charm customers serve as indicators that he will succeed in business.

Dick is also mentored by Mr. Greyson, a merchant who introduces him to Christianity – an important aspect of the American capitalist ideal – and who opens his house to him on various occasions so that Dick can become acquainted with the niceties of drawing-room society. Mr. Greyson also provides Dick with a bankbook, an action that inspires Dick to focus on capital accumulation. When Dick's bank account tops one hundred dollars, Alger tells his readers that Dick felt "like a capitalist when he looked at the long row of deposits in his little bankbook. There were other boys in the same business who had earned as much money, but they had had little care for the future, and spent as they went along, so that few could boast a bank-account, however small" (1990: 136–7). By the novel's conclusion, Dick's ability to accrue funds – and spend them wisely – enables him to rise to the level of clerk in a counting house, win the love of Mr. Greyson's daughter Ida, and establish himself as a "respectable gentleman" of means.

A central characteristic of the conventional novel is its structural and thematic predictability, which results in the virtual elimination of narrative tension. For instance, on a number of occasions, through the use of authorial intrusion, Alger reminds his readers that Richard Hunter's "nature was a noble one, and had saved him from all mean faults" (Alger 1990: 8). When Dick begins to earn a decent wage as an errand boy, Alger assures readers that he will not become corrupted by wealth, and when Dick's life is threatened after turning in a thief to the police, Alger quickly diminishes suspense by informing the reader that Jim Travis, the thief,

> was duly tried, and his guilt being clear, was sent to Blackwell's Island for nine months. At the end of that time, on his release, he got a chance to work his passage on a ship to San Francisco, where he probably arrived in due time. At any rate, nothing more has been heard of him, and probably his threat of vengeance against Dick will never be carried into effect. (p. 161)

The absence of narrative tension may explain why many of the "classics" of children's literature, including *Elsie Dinsmore*, *Pollyanna*, and *Ragged Dick*, appealed more to nostalgic adults than to actual child readers, most of whom – to use dime novelist Edward Stratemeyer's phrase – craved novels that provided "a fair proportion of legitimate excitement" (quoted in Johnson 1993: 5).

Speculative narratives, which emerged during a period when controversial ideas such as women's suffrage and racial desegregation began to gain cultural legitimacy, were far more likely to produce the type of narrative tension that would attract young readers. Louisa May Alcott's *Little Women* (1868–9) and Susan Coolidge's *What Katy Did* (1872), the first speculative novels written for children, feature debates regarding the extent to which young women should pursue careers in traditionally male occupations – a topic that captivated the nation during the postbellum era. The 1860s, in particular, represent a pivotal decade in the struggle for women's equality.

The clubwomen's movement, which gained momentum during the antebellum era, propelled middle-class women into the public realm in unprecedented numbers. In addition to agitating for suffrage, abolition, and municipal improvements, club-women banded together to call for educational and vocational opportunities for girls. In 1865 Vassar College admitted its first undergraduate class, and by 1870 over 11,000 women were enrolled in four-year colleges or normal schools. Despite rigorous opposition, girls were gaining a foothold in the public realm, and their struggle for self-fulfillment became a logical topic for children's fiction.

Louisa May Alcott's *Little Women* concerns the maturation of the March sisters – Meg, Jo, Beth, and Amy – whose lives become unsettled when their father leaves home to serve as a chaplain for the Union forces in the Civil War. Each girl promises her father that she will strive to become a "little woman," and each girl faces a number of life lessons as she moves toward that goal. Jo March, the tomboy of the family, faces the greatest challenge because, unlike her more conventional sisters, she possesses a rebellious temperament that resists Victorian attitudes regarding appropriate female behavior. Jo's desire to lead an adventurous life as a famous author places her in constant conflict with her family and with the larger culture. When her friend Theodore Laurence asks Jo about her plans for the future, she replies, "If I was a boy, we'd run away together, and have a capital time; but as I'm a miserable girl, I must be proper and stay at home" (Alcott 1995: 164). Jo's desire to remain an adolescent – humorously expressed in her wish that she could wear a flatiron on her head to keep her from growing up – is the result of her recognition that once she becomes a woman, she will be confined to the domestic realm.

However, in a very daring move, Alcott alters the traditional romantic trajectory of Jo's relationship with Teddy Laurence. Rather than marrying her wealthy neighbor, Jo moves to New York City in order to advance her literary career. Because Alcott had carefully and methodically built up the romantic tension in her novel, it is all the more shocking when she deflates that plot line and turns in a direction designed to question the culture's attitude towards women's roles. This shift is paralleled in Jo's decision to leave off writing sentimental romances in order to write semi-autobio-graphical fiction – a move that enables her to grow as an artist and to receive critical acclaim. However, the person to encourage Jo in her literary maturation is Professor Bhaer, the elderly German immigrant who becomes Jo's mentor and husband. Ultimately, Alcott returns Jo to the more traditional role of wife and helpmate; but before doing so she opens the door – albeit briefly – to the idea that a woman's destiny might lie beyond the domestic realm.

Although many contemporary scholars have rightly labeled *Little Women* as a proto-feminist narrative, it is important to remember that Jo's success is contingent upon her willingness to take the advice of a male mentor and that her quest for self-fulfillment ends in marriage. Hers is the first of many narratives in which young women attain literary success only after receiving advice from men and after setting their texts within the domestic realm – L. M. Montgomery's *Anne of Green Gables* (1908) and Maud Hart Lovelace's *Betsy/Tacy* series come immediately to mind. For her part, Alcott links her own growth as an author to the decision to write predominantly in the "conventional" mode. In an article written in 1888 for the *Youth's Companion*, Alcott reflects upon the keys to her success:

> At sixteen I began to teach twenty pupils, and for ten years learned to know and love children. The story writing went on all the while with its usual trials of beginners. Fairy tales told to the Emersons made the first printed book, and "Hospital Sketches," the first successful one. Every experience went into the cauldron and came out as froth, or evaporated in smoke, till time and suffering strengthened and clarified the mixture of truth and fancy, and a wholesome draught for children began to flow pleasantly and profitably. (Alcott 1988: 261)

Although *Little Women* solidified Alcott's reputation, her subsequent novels for girls, *An Old Fashioned Girl* (1870) and *Jack and Jill* (1880), both can be termed "taming narratives," in which a young girl experiences increasingly acute social pressure to put aside personal ambition and to accept her role within the domestic realm.

Susan Coolidge, Alcott's contemporary, also tested the public's willingness to accept a heroine who challenges the status quo. In *What Katy Did*, Katy Carr, the twelve-year old heroine of the title, is described by Coolidge as being the very epitome of a tomboy: "her hair was forever in a snarl; and her gowns were always catching on nails and tearing themselves, [and she] didn't care a button about being called 'good'" (Coolidge 1976: 9). Left motherless at an early age, Katy and her five brothers and sisters are raised by their tolerant father and his sister, Aunt Izzie. Although Katy is shown to "have fits of responsibility about the other children, and longed to set a good example," she is much more concerned with carrying out "the many delightful schemes rioting in her brain" (p. 19). In an amusing nod to the conventional novels that were readily available at that time, Aunt Izzie is shown to wonder why Katy is "so little like the good boys and girls in Sunday-school memoirs, who were the young people she liked best, and understood the most about" (p. 11). Despite this critique, however, Coolidge's sympathies eventually mirror Aunt Izzie's. *What Katy Did* is a story of crime and punishment. Katy's crime is her desire to question the status quo; her punishment reflects the predicament of an author who could go only so far in challenging traditional attitudes regarding female behavior.

Katy's desire for a career that will enable her to enter the public realm puts her in conflict with established notions regarding appropriate female vocational choices. Early in the novel, she outlines her unconventional plans to her siblings:

> "I mean to do something grand," she said. "I don't know what yet; but when I'm grown up I shall find out. . . . Perhaps," she went on, "it will be rowing out in boats, and saving peoples' lives . . . or perhaps I shall go and nurse in the hospital, like Miss Nightingale. Or else I'll head a crusade and ride on a white horse, with armor and a helmet on my

head, and carry a sacred flag. Or if I don't do that, I'll paint pictures, or sing, or scalp – sculp – what is it? you know – make figures in marble." (Coolidge 1976: 31–2)

Most of Katy's ideal occupations – rescuer, crusader, and artist – are traditionally ones held exclusively by men; only teaching and nursing were thought to be acceptable occupations for women during the postbellum era. Added to the crime of ambition is Katy's insistence on questioning adult authority. At a key moment midway through the text, Katy participates in an act of defiance and empowerment that alters her life in substantial ways. Forbidden to use a brand new swing that the hired hand has installed in the woodshed, Katy rebels, muttering to herself: "How exactly like Aunt Izzie ordering children not to swing till she gives them leave.... I sha'n't mind her, anyhow" (Coolidge 1976: 152). On the heels of the declaration, Katy unleashes her repressed desire for autonomy and control in a passage full of suggestion:

> The motion of the swing seemed to set the breeze blowing. It waved Katy's hair like a great fan, and made her dreamy and quiet.... Swinging to and fro like the pendulum of a great clock, she gradually rose higher and higher, driving herself along by the motion of her body, and striking the floor smartly with her foot, at every sweep.... She had never swung so high before. It was like flying, she thought, and she bent and curved more strongly in the seat, trying to send herself yet higher, and graze the roof with her toes. (Coolidge 1976: 153)

Moments after experiencing the euphoria of physical and emotional freedom, Katy is brought to earth in a stunning crash that leaves her paralyzed and on the brink of death.

During her convalescence Katy is cared for by Helen Carr, her angelic cousin, who had, in the past, attempted to teach Katy the tenets of "true womanhood," but with little success. After the accident Helen gains the upper hand, principally because Katy is a "captive audience." At their first meeting Helen puts forth her plan for Katy's reformation by encouraging her to enroll in "God's school":

> "It is called The School of Pain," explained Cousin Helen, with her sweetest smile. "And the place where the lessons are to be learned is this room of yours. The rules of the school are pretty hard, but the good scholars, who keep them best, find out after a while how right and kind they are.... There's the lesson of Patience ... and the lesson of Making the Best of Things ... and the lesson of Neatness. School-rooms ought to be kept in order, you know. A sick person ought to be as fresh and dainty as a rose." (Coolidge 1976: 175–7)

In the year that follows, Katy leaves off questioning her diminished status within the culture; instead, she focuses exclusively on directing the domestic affairs of her household. By practicing self-control and suppressing any desires she may have once had for public life, Katy becomes so useful and efficient that her sister Clover says,

"Sometimes I think I shall really be sorry if she ever gets well. She's such a dear old darling to us all, sitting there in her chair, that it wouldn't seem so nice to have her anywhere else" (Coolidge 1976: 257). Indeed, Coolidge seems to share Clover's anxiety that, once mobile, Katy might revert to her old ambitions and desires. It is a full four years before Katy is able to walk again, and by this time she has proven by her gentle expression and her womanly voice that her transformation into a "true woman" is permanent.

From the standpoint of narrative form, speculative novels such as *Little Women* and *What Katy Did* are inherently realistic: the conflicts depicted in speculative novels are predicated upon issues that remain unresolved in the contemporary society as a whole. If the issues were easily brooked, then narrative tension would disappear. For example, once the issue of women's suffrage was resolved with the passage of the Nineteenth Amendment in 1920, the entire genre of girls' fiction was altered significantly. Narratives in which young women entered the public realm became commonplace – conventional, in fact – and authors who were interested in questioning the status quo concerned themselves with more controversial subjects, such as premarital sex. However, the original intended audience for Alcott's and Coolidge's novels could identify with the concerns and frustrations experienced by protagonists such as Jo March and Katy Carr. As a result, reading *Little Women* or *What Katy Did* compelled these readers to ask what I call the *speculative question*, namely, "Will the protagonist 'get away' with behavior that contests the status quo?" While the answer to this question was mixed in the case of *Little Women* and solidly negative in the case of *What Katy Did*, the very fact that such a question was being raised added to the speculative novel's relevance as a harbinger of cultural change.

Mark Twain and Emma Dunham Kelley-Hawkins, two of the prominent authors of insurgent novels, turned to this narrative tack only after launching their careers as authors of well-received speculative novels. Given that Twain fashioned *Adventures of Huckleberry Finn* (1884) as an indictment of Jim Crow society and Kelley-Hawkins viewed *Four Girls at Cottage City* (1898) as a critique of mainstream Christianity, it is not surprising that both authors relied upon strong moral conviction and an established reputation to buffer the potentially explosive response that their insurgent novels promised to generate.

The Adventures of Tom Sawyer, published in 1876, was a speculative novel that solidified Twain's standing as a writer whose wit appealed as much to adults as it did to young readers. By the early 1870s Twain had transplanted his family to the Nook Farm neighborhood of West Hartford, Connecticut, where he lived alongside a number of established authors of children's literature, including Harriet Beecher Stowe and Charles Dudley Warner, who helped to encourage his interest in the genre. *The Adventures of Tom Sawyer* had its antecedent in what Albert E. Stone, Jr. labels the "Bad Boy" narrative tradition, begun with the publication of Thomas Bailey Aldrich's *The Story of a Bad Boy* in 1869 and followed by George W. Peck's popular series, *Peck's Bad Boy* (1883). In addition to portraying the mischievous exploits of young boys, one of the key features of the "Bad Boy" narrative was its evocation of nostalgia that adult readers might feel regarding their younger, less polished selves. Although Stone places *The Adventures of Tom Sawyer* within this tradition, he goes on to argue that the novel is "more than a nostalgic re-creation of Mississippi River life before the War, though it is this, too. Mark Twain pays boyhood the ultimate compliment by using Tom as the vehicle for a full-dress study of personality, community, and the anatomy of social evil" (Stone 1961: 63).

Early in the narrative, Twain offers a series of interlocking vignettes that critique the content of conventional novels and present Tom Sawyer as someone more interesting and genuine than "the model boy of the village." In the first episode, Tom is ordered to whitewash his Aunt Polly's fence as punishment for playing hookey from school and for fighting with another boy. In a conventional novel, this punishment would compel Tom to recognize the wisdom of his elders and to amend his behavior. The moral lesson that Tom is shown to realize, however, is that he can get out of work quite easily by conning his friends into believing that whitewashing a fence is a rare and enjoyable activity. Twain equates Tom's ability to manipulate his peers to "the slaughter of the innocents," and he concludes the episode with Tom counting up the toys and trinkets that he has received from his playmates, all the while mulling over the idea that "to make a man or boy covet a thing, it is only necessary to make the thing difficult to attain" (Twain 1994: 17). The entire chapter provides a commentary on how conventional novels – especially Horatio Alger's "rags to riches" homilies – whitewash the truth about human nature.

In the second episode, Twain questions the value of religious education for the young. Rather than encouraging true spirituality in his students, the Superintendent who runs the town's Sunday School provides incentives for children to memorize biblical passages in the form of a prize competition. Twain mocks the exercise in a passage that encourages his readers to question both the prize itself and the children who compete for it:

> How many of my readers would have the industry and the application to memorize two thousand verses, even for a Doré Bible? And yet . . . a boy of German parentage had won four or five. He once recited three thousand verses without stopping; but the strain upon his mental faculties was too great, and he was little better than an idiot from that day forth. (Twain 1994: 32)

Although Tom is shown to loathe the memorization of verses, he does wish to gain the acclaim of having won a prize. By using the trinkets he earned from the whitewashing episode, he is able to barter his way into the possession of enough Sunday School tickets to win a Doré Bible. As Tom heads up to the podium at church to bask in the approval of the assembled congregation, his friends are "all eaten up with envy; those that suffered the bitterest pangs were those who perceived too late that they themselves had contributed to this hated splendour by trading tickets to Tom for the wealth he had amassed in selling whitewashing privileges" (Twain 1994: 36).

During the presentation ceremony, Judge Thatcher tells Tom:

> Two thousand verses is a great many – very, very great many. And you never can be sorry for the trouble you took to learn them; for knowledge is worth more than anything there is in the world; it's what makes great men and good men; you'll be a great man and a good man yourself, some day, Thomas, and then you'll look back and say, it's all owing to the precious Sunday-school privileges of my boyhood. . . . That is what you will say, Thomas – and you wouldn't take any money for those two thousand verses, then – no, indeed you wouldn't. (Twain 1994: 32)

The irony in Judge Thatcher's speech is two-fold; for Tom has certainly "paid" for his knowledge, and later in the text, Judge Thatcher's own greedy nature will shine through after Tom and Huck come into possession of buried treasure.

In a distinct shift in emphasis and mood that occurs midway through *The Adventures of Tom Sawyer*, Twain converts what has been an episodic evocation of childhood into a proper bildungsroman, as Tom engages in a number of encounters that initiate him into the adult world. The murder of Doc Robinson, the death of Injun Joe, and the discovery of an actual treasure combine to alter Tom's relationship with his community. As Walter Blair has noted, Tom's summer of adventures combine to push him towards "respectability" – a state that is prized by conventional heroes such as Ragged Dick. Blair is particularly interested in the transformation of Tom's attitude towards his friend Huckleberry Finn, an unkempt, somewhat rough boy who, up until the latter section of the novel, was considered to be an appropriate playmate by Tom. However, Blair points out that when Tom comes into money, he ends up threatening Huck with expulsion from "the gang" if he doesn't become "civilized." In Blair's opinion, "something has happened to Tom. He is talking more like an adult than like an unsocial child. He has, it appears, gone over to the side of the enemy" (Blair 1939: 88) – in this case, to the world of propriety into which Aunt Polly has attempted to usher Tom from the outset.

Tom's increased inability to question the status quo is further explained by his need for an appreciative audience. The desire to stand out among the other children manifests itself in the Sunday School episode, in which Tom is described as longing "for glory and the *éclat*" from the church community, and in the Jackson Island prank, in which the townsfolk's sincere anxiety over the presumed death of a number of its young citizens enables Tom to make a grand, dramatic entrance at his own funeral. If Tom were to pose a serious challenge to the status quo, he would forfeit his ability to gain public recognition for his escapades. As Stone has observed, after the boys find the buried treasure, Huck seems to understand the manner in which the townsfolk hope to exploit the boys' sudden financial windfall, while Tom – who once took advantage of others' naïveté – seems fated to share in it.

Of course, Huck Finn has far more reason to feel distanced from his community. His father is abusive, and Judge Thatcher, who ends up controlling Huck's finances, is conniving and greedy. Even the pious townspeople who weep openly at the return of Tom from the dead must be reminded that Huck, too, has returned unscathed.

The sense of alienation that initially exists at the margins of Huck's consciousness in *The Adventures of Tom Sawyer* is brought firmly into the foreground in Twain's companion text, *Adventures of Huckleberry Finn*, as Huck bears witness to the struggles of Jim, the escaped slave, whose poignant humanity is repeatedly contrasted with the depraved selfishness of the Southern "aristocracy" and of the fledgling middle class whom both Huck and Jim meet as they travel through the river towns along the Mississippi.

Twain's attitude toward his country – and especially towards the South – had soured considerably in the years between the publication of *Tom Sawyer* and of *Huckleberry Finn*. By 1882, when Twain was scheduled to return to the Mississippi on a fact-finding trip, he had begun to attack the South in his private journals: "The South was poverty-stricken, barren of any progress, he wrote in his notebook. Except in the arts of war, murder, and massacre, the South had contributed nothing. It had no architecture, it was sophomoric, its speech was 'flowery and gushy'" (Kaplan 1966: 243). This sense of disillusionment colors every aspect of *Adventures of Huckleberry Finn*. While James Osgood, Twain's editor for *Life on the Mississippi*, had removed many of the scathing anti-Jim Crow passages from that novel, by the time Twain finished *Huckleberry Finn* he was acting as his own editor and publisher. Freed from the censors and armed with righteous anger, Twain forged what has long been considered one of the key texts in the canon of American literature.

The two experiences that most attune Huck Finn to the darker side of society both involve extreme human suffering. The first occurs when Huck witnesses the murder of Buck Grangerford, a thirteen-year-old boy who becomes caught up in his family's longstanding feud. When the supposed exemplars of Southern gentility race through the swamp land, yelling "Kill them, kill them!" just prior to attacking Buck, Huck is appalled: "It made me so sick I most fell out of the tree. I ain't a-going to tell *all* that happened – it would make me sick again if I was to do that" (Twain 1996: 160). Although Twain spares his readers the entire grisly scene, he is much more forthcoming in his description of Jim's agony over leaving his family behind in his escape from slavery. Huck's realization of Jim's suffering, made manifest in the observation that Jim "cared just as much for his people as white folks does for their'n" leads him to a further understanding that Jim loves him in a manner that no person – white or black – has ever hitherto done. Ultimately, when Huck believes that it is in his power to help Jim escape, he does so, regardless of the consequences.

Huck's brave insurgency, when juxtaposed with Tom Sawyer's casual disregard for Jim's humanity expressed in the later chapters of the novel, provides a further indictment of a society in which disenfranchised black men owe their liberty to the caprice of whites, regardless of their age or social status. The elaborate Evasion that Tom plans, during which he dupes Jim into thinking that he has returned to his slave status and must be held prisoner by the boys, has puzzled critics, leading many to wonder why Twain would divert the reader's attention away from the trope of Huck's maturation and back into the pranks and follies of youth that characterized *The Adventures of Tom Sawyer*. My belief is that Twain uses this interlude to draw a stark contrast between the speculative nature of his first novel and the insurgency of his second. While Tom has remained fixed in an adolescence that mirrors the limitations of his culture, Huck is shown to have matured sufficiently to realize that only by "light[ing] out for the territories" can he outgrow the impotency of conventional childhood.

The publication of *Adventures of Huckleberry Finn* marked a turning point in American children's narrative. In March 1885 the Library Committee of Concord, Massachusetts banned the novel, and Louisa May Alcott, whose early insurgency had faded into a prim conservatism, wrote that "if Mr. Clemens cannot think of something better to tell our pure-minded lads and lasses, he had best stop writing for them" (quoted in Vogelback 1939: 270). The fury of the intelligentsia actually spurred the sales of the novel; the fact that the book was banned from most libraries meant that purchases increased exponentially. As Twain noted years later, "The truth is that when a library expels a book of mine and leaves an unexpurgated Bible around where unprotected youth and age can get hold of it, the deep unconscious irony of it delights me and doesn't anger me" (Twain 1917: 805). Given Twain's financial and editorial power, he was able to withstand the onslaught of criticism, and in so doing, pave the way for other authors who wished to use children's narrative to question the status quo.

Like Twain before her, Emma Dunham Kelley-Hawkins, an African American schoolteacher from Boston, changed direction in mid-career, moving from writing speculative to insurgent narratives. Her first novel, *Megda* (1891), focuses on a young woman's struggle to maintain her individuality and her vocation in the face of extreme societal pressure. Through humiliation and intimidation, Megda Randall gives up her career as an actress, joins a conservative, patriarchal sect of the Baptist church, and marries a distant, imperious minister. Like Katy Carr, Megda is forced to suffer because she questions the status quo.

Megda is introduced to the reader as a free-spirited and opinionated girl. In addition to pursuing an acting career, Megda argues passionately for the rights of women: "I hold that there is more real moral character in a woman's little finger than in a man's whole body," she tells her brother Hal. "[I] speak of men and women collectively now, not individually, putting woman where she ought always to be put — on an equal basis with man" (Kelley-Hawkins 1988b: 60). Comparing herself to her female friends, she notes that " 'they are too dependent; they let other people think for them; they have no settled ideas of their own about anything, or if they have they do not give expression to them' " (p. 69).

At the beginning of the novel, Megda is the most popular girl in her high school; however, her status changes once a new minister, Reverend Arthur Stanley, starts a youth group at the local Baptist church. First, her friend Ethel Lawton joins the group, and soon all of Megda's friends follow. Once Megda is the only hold-out, Arthur Stanley tries to break her spirit, telling her, "you have tested your own strength, and it has failed you. You will be glad now to lean on Him whose strength is all-sufficient" (Kelley-Hawkins 1988b: 309). After weeks of painful social isolation and intimidation, Megda agrees to leave off her career and join the church. Almost immediately, her unique and forceful way of speaking is replaced by simple expressions of piety or by silence. When Megda accepts Arthur Stanley's marriage proposal, Kelly-Hawkins assures her readers that Megda is "glad to have a tender loving husband to guide and to protect her" (p. 394) and a "Heavenly Father" to watch over her, implying that the best way to worship God is to be submissive and obedient to the patriarchy. By the end of the narrative, Megda's entire life is circumscribed within the narrow bounds of a conservative society.

In 1895, Kelley-Hawkins obtained the copyright on her second novel, *Four Girls at Cottage City*, which was published in 1898. Written at a time when African American women were congregating in Boston to form the National Association of Colored Women, *Four Girls at Cottage City* provides readers with a fictive reality in which African American teenagers form what could be termed a "junior" version of the NACW, a girls' society that enables the young women to question every element of their culture – including patriarchal religion – without facing the sort of psychological anxiety experienced by Megda Randall. The novel offers evidence of Emma Dunham Kelley-Hawkins's eagerness to break with her earlier, conventional view of ideal womanly behavior. *Four Girls at Cottage City* is an insurgent novel in which the very foundation of African American cultural life is open to criticism.

Kelley-Hawkins's second novel begins as a group of young friends leave their comfortable Boston homes to spend two weeks at the African American resort town of Cottage City. Vera Earle, the eldest at twenty-three, is a responsible, practical feminist. When the girls discuss Tennyson, Vera argues that the poet "'makes his women too weak'" (Kelley-Hawkins 1988a: 60). Allison Hunt, the quietest of the girls, shares with Vera a clear desire to find spiritual happiness. The foursome is made complete by the aptly named Dare sisters, Garnet and Jessie, who, as their surname implies, are the boldest of the group. At twenty-one, Garnet is a promising academic, interested in Romantic philosophy and popular forms of spiritualism. Jessie, her junior by three years, is loud, impetuous, and independent.

A few days into their vacation at Cottage City, the girls recognize that the room they have rented for their holiday is the same one used by Megda Randall and her friends in a novel by Emma Dunham Kelley-Hawkins. In addition to creating a rather humorous, self-parodic moment in her second narrative, Kelley-Hawkins draws her readers' attention to the significance of place. In her first novel, Megda and her friends decide to rent the cottage because of its location directly across the street from a Tabernacle, and they are deeply moved by a sermon given at the church. In *Four Girls at Cottage City*, the focal point is not the church, a representative of organized, patriarchal religion that becomes central to the girls' growth; rather, it is the girls' community that is fostered within the cottage itself. Together, the girls create impromptu spiritual ceremonies that emphasize active faith, rather than passive submission to a patriarchal creed.

At the cottage, the landlady, Mother Atherton, encourages the girls' community by prohibiting her husband from intruding into their discussion on religion. Whenever both of them visit the upstairs room, Mother keeps "Grandpa" in check, leading Vera to wonder how long Mother has "been holding 'Grandpa' back with that little slender hand of hers?" (Kelley-Hawkins 1988a: 42). Of all the girls, Jessie is the most anxious to protect the women's space. When her cousin Fred Travers and his friend Erfort Richards begin to spend time with the girls, Jessie resents their interference. As she tells Vera, "I'm not going [out with you all tonight] because I'm tired to death of having those two fellows tied to our apron strings everywhere we go. We can't move but what 'the gen-tle-men will call for us at such and such a time.' When we came down here I thought we four girls were going around together and have a good time. There's no fun when there's a parcel of men around" (p. 129).

On the first Sunday that the girls are in Cottage City, they drag themselves to church, not expecting to enjoy the sermon at the Tabernacle. As they walk to the service, the girls pause to enjoy the beauty of the crisp summer morning. Lost in a reverie of nature, "the loud notes of [the church] bell startle them" (Kelley-Hawkins 1988a: 48), disrupting their spiritual experience. Once in church, they spend their time trying to not to fall asleep. "What a heartlessly long sermon!" Jessie complains. "I do think that minister ought to be arrested for cruelty to animals" (p. 54). This open disregard for patriarchal religion never appeared in *Megda*, even when Megda attempts to argue against the strictures of the creed. Instead, the Baptist faith is held up as an ideal; in *Four Girls*, its adherents are criticized. As Vera observes, "They stay at home from all [types of amusements] from one year's end to the other. If a member of their church went to such places their names would be crossed off the church book. How is that? Aren't one class just as good as another? If it is right for people of one denomination to go, why isn't it right for those of another?" (p. 106).

At a time when religious awakening was synonymous with self-actualization and empowerment, Vera and the other girls are looking for an experience that will satisfy the spiritual needs of natures diverse as their own. A chance encounter with a female evangelist named Charlotte Hood propels the girls into a complete disavowal of organized religion in favor of a religious ideal in which women, not men, are favored by God. In an extremely radical segment of the text, Charlotte Hood shares with the girls a vision in which a local woman, Hester Norton, is personally selected by Jesus to sit at his side, while the minister of the Tabernacle is cast into Hell:

> "I thought when the minister went forward he would be assigned a place among the many standing about the throne, but what was my surprise to see him turn, with his form bent, in an agony of shame and humiliation, and pass slowly out of sight.... Hester went next.... [Christ] cast over her a robe of snowy whiteness...and on her head he put a plain gold crown. 'Stand at my right hand, for thou art one of my well-beloved,' He said." (Kelley-Hawkins 1988a: 304)

At the novel's conclusion, the girls have formed their own charitable organization, and Garnett has gone on to pursue a career in academia. Unlike Megda, who must stifle her individuality in order to align herself with her community and her religious faith, the four girls experience deep spiritual and emotional satisfaction from casting off conventional religion.

By the early twentieth century, insurgent ideas also began to appear in the "lowbrow" series fiction that enjoyed increasing popularity among young readers. Edward Stratemeyer, who began his career as a ghostwriter for Horatio Alger, Jr., established his own series syndicate in the 1890s and went on to publish some of the most popular children's books on record, including *The Hardy Boys*, *The Bobbsey Twins*, and *The Nancy Drew Mystery Stories*. As he told an interviewer in 1904: "This is a strenuous age. Children of today are clever and up-to-date and appreciate that which is true to life as much as their elders. They love incident and adventure... [and] the best an author can do is to give them a fair proportion of legitimate excitement" (quoted in Johnson 1993: 5). Although Stratemeyer himself was a noted social conservative, he was more than happy to set aside his own beliefs in the interest of profit.

One of Stratemeyer's most popular early series was *The Outdoor Girls of Deepdale* (1911), ghostwritten under the pseudonym of Laura Lee Hope by Lilian Garis – a college-educated journalist and advocate of women's rights – and her husband, Richard Garis. Targeted at young girls who were involved in the Girl Scouts and the Campfire Girls, the series followed the adventures of four high-school students who embark on a series of adventures, unescorted by parents and free from the typical constraints on female behavior that were current during the Progressive era.

In the first installment of the *The Outdoor Girls* series, Betty Nelson, Amy Stonington, Grace Ford, and Mollie Billette are inspired to spend two weeks of their summer vacation on a 200-mile hike, after reading a book on women's exercise. Every aspect of their journey, from choosing sensible hiking clothes to camping out-of-doors, provides an opportunity for the Garises to challenge the status quo. For instance, consider their description of the girls in hiking gear: "Clad in their new suits of olive drab, purposely designed for walking, with sensible blouses, containing pockets, with skirts sufficiently short, stout boots and natty little caps, the outdoor girls looked their name. Already there was the hint of tan on their faces, for they had been much in the open of late" (Hope 1911: 90). Gone is the idealized image of the pale, fragile "angel of the house"; in its place is a portrait of young women who are prepared to lead "the strenuous life."

Lilian and Richard Garis also describe how the girls overcome the objection of their brothers and male friends, who claim that girls are too timid to go hiking on their own. Betty's brother puts his objections quite succinctly: "I think you'll run at the sight of the first tramp – or cow," he says. "And as for a storm – good night!" (Hope 1911: 66). So he and the girls' other male friends plot to accompany them on their trip. In order to escape their unwelcome counsel and companionship, the girls manage to dupe the boys by arranging to have them babysit neighborhood children – an ironic role reversal – while they sneak out of town.

Once on the open road, the girls cause quite a stir. As the authors describe it, "the girls passed farm houses, in the kitchen doors of which appeared the women and girls of the household, standing with rolled-up sleeves, arms akimbo, looking with no small wonder at the four travelers" (Hope 1911: 98–9). As they walk through a town, one boy yells, "Ma-ma! Come an' see the suffragists," while other men cry out, "What be you – suffragists?" or "Are you a votes for Women crowd?" (pp. 99–100). Whenever such outbursts occur, the girls "bravely march along, with a confident swing and firm tread" (p. 99). Beyond these brief interactions with the public, the girls are left alone to carry out a number of daring adventures, including the capture of a railway thief and a showdown with an escaped circus bear.

Another popular series, Josephine Chase's *Grace Harlowe at Overton College*, follows the progress of a young collegian as she attempts to fashion a life for herself after college that involves work, not matrimony. When she tells her mother of her unconventional plans, she is surprised to learn that she has an ally: "Your college life is only the beginning," Mrs. Harlowe tells Grace. "You are likely to discover that your work lies far from [your hometown of] Oakdale, but you know that your father and I will wish you Godspeed. You are to be perfectly free in the matter of choosing your business of life" (Chase 1914: 153). While many of her college friends eventually marry, Grace continues to refuse the proposals made by her childhood friend, Tom Gray. For three years after graduation, he makes periodic attempts to win Grace away from her work as a school counselor by calling into question her self-confidence. This interchange between the couple is typical:

> Tom's eyes were full of pain. "I am a man now, with a man's devoted love for you," he said. "The whole trouble lies in the sad fact that you are just a dreaming child without the faintest idea of what life really means."
>
> "You are mistaken, Tom." There was a hint of offended dignity in Grace's tone. "I do understand the meaning of life, only it doesn't mean love to me. It means work. The highest pleasure I have in life is my work....I feel so free and independent. It's my freedom I love. I don't love you." (Chase 1914: 153)

Although Grace eventually marries Tom in the eleventh book of the series, she leaves him behind so that she can travel to Europe and other places to solve mysteries. Despite her married status, Grace is never forced to relinquish her public identity. In Chase's *Grace Harlowe* series, young women view their college years as a rehearsal for a public life that is actually within their reach. On graduation day, Grace and her friends are said to be "deeply conscious of the fact that their diplomas were their passports into the real world of work and endeavor that was now about to open before them" (Chase 1914: 236).

Many of these popular insurgent novels, especially those that focused on characters whose freedom from convention is never confronted, were obviously utopian in nature. The protagonists in *The Outdoor Girls of Deepdale* or *The Grace Harlowe at Overton College* series were rewarded for behavior that would have brought censure upon the heads of actual readers if they were to initiate such activity in their own communities. Simply put, utopian insurgent novels transferred the narrative tension *away from the text itself and into the world of the reader.* The speculative question, "Will the protagonist 'get away' with behavior that contests the status quo?" might be followed by a more personal and insurgent question, "Why can't I, the reader, 'get away' with such behavior?" While the latter question may have occurred to the intended audience of speculative novels – after all, many nineteenth-century readers might have hoped to emulate Jo March's career as a writer – authors of speculative novels always provided an ambivalent answer, at best. Alcott's Jo March marries a classic representative of the patriarchy, and Coolidge's Katy Carr becomes a domestic angel. However, the authors of insurgent novels always answered the *insurgent question* in the affirmative, and once the precedent for a certain mode of revolutionary behavior was set on the page, could its realization in the actual world be far behind?

The response of critics to all insurgent novels, be they realistic or utopian, included shrill invective that carried with it the thinly disguised fear that adult authority figures were beginning to feel towards youth culture. Walter Taylor Field, author of *A Guide to Literature for Children* (1928), argued that "much of the contempt for social conventions for which the rising generation is blamed is due to the reading of this poisonous fiction" (Field 1928: 7). In a similar vein, Elizabeth Wisdom argued that characters in series fiction were continuously "flouting authority and acting as adults," behavior that would, of course, tempt young readers to do the same (quoted in Deane 1991: 28).

By the first decades of the twentieth century, children's literature had earned a reputation as an important vehicle for social commentary and literary innovation. L. Frank Baum, Jr.'s *The Wonderful Wizard of Oz* (1900), for instance, functioned simultaneously as an allegory for the struggles of William Jennings Bryant's Populist Party, as a commentary on girls' culture, and as a parable concerning childhood development. Gene[va] Stratton-Porter's *A Girl of the Limberlost* (1909) provided a nuanced treatment of women's lives in rural America, placing the text in a direct dialogue with Gertrude Stein's *Three Lives* (1909) and Willa Cather's *O Pioneers!* (1913). Long before Stephen Crane, Jacob Riis, or Upton Sinclair fueled social change through their depictions of the suffering of the working class, Horatio Alger, Jr. and Mark Twain were bringing issues of child labor and poverty to the attention of the reading public, just as Emma Dunham Kelley-Hawkins and Josephine Chase were advocating women's rights. Given that so many notable American authors of the postbellum and Progressive eras chose to write children's literature, to reference it in their mainstream literary texts, or to borrow from its traditions, no serious commentary on nineteenth- and twentieth-century American narrative can be complete without taking the genre, and its role as social criticism, into consideration. The rise of the insurgent novel, in particular, anticipated the increasing politicization of youth and youth culture that would characterize the twentieth century. Although J. D. Salinger's *The Catcher in the Rye* (1951) has been heralded by contemporary critics as the first truly revolutionary adolescent novel, it marked only a new phase in what was actually a lengthy tradition that began with the speculative and insurgent novels written in the nineteenth and early twentieth centuries.

PRIMARY TEXTS

Alcott, Louisa May. *Little Women*. 1868–9.

Alcott, Louisa May. "Reflections of My Childhood." 1888.

Alger, Horatio, Jr. *Ragged Dick; or, Street Life in New York with the Boot Blacks*. 1868.

Chase, Josephine. *Grace Harlowe's Fourth Year at Overton College*. 1914.

Coolidge, Susan [Sarah Chauncey Woolsey]. *What Katy Did*. 1872.

Finley, Martha. *Elsie Dinsmore*. 1867.

Hope, Laura Lee [Lilian Garis]. *The Outdoor Girls of Deepdale*. 1911.

Kelley-Hawkins, Emma Dunham. *Four Girls at Cottage City*. 1898.

Kelley-Hawkins, Emma Dunham. *Megda*. 1891.

Montgomery, L. M. *Anne of Green Gables*. 1908.

Porter, Eleanor H. *Pollyanna*. 1913.

Stowe, Harriet Beecher. *Uncle Tom's Cabin; or, Life among the Lowly*. 1852.

Stratton-Porter, Gene. *A Girl of the Limberlost*. 1909.

Twain, Mark. *The Adventures of Tom Sawyer*. 1876.

Twain, Mark. *Adventures of Huckleberry Finn*. 1884.

REFERENCES AND FURTHER READING

Alcott, Louisa May (1888). "Reflections of My Childhood." *The Youth's Companion*, May 24, 261.

Alcott, Louisa May (1995). *Little Women*. New York: Scholastic.

Alger, Horatio, Jr. (1990). *Ragged Dick; or, Street Life in New York with the Boot Blacks*. New York: Signet Classics.

Avery, Gillian (1994). *Behold the Child: American Children and their Books, 1621–1922*. Baltimore: Johns Hopkins University Press.

Baum, L. Frank, Jr. (1900). *The Wonderful Wizard of Oz*. Chicago: G. M. Hill.

Blair, Walter (1939). "On the Structure of *Tom Sawyer*." *Modern Philology* 37, 85–96.

Chase, Josephine (1914). *Grace Harlowe's Fourth Year at Overton College*. Philadelphia: Altemus.

Clark, Beverly Lyon (2003). *Kiddie Lit: The Cultural Construction of Children's Literature in America*. Baltimore: Johns Hopkins University Press.

Coolidge, Susan [Sarah Chauncey Woolsey] (1976). *What Katy Did*. New York: Garland.

Deane, Paul (1991). *Mirrors of American Culture: Children's Fiction Series in the Twentieth Century*. Meuchen, NJ: Scarecrow.

Emerson, Ralph Waldo (1983). *Essays and Lectures*, ed. Joel Porte. New York: Library of America.

Field, Walter Taylor (1928). *A Guide to Literature for Children*. Boston: Ginn & Co.

Finley, Martha (1896). *Elsie Dinsmore*. New York: Grosset & Dunlap.

Harte, Bret (1871). "Current Literature." *The Overland Monthly and Out West Magazine* 6: 2, 192–200.

Heininger, Mary Lynn, ed. (1984). *A Century of Childhood, 1820–1920*. Rochester, NY: Margaret Woodbury Strong Museum.

Hiner, N. Ray, and Hawes, Joseph M. (1985). *Growing Up in America: Children in Historical Perspective*. Urbana: University of Illinois Press.

Hope, Laura Lee [Lilian Garis] (1911). *The Outdoor Girls of Deepdale*. New York: Grosset & Dunlap.

Janeway, James (1977). *A Token for Children*. New York: Garland. (First publ. 1642.)

Johnson, Dianne (1990). *Telling Tales: The Pedagogy and Promise of African American Literature for Youth*. New York: Greenwood.

Johnson, Deidre (1993). *Edward Stratemeyer and the Stratemeyer Syndicate*. New York: Twayne.

Kaplan, Justin (1966). *Mr. Clemens and Mark Twain*. New York: Simon & Schuster.

Kelley-Hawkins, Emma Dunham (1988a). *Four Girls at Cottage City*. New York: Oxford University Press.

Kelley-Hawkins, Emma Dunham (1988b). *Megda*, intr. Molly Hite. New York: Oxford University Press.

Lurie, Alison (2003). *Boys and Girls Forever: Children's Classics from Cinderella to Harry Potter*. New York: Penguin.

Lystad, Mary (1980). *From Dr. Mather to Dr. Seuss: 200 Years of American Books for Children*. Boston: Hall.

McGavran, James Holt (1999). *Literature and the Child: Romantic Continuations, Postmodern Contestations*. Iowa City: University of Iowa Press.

MacLeod, Anne Scott (1994). *American Childhood: Essays on Children's Literature of the Nineteenth and Twentieth Centuries*. Athens, Ga.: University of Georgia Press.

Murray, Gail S. (1998). *American Children's Literature and the Construction of Childhood*. New York: Twayne.

Plotz, Judith (2001). *Romanticism and the Vocation of Childhood*. New York: Palgrave.

Porter, Eleanor H. (1913). *Pollyanna*. Boston: L. C. Page.

Stone, Albert E., Jr. (1961). *The Innocent Eye: Childhood in Mark Twain's Imagination*. New Haven: Yale University Press.

Stowe, Harriet Beecher (1996). *Uncle Tom's Cabin; or, Life among the Lowly*. New York: Modern Library.

Tarbox, Gwen Athene (2000). *The Clubwomen's Daughters: Collectivist Impulses in Progressive-era Girls' Fiction*. New York: Routledge.

Thacker, Deborah Cogan, and Webb, Jean (2002). *Introducing Children's Literature: From Romanticism to Postmodernism*. New York: Routledge.

Twain, Mark (1996). *Adventures of Huckleberry Finn*. New York: Oxford University Press.

Twain, Mark (1994). *The Adventures of Tom Sawyer*. New York: Penguin.

Twain, Mark (1917). *Mark Twain's Letters*, ed. Albert Bigelow Paine, 2 vols. New York: Harper & Bros.

Vogelback, A. L. (1939). "The Publication and Reception of *Huckleberry Finn* in America." *American Literature* 11: 3, 260–72.

West, Elliott, and Petrik, Paul, eds. (1992). *Small Worlds: Children and Adolescents in America, 1850–1950*. Lawrence: University of Kansas Press.

West, Mark I. (1989). *Before Oz: Juvenile Fantasy Stories from Nineteenth-Century America*. Hamden, Conn.: Archon.

Zipes, Jack David (2001). *Sticks and Stones: The Troublesome Success of Children's Literature from Slovenly Peter to Harry Potter*. New York: Routledge.

PART III
Major Authors

23

An Idea of Order at Concord: Soul and Society in the Mind of Louisa May Alcott

John Matteson

"I desire to know the one just thing to be done, and to be made brave enough to do it, though friends lament, gossips clamor, and the heavens fall." (Louisa May Alcott, *Moods*, ch. 19)

Louisa May Alcott (1832–88) was fond of observing that everything went by contraries with her, and her career was, indeed, a litany of paradoxes. Raised in the epicenter of Transcendentalism, she rejected her father's spiritualized asceticism in favor of worldly ambition, and countered Emersonian self-reliance with a moral vision rooted in community. Essentially resistant to the constraints of conventional femininity, she wrote books that were held up for generations as models for young female behavior. After years of striving to become a respected writer of adult fiction, she instead won fortune and renown for a book she described as "very hastily written to order" and which she was reluctant to write because works for juveniles, in her experience, did not "pay as well as rubbish." She raised her family out of chronic indebtedness by evoking a glorified vision of genteel poverty. Some of these paradoxes arose from a disjunction between the kind of books she wanted to write and the kind she discovered would sell. Others emerged predictably from the difficulties confronted by a woman seeking credibility in a masculine society. However, the most powerful conflicts in Alcott's life were more intimate and personal. She strove to come to terms with a family life that simultaneously nurtured her and subjected her to intolerable judgments, and she struggled, as she described it in *Moods*, "to live by principle, not impulse, [making] it both sweet and possible for love and duty to go hand in hand."

Knowledge of a writer's early life almost always offers clues to the later artistic development. In the case of Louisa May Alcott, these childhood influences are particularly inescapable, both because her work returns perpetually to the subject of the home and because she was born into a household in which the proper moral education of children was an obsessive concern. Louisa's father, A. Bronson Alcott, achieved both fame and notoriety as an educator and as a radical theorist in the field of child development. A member of the august Concord, Massachusetts circle that included Emerson, Thoreau, and Hawthorne, the elder Alcott is still remembered for his innovative but short-lived Temple School, so named because it was housed in Boston's Masonic Temple. Bronson believed that children entered the world with a spark of divine wisdom and spirituality that was typically repressed and contorted by contact with an unfeeling social order. He theorized that, if children could be exposed from birth only to loving and morally strengthening influences, their innate divinity might flourish in a way that could enlighten and redeem the world.

With this lofty objective in mind, and with the patient support of his wife Abba, whom Louisa later immortalized in the character of Marmee in *Little Women*, Bronson set about rearing his own four daughters in an environment that had some of the flavor of a behaviorist science experiment. For each of his three eldest girls, Bronson kept notebooks in which he tried to chronicle their every infantile development. As they grew older, the Alcott girls were admonished to resist every selfish, worldly impulse and to indulge every creative one. On the one hand, youngest daughter May, who showed artistic talent, was allowed to draw on the walls of her bedroom. On the other, four-year-old Louisa was forced to surrender the last piece of cake at her birthday party to an unexpected guest.

In 1843, as Louisa approached her teens, Bronson elevated self-denial to its own form of excess, co-founding a utopian community called Fruitlands, whose members vowed to forswear all animal products, as well as coffee, tea, and any commodity that had been created in exploitative labor conditions. More significantly for Louisa, the community attempted to constitute itself as a "Consociate Family," in which blood ties were supposed to count for nothing and all members were entitled to an equal claim on one another's loyalties and affections. Ill-planned and precariously financed, the venture collapsed less than a month into its first winter, but not before Bronson, in a last-ditch plan to save the community, proposed that he should permanently segregate himself from Abba and their daughters in imitation of a nearby Shaker colony. Eleven-year-old Louisa responded to this threat to her security with tearful prayers; she wrote in her journal of pleading with God to keep the family together. The Alcotts did not divide. However, the Fruitlands experience of first gaining a larger family and then seeing her own family nearly dissolve profoundly affected Louisa. It both convinced her of the crucial importance of family unity as a bulwark against misfortune and showed her the possibility of forming intimate spiritual attachments on a basis other than blood or romance. Both the centrality of family and the willingness to redefine family on more inclusive terms were to characterize much of Alcott's mature thinking about social arrangements.

Much more than any of her sisters, Louisa resisted her father's efforts to fashion her into a model child. Her innate wildness was more than personally irritating to her father; it was a living refutation of his theory that a soul could be molded into perfection by behavioristic means. Louisa's earliest surviving journal entries, dating from the Fruitlands period, tell of her efforts to master her volatile temper and her struggles to accept the Spartan regimen that her father had imposed. Family documents suggest that she loved Bronson with the desperate feelings of many daughters toward their fathers, but that decades passed before she finally won his favor. In the meantime, her life was a dissonant combination of lavish intellectual opportunities and demeaning material poverty. Hawthorne was a longtime family acquaintance and eventually became a next-door neighbor. Thoreau played his flute for Louisa and took her on long, roving walks in the woods. Emerson, whom Louisa called her "beloved Master," and "the man who has helped me most," opened his library to her. But at the end of the day she returned to a home where the father was chronically unemployed, the mother ruminated upon her disappointments, and all were, in Louisa's words, "poor as rats." Bronson hoped to teach his daughter the meaninglessness of worldly wealth; its very absence convinced her of its necessity.

The conditions of her formative environment instilled in Alcott a passionate moral sense, a fascination with the written word, and a consuming dread of financial hardship. As she began to emerge both as an adult and as a writer, another factor in her creative life began to assert itself: a pattern of behavior that might in later times have been described as manic-depressive. Alcott referred to her most exuberantly creative periods as "vortices." In the midst of a vortex, she would retreat from family life for weeks at a time, denying herself food and sleep to turn out as many pages as her endurance allowed. Then, exhausted, she would sink into a period of relative dullness and despondency. At least once, in her mid-twenties, she paused tremulously by the Mill Dam in Boston, debating whether to plunge into the waters below. Alcott's emotional difficulties were certainly not eased by her father's insistence that character was a question of ethics and that moody, anti-social behavior was merely evidence of a lack of self-discipline. Alcott's creative habits may in one sense be seen as a response to her familial environment, combining the values of physical self-denial and creative and intellectual excess. Her parents' ascetic leanings may also help to explain why Alcott's bildungsromans tend to progress, not from innocence to disillusionment, but from self-absorption to self-sacrifice.

With Alcott, however, self-sacrifice was not a matter of passive surrender. Her response to perceived injustice was always to fight it, and she fought resolutely. The fight that most powerfully influenced her life, the Civil War, also produced her first literary success, *Hospital Sketches* (1863), based on Alcott's own experience as a Union Army nurse. With its beginning declaration, "I want something to do," *Hospital Sketches* announces a theme to which Alcott would tirelessly return for the next thirty years: a woman's search to make herself useful, and therefore happy, in a world that underestimates or misconceives her true utility. Through her thinly disguised *alter ego*, Tribulation Periwinkle, Alcott avers that a woman's "something to do" should be nothing less than throwing oneself into the highest, most challenging cause available. Not only does Nurse Periwinkle go off to war, but she leaves no doubt that her war is only secondarily to save the Union. It is above all a struggle for liberation, both for African Americans and for women who have not heretofore been given sufficient scope for their energies. Although Periwinkle acquits herself bravely in the chaotic wards of Hurly-burly House Hospital, some of her most triumphant moments come in her striving toward interracial unity, as when she exchanges whoops of joy with a group of black men who are lighting firecrackers to celebrate the Emancipation Proclamation, or when she hugs and kisses a black baby to the astonishment of a bigoted colleague. Perhaps Alcott's most significant concern, however, is to depict herself, and, by extension, other women, as being capable of heroic, self-reliant action. Early in her narrative, Periwinkle proclaims, "I am a woman's rights woman, and if any man had offered help...I should have condescendingly refused it, sure that I could do everything as well, if not better, myself."

Nevertheless, Alcott does not claim complete independence for herself or for women in general. Moments after Periwinkle proclaims herself a "woman's rights woman," she swallows her pride and accepts needed help from her brother-in-law. Later, called upon to assist a surgeon in a series of grisly operations, she "fell to work with a vigor which soon convinced me that I was the weaker vessel, though nothing would have induced me to confess it then." Periwinkle concedes her limitations; what she asks is that women have the chance to discover those limitations for themselves, in the firm expectation that they will find them far less confining than even they themselves imagined.

The central episode of *Hospital Sketches* tells of the last days of a Virginia blacksmith, John, who has taken a mortal wound at the battle of Fredericksburg. John not only embodies an ideal of stoical courage, but also offers Nurse Periwinkle the chance to experience what Alcott sees as perhaps the *summum bonum* of earthly experience: the sweetness of sharing another's adversity. One night, when Periwinkle sees the blacksmith weeping silent tears, she is profoundly moved:

> ...straightway my fear vanished, my heart opened wide and took him in, as, gathering the bent head in my arms, as freely as if he had been a little child, I said, "Let me help you bear it, John."
>
> Never, on any human countenance, have I seen so swift and beautiful a look of gratitude, surprise and comfort, as that which answered me more eloquently than the whispered –
>
> "Thank you, ma'am, this is right good! this is what I wanted!"

Similar expressions of desire to bear the suffering of another pass from Jo to the dying Beth in *Little Women* (1868–9), from Fanny Shaw to her suddenly bankrupted father in *An Old-Fashioned Girl* (1870), and from Christie to the disgraced Rachel in *Work* (1873). Within misfortune, Alcott heroines tend to be quick to perceive the chance to transcend self-interest. It is an opportunity they almost invariably embrace.

The success of *Hospital Sketches* came at an enormous personal price for Alcott. The nursing experience that provided her with the factual material for the book also exposed her to typhoid pneumonia. Her doctors treated the condition with calomel, a mercury compound that poisoned her. Alcott never again knew perfect health, and when she wrote in *A Modern Mephistopheles* (1877) of "that long discipline of pain [that] failed to conquer the spirit . . . and . . . the slow ruin of the body that imprisoned it," she wrote from harrowing experience.

Alcott claimed that writing *Hospital Sketches* showed her her style. It is difficult to know precisely what she meant, since one sees in her work not one dominant mode of expression, but rather three distinct voices. Even before her breakthrough with *Hospital Sketches*, she had enjoyed some anonymous success as a writer of thrillers, many penned under the pseudonym of A. M. Barnard. As everyone knows, she won lasting fame as an author of books for girls. Yet the literary identity she most coveted – as a writer of serious fiction for adults – was the one that circumstances made it most difficult for her to achieve. Her first effort in this line, arguably her best, was *Moods*.

In *Little Women*, Alcott disavows the first novel of her fictional counterpart, Jo March, insisting that Jo's book is the product of an unhappy compromise. Attempting to strike a balance among her own creative impulses, the market-driven requirements of her publisher, and the well-intentioned but muddled suggestions of the March family, Jo turns her promising manuscript into a hash that neither accurately expresses her mind nor wins commercial favor. Alcott writes of Jo's failed effort to produce a masterpiece, "In the hope of pleasing every one, she took every one's advice; and, like the old man and his donkey in the fable, suited nobody." The analogous book in Alcott's actual career was *Moods*, a book whose tangled textual history and complex authorial motivations continue to generate controversy.

True to her usual impulsive habits of composition, Alcott produced the first draft of *Moods* in one vortex in late 1860 and revised it during a three-week jag, at the end of which she "found that my mind was too rampant for my body . . . my head was dizzy, legs shaky." But, unlike the case with many of her other projects, the vortex did not suffice for *Moods*. Alcott wrote many of her most noteworthy books, *Little Women* included, with virtually no revision; as a writer deeply accustomed to the demands of the marketplace, she was typically able to tackle a book or story head-on, and quickly turn her attentions elsewhere. However, Alcott not only rewrote *Moods* before its initial publication in 1864; she also, still not satisfied with it, published another substantially reworked version in 1882. (Except where otherwise noted, this essay's observations are based on the 1882 text.) *Moods* was a project Alcott could neither perfect nor abandon. Arguably, *Moods*, rather than anything she ever wrote about the March family, was her most earnest attempt to get her own spirit onto paper.

The 1864 edition of *Moods* is prefaced by an epigram from Emerson: "Life is a train of moods like a string of beads; and as we pass through them they prove to be many colored lenses, which paint the world their own hue, and each shows us only what lies in its own focus." *Moods* is indeed Alcott's attempt to elaborate in fiction some of Emerson's reflections on the life of the emotions. Alcott takes as her model, however, not the confident, ebullient Emerson of *Nature* and "Self-Reliance," but the chastened, skeptical Emerson of "Experience," who regarded life as a maze of contingencies, in which we must continually ask, "Where do we find ourselves?" Concerned less with the glories of the individual spirit than with its sometimes self-defeating contradictions and illogic, *Moods* contains Alcott's most subtly shaded psychological portrait in the person of Sylvia Yule, whose efforts to triumph over her impulsive nature and to discover inner tranquility closely resemble Alcott's own. Like Alcott, Sylvia has absorbed "pride, intellect, and will" from her father, while inheriting from her mother "passion, imagination, and the fateful melancholy of a woman defrauded of her dearest hope." These influences conspire to produce in Sylvia a nature "ambitious yet not self-reliant; sensitive, yet not keen-sighted." Those who have tended to read hostility toward Bronson into Louisa's almost complete exclusion of Mr. March from the world of *Little Women* should observe that in *Moods*, a book much closer to Alcott's heart, it is the maternal figure who is summarily dismissed. Sylvia's mother has died in child-birth, and it is the Bronson-like father who, after years of emotional remoteness, at last becomes uniquely dear to his daughter. As Alcott describes it, "No one was so much to her as he; no one so fully entered her thoughts and feelings. . . . As man and woman they talked, as father and daughter they loved; and the beautiful relation became their truest solace and support."

Sylvia, like the young Louisa, struggles to be good, but her mercurial temperament prevents her from keeping her resolutions to be better. Her self-descriptions express frustration and plead for understanding: "I don't try to be odd; I long to be quiet and satisfied, but I cannot; and when I do . . . wild things, it is not because I am thoughtless or idle, but because I am trying to be good and happy. . . . [S]ometimes I think I am a born disappointment." Although the narrator suggests that many of Sylvia's failings would be cured by the presence of "a wise and tender mother," Sylvia herself makes no attempt to blame her volatile nature on external forces, either rooted within her family or emanating from a constricting, gender-biased society. Indeed, broader social relations impose but little upon the Yule family and its circle, and Sylvia's own friends and relatives respond to her emotional instabilities with concern instead of condemnation. Sylvia insists that her problems are her own: "I know I'm whimsical, and hard to please, and have no doubt the fault was in myself." She understands that to deny responsibility for her condition would also be to forfeit her claim to autonomy.

In important respects, *Moods* critiques the romantic notions of the Transcendentalist movement, particularly its faith in nature as a benevolent and restorative influence. Sylvia is magnetically drawn to nature in its most tempestuous aspects, and her attraction repeatedly threatens to annihilate her. On a boating excursion, as her companions desperately seek shelter from a violent thunderstorm, Sylvia sits erect, impervious to the danger and eager to share in the elemental fury. In earlier chapters, she has been nearly consumed by a brushfire and almost drowned by a fast-rising ocean tide. Overall, the novel evinces an understanding that Alcott's father and other Transcendentalist mentors seldom acknowledged: that nature is a fitful, savage force, and sympathetic conformity with its energies can physically and psychologically shatter a human being.

In each of Sylvia's nearly disastrous encounters with nature, the same man rescues her. He is Adam Warwick, a figure modeled on Henry David Thoreau. Warwick is a "violently virtuous" man who "always takes the shortest way, no matter how rough it is." Warwick sympathizes strongly with Sylvia from the outset, and, even though he has witnessed the perils that await her if she fails to check her impulses, he seems to sense that less repression, not more, holds the most probable cure. He advises, "Let her alone, give her plenty of liberty, and I think time and experience will make a noble woman of her." Warwick's formidable integrity appears at first to offer Sylvia the balance she requires. However, his dedication to principle proves every bit as extreme as Sylvia's emotionalism, and the mind preoccupied by ideas stands revealed as no more satisfactory than the heart absorbed by feeling. As another character observes, "Adam has only the pride of an intellect which tests all things and abides by its own insight. He clings to principles; persons are but animated facts or ideas; he seizes, searches, uses them, and when they have no more for him, drops them like the husk, whose kernel he has secured."

The love triangle is a staple plot device in Alcott's fiction. An Alcott heroine is typically called upon to choose between a man who, like Warwick, speaks compellingly to her soul, and one who stands for some more practical principle. The safer choice in *Moods* is Geoffrey Moor. An essentially bland, forgettable character, Moor appeals to Sylvia precisely because he inspires no passion. He has also just spent five years caring for a dying sister, a service that appears to qualify him to help Sylvia conquer her mental ills. She reaches out to him in search of a Platonic friend, little imagining the difficulties of preventing such an attachment from edging toward marriage, with all its daunting implications of sex and permanence. Incapable of understanding her intentions, Moor proposes. Sylvia at first rebuffs him, but then, in the mistaken belief that Warwick has left never to return, she consents. Warwick resurfaces soon after the two are married, and all three characters ruminate upon the injustice of an institution that presumes to confer lifelong exclusive rights to another's love and loyalty.

Perhaps echoing the consociate spirit of Fruitlands, Warwick argues that unhappy marriages will remain "the tragedies of our day . . . till we learn that there are truer laws to be obeyed than those custom sanctions." Although speeches like these prompted some to accuse Alcott of advocating free love, *Moods* retreats from the tantalizing possibilities of following such "truer laws." Moor and Warwick sportingly consent to travel together to Europe for a year-long sabbatical while Sylvia decides whether she can love her husband. While away, the two achieve a literary rapprochement, co-authoring a book to which Moor contributes poems and Warwick supplies essays. The production of literature becomes a means of reconciliation. On the return voyage, the boat in which the two men are traveling sinks, and Warwick heroically and conveniently drowns. In the 1864 text, Sylvia dies of consumption. In the 1882 version, however, inspired by the advice that "in making the joy of others we often find our own," Sylvia gives up morbid self-contemplation in order to serve others. She dedicates herself first to her father and later, after her father's death, to Moor. Alcott presents her heroine's self-conquest as a happy ending, although it is easy to regret the reform of the younger, more impulsive Sylvia, who, for all her mental disturbance, was a good deal more fun.

As a woman long tormented and betrayed by her emotions, Sylvia Yule is more than happy to submerge the mercurial aspects of her temperament in contented marriage. But in Alcott's other most critically significant works, *Little Women* and *Work*, her heroines approach marriage at greater personal risk. They stand to lose not only their troublesome restlessness, but also the opportunity to develop their positive talents and energies. Alcott published *Little Women* in two parts, the first appearing in October 1868 and the conclusion making its debut the following spring. Although both parts obviously relate the experiences of the same characters, they are two different books in terms of their central thematic concerns. Part One is about the formation of character; it presents the March sisters as young girls struggling to develop their talents, to achieve emotional maturity, and to master their initially egocentric desires. Part Two is about young women who, having achieved a sense of self, must struggle against external forces – for example, mortality and phallocratic social conventions – that threaten to diminish or destroy those selves.

Little Women, or Meg, Jo, Beth and Amy (1868, 1869) is about growing up. However, as Mark Adamo has shown in his recent operatic adaptation of the novel, it is also about the dread of growing up. Eager to lead her siblings forward into almost every other kind of adventure, Jo not only resists her own coming of age, but also resents the comparative ease with which her sisters appear to be making the transition. Her reasons for seeking an artificially prolonged childhood arise in part from Louisa's contradictory experiences in growing up as an Alcott. While they lavished intellectual and moral stimuli upon their daughters, Bronson and Abba were not precisely clear as to what ought to become of all that knowledge and training when its recipients reached womanhood. The two daughters Bronson loved best, Anna and Lizzie, never achieved a life outside the domestic sphere. And if success within the home seemed a satisfactory culmination to many nineteenth-century women, Louisa May Alcott found it a barely tolerable anti-climax. In *Little Women*, even the meek and accommodating Beth admits in despair that her choice of a domestic life has resulted more from a failure of talent and imagination than a vision of fulfillment: "I'm not like the rest of you; I never made any plans about what I'd do when I grew up. . . . I couldn't seem to imagine myself anything but stupid little Beth, trotting about at home, of no use anywhere but there." The Alcott family emphasis on juvenile self-culture would seem to have been largely futile, even absurd, if it necessarily gave way to mature self-sacrifice. If childhood were all about self-discovery and adulthood were all about self-denial, who indeed would want to grow up?

Alcott herself was initially reluctant to end the novel with the matrimonial frenzy that characterizes the dénouement of Part Two of *Little Women*; she decided to marry off all the surviving sisters only after the opinions of publisher and public alike convinced her that a less conventional ending would damage the book's popularity. At the novel's close, characters pair off with such determination that one of Alcott's more waggish friends suggested that Part Two be christened "Wedding Marches." In the last chapter, as Meg, Jo, and Amy look back on their lives, their memories bear them back neither to any of their more celebrated adventures nor to the passing of Beth. Rather, they recall the events of a chapter from Part One titled "Castles in the Air," in which each of the girls and their male friend Laurie confided their secret hopes for the future. In this moment of nostalgia, a curious fact arises. Marriage is perhaps the quintessential happy ending to a children's tale; yet Alcott treats Jo's marriage in a single sentence. As a single woman, Jo has been forthright and energetic. Her wedding, to the contrary, finds her dazed and passive. All we are told is: "Almost before she knew where she was, Jo found herself married and settled at Plumfield." Moreover, none of the ostensibly happily married March sisters has achieved the dream she described earlier in the novel. Materialistic Meg, who imagined "all sorts of luxurious things," has married the poor but virtuous John Brooke. Jo and Amy, who looked forward to brilliant careers in literature and art, have deferred these dreams and settled down with their respective husbands. Even Beth, who modestly wished only "to stay safe at home with mother and father," has been denied her fancy by death. Jo and Amy both imply that their actual lives have brought them more contentment than their professional dreams could have given them, although neither has given up her artistic hopes. Nevertheless, *Little Women* appears to end as a story not of dreams come true, but of dreams at best compromised and at worst thwarted.

As Angela M. Estes and Kathleen Lant have observed, in the cases of both Jo and Laurie, the impossibility of fulfillment is due in large part to their discomfort with the expectations imposed on them by gender. Even youthful readers may recognize with a giggle that Laurie has a girl's name and Jo a boy's name. Only upon reading the story to our own children, however, are we likely to interpret Alcott's naming of the two as part of a larger scheme of transgender fantasy. Part of Laurie's castle in the air is "never to be bothered about money and business," that is, to circumvent the manly domain of commerce that Bronson Alcott, too, had found so alien and threatening. Jo's yearnings are more overt. She openly proclaims her "disappointment in not being a boy," and she snatches eagerly at her chance to be "the man of the family now papa is away." Her most memorable self-sacrifice, selling her hair to finance Marmee's journey to the bedside of the seriously ill Mr. March, is obliquely an act of self-assertion, since it renders her appearance more boyish. Jo's haircut also affords her some relief from the frustrations of being an intellectual woman in the nineteenth century; she asserts, "It will do my brains good to have that mop taken off." The brain, of course, has not changed, but with a boy's haircut to cover it, Jo feels less freakish and unnatural.

Jo and Laurie are both reluctant to grow up, because growing up means that the disquieting subject of gender identity can no longer be treated as a game. But Jo eventually recognizes, as Laurie does not, that the game must end, and it is this recognition that compels her to reject him as a suitor. Were they lifelong partners, he would continue to confirm her masculine side, and she would encourage his feminine proclivities; little wonder, then, that Jo tells Laurie, "I don't believe it's the right sort of love, and I'd rather not try it." Jo's acceptance of the unambiguously masculine professor, her bearded, large-handed "Papa Bhaer," is part and parcel of her belated acceptance of mature womanhood. Paradoxically, Jo's literary side is represented both as a means of romantic attraction and as a potential impediment to an enduring relationship. Bhaer is emboldened to court her by reading one of her poems. At almost the same moment that he declares his intentions, however, Jo tears the poem to shreds.

Even though her acceptance of Professor Bhaer seems to represent the defeat of her personal ambitions, Jo seems not to think so. She believes that her dreams have been not lost, but rather transmuted into a more charitable form. She gives her husband essential help in establishing his "school for little lads" at Plumfield, where the students are encouraged to call her "Mother." If, as Alcott says we must, we regard Jo's matronly life at Plumfield as a triumph, we can understand a key tenet of Alcott's feminist ideal. Women's rights, for Alcott, was never an end in itself. Rather, expanding opportunities for women was the great and necessary means by which previously neglected talents and energies might be made available to benefit the entire societal family. Jo learns that abilities used to benefit only oneself are thrown away. Used to advance only one's biological family, they remain largely wasted. Only when one gives freely to all do talent and effort attain their highest value. Although this altruism lies at the root of Alcott's feminism, it is also the reason modern readers sometimes misconceive her as anti-feminist. It can be argued that women historically accepted a subservient position precisely because of their willingness to sacrifice for the perceived greater good of the family. If Alcott was proposing a social order in which women were educated to feel a sense of family obligation to the entire community, might not her vision deepen, rather than diminish, the problem of sexual inequality? Perhaps the best answer is that Alcott expected the self-sacrifice of good men as well as good women. Her ideal of equality touched principally on opportunities to serve rather than any presumed right to seek one's individual happiness.

Little Women is undeniably driven by a Christian sensibility. Marmee equips each of her daughters with a New Testament and shares with them the glories of "the greatest life ever lived." The growth of the March girls toward adulthood is explicitly analogous to the journey of Christian in *The Pilgrim's Progress*, a text that had been central to the intellectual and moral formation of both Louisa and her father. The influence of Bunyan on *Little Women* is everywhere apparent, from the adapted epigram that precedes the story to Alcott's allegorical labels for the ethical trials through which the girls must pass: Vanity Fair, the Valley of Humiliation, and so on. But *Little Women*'s larger commentary on Bunyan is principally ironic; Alcott resists imitating the trajectory of the earlier work and wryly questions its moral conclusions. Like *Little Women*, *The Pilgrim's Progress* was published in two parts. The first describes an assertively individual journey, which Christian can begin only after he severs his ties with his family, whom he cannot persuade to believe in his apocalyptic vision. Only in the second part do Christian's wife and four children – all boys – belatedly follow in the Pilgrim's footsteps to the Celestial City. Whereas Alcott's work adopts Bunyan's basic premise that life is a moral journey, she parts company from him to argue that the journey is most successful when it is shared. Moreover, although Part One of *Little Women* tells of a family with a father who has departed for religious reasons, it is the family he leaves behind whose moral struggles are most powerfully relevant. Moreover, the two March sisters for whom life's journey ranges widest, Jo and Amy, cannot rely upon the family to follow; rather, their journeys outward are only prologues to their returns to the domestic center. From the outset of *The Pilgrim's Progress*, Bunyan is clear that, if the hero remains enmeshed in domestic life, he will perish. In *Little Women* the home is the only place where life is ultimately sustained; it is the Celestial City toward which the March sisters have always unconsciously striven.

For all its awareness of the Bible and Bunyan, however, Alcott's work shows signs of the struggles for moral equilibrium that engaged American writers as their nation turned away from conventional theism and toward more material concerns after the Civil War. It has been aptly observed that, in *Little Women*, even though their father is a clergyman, the March sisters never set foot in church. Moreover, Jo's famous opening grumble, "Christmas won't be Christmas without any presents," is the lament of a child who needs no persuading that the true spirit of her culture is commercial, not ecclesiastic. Of course, Alcott's father and his Transcendental brethren had striven to retain a reverential view of the world while discarding outward forms and unbending dogmas. Louisa was bound to inherit the philosophical problem that their heresies had raised: how, in the absence of a sturdily organized faith, does one preserve both the feel of a religious life and the idea of an ethical existence? Lacking a system of either rituals or sacraments through which to practice their piety, the March sisters are pressed repeatedly in the direction of good works. Lacking the deep pockets essential to large-scale charity, they must continually give of themselves. Indeed, few books narrate more acts of unselfish generosity than *Little Women*. However, it is this impulse toward charity that exposes Beth to scarlet fever, and the power of the Marches to do good is generally restricted by their limited means. Although one feels deep admiration when the girls give up their Christmas breakfasts to a more abject family, the greatest acts of philanthropy in the novel, for instance the founding of Plumfield, are made possible only by the accumulated capital of wealthy people like Grandfather Laurence and Aunt March.

After *Little Women*, Alcott never again had to dream of a Mr. Laurence or an Aunt March coming to the financial rescue of her real-life family. The novel's royalties paid the debts that Bronson had accumulated over decades. When the sequel, *Little Men: Life at Plumfield with Jo's Boys* (1871), sold 50,000 advance copies, it was evident that the impecunious days of the Alcotts were over. Another author might have converted this financial freedom into an aesthetic emancipation, choosing thereafter to take on only those projects she found artistically appealing. Alcott did not pursue this path. She had fallen prey, it seems, to what post-1930s generations would call a Depression mentality. Haunted by the memories of childhood indigence, she could never reach a level of security that she found sufficient. Habituated to being her family's financial savior, she continued to turn out lucrative children's books, which she personally disparaged as "moral pap for the young," long after the family no longer needed saving. Only once after *Little Women* did Alcott put her name to a piece of published adult fiction, and that novel, *Work*, she had begun drafting in the early 1860s.

Despite having turned largely away from the adult market, Alcott continued to refine her vision of the possibilities for women in American life. On the whole, this vision becomes increasingly optimistic. Although her later works only intermittently rival the artistic achievement of *Little Women*, they offer a number of instances in which women characters arrive at levels of fulfillment, autonomy, and professional success that Alcott had pointedly denied Jo March in that book. In one of Alcott's best children's fictions, the underrated *An Old-Fashioned Girl* (1870), the heroine, Polly Milton, is again a girl of modest means who comes into contact with the upper classes. Unlike in *Little Women*, however, the largesse of the gentry is not required to finance a happy ending. Rather, the book's prosperous family, undermined by its own vanity and extravagance, goes bankrupt, and it is Polly who rescues them with her unselfish compassion. Through her example of thrift and self-reliance, she inspires even the family's profligate son to declare that redemption is still possible as long as he has "a conscience and a pair of hands."

In the book's most memorable chapter, "The Sunny Side," Polly takes her socialite friend Fanny to visit two young women who share an apartment that resembles a feminist artists' colony in miniature. One of the women is at work on an imposing statue of "the coming woman," a figure that combines the attributes of saint, muse, goddess and fate. The new woman possesses "broad shoulders [that] can bear burdens without breaking down," eyes that see clearly, and lips that can "do something besides simper and gossip." The women decide that the base of the statue should be adorned with a ballot box. Into the scene Alcott interjects a self-portrait far more starkly accurate than Jo March; she represents herself in the person of Kate King, an author who has written a successful book by accident and has suddenly become fashionable. A focus of reverence among the aspiring new women, King is glad to encourage them in their artistic dreams; but she takes no pleasure in her own popularity, and looks tired and old before her time. She causes Fanny to wonder if the time will ever come "when women could earn a little money and success, without paying such a heavy price for them."

A heavier price is almost exacted from Christie Devon, the heroine of *Work: A Story of Experience* (1873). Christie's failed attempts to find a secure place in the working world bring her within moments of committing suicide. Two of Alcott's philosophical heroes, Emerson and Thomas Carlyle, from whose writings the epigraph for *Work* is taken, urged that labor is the process by which a person achieves full humanity. While Alcott agreed that work could be ennobling, she had also learned at first hand that undercompensated, unappreciated work could wear down and diminish the laborer. As Christie discovers, performing the very tasks that strengthen her competence and character leads a leisure-loving society to regard her as an inferior. Almost throughout *Work*, Alcott's female characters either possess practical knowledge and strength of character but lack the worldly means to make a difference in society, or vice versa.

During her picaresque wanderings in the first third of the novel, Christie performs with reasonable skill the tasks of maidservant, actress, governess, hired companion, and seamstress. She is driven from each occupation in turn, but never by an inability to do her work well. Most often, the change is necessitated by the impossibility of remaining under employers who have infected the employment relation with their own character flaws. While others decried the impersonal nature of the workplace, Christie's history indicates that, at least in the occupations available to women who wish to avoid factory work, employment relations were often *too* personal, and that the need for cash too frequently meant exposure to the whims and cruelties of careless or obdurate employers. Economic relations in the book are unsatisfactory so long as they involve either the mere exchange of money for service or the flaunted superiority of one class over another. Alcott writes: "There are many Christies, willing to work, yet unable to bear the contact with coarser natures which makes labor seem degrading, or to endure the hard struggle for the bare necessities of life when life has lost all that makes it beautiful." Hepsey Johnson, a black domestic who becomes Christie's first friend in the novel, puts the matter simply: "Folks don't seem to 'member dat we've got feelin's."

And yet, where the relationship is graced by mutual respect and sympathy, no task is truly distasteful. As Christie's benefactor Mrs. Wilkins puts it, "There warn't never a hard job that ever I'd hated but what grew easy when I remembered who it was done for." Mrs. Wilkins – whose occupation as a laundress and "clear-starcher" reflects both upon the clear, simple terms with which she regards life and the purifying, strengthening influence she exerts on those around her – is almost always shown working in her kitchen; Hepsey is employed as a cook. Both of them are, in more ways than one, nurturing characters, and their shared association with food illustrates that work must not only produce wealth; it must nourish both body and soul. In *Work*, Alcott explores the possible connection between love and money in both its highest and lowest forms. When Christie gives a hundred hard-earned dollars to Hepsey to help her guide slaves to freedom, Alcott invokes the language of the marketplace to highlight the act of charity. She calls the gift an "investment" and observes that "shares in the Underground Railroad pay splendid dividends that never fail." The other side of the love–cash nexus is personified in Rachel, a former prostitute whom Christie befriends while the two are working as seamstresses, and whose experience illustrates the tragedies that result when physical intimacy becomes commodified. Christie's kindness to Rachel is more than repaid when the latter appears in the nick of time to save her from throwing herself in the river.

Rescued from suicide, Christie does not take the easy way out. But at this juncture in the plot, Alcott almost does. Soon after Christie's brush with death, the story veers into a love triangle somewhat stalely reminiscent of *Moods*. Again, one of the candidates for Christie's affections, a florist named David Sterling, is modeled on Thoreau. Christie rejects a wealthy suitor and accepts Sterling, and the story teeters on the brink of predictability until the outbreak of the Civil War inspires both Sterling and Christie to enlist, he in the army, she in the nursing corps. At their hastily planned wedding, both are in uniform. David is killed, leaving Christie to raise their baby daughter and to wonder whether she will ever find the work for which her life of struggle and trial has prepared her. The question is answered when, near the eve of her fortieth birthday, Christie attends a women's rights meeting. It soon becomes painfully apparent that the wealthy women in attendance and their working comrades have no idea of how to understand or reach out to each other. Standing at the lowest step of the speakers' platform, symbolically bridging the space between high and low, Christie gives an eloquent, impromptu address whose spirit unites and inspires the crowd. Her sufferings have shaped her unawares into a potent feminist activist.

The closing tableau of *Work* reunites many of the women whom Christie has met upon her journey, including Hepsey, Mrs. Wilkins, and Rachel, who, it has been revealed, is actually Sterling's sister, long presumed dead. Gathered together in the name of creating a better place for women in American life, Christie's friends join hands as "a loving league of sisters, old and young, black and white, rich and poor." The scene is one of many in Alcott's writings that redefine family according to shared mission rather than bloodlines. Although it calls to mind Bronson Alcott's ideal of the consociate family, this alliance is different in that it excludes any masculine presence. The war has made casualties of both Christie's lovers, making room for the higher love of sisterhood. At age eleven, Louisa had cried when her father suggested dividing their family along gender lines. Now, only a few years younger than her father had been at Fruitlands, Alcott saw intriguing possibilities in single-sex community. The ending of the novel reconstructs not only the idea of family but also the meaning of the book's title. Whereas "work" had once signified to Christie the grubbing, lonely life of a menial laborer, the word is at last made synonymous with the holy labors of reform.

After *Work*, Alcott completed only one more piece of adult fiction: *A Modern Mephistopheles*, one of her longest and best thrillers, was published anonymously in 1877. Alcott's illness and compulsive work habits aged her before her time, and she struggled to finish her last novel. *Jo's Boys, and How They Turned Out* (1886), which completes the March family trilogy, is somewhat deceptively named. *Jo's Boys* does indeed tell of the further adventures of characters introduced in the middle volume of March trilogy, the highly successful but stylistically bland *Little Men*. However, it is perhaps most noteworthy for its redemption of the feminine ambitions that had seemed close to annihilation at the end of *Little Women*. Jo, whose literary future seemed in grave doubt when she married Professor Bhaer, has surmounted the distractions of motherhood and the jocular turmoil of Plumfield to write her break-through novel, which has brought her "an unexpected cargo of gold and glory." Amy has resumed her work as an artist and has likewise proven "that women can be faithful wives and mothers without sacrificing [a] special gift." The most radical developments, however, concern Plumfield itself. Founded as a boys' academy at the end of *Little Women*, the school has, by the time of *Jo's Boys*, evolved into the fully co-educational Laurence College, where a faculty of "cheerful, hopeful men and women" minister to youths of "all sexes, colors, creeds and ranks." Now a somewhat elder stateswoman of progressive education, Jo inveighs against those who predict "nervous exhaustion and an early death" for girls who use their brains. Meg's daughter Josie anticipates Billie Jean King in besting visiting Harvard boys at tennis, and Nan cheerfully chooses spinsterhood so that she may better pursue her career in medicine.

A far cry from the earnest struggles to subdue the self that abound in *Little Women*, *Jo's Boys* may deserve to be classified as utopian fiction. Although Dan may need to curb his impulsiveness and Nat may require strengthening against temptation, the most daunting enemies of the self are no longer primarily situated in the internal workings of character, but in the "prejudice, ridicule [and] neglect" that uglify the outside world. If these foes have yet to be vanquished in *Jo's Boys*, they have at least been driven outside Plumfield's gates. The book offers a wealth of inspiration for girl readers seeking visions of identity and independence. However, with the exception of the story of Dan, who discovers fortune, violence, and adventure in the West, far beyond the reforming reach of Plumfield, *Jo's Boys* suffers on a dramatic level from a flaw that drains excitement from most fictional Arcadias: the lack of a compelling source of *agon*. Also absent from the novel, as from most of Alcott's writing, is any meaningful sense of moral ambiguity. Whereas many of her great contemporaries returned continually to the tendency of good and evil to overlap and interpenetrate in perplexing fashion, Alcott was personally quite certain of her ability to tell right from wrong, and she took it as her task as a writer to provide moral encouragement, not to explore the gray areas of human motivation. Her lack of philosophical ambivalence costs her something as a literary artist, though it is perhaps precisely this firmness that underlies her appeal for young readers who crave an ethically stable universe.

Sensing her book's aesthetic flatness, Alcott wrote a preface to *Jo's Boys* calling it "more faulty than any of its imperfect predecessors," and she was heartily glad to have done with writing it. With a sarcastic turn on the obligatory "they lived happily ever after," Alcott told her readers that she was closing the March family saga with as "many weddings, few deaths, and as much prosperity as the eternal fitness of things will permit." In the last chapter, she wrote, "It is a strong temptation to the weary historian to close the present tale with an earthquake which should engulf Plumfield and its environs so deeply in the bowels of the earth that no youthful Schliemann could ever find a vestige of it." But Plumfield does not really deserve to be buried. It is in many ways Alcott's attempt to reinvent in fiction her father's Fruitlands experiment, adding to it the gender equality that had been conspicuously absent from his ideal. But whereas Fruitlands was experienced only by a handful of impractical dreamers, Plumfield has left its gentle mark on the imaginations of generations of children, sowing seeds of idealism to sprout where they may.

The eternal fitness of things decreed an ironic end for Alcott herself. She had been born on her father's thirty-third birthday. Fifty-five years later, they nearly shared the same death date. In late 1882 Bronson had suffered a paralyzing stroke. Under the watchful care of Anna and Louisa – then the only two surviving little women – he clung to life until the late winter of 1888. When Louisa paid him her last visit, Bronson spoke of his approaching death and, in words both gentle and macabre, invited his daughter to "come up" with him. Louisa replied that she wished she could. On March 4, 1888, Bronson Alcott died. Only two days later, Louisa, who, like one of her heroines had devoted her life to serving others but now could serve no more, did, indeed, "come up."

SELECTED PRIMARY TEXTS BY LOUISA MAY ALCOTT

The Inheritance. 1849 (first publ. 1997).

Flower Fables. 1855.

Hospital Sketches. 1863.

Moods. 1864, rev. 1882.

Little Women, or Meg, Jo, Beth and Amy, Part One. 1868.

Little Women, or Meg, Jo, Beth and Amy, Part Two. 1869.

An Old Fashioned Girl. 1870.

Little Men: Life at Plumfield with Jo's Boys. 1871.

Work: A Story of Experience. 1873.

"Transcendental Wild Oats." 1874.

Eight Cousins; or, The Aunt-Hill. 1875.

Rose in Bloom: A Sequel to Eight Cousins. 1876.

A Modern Mephistopheles. 1877.

Under the Lilacs. 1878.

Jack and Jill: A Village Story. 1880.

Jo's Boys, and How They Turned Out. 1886.

COLLECTIONS OF SHORTER TEXTS

Alcott, Louisa May (1975). *Behind a Mask: The Unknown Thrillers of Louisa May Alcott*, ed. Madeleine B. Stern. New York: Avenel.

Alcott, Louisa May (1976). *Plots and Counterplots: More Unknown Thrillers of Louisa May Alcott*, ed. Madeleine B. Stern. New York: Avenel.

Alcott, Louisa May (1987). *The Selected Letters of Louisa May Alcott*, ed. Joel Myerson and Daniel Shealy with Madeleine B. Stern. Boston: Little, Brown.

Alcott, Louisa May (1988a). *Alternative Alcott*, ed. and intr. Elaine Showalter. New Brunswick: Rutgers University Press.

Alcott, Louisa May (1988b). *A Double Life: Newly Discovered Thrillers of Louisa May Alcott*, ed. Madeleine B. Stern with Joel Myerson and Daniel Shealy. Boston: Little, Brown.

Alcott, Louisa May (1989). *The Journals of Louisa May Alcott*, ed. Joel Myerson and Daniel Shealy with Madeleine B. Stern. Boston: Little, Brown.

Alcott, Louisa May (1991). *Freaks of Genius: Unknown Thrillers of Louisa May Alcott*, ed. Daniel

Shealy with Madeleine B. Stern and Joel Myerson. New York: Greenwood.

Alcott, Louisa May (1992). *Fairy Tales and Fantasy Stories*, ed. Daniel Shealy. Knoxville: University of Tennessee Press.

Alcott, Louisa May (1993). *From Jo March's Attic: Stories of Intrigue and Suspense*, ed. Madeleine B. Stern and Daniel Shealy. Boston: Northeastern University Press.

Alcott, Louisa May (1995). *Louisa May Alcott Unmasked: Collected Thrillers*, ed. Madeleine B. Stern. Boston: Northeastern University Press.

Alcott, Louisa May (1996). *A Whisper in the Dark: Twelve Thrilling Tales by Louisa May Alcott*, ed. Stefan Dziemianowicz. New York: Barnes & Noble.

Alcott, Louisa May (1997). *Louisa May Alcott on Race, Sex, and Slavery*, ed. Sarah Elbert. Boston: Northeastern University Press.

Alcott, Louisa May (2002). *L. M. Alcott, Signature of Reform*, ed. Madeleine B. Stern. Boston: Northeastern University Press.

References and Further Reading

Bedell, Madelon (1980). *The Alcotts: Biography of a Family*. New York: Charles N. Potter.

Cheney, Ednah D. (1889). *Louisa May Alcott: Life, Letters and Journals*. Boston: Roberts Bros.

Clark, Beverly Lyon, and Alberghene, Janice M., eds. (1998). Little Women *and the Feminist Imagination*. New York: Garland.

Elbert, Sarah (1984). *A Hunger for Home: Louisa May Alcott and* Little Women. Philadelphia: Temple University Press.

Estes, Angela M., and Lant, Kathleen Margaret (1989). "Dismembering the Text: The Horror of Louisa May Alcott's *Little Women*." *Children's Literature* 17: 98–123.

Keyser, Elizabeth Lennox (1999). *Little Women: A Family Romance*. New York: Twayne.

Keyser, Elizabeth Lennox (1993). *Whispers in the Dark: The Fiction of Louisa May Alcott*. Knoxville: University of Tennessee Press.

MacDonald, Ruth K. (1983). *Louisa May Alcott*. Boston: Twayne.

Saxton, Martha (1977). *Louisa May: A Modern Biography of Louisa May Alcott*. Boston: Houghton Mifflin.

Stern, Madeleine B. (1996). *Louisa May Alcott: A Biography*. New York: Random House.

Stern, Madeleine B., ed. (1984). *Critical Essays on Louisa May Alcott*. Boston: Hall.

Strickland, Charles (1985). *Victorian Domesticity: Families in the Art and Life of Louisa May Alcott*. University, Ala.: University of Alabama Press.

24

America Can Break Your Heart: On the Significance of Mark Twain

Robert Paul Lamb

Some think they're strong, some think they're smart,
Like butterflies they're pulled apart,
America can break your heart.
You don't know all, sir, you don't know all. (W. H. Auden, 1939)

Critics frequently speak of Mark Twain as the quintessential American author, but what does such a statement mean? Does it have something to do with his rise from humble origins, his staunchly egalitarian values, or his assaults on racism, imperialism, hypocrisy, and social injustice? Is it the accessibility of his books or that he was the first major American novelist to write in the vernacular and fill his pages with the voices of common folk? Could it be the appeal of his imagination, one arguably unsurpassed in literary history? Is it his extraordinary humor, his common sense, his genius with language, or the cultural richness of his works, not to mention their variety: realist novels, historical novels, science fiction, children's books, travel literature, speeches, essays, plays, sketches, short stories, satires, detective fiction, journalism, and literary criticism? All of this is true, yet it barely tells the story of Twain's place in American literature and culture, or of the abiding love that so many feel for him.

Samuel Langhorne Clemens (1835–1910) was a complex man whose inner divisions fueled, deepened, and enriched his writings. Born into a life of poverty and provincial ignorance, and forced to earn a living from age twelve after his father's death, he grew up in a racist culture permeated by the evil of slavery. But he shed these culturally imposed limitations through a lifelong journey of self-education, becoming an advocate of racial justice and one of the most learned persons of his age. This self-taught itinerant newspaperman, accomplished pilot, and homespun author, who first came to national attention as "the wild man of the Pacific slope," was fluent in French and German, an expert on Shakespeare and Elizabethan literature, the friend of powerful politicians and businessmen, and a recipient of honorary degrees from Yale and Oxford. Possessed of a profound *wanderlust* (between the ages of seventeen and twenty-one he worked as a printer in St. Louis, New York, Philadelphia, Keokuk, and Cincinnati), Clemens was a Southerner who moved north, a Westerner who went east, an American who spent over a decade living abroad, a vagabond turned Victorian gentleman, and a product of the rough worlds of the Mississippi River and Nevada mining camps who fell in love with the daughter of wealthy Elmira, New York abolitionists, entered genteel New England society, and tried not to look too out-of-place. Born and raised in a border state, for him living on the border became a state of mind. He was the perpetual outsider looking in and the perpetual insider looking out, never fully at home wherever he happened to be.

Clemens's powerful need for freedom, personal and imaginative, and his equally insistent hunger for social stability and moral order, created in him a double impulse to join and to separate that manifested itself in a paradoxical nature. He was a foremost advocate of America, progress, and the nineteenth century, but also their most bitter and effective critic. He was both idealist and cynic, dreamer and pragmatist, believer and skeptic. He hated power and its abuses, but was fascinated by powerful men, and his works are filled with such characters, toward whom he shows a maddening ambivalence. He was shrewd and foolhardy, generous and mean-spirited, self-promoting and self-defeating, mercurial in temperament, and he could be a loyal friend or a terrible foe. Brave and cowardly, arrogant and penitent, self-inflating and self-hating, an accomplished liar and a champion of truth, both in life and in art, Clemens was a person of gargantuan contradictions. Although his notebook jotting – "I am not *an* American. I am *the* American." – was not about himself, it was nonetheless appropriate, for, at his best and worst, he was the ideal representative of what was good and what was not so good about his nation and its citizens. American genius and American jester, he understood his own contradictoriness and uttered it with typical Twainian irony: "Ah, well, I am a great & sublime fool. But then I am God's fool, & all His works must be contemplated with respect" (Twain and Howells 1960: 215).

Twain first leaped to national attention as a California humorist with the title story of *The Celebrated Jumping Frog of Calaveras County and Other Sketches* (1867), but his initial critical success was *The Innocents Abroad* (1869), a satire about Americans traveling across Europe and into the Holy Land based upon his own 1867 journey as a roving correspondent. Notable were its uniquely irreverent attitude toward European culture, its brilliant satire on the "ugly American" abroad, its eloquent passages of description, and, of course, its humor, with everyone, most especially the author, serving as the butt of the joke. Yet it also evidenced what would be one of Twain's lifelong problems, that of composition or structure. Inexperienced in writing books, he adopted the "narrative plank" method of his public lectures, alternating set pieces of serious and humorous material, with the two commenting on each other by means of juxtaposition. (This is what lay behind his tendency toward the episodic in later narratives.) Forced to complete a 600-page subscription book contract, he ran out of interest and filled it with padding, and his resentment seeped into the text in scenes of disaffection and morbidity. Twain would return to the travel book through-out his career, in works like *A Tramp Abroad* (1880) and *Following the Equator* (1897).

The structure of *The Innocents Abroad* had derived from Twain's recent excursion and his newspaper reports. But *Roughing It* (1872), another lengthy subscription book, lacked a ready-made form, challenging a writer whose enormous imagination out-stripped his compositional talents. Roughly autobiographical, this story of Twain's Western years as a miner and reporter in Nevada, San Francisco, and Hawaii (1861–6) combined picaresque travelogue, bildungsroman, a parody of the tradition of Western writing, and journalistic accounts of a vanishing era in a realist text where the voices of high rhetoric, reportage, and the vernacular alternate and collide, with the last emerging as dominant. In the first part (chapters 1–33), written while Twain was struggling with newfound familial responsibilities (he had married Olivia Langdon in 1870) and fondly recalling his shiftless Western years, the outsider narrator/protag-onist (Sam) views the West as an idyllic place of freedom, adventure, and easy riches, and "the States" as oppressive and boring. In the second part (chapters 34–41), written while Twain was perusing old letters and editorials and recalling his actual experiences in Nevada, Sam as an insider discovers the real West is chaotic, violent, and bereft of economic opportunity. In the third part (chapters 42–77), Sam is an outsider again, but by choice, and as a journalist his critique cuts both ways: Western freedom is anarchic and civilization is tyrannical. He can find no society that accommodates individual freedom within the matrix of a stable social order. *Roughing It* thus commences as a flight from order, turns into a flight from freedom, becomes a quest for a social order in which meaningful freedom can flourish, and concludes with the narrator's realization of the futility of this search and his consequent alienation. Since this quest mirrors the nation's century-old attempt to reconcile "liberty and union," *Roughing It* represents the main current of American political thought.

In the first part, Sam is initiated into the West during a 1,700-mile stage drive and his first year in Washoe (Nevada). Throughout, romantic expectation is punctured by disappointing reality, and excitement declines into boredom. The Great Plains begin as a "grand sweep . . . like the stately heave and swell of the ocean's bosom" but quickly turn into a monotonous 700-mile stretch of level land (Twain 1993: 6–7). The alkali desert is "romantic" and "dramatically adventurous" but the poetry is "all in the anticipation" and soon it becomes a "thirsty, sweltering, longing, hateful reality" (pp. 122–4). The Goshoot Indians are decidedly un-Cooperesque, and the legendary desperado Slade is disappointingly polite and commonplace (p. 67). The pattern can even be glimpsed in one sentence on Western speech: "Its western freshness and novelty startled me, at first, and interested me; but it presently grew monotonous, and lost its charm" (p. 25). In Nevada, he discovers "that *nothing* that glitters is gold" (p. 188); precious metals are difficult to locate, require much labor and money to extract, and are "tedious and costly" to process (p. 191). Like the "Sphinx" who turns unbearably talkative (pp. 8–9), nothing in the West is what it seems. Furthermore, like the runaway dictionary in the stagecoach (p. 19), his inherited knowledge and values are useless, even dangerous: relying on books during a snowstorm almost gets him killed (pp. 211–13). His understanding of the West evolves in its symbols, from the innocuous jackass rabbit that entertains him (p. 13), to the trickster coyote who fools the well-fed town dog (pp. 30–3), to the buffalo that charges him (p. 42), and he is the target of pranksters (like the stagecoach driver who feigns an "Indian attack": pp. 57–8) and of horse swindlers who sell him "a Genuine Mexican Plug" (pp. 158–9).

When, after the snowstorm debacle, Sam and his companions resume their vices of smoking, drinking, and card-playing, they figuratively enter into Western society (Twain 1993: 219). Significantly, in recounting the Great Landslide Case (chapter 34), Sam does not employ the first-person, and the arrogant "town dog/victim" is an Easterner other than himself. In this second part of the book, he realizes that in the West status is based on usefulness, best exemplified in the competent figure of Captain John Nye, whose memory, "conversational powers," and "handiness" create a "spirit of accommodation" in an unfriendly inn they visit (pp. 228–9). But he also learns what the real West is like: the drudgery of working in a quartz mill, the curse of gold fever (p. 239). On the mining frontier, labor is horizontal but success is vertical, producing a lottery-like mindset of expectation and disappointment, and anticipatory selves (prefiguring naturalism's characters) who live in the future while ignoring the present. This speculatory psyche was something Twain possessed throughout his life; bequeathed to him by his father, it would lead him close to financial ruin in the 1890s. When Sam and Cal Higbie discover a "blind lead" worth millions, they can discuss what they will do with their riches but cannot focus on the present long enough to do a few hours' work to establish the claim (chapters 40–1). Sam fails because, unlike their third partner, he is incapable of resorting to violence to get his share (p. 268), and because, on a larger level, pure freedom leads to aimlessness.

The third part begins with Sam symbolically discarding his Western garb and revolver and becoming a reporter; henceforth he will make his living with his pen. With both Twain and the bildungsroman exhausted, the book's subscription length unfilled, and the author recalling the despair that led him to the brink of suicide in 1866, his mood turns increasingly bitter and he finishes by filling the narrative plank with tall tales, anecdotes, his old reportage, and the landscape descriptions from his 1866 Hawaii letters to the Sacramento *Union*. In the sketch in which a coyote tricks a town dog (chapter 5), he had privileged Western vernacular over Eastern genteel values (Smith 1962: 54–6), but in the humorous "conversation" between Scotty Briggs and the minister over Buck Fanshaw's funeral (Twain 1993: 310–16), he mocks both rhetorics, and follows with: an attack on desperadoes, corrupt lawmen, and a jury system that places a "premium upon ignorance, stupidity, and perjury" (p. 321); a parody of Eastern literary conventions and sentimental fiction; a grotesque description of the tomblike Nevada mines; and a denunciation of nativist hostility toward the Chinese – "Only the scum of the population do it . . . and . . . the policemen and politicians, likewise, for these are the dust-licking pimps and slaves of the scum, there as well as elsewhere in America" (p. 375). His attitude toward Western violence is unambiguous as he reports that the "first twenty-six graves" in the cemetery "were occupied by *murdered* men" (p. 318), a number metonymically linked to Slade, who killed his first man at age twenty-six (p. 60) and who, Twain falsely claims, "*had taken the lives of twenty-six human beings*" by the time they met (p. 67).

Like his author, Sam is one of Tocqueville's restless Americans, "forever brooding over" what he does not possess, who "clutches everything" but "holds nothing fast" (Tocqueville 1989: 136). With his "vagabond instinct" upon him (Twain 1993: 421) – like Emerson's "traveler, who says, 'Anywhere but here'" (Emerson 1983: 1090) – Sam begins "to get tired of staying in one place so long" and wants "a change" (Twain 1993: 376) for its own sake. For Twain, things always look best either when they are new, or else at a distance, whether spatial or temporal. He longs for Nevada just as he leaves it (significantly, as it stands on the verge of statehood: p. 382); the illuminated flag looks best as the sun sets (p. 383); California's plains and forests are "best contemplated at a distance" (p. 385); and he even waxes nostalgic about mining once that world has passed from the scene (pp. 390–2). His thirst for change and excitement perversely causes him to "enjoy" the great San Francisco earthquake (chapter 58), which tears the veneer off civilization just as the cave-ins of Nevada exposed the illusion of Western freedom.

Sam's journey to Oahu and Hawaii becomes a descent into history and into hell as he explores primitive civilization and the despair in his own soul. Hoping to discover some clue to the evolution of human society from its prelapsarian origins to its current unsatisfactory state, he is fascinated with President Kekuanoa, who began life as a bloodthirsty pagan warrior and is now an "educated Christian" at "the reins of an enlightened government" (Twain 1993: 457–8). But phylogeny does not follow ontogeny; in times of trouble, the natives return to their old ways, and the downside of progress is extermination (p. 454). Native culture has been degraded by contact with Western civilization, leaving behind a people caught between their dying past and their poorly assimilated future. They are homologous to Twain, himself caught between the vernacular and genteel worlds, and this leads to inconsistency in his otherwise devastating critique of the consequences of Western imperialism. In a space of four paragraphs, he criticizes the natives for human sacrifice and the missionaries for ending it, enthusiastically recreates a scene of sacrifice, and offers a sincere tribute to the missionaries for bringing clothing, education, and law to the islands (pp. 439–41). Wherever Twain turns for answers, history is mute. The story of the battleground bone-yard "is a secret that will never be revealed" (p. 442); the natives' description of their immolation of Captain Cook is illegible (p. 492); the building of the temple to Lono by ghosts remains a puzzle (p. 494); and who built the City of Refuge, "how it was built, and when, are mysteries" (p. 503).

Twain typically reveals his feelings by projecting them upon the landscape. Early in *Roughing It*, on the Continental Divide at South Pass, he expresses his double impulse to join and separate in the figure of the spring that sends its water in opposite directions, one "starting on a journey westward" through "miles of desert solitudes" and the other heading east to "join the broad Missouri" and "enter the Mississippi"

(Twain 1993: 81). Later in the first section, his exhilaration in Western freedom is depicted in the idyl at Lake Tahoe, where the water, a synecdoche for nature and metaphor for his own sense of self, "was not *merely* transparent, but dazzlingly, brilliantly so" (p. 153). But Mono Lake, in the second section, is the "lonely tenant of the loneliest spot on earth" (p. 245); the "venomous water" (p. 250) is murky with alkali, and though many brooks flow into it, no "*stream of any kind flows out*" (p. 248). In Hawaii his despair grows more intense. With nature writ large and humans sparse, Twain finds the perfect symbol for his emotional state – the volcano. Thrill-seeking with a vengeance, Sam descends into the "yawning pit" of the great volcano of Kilauea. Twain describes the perilous journey across the crater floor in hellish imagery and, in another self-reflexive passage, recounts how the fiery lava lake would occasionally spew forth, out of which a "film of vapor" would "float upward and vanish in the darkness – a released soul soaring homeward from captivity with the damned" (p. 515). Later, atop the volcano of Haleakala, as a cloud bank obscures land, sea, and sky, Twain's alienation from society is complete. In an eerie anticipation of the embittered solipsism of his final years, he writes: "I felt like the Last Man, neglected of the judgment, and left pinnacled in mid-heaven, a forgotten relic of a vanished world" (p. 524).

Twain's co-authored first novel, *The Gilded Age* (1873), which gave its name to the postwar era, contains two main plots: the story of a Missouri family destroyed by its pursuit of riches and faith in the American dream; and a blistering satire on corrupt Washington politics, society, and the court system. For the first time, Twain drew upon his childhood, using his family's move to Missouri and his father's self-destructive faith in his worthless Tennessee lands. Shortly thereafter he commenced the great Mississippi books published during his forties. He began *Tom Sawyer* in late 1872 or early 1873 and finished it in 1875; wrote "Old Times on the Mississippi" for W. D. Howells's *Atlantic Monthly* in 1875; started *Adventures of Huckleberry Finn* in 1876, returned to it in 1879, and completed it in 1883; and extended "Old Times" into *Life on the Mississippi* in 1883. During this decade, he also published seven other books and co-authored two plays, including a lengthy travelogue, *A Tramp Abroad* (1880); a scatological satire on Elizabethan England, *1601* (1880); a children's book, *The Prince and the Pauper* (1881); a story collection, *The Stolen White Elephant, Etc.* (1882), and the original play version of *The American Claimant* (1883). This compositional process made the Mississippi books highly intertextual. For example, John Murel's thrice-stolen loot is in *Tom Sawyer* and the Murel Gang's history appears in *Life* (chapter 29); the Watson–Darnell feud of *Life* (chapter 26) is fictionalized as the Grangerford–Shepherdson feud in *Huck Finn*; Southern "crockery culture" is lampooned in *Life* (chapter 38) and revisited at the Grangerfords; and Colonel Sherburn's speech on mobs, cowardice, juries, and lynchings in *Huck Finn* is reworked from *Life* (chapter 47).

Life on the Mississippi (1883) explores and contrasts antebellum and postbellum America, focusing on the cultures of piloting and the Mississippi Valley. The 1875 "Old Times" section (chapters 4–17) constitutes an autobiographical bildungsroman in which Sam Clemens learns his trade as a cub pilot apprenticed to the legendary Horace Bixby in 1857–9. The bulk of the extended book (chapters 1–3, 18–60) is a picaresque travelogue based on Twain's own return to the river in 1882 after an absence of 21 years. The book's style is Twain's unique combination of what James Cox terms humorous deviation and reportorial clarity, both of which effectively expose things for what they are: the former employing outlandish vernacular exaggeration, deadpan hoax, satire, parody, burlesque, impersonation, and jokes to expose through comic caricature; the latter using direct, clear depiction and factual details to expose through accurate representation (Cox 1984: 11). Both styles are literary performances, the first of pure imagination and the second of reportorial accuracy. They also express the two sides of Twain's psyche: humorous deviation is the verbal freedom of the centrifugally unfettered imagination; reportorial accuracy is the centripetal verbal order of realist depiction.

The narrative thread of "Old Times" follows the Twainian pattern of romantic expectation continually punctured by reality as the naïve Sam progressively discovers that he must stand watch every four hours; memorize all points of the river, "every old snag and one-limbed cottonwood" (Twain 1984: 81), in every kind of light, upstream and downstream; and memorize the leadsmen's calls and bank heights both ways. The river constantly shifts, so this information continually changes. Even worse, the river lies: there is no way to distinguish between a harmless wind reef and a deadly bluff reef except by instinct (p. 94). The hero of "Old Times" is Bixby – Twain's ultimate competent man – whose freedom derives from his expertise in the "science of piloting" (p. 115), requiring perfect memory, "good and quick judgment," and "cool, calm courage" (pp. 118–19). These qualities make the pilot "the only unfettered and entirely independent human being" who ever lived (p. 122).

As Bixby "learns" Sam to read the river as a text, in chapter 9 – a realist manifesto – Twain distinguishes between the pilot and the passenger. The latter possesses a romantic point of view, reads only the surface of the river, values beauty and the ideal, and depicts the world in a genteel rhetoric that is of no practical use. But the pilot has a realist perspective, can read the surface of the river to discover the underlying reality, values truth and the actual, and employs a functional vernacular discourse. To the passenger, the world is static, a painting upon which s/he projects human emotions; but the pilot views the world as process, epistemologically accessible through the accretion and application of experience. For Twain, the appreciation of difference is essential to knowledge, whether of people or of the world, for life is constant flux; as Bixby says, "If the shapes did n't change every three seconds they would n't be of any use" (Twain 1984: 89). Like Howells's businessmen and Hemingway's matadors, Twain's pilot becomes a metaphor for the realist writer, one whose art is functional rather than idealizing, a matter of well-hidden craft rather than, as for Walter Scott and Fenimore Cooper, rhetorical flourish. In the final analysis, writing and piloting are expressions of character.

In expanding "Old Times" into *Life*, Twain completed the bildungsroman with the heroic death of his younger brother Henry in the explosion of the *Pennsylvania*, an event that lay behind Twain's lifelong feelings of survivor guilt and his obsession with physical catastrophes in his writings. Henry's death halts the nostalgic tone of *Life*; Twain barely mentions his own notable career as a full pilot, quickly summarizes the years from 1859 to 1881, and expresses the loss of his great love in understatement: "by and by the war came...my occupation was gone" (Twain 1984: 166). Like Whitman returning to the scene of his strength on Paumanok (Long Island) and discovering but "a little wash'd-up drift" (Whitman 1982: l. 22), Twain returns to the Mississippi to find "lifeless steamboats," "empty wharves," and river men "absorbed into the common herd" (Twain 1984: 172). Government engineers have equipped the boats with electric lights and derricks, turned the river into a "two-thousand-mile torch-light procession" (p. 201), removed snags, and built wing-dams, dikes, and jetties. Piloting is now "nearly as safe and simple as driving [a] stage," taking "away its state and dignity" (pp. 204–5) and making pilots into hired hands. If Bixby was the competent man who negotiated the "eluding and ungraspable" (p. 88) river by respecting it, the engineer is the powerful man who views the river as an object to be conquered. The internal improvements have helped end steamboating, making the Mississippi a "watery solitude" (p. 198) on a once busy stretch, Twain sees a single steamboat, the "Mark Twain," symbolizing his sense of isolation and loss in the midst of his growing fame. But whether the engineers can tame "that lawless stream" (p. 205) is another matter. The river continues to shorten itself, create new cut-offs, overrun islands, shift state boundaries, and flood its banks well into the interior. The shore beacons below Memphis stand "in water three feet deep" (p. 225) and Bixby's charts become instantly obsolete (p. 355). Ship Island, where Henry was scalded trying to help the wounded, has disappeared; Hat Island, scene of Bixby's great piloting feat in "Old Times," is gone; the Confederate stronghold of Vicksburg is no longer on the river; and New Orleans is flooded during the bicentennial of its discovery.

The region has progressed economically but not socially, and Twain launches a devastating critique on both the South and America as a whole. The horrors of Vicksburg during the siege (chapter 35) give way to a burlesque of high-toned Southern kitsch culture (chapter 38); two swindling salesmen exchange trade secrets ("dollar their god, how to get it their religion": p. 282) as Twain's boat passes Port Hudson, wartime scene of slaughter and sacrifice (chapter 39). In chapter 40, past Baton Rouge "in the absolute South" of large sugar plantations and at the start of the "pilot's paradise" of wide river (Twain 1984: 282) – the juxtaposition of the thing he hated, slavery, and the love he lost, piloting, causes Twain to break into his most furious assault. He blames Walter Scott's medieval "romantic juvenilities" for their "debilitating influence" on Southern culture, as seen in the South's "inflated language" and "windy humbuggeries" (p. 286), juxtaposing an advertisement for a Kentucky female college that stresses Southern values with extended footnotes detailing homicidal duels by leading citizens in the contemporary South. He segues to a condemnation of antebellum New York, Philadelphia, Cincinnati, Boston, and Hartford for their nativist hatred of immigrants, anti-abolitionist violence, mistreatment of paupers and the insane, anti-semitism, chauvinist bluster, religious hypocrisy, and bellicosity. Antebellum America "was good rotten material for a burial" (p. 295), but contemporary America is hardly better; corruption in Washington shows "that the nation of moral cowards still exists" (p. 297).

Twain's greatest contempt is reserved for the South, whose four main sports are talking about the war, cock fights, mule races, and describing "the beauty and chivalry" (women and men) of the South *ad nauseam* (Twain 1984: 322). The French Revolution instituted meritocracy and paved the way for "liberty, humanity, and progress." But Walter Scott forestalled this evolution in the South, enchanting it with "the jejune romanticism of an absurd past that is dead" (p. 327). Scott created "reverence for rank and caste" (p. 328), buttressing among whites the class distinctions that slavery brought into existence. This hegemony in a "region that purports to be free" is what keeps the white half of the South "as far from emancipation as ever" (p. 332), and two apt symbols of Southern futility are the inhabitants of the "migrating negro region" who move about in order to demonstrate for themselves their freedom (p. 225) and the superannuated pilot who confusedly circles the same chute endlessly, only to return to the spot where he had started (p. 226). Southerners are "timid" (p. 334), and in one final juxtaposition Twain contrasts them with the now vanished steamboat pilot. First, he observes that *"there is no instance of a pilot deserting his post to save his life while by remaining and sacrificing it he might secure other lives from destruction"* (p. 346); and then he follows with a list of heroic deeds of former colleagues – many of whom died or were injured on the river – a list that implicitly includes Henry.

The emotional climax of *Life* is Twain's return after three decades to his home town of Hannibal, the tone of which is by turns nostalgic and morbid as he discovers the fate of old friends and recalls two drownings, a dead girl preserved in a cylinder, the death of Jimmy Finn in a tan vat, and a drunken tramp who burned to death in the jail after young Sam lent him matches. Like the river, Hannibal is utterly changed, and Twain feels like "one who returns out of a dead-and-gone generation" (Twain 1984: 370). As a pilot, he can no longer steer by the river in his head. However, as a writer the past in his head is "still as clear and vivid . . . as a photograph" and what he gazes upon does "not affect the older picture in [his] mind" (pp. 370–1). Between 1872 and 1883, the recreation of his youth had become Twain's main authorial project, beginning with the fictionalized Hannibal (St. Petersburg) in *Tom Sawyer*, that representative antebellum village fast disappearing from the American scene.

Begun in winter 1872–3, *The Adventures of Tom Sawyer* (1876) was Twain's first sustained representation of the world of children, written from the nostalgic perspective of an author just entering fatherhood in his mid-thirties. (His daughter Susy was born in March 1872, a few months before the death of his first child and only son, Langdon, at the age of a year and a half.) Typical in Twain and reflecting the high mortality rate of his time and region, Tom lives in a hybrid family with his deceased mother's sister Polly, half-brother Sid, and older cousin Mary. A realist character, socially constructed but capable of agency, Tom's "adventures" serve to plot a novel structured around "deaths." The first section (chapters 1–7) consists of Tom's endless antics, as Twain presents the complex cultural codes of a boy's world and Tom's relation to others: matriarch Polly and domestic angel Mary; friends Joe, Ben, and Huck; rivals Sid and Alfred Temple; girlfriends Amy Lawrence and Becky Thatcher; desirable, ineffectual, and sadistic patriarchs Judge Thatcher, Sunday school superintendent Walters, and schoolmaster Dobbins. At the quarter-point, chapter 8, as Tom becomes bored, he and Huck witness Injun Joe's graveyard murder of Dr. Robinson, triggering the hermeneutic code of suspense. But the second section (chapters 9–17) defers any development of this drama because of Tom and Huck's blood oath not to tell, and Tom again drifts into boredom, followed by his runaway plot to Jackson's Island. When this adventure, too, dissipates into boredom (Huck's and Joe Harper's), at the midway point of the book, we get the boys' assumed deaths and Tom's staged "resurrection" in church.

Twain had intended a picaresque, taking Tom on the road (or river), but realized that he would be a poor character for it, and forthwith turned to the bildungsroman. In the third section (chapters 18–24), Tom grows up. He apologizes to Aunt Polly; he apologizes to Becky, takes her whipping from Dobbins for tearing his pornographic book, and forgives her; he refrains from beating up Alfred for his treachery; though once again bored, he does not participate in the best prank in the book when the students publicly remove Dobbins's hairpiece; and, after a chapter of unbearable boredom, he breaks his pact with Huck, testifying at the Robinson murder trial in order to save Muff Potter. With Tom's "maturation," previous tensions are no longer operative, and so in the final section (chapters 25–35) Twain/Tom activates the treasure plot, which begins with Tom and Huck's near-death in the haunted house at the novel's three-quarter point and ends with Tom's and Becky's assumed deaths, their "resurrection," and Injun Joe's real death in the cave. Thus the novel's various storylines are resolved: the novel of manners (Tom's rebellious relations with family, peers, and town) and bildungsroman; the courtship plot (Tom and Becky); the runaway plot (Jackson's Island); the crime and punishment plot (Robinson's murder, Muff's trial, Injun Joe's death); and the adventure plot (the quest for Murel's stolen treasure).

The irony of a novel of manners is that society scapegoats transgressors (e.g. Wharton's Lily Bart), yet without transgressors everyone would die of boredom. Tom performs eight types of transgression: *pranks* to entertain himself (e.g. feeding the cat his medicine); *cons* to deceive for gain (e.g. getting others to whitewash Polly's fence in exchange for booty that he trades for Bible tickets); *evasions* to avoid responsibility or punishment (e.g. playing hooky); *small acts of disobedience* to assert individuality or relieve boredom (e.g. carving up Polly's cupboard); *lying* to avoid consequences (e.g. deceiving Polly about her "dream"); *violence* to assert dominance (e.g. pelting Sid with dirt); *stealing* (e.g. a ham, raft, boat, treasure); and *showing off* to get attention and/or win approval (e.g. "winning" the Doré Bible, the two "resurrections," testifying at Muff's trial, revealing the money). Significantly, he is punished for all transgressions except showing off and stealing (he is even allowed to keep

Murel's thrice-stolen loot). Forrest Robinson terms this "bad faith," that is, the deceptions "that may seem to violate the laws, rules or customs – but that, in fact, enjoy the tacit and often unconscious approval of society." Such bad faith exists in St. Petersburg/Hannibal and, by extension, in small-town America. Tom is the "give" in an otherwise stifling society (Robinson 1984: 11–12). His behavior is not only tolerated but appreciated, because he provides entertainment, relief from boredom, and opportunities for adults to feel virtuous. Moreover, Tom's behavior, whether in showing off or in getting others to do his work for him, is an imitation of how adults act – for instance, the orgy of showing off in Sunday School by Walters, the teachers, the librarian, and Judge Thatcher (Twain 1982: 33–4). Far from being at odds with the town, he is its finest product.

Tom's bildungsroman in the second half of the novel is enabled by such earlier exemplifications of adult values, and Twain insightfully links this maturation to race, gender, and class. Injun Joe, the book's "racial other," although at one point passing for a Spaniard, is deemed unassimilable, relieved of his money, and buried alive in the same sequence in which Tom emerges from the cave. Until that scene, as Glenn Hendler observes, Becky is highly active, and Tom is the one who speaks in sentimental language, as in his daydreaming death fantasies. But in the cave Becky is transformed into the dying child heroine of the sentimental novel (e.g. Stowe's Little Eva) who is too good for the world. While Becky turns passive, frail, and helpless, Tom finds the exit, eludes Injun Joe, discovers the hidden treasure, and ceases to express feelings of self-doubt, weakness, or melancholy. The two mature by becoming fixed in nineteenth-century gender roles: Becky takes to her bedroom while Tom becomes the subject of a Horatio Alger-like biographical sketch and, in the Judge's opinion, a proper candidate for the military academy or law school (Hendler 1993: 47–8).

Most telling is the evolution of the relationship between Tom and Huck. Swinging a dead cat, Huck strolls into American literature as a "romantic outcast," dreaded by mothers and envied by Tom and other "respectable boys" (Twain 1982: 47–9). In their first encounter, they stand as equals, almost as exemplars of parallel universes, and they make the only honest, mutually fair exchange in the book, trading Tom's tooth for Huck's tick. Tom is proud to be seen with Huck and share in his exotic aura, but in the aftermath of Robinson's murder Huck's illiteracy enables Tom to assert his cultural authority by writing the blood oath. When Tom goes searching for treasure, Huck is only his third choice for a partner, and Tom's "knowledge" of the codes of robbery, gleaned from books, further places Huck in his thrall. With his share of the loot, Huck can envision nothing more than buying pie and soda, but Tom, a bourgeois subject, plans to invest for the future, purchase consumer items, and get married. Tom now views Huck as beneath him, and in their joint (ad)venture, "[h]e did not care to have Huck's company in public places" (p. 195). By the end of the novel, Huck is placed under Widow Douglas's protection and "dragged" into society: "the bars and shackles of civilization shut him in and bound him hand and foot" (p. 255). When Huck runs off, his flight sets up the final stage in Tom's bildungsroman. Finding Huck living in an empty hogshead, Tom tricks him into returning by offering to let him into his new gang of robbers, but only if he returns to the Widow and is "respectable" (p. 258). Tom brings Huck back into society for two reasons: Huck *should* be civilized and he should be *under* Tom in the gang's hierarchy.

Tom defends the Widow's civilized ways as normative – "everybody does that way, Huck" – but Huck asserts, "I ain't everybody" (Twain 1982: 257). Earlier, Huck had been an outcast because of his poor white class status; now, however, he is an outsider because he rejects society. Robert Regan identifies in these characters "two radically opposed impulses" (1966: 89). The first is the Tom Sawyer impulse of the "unpromising hero" ("Twain's most persistent wish-fulfillment fantasy") who outdoes his brothers, shows up his enemies, undergoes a moral test and a trial of courage, wins the admiration of the formerly derisive community, symbolically sheds his unworthy father, and is rewarded with a new surrogate father (Judge Thatcher/Jervis Langdon), the hand of the princess (Becky Thatcher/Olivia Langdon), and riches. But the Huck Finn "antipodal impulse" embodies a vision that such a society is not worth succeeding in because to accept its "shoddy values amount[s] inevitably to moral failure" (Regan 1966: 89–91). These two impulses correspond to Twain's double impulse to join and to separate, and his tendency to both champion and criticize his culture. Tom Sawyer may have matured into a man, but to be a man in such a world is to be nothing more than a grown-up boy. That is why, in the middle of writing the book, Twain realized he could not take Tom into manhood; as he told Howells, Tom "would just be like all the one-horse men in literature" (Twain and Howells 1960: 91). In Huck, however, he would discover an alternative.

When Ernest Hemingway stated, "All American literature comes from . . . *Huckleberry Finn*" (1963: 22), he meant that the American vernacular in fiction reached its apogee when Twain boldly allowed Huck to speak uninterrupted without authorial commentary. Huck's heteroglossic voice is a uniquely American mix of the many dialects, including African American, that comprised the rural white speech of the Mississippi Valley (Fishkin 1993: *passim*; Carkeet 1979: 331–2; Jones 1999: 55–62). When Huck says he prefers food "where things get mixed up, and the juice kind of swaps around" (Twain 2001: 2) or when he describes a sunrise as paleness softening up the blackness of the river and turning it to gray (p. 156), he unknowingly expresses Twain's own preference for, and understanding of, American language and culture as richly hybrid and multi-racial.

Huck is also a classic example of the realist socially constructed character, hegemonically formed by the ideological beliefs of his society but nevertheless retaining a small core of self that is originary, unique, and capable of autonomous moral choice. Huck's subjectivity is constructed by three worlds: he was born into the poor uncivilized margin represented by Pap; adopted into the genteel respectable world of the Widow; and wants desperately to enter the transient childhood world of Tom Sawyer that he missed out on. He fully understands the codes of Pap's world – as seen in the practical, calculated way he deals with Pap and later with the Duke and King, whom he identifies as Pap's "kind of people" (Twain 2001: 165). But he has trouble grasping the codes of his other worlds, particularly those dealing with the impalpable, though he shrewdly connects the Widow's "spiritual gifts" (p. 13) with Tom's world of play: "I reckoned he [Tom] believed in the A-rabs and the elephants, but . . . I think different. It had all the marks of a Sunday school" (p. 17). Throughout his picaresque journey downriver, Huck encounters variations of these three worlds: the Wilks sisters and the Phelpses are like the Widow; the Duke, King, raftsmen, and townspeople of Bricksville are like Pap; the Grangerfords are like Tom with live ammunition.

At different times, Huck thinks in accordance with, and speaks in the voice of, each of the three worlds that construct him, and often they come into conflict in his mind. For example, one short sequence begins with his justifying stealing food through "Pap-logic" ("Pap always said, take a chicken when you get a chance": p. 79); this is immediately undercut by the Widow's ideology ("but the widow said it warn't anything but a soft name for stealing": p. 80); the conflict in Huck's socially created conscience is smoothed over by Jim to allow them to continue appropriating food ("Jim said he reckoned the widow was partly right and pap was partly right": p. 80); then Huck shifts into Tom's world when he sees the wrecked steamboat ("Do you reckon Tom Sawyer would ever go by this thing?": p. 81); and, after executing a ruse to save the ruffians aboard, he assesses himself from the Widow's perspective ("I judged she would be proud of me": p. 91). These worlds have in common their racism and belief in the morality of slave-owning, and whenever Huck, because of his moral core, helps Jim elude capture, he ironically justifies his action by Pap-logic, as when he fools the slave-hunters ("what's the use you learning to do right, when it's troublesome to do right and ain't no trouble to do wrong, and the wages is just the same?": p. 128) or when he decides to free Jim from the Phelps farm ("I would take up wickedness again, which was in my line, being brung up to it": p. 271).

In response to Jim, a fourth world slowly emerges, the world of the raft, best glimpsed in the opening five paragraphs of chapter 19 that form the idyllic normative center of the text – a black and a white American harmoniously coexisting in, significantly, the natural world. The longstanding controversy over the character of Jim – so often mistaken for a racist stereotype – is itself a tribute to Twain's knowledge of antebellum slave culture. Twain was the first major white author to create a non-essentialist African American character, one who wears the minstrel mask so effectively that he deceives the novel's white characters and, for a century, has deceived white readers and critics as well. But African American critics like Jocelyn Chadwick-Joshua were not fooled, observing that "Jim is a man, a father, a husband, a slave who decides to run toward an ideal – freedom – in a country where his mask and double voice are his survival tools" (Chadwick-Joshua 1998: xxii). Nor were African American authors like Charles W. Chesnutt, Langston Hughes, Ralph Ellison, Richard Wright, and Toni Morrison fooled, holding Twain and Jim in the highest regard. Chesnutt proudly displayed a bust of Twain in his library; Ellison kept a framed photograph of him on his desk; and David Bradley called *Huck Finn* the precursor of twentieth-century black fiction (Fishkin 1997: 110–11).

Twain introduces Jim and white ignorance of blacks simultaneously. With Jim backlit in the kitchen door, Huck says, "we could see him pretty clear, because there was a light behind him" (Twain 2001: 6). The silhouette Huck sees is figuratively both the phenomenon of black invisibility to whites and the minstrel mask that slaves wore for protection. An example immediately follows. When Tom hangs the sleeping Jim's hat on a tree and leaves a five-cent piece, Jim responds by feigning ignorance of the prank and inventing a story of being bewitched. To Huck, Jim and the "super-stitious" slaves he regales with his story are both fooled and foolish: "Jim was most ruined, for a servant, because he got so stuck up on account of having seen the devil and been rode around by witches" (p. 8). However, Jim has seized the opportunity afforded by Tom's prank (Smith 1992: 108–9); he increases his status in the slave community, earns gifts from the other slaves for telling his story, keeps Tom's five-cent piece, and gets out of work. The other slaves also cleverly avoid work, but, because they all play the minstrel part, Huck sees none of this.

Jim possesses what W. E. B. Du Bois would later term the African American "double-consciousness": viewing everything through both his own eyes and those of his white oppressors. Assuming the role of the loyal, lazy, ignorant, unthinking slave, he carefully operates behind this minstrel mask, sifting through his options and choosing the best available one. Whenever Huck reports that Jim "didn't say nothing for a minute" (Twain 2001: 52) or "studied it over" (p. 66) or "grumbled a little, but give in" (p. 81), Jim is thinking prior to manipulating Huck; but because Huck assumes that black people are incapable of complex thought, he never realizes that he's being played. And Jim's manipulations virtually emplot the novel. Upon first encountering Huck on Jackson's Island, Jim shrewdly extracts Huck's promise not to tell on him, knowing the significance of a white Southerner's word of honor, before he reveals that he's escaped (p. 52). When Jim finds Pap dead in the floating house, he keeps Huck away out of feigned concern for Huck's sensibilities, when in fact he wishes to prevent Huck from discovering that he can now safely return home (p. 61). After Huck leaves a dead snake by Jim's blanket and Jim gets bitten by its mate, Jim attributes the misfortune to Huck's having earlier handled a snakeskin – which Jim had warned him would bring bad luck – rather than telling Huck that he was aware of the prank and thereby revealing his intelligence (pp. 63–5). Huck feels no remorse for hurting Jim, only embarrassment for having forgotten that a snake will curl up around its dead mate. When Huck plays another prank on Jim in chapter 15 – insisting that their separation in the fog was only something Jim dreamed – Jim thinks for five minutes and then interprets the "dream" in a way that warns Huck to behave. But when Huck reveals the prank and ridicules him, Jim snaps and drops his mask for the first time, calling Huck "trash" (pp. 104–5). Although Huck apologizes, vowing to himself never to play another prank on Jim, having to humble himself to a slave will shortly lead to resentment.

In chapter 16, Huck's socially constructed conscience pricks him as Jim – his mask still down as they approach the critical location of Cairo – speaks openly about stealing his family out of slavery (Twain 2001: 123–4). Huck paddles off in the canoe toward the slave-hunters, secretly intending to turn Jim in, and what ensues is Jim's finest use of the minstrel mask. Suspecting Huck's motives, Jim calls out: "Pooty soon I'll be a-shout'n for joy, en I'll say, it's all on accounts o' Huck; I's a free man, en I couldn't ever ben free ef it hadn' ben for Huck; Huck done it. Jim won't ever forget you, Huck; you's de bes' fren' Jim's ever had; en you's the *only* fren' ole Jim's got, now" (p. 125). Beneath his seeming gratitude, he is threatening to reveal that Huck has helped a fugitive slave, and Huck grasps the threat, if not the conscious intention. Huck admits, "I was paddling off, all in a sweat to tell on him; but when he says this, it seemed to kind of take the tuck all out of me" (p. 125). Jim follows with: "Dah you goes, de ole true Huck; de on'y white genlman dat ever kep' his promise to ole Jim" (p. 125) – slyly elevating Huck from "white trash" to "white gentleman" and reminding him of his earlier promise. These words hit their mark, as Huck confesses, "I just felt sick" (p. 125). When Huck returns to the raft, after deceiving the slave-hunters, Jim lavishes him with compliments and explains that he's in the water in case he had to make a quick escape; but in fact he heard Huck pause when asked by the men whether his companion was white or black, and he didn't trust Huck to lie to them. They miss Cairo, and Jim attributes this misfortune to Huck's handling the snakeskin, which makes Huck think about the snake prank and, now that he's seen Jim has human feelings, feel guilty, with Jim increasing this guilt by saying, "It ain't yo' fault, Huck; you didn' know" (p. 129). Jim never again lowers his mask until the end of the novel – when he is free and reluctantly tells Huck that the dead man in the floating house was Pap – and he wears it with a vengeance in front of the Duke and King, in captivity on the Phelps farm, and when he plays the faithful slave by seeming to give up his freedom to save the wounded Tom Sawyer (Robinson 1988: 388) – an action that elicits Huck's praise ("I knowed he was white inside": Twain 2001: 341) and saves him from the would-be lynch mob ("a nigger like that is worth a thousand dollars – and kind treatment, too," argues the doctor: p. 353).

Although Huck's racism runs too deep ever to vanish, he increasingly exempts Jim from the category of "nigger" and even comes to see other blacks in a different light as Jim both consciously and inadvertently reveals his humanity. Examples include Jim's response to the fog prank; Jim's story of his mistreatment of his daughter (Twain 2001: 201–2), in which Huck views Jim as a complex patriarch within his own family and – unlike Pap – a father capable of remorse; and the times Jim protects Huck and extends his own watch to allow the boy to sleep. Huck glimpses the phenomenon of slave cooperation at the Grangerfords as his slave Jack uses plausible deniability to reunite him with Jim in the swamp (p. 151), and he is tormented by the memory of the Wilks slave auction (p. 234). All of this comes to a head in a central realist scene of deliberation and choice (Mitchell 1989: 5) in chapter 31 after Jim has been sold to the Phelpses – arguably the most moral moment in American literature – when Huck finally has to confront "what this thing was that I was doing" (Twain 2001: 123) in helping Jim.

Huck's crisis over whether to send the letter to Miss Watson begins with his thinking like the Widow. Without Jim present to attribute bad luck to the snakeskin, he sees "the plain hand of Providence" punishing him for "stealing a poor old woman's nigger" (Twain 2001: 268–9). He briefly shifts into Pap's world and tries to rationalize that he was "brung up wicked" and "warn't so much to blame," but his Widow's voice responds that he could have gone to Sunday School. He attempts to pray but cannot, acknowledging, "You can't pray a lie" (p. 269) – a critical point since this revelation that he has internalized the Widow's religion makes his eventual decision much more impressive. He writes the letter and feels "washed clean of sin," but gets to thinking – and all he can think about is Jim: their friendship on the raft, Jim standing Huck's watch, Jim's joy when they were reunited in chapter 15, Jim's gratitude when Huck foiled the slave-hunters. Then, for the first time ever, Huck fully adopts Jim's perspective, repeating Jim's exact words from chapter 16, right down to the emphasis – "[he] said I was the best friend old Jim ever had in the world, and the *only* one he's got now" (p. 270). His moral core self responds to Jim's world and chooses – "All right, then, I'll *go* to hell" (p. 271) – and he tears up the letter.

On one side of this decision lie all three worlds that have formed him, every white friend and family member he has, every social institution in his culture – school, church, state – and his very real fears of both legal and divine retribution: the hell he accepts is a Presbyterian hell of eternal fire and damnation. On the other side is simply Jim. What makes the scene remarkable is not that Huck makes this decision, but that Twain makes it believable. He also makes it triply ironic. The words Huck recalls were actually Jim's attempts to manipulate him from behind the mask; Jim said them as Huck was paddling toward the slave-hunters to turn him in, not, as Huck recalls, after he returned to the raft following his ruse; and Huck justifies his decision here, as always, through Pap-logic – he sees his moral act as a sign that he is hopelessly degenerate by birth.

In 1935 Hemingway called chapter 31 "the real end" of the novel and the rest "cheating" (1963: 22), and nearly twenty years later Leo Marx laid the foundation for subsequent scholarly critiques of the ending, which has come to be termed "the evasion," observing that Miss Watson's freeing of Jim is "a flimsy contrivance," that both Huck and Jim regress as characters, and that the entire ending is simply bad burlesque (Marx 1953: 426–30). However, in his seeming acceptance of Tom's idiotic schemes for his escape, Jim continues to choose his best available options while wearing the minstrel mask (a mask worn as well by the Phelps slave, Nat). And Huck has always been enthralled by Tom, unaware of how much he himself has changed until the very end when Tom reveals what he had planned for after Jim's escape and Huck understatedly says, "But I reckoned it was about as well the way it was" (Twain 2001: 360).

Huck Finn was written between 1876 and 1883, and the ending is best viewed as a symbolic representation of the post-Reconstruction era. Since Jim is already free throughout the Phelps episode, the problem of freeing a free man that Tom and Huck confront is the same as that faced by Americans after the war (Schmitz 1971: 60–2): how can technically free people achieve actual freedom when they remain in political, economic, and social bondage? As Shelley Fishkin observes, it "dramatizes...both the dream and the denial of the dream, both the spectacular boldness of a national experiment based on the idea that 'all men are created equal' and our spectacular failure to fulfill our promise" (Fishkin 2002b: 144). The Phelps episode is indeed a burlesque, but of postwar racial accommodations: one in which Jim receives forty dollars from Tom rather than the forty acres and a mule that the freedmen required to make their "liberty" meaningful. In addition, it symbolizes the post-Reconstruction sell-out of former slaves after the 1877 compromise – in which Tom's class was allowed to decide the fate of the freedmen, Huck's (and Twain's) class (which had sacrificed itself defending the interests of Southern planters) was shunted aside, and Jim's class was subject to sharecropping, Jim Crow legislation, and lynchings (Nilon 1992: 70). When Tom says of freeing Jim, "You got to invent *all* the difficulties.... there's more honor in getting him out through a lot of difficulties and dangers" (Twain 2001: 298), Twain not only ties Tom's evasion to Southern strategies of "gradualism" in delaying the freedmen's full citizenship (Nilon 1992: 66), he also ties it to Southern honor (see Scott 2005), that peculiar ethos of white male militancy, white female passivity, and the imaging of black men as sexual threats. Tom's sense of honor, within the context of his "boy-play world" in which he views Jim as a noble figure out of a Dumas novel, is at least consistent and, in its own way honorable; in this, it serves as a criticism of actual southern honor, which is neither (Scott 2005: 189–94, 198–204). The Phelps farm episode may not be verisimilar – in real life Huck would have been hanged and Jim sold down the river – but it is frustrating and ridiculous, mimetically reproducing in the reader what Jim is feeling behind his mask, what African Americans were feeling in postbellum America, and what Twain felt about the inhuman treatment of ex-slaves by his fellow Southerners. As Colonel Sherburn/Mark Twain (both born and raised in the South and having lived in the North) derides the crowd that has come to hang him: "If any real lynching's going to be done, it will be done in the dark, southern fashion; and when they come, they'll bring their masks" (Twain 2001: 191).

Twain would try to resurrect Jim, Huck, and Tom in later works, but his efforts were unsuccessful and often embarrassing. A serious treatment of Jim's future was too tragic for him to attempt, and *Huck Finn* had left its protagonist in a cul-de-sac. The world of Pap is as dead as Pap, and the world of the Widow lies discredited; Huck's final words are "aunt Sally [Phelps] she's going to adopt me and sivilize me and I can't stand it. I been there before" (Twain 2001: 362). The world of Tom was never more than a childhood version of the same – Huck never even considers returning to it – and the dividing line of race separates him from the world of Jim. As Toni Morrison observes, "Huck cannot have an enduring relationship with Jim; he refuses one with Tom" (1996: xli). Although readers often find Huck's declaration to "light out for the Territory" (Twain 2001: 362) inspiring, his creator had "been there before" in *Roughing It*, and well knew that the frontier held no better promise than civilization. Twain's only realistic plan for Tom and Huck would come in a 1891 notebook entry in which Huck, sixty years old and his wits gone, returns to Hannibal and reconnects with Tom: "both are desolate, life has been a failure, all that was lovable, all that was beautiful is under the mould. They die together" (Twain 1975–9: vol. 3, 606).

The years after *Huck Finn* were also increasingly tragic for Twain, leading to a growing bitterness and despair in his writing. His disastrous investments in the Paige typesetter from 1880 to 1895 and the failure of his publishing house placed his family in dire financial straits, compelling him to undertake a grueling year-long, worldwide lecture tour in 1895–6 to avoid the dishonor of personal bankruptcy. His final two decades were punctuated by deaths, many untimely, that obliterated his family circle: his mother and mother-in-law (1890); eldest daughter Susy at age 24 (1896); older brother Orion (1897); wife Livy, sister-in-law Molly, and remaining sibling Pamela (1904); nephew and namesake Sam (1908); and youngest daughter Jean at age 29 (1909). Too ill to travel to the family cemetery in Elmira, Twain watched Jean's hearse pull away on Christmas day, observing, "I have never greatly envied any one but the dead" (quoted in Kaplan 1966: 387). After setting down an account of her life and death, he declared his writing career over.

Twain was prolific during this later, darker phase, producing nearly two dozen books and a massive amount of unpublished writing, much of it devoted to metaphysical questions focused on his lifelong argument with God. Increasingly pessimistic, he began to doubt the human capacity for moral progress: "there is no such thing as nature; what we call by that misleading name is merely heredity and training. We have no thoughts of our own, no opinions of our own: they are ... trained into us" (Twain 1983: 162). Elsewhere he wrote, "To create man was a quaint and original idea, but to add the sheep was a tautology" (Twain 1992b: 946).

His two most important novels of the period – *A Connecticut Yankee in King Arthur's Court* and *Pudd'nhead Wilson* – extend his earlier critiques of imperialism and race at a time when America's belief in "Manifest Destiny" turned international and race relations in the United States had reached their nadir. Astutely connecting "conquest abroad and suppression of blacks at home" (Pettit 1974: 134–5), in anti-imperialist essays like *King Leopold's Soliloquy* (1905) and "To the Person Sitting in Darkness" (1901) his satiric edge grew sharper, his anger more acute, his despair over "the damned human race" more evident. In a "salutation-speech" from the nineteenth century to the twentieth, published in the New York *Herald* on December 31, 1900 and widely reprinted in the anti-imperialist press, he wrote: "I bring you the stately matron named Christendom, returning bedraggled, besmirched, and dishonored from pirate-raids in Kiao-Chow, Manchuria, South Africa and the Philippines, her mouth full of pious hypocrisies. Give her soap and a towel, but hide the looking-glass" (Twain 1992b: 456).

A Connecticut Yankee in King Arthur's Court (1889) is arguably Twain's most startling imaginative performance: an anatomy of imperialism; a celebration and critique of the nineteenth century's cherished notion of moral and technological progress; a contrastive study of the mindsets of oral versus written culture; a blueprint for the creation of "civilization," from patent offices and newspapers to baseball and genocide; a study of ethnicity; a pioneering work in "time travel" science fiction; a modern revision of

Malory's *Morte D'Arthur* in which Launcelot's insider trading on the stock market leads to the fall of Camelot; a parody of Horatio Alger's novels; an early example of American literary naturalism; and, in a period of utopian novels, a dystopia. Like many Twain texts, it begins innocuously – as a gentle satire on the sixth century – but then engages his deeper conflicts and turns into a serious double-edged critique of both that century and his own: first on the barbarism of the feudal world and the corruption of absolute power concentrated in the aristocracy and church, and then on the dehumanizing consequences of uncontrolled technological power. It commences with the narrator appalled by the mistreatment of a man and ends with him gleefully electrocuting 11,000 men with the flick of a switch.

A remarkably predictive novel, *Connecticut Yankee* depicts the processes by which secular dictators rise to power, a phenomenon that would plague the twentieth century (in German and Italian editions, Hank Morgan's title, "The Boss," is translated as "Der Führer" and "Il Duce"). Hank's "man-factories," paramilitary academies, and uses of advertising as propaganda prefigure methods of later totalitarian regimes, and the novel's conclusion chillingly anticipates the massive death by technology of the First World War and of twentieth-century campaigns of genocide. A decade before Conrad's Kurtz in *Heart of Darkness* scribbles on his earlier plan to bring civilization to the natives, "Exterminate all the brutes!" (Conrad 1971: 51), Hank addresses his men as "CHAMPIONS OF HUMAN LIBERTY AND EQUALITY" and announces to loud applause, "We will kill them all" (Twain 1983: 433). Hank even says of his eerie and unprecedented power, "I stood with my finger on the button . . . ready to press it and flood the midnight world with intolerable light at any moment" (p. 83). But he also attacks the unequal distribution of wealth and labor in Camelot, preceding Franklin Roosevelt in calling his democratic political program "a new deal" for the people (p. 114).

This superintendent in the Hartford Colt firearms factory, who gets knocked unconscious and awakens thirteen centuries earlier in Camelot, has in common with his author and with many other Twain protagonists that he is a consummate liar and public performer obsessed with power. Yet, because he is delightfully imaginative and so often voices nineteenth-century values – democracy, meritocracy, egalitarianism, and pragmatism – it is easy for readers to identify his voice with Twain's and thus to become increasingly disturbed when he commits acts of gratuitous violence like hanging the band at Morgan le Fay's castle, or when he calls the populace "white Indians," "animals," or "human muck" (Twain 1983: 20, 40, 427). Hank may reflect Twain's increasing misanthropy, but he is also a character who defies the realist aesthetics of consistency. Unlike the realist socially constructed subject who contains a unique, moral inner core (e.g. Huck Finn), or even the naturalist subject, who is a consistent social construction lacking any core and at the mercy of heredity and environment (e.g. Norris's McTeague or Crane's Henry Fleming), Twain's obtuse narrator predates by nearly a century what has come to be known as the postmodern subject: a socially constructed "self" that is no more than a site upon which different and often incompatible voices and ideologies contend.

This is a major innovation. Hank's character undergoes virtually no development during his six years in Camelot, but at various points in the book he voices and acts upon the following subject positions and ideologies, many of which are mutually exclusive: racist (Twain 1983: 20, 40, 54, 108, 427); imperialist (pp. 323, 398); colonialist (pp. 54, 74, 138–9); totalitarian dictator (pp. 17, 45, 63, 83, 152, 272, 397, 399, 433); genocidal anti-humanist (pp. 302, 432–3); nineteenth-century liberal (pp. 74, 81, 161, 182–3, 298, 323, 330); egalitarian democrat (pp. 64, 67–9, 113–14, 162, 166–7, 239, 242, 322, 398); social reformer (pp. 64, 84, 114, 153, 228, 249, 279, 300, 365, 398); abolitionist (pp. 199–200, 297); advocate of women's suffrage (p. 398); bourgeois subject (pp. 52–3); inventor (pp. 4, 54, 72, 323); entrepreneur (pp. 31, 45, 49, 56, 81, 119, 142, 181, 292); middle manager (*passim*); technocrat (pp. 81, 103, 150, 157, 214); monopolist (pp. 59, 63, 205, 413); proto-Marxist economist (pp. 109–10, 279, 330); humanist, naturalist, and nihilist (*passim*); essentialist (pp. 157, 204, 297, 284–5, 298–300, 349); existentialist (pp. 65, 162, 292, 297); utilitarian pragmatist (pp. 65, 162–4, 177, 214); sentimentalist (pp. 406–8, 440); and performer/ showman (the eclipse, blowing up Merlin's tower, fixing the holy fountain, defeating the rival magician, various public battles with knights, humiliating Dowley, the battle of the Sand Belt, and "getting up his last effect").

Some of these subject positions go together, others are related, and many are culturally revealing. For instance, in showing how Hank's failure to win over the hearts and minds of the people to his democratic political and social reforms leads him to violence, Twain brilliantly connects liberalism and social reform with imperialism and genocide (a link that eluded him in *Roughing It*). Yet many of these positions are also antipodal. For example, in chapter 40, while in the midst of bragging about the spread of schools and newspapers, and his institution of proportional taxation and equality before the law, Hank also boasts that he suppressed a book he disliked and had the author hanged. He then claims that armored knights are his "most effective spreaders of civilization" but "if they couldn't persuade a person to try a sewing machine on the instalment plan, or a melodeon, or a barbed wire fence, or a prohibition journal, or any of the other thousand and one things they canvassed for, they removed him and passed on" (Twain 1983: 398). In the very next paragraph he reveals two new reforms he will attempt: replacing the established state church with religious denominationalism and "unlimited suffrage" for "men and women alike" (p. 398). Never does he see the contradictions in his philosophy or actions. But what makes Hank a puzzle to realism and a failure of characterization to many traditional critics is exactly what should make him a stunning achievement to students of the postmodern condition. When Hank blows up Merlin's tower and replaces it with his own figurative tower of Babel, it speaks to a new view of the human self.

The slaves in *Connecticut Yankee* are white, but the novel contains Twain's most horrific scenes of the "peculiar institution." As a boy, Clemens "had no aversion to slavery" (Twain 1990: 115) but had much contact with African Americans: young comrades and also older mentors like his uncle's slave Dan'l, upon whom Jim was partially based. From this intimacy with African Americans came his early love of black speech, storytelling, and music. Along with his adult recollections of cruelty toward slaves, it transformed his views on race, which accelerated when he married into a family of former abolitionists who were now funding the education of freedmen. Clemens, too, would engage in such altruism, donating money to Lincoln University for black scholarships and financing the Parisian education of a young black artist (Pettit 1974: 125–26). In 1885 he began paying board for Warner McGuinn, a black student at Yale Law School, writing to the school's dean, "We have ground the manhood out of them, & the shame is ours, not theirs, & we should pay for it." McGuinn later edited an important black newspaper, co-founded the NAACP's Baltimore branch, and was mentor to young Thurgood Marshall (Fishkin 1997: 101–6). Twain also wrote scathing indictments like "The United States of Lyncherdom" (1901), collected clippings for a posited multivolume history of lynching in America, and created one of the most militant black characters in literature in *Which Was It?* (unfinished, *c.*1899–1903). In the main plot, akin to Melville's *Benito Cereno*, an abused mulatto enslaves a white man while pretending to be his slave, claiming, "it's my turn now; dey's a long bill agin de low-down ornery white race" (in Twain 1967b: 415). But irony was always Twain's most effective method of attacking such evils as nativism and race, and in *Pudd'nhead Wilson*, his most ironic novel, he went beyond his perspective in *Huck Finn* to expose race as a completely arbitrary social construction, "a fiction of law and custom" (Twain 1980: 9) that is devastating in its effect on all members of society. In so doing, he laid the groundwork for the race fiction of such authors as Chesnutt and Faulkner.

Pudd'nhead Wilson (1894) is a tragic farce about false, mistaken, constructed, unanchored, displaced, and ultimately unknowable identities that undercuts all attempts to place human beings into categories, racial or otherwise. The title character, attorney David Wilson, is a resident of interior New York State who travels to the Mississippi river town of Dawson's Landing in 1830 "to seek his fortune," makes an ironic "fatal remark" that gets him labeled a "pudd'nhead," and spends the next twenty years trying to emerge from this stigma (Twain 1980: 5–6). Twain wrote Livy that he never viewed Wilson as "a *character*, but only as a piece of machinery – a button or a crank or a lever, with a useful function to perform in a machine, but with no dignity beyond that" (Twain 1949: 291). Yet Wilson, however two-dimensional, is also an impenetrable mystery. We have no clue as to why he moves to a slave state from a region that Twain well knew was historically an abolitionist stronghold, nor why he remains there long after he is relegated to obscurity; his one close friend is, oddly, the town's chief citizen, Judge York Driscoll; he writes sardonic, misanthropic aphorisms in his calendar that sound much like Twain and that serve as epigraphs to the book's chapters; and his triumphant moment comes in court when, through his knowledge of fingerprints, he exposes the Judge's nephew and heir Tom as the child of the Judge's brother's slave Roxy – whom she switched as an infant with the real heir, Chambers – thus restoring the (by now thoroughly discredited) status quo.

If Wilson's identity is a mystery to the reader, the identities of the putative "black" characters are – until Wilson's motivationally suspect identification of Tom puts an

Figure 24.1 *"Huck and Jim in their final years"*

In 1903, on his last visit to his sister-in-law, Susan Langdon Crane, and her family at Quarry Farm in Elmira, New York, Mark Twain posed for this photograph with his friend John T. Lewis (1835–1906), a free-born African American who had migrated to upstate New York. They had met in 1877 after Lewis saved the lives of Susan Crane and her daughter by courageously stopping their runaway carriage at no small risk to his own safety. Lewis was an Elder in the Church of the Brethren (the Dunkers), and he and Twain often talked about religion and other such matters. After Lewis retired, Twain and his in-laws arranged to have him receive a pension. When Twain returned to writing *Huckleberry Finn*, in 1879 while at Elmira, Lewis was one of the real-life people upon whom he based the character of Jim, and it is even possible that his acquaintance with Lewis caused Twain to continue working on the novel after having earlier set it aside.

Twain's friendship with Lewis was hardly atypical; of all the white authors in this period, he was the one most fully immersed in and appreciative of African American culture and the one most at home in the company of African Americans. Near the end of his life he recalled a time in New York City when he was walking with another black friend, George Griffin, and people stared at them: "a 'white man' & a negro walking together was a new spectacle to them. The glances embarrassed George, but not me, for the companionship was proper: in some ways he was my equal, in some others my superior." Published in 1884, *Huckleberry Finn* is about a racist boy's realization of the full humanity of a fugitive slave. Ten years later, in *Pudd'nhead Wilson*, Twain would deconstruct the very idea of race itself as nothing more than "a fiction of law and custom." (Photograph by permission of the Library of Congress, Prints and Photographs Division, LC-USZ62–60538.)

end to the masquerade – mysteries to the townspeople. The one truly three-dimensional character of the book, Roxy, is "as white as anybody, but the one-sixteenth of her which was black out-voted the other fifteen parts and made her a negro" (Twain 1980: 8–9). At various points, she is a "black" woman, a "free black" woman pretending to be a "black" slave (ch. 16), a free "black" woman pretending to be a kidnapped "free black" woman (ch. 18), a "free black" woman disguised as a "white" man (ch. 18), and Tom Driscoll's mother pretending to be Tom Driscoll's slave. Chambers, the real Driscoll heir mistaken for a Driscoll slave, is a "white" man mistaken for a "black" man. The most unanchored identity in the book belongs to Roxy's son, the false Tom Driscoll, who is, chronologically, a "black" baby (ch. 2), a "white" baby (ch. 3), a "black" man who thinks he's a "white" man (chs. 4–9), a "black" man who pretends to be a "white" man (chs. 9–21), a "black" man pretending to be a "white" man pretending to be a young "white" woman (ch. 7) , a "black" man pretending to be a "white" man pretending to be an old "white" woman (ch. 13), a "black" man pretending to be a "black" man (ch. 19), a "black" man pretending to be a "black" woman (ch. 19), a "black" man pretending to be a "white" tramp (ch. 19), and finally, simply a "black" man (ch. 20). By the time he is exposed and the status quo restored, however, the idea of such a thing as "simply a black man" is untenable – except to the townspeople, who proceed to sell him down the river.

As in *Huck Finn*, Twain's meaning emerges from the difference between the characters' and the thoughtful reader's perspectives. Blue-eyed, flaxen-haired Tom is a villain – he treats Chambers viciously, wantonly gambles, steals from his benefactor, burgles the neighbors' houses, and later sells his own mother down the river into slavery and murders his supposed "uncle." Roxy blames this on his "black" blood. Disgusted when he refuses to defend his honor in a duel, she assesses the reason: "It's the nigger in you, dat's what it is. Thirty-one parts o' you is white, en on'y one part nigger, en dat po' little one part is yo' *soul*" (Twain 1980: 70). "What ever has 'come o' yo' Essex blood?" (p. 70) she asks him, ashamed that he has disgraced the lineage of his father, the man who raped her. Falling into blackness, Tom at first questions the justice and even the reality of race: "Why were niggers *and* [emphasis in original] whites made? What crime did the *uncreated* [emphasis added] first nigger commit that the curse of birth was decreed for him? And why this awful difference between white and black?" (p. 44). In a passage deleted probably because Twain wanted to keep Tom's perspective aligned with that of the other characters, Tom continues: "Yesterday I hated nobody very much, but now I hate the whole human race..... [...]Yesterday I was ashamed of my thefts – but now, why now, I am not, for I stole from the whites [...] ...... And that poor lowly and ignorant creature is my mother! ...... Well, she has my respect for one thing – she has never owned a slave. All the white respectability of this town is shabby and mean, beside that one virtue" (p. 191 fn).

Tom's knowledge unnerves him – he is ashamed to shake hands with white friends, defers to the lowest of whites, and takes on "a hunted sense and a hunted look" (Twain 1980: 45). Although he later learns that he descends from Captain John Smith and an African king (p. 70), he still finds himself involuntarily imitating the behavior of a slave. In another deleted passage, he tries to understand his racial character as biologically determined, but ends up interpreting it as environmentally acquired:

> Why was he a coward? It was the "nigger" in him. The nigger *blood*? Yes, the nigger
> blood degraded from original courage to cowardice by decades and generations of insult

and outrage inflicted in circumstances which forbade reprisals, and made mute and meek endurance the only refuge and defence.

Whence came that in him which was high, and whence came that which was base? That which was high came from either blood, and was the monopoly of neither color; but that which was base was the *white* blood in him debased by the brutalizing effects of a long-drawn heredity of slave-owning, with the habit of abuse which the possession of irresponsible power always creates and perpetuates, by the law of human nature. So he argued. (p. 191fn)

Twain probably removed this passage because it expresses the author's thoughts rather than those of the character, despite the use of free indirect speech and the assertion of the final sentence. For Twain, race was no longer a biological reality to be subsumed under his larger belief in human equality and justice, but a shared historical experience with no basis in biology – which is the position that enlightened persons would embrace a century later. But *Pudd'nhead Wilson*'s final scenes take place in 1853 in a place where such a view would seem absurd; the fingerprints that identify Tom as a "murderer" also identify him as a "negro and slave" (p. 112), and, for the citizens of Dawson's Landing, the latter explains the former.

Dawson's Landing, named after a Hannibal schoolteacher, is Twain's final extended incarnation of his boyhood home. The town is farther south than Hannibal, where slavery was of the "milder" sort, and thus it is fully implicated in slavery's economics. After a sentimental opening description of the town symbolized by a sleeping cat, a sign of "contentment and peace" (Twain 1980: 3), we read, "Dawson's Landing was a slave-holding town, with a rich slave-worked grain and pork country in back of it" (p. 4), after which the nostalgic tone is permanently mocked by an ironic one. In this land where a slave is "daily robbed . . . of an inestimable treasure – his liberty" (p. 12), the constant threat of being "sold down the river" (mentioned 26 times and implied twice) into the most hellish form of slavery hangs over the heads of the slaves, and is the reason why Roxy switched the babies. Tom is nevertheless "sold down the river" in the last line of this American-style Greek tragedy/Renaissance farce. Had he been a "white" man, it would have been "unquestionably right to punish him – it would be no loss to anybody; but to shut up a valuable slave for life – that was quite another matter" (p. 115). Twain well understood that slavery was, at base, the most extreme form of power in which the few rob the many, different in degree but not in kind from other forms found in capitalism. As Nancy Fredericks points out, in a book filled with felonies, "the one thing this proto-totalitarian society will not tolerate is faulty bookkeeping. . . . [T]he real guilt lay not with 'Tom,' but with the 'erroneous inventory'" that did not list Tom with the rest of the Driscoll property when it was settled (Fredericks 1989: 497).

In the middle of the first of his three classic autobiographies, Twain's friend Frederick Douglass told his readers, "You have seen how a man was made a slave; you shall see how a slave was made a man" (Douglass 1986: 107). These are precisely the two narratives that *Pudd'nhead Wilson* leaves untold. Much like Jim's subsequent efforts to reunite his family, they are narratives that Twain, even with his boundless imagination and wealth of sympathy, had no authority to tell. As Zora Neale Hurston's Janie would later say of her ascent from gender slavery into womanhood, "you got tuh *go* there tuh *know* there" (Hurston 1998: 192). Tom is sold down the river, and Chambers is forever lost between the slave world he was trained into and the white world he is unequipped to enter; his would be, Twain notes, "a long story" (Twain 1980: 114). Even less optimistic is David Wilson's final calendar entry: "It was wonderful to find America, but it would have been more wonderful to miss it" (p. 113).

In *Connecticut Yankee* and *Pudd'nhead Wilson*, as in "The Man That Corrupted Hadleyburg" (1900), a stranger enters a new society and reveals dark truths about it. The most extreme of these figures appears in four versions of a novel Twain attempted between 1897 and 1908. In the second version, *The Chronicle of Young Satan* (left unfinished in 1900), a young angel who turns out to be Satan comes to an early eighteenth-century Austrian village. Having no moral sense, he views human beings as machines since they have no ability to create, and amuses himself by tampering with their fates. In the third version, "Schoolhouse Hill" (abandoned in 1898), the setting is St. Petersburg *circa* 1850 and the stranger is more benign, a sort of Tom Sawyer run amuck. In the final version, *No. 44, The Mysterious Stranger* (written 1908, published 1969), set in late fifteenth-century Austria, the stranger is a sensitive and seemingly naïve boy, poorly treated by the printers with whom he works, and his appearance and extraordinary powers are left unexplained. As he departs, he tells the young narrator: "there is no God, no universe, no human race, no earthly life, no heaven, no hell. It is all a Dream, a grotesque and foolish dream. Nothing exists but You. And You are but a *Thought* – a vagrant Thought, a useless Thought, a homeless Thought, wandering forlorn among the empty eternities!" His only advice for his horror-stricken friend is, "Dream other dreams, and better!" (Twain 1969a: 404–5). Posthumously published, Twain's last words to his readers can be viewed as the summa statement of the philosophical autism into which he sank at the end of his career, or they can be viewed as affirming and empowering – change, after all, begins in better dreams. Thus, Twain's final note is neither satirical nor humorous but, characteristically, expressive of contrary impulses.

Samuel Langhorne Clemens was born in Florida, Missouri on November 30, 1835, two weeks after the appearance of Halley's Comet, and often joked that he would exit with that celestial body on its next visit. True to his word, he died in Stormfield, Connecticut on April 21, 1910, the day after the returning comet reached its perihelion. It was the final performance of a master showman. On April 23, Shakespeare's birthday, a tearful Reverend Joseph Twitchell, the former Hartford neighbor who had officiated at Clemens's wedding 40 years earlier, presided over his funeral. Thousands of mourners filed past the casket in the Presbyterian Brick Church in New York City to bid farewell, and on its front page the *New York Times* duly reported the deceased author's artistic triumphs and personal tragedies. But the most fitting eulogy came in a memoir written several months later by William Dean Howells, the dean of American letters and, for four decades, Clemens's best friend. Personally acquainted with nearly every important writer of the age, Howells offered an assessment that has stood the test of time: "I knew them all and all the rest of our sages, poets, seers, critics, humorists; they were like one another and like other literary men; but Clemens was sole, incomparable." He was, the dean concluded, "the Lincoln of our literature" (Howells 1967: 84).

AUTHOR'S NOTE

This essay is dedicated in loving memory to Charlie Mushaw of Brooklyn, New York, who taught me when I was a boy that race is a lie and that racism is a lie told by bullies, and to the beloved memories of Nicky, Wendy, Percy, Syd, and Homer Lamb, who made me into a much better person than I ever would have become on my own. Until we meet again.

SELECTED PRIMARY TEXTS BY MARK TWAIN

The Celebrated Jumping Frog of Calaveras County and Other Sketches. 1867.

The Innocents Abroad, or The New Pilgrim's Progress. 1869.

Roughing It. 1872.

The Gilded Age: A Tale of To-day (co-authored with Charles Dudley Warner). 1873.

"Old Times on the Mississippi." 1875.

Mark Twain's Sketches, New and Old. 1875.

The Adventures of Tom Sawyer. 1876.

Ah Sin, the Heathen Chinee (a play, co-authored with Bret Harte). 1877.

A Tramp Abroad. 1880.

1601. Conversation as it was by the Social Fireside, in the time of the Tudors. 1880.

The Prince and the Pauper: A Tale for Young People of All Ages. 1881.

The Stolen White Elephant, Etc. 1882.

Life on the Mississippi. 1883.

Adventures of Huckleberry Finn. 1884.

A Connecticut Yankee in King Arthur's Court. 1889.

Merry Tales. 1892.

The American Claimant. 1892. (A much different version of this novel was first written as a play in 1883, in collaboration with W. D. Howells.)

The £1,000,000 Bank-Note and Other New Stories. 1893.

Extracts from Adam's Diary: Translated from the Original MS. 1893.

Pudd'nhead Wilson and Those Extraordinary Twins. 1894.

Tom Sawyer Abroad. 1894.

Tom Sawyer, Detective. 1896.

Personal Recollections of Joan of Arc. 1896.

How to Tell a Story and Other Essays. 1897.

Following the Equator: A Journey Around the World. 1897.

The Man That Corrupted Hadleyburg and Other Stories and Essays. 1900.

King Leopold's Soliloquy: A Defense of His Congo Rule. 1905.

The $30,000 Bequest and Other Stories. 1906.

Eve's Diary: Translated from the Original MS. 1906.

Mark Twain's Own Autobiography: The Chapters from the North American Review. 1906–7.

Christian Science. 1907.

Extract from Captain Stormfield's Visit to Heaven. 1909.

Is Shakespeare Dead? From My Autobiography. 1909.

Mark Twain's Speeches. 1910.

LATER COLLECTIONS

Twain, Mark (1917). *Mark Twain's Letters*, 2 vols., ed. Albert Bigelow Paine. New York: Harper & Bros.

Twain, Mark (1949). *The Love Letters of Mark Twain*, ed. Dixon Wecter. New York: Harper.

Twain, Mark (1957). *Mark Twain of the* Enterprise: *Newspaper Articles & Other Documents, 1862–1864*, ed. Henry Nash Smith and Frederick Anderson. Berkeley: University of California Press.

Twain, Mark (1962). *Letters from the Earth*, ed. Bernard DeVoto. New York: Harper.

Twain, Mark (1966). *Mark Twain's Letters from Hawaii*, ed. A. Grove Day. New York: Appleton-Century.

Twain, Mark (1967a). *Mark Twain's Satires & Burlesques*, ed. Franklin R. Rogers. Berkeley: University of California Press. (The Mark Twain Papers.)

Twain, Mark (1967b). *Mark Twain's Which Was the Dream? and Other Symbolic Writings of the Later Years*, ed. John S. Tuckey. Berkeley: University of California Press. (The Mark Twain Papers.)

Twain, Mark (1968). *Mark Twain's Hannibal, Huck & Tom*, ed. Walter Blair. Berkeley: University of California Press. (The Mark Twain Papers.)

Twain, Mark (1969a). *The Mysterious Stranger*, ed. William M. Gibson. Berkeley: University of California Press. (The Mark Twain Papers.) (*Note:* This volume contains the three extant manuscripts of the novel. A horribly inaccurate version of this novel, combining parts of two of the different manuscripts, was published in 1916.)

Twain, Mark (1969b). *Clemens of the* Call: *Mark Twain in San Francisco*, ed. Edgar Marquess Branch. Berkeley: University of California Press.

Twain, Mark (1972). *Mark Twain's Fables of Man*, ed. John S. Tuckey. Berkeley: University of California Press. (The Works of Mark Twain.)

Twain, Mark (1973). *What Is Man? and Other Philosophical Writings*, ed. Paul Baender. Berke-ley: University of California Press. (The Works of Mark Twain.)

Twain, Mark (1975–9). *Mark Twain's Notebooks and Journals*, 3 vols., ed. Frederick Anderson et al. Berkeley: University of California Press. (The Mark Twain Papers.)

Twain, Mark (1979–81). *Early Tales and Sketches, 1851–1865*, 2 vols., ed. Edgar Marquess Branch and Robert H. Hirst. Berkeley: University of California Press. (The Works of Mark Twain.)

Twain, Mark (1988–2004). *Mark Twain's Letters, 1853–1880*, 6 vols., ed. Edgar Marquess Branch et al. Berkeley: University of California (ongoing project of The Mark Twain Papers).

Twain, Mark (1992a). *Mark Twain: Collected Tales, Sketches, Speeches, & Essays, 1852–1890*, ed. Louis J. Budd. New York: Library of America.

Twain, Mark (1992b). *Mark Twain: Collected Tales, Sketches, Speeches, & Essays, 1891–1910*, ed. Louis J. Budd. New York: Library of America.

Twain, Mark (1995). *Mark Twain's Weapons of Satire: Anti-Imperialist Writings on the Philippine–American War*, ed. Jim Zwick. Syracuse, NY: Syracuse University Press.

Twain, Mark (1996). *The Oxford Mark Twain*, 29 vols., ed. Shelley Fisher Fishkin. New York: Oxford University Press. (Facsimiles of the first American editions of Mark Twain's works.)

Twain, Mark (2004). *Is He Dead? A Comedy in Three Acts* (written 1898), ed. Shelley Fisher Fishkin. In *Jumping Frogs: Undiscovered, Rediscovered, and Celebrated Writings of Mark Twain*. Berkeley: University of California Press.

Twain, Mark, and Howells, W. D. (1960). *Mark Twain–Howells Letters: The Correspondence of Samuel L. Clemens and William D. Howells, 1872–1910*, 2 vols., ed. Henry Nash Smith and William M. Gibson. Cambridge, Mass.: Harvard University Press.

REFERENCES AND FURTHER READING

Andrews, Kenneth R. (1950). *Nook Farm: Mark Twain's Hartford Circle*. Cambridge, Mass.: Harvard University Press.

Baetzhold, Howard G. (1970). *Mark Twain and John Bull: The British Connection*. Bloomington: Indiana University Press.

Beaver, Harold (1987). *Huckleberry Finn*. London: Unwin Hyman.

Blair, Walter (1960). *Mark Twain & Huck Finn*. Berkeley: University of California Press.

Blair, Walter (1993). *Essays on American Humor: Blair through the Ages*, ed. Hamlin Hill. Madison: University of Wisconsin Press.

Bridgman, Richard (1987). *Traveling in Mark Twain*. Berkeley: University of California Press.

Branch, Edgar Marquess (1950). *The Literary Apprenticeship of Mark Twain, with Selections from his Apprenticeship Writings*. Urbana: University of Illinois Press.

Brooks, Van Wyck (1970). *The Ordeal of Mark Twain*. New York: Dutton. (First publ. 1920.)

Budd, Louis J. (1962). *Mark Twain: Social Philosopher*. Bloomington: Indiana University Press.

Budd, Louis J. (1983). *Our Mark Twain: The Making of his Public Personality*. Philadelphia: University of Pennsylvania Press.

Budd, Louis J., ed. (1985). *New Essays on* Adventures of Huckleberry Finn. Cambridge and New York: Cambridge University Press.

Camfield, Gregg (1994). *Sentimental Twain: Samuel Clemens in the Maze of Moral Philosophy*. Philadelphia: University of Pennsylvania Press.

Camfield, Gregg (2003). *The Oxford Companion to Mark Twain*. New York: Oxford University Press.

Carkeet, David (1979). "The Dialects in *Huckleberry Finn*." *American Literature* 51: 3, 315–32.

Chadwick-Joshua, Jocelyn (1998). *The Jim Dilemma: Reading Race in* Huckleberry Finn. Jackson: University of Mississippi Press.

Champion, Laurie, ed. (1991). *The Critical Response to Mark Twain's* Huckleberry Finn. New York and Westport, Conn.: Greenwood.

Clemens, Clara (1931). *My Father Mark Twain*. New York: Harper & Bros.

Clemens, Susy (1985). *Papa: An Intimate Biography of Mark Twain*, ed. Charles Neider. Garden City, NY: Doubleday.

Conrad, Joseph (1971). *Heart of Darkness*, ed. Robert Kimbrough. New York: Norton Critical Edition. (First publ. 1899.)

Covici, Pascal, Jr. (1962). *Mark Twain's Humor: The Image of a World*. Dallas: Southern Methodist University Press.

Cox, James M. (1966). *Mark Twain: The Fate of Humor*. Princeton: Princeton University Press.

Cox, James M. (1984). "Introduction." In Mark Twain, *Life on the Mississippi*. New York: Penguin.

Cummings, Sherwood (1988). *Mark Twain and Science: Adventures of a Mind*. Baton Rouge: Louisiana State University Press.

DeVoto, Bernard (1932). *Mark Twain's America*. Boston: Little, Brown.

DeVoto, Bernard (1942). *Mark Twain at Work*. Cambridge, Mass.: Harvard University Press.

Dolmetsch, Carl (1992). *"Our Famous Guest": Mark Twain in Vienna*. Athens, Ga.: University of Georgia Press.

Douglass, Frederick (1986). *Narrative of the Life of Frederick Douglass, An American Slave*, ed. Houston A. Baker, Jr. New York: Penguin Classics. (First publ. 1845.)

Doyno, Victor A. (1991). *Writing* Huck Finn: *Mark Twain's Creative Process*. Philadelphia: University of Pennsylvania Press.

Emerson, Everett (2000). *Mark Twain: A Literary Life*. Philadelphia: University of Pennsylvania Press.

Emerson, Ralph Waldo (1983). *The Conduct of Life*. In *Ralph Waldo Emerson: Essays and Lectures*, ed. Joel Porte, 937–1124. New York: Library of America.

Ensor, Allison (1969). *Mark Twain and the Bible*. Lexington: University of Kentucky Press.

Fatout, Paul (1960). *Mark Twain on the Lecture Circuit*. Bloomington: Indiana University Press.

Fatout, Paul (1964). *Mark Twain in Virginia City*. Bloomington: Indiana University Press.

Fishkin, Shelley Fisher (1993). *Was Huck Black? Mark Twain and African-American Voices*. New York and Oxford: Oxford University Press.

Fishkin, Shelley Fisher (1997). *Lighting Out for the Territory: Reflections on Mark Twain and American Culture*. New York: Oxford University Press.

Fishkin, Shelley Fisher, ed. (2002a). *A Historical Guide to Mark Twain*. Oxford: Oxford University Press.

Fishkin, Shelley Fisher (2002b). "Mark Twain and Race." In Shelley Fisher Fishkin (ed.), *A Historical Guide to Mark Twain*, 127–62. Oxford: Oxford University Press.

Fredericks, Nancy (1989). "Twain's Indelible Twins." *Nineteenth-Century Literature* 43: 4, 484–99.

Fulton, Joe B. (1997). *Mark Twain's Ethical Realism: The Aesthetics of Race, Class, and Gender.* Columbia: University of Missouri Press.

Gibson, William M. (1976). *The Art of Mark Twain.* New York: Oxford University Press.

Gillman, Susan (1989). *Dark Twins: Imposture and Identity in Mark Twain's America.* Chicago: University of Chicago Press.

Gillman, Susan, and Robinson, Forrest G., eds. (1990). *Mark Twain's* Pudd'nhead Wilson: *Race, Conflict, and Culture.* Durham, NC: Duke University Press.

Griffith, Clark (1998). *Achilles and the Tortoise: Mark Twain's Fictions.* Tuscaloosa: University of Alabama Press.

Hendler, Glenn (1993). "Tom Sawyer's Masculinity." *Arizona Quarterly* 49: 4, 33–59.

Harris, Susan K. (1982). *Mark Twain's Escape from Time.* Columbia: University of Missouri Press.

Harris, Susan K. (1996). *The Courtship of Olivia Langdon and Mark Twain.* New York: Cambridge University Press.

Hemingway, Ernest (1963). *Green Hills of Africa.* New York: Scribner's. (First publ. 1935.)

Hill, Hamlin (1973). *Mark Twain: God's Fool.* New York: Harper & Row.

Howe, Lawrence (1998). *Mark Twain and the Novel: The Double-Cross of Authority.* Cambridge: Cambridge University Press.

Howells, William Dean (1967). *My Mark Twain: Reminiscences and Criticisms.* Baton Rouge: Louisiana State University Press. (First publ. 1910.)

Hurston, Zora Neale (1998). *Their Eyes Were Watching God.* New York: Harper Perennial Classics. (First publ. 1937.)

Inge, Thomas M., ed. (1985). *Huck Finn among the Critics: A Centennial Selection.* Frederick, Md.: University Publications of America.

Johnson, James L. (1982). *Mark Twain and the Limits of Power: Emerson's God in Ruins.* Knoxville: University of Tennessee Press.

Jones, Gavin (1999). *Strange Talk: The Politics of Dialect Literature in Gilded Age America.* Berkeley: University of California Press.

Kahn, Sholem J. (1978). *Mark Twain's* Mysterious Stranger: *A Study of the Manuscript Texts.* Columbia: University of Missouri Press.

Kaplan, Fred (2003). *The Singular Mark Twain: A Biography.* New York: Doubleday.

Kaplan, Justin (1966). *Mr. Clemens and Mark Twain.* New York: Simon & Schuster.

Krause, Sydney J. (1967). *Mark Twain as Critic.* Baltimore: Johns Hopkins University Press.

Krauth, Leland (1999). *Proper Mark Twain.* Athens, Ga.: University of Georgia Press.

Lauber, John (1985). *The Making of Mark Twain: A Biography.* New York: Farrar, Straus & Giroux.

Lauber, John (1990). *The Inventions of Mark Twain.* New York: Hill & Wang.

Leonard, James S.; Tenney, Thomas A.; and Davis, Thadious M., eds. (1992). *Satire or Evasion? Black Perspectives on* Huckleberry Finn. Durham, NC: Duke University Press.

Lowry, Richard S. (1996). *"Littery Man": Mark Twain and Modern Authorship.* New York: Oxford University Press.

Lynn, Kenneth S. (1959). *Mark Twain and Southwestern Humor.* Westport, Conn.: Greenwood.

Lystra, Karen (2004). *Dangerous Intimacy: The Untold Story of Mark Twain's Final Years.* Berkeley: University of California Press.

Marx, Leo (1953). "Mr. Eliot, Mr. Trilling, and *Huckleberry Finn.*" *American Scholar* 22: 4, 423–40.

Marx, Leo (1988). *The Pilot and the Passenger.* New York: Oxford University Press.

Messent, Peter B. (2001). *The Short Works of Mark Twain: A Critical Study.* Philadelphia: University of Pennsylvania Press.

Michelson, Bruce (1995). *Mark Twain on the Loose: A Comic Writer and the American Self.* Amherst: University of Massachusetts Press.

Mitchell, Lee Clark (1989). *Determined Fictions: American Literary Naturalism.* New York: Columbia University Press.

Morrison, Toni (1996). "Introduction." In Mark Twain, *Adventures of Huckleberry Finn*, ed. Shelley Fisher Fishkin. New York: Oxford University Press. (The Oxford Mark Twain.)

Nilon, Charles (1992). "The Ending of *Huckleberry Finn*: 'Freeing the Free Negro.'" In James S. Leonard, Thomas A. Tenney, and Thadious Davis (eds.), *Satire or Evasion? Black Perspectives on* Huckleberry Finn, 62–76. Durham, NC: Duke University Press.

Paine, Albert Bigelow (1912). *Mark Twain: A Biography*, 3 vols. New York: Harper & Bros.

Pettit, Arthur G. (1974). *Mark Twain and the South.* Lexington: University of Kentucky Press.

Powers, Ron (1999). *Dangerous Water: A Biography of the Boy Who Became Mark Twain*. New York: Basic Books.

Quirk, Tom (1993). *Coming to Grips with* Huckleberry Finn: *Essays on a Book, a Boy, and a Man*. Columbia: University of Missouri Press.

Quirk, Tom (1997). *Mark Twain: A Study of the Short Fiction*. New York: Twayne.

Railton, Stephen (2004). *Mark Twain: A Short Introduction*. Oxford: Blackwell.

Rasmussen, R. Kent (1996). *Mark Twain A to Z: The Essential Reference to His Life and Writings*. New York: Oxford University Press.

Regan, Robert (1966). *Unpromising Heroes: Mark Twain and his Characters*. Berkeley: University of California Press.

Robinson, Forrest G. (1984). "Social Play and Bad Faith in *The Adventures of Tom Sawyer*." *Nineteenth-Century Literature* 39: 1, 1–24.

Robinson, Forrest G. (1986). *In Bad Faith: The Dynamics of Deception in Mark Twain's America*. Cambridge, Mass.: Harvard University Press.

Robinson, Forrest G. (1988). "The Characterization of Jim in *Huckleberry Finn*." *Nineteenth-Century Literature* 43: 3, 361–91.

Robinson, Forrest G., ed. (1995). *The Cambridge Companion to Mark Twain*. Cambridge, UK: Cambridge University Press.

Rogers, Franklin R. (1960). *Mark Twain's Burlesque Patterns, as Seen in the Novels and Narratives, 1855–1885*. Dallas: Southern Methodist University Press.

Salomon, Roger B. (1961). *Twain and the Image of History*. New Haven, Conn.: Yale University Press.

Sattelmeyer, Robert, and Crowley, J. Donald, eds. (1985). *One Hundred Years of* Huckleberry Finn: *The Boy, His Book, and American Culture. Centennial Essays*. Columbia: University of Missouri Press.

Schmitz, Neil (1971). "Twain, *Huckleberry Finn*, and the Reconstruction." *American Studies* 12: 59–67.

Scott, Kevin Michael (2005). " 'There's More Honor': Reinterpreting Tom and the Evasion in *Huckleberry Finn*." In *Studies in the Novel* 37: 2, 186–206.

Sewell, David R. (1987). *Mark Twain's Languages: Discourse, Dialogue, and Linguistic Variety*. Berkeley: University of California Press.

Skandera-Trombley, Laura E. (1994). *Mark Twain in the Company of Women*. Philadelphia: University of Pennsylvania Press.

Sloane, David E. E. (1979). *Mark Twain as a Literary Comedian*. Baton Rouge: Louisiana State University Press.

Smith, David L. (1992). "Huck, Jim, and American Racial Discourse." In James S. Leonard, Thomas A. Tenney, and Thadious Davis (eds.), *Satire or Evasion? Black Perspectives on* Huckleberry Finn, 103–20. Durham, NC: Duke University Press.

Smith, Henry Nash (1962). *Mark Twain: The Development of a Writer*. Cambridge, Mass.: Harvard University Press.

Smith, Henry Nash, ed. (1963). *Mark Twain: A Collection of Critical Essays*. Englewood Cliffs, NJ: Prentice-Hall.

Steinbrink, Jeffrey (1991). *Getting to Be Mark Twain*. Berkeley: University of California Press.

Stone, Albert E. (1970). *The Innocent Eye: Childhood in Mark Twain's Imagination*. New Haven, Conn.: Yale University Press.

Stoneley, Peter (1992). *Mark Twain and the Feminine Aesthetic*. Cambridge: Cambridge University Press.

Sundquist, Eric J. (1993). *To Wake the Nations: Race in the Making of American Literature*. Cambridge, Mass.: Belknap Press/Harvard University Press.

Sundquist, Eric J., ed. (1994). *Mark Twain: A Collection of Critical Essays*. Englewood Cliffs, NJ: Prentice-Hall.

Tocqueville, Alexis de. (1989) *Democracy in America*, vol. 2, ed. Phillips Bradley. New York: Knopf. (First publ. 1840.)

Tuckey, John S. (1963). *Mark Twain and Little Satan: The Writing of* The Mysterious Stranger. West Lafayette, Ind.: Purdue University Press.

Twain, Mark (1980). *Pudd'nhead Wilson and Those Extraordinary Twins*, ed. Sidney E. Berger. New York: Norton Critical Edition.

Twain, Mark (1982). *The Adventures of Tom Sawyer*, ed. John C. Gerber and Paul Baender. Berkeley: University of California Press, 1982. (The Mark Twain Library.)

Twain, Mark (1983). *A Connecticut Yankee in King Arthur's Court*, ed. Bernard L. Stein. Berkeley: University of California Press. (The Mark Twain Library.)

Twain, Mark (1984). *Life on the Mississippi*. New York: Penguin Classics.

Twain, Mark (1990). *Mark Twain's Own Autobiography: The Chapters from the* North American Review, ed. Michael J. Kiskis. Madison: University of Wisconsin Press.

Twain, Mark (1993). *Roughing It*, ed. Harriet Elinor Smith and Edgar Marquess Branch. Berkeley: University of California Press. (The Works of Mark Twain.)

Twain, Mark (2001). *Adventures of Huckleberry Finn*, ed. Victor Fischer et al. Berkeley: University of California Press. (The Mark Twain Library.)

Wecter, Dixon (1952). *Sam Clemens of Hannibal*. Boston: Houghton Mifflin.

Whitman, Walt (1982). "As I Ebb'd with the Ocean of Life" (first publ. 1860). In *Walt Whitman: Complete Poetry and Collected Prose*, ed. Justin Kaplan, 394–6. New York: Library of America.

Wonham, Henry B. (1993). *Mark Twain and the Art of the Tall Tale*. New York: Oxford University Press.

25

William Dean Howells and the Bourgeois Quotidian: Affection, Skepticism, Disillusion

Michael Anesko

Size matters – to most Americans. At least since the appearance of Tocqueville's penetrating critique of democracy in the young Republic, cultural historians have remarked upon Americans' apparently endemic fondness for the big, the enormous, the monumental, the spectacular. Familiar and easily recognizable examples readily confirm the continuing significance of this criterion: from the scale of our public architecture (the Capitol, the Statue of Liberty, Mount Rushmore) to the inflated dimensions of our so-called media events (Superbowl Sunday, the Simpson trial, Powerball jackpots), the national passion for the superlative seems forever unassuaged. This outwardly harmless aspect of democratic culture brings with it, however, an implicit (and less benign) corollary; for if we love to see things writ large, we also take perverse pleasure in watching them collapse. Large-scale implosions of sports arenas and towering buildings – let us confess it, even the World Trade Center – always captivate attention and usually fetch a crowd.

Not many other American writers have felt the pulse of our society more acutely than William Dean Howells (1837–1920). His most representative protagonist, Silas Lapham, embodies the national love of bigness, and the story of that character's financial collapse (and moral rise) gives narrative form to what might be called the melodrama of scale that has always captivated Americans' collective consciousness. In its own peculiar way, however, the literary standing of Howells himself demonstrates even more forcefully the pertinacity of Tocqueville's observations about the fickleness of popular opinion in democratic societies. Celebrated for much of his lifetime as the nation's foremost man of letters, Howells lived long enough to watch his reputation begin to erode in the first decades of the twentieth century. With characteristic serenity, he recognized the symptoms of his own cultural deflation and stoically accepted them. He already understood what later critics claim to have discovered – that, careless of history and indifferent to taste, American culture ruthlessly discards what it doesn't know how to use.

From very modest beginnings on the Ohio frontier, Howells came to occupy a position of remarkable cultural prestige – first in Boston, where he rose to edit the *Atlantic Monthly*, the nation's premier literary magazine, and ultimately in New York, where he became a conspicuous mainstay of the vast Harper publishing empire. Howells was, of course, the most unlikely of celebrities. As many of his critics liked to point out, his whole career testified to the virtues of plainness and the attractions of the ordinary. In deliberate contrast to the roll-call of New England worthies – Ralph Waldo Emerson, Oliver Wendell Holmes, James Russell Lowell, Henry Wadsworth Longfellow – whose title-pages broadcast their sonorously triple-barreled names in apparent affirmation of their cultural worth, W. D. Howells used *that* abbreviated appellation on almost all the titles he published during his lifetime. He became "William Dean Howells" only through a deliberate campaign of cultural inflation, largely orchestrated by the public relations department of Harper & Brothers, the firm with which he was uninterruptedly affiliated after 1900.

The capstone of Harper's efforts, ironically, was an *extra*literary event – a confabulation to celebrate the Dean's seventy-fifth birthday in 1912: an invitation to which even the President of the United States felt proud to accept. Hundreds of others did, too, and newspapers across the country filled their columns with stories and panoramic photographs of the luxurious spread at Sherry's, then the poshest restaurant in Manhattan. But, as one recent observer cleverly remarks, Howells the famous author was forced to endure "the slings and arrows of outrageous reception": his books "suffered mortally as they came less and less to be read while their author came more and more to be lionized" (Crowley 1999: 49). One of W.D.'s saving graces, surely, was his ability to understand and even to accept the grim fate that awaited his posthumous career. Heralded for much of his lifetime as the Dean of American letters, the literary standard-bearer of his age, the man with the providentially inspired middle name lived long enough to see his fame falter and his sales diminish – so much so that he could even prophesy his own canonical extinction. "I am comparatively a dead cult," he told Henry James in 1915, "with my statues cast down and the grass growing over them in the pale moonlight" (Anesko 1997: 460). With characteristic understatement, Howells grimly confirms Tocqueville's trenchant conclusion about intellectual labor in the United States. "A democratic public often treats its authors much as kings usually behave toward their courtiers," the Frenchman declared: "it enriches and despises them" (Tocqueville 1969: 475). Howells surely made a comfortable living from literary work, but the security of his reputation has proven vulnerable to challenge.

Those coming not to praise Howells but to bury him quickly made their views known in the first decade after his death. The withering wit of H. L. Mencken already had inserted inverted commas around "The Dean" in a 1917 review of *The Leatherwood God*, just one of several occasions that acerbic critic found to pillory Howells as the prissy figurehead of an inert puritanical culture, a writer "enveloped in a web of superstitious reverence," whose flatulent books were "merely fawned over" by newspaper eunuchs who could "no more bring themselves to question them than they could question Lincoln's Gettysburg speech...or their own virginity" (Mencken 1949: 490, 489). Mencken's merciless jabs made it easier for Van Wyck Brooks and Sinclair Lewis to continue the assault, which culminated (more or less) with Lewis's notorious acceptance speech when he became the first American to receive the Nobel Prize for Literature in 1930. "Mr. Howells was one of the gentlest, sweetest and most honest of men," Lewis conceded at Stockholm, "but he had the code of a pious old maid whose greatest delight was to have tea at the vicarage." In contrast, presumably, to the more courageous work of writers like Theodore Dreiser and Sherwood Anderson – even Willa Cather – Howells's books betrayed the conformist's fear of anything "which is not a glorification of everything American, a glorification of our faults as well as our virtues" (Lewis 1953: 15, 6).

Lewis and most of the other moderns conveniently forgot – or, more likely, never knew – that in his prime Howells had provoked considerable censure from influential sectors of the literary establishment. To genteel critics of polite letters, the "realism" Howells advocated seemed commonplace and dingy, incompatible with the cultural imperative that literature provide inspiration through the evocation of ideal states of feeling. Though frequently derided by twentieth-century critics as timid and sexually naïve, Howells in his own day scandalized many readers because of his willingness to tackle subjects like divorce (*A Modern Instance* [1882]), the corruption of business ethics (*The Rise of Silas Lapham* [1885]), social inequality (*A Hazard of New Fortunes* [1890]), and interracial marriage (*An Imperative Duty* [1892]). In his monthly columns for *Harper's Magazine*, Howells waged a war for realism and its political concomitant, humane social justice, that established him as the nation's most respected (if not its most popular) man of letters. To a new generation of literary aspirants, his example was invaluable. "You have thrown a wonderfully clear light into problems which must vex every young writer," a youthful disciple named Henry Harland (who later edited the *Yellow Book*) remarked in 1887.

> The contemptible flings at your utterances in which newspaper critics, and third-rate literary folks are fond of indulging have made me feel very sore and indignant sometimes; though I have comforted myself by remembering that the crowd has always visited its wrath upon the head of the man who has had the courage to stand out and proclaim hitherto unrecognized and therefore unpopular truths. (Harland 1887)

As literary realism's most prolific crusader and champion in America, Howells fathered a multitude of heirs who inherited his treasures but forgot their paternity. Surely one of them was Sinclair Lewis himself. If not a lineal descendant of Silas Lapham, George Babbitt has got to be his second cousin.

Dozens of other echoing tributes besides Harland's could be drawn from the Howells archive at Harvard, and in their range of authorship we can glimpse the outlines of an extraordinarily large and important chapter in American literary history. Even the index of Howells's correspondents (from George Ade to Israel Zangwill) testifies to a catholicity of taste and temperament that remains unparalleled in nineteenth-century American letters. The young man from Ohio whom Hawthorne once judged "worthy" of an introduction to Emerson was destined to become an arbiter of literary reputation no less exacting, though possibly more impartial, than the New England worthies to whom he first paid tribute in *Literary Friends and Acquaintance* (1900). "When the fussy and noisy accidents of our crowded day come to be left behind," wrote Henry Blake Fuller in 1907, "it will be perceived that for one full generation in American annals the dominant influence has been yours – and always for the good. The Age of Howells – isn't that, some time, possible and likely?" (Fuller 1907). Though Fuller's rosy prophecy has not been consistently realized, it is worth remembering that the uncanny symmetry of affection that placed Howells squarely between Mark Twain and Henry James – those other two great contemporaries who had nothing in common but his large admiration – remains for us an emblem of his central role in the development of a distinctively American literature.

Howells was born on March 1, 1837, in the Western Reserve region of Ohio. From the age of nine he helped his father, an itinerant newspaperman, in the printing shop – first setting type and, not long after, reading proof, and eventually contributing stories and verses from his own pen. Like Melville's whaling ship, the pressroom was his Harvard and his Yale. At nineteen Howells began his own journalistic career, sending weekly letters from the state capital to the *Cincinnati Gazette*. Soon, other newspapers in Ohio were printing his stories. When the Republican party assumed control of the *Ohio State Journal* in Columbus, Howells quickly found a place on the masthead. Never comfortable with the job of street reporting, he refined his talents at the editorial desk and collaborated with John James Piatt, a fellow journalist, on *Poems of Two Friends* (1859), his first published book. With a national election – and civil war – looming, the Republicans engaged Howells to write a campaign biography for their standard-bearer, another Midwesterner named Abraham Lincoln.

His royalties on *Lives and Speeches of Abraham Lincoln and Hannibal Hamlin* (1860) amounted to less than two hundred dollars, but, with a Republican victory that November, Howells gained immeasurably when he was rewarded for his labors with the American consulship to Venice. Prior to his appointment and departure for Europe, the aspiring young writer made a pilgrimage to New England, where (astonishingly) he met virtually all the luminaries of the nation's literary life – Emerson, Lowell, Holmes, Longfellow, Thoreau, Hawthorne. Lowell had already accepted a few of Howells's poems for the prestigious *Atlantic Monthly*, but the Western writer's reputation in Boston assumed a firmer footing with the appearance of travel sketches that he began sending from Venice in 1863. Collected in *Venetian Life* (1866) and *Italian Journeys* (1867), these pieces won Howells the esteem of the Brahmin custodians of literary culture. Even young Henry James would concede that these two books belonged "to literature and to the center and core of it, – the region where . . . the classics stand on guard" (Anesko 1997: 61).

Four months after Lee's surrender at Appomattox Courthouse, Howells returned from Italy to New York, where he joined the staff of Edwin L. Godkin's new periodical, the *Nation*. Shortly thereafter, James T. Fields invited Howells to become assistant editor of the *Atlantic*, an offer that must have seemed to fulfill a lifelong dream of literary ambition. When Howells first came to Boston in 1860, the venerable Oliver Wendell Holmes had quipped rather sharply to Lowell, "Well, James, this is something like the apostolic succession; this is the laying on of hands" (*Literary Friends and Acquaintance*). In little more than a decade, this subtle sarcasm would become a social fact. After Fields retired in 1871, Howells assumed the editorship of the nation's foremost literary magazine. The apostolic succession was complete.

Though Howells would continue to write verse until the end of his life, his experience as a journalist and editor easily persuaded him that mastering prose narrative was the cornerstone of a modern literary career. With a growing family to support (while abroad, Howells had married Elinor Mead, who bore him three children), he was anxious to secure his hard-won literary status and maintain a middle-class standard of living. To do that meant he had to write novels – first serializing them in magazines (to establish readership and generate publicity) and then bringing them to consumers as attractively bound volumes. With almost incessant regularity, Howells composed at least one novel annually for almost fifty years, beginning with *Their Wedding Journey* (1872) and ending with the posthumously published *The Vacation of the Kelwyns* (1920). To this already bulging bibliography he added an editor's considerable day-work of book reviews, prefaces, critical essays, travel sketches, and parlor theatricals. His was truly a writing life.

Though Howells remained a religious agnostic for all of his life, his early experience with frontier democracy and anti-slavery zeal had a lasting impact upon his social and political outlook. During his term as editor of the *Atlantic* (1871–81) he expanded the magazine's reach beyond the accustomed boundaries of New England, actively seeking out contributions from other regions and other voices. Despite Howells's own rise to a position of relative eminence within the literary establishment, his elected affinity for New England culture was always undermined by a nagging sense of its illiberal social origins. His first major novel, *A Chance Acquaintance* (1873), contrasts the democratic freedom of a young woman from upstate New York with the staid conventionality of "a Boston that would rather perish by fire and sword than be suspected of vulgarity." The novel of manners in the United States could not have flourished without the central figure of "the American girl," and she was largely Howells's creation.

By transporting that character to Europe, Howells could extend the implications of his basic theme and make good use of his own first-hand experiences. *A Foregone Conclusion* (1875), *The Lady of the Aroostook* (1879), and *A Fearful Responsibility* (1881) each chart this migration, shifting the axis for the contrast of manners from West vs. East to New World vs. Old. Howells soon recognized, however, that the "International Theme" probably was better left to his friend Henry James, whose deliberate expatriation to Europe assured him a firmer claim on that material. In 1879 James himself had given Howells strict orders – "Continue to Americanize & to *realize*: that is your mission" – advice well taken and received (Anesko 1997: 137). The solid achievements of *A Modern Instance* and *The Rise of Silas Lapham* confirm the extent to which Howells's imagination found its surest promptings on native ground. Neither of these titles has ever gone out of print, a testament to their enduring relevance as documentary narratives of distinctively American conditions.

Howells's contemporaries immediately recognized the importance of these works, the latter in particular eliciting superlatives from readers here and abroad. Contrasting Howells's depth of national feeling with Henry James's pallid cosmopolitanism, the blunt assessment of London's *Saturday Review* still rings true. "Mr. Howells knows his America, and he feels it; he is in sympathy with it; he knows what it means; he enjoys it, and he loves it" (Anon. 1885: 517). Edmund Gosse distinguished *The Rise of Silas Lapham* as *a* – if not *the* – great American novel, "the high-water mark" of a "great and unique photographic genius" (Gosse 1885: 8). Even the expatriate James found the book "tremendously good – life & reality caught in the very fact," a compliment not often heard from that quarter (Anesko 1997: 182).

Though it has become almost tiresomely familiar to classify Howells as the quintessential American prude (Queen Victoria with a handlebar mustache), stepping aside from the conventional view can allow us to see *The Rise of Silas Lapham* as a novel of seduction. The virtue at risk of compromise, however, is not titillatingly virginal but, rather, political and moral; for Howells carefully constructs the novel to entice the reader to assume a point of view superior to that of his lumbering protagonist, the country farmer turned mineral-paint millionaire, blessed with fistfuls of money but still equipped with "hairy paws" with which to grab them. Almost all of the text's references to Silas Lapham's physical characteristics share this taint of biological recidivism, which should help us to remember that the simian shadow of Darwin's *Descent of Man* (1871) already was creeping across the nation's literary landscape. At the same time that other American intellectuals were appropriating the concept of evolution to justify (yet again) a supposedly preordained hierarchy of ethnic status and the increasing concentration of wealth, Howells slyly weaves the trope of the "rise" from primitivism to civilization into the fabric of his outwardly Horatio Algeresque plot to subvert – or at least complicate – that simplistic formula. (It should come as no surprise that the author of *Ragged Lady* [1899] was familiar with the author of *Ragged Dick* [1868], which canonized the rags-to-riches fable in juvenile literature.)

The opening scene of the novel plays with all these possibilities, as Lapham greets a slick newspaperman (Bartley Hubbard, of *Modern Instance* notoriety), intent upon getting the paint king's story for the "Solid Men of Boston" series that his lowbrow rag is featuring. Set, appropriately, in the businessman's downtown office, the first chapter offers a wonderful emblem of the book's meaning, as it immediately confronts us with one of the keenly pathetic paradoxes of our bourgeois culture – namely, the extent to which the self-made man is, in fact, made and controlled by others. Individual success helps to foster the illusion of self-mastery and a kind of virtuous authenticity (these are crucial elements in Lapham's sense of his own democratic dignity); yet, from the very beginning, we see that Lapham's understanding of himself is not wholly reliable. The narrative device of the interview allows the reader to shape his own view of Silas, because it forces us to separate and sift through competing perceptions of his character – those of himself and those of the interviewer. Before long the reader senses (as, crucially, Lapham does, too) that Hubbard has come for the purpose of confirmation rather than discovery: his story has, essentially, already been written (first by Benjamin Franklin, then sanitized by Alger). The real particulars of Silas's life history would only interfere with the replication of a type; idiosyncrasy has no place in a "series."

While Lapham seems disconcerted by the interviewer's irreverent interjections as he attempts to fill in his biographical sketch, his reactions simply confirm the extent to which he subscribes to a romanticized version of the success story. His innocent faith in the mythology of the self-made man (together with his lack of self-awareness) betrays him into making all kinds of accidental disclosures that reveal a string of discrepancies between the cultural archetype and his own life history. It is clear, for example, that Silas needs to think of himself as a devoted family man, yet the memento he reaches for to prove it is "a large warped, unframed photograph" covered with dust. In spite of his professed devotion to the family farm in Vermont (where he "hung on . . . not because the paint-mine was on it, but because the old house was – and the graves"), we soon learn that, just like all the rest, he deserted New England to try his luck out West and only came back because he got tired of Texas. As the conversation continues, realistic details and facts continue to intrude upon Silas's sentimentalized version of himself; he trips himself up in unselfconscious contradiction because he does not really know who he is. Hubbard, on the other hand, sees right through him – or thinks he does – and writes up his story as a kind of parody of the commonplace sublime, confident all the while that Lapham's stupidity will blind him to the writer's malevolent intentions. " 'Bartley! you *won't* make fun of him as you do some of those people? *Will* you?' " his wife implores. " 'Nothing that *he*'ll ever find out,' " is Hubbard's snide answer.

At the very start, then, Howells encourages us to think of *Silas Lapham* as a novel about perception and narration, about manners of seeing and saying – in short, about style. As the book proceeds, the question of style takes on a certain political and moral dimension, first underscored by our recognition that the journalist employs the engine of publicity as a means to vent resentment and envy against his subject. To all of which, as Hubbard cynically foretells, Lapham is largely oblivious:

> He had not much to complain of in Bartley's treatment, unless it was the strain of extravagant compliment which it involved. But the flattery was mainly for the paint, whose virtues Lapham did not believe could be overstated, and himself and his history had been treated with as much respect as Bartley was capable of showing any one. He made a very picturesque thing of the discovery of the paint-mine. "Deep in the heart of the virgin forests of Vermont, far up toward the line of the Canadian snows, on a desolate mountain-side, where an autumnal storm had done its wild work, and the great trees, strewn hither and thither, bore witness to its violence, Nehemiah Lapham discovered just forty years ago, the mineral which the alchemy of his son's enterprise

and energy has transmuted into solid ingots of the most precious of metals. The colossal fortune of Colonel Silas Lapham lay at the bottom of a hole which an uprooted tree had dug for him, and which for many years remained a paint-mine of no more appreciable value than a soap-mine." (Howells 1982: 876–7)

The newspaperman's parodic manner contrasts not only with Lapham's grossly utilitarian outbursts ("I never saw anything so very sacred about a big rock, along a river or in a pasture, that it wouldn't do to put mineral paint on it in three colours," he declares), but also, and more significantly, with the patient recording voice of the narrative itself. The invisible eye of the narrator champions keen observation of detail; unlike Lapham, he has no desire to paint over nature's hues; and unlike Hubbard, he has no interest in exaggerating or distorting their symbolic value. Howells's description of the business district through which Lapham drives his horse-drawn buggy exemplifies a confident clarity of perception that foils the misperceptions of most of his characters:

> The streets were all narrow, and most of them crooked, in that quarter of the town; but at the end of one the spars of a vessel penciled themselves delicately against the cool blue of the afternoon sky. The air was full of a smell pleasantly compounded of oakum, of leather, and of oil. It was not the busy season, and they met only two or three trucks heavily straggling toward the wharf with their long string teams; but the cobblestones of the pavement were worn with the dint of ponderous wheels, and discoloured with iron-rust from them; here and there, in wandering streaks over its surface, was the grey stain of the salt water with which the street had been sprinkled. (p. 876)

No wonder Gosse could remark upon Howells's "photographic genius." His style vividly captures the qualities of atmosphere and light that make the felt impression of life attractively compelling.

In the rarefied air of cultured Boston, Lapham's occasionally brusque manner of speaking and relish for colloquial speech work to remind us of his primitive origins and of how far he has yet to ascend in his quest for social recognition. Importantly, though, Howells has no wish to catalogue all of his protagonist's elocutionary peccadilloes. Silas's vernacular sets him apart from the novel's more privileged characters (notably the Coreys, whose son, Tom, applies for a job in Lapham's business and eventually falls in love with one of his daughters); but, as Elsa Nettels carefully discerns, it does not make him "grotesque" (Nettels 1980: 320). Because Howells carefully selects and limits our exposure to the excesses of Lapham's speech, his phrasings leave an impression of vigor rather than of barbarism.

Still, the narrator takes pains to distinguish Lapham's slangy colloquialisms from his own stylistic preference by disclaiming responsibility for them. The repeated use of parenthetical attribution (e.g., "as he would have expressed it," "as he always called them") in transcribing indirect discourse establishes a discursive breach between Howells and his semantically challenged hero; and, through this kind of narrative wink, the novelist invites the reader to join him on the side of idiomatic propriety. That solicitation, however, is exactly what makes *Silas Lapham* so brilliant. Howells deliberately encourages us to adopt a condescending attitude toward his central character only to turn the tables once we inescapably have committed ourselves to a position of presumed superiority.

The architecture of *Silas Lapham* also affirms the centrality of style to the novel's narrative design, as its twenty-seven chapters divide evenly around the pivotal dinner party at the Coreys' Brahmin mansion. To Silas, of course, an invitation to appear at this event savors of the social victory he all along has relished for himself and his family. If he were more philosophical, perhaps, Lapham might appreciate the occasion as a sign of the democratic transcendence of class distinctions, but it has to be confessed that his immediate reaction is tinged with retributive pride. When Lapham tells his wife that Tom's father has come down to his office to introduce himself, the narrator discloses that, "in his averted face," Silas does not let her see "the struggle that revealed itself there – the struggle of stalwart achievement not to feel flattered at the notice of sterile elegance, not to be sneakingly glad of its amiability, but to stand up and look at it with eyes on the same level" (Howells 1982: 894). Howells orchestrates the scenes leading up to the dinner party with consummate skill, allowing the reader hungrily to anticipate the humiliations that await.

The surest sign of impending catastrophe, needless to say, is the last-minute acquisition of an etiquette book – the ultimate symptom of class-bound despair. A crash course in manners can only result in a crack-up. Lapham falsely imagines that this supposedly peerless reference work will answer the host of questions that anxiously beset him, especially with regard to his proper manner of dress. But his clothbound authority is silent on the finer points, and beads of perspiration appear on Lapham's forehead as he ponders the perplexing choices among waistcoats, cravats, and gloves. Tension in the household rises to a fever pitch on the eve of the now-dreaded occasion, and retributive accusations fly. " 'Look here!' " Lapham exclaims to his wife, Persis, " 'Who wanted to go in for these people in the first place? Didn't you come home full of 'em last year, and want me to sell out here and move somewheres else because it didn't seem to suit 'em? And now you want to put it all on me! I ain't going to stand it' " (Howells 1982: 1032). The unconscious eruption of solecisms betrays Lapham's morbidly self-conscious class anxiety, further admonishing the reader to stand clear.

Through this crescendo of depressing revelations, Howells cleverly encourages us to imagine that, if the Coreys' elegant invitation had arrived in *our* postbox, we would not comparably be driven to wince in trepidation. Of course, the proper clothes already would hang in our wardrobe. Of course, we already would anticipate what topics of the day would most likely arise in the leisurely course of dinner conversation. Of course, we instinctively would reach for the proper fork at the proper time, know where to rest our knife and whose salad plate belonged to whom. An exclusive standard, naturally, would be our standard, too: why settle for anything less? Through this latent mechanism for cementing the reader's class allegiance within the novel's projected social field, Howells radically reverses the logic of retributive melodrama that his plot has set in motion. Lapham all along has hated the Corey name "as a symbol of splendour" possessing an aura that his own fortune cannot buy; and his aggressive eagerness to be accepted by Brahmin society as a deserving equal gives the first half of the book a kind of avenging energy. That force dissipates, literally, in chapter 14, as Lapham nervously drinks his way through the evening as the Coreys' dinner guest. Inexperienced with alcohol and indifferent to epicurean taste in wine, Lapham keeps a glass to his lips as a means for avoiding conversation with people whose badinage he doesn't understand. But vast quantities of sauterne and Madeira eventually unhitch his jaw, releasing a torrent of tasteless, bourgeois braggadocio:

> He told Charles Bellingham that he liked him, and assured James Bellingham that it had always been his ambition to know him, and that if anyone had said when he first came to Boston that in less than ten years he should be hobnobbing with Jim Bellingham, he should have told that person he lied. He would have told anybody he lied that had told him ten years ago that a son of Bromfield Corey would have come and asked him to take him into the business. Ten years ago he, Silas Lapham, had come to Boston a little worse off than nothing at all . . . and here he was now worth a million, and meeting you gentlemen like one of you. (Howells 1982: 1052)

Like the cruel conclusion of *Huckleberry Finn*, chapter 14 seems interminable, sinking Lapham ever deeper in a hopeless mire of embarrassment. As with Twain's masterpiece, however, the reader is likely to take perverse pleasure in the meanness of its comedy. By appealing to our most conservative instincts, the author cunningly has set his trap, baited with the prospect not of Lapham's triumph but of his humiliation.

Howells mercifully spares us from listening to the worst excesses of Lapham's debauch by employing (mostly) indirect discourse, but this narrative mode also shields his protagonist from irredeemable disgrace. (An unabridged, phonetically spelled transcription of Silas's slurred boasting surely would put him beyond the pale of any reader's sympathy.) Consequently, Lapham's morning-after conviction that he has made a fool of himself and his helpless need to abase himself before Tom Corey (an employee, after all) seem disproportionate to the actual nature of his social offense. Because young Corey still hopes to marry the boss's elder daughter, witnessing Lapham grovel only aggravates the injuries his Brahmin self-respect has already sustained.

> It had become a vital necessity with him to think the best of Lapham, but his mind was in a whirl of whatever thoughts were most injurious. He thought of him the night before in the company of those ladies and gentlemen, and he quivered in resentment of his vulgar, braggart, uncouth nature. He recognised his own allegiance to the exclusiveness to which he was born and bred, as a man perceives his duty to his country when her rights are invaded. . . . Amidst the stings and flashes of his wounded pride, all the social traditions, all the habits of feeling, which he had silenced more and more by force of will during the past months, asserted their natural sway, and he rioted in his

contempt of the offensive boor, who was even more offensive in his shame than in his trespass. (Howells 1982: 1057)

Inwardly, Corey explicitly names what we covertly have just experienced in finishing chapter 14 – a riot of contempt. Within the space of a paragraph, however, the young Bostonian quickly repudiates his prejudices and his sneering conclusions, thereby shaming himself and the reader simultaneously. Still aware of his love for Penelope, a stronger force than social caste, Corey can almost hear her voice pleading with him to see things in a fairer light, and he is pierced "with a thrill of sudden remorse." *His* failure of sympathy for an essentially innocent victim now seems more wrongful than Lapham's oafish transgressions – which, after all, were only to be expected from a newcomer to "society" (not to say wine). As eager witnesses to the scene of Lapham's downfall, we now find ourselves incriminated by the act of reading itself.

To discover that Howells was an early experimenter with reader-response theory should not come as much of a surprise, considering how many of his stories (including *Silas Lapham*) concern themselves with the social consequences of literacy and the shifting currents of popular taste. (That novel's romantic sub-plot hinges, in fact, on the characters' reading – or, more accurately, *mis*reading – of a drivel called *Tears, Idle Tears*.) Throughout the author's long career as a commentator on books as works of art and vehicles of acculturation, he displayed unflagging wariness about the debasing effect that popular fiction had on the nation's collective consciousness. Most notably in his monthly columns for *Harper's Monthly*, Howells relentlessly attacked the puerile romanticism of conventional novels and pleaded with readers to reject the excesses of passion and violence upon which formulaic fiction depends. As he concluded in *Criticism and Fiction* (1891), "It may be safely assumed that most of the novel-reading which people fancy an intellectual pastime is the emptiest dissipation, hardly more related to thought or the wholesome exercise of the mental faculties than opium-eating; in either case the brain is drugged, and left weaker and crazier for the debauch."

It just might be true, however, that publishing *Criticism and Fiction* was the biggest mistake that Howells ever made, since a handful of passages from it goaded the writers who later attacked him and precipitated his fall from grace. Even when Howells had occupied the "Editor's Study" for only two years, one of his oldest friends urged him to tone down his "monthly polemics." "It seems to me," Henry James advised, "that on occasions you mix things up that don't go together, sometimes make mistakes of proportion, & in general incline to insist more upon the restrictions & limitations, the *a priori* formulas & interdictions, of our common art, than upon that priceless freedom which is to me *the* thing that makes it worth practising" (Anesko 1997: 266). When Howells hurriedly pasted his book together from bits and pieces of his *Harper* columns, he did not altogether compensate for certain accidents of tone and implication that sharp-eyed readers might discover. The most notorious of Howells's apparently glib pronouncements averred that, in contrast to European novelists (who necessarily were burdened by the brutal legacy of feudal and aristocratic institutions), "our novelists . . . concern themselves with the more

Figure 25.1   The Dean of American letters

William Dean Howells – pictured here in 1874 while he was the editor of the *Atlantic* – was for nearly half a century synonymous with literary realism in America. He promoted the cause of realism in a prodigiously productive career as a novelist, playwright, essayist, reviewer, editor, and critic. His prolific criticism and reviews virtually delineated what realism could and should be, and although his own many novels are quite varied, they include books – like *A Modern Instance, A Hazard of New Fortunes*, and most especially *The Rise of Silas Lapham* – that are perhaps the purest examples of the genre. Howells was the single most powerful and influential literary critic of the period and the friend, adviser, and/or champion of a diverse range of American authors, including his oddly matched best friends, Mark Twain and Henry James, as well as Edith Wharton, George Washington Cable, Hamlin Garland, Sarah Orne Jewett, Stephen Crane, Charlotte Perkins Gilman, Henry Blake Fuller, Frank Norris, Charles W. Chesnutt, Mary E. Wilkins Freeman, and Abraham Cahan. He was even among the first to recognize the genius of Emily Dickinson. Like his friend James, he was well versed in the works of his European contemporaries, and his reviews brought to the attention of American readers such authors as Ivan Turgenev, Leo Tolstoy, George Eliot, Henrik Ibsen, Émile Zola, and Thomas Hardy. Although distinctly middle-class, both in his life and in his art, he possessed a great generosity of spirit toward writers unlike himself, and he was one of the few major authors to risk his reputation on behalf of the working classes and the downtrodden, as in his highly public defense of the workers arrested and executed after the Haymarket Riot.

By the time of his death, a new generation of writers, many of whom he had helped, had turned against him, considering him too timid, and today he has fallen into a relative, and unjust, neglect – a situation Howells himself somewhat anticipated and one that he would certainly have viewed with a customary sense of irony and stoic calm. (Photograph by permission of the Houghton Library, Harvard University.)

smiling aspects of life, which are the more American, and seek the universal in the individual rather than the social interests." Even writers who cut their teeth on Howells's novels – notably Dreiser and Lewis – choked when they got to *that* line. Howells's admittedly squeamish views on the representation of sex didn't help, either. Ironically, the critical vehicle through which Howells made the best case for expanding the range of our literary canon has been used to expel him from it.

Howells was neither ashamed nor afraid of using his editorial position to educate the public and expand its literary horizons. His monthly columns commented on a wide range of topics, books, and authors, and he frequently championed younger artists whose work probably overstepped some of his own self-prescribed bounds. Twain and James, of course, could count upon his steadfast endorsement (the latter very much in need of it, too). But Howells also brought many newer writers to the public's attention (Hamlin Garland and Harold Frederic, for example) and frequently discussed continental works of fiction that otherwise might have escaped notice altogether. In the process, it should be said, Howells also educated his own taste somewhat. In spite of – or, possibly, because of – James's chafing, Howells gradually did adopt a more open-minded critical point of view as his columns progressed, and he would demonstrate an even more catholic attitude toward innovative work in the decade ahead. The early American naturalists (Crane and Norris) benefited from his support; and he would even, at last, put in a good word for Zola.

Though one might not imagine it, considering the sheer volume of his critical output during these years, Howells did not spend all his time reading books. The turbulent social history of the 1880s had a profound effect on his artistic priorities. When the State of Illinois executed four suspected anarchists for the bombing of Chicago's Haymarket Square in 1886, Howells feared that his beloved Republic was collapsing. Not even circumstantial evidence could link the accused prisoners to the scene of violence, but a frenzied public, eager for retribution, discounted their alibis. Trial by newspaper supplanted trial by jury. Utterly alone among American men of letters, Howells made a public appeal for clemency; but the hangman had his day. A grim awareness of this grotesque inversion of civic values pervades the later novels of this decade – particularly *Annie Kilburn* (1889) and the urban panorama, *A Hazard of New Fortunes* (1890) – both of which address the theme of economic inequality and the complicity of middle-class Americans in the destructive tendencies of the nation's social life.

Howells's lonely gesture on behalf of the defendants in the Haymarket Affair should remind us that the vital link between his literary and social priorities has not always been properly appreciated. What Howells (in *Criticism and Fiction*) demanded of the artist – "the truthful treatment of material" – was precisely what he expected of a court of law or any other democratic institution: a proper regard for the evidence in conducting its proceedings. Howells denigrated romance and senti- mentality because their promiscuous indulgence by popular writers paralleled, in a literary sense, the violation of public trust that he witnessed in the nation's economic and political life. The four men hanged in Chicago on November 11, 1887, "would be alive today," he wrote, "if one thousandth part of the means employed to compass their death had been used by the people to inquire into the question of their guilt; for, under the forms of law, their trial has not been a trial by justice, but a trial by passion, by terror, by prejudice, by newspaper." The same agencies – passion and terror – that Howells decried in bestselling novels, he also held responsible for the gravest miscarriage of justice the nation had yet seen. On that November day in 1887 four men died, "in the prime of the first Republic the world has ever known, for their opinions' sake" (Howells 1968– : vol. 3, 201–4). Howells's courage waned before he could make *that* opinion public, but he preserved it for a time when journalism would cease and history could begin.

Not very long after Howells conceded that American conditions conspired to invite the country's writers to focus on the more smiling aspects of life, he felt obliged to register his own dissent. Responding to one of Henry James's perpetual complaints about their native land, Howells confessed:

> I'm not in a very good humor with "America" myself. It seems to me the most grotesquely illogical thing under the sun; and I suppose I love it less because it wont let me love it more. I should hardly like to trust pen and ink with all the audacity of my social ideas; but after fifty years of optimistic content with "civilization" and its ability to come out all right in the end, I now abhor it, and feel that it is coming out all wrong in the end, unless it bases itself anew on a real equality. (Anesko 1997: 272)

That view, expressed privately to James in October 1888, assumed narrative form in *A Hazard of New Fortunes*, which began its serial run in *Harper's Weekly* the following year. Howells's semi-autobiographical protagonist, Basil March, gradually discovers the grotesque illogic of modern America after he moves his family from Boston to New York, where he intends to pursue a new career as the editor of an upstart literary magazine, *Every Other Week*. March's removal from New England to Manhattan parallels Howells's transfer of allegiance from the stolid publishing world of Boston to Franklin Square, where he had signed what was to be the first of several long-term contracts with Harper & Brothers in 1885. Committed by long practice to make novelistic use of his own private and professional experiences, Howells pursued a similar strategy in his new novel, but arguably with a greater degree of honest self-criticism. The author had first created Basil and Isabel March as he recorded the romantic itinerary of *Their Wedding Journey* in 1872, and he continued the serial chronicle of their married life through many other stories and novels. The jarring material circumstances of *Hazard* deliberately disturb the moral and social complacency to which the Marches have become accustomed among their genteel peers in Boston. New York exposes them to brutal new facts – forms of poverty that can no longer be viewed as picturesque, inequalities of status that make a mockery of democratic ideals, the real power of money to corrupt whatever it touches. March comes to see that even the world of letters offers no refuge from these facts – and that, in fact, it shouldn't. He wants the magazine to become the voice of his aggrieved liberal conscience, and for his readers to understand that the real function of literature is to help them be kinder to their fellows, juster to themselves, and truer to all. That credo does not literally appear in *Hazard*'s text (it comes from Howells's 1899 lecture, "Novel-Writing and Novel-Reading"), but its implications are felt on almost every page.

Interfering with March's generous goal is the fact that the principal patron of *Every Other Week* is a hard-driving businessman who wants to exploit the cultural capital of the magazine as a means to win social approval for his *arriviste* family. Jacob Dryfoos is no Silas Lapham, however. No residuum of agrarian virtue or respect for honest labor survives his transplantation to the city. Once natural gas is discovered on his Indiana farmland, the mercenary poison of unearned wealth infiltrates his very nature. After meeting the magazine's owner for the first time, March cannot repress his reservations when describing him to Isabel:

> "I don't believe a man's any better for having made money so easily and rapidly as Dryfoos has done, and I doubt if he's any wiser. I don't know just the point he's reached in his evolution from grub to beetle, but I do know that so far as it's gone the process must have involved a bewildering change of ideals and criterions. I guess he's come to despise a great many things that he once respected, and that intellectual ability is among them – what *we* call intellectual ability. He must have undergone a moral deterioration, an atrophy of the generous instincts, and I don't see why it shouldn't have reached his mental makeup. He has sharpened, but he has narrowed; his sagacity has turned into suspicion, his caution to meanness, his courage to ferocity." (Howells 1994: 193–4)

From this first encounter with his grizzled employer (who bears a rather striking resemblance to John D. Rockefeller), March intuits that, sooner or later, his editorial freedom will be compromised. As he humbly puts it to his wife, "the man that holds the purse holds the reins" (Howells 1994: 194). Anticipating that inevitable challenge – and March's response to it – Howells sustains dramatic interest while enabling his various characters to fill in a sweeping canvas of late nineteenth-century urban life.

In contrast to many of Howells's other books, in which the reader's attention gravitates toward a relatively small number of figures, *Hazard* is almost prodigal in its creation of vivid people, all spread across a surprisingly diverse social field. No one understood this better than Henry James, who wrote Howells at great length to congratulate him on his imaginative triumph. "*Hazard* is simply prodigious," James averred. "The life, the truth, the light, the heat, the breadth & depth & thickness . . . are absolutely admirable" (Anesko 1997: 275). Besides Basil and Isabel (already familiar but still with recesses of character to yield up), Howells introduces us to a host of others who occupy strategic positions along what might be called a rhetorical spectrum. (Howells, too, could do the police in different voices.) Since few of the novel's New Yorkers are genuine natives, their speech reflects the various regions from which they come. Piles of money cannot flatten the hard country accents of the Dryfooses; and phonetic spelling helps Howells recreate the Southern drawl of

Colonel Woodburn and his daughter. More interesting, though, and more central to the novel's thematic preoccupations, is the character of Fulkerson, the irrepressible business manager of *Every Other Week*, whose flare for vernacular and disarming personality work to keep the unstable enterprise afloat. An advertising man at heart, Fulkerson embodies and gives voice to a style that brims with exaggerated confidence in the virtues it professes. Without really knowing it, he uses language as a cloak for the power of Capital, mystifying its origins while effectively doing its bidding. Without his genial solicitation in the opening chapter, March would never have been persuaded to abandon the security of his insurance job in Boston for the hazards of New York. It is only fitting that, in the novel's climactic scene (again, a dinner party), Fulkerson literally speaks for Dryfoos, colorfully narrating his rags-to-riches story, one episode of which involves a cunning maneuver in strike-breaking. "'No, no!' cried Fulkerson. 'Let *me* tell that! I know you wouldn't do yourself justice, Mr. Dryfoos, and I want 'em to know how a strike can be managed, if you take it in time'" (Howells 1994: 295–6). Fulkerson's magic phrasing transforms social tragedy into an exalted flight of Western humor; his subject's human cost evaporates in a cloud of laughter. "'Such a *coup* as that would tell tremendously in a play,'" one auditor tellingly exclaims. Why should art imitate life when, instead, it can simply imitate art?

Another listener, who is *not* amused, is the German immigrant Lindau, a man who came to America in order to help Lincoln free the slaves and sacrificed one of his arms in the process. "That was vile treason," he says – in German – to his friend, Basil March. "He's an infamous traitor! I cannot stay here. I must go." In stark contrast to Fulkerson's humorous euphemisms, Lindau's unvarnished words express unflattering truths, but his rhetorical standing in the text is curiously unstable. Only in fluent *Hochdeutsch* can he express American ideals (rendered by Howells in standard English). When Lindau speaks the language of his adopted country, however, his impassioned words come out as guttural distortions. Frustrated by the business manager's glib complacency, Lindau lashes out at his easy tolerance for the concentration of wealth that was becoming more and more conspicuous in the streets (and slums) of New York. "'Hold on; hold on now, Lindau!'" Fulkerson objects,

> "Ain't that rather un-American doctrine? We're all brought up, ain't we, to honor the man that made his money, and look down – or try to look down; sometimes it's difficult – on the fellow that his father left it to?"
>
> The old man rose and struck his breast. "On-Amerigan!" he roared, and as he went on, his accent grew more and more uncertain. "What iss Amerigan? Dere *iss* no Ameriga anymore! You start here free and brafe, and you glaim for efery man de righdt to life, liperty, and de bursuit of habbiness. And where haf you entedt? No man that vorks vith his handts among you hass the liperty to bursue his habbiness." (Howells 1994: 276)

When Howells told Henry James that he could barely trust his pen to paper to express his disillusion with "America," he wasn't kidding. Instead, he displaced his most profound discontent through Lindau's fractured idiom, the crippled speech of a crippled man. The cherished Jacksonian democracy of his Ohio boyhood seemed gone forever. As he lamented in *A Boy's Town* (1890), "I have tried to give some notion of the general distribution of comfort which was never riches in the Boy's Town; but I am afraid that I could not paint the simplicity of things there truly without being misunderstood in these days of great splendor and great squalor. Everybody had enough, but nobody had too much. . . . "

Und dann gab es kein Amerika mehr.

Howells lived another thirty years, but he never wrote another novel equal to *A Hazard of New Fortunes*. At his memorial service in New York City on May 12, 1920, the *Times* noted that an "outpouring of representative men and women in the world of American letters" crowded the solemn chapel to pay their respects. "But, as if by common consent, those in charge of the arrangements had decided that Howells's place in both literature and life was too well established and too adequately granted to require further stress," and so no eulogy was offered (Anon. 1920: 11). Surely Howells, secure within his coffin, would have known that the newspaper got it wrong.

SELECTED PRIMARY TEXTS BY WILLIAM DEAN HOWELLS

Poems of Two Friends (with John James Piatt). 1859.

Lives and Speeches of Abraham Lincoln and Hannibal Hamlin (with John L. Hayes). 1860.

Venetian Life. 1866.

Italian Journeys. 1867.

Suburban Sketches. 1871.

Their Wedding Journey. 1872.

A Chance Acquaintance. 1873.

A Foregone Conclusion. 1875.

The Lady of the Aroostook. 1879.

The Undiscovered Country. 1880.

A Fearful Responsibility. 1881.

A Modern Instance. 1882.

The Rise of Silas Lapham. 1885.

Indian Summer. 1886.

The Minister's Charge. 1887.

April Hopes. 1888.

Annie Kilburn. 1889.

A Boy's Town. 1890.

A Hazard of New Fortunes. 1890.

The Shadow of a Dream. 1890.

Criticism and Fiction. 1891.

An Imperative Duty. 1892.

The Quality of Mercy. 1892.

The Coast of Bohemia. 1893.

The World of Chance. 1893.

A Traveler from Altruria. 1894.

My Literary Passions. 1895.

The Landlord at Lion's Head. 1897.

Their Silver Wedding Journey. 1899.

"Novel-Writing and Novel-Reading." 1899.

Literary Friends and Acquaintance: A Personal Retrospect of American Authorship. 1900.

Literature and Life. 1902.

Letters Home. 1903.

The Son of Royal Langbrith. 1904.

Through the Eye of the Needle. 1907.

Fennel and Rue. 1908.

My Mark Twain: Reminiscences and Criticisms. 1910.

New Leaf Mills: A Chronicle. 1913.

The Leatherwood God. 1916.

Years of My Youth. 1916.

The Vacation of the Kelwyns. 1920.

Mrs. Farrell. 1921. (Publ. in *Atlantic Monthly*, 1875–6, as *Private Theatricals*.)

LATER COLLECTIONS

Howells, W. D. (1928). *Life in Letters of William Dean Howells*, 2 vols., ed. Mildred Howells. Garden City, NY: Doubleday, Doran.

Howells, W. D. (1968–). *A Selected Edition of W. D. Howells*, 25 vols. to date, ed. David J. Nordloh and Christoph K. Lohmann. Bloomington: Indiana University Press. (Includes 6 vols. of *Selected Letters* published jointly with Twayne.)

Howells, W. D. (1983). *Editor's Study*, comp. James W. Simpson. Troy, NY: Whitson.

Howells, W. D. (1994). *Staging Howells: Plays and Correspondence with Lawrence Barrett*, ed. George Arms, Mary Bess Whidden, and Gary Scharnhorst. Albuquerque: University of New Mexico Press.

Howells, W. D., and Twain, Mark (1962). *Mark Twain–Howells Letters*, 2 vols., ed. Henry Nash Smith and William H. Gibson. Cambridge, Mass.: Harvard University Press.

REFERENCES AND FURTHER READING

Anesko, Michael (1997). *Letters, Fictions, Lives: Henry James and William Dean Howells*. New York: Oxford University Press.

Anon. (1885). Review of *The Rise of Silas Lapham*. *Saturday Review*, Oct. 17, 517–18.

Anon. (1920). "Simple Rites Mark Howells Funeral." *New York Times*, May 13, p. 11, col. 3.

Cady, Edwin (1956). *The Road to Realism: The Early Years 1837–1885 of William Dean Howells*. Syracuse, NY: Syracuse University Press.

Cady, Edwin (1958). *The Realist at War: The Mature Years 1885–1920 of William Dean Howells*. Syracuse, NY: Syracuse University Press.

Cady, Edwin, and Cady, Norma, eds. (1983). *Critical Essays on W. D. Howells, 1866–1920*. Boston: Hall.

Cady, Edwin, and Budd, Louis G., eds. (1993). *On Howells*. Durham, NC: Duke University Press.

Carter, Everett (1954). *Howells and the Age of Realism*. Philadelphia: Lippincott.

Crowley, John W. (1985). *The Black Heart's Truth: The Early Career of W. D. Howells*. Chapel Hill: University of North Carolina Press.

Crowley, John W. (1989). *The Mask of Fiction: Essays on W. D. Howells*. Amherst: University of Massachusetts Press.

Crowley, John W. (1999). *The Dean of American Letters: The Late Career of William Dean Howells*. Amherst: University of Massachusetts Press.

Davidson, Rob (2005). *The Master and the Dean: The Literary Criticism of Henry James and William Dean Howells*. Columbia: University of Missouri Press.

Fryckstedt, Olov W. (1958). *In Quest of America: A Study of Howells's Early Development as a Novelist*. Cambridge, Mass.: Harvard University Press.

Fuller, Henry Blake (1907). ALS to William Dean Howells, Feb. 27. Howells Papers, Houghton Library, Harvard University.

Gibson, William M., and Arms, G. (1948). *A Bibliography of William Dean Howells*. New York: New York Public Library.

Gosse, Edmund (1885). "A Great American Novel." *Pall Mall Gazette*, Sept. 11, 8.

Harland, Henry (1887). ALS to William Dean Howells, Aug. 3. Howells Papers, Houghton Library, Harvard University.

Higginson, Thomas Wentworth (1880). *Short Studies of American Authors*. Boston: Lee & Shepard.

Howells, Elinor Mead (1988). *If Not Literature: Letters of Elinor Mead Howells*, ed. Ginette de B. Merrill and George Warren Arms. Columbus: Ohio State University Press for Miami University.

Howells, William Dean (1982). *The Rise of Silas Lapham*. In *Novels 1875–1886*, ed. Edwin H. Cady. New York: Library of America.

Howells, William Dean (1994). *A Hazard of New Fortunes*. New York: Meridian.

Lewis, Sinclair (1953). "The American Fear of Literature" (first publ. 1930). In Harry E. Maule and Melville H. Cane (eds.), *The Man from Main Street: A Sinclair Lewis Reader*, 3–17. New York: Random House.

Lynn, Kenneth S. (1971). *William Dean Howells: An American Life*. New York: Harcourt Brace Jovanovich.

Mencken, H. L. (1949). "The Dean" (first publ. 1917). In *A Mencken Chrestomathy*, 489–92. New York: Knopf.

Nettels, Elsa (1980). "William Dean Howells and the American Language." *New England Quarterly* 53, 308–28.

Nettels, Elsa (1988). *Language, Race, and Social Class in Howells's America*. Lexington: University Press of Kentucky.

Olson, Rodney D. (1991). *Dancing in Chains: The Youth of William Dean Howells*. New York: New York University Press.

Pease, Donald E., ed. (1991). *New Essays on* The Rise of Silas Lapham. New York: Cambridge University Press.

Prioleau, Elizabeth Stevens (1983). *The Circle of Eros: Sexuality in the Work of William Dean Howells*. Durham, NC: Duke University Press.

Simpson, Lewis P. (1973). "The Treason of William Dean Howells." In *The Man of Letters in New England and the South*, 85–128. Baton Rouge: Louisiana State University Press.

Tocqueville, Alexis de (1969). *Democracy in America*, ed. J. P. Mayer, trans. George Lawrence. Garden City, NY: Doubleday-Anchor. (First publ. 1835, 1940.)

Vanderbilt, Kermit (1968). *The Achievement of William Dean Howells*. Princeton, NJ: Princeton University Press.

26

Henry James in a New Century
John Carlos Rowe

The revival of interest in Henry James's writings in the 1990s and into the new century has attracted considerable comment from scholars and public intellectuals. Feature films based on *The Portrait of a Lady*, *Washington Square*, *The Wings of the Dove*, and *The Golden Bowl* have been accompanied by republication of virtually all of Henry James's writings, including minor novels, for example *The Outcry*, and such nonfiction as his travel writings and literary criticism. One reasonable explanation is that Henry James (1843–1916) so exemplifies high culture at the turn of the nineteenth to twentieth centuries that the revival of interest in his work must suggest some return to the sophisticated aesthetic values of a more cultivated age. In our era of overnight celebrities, video-game and computer obsessions, television news soundbites, sitcom humor, and standup one-liners, the difficulty of Henry James's prose may present a refreshing alternative to the superficiality of postmodern culture. Indeed, this renewed interest in James may be extended to some of his most important modernist heirs, including James Joyce, Gertrude Stein, and T. S. Eliot, each of whom explicitly acknowledged Henry James's formative influence (Rowe 2000b: 190–1).

Yet such an explanation can only be partial, because it implies that Henry James and many other moderns hold interest for us because they represent a neo-conservative, even politically reactionary, desire to recall the aesthetic values of an earlier period, when culture had substance and literary celebrity was built upon enduring traditions. The legend of Henry James as the "master" of the modern novel certainly reinforces this idea, and virtually every reader of Henry James can testify to that literary authority by recalling his or her first encounter with his daunting prose style. In 1913 John Singer Sargent painted the famous portrait of Henry James today displayed in the National Gallery in London. The portrait had been commissioned by James's friends in celebration of the author's seventieth birthday, and it was publicly exhibited in Sargent's studio and then in the Spring Exhibition of the Royal Academy (Edel 1972: 490). Yet in "May 1914,...a militant suffragette broke the glass protecting his portrait...," drew "a meat cleaver concealed under her coat, . . . [and] made three long slashes in the painting" (Kaplan 1992: 551). Mrs. Mary Wood knew nothing about Henry James's writings, but claimed to be protesting the disparity in value between portraits by men, especially famous artists like Sargent, and women: "A woman painter, she said, would not have received anywhere near" the £700 at which Sargent's portrait was valued (Edel 1972: 490). This bizarre attack on James's image may not have been targeted at Henry James or his writings, but it is reasonable to conclude that Mrs. Wood was also attracted to the imposing authority Sargent rendered in James's head and vested torso. As an icon, James's portrait must have seemed the exemplification of upper-class patriarchy in Georgian England.

Yet behind that familiar facade of the "Master," whose intricate style and deft manipulation of the formal properties of the modern novel have often frustrated readers, Henry James was a figure of enormous contradictions and personal self-doubts. An admirer of eighteenth-century architecture and cultural styles, he was one of the great avant-garde experimentalists of the late nineteenth and early twentieth centuries. Prone to mock new technologies like the automobile, telegraph, and typewriter, he invariably included references to the most modern conveniences in his writings and used many of them on a daily basis. Anxious about changing attitudes toward women's rights and their growing visibility in the public sphere, James nonetheless produced literature that still deserves its reputation as supportive of feminist issues, especially as far as the complexity and sophistication of his women characters are concerned. Few writers of his generation can compete with his extraordinarily nuanced accounts of what it meant and felt to be a woman in many different social contexts in England and America. Contemptuous of more outspoken and politically radical artists, like the Decadents and Symbolists, James published in the *Yellow Book* and seems often to be competing with the extremity of such writers as Oscar Wilde, John Addington Symonds, and Algernon Charles Swinburne. Sexually ambivalent in his private life and reluctant to identify with the affirmative homosexuality of Wilde and Symonds, James nonetheless addresses homosexual themes positively throughout his career (Rowe 1998: 27–37). Finally, James is celebrated as one of the great American authors, whose works explore consistently the contact zone between US and European cultures; but James was made a British subject by King George V in 1915 and wrote often in apparent support of British cultural and at times political superiority over other nations, including the United States (Edel 1972: 531).

These problems and contradictions in Henry James's life and work have made him a topic of the greatest interest to scholars. He ranks with William Shakespeare, James Joyce, and William Faulkner as one of the most frequently discussed authors. Yet for these same reasons, he is often baffling and daunting to students and other readers unfamiliar with his works. Some of these difficulties can be attributed to Henry James's very difficult prose style, which grew more complex and involuted as he matured as a writer and late in his career experimented with modernist techniques of narration, especially in the three novels of his so-called "Major Phase": *The Wings of the Dove* (1902), *The Ambassadors* (1903), and *The Golden Bowl* (1904). Although well known as an important literary realist, especially in his novels and stories from *The Portrait of a Lady* (1881) to *What Maisie Knew* (1897) and *The Awkward Age* (1899), he was also profoundly influenced by his Romantic predecessors, especially Nathaniel Hawthorne, and began his literary career writing modern versions of such familiar romantic plots as star-crossed lovers (*Daisy Miller* [1879]) and the hero resisting implacable destiny (*The American* [1877]). Throughout his career James relied on Romantic themes and motifs, even formal characteristics of the nineteenth-century romance, in numerous ghost stories and tales of the supernatural, including such celebrated works as *The Turn of the Screw* (1898), "The Beast in the Jungle" (1903), and "The Jolly Corner" (1908). The famous "difficulty" of Henry James's work is thus not solely a consequence of his avant-garde use of different points of view, stream-of-consciousness narration, and deliberately disjointed fictional temporality; it is also a consequence of the great variety of literary forms and genres he employed in a long career during which he published twenty-two novels and novellas (with two others, *The Sense of the Past* [1917] and *The Ivory Tower* [1917], published posthumously), 114 short stories, three volumes of autobiography, five volumes of travel writings (including his social criticism of America in *The American Scene* [1907]), several volumes of literary criticism (including *Nathaniel Hawthorne* [1879]), and countless book reviews, journalism, and uncollected essays on a wide range of artistic and literary topics.

Social, economic, political, and cultural changes in James's lifetime must also contribute to the difficulty of his works for today's reader. His father, Henry James, Sr., was a member of the New England Transcendentalists and the author of numerous philosophical writings, many deeply influenced by Immanuel Swedenborg. Henry James grew up in the world of the American Romantics, such as Emerson, Fuller, and Thoreau, many of whom were deeply suspicious of modernization and insistently American in their commitments. Yet the James family traveled widely, taking up residence in various European cities during James's youth and adolescence, so that he was imbued with European cultural values. By 1875 James was a permanent resident of Europe; when he returned to the United States for a lecture tour in 1904–5, recording his impressions in *The American Scene*, it was not unlike Spencer Brydon's "strangely belated return," full of "unattenuated surprises" in "The Jolly Corner" (James 1909d: 435). Many scholars have noted that Henry James found Europe attractive for its long cultural history, perhaps even for its repudiation of the modernity so relentlessly represented by US commercialism in the post-Civil War era. By the same token, Europe was changing dramatically, as James himself recorded in his foreign correspondence from Paris for the *New York Tribune* between 1875 and 1876 (collected posthumously in *Parisian Sketches* [1957]), in the aftermath of the Franco-Prussian War (1871–2) and at the beginning of a new European geopolitical map (Rowe 1997: 190–1).

Drawn to the historical density of European culture, raised in a family deeply influenced by the values of the late Enlightenment and the early nineteenth-century Romantics, Henry James also had to adapt to an increasingly international and cosmopolitan culture. More than any writer of his generation, James attempted to respond to social and political transformations that often baffled and confused him, and thus his amazing literary output is characterized by numerous formal as well as intellectual changes. Previous scholars have often addressed the variety of James's career by strictly periodizing it into the "early" Romantic writings, deeply influenced by New England Transcendentalism, his "middle" period of committed psychological realism, and a "late" (or Major Phase) devoted to experiments in the novel today considered fundamental to Anglo-American literary modernism. Contemporary scholars have continued this work by extending James's career to include a "fourth phase," as it is sometimes called, in which such later works as his cultural criticism in *The American Scene* and his posthumously published novels, *The Ivory Tower* and *The Sense of the Past*, as well as such previously neglected works as *The Outcry* (1911), are treated as indications of James's response to the new phase of global modernization launched abruptly by the outbreak of World War I. There are many advantages to dividing James's literary career into manageable and describable periods, especially for the reader daunted by its complexity and volume. On the other hand, this scholarly desire for order may unintentionally falsify what makes Henry James so compelling to us today in the twenty-first century: his personal ambivalence, intellectual changes, and even contradictions anticipate our own continuing problems with a modernization process that is now thoroughly global and by most accounts postmodern. Reconsidering Henry James from the perspective of our new century and understanding how he struggled with his own new century, we can find some common concerns that run consistently through his career, especially with regard to the United States as a global power and to the well-educated citizen as inevitably cosmopolitan.

I

In the general context of James's notorious "difficulty," then, I propose to answer the question asked by most readers who are not specialists: "Why should I read Henry James?" Many scholars answer this question directly by demonstrating that Henry James is among the best novelists of his time and arguing that his aesthetic values are much needed in our culturally superficial era. I wish to take seriously the image I have outlined above of Henry James as often contradictory, sometimes confused, and yet always intelligent and curious about the modern world that changed dramatically in his lifetime. How Henry James responded to the modernization process, even when he was thoroughly baffled by it, provides an analogy with how we might understand our often confusing circumstances at the beginning of the twenty-first century. I do not mean to argue that James's modern and our postmodern eras are the same; I do mean to show that these two eras are intimately connected and that, by reading Henry James carefully, we can better understand that crucial history. In these respects, Henry James still has relevance for us today.

There are, then, three equally important ways to discuss Henry James and modernity. First, James's responses to the modernization process anticipate many of our concerns with the one-way globalization practiced by first-world nations and transnational corporations, and the concomitant reconfiguration of second- and third-world economies as they are made to serve this process in increasingly inequitable ways. Second, James was a witness to and participant in the early stages of today's globalization, wherein second-stage modernization, characterized by Taylorism and Fordism, developed together with the consolidation of the British empire in its growing competition with lesser European imperial powers and the emergence of the United States and Japan as colonial forces, if not outright imperial powers. Third, James has become a typical commodity of postmodern cultural capital, and the very process through which he has been commodified as a status symbol (high culture) or social critic (feminist, gay, Marxist) is an interesting example of how culture contributes to a system of value tied to the global circulation, rather than consumption, of its products. All three of these approaches are related if we take the longer view of globalization as a process of modernization traceable to the European desire to "discover" new lands. In short, the discussion of globalization begins properly with the European effort to conquer and then colonize the western hemisphere, and the long cultural history through which this violent origin for modernity has been rationalized (Rowe 2002: xx).

James traces many modern problems back to the conquest and colonization of the Americas. Christopher Newman's name in *The American* has prompted a great variety of critically ingenious interpretations, but at a basic level James links Columbus's given name, Christianity's complicity in European colonialism, and the Enlightenment's dream of the "new man" merely to remind us of a history we repeat precisely because we won't remember its horrors. The irony of Newman's pioneering journey east to France, rather than to the West, also reminds us that the feverish desire to escape the old, dark, sinful Europe generally ends up repressing our responsibility for it. Newman acts out that European colonial destiny in the United States before heading for France, so the irony turns out to be illusory and the serious argument remains. As he takes that "immortal historical hack" to wreak vengeance on some Wall Street competitor who has done him a business injury, and as he builds a fortune in those vaguely described entrepreneurial ventures in washtubs and railroads in the equally sketchy Midwest and San Francisco, Newman announces to the reader that the legacy of European colonialism is not only alive and well in his new world, but is morphing into a new, potentially even more poisonous version in the figure of the cosmopolitan capitalist (James 1907: 30; Rowe 1997: 179–84).

Christopher Newman, even though he is thoroughly American, nevertheless displays a capacity for colonial conquest, at least at the imaginary and psychological levels, that Henry James quite consistently analyzes and criticizes throughout his long literary career. Prince Amerigo in *The Golden Bowl* appears long after Christopher Newman and has a radically different lineage. Adam Verver is Newman's equivalent and even namesake (if we equate "Adam" with "Newman") in this novel, and the

Prince's mushy moral sense is modeled on the Victorian type of the shabby Italian aristocrat, who would appear to have little in common with the robust, innocent, albeit deluded Yankee, Christopher Newman. But the Prince's vaguely identified, perhaps apocryphal ancestor Amerigo Vespucci is the early explorer who truly conquers America, because his name is adopted. Mapping America, it would seem, has more lasting value than mere physical discovery, because for James it refers to the cultural appropriation he so often criticizes as neo-colonial even as he owns his part in it. In *The Golden Bowl*, there are numerous connotations of Prince Amerigo's historical name, but the simple meaning is that the Italian culture James and his readers so love is implicated in the more violent history of colonization. W. E. B. Du Bois puts this matter much more bluntly in "Africa and the Slave Trade" (1915): "Such is the story of the Rape of Ethiopia – a sordid, pitiful, cruel tale. Raphael painted, Luther preached, Corneille wrote, and Milton sung; and through it all, for four hundred years, the dark captives wound to the sea amid the bleaching bones of the dead. . . . for four hundred years America was strewn with the living and dying millions of a transplanted race . . . " (Du Bois 1996: 637).

James is by no means as explicitly political as Du Bois, but the ambivalence of his love for Italy throughout his life is explained in part by the warning the "ruins" so loved by his Victorian predecessors seem to offer him of the new American empire and its tendency to repeat the mistakes of previous empires. Thus James's famous international theme frequently enacts the new US will-to-power in the polite drawing rooms, public gardens, galleries, and artists' workshops of American expatriates in Italy, where they have traveled to study how to recapture the glory that was Rome and forget just what horrors are inscribed dimly on those pillars and capitals in the Forum and the Colosseum. In *Daisy Miller*, Rome is not just a cultivated setting for the psychological drama between Daisy and Winterbourne; James also uses it as a landscape of the soul for both of these Americans. For Winterbourne, Rome represents moral rot, probably tangled up with his contempt for Catholics, loose morals, and the city's poor public hygiene in the late nineteenth century. Legitimate tourist concerns to be sure, especially for the Protestant expatriate visiting from Geneva by way of Salem; but they happen to be disturbingly similar to the anxieties of so many US travelers in the tropics of South America and Africa to this day.

On the other hand, Daisy seems to thrive in this unhealthy moral climate, however briefly. Daisy's sexuality hardly seems threatening in the era of internet pornography and the global sex trade, but for Winterbourne it represents the transgression of proper social boundaries, notably those regulating class and gender. Daisy does not behave as a lady should, and Winterbourne first notices this impropriety when she fraternizes with people from the working class. Although she apparently does not remember Byron's "The Prisoner of Chillon" and its democratic sentiments, she wants to travel to Chillon by steamer to be with other people (whereas Winterbourne wants to take a private carriage and does so on their return). When Winterbourne meets her in the lobby of the hotel in Vevey for the trip to Chillon, James describes it as a public place where "the couriers, the servants, the foreign tourists were lounging about and staring. It wasn't the place he would have chosen for a tryst, but she had placidly appointed it" (James 1909c: 158). Winterbourne's "stiff," Calvinistic individualism is elitist, whereas Daisy's openness and social gregariousness have a democratic aura. We are reminded, then, of a certain linkage between the feminine, the crowd and mob, democratic freedom, and how they provoked ruling-class anxieties in the nineteenth century. In the early days of the US republic, these anxieties about the democratic mob were often projected onto specific groups, ranging from the traveling "Illuminati" to the dreaded "Free Masons," radical French intellectuals (a persistent anxiety, it seems, in the United States), and "Indians" (Rowe 2000a: 38–9). In the last quarter of the nineteenth century, these sources of anxiety included women, homosexuals, immigrants, free African Americans, and Mexicans. Daisy's identification with some sort of populist solidarity, albeit left undeveloped in *Daisy Miller*, suggests one way James imagined how groups differently marginalized in different eras might take a historically long view that would allow them to build effective coalitions.

But the serious global implication of *Daisy Miller* is that the political issues in 1878 are increasingly transnational, given not only the imperial expansion of nations but also the mobility of their ruling citizens and the peoples who work for them. Future political causes, James seems to hint in *Daisy Miller*, will involve more global consciousness, which of course he is happy to provide as the guiding spirit of a critical cosmopolitanism. Daisy appears to be a somewhat tamer fictional version of Louisa Lander, the American woman sculptor in Rome chastised by William Wetmore Story (head of that fussy clan of American expatriate artists in Rome) for posing in the nude and living out of wedlock with an Italian (Rowe 2002: 86–8). James's ambivalent account in *William Wetmore Story and His Friends* (1903) of the American colony in Rome criticizes its members for cultural colonialism and indicts himself for enjoying so thoroughly their cultivation. Story reading "so richly and forcibly" from his neoclassical drama *Nero*, a chapter from "the more 'lurid' Roman past," seems almost comical in James's account, were it not for James's fond memories of Fanny Kemble, to whom Story dedicated *Nero*, in that intimate audience, "whose admirable face was less at play than when it accompanied her admirable voice" (James 1903: vol. 2, 254–5). Thus as the moral leader of this little American colony abroad thunders warnings about ancient Roman despotism and decadence, the young James of the 1870s dreamily fantasizes about the alluring Anglo-American actress. The scene might have been lifted directly from *Daisy Miller*.

James hopes to avoid the fate of those American expatriates whom Madame Merle dismisses in her own self-condemnation: "We're mere parasites, crawling over the surface; we haven't our feet in the soil" (James 1908a: 280). She does not escape this criticism, but James claims to do so insofar as he refuses to worship either the European past or American futurity, seeing them instead as parts of the same cultural history. On the one hand, the American abroad may fetishize European culture, as Gilbert Osmond of *The Portrait of a Lady* does with his careful copies of old Roman coins and Adam Verver does with his purchases of European art for his museum in American City. On the other hand, the future of artistic success and innovation may well end up serving a new imperium, either British or American. Maud Lowder wields her power over the social relations in *The Wings of the Dove* as an explicit "Britannia," the allegorical figure of British authority. In *The Tragic Muse* (1890), Peter Sherringham wants to marry the actress Miriam Rooth and adapt her theatrical talents to the social role of the diplomat's wife in some "little hot hole in Central America," where the Foreign Office is posting him. His plan is on the face of it ridiculous, but James makes the more serious point that the new influence of art will be global in scope and political in its effects. Even in those passages where he admires Miriam's international reputation (and cosmopolitan identity), James expresses anxiety about unbounded powers of the imagination, once they are unmoored from their representative locale, whether it be the "New England charm" of his cultural fathers or his adopted England. James is as dazzled and confused as Peter Sherringham by Miriam's performance of Constance in Shakespeare's *King John*: "Miriam was a beautiful actual fictive impossible young woman of a past age, an undiscoverable country, who spoke in blank verse and overflowed with metaphor, who was exalted and heroic beyond all human convenience and who yet was irresistibly real and related to one's own affairs" (James 1908b: vol. 8, 327).

II

Edward Said has demonstrated how the novel's contribution to nationalism is always entangled with the nation's reliance on foreign wealth, labor, and culture. In Jane Austen's lovely British romance *Mansfield Park*, Sir Thomas Bertram's plantations in Antigua provide the borders of the fictional gardens (Said 1993: 85). Austen and Charlotte Brontë in *Jane Eyre* used the Caribbean contexts of slavery and feudalism primarily as factual backgrounds rather than for purposes of political critique, requiring Said and Jean Rhys's *Wide Sargasso Sea* (1962) respectively for us to understand the ideological consequences of these famous love stories, but James consistently implicates culture in the work of imperial expansion and domination. Said observes that "Henry James's Ralph Touchett in *Portrait of a Lady* travels in Algeria and Egypt," but James uses such scenic details for far more critical purposes than such contemporaries as Kipling, Haggard, and Arthur Conan Doyle who imagined the East (Said 1993: 63). How else are we to understand John Marcher's Orientalized "beast," that "tiger" he avoids even in "the depths of Asia," where he spends "himself on scenes of romantic interest, of superlative sanctity" (James 1909b: 199)? To be sure, James could be charmed by the lure of the exoticized "Orient," as he confesses in his introduction to Pierre Loti's *Impressions*, even identifying it with the lure of forbidden sexuality: "Loti's East is, throughout, of all Easts the most beguiling, though, for the most part – unless perhaps in the case of *Au Maroc*, where he appears to have been peculiarly initiated – it seldom ceases to be the usual, accessible East . . . of the English and American swarm" (Loti 1898: 17). Yet even in such moments, he seems to understand how the exotic and ordinary are two sides of the same imperial coin.

James paid relatively little attention to the peoples and societies beyond the Euro-American center of his modern era, but within this territory he understood the consequences of cultural imperialism. The colonial imagination is at the heart of the immorality of the narrator of *The Aspern Papers* (1888), that "publishing scoundrel" who betrays human affection for letters made valuable simply by their celebrity association with the American Byron, and more so for their hint of his scandalous relationship with Juliana Bordereau so many years earlier. *The Aspern Papers* is full of references to more obvious conquerors with whom the narrator is compared in mock-heroic mode: Admiral Nelson at Trafalgar, Napoleon at Austerlitz, the treasonous *condottiere* Bartolommeo Colleoni (sculpted by Verrocchio and Leopardi), and the Roman Emperor Marcus Aurelius (James 1909a: 6, 138). In love with Italy and its cultivated history, James also knows that his affection for it can become a similar kind of sickness, a passion to possess the past that destroys its charm and value. Jane Campion's film of *The Portrait of a Lady* brilliantly captures the nineteenth-century woman's experience of alienation and fragmentation in the morcellized fragments – giants hands, ancient heads, broken trunks – of the human body that litter her Roman cityscapes (Rowe 2000b: 197–201). She learned this technique from James himself, who uses it effectively in early stories like "Adina" and "The Last of the Valerii" as well as in *Roderick Hudson* (1875) and *Portrait of a Lady* to suggest the more general economy of commodification and fetishism characteristic of modernity's misuses of the past (Rowe 1998: 49–54).

James's celebrated historical consciousness thus takes the long view of the history in which nation states have emerged and claimed discrete and competitive authorities only by ignoring their common origins and motives. To be sure, James's complex sense of history also has its high-cultural aura; to understand the interconnectedness of different communities in their mutually entangled histories gives you special authority, even prestige. Story reading aloud from his *Nero* is mildly comic because he seems unaware of how he himself is repeating that past, albeit on the much smaller stage of the American artists' community in Rome. The fragments of the past are symptomatic of our failure to read history, and James is always providing the hints to help us fill in the details. One should not visit Chillon, as Daisy and Winterbourne do, without reading Byron's "The Prisoner of Chillon" and understanding this shrine to the medieval Swiss peasant revolts as also one of the Romantics' "origins" for subsequent democratic revolutions in America and France. The ligaments of history are also the points of contact between different nations and cultures, exemplified in James's own passionate cosmopolitanism, as his copious travel writings and literary criticism from *French Poets and Novelists* (1878) to *Italian Hours* (1909) and *The American Scene* attest. Henry James achieved the modernist ideal of cosmopolitan, albeit in the manner of the high-cultural standard set by Matthew Arnold.

The most provincial settings in Henry James often turn out weirdly to be the most transnational. What could be more deliberately regional than *The Turn of the Screw*'s country house of Bly and the isolation of Miles and Flora with the Governess, Mrs. Grose, and those specters, Peter Quint and Miss Jessel? But it is the death of the Uncle's parents in India, with its evocation of British imperial power and foreign service, that forces him reluctantly to take charge of Miles and Flora after they are orphaned by his "military" brother's untimely death (James 1909e: 153). And the Irish background of Peter Quint – that red hair seems to clinch it – suggests that the children are haunted by far more than the sexually illicit. An aura of the political legacy of British imperialism shimmers along the boundaries of this contested property (Rowe 1984: 132–5). James knew well enough how the English countryside, however charmingly rural, still hid the secrets of a violent past in which theft, murder, invasion, and brigandry structured its landscape. Winchelsea, Rye, and other English coastal towns formed the center of the late eighteenth- and early nineteenth-century smuggling trade, as James points out in *English Hours*: "These communities appear to have had, in their long decline, little industry but their clandestine traffic with other coasts, in the course of which they quite mastered the art of going... 'one better' than the officers of the revenue" (James 1905a: 281). The growth of the metropolitan center of London as the contact zone linking the British empire with the countryside is a subject of considerable interest to James. Filled with the spoils of ancient imperial power, country houses like Lord Mark's Matcham imitate the architecture of the Romans and the art collections of the quattrocento princes. Bronzino's *Lucrezia Panciatichi* provides Milly's mirror-stage in *The Wings of the Dove* in a double sense: Lucrezia is "dead, dead, dead," not only because James (and Milly) find Bronzino's mannerism to be stiff and stylized, nor only because Milly sees in the painting her own biological and psychological destiny. The Renaissance aristocracy represented by Bronzino has been replaced by American power and wealth, so that Milly's comment, now filtered through James, may be said to apply to Lord Mark as well (Rowe 1976: 185–90). Desperate for an American match, the British aristocracy is rapidly moving in the direction of its Italian and Spanish predecessors. Gardencourt is owned by Americans, as are an increasing number of the valuable paintings and cultural artifacts of the European past.

Metropolitan London is ineluctably transformed by the diasporas of the peoples colonized by the British. The "brown lady" in *What Maisie Knew* first appears at one of those bazaars that became tourist attractions for Victorians curious about the peoples and places of the empire. The "American countess" suggests some new, unrecognized aristocracy: a future ruling class. James is not entirely comfortable with her "darkness" or with Miriam Rooth's "Jewishness," even if he renders both so ambiguous as to make any decisive judgement of African American or Jewish identity impossible (Rowe 1998: 143–50). James is ambivalent about the new "mob" composed of peoples not only from different classes but from communities traditionally ignored by the historical consciousness he himself favors. Like Hegel, James treats Africa as having "no historical part" in world history, "no movement or development to exhibit," and thus awaiting only the "civilizing" influences of Europe and the United States (Hegel 1956: 99). To be sure, such a view is very much part of the imperial imaginary in the late nineteenth and early twentieth centuries, and James cannot be absolved of his part in such modernism, no matter how hard some critics have tried to do so. When James addresses women undergraduates at Bryn Mawr in "The Question of Our Speech" (1905) and appeals to immigrants in the Bowery in *The American Scene*, his moral view supports adaptation to Euro-American civilization. For the young graduates as much as for the immigrants, learning to use English in all its cultivated subtlety is their best opportunity for democratic equality (Rowe 1998: 31–6).

In many respects, James endorses the assimilationist positions prevalent at the turn of the nineteenth to twentieth centuries, but there is a certain residuum that complements more precisely his advocacy of a historical consciousness that depends more on the *uses* of the past than on its commodification. Women and immigrants will *change* English, James argues, and as long as such change occurs within certain acceptable bounds, then it is one of the positive consequences of modernization. Language thrives on such changes, as James the technical innovator and modern experimenter knows so well. Of course, English remains the primary language, and James seems in this regard to anticipate the monolingualism of E. D. Hirsch, Jr.'s *Cultural Literacy*, if not the more strident politics of the "English-Only" movement of Ron Unz, S. I. Hayakawa, and others in California in the 1980s. Monolingualists usually fall into their own contradictions, as James does in his frequent use of Italian and French phrases to adapt English to his special cosmopolitanism. Indeed, the best English seems polyglot, inflected with the spirit of Italian *conversazione* and the rhetorical subtlety of French *points des repères* ("reference points"), a phrase Henry James uses in his Prefaces (1907–9) to the New York Edition to refer simultaneously to the protagonist and the different points of view through which she is so often represented. Just as American culture is broadened and enriched by its many different cultural sources, so English is itself truer to its essence only insofar as it draws on other languages.

Living elsewhere is sometimes just parasitic tourism, sometimes mindless worship of the past, occasionally an emancipatory experience of your own freedom. In part, these rare moments of liberation are the consequence of alienation, such as James's feminine protagonists experience from the outset of their fictional journeys. When it accomplishes magical transformations, such alienation depends on the character's recognition of the social constructedness of all human values and relations – a radical relativism that allows the character a moment of vision outside her conventional role. When Milly Theale walks through London following her visit to Dr. Luke Strett, she wanders into strange neighborhoods only to identify with the prostitutes of London and New York (James 1909f: vol. 20, p. 248). This surreal episode foreshadows, of course, how she will be commodified and dehumanized by Kate and Merton, but it also indicates how her existential predicament enables her to step outside class, race, and nation to achieve a sympathetic identification with other victimized people. Such literary moments, infrequent as they are in James's fiction, anticipate the trans-national political and cultural coalitions often imagined today as alternatives to one-way, corporate globalization.

Of course, the cosmopolitanism endorsed by Henry James is best exemplified in his own life, and it has a certain *Americanness* to it, even when James is at his most European. The ideal American for James is precisely the modern cosmopolitan, who is always on the verge of turning into an Osmond or Adam Verver and yet strives to maintain his or her balance as interested in other cultural influences and willing to incorporate them into work or life in ways that change both. It is an American exceptionalism, even though it is also epitomized by a wide variety of characters who are decidedly *not* American, such as Gabriel Nash and Miriam Rooth in *The Tragic Muse*, Maisie Farange in *What Maisie Knew*, Maria Gostrey in *The Ambassadors*, Fleda Vetch in "The Spoils of Poynton" (1897), Mr. Drake in *In the Cage* (1898), and May Bartram in "The Beast in the Jungle." All of these characters are variants on such tragic heroes as Christopher Newman, Daisy Miller, Isabel Archer, Lambert Strether, Maggie Verver, and Milly Theale, who fail to connect their American identities with their international destinies. Returning to the United States in 1904–5, James would be impressed by how "American civilization... had begun to spread itself thick and pile itself high, ... in proportion as [Europe] had taken to writing itself plain" (James 1968: 366). James represents in *The American Scene* the shift in global power from Europe to America, with respect to both political and cultural economies. Even as he criticizes American cultural deficiencies and capitalist excesses, James still takes pride in the growing centrality of the American as the type of the cosmopolitan, as the Italian had been in the quattrocento and the Englishman in the Victorian era.

From *The Tragic Muse* (1890) on, James's writings seem to identify such cosmopolitanism not only with understanding different cultures' achievements but also with a certain latitude in regard to social, sexual, and personal identities. The sexually ambivalent Gabriel Nash, James's fictional caricature of Oscar Wilde, is by no means an unequivocal hero in *The Tragic Muse*, but by the end he can become Nick Dormer's "muse" and be saved by James as a ghostly, symbolic figure of the confused possibilities of sexual and aesthetic freedom (Rowe 1998: 96–8). In many respects, James identifies with people marginalized, especially by the modernization process, although he takes relatively little account of how peoples of color were displaced by Euro-American colonialism. Miriam Rooth's ambivalent Jewish background recalls the popular identification of cosmopolitanism with Jewishness in the late nineteenth century, but James appears to transform such anti-semitism – the myth of the wandering, displaced Jew – by dramatizing Miriam's success on the English stage. By the end of the novel, Gabriel Nash can imagine Miriam as a global figure, who will brighten "up the world for a great many people" and bring "the ideal nearer to them," working as an aesthetic counter-force to the exploitative globalization of British imperialism (James 1908b: vol. 8, 198). In general, James follows the logic of Freudian sublimation by incorporating minority and marginal social identities into an aesthetic cosmopolitanism, which epitomizes his own authorial position and disguises any more personal identification with gay men, lesbians, straight women, Jews, immigrants, peoples of color, prostitutes, and children.

In many respects, these very groups are consequences of the modernization process, which James criticizes and fears throughout his career. The legal demonization of homosexuality with the British Criminal Law Amendment Act of 1885, the rise of anti-semitism in the late nineteenth century, growing fears of the "New Woman," riots in the United States against minority and immigrant competition in the labor force, and the rapid growth in the same period of what today we recognize as the global "sex industry" are social phenomena traceable directly to urbanization, the accelerated movement of peoples and goods across national borders (especially imperialism's multidirectional traffic), growing disparities in the distribution of wealth, and the cheapening of labor. "The future belongs to crowds," Don DeLillo writes in *Mao II* (1991), and Henry James anticipates how this postmodern consequence would develop out of the ideological construction of the mob from women, sexual "deviants," Jews, and other immigrants and displaced persons (DeLillo 1991: 16). It would require little imagination on the part of European fascists in Germany, Italy, and Spain to add communists, gypsies, and avant-garde artists to their definition of the "masses."

Miriam Rooth's artistic destiny does not lead unequivocally to the triumph of the ideal over the commercial drive for new products and new markets James elsewhere condemns. The imagination and aesthetic sensibility of James's most humane characters are always subject to commodification, threatened on all sides by traders in psychic and monetary currency. From the members of the audience, like Peter Sherringham, who see in Miriam's roles something to be desired and possessed, to art collectors like Christopher Newman and Adam Verver, who try to buy imagination and taste, James's characters foreshadow the postmodern economy in which the uniqueness and originality of art command astounding prices even as their true value is neglected.

In his last novel, *The Outcry* (1911), James returns to the subject of an American businessman, Bender Breckenridge (modeled after J. P. Morgan), trying to buy pieces of the British cultural heritage. Critical as ever of our "priggish, precious modernity," as the art historian Hugh Crimble puts it, James nonetheless reminds his readers that the phenomenon of "people . . . trafficking all round" is by no means an exclusively modern or even American phenomenon (James 2002: 37, 34). Lady Grace points out that British "art-wealth came in – save for those awkward Elgin Marbles! – mainly by purchase too. . . . We ourselves largely took it away from somewhere, didn't we? We didn't *grow* it all" (p. 35). Of course, those "awkward Elgin Marbles" were stolen, and most of the British purchases were one-sided, imperial bargains. From the neo-classical architecture of London's government buildings to the far-flung outposts of the remotest colonies, imperial Britain borrowed, stole, or bought other cultures' aesthetic traditions to bolster its own authority. Henry James understood America to be following this lead and refining even further the extent to which the aesthetic aura might be used to disguise its conquering will.

Today the cosmopolitan ideal Henry James typified in his person and work has been extensively commodified by the academic and mass media veneration of his genius. Along with William Shakespeare and James Joyce, Henry James contributes regularly to an aesthetic ideology that is integral to a postmodern economy intent upon the production and circulation of representations ranging from artistic styles to computer programs. In our culture of simulation and hyper-reality, Henry James is at once a valuable product and a nostalgic token of an earlier period, in which art survived on the margins of a more material economy governed by physical labor, tangible commodities, and identifiable markets. In our contemporary world, celebrity voices and bodies are legally protected intellectual properties, website names command high prices, and webpage design is an alternative career for struggling artists. In the global economy, there is "no there there," as Gertrude Stein complained of Oakland, but an increasingly homogenized "everywhere" of malls, multiplex theaters, and ceaseless traffic. Throughout his long career, Henry James resisted the incipient commercialization of the aesthetic process, insisted upon the intangible, spiritual values of art, and damned the confusion of culture and economics. He would not be at home in our postmodern, commodified, globalized world, but he helps us understand it.

Selected Primary Texts by Henry James

A Passionate Pilgrim and Other Tales. 1875.

Roderick Hudson. 1875.

Transatlantic Sketches. 1875.

The American. 1877.

The Europeans. 1878.

French Poets and Novelists. 1878.

Watch and Ward. 1878.

Confidence. 1879.

Daisy Miller. 1879.

An International Episode. 1879.

The Madonna of the Future and Other Tales. 1879.

Nathaniel Hawthorne. 1879.

The Diary of a Man of Fifty and a Bundle of Letters. 1880.

The Portrait of a Lady. 1881.

Washington Square. 1881.

Portraits of Places. 1883.

The Siege of London. 1883.

A Little Tour in France. 1884.

Tales of Three Cities. 1884.

The Bostonians. 1886.

The Princess Casamassima. 1886.

The Aspern Papers. 1888.

Louisa Pallant. 1888.

The Modern Warning. 1888.

Partial Portraits. 1888.

The Reverberator. 1888.

A London Life. 1889.

The Tragic Muse. 1890.

The Lesson of the Master. 1892.

Essays in London and Elsewhere. 1893.

Picture and Text. 1893.

The Private Life. 1893.

The Real Thing and Other Tales. 1893.

The Wheel of Time. 1893.

Terminations. 1895.

Embarrassments. 1896.

The Other House. 1896.

The Spoils of Poynton. 1897.

What Maisie Knew. 1897.

In the Cage. 1898.

The Two Magics. 1898.

The Turn of the Screw. 1898.

The Awkward Age. 1899.

The Sacred Fount. 1901.

The Wings of the Dove. 1902.

The Ambassadors. 1903.

The Better Sort. 1903.

William Wetmore Story and his Friends. 1903.

The Golden Bowl. 1904.

English Hours. 1905.

The Question of Our Speech, and The Lesson of Balzac. 1905.

The American Scene. 1907.

Views and Reviews. 1908.

The Altar of the Dead. 1909.

Italian Hours. 1909.
Julia Bride. 1909.
The New York Edition, 24 vols., 1907–9.
The Finer Grain. 1910.
The Outcry. 1911.
A Small Boy and Others. 1913.
Notes of a Son and Brother. 1914.

Notes on Novelists. 1914.
The Ivory Tower. 1917.
The Middle Years. 1917.
The Sense of the Past. 1917.
Within the Rim and Other Essays. 1918.
Travelling Companions. 1919.
Notes and Reviews. 1921.

LATER COLLECTIONS

James, Henry (1957). *Parisian Sketches: Letters to the "New York Tribune" 1875–1876*, ed. Leon Edel and Ilse Dusoir Lind. New York: New York University Press.

James, Henry (1962). *The Art of the Novel: Critical Prefaces*, ed. R. P. Blackmur. New York: Scribner. AN.

James, Henry (1974–84). *Letters*, ed. Leon Edel, 4 vols. Cambridge, Mass.: Harvard University Press.

James, Henry (1984a). *Henry James: Literary Criticism*, vol. 1: *Essays on Literature, American Writers, English Writers*, ed. Leon Edel. New York: Library of America.

James, Henry (1984b). *Henry James: Literary Criticism*, vol. 2: *French Writers, Other European Writers, The Prefaces to the New York Edition*, ed. Leon Edel. New York: Library of America.

James, Henry (1987). *The Complete Notebooks of Henry James*, ed. Leon Edel and Lyall H. Powers. New York: Oxford University Press.

James, Henry (1996–9). *Henry James: Complete Stories*, 5 vols. New York: Library of America.

REFERENCES AND FURTHER READING

Anderson, Charles R. (1977). *Person, Place, and Thing in Henry James's Novels*. Durham, NC: Duke University Press.

Anesko, Michael (1986). *"Friction with the Market": Henry James and the Profession of Authorship*. New York: Oxford University Press.

Anesko, Michael (1997). *Letters, Fictions, Lives: Henry James and William Dean Howells*. New York: Oxford University Press.

Banta, Martha (1972). *Henry James and the Occult: The Great Extension*. Bloomington: Indiana University Press.

Bell, Millicent (1991). *Meaning in Henry James*. Cambridge, Mass.: Harvard University Press.

Blair, Sara (1996). *Henry James and the Writing of Race and Nation*. Cambridge, UK: Cambridge University Press.

Brooks, Peter (1995). *The Melodramatic Imagination: Balzac, Henry James, Melodrama, and the Mode of Excess*. New Haven, Conn.: Yale University Press.

Buitenhuis, Peter (1970). *The Grasping Imagination: The American Writings of Henry James*. Toronto: University of Toronto Press.

Cameron, Sharon (1989). *Thinking in Henry James*. Chicago: University of Chicago Press.

Cannon, Kelly (1994). *Henry James and Masculinity: The Man at the Margins*. New York: St. Martin's.

Chatman, Seymour (1972). *The Later Style of Henry James*. Oxford: Blackwell.

Cross, Mary (1993). *Henry James: The Contingencies of Style*. New York: St. Martin's.

Davidson, Rob (2005). *The Master and the Dean: The Literary Criticism of Henry James and William Dean Howells*. Columbia: University of Missouri Press.

De Lillo, Don (1991). *Mao II*. New York: Penguin.

Du Bois, W. E. B. (1996). *The Oxford W. E. B. Du Bois Reader*, ed. Eric J. Sundquist. New York: Oxford University Press.

Dupee, F. W. (1974) *Henry James*, rev. edn. New York: Morrow. (First publ. 1951.)

Edel, Leon (1972). *Henry James. The Master: 1901–1916*. Vol. 5 in *The Life of Henry James*, 5 vols., 1953–72. Philadelphia: Lippincott.

Freedman, Jonathan (1990). *Professions of Taste: Henry James, British Aestheticism, and Commodity Culture*. Stanford, Calif.: Stanford University Press.

Freedman, Jonathan, ed. (1998). *The Cambridge Companion to Henry James*. Cambridge, Mass.: Cambridge University Press.

Fussell, Edwin S. (1993). *The Catholic Side of Henry James*. Cambridge, Mass.: Cambridge University Press.

Gordon, Lyndall (1999). *A Private Life of Henry James: Two Women and his Art*. New York: Norton.

Graham, Kenneth (1996). *Henry James: A Literary Life*. New York: St. Martin's.

Griffin, Susan (1991). *The Historical Eye: The Texture of the Visual in Late James*. Boston: Northeastern University Press.

Habegger, Alfred (1989). *Henry James and the "Woman Business."* Cambridge, UK: Cambridge University Press.

Hadley, Tessa (2002). *Henry James and the Imagination of Pleasure*. Cambridge, UK: Cambridge University Press.

Hagberg, Garry (1994). *Meaning and Interpretation: Wittgenstein, Henry James, and Literary Knowledge*. Ithaca, NY: Cornell University Press.

Hegel, Georg Wilhelm Friedrich (1956). *The Philosophy of History*, trans. J. Sibree. New York: Dover.

Hirsch, E. D., Jr. (1987). *Cultural Literacy*. Boston: Houghton Mifflin.

Hocks, Richard A. (1974). *Henry James and Pragmatic Thought: A Study in the Relationship between the Philosophy of William James and the Literary Art of Henry James*. Chapel Hill, NC: University of North Carolina Press.

Hocks, Richard A. (1990). *Henry James: A Study of the Short Fiction*. New York: Twayne.

Holland, Laurence B. (1982). *The Expense of Vision: Essays on the Craft of Henry James*. Baltimore: Johns Hopkins University Press. (First publ. 1964.)

Holley, Carol (1995). *Intensely Family: The Inheritance of Family Shame and the Autobiographies of Henry James*. Madison: University of Wisconsin Press.

Horne, Philip (1990). *Henry James and Revision*. Oxford: Clarendon.

Hughes, Clair (2001). *Henry James and the Art of Dress*. New York: Palgrave.

James, Henry (1903). *William Wetmore Story and his Friends: From Letters, Diaries, and Recollections*, 2 vols. Boston: Houghton Mifflin.

James, Henry (1905a). *English Hours*. London: Heinemann.

James, Henry (1905b). *The Question of our Speech, and the Lesson of Balzac*. Boston: Houghton Mifflin.

James, Henry (1907). *The American. The Novels and Tales of Henry James*, vol. 2. New York: Scribner, 1907.

James, Henry (1908a). *The Portrait of a Lady. The Novels and Tales of Henry James*, vols. 3–4. New York: Scribner.

James, Henry (1908b). *The Tragic Muse. The Novels and Tales of Henry James*, vols. 7–8. New York: Scribner.

James, Henry (1909a). *The Aspern Papers*. In *The Novels and Tales of Henry James*, vol. 12, 1–143. New York: Scribner.

James, Henry (1909b). "The Beast in the Jungle." In *The Novels and Tales of Henry James*, vol. 17, 59–127. New York: Scribner.

James, Henry (1909c). *Daisy Miller*. In *The Novels and Tales of Henry James*, vol. 18, 1–94. New York: Scribner.

James, Henry (1909d). "The Jolly Corner." In *The Novels and Tales of Henry James*, vol. 17, 433–85. New York: Scribner.

James, Henry (1909e). *The Turn of the Screw*. In *The Novels and Tales of Henry James*, vol. 12, 145–309. New York: Scribner.

James, Henry (1909f). *The Wings of the Dove. The Novels and Tales of Henry James*, vols. 19–20. New York: Scribner.

James, Henry (1968). *The American Scene*. Bloomington: Indiana University Press.

James, Henry (2002). *The Outcry*. New York: New York Review of Books.

Jolly, Roslyn (1993). *Henry James: History, Narrative, Fiction*. Oxford: Clarendon.

Kaplan, Fred (1992). *Henry James: The Imagination of Genius. A Biography*. New York: Morrow.

Kress, Jill M. (2002). *The Figure of Consciousness: William James, Henry James, and Edith Wharton*. New York: Routledge.

Krook, Dorothea (1962). *The Ordeal of Consciousness in Henry James*. Cambridge, UK: Cambridge University Press.

Levine, Jessica (2003). *Delicate Pursuit: Discretion in Henry James and Edith Wharton*. New York: Routledge.

Lewis, R. W. B. (1991). *The Jameses: A Family Narrative*. New York: Farrar Straus.

Loti, Pierre (1898). *Impressions*, intr. Henry James. Westminster: Archibald Constable and Co.

Lustig, T. J. (1994). *Henry James and the Ghostly*. Cambridge, UK: Cambridge University Press.

McWhirter, David M. (1989). *Desire and Love in Henry James: A Study of the Late Novels*. Cambridge, UK: Cambridge University Press.

McWhirter, David M., ed. (1996). *Henry James's New York Edition: The Construction of Authorship*. Stanford, Calif.: Stanford University Press.

Matthiessen, F. O. (1944). *Henry James: The Major Phase*. New York: Oxford University Press.

Meissner, Collin (1999). *Henry James and the Language of Experience*. Cambridge, UK: Cambridge University Press.

Mizruchi, Susan L. (1983). *The Power of Historical Knowledge: Narrating the Past in Hawthorne, James, and Dreiser*. Philadelphia: University of Pennsylvania Press.

Novick, Sheldon M. (1996). *Henry James: The Young Master*. New York: Random House.

Perosa, Sergio (1983). *Henry James and the Experimental Novel*. New York: New York University Press.

Pippen, Robert B. (2000). *Henry James and Modern Moral Life*. Cambridge, UK: Cambridge University Press.

Poirier, Richard (1960). *The Comic Sense of Henry James: A Study of the Early Novels*. New York: Oxford University Press.

Posnock, Ross (1991). *The Trial of Curiosity: Henry James, William James, and the Challenge of Modernity*. New York: Oxford University Press.

Powers, Lyall (1971). *Henry James and the Naturalist Movement*. East Lansing: Michigan State University Press.

Reeve, N. H., ed. (1997). *Henry James: The Shorter Fiction, Reassessments*. New York: St. Martin's.

Rimmon, Shlomith (1977). *The Concept of Ambiguity: The Example of James*. Chicago: University of Chicago Press.

Rowe, John Carlos (1976). *Henry Adams and Henry James: The Emergence of a Modern Consciousness*. Ithaca, NY: Cornell University Press.

Rowe, John Carlos (1984). *The Theoretical Dimensions of Henry James*. Madison: University of Wisconsin Press.

Rowe, John Carlos (1997). *At Emerson's Tomb: The Politics of Classic American Literature*. New York: Columbia University Press.

Rowe, John Carlos (1998). *The Other Henry James*. Durham, NC: Duke University Press.

Rowe, John Carlos (2000a). *Literary Culture and U.S. Imperialism: From the Revolution to World War II*. New York: Oxford University Press.

Rowe, John Carlos (2000b). "For Mature Audiences: Sex, Gender and Recent Film Adaptations of Henry James's Fiction." In John R. Bradley (ed.), *Henry James on Stage and Screen*, 190–211. Basingstoke: Palgrave.

Rowe, John Carlos (2002). *The New American Studies*. Minneapolis: University of Minnesota Press.

Said, Edward (1993). *Culture and Imperialism*. New York: Random House.

Salmon, Richard (1997). *Henry James and the Culture of Publicity*. Cambridge, UK: Cambridge University Press.

Sears, Sally (1968). *The Negative Imagination: Form and Perspective in the Novels of Henry James*. Ithaca, NY: Cornell University Press.

Seltzer, Mark (1984). *Henry James and the Art of Power*. Ithaca, NY: Cornell University Press.

Tambling, Jeremy (2000). *Henry James*. New York: St. Martin's.

Tanner, Tony (1995). *Henry James and the Art of Nonfiction*. Athens, Ga.: University of Georgia Press.

Teahan, Sheila (1995). *The Rhetorical Logic of Henry James*. Baton Rouge: Louisiana State University Press.

Tintner, Adeline R. (1993). *Henry James and the Lust of Eyes: Thirteen Artists in his Work*. Baton Rouge: Louisiana State University Press.

Tintner, Adeline R. (2000). *The Twentieth-Century World of Henry James: Changes in his Work after 1900*. Baton Rouge: Louisiana State University Press.

Veeder, William (1975). *Henry James – The Lessons of the Master: Popular Fiction and Personal Style in the Nineteenth Century*. Chicago: University of Chicago Press.

Wallace, Ronald (1975). *Henry James and the Comic Turn*. Ann Arbor: University of Michigan Press.

Walton, Priscilla L. (1992). *The Disruption of the Feminine in Henry James*. Toronto: University of Toronto Press.

Wegelin, Christof (1958). *The Image of Europe in Henry James*. Dallas: Southern Methodist University Press.

Williams, Merle A. (1993). *Henry James and the Philosophical Novel: Being and Seeing*. Cambridge, UK: Cambridge University Press.

Winner, Viola Hopkins (1970). *Henry James and the Visual Arts*. Charlottesville: University Press of Virginia.

Yeazell, Ruth Bernard (1976). *Language and Knowledge in the Late Novels of Henry James*. Chicago: University of Chicago Press.

27

Toward a Modernist Aesthetic: The Literary Legacy of Edith Wharton

Candace Waid and Clare Colquitt

Edith Wharton (1862–1937) was restless in 1902, a watershed year in which she would publish her first novel, the well-researched and woodenly historical *Valley of Decision*, burdened with the philosophical and actual furniture of the Italian eighteenth century. Two years earlier she had published a revelatory novella, *The Touchstone*, a work that focuses on the betrayal of a dead woman novelist whose love letters – "unloved letters" – are published to fund the marriage of the man to whom they were written. On January 24, 1902, her fortieth birthday, Wharton was fitful and impatient as she awaited the February publication of *The Valley of Decision*. She lamented to a friend: "Don't I know that feeling you describe, when one longs to go to a hospital & *have something cut out*, and come out minus an organ, but alive & active & like other people, instead of dragging on with this bloodless existence!! Only I fear you & I will never find a surgeon who will do us that service" (Wharton 1998: 55). Writing six years later to the same friend, Sally Norton, who had given over her life to the care of her elderly and now dying father, Wharton sends thoughts of "deep sympathy" along with a rash fantasy of female social intervention: "[A]las, I should like to get up on the house-top & cry to all who come after us 'Take your own life, every one of you!'" (Oct. 17, 1908, in Wharton 1998: 163). Wharton's words echo the infamous advice given by Henry Adams to Henry James to "take your own life . . . to prevent biographers from taking it in theirs" (May 6, 1908, in Levenson et al. 1988: vol. 6, 136).

In 1914 Wharton was at work on a coming-of-age novel entitled "Literature," a manuscript that incorporated events of her own intimate past to tell the story of the artist figure as a young man. Interrupted by the outbreak of war in Europe, such a work became impossible not just because of the immediacy of the violence – she had become a permanent resident of France in 1909 and was taken on numerous occasions to bear witness through her writing to the body-strewn horror of the front – but also because Wharton, conscious of history, had become increasingly aware of her place in history. Even before she was given the highest honor awarded by the French to the foreign-born for her humanitarian efforts in organizing charitable relief for the refugees pouring into Paris – many of them Belgian orphans – Wharton had already become an historical figure. Twenty years later, in 1934, as she "hear[d] close underfoot the growling of the volcano" (1998: 379) that would give way to another world war, Wharton took her life in her own words when her autobiography, *A Backward Glance*, appeared. She left other, more revelatory stories to her anticipated biographers, most notably R. W. B. Lewis, who in 1975 opened Wharton's long-closed life to the world through his Pulitzer Prize-winning *Edith Wharton*.

I

Edith Wharton, born Edith Newbold Jones in 1862, entered into the careful and closed ranks of the New York aristocracy, defied the limitations of a society that did not condone the practice of art for men or women, and for over forty years seized her life through writing. The internationally acclaimed author of nearly fifty books, an acknowledged expert in the visual arts (the history of painting, sculpture, architecture, and gardens), and a generative reader of almost unimaginable proportions and range, Wharton is best known for her fiction, which took the form of twenty-two books, equally divided between novels and novellas, and nearly a hundred published short stories, including such oft-anthologized tales as "Souls Belated," "The Other Two," "The Eyes," and "Roman Fever." Among her novellas, *Ethan Frome* (1911) and *Summer* (1917) have been acclaimed as masterpieces of the genre, while of her novels the best known and most critically admired are *The House of Mirth* (1905), *The Reef* (1912), *The Custom of the Country* (1913), and *The Age of Innocence* (1920). From the outset, Wharton's startling creativity and productivity have brought critics back to the quandary posed by her peculiar origins: How could so luminous a figure emerge from a "provincial society" that saw the writing of fiction, "authorship," as an activity located (in her words) somewhere "between a black art and a form of manual labour" (Wharton 1998: 69)? The sixteen-year-old girl-poet's work was presented by the elderly Longfellow to William Dean Howells; early poems of hers were published in the *Atlantic* and a New York newspaper; and a bound volume of her poems and translations from German, *Verses*, was privately and anonymously printed in 1878, an unusual event that has been seen as part of her mother's efforts to mark a conclusion to her daughter's youthful obsessions.

The image of Wharton as a *rara avis* in terms of her literary inclinations is much more than a retrospective version of her youth seen through the lens of her productive career. Indeed, the past was present as the young Edith Jones, already described as having the eyes of a "young hawk" (quoted in Lewis 1975: 35), returned from a sojourn of six years in the cultural capitals of Europe. A veteran of the well-traveled roads of the Grand Tour (the pilgrimage to sites of cultural interest identified by august figures such as Goethe and James), the ten-year-old Edith who came back to America had been transformed by her near-death from typhoid fever in Germany and the wild sights seen from the stagecoach window as the Jones family traveled south into Spain, a trip the noted travel writer would later recall in her own adventurous journeys into the northern Africa of Tunisia and Morocco. The word *inflation* had entered American English as an economic term in 1864, a sign of the forces that encouraged George Frederic Jones to glean the high rents procurable from the family's US properties while enjoying the palatial elegance that was remarkably affordable in Rome, Florence, and Paris. During these early years abroad, the child who was destined to become a celebrated author demonstrated what in retrospect would be read as clear signs of her telling difference.

Too young to read, Edith Jones held a book in her hands (it was equally helpful upside down) as she enacted a ritual of her own devising in which she would, in her phrasing, "make up" stories. Entering into a storytelling trance that held her in its thrall, she would leave invited playmates, asking her mother to explain her absence when she felt compelled to declaim her stories "about grown-up people, 'real people,' I called them," while pacing back and forth in a frenzied fashion (Wharton 1998: 33). Her mother, noted for a prosaic nature that found its aesthetic outlet in a dedication to dress and the collection of old lace, was still amused by her precocious child. Lucretia Jones is known to have tried – without success – to record these verbal outpourings that had only begun to suggest the narrative drives that raged in what was for her an increasingly bewildering daughter. Wharton, who would entitle her first collection of stories *The Greater Inclination* (1899), initially expressed a wish to be like her mother, a desire she articulated simply as becoming "the best-dressed woman in New York" (Wharton 1998: 20). This was before she acknowledged that she wanted to become a writer, the greater inclination that was all the more strange because she had "never even seen one in the flesh!" (Wharton 1998: 76).

Wharton was the witness from within to a world that adhered to and cohered through strict rituals of social inbreeding that favored cousin–cousin marriages and other forms of enforced exclusion. Following the mandated seasonal migrations alternating between the fashionable resort town of Newport, Rhode Island in summer and fall and Manhattan in the winter social season, the Jones family was part of the hereditary elite that came to be known in Ward McAllister's phrase as "the New York Four Hundred." This hereditary "social aristocracy" was defined by the limits of the capacity of Mrs. Astor's ballroom (Wharton 1998: 5). Part of the established elite (Wharton's father was Mrs. Astor's first cousin), Edith attended the exclusive Assemblies (invitational balls organized by the Patriarchs Society), young ladies' social debuts, and other more explicitly staged events, including sonorous Sunday sermons that drew heavily on the poetry from the King James Bible, contemporary as well as classical plays, and yearly performances of the same favored operas such as Gounod's *Faust*. The social responsibilities of Wharton's parents and the legacy that was passed on to their daughter as a young society matron included regular carriage outings, promenades in the newly designed Central Park, the passive leaving of calling cards (a ritual that could lead to actual visits during the afternoons when one was formally "at home" for those to whom one was "at home"), and an elaborate system of reciprocal recognition and social exchange based on private dinner parties and the newly fashionable custom of afternoon tea (see Waid 2003).

Whether in church listening to the voice of her Episcopalian minister, the Reverend Dr. Washburn, or reading Goethe's poem about the seductive call of the Erlkönig's (Earl-King's) daughters, Wharton's childhood, as she later described it, always concealed a secret life. Edith, who extolled the pleasures of her father's library, was actually able to study Old Norse and older forms of English in her visits with the minister's daughter. It is no accident that a significant number of the most distinguished women writers of the nineteenth century – Jane Austen, the Brontë sisters, and Harriet Beecher Stowe – were clergymen's daughters from an emerging middle class. Wharton came from a world that collected and appreciated art while disdaining the practice of its craft. This world saw writing as a highly questionable vocation for men. (The culturally respected icon Washington Irving was a notable exception.) In terms of the possibilities for women, Wharton would recall the "commonness" that her own mother managed to intone in the very pronunciation of the name "Mrs. Beecher Stowe" (Wharton 1998: 68). Calling the chapter in her autobiography devoted to her writing "The Secret Garden," Wharton acknowledges that the call of art was from the outset a forbidden fruit that took the form of voices, "teeming visions" (Wharton 1998: 197) that lured her away from what she experienced as a mundane life ruled by social convention to an underworld of language that trembled with the mysteries of words (Waid 1991: 13–14).

Profoundly shy throughout her life, a shyness effectively cloaked in a formal coldness that was seen as *hauteur*, Wharton was criticized (not always without reason) for snobbishness. Born late to parents who had two significantly older sons, the Joneses' daughter was an isolated child who satisfied her intense narrative needs through reading. At age fourteen, Edith found an outlet for her insatiable desire for voice in daily writing, secret writing that culminated in a thirty-thousand-word novella with the racy title "Fast and Loose." Inscribed on stolen paper in stolen time, this carefully preserved manuscript, documenting the narrative impulse that had once gone into "making up," must be read as a daring act of escape performed by a young girl who had been explicitly forbidden to read the novels that were the staple form of private recreation among literate women, a group that included Wharton's mother, her aunts, and her grandmother – and no doubt Wharton herself. Set in the present of the 1870s, "Fast and Loose" treats a high-profile contemporary subject that was fodder for the society columns featuring real-life fairy-tales gone awry as New York socialites suffered unhappy marital alliances with men from the European aristocracy. Clearly topical in its decision to present a fairy-tale *manqué*, Wharton's first concerted effort at writing longer fiction reveals a knowledge of the conventions of the sentimental novel and, perhaps more alarmingly, the ways in which such formulas of unrequited love had become the models for lived realities. As the ill-fated and dying heroine of this early novella confesses her love to the man whom she regrets not having married, the sentimental scene marks the harsh reality that often divided the business of marriage from the dream of romance.

Born into a culture that fetishized female innocence, Wharton appears to have breathed in the sentimental scenarios that had long provided scripts for female emotions and fantasies. Such plots joined Christian domesticity to an ethos of feminine sacrifice that found its highest expression in such influential novels as Richardson's *Clarissa* (1747–8). Looking back to this tradition, "Fast and Loose" focuses on the consequences of female sacrifice and offers a suggestive account of the class-driven interests that set the terms of the exchange in women. In her most powerful works, Wharton would underline the inherent feminization that marked scenes of sacrifice, often exacted in marriages, whether its purported victims were male or female. Although traditional comedies end in the celebration of a marriage, such an ending does not provide closure, and such conclusions cannot close off the tragic and troubling events that remain unresolved. Indeed, failed rituals of erasure, the silence of marriage echoing in the falling of the curtain rather than death, are essential to the complexity of Wharton's social critiques and her articulation of tragedy. This narrative of a failed marriage whose cost is measured in the sacrifice of art becomes a crucial plot that forms the emotional center of Wharton's most sharply realist, that is to say, her most unswervingly naturalist fictions.

"Fast and Loose," finished just after Wharton's fifteenth birthday, suggested the family's problem of reining in the passions of this quiet and driven daughter. Two years before the twenty-three-year-old Edith Jones married the congenial sportsman, Edward Wharton, in 1886 (the act that Henry James years later would declare the "inconceivable thing" [quoted in Lewis 1975: 52]), this debutante from the highest social circle had suffered a humiliatingly brief engagement to Henry Stevens. In a social first in terms of public explanations for behavior among the elite, the Newport *Daily News* reported that "the only reason for the breaking of the engagement . . . is an alleged preponderance of intellectuality on the part of the intended bride," who is "an ambitious authoress" (quoted in Lewis 1975: 45). While conflicts over social insults and questions of inheritance that were taking place among the parental generation have in retrospect been given pride of place in biographical treatments, this strangely direct account of female ambition underlines the visible quality of Wharton's difference.

Wharton's seriousness about her writing, her sophistication about the exposure entailed in acts of publication, had already been articulated seven years earlier in mock reviews she appended to "Fast and Loose." The review the aspiring author attributed to the *Nation* was particularly trenchant: "It is false charity to reader and writer to mince matters. The English of it is that every character is a failure, the plot a vacuum, the style spiritless, the dialogue vague, the sentiments weak, & the whole thing a fiasco." Castigating the author to whom she herself had given a male pseudonym, the "disgusted" reviewer questions whether "David Olivieri" "is not . . . very, very like a sick-sentimental school-girl who has begun her work with a fierce & bloody resolve to make it as bad as Wilhelm Meister, Consuelo and '*Goodbye Sweetheart*' together, & has ended with a blush, & a general erasure of all the naughty words which her modest vocabulary could furnish?" (Wharton 1993: 117). This review, with its gendering of genre, obliquely gestures to the prohibitions against authorship enforced by the New York elite, "the old New York" Wharton would satirically remember in *The Age of Innocence* and in the four novellas she collected as *Old New York* (1924). Aesthetic callings or, for that matter, any distinguishing obsessions could not only ruin engagements, they could also ruinously mark men, a prospect Wharton detailed in her portrayal of the ill-fated poet of *The Custom of the Country*, the aptly named Ralph Marvell. As Wharton's first bestseller, *The House of Mirth*, suggests, even an unarticulated yearning for beauty can lead away from marriage to the virgin sacrifice of a thirty-year-old heroine, Lily Bart.

Despite efforts to place Wharton as a "female Henry James," or, as a more witty and astute reviewer asserted, a positively "masculine H. J." (quoted in Lewis 1975: 132), gender was only part of the quandary Wharton posed to a world that increasingly realized there was really no one remotely like her. From a socially conservative realm where any type of appetite aside from the maternal might be seen as a masculine proclivity, this lady author of a few stories and sonnets was far from famous when she was described as an oddity by the well-known French novelist Paul Bourget in his series for the New York *Herald*. Bourget (later a friend) was introduced to the Whartons in the Newport of 1893 and subsequently penned a recognizable account of an anxiety-provoking woman:

> the intellectual tomboy...has read everything, understood everything, not superficially, but really, with an energy of culture that could put to shame the whole Parisian fraternity of letters.... Though like the others she gets her gowns from the best houses of the Rue de la Paix, there is not a book of Darwin, Huxley, Spencer, Renan, Taine, which she has not studied, not a painter or sculptor of whose works she could not compile a catalogue, not a school of poetry or romance of which she does not know the principles. (Quoted in Lewis 1975: 69)

While Bourget goes on to criticize the precision of Wharton's intellect, suggesting that it appeared to have been "ordered...as we would order a piece of furniture,...with as many compartments as there are branches of human knowledge," he frames his response in an unabashedly gendered economy in which the American "tomboy" shames "the whole Parisian brotherhood of letters" (quoted in Lewis 1975: 70). In many ways, this was a response that Wharton experienced throughout her life as her increasingly remarkable fictions and her daunting intelligence provoked defensive posturing even from friends.

The intensity which Wharton brought to her early conversations with Bourget illumines her desire to break through the intellectual isolation that had always characterized her life. The Wharton who articulated her most comprehensive view of aesthetics in her manual on interior decoration, the co-authored *Decoration of Houses* (1897), produced her "own first-born" (Wharton 1998: 124), the story collection *The Greater Inclination*, just two years later. In Wharton's words, this volume "broke the chains that had held me so long in a kind of torpor. For nearly twelve years, I had tried to adjust myself to my marriage; but now I was overmastered by the longing to meet people who shared my interests" (Wharton 1998: 122). Having belatedly determined that her first allegiance was to her art, Wharton would cultivate relationships with like-minded friends such as Henry James, Bernard Berenson, and Gaillard Lapsley who, among others, came to comprise what Susan Goodman has evocatively termed *Edith Wharton's Inner Circle* in her book by that title.

Writing to the man who was arguably her first lover (scholars believe that her twenty-six-year marriage to Edward Wharton may never have been consummated), the emotionally weary Wharton turned to the fullness of life that had always resided for her in art. As she perceived that, for unrelated reasons, both her love affair with Morton Fullerton — her sole experience of life "*in the round*" ([May 1910], in Wharton 1988: 216) — and her marriage were drawing to a close, Wharton proclaimed: "The tiresome woman is *buried*, once for all, I promise, & only the novelist survives!" (May 10, 1909, in Wharton 1988: 179). Wharton's understanding of what it meant to bury herself as a woman allowed her to speak from beyond the grave, to incorporate that experience of passion and the necessity of renunciation into her consummate art: an already structurally evolved and convincing narrative that recognized repression — individual sacrifice and sacrifice of individualism — as fundamental to a master narrative of civilization.

II

If Wharton's fictional past includes a drunken character named "Poe" and a bearded comforter walking among wounded men, a direct allusion to a Civil War Whitman, her fictional universe is also peopled by other drunken, poetry-mad, and wounded men who assume the female status of caretakers. Clearly, men as well as women may be victims of other characters' appetites. Some of the most insatiable predators wreaking destruction for their continued succor in lives of pleasure are unscrupulous women, including the socially prominent Bertha Dorset of *The House of Mirth* and the socially ambitious Undine Spragg of *The Custom of the Country*. In this field of moral action, Old New York is pictured practicing its rituals of cohesion through acts of exclusion and individual sacrifice while the world of Wharton's childhood is also shown destroying itself from within. Destruction may come from opening its marital doors to the socially calculating ranks of the newly moneyed or from blocking such entry by closing off the outer world, entombing the remnant in an airless vault where preservation of the past leads to infertility and death. The "carnivorous" predator, Gus Trenor of *The House of Mirth*, who exposes the ethos of consumption that rules the exchange of unprotected female beauty and money is (seen through his appetites) close kin to the survival-conscious and art-loving Mrs. Manson Mingott of *The Age of Innocence*, "the carnivorous old lady" who declares that the moribund world of Old New York needs "new blood and new money" (Wharton 2003a: 20) Wharton compared *The House of Mirth* to the lifting of a "little corner of ... [a] garment," explaining that she intended "to show only that little atrophied organ — the group of idle & dull people – that exists in any big & wealthy social body" (Nov. 11, [1905], in Wharton 1988: 97). Later she justified her choice of subject with a critical maxim: "a frivolous society can acquire dramatic significance only through what its frivolity destroys." Explicating the tragic "power [that lies in] debasing people and ideals," Wharton concluded, "[t]he answer, in short, was my heroine, Lily Bart" (Wharton 1998: 207).

Known for her novels of manners and seen from the outset as a figure who could expose the mysteries of the most exclusive society America would ever know, Wharton inhabited both sides of a seemingly irreconcilable divide. Sought after as an informant and admired for the perspective provided by characters who display fatal detachment in their roles as participant observers, Wharton emerged as a writer of profound works of fiction that were remarkable for their ability to define the significance of what she called "frivolous society" while interrogating the relationship between culture and history. She did this in prose that used myth and parable to construct historically realist and sharp-edged fictions.

Wharton's late-life knowledge of bodily passion, an experience of the primal that she soon saw echoed and exposed in the violence of war, led her to create the highly embodied psychological landscapes of her New England novellas. The New England worlds of *Ethan Frome* and *Summer* represent places that allow anxious and urbane strangers (respectively, the unnamed narrating engineer and the fertilizing sketch-artist, Lucius Harney) access to – and escape from – goblin markets of desire. These rural settings embody a past that despite its pregnability – its explicit violability – remains at a distance. Place in Wharton's best work is profoundly linked to time, and the New England of Wharton's fiction – with its desiccating cartography dominated by villages with such names as Starkfield, North Dormer, and Nettleton – becomes the space of a visceral past. As she herself moved to the foothills of the northern Appalachians, shifting her summer "cottage" from Newport to the upland Berkshire air, Wharton entered into psychological landscapes that she insisted were the denied realities concealed by the celebrated stories that had comprised "the New England of fiction" (Wharton 1996: 259) as "seen through the rose-coloured spectacles of [her] predecessors, Mary Wilkins [Freeman] and Sarah Orne Jewett" (Wharton 1998: 293). The past glimpsed by Hawthorne was present in what Wharton perceived as "still grim places, morally and physically," where "insanity, incest and slow mental and moral starvation were hidden away behind the paintless wooden house-fronts or in the isolated farm-houses on the neighbouring hills" (Wharton 1998: 294).

Continuing to map her parables of time and change onto place, Wharton located the future in the Midwest, a vacuous region in fiction that situates American soullessness in the insatiable female belly. For Wharton, the interior of the United States remains spiritually childless, embodying the vacuity of a materialism that is not and cannot be filled. Willa Cather would follow Wharton's lead as she critiqued technological modernity and the emptiness of materialism in her invention of the "Outland Vacuum" for *The Professor's House* (1925). Among Wharton's characters, this

Midwest is bodied forth most ravenously in Undine Spragg, the devouring muse of *The Custom of the Country*. However, this region evolves in Wharton's concluding novels to suggest the possibility that a genuinely gifted, if culturally unsated, individual may emerge from this interior. Imagined as a vast flat place ruled by lax divorce laws and desires for material acquisition, accessible by the fast train that was in historical fact called "The Twentieth Century," the Midwest produces the striving artist figure, Vance Weston, auspiciously named after a real estate sub-division, "Advance West." Fleeing cultural shallowness (and his hometown of Euphoria, Kansas) and traversing every maligned fad and fashion in contemporary literature (ridiculing along the way the regional politics governing the awarding of what is called "the Pulsifer Prize"), Vance Weston goes to New England and Europe in the course of two long books (*Hudson River Bracketed* [1929] and *The Gods Arrive* [1932]) looking for the depth of the past in places associated with art and libraries. The impending birth that closes *The Gods Arrive* (the last novel Wharton completed) does not suggest an act of sacrificial incarceration that assures the survival of civilization. The returning protagonist Vance Weston is welcomed by a vision of apotheosis as his previously abandoned, fully pregnant, and art-loving female muse, "Halo" Spear, opens the door of celestial ascent to the errant artist. This long-awaited scene where man and muse – art and fertility – are at last made one is related to "crucial moments" from earlier tales: the final door that opens for the male artist in *The Gods Arrive* re-imagines the door that opens for the narrator onto the infertile witches of *Ethan Frome*, revisits the door that opens into the red house for the pregnant Charity of *Summer*, and redefines the meaning of pregnancy and return as the window that closes for Newland Archer, the father-to-be of *The Age of Innocence*. Indeed, only by opening this door does the allegorically named artist figure, Vance Weston, like Wharton herself, advance east into the "old" (the western) world of book-lined houses. Finding a place for the artist on earth was the motive force for Wharton's life and art. She wrote and rewrote stories – her own and those of others – as if her own life and the fate of civilization depended on words themselves.

Counterposing the old world to the new, the past to the present, a sense of ethical depth to social shallowness, Wharton structured an imaginative territory that insisted on binary oppositions, a vision that allowed her to mount revelatory epiphanies through her use of paradox, the sharp, almost surgical, treatment that distinguishes her critiques of class and of gender. Some of Wharton's gentlest men, the dedicated caretakers such as Ethan Frome with his "red gash" in his forehead and the sensitive son-loving poet Ralph Marvell, are sacrificed on the protean yet strangely fixed altar of gender by complaining and voracious women. In Wharton's paradoxically gendered binary, loss itself is feminized, and there is a sense of ritualized female sacrifice in the tragic fate that befalls failed artists as well as caretakers, wounded men as well as vulnerable women. While the source of destruction may lie in the exacting appetites of feminine and shallow characters – Bessy Westmore (*The Fruit of the Tree* [1907]), Mattie Silver (*Ethan Frome*), and Undine Spragg (*The Custom of the Country*), to name a few – those who suffer in the fullness of consciousness assume the female or, more precisely, sacrificial position in a culture and a civilization that is by definition created through the sacrifice of the individual.

Lawyers, from the suicidal Ralph Marvell of *The Custom of the Country* to the drunken Mr. Royall of *Summer* to the tradition-bound Newland Archer of *The Age of Innocence*, move within established ethical structures to protect women, regardless of whether these female characters are sexually innocent. In contrast to these flawed lawgivers who valorize protection over passion in their roles as conservers of civilization, the emerging male artist figure (associated with the fatally self-divided Ralph Marvell) becomes the life-creating, art-engendering, younger generation whose proclivities take the form of a commitment to architecture by introducing new structures to the cultural drawing board. *Summer*'s child sired by the outsider named Harney (a descendant of Twain's violent exogamist, Harney Shepherdson of *Huckleberry Finn* [1884]) would have been a bastard if the mother's (Charity's) guardian, the reformed drunkard Lawyer Royall, had not married his own charge. Here, the older, more responsible man assumes responsibility as the caretaker of the new life infused by the architectural sketcher, the local colorist from the city whose interests lie in the past.

Problems raised in one Wharton novel have the generative power – an impetus that carried the urgency of a necessity – to provoke resolutions that are enacted in later novels. Yet rather than a recycling of plots, Wharton's *œuvre* insists on a nexus of vital relationships among works that display an obsession with finding resolutions to previously plotted dangers that seem to have attained a life of their own. In a profound connection characteristic of Wharton's fiction, the problem introduced by the failed architect of *Summer* – the stranger from the city who sketches abandoned and fallen houses rather than taking responsibility for building new structures – is resolved in *The Age of Innocence*, a novel where the lawyer-father remains because of his wife's announcement of her pregnancy. Arguably a better father than a lawyer, Newland Archer succeeds in rearing a socially liberated architect son, Dallas, who plans to marry Fanny Beaufort, the once illegitimate child that the novel elsewhere refers to in the ominous plural as "Beaufort's bastards." Although Fanny Beaufort's love-match rewrites Charity's story by redefining the specter of illegitimacy, *Summer*'s troubling truth remains. Denied romantic love in the season's turn toward the cold facts of marriage, the illegitimate Charity weds in a rural society where widowers of this era (often significantly older) were serially mated with women of childbearing age who tended to live close by, if not already within, their households.

Figures as seemingly distant as the suicidal Ralph Marvell and laudanum-addicted Lily Bart (who gambles between sleep and death) are replaced by characters who are not only "doomed to live" (Faulkner, *Absalom, Absalom!*), but who (like the Countess Olenska and even her thwarted lover, Newland Archer) manage to live well whether close to or at a sanctified distance from the life's blood of a clearly vital art. Never consummated, Newland and Ellen's relationship of renunciation nonetheless bears fruit, and there is the vital legacy of future fulfillment bodied forth through "their" children, spawned by an age that was not innocent of desire. While Ellen Olenska never has an affair with either the scurrilous Julius Beaufort or the respectable

Newland Archer, she is the family figure who scandalously comforts Beaufort's wife, her own cousin Regina Dallas (shunned by society after Beaufort's soiling financial scandal). The Countess also adopts the orphaned Fanny Beaufort (the illegitimate daughter of Beaufort and the notorious Fanny Ring) as her protégée when she is sent to convent school in Paris. Underlining the intensity of Fanny's entry into May's family, this once-rejected child returns to New York as the legal charge of Jack Welland, May's brother and an otherwise almost invisible character. When Newland and May's son Dallas (a baby whose very naming marks a rehabilitation of the dishonored family name borne by the ostracized Regina Dallas) marries Fanny Beaufort, all the unconsummated and childless relations of the novel will have become fulfilled through what Goethe elsewhere called "elective affinities." Just as Mrs. Manson Mingott's father, himself a notorious embezzler, has long ago abandoned her and her mother, Julius Beaufort in his exodus following his own fiduciary scandal effects a timely escape with his mistress and their illegitimate daughter that will also take them on an itinerary that includes the Spanish south of the new world. Indeed, the resilient plot vector that returns to the stories of orphaned rather than abandoned daughters centers on the childless Medora Manson who, at two different moments in her own extravagant marital career, takes care of an orphaned girl and oversees her financially lucrative and emotionally disastrous marriage. Arguably, Regina Dallas and Ellen Mingott are closer than sisters in their shared fates. Near the conclusion of *The Age of Innocence*, a second-generation orphaned girl-child, born into illegitimacy yet never abandoned, is legitimately embraced into the family fold. Progress evolves and meaning is generated as the same things happen over and over again until they can be repeated with a difference. Indeed, the genealogically overdetermined plot of *The Age of Innocence* has a compelling resonance with the revisited plots and intense acts of return that characterize the charged emotional landscape within, between, and among Wharton's most powerful fictions. Read as a dynamic narrative whole, Wharton's fiction, having begun by focusing on the sacrifice of art that embodies the specter of a culture's fall, ultimately comes to insist on the necessity of sacrifice for the survival of civilization.

As Wharton consciously made notes, proposing and sometimes writing books begotten by her own troubling creations – what might be called the "unquiet ghost[s]" ("A Bottle of Perrier," *Ghosts* [1937]) of other books – she imagined, among other things, a sequel to *The Age of Innocence* to be called "The Age of Wisdom" (Greeson 2003: 421). Proclaiming an optimistic turn into the new century by focusing on Fanny and Dallas, the proposed "Age of Wisdom" had no need to resolve problems articulated in the past, no compelling impetus to provoke it into being. Having lived through the wounding reality of the First World War, Wharton could *announce* the coming of the "age of wisdom," but even her well-matched couple, in historical as well as biblical terms, is destined to occupy an unfolding twentieth century that will march ineluctably toward 1914 while seeking titular shelter in a so-called "Age of Wisdom." If the fools described in Ecclesiastes are destined to dwell in "the house of mirth," those who seek refuge in the "age of wisdom" are fated to arrive with the wise at their biblically determined destination: "the house of mourning." Even as Dallas and Fanny's approaching marriage anticipates the embrace of the pregnant "Halo" Spear as she opens the door to Vance Weston at the close of *The Gods Arrive*, the proposed union at the close of *The Age of Innocence* functions as a veritable apotheosis, bringing together four significant triangles. This miraculous marriage retrospectively reconfigures, justifies, and serves to consummate the vexed triangulated relationships between and among Ellen, Newland, and May; Newland, Ellen, and Beaufort; Regina Dallas, Beaufort, and Fanny Ring; and May, Ellen, and Regina Dallas. The couple of the future, Dallas and Fanny, are the spiritual children of so many impulses and sacrifices that even as they inherit a changed world, their union consecrates the advent of an altered society in which former outlaws have become in-laws. Both born of erotic desire and fed by the harvests of life-affirming renunciation, Fanny and Dallas are finally joined by their shared affinity for the arts, an aesthetically driven love that consummates the legitimate union of so many once thwarted, spurned, and orphaned passions.

III

Briefly neglected in the decades following her death, Wharton has increasingly been recognized as one of the most imaginative and creative intellectual forces in English in the late nineteenth and early twentieth centuries. Her novels, novellas, and short stories were driven by ideas and by the psychological necessity to solve the problems that her own past creations had posed. Linking art to survival (both her own survival and that of the larger world), Wharton's fiction succeeds by evoking troubling realities in monitory parables. Joining raucous and unexpected humor to profound sadness, her finest work returns again and again to the place of sacrifice in the violent forging of civilization itself. Used historically, the word *civilization* might appear in the plural, but it was her understanding that the word *culture* could be understood in anthropological as well as aesthetic terms that was one of her major leaps into the new century. Less than a decade before her death and following a spate of writing that included her weakest as well as some of her strongest work, Wharton (flanked only by the younger figure of Willa Cather) was formally recognized as standing at the head of the American mainstream. Indeed, the critical insistence on the propriety of her class background and the habit of including a review of her *haute couture* clothes in early responses to her fiction belie the fact that Wharton herself (despite her formal manners and her unwavering fealty to the classics) was a radical experimentalist who *malgré lui* became a major influence on the literary modernism that she dismissed with such productive sound and fury.

Amid the tropes of literary descent sung on the open road, the Mississippi, and other major arteries of circulation, it is arguably the formally innovative, acutely intellectual, and theoretically astute Wharton who, in retrospect, can be seen as a figure of influence. In a 1931 essay, "My First Novels (There Were Two)," Cather explicitly blamed Wharton for the wrong path of her first novel, *Alexander's Bridge* (1912), a novel that from its choice of a protagonist who is a cultured engineer to the cultural crisis mapped onto two women reveals itself as a tame version of Wharton's *Ethan Frome*. Yet Cather drew formal inspiration from the experimental challenge posed by the same book in *The Professor's House*, a work whose dead man talking at its center mirrors the form of Wharton's *Ethan Frome* while insisting on repeating that novel's crucial image of a feminized man who is wounded on the forehead. Faulkner, who may have turned to Cather's *Professor's House* for his image of a dead mother careening downhill in an unwieldy box dragging a mule to its death in *As I Lay Dying* (1930), creates a work where a dead character also speaks into the central emptiness of a novel haunted by the vacuity of materialism. Cather's *Professor's House* and Faulkner's *As I Lay Dying* also glance backward to an even more direct descendant of *Ethan Frome*, specifically, the frozen burial of the grotesque mountain mother ("like a dead dog in a ditch") in *Summer*, the erotically explosive sequel that Wharton privately referred to as the "Hot Ethan." Cognizant of stagnation and the ominous presence of dead or infertile mothers, Wharton's work entered the stream, shaping the main currents of American literature in which her contributions became a formal force that linked death to the objectification born of materialism, and survival with the revivification that lay in the inanimate materials of art.

While Wharton's precocious modernist work, the *Ethan Frome* of 1911, was clearly influential as a work of fiction, her 1922 introduction to that same work must be read as a generative, critical manifesto that insists on the sculptural power of the spoken word. Arguing that truth may be produced by different characters who see a situation from varying points of view to create " 'roundness' in the plastic sense," Wharton's novel, which begins "I had the story, bit by bit, ... and ... each time it was a different story" (Wharton 1995: 3), articulates the narrative process behind such monumental works of modernist voice as Faulkner's *The Sound and the Fury* (1929), *As I Lay Dying*, and *Absalom, Absalom!* (1936). While there are signs of her influence throughout Faulkner's novels on the level of quoted words as well as shared thematic obsessions, Wharton's impact on a then unknown writer is audible in her most influential and provocative critical diatribe: *The Writing of Fiction* (1925). Here Wharton locates modernist fiction in "a pathological world where the action, taking place between people of abnormal psychology, and not keeping time with our normal human rhythms, becomes an idiot's tale, signifying nothing."

Like George Eliot, Wharton was fully immersed in the evocative poetry of aesthetics and the dream of realism as she inhabited a tough-minded world that compelled her to respond to, converse with, and finally give structural form to the questions she continued to hear in her profound acts of reading. Indeed, the challenge of reading Wharton is to enter a frame of reference gathered through a lifetime by a woman with one of the most extensive, discerning, and indiscriminate reading habits in the history of the book. Wharton alluded to literature from the four languages she spoke as well as from classical texts in translation. She quoted playfully from popular music and opera; she played with form, performing jazz riffs in relation to magazine advertisements and the debased mercantile language that spoke for an emerging mass culture. She used paintings and sculpture as imagined illustrations for scenes that fleshed out her fiction, and she even incorporated key scenes of female demise from once flashy, now largely forgotten, thrillers, notably Anna Katherine Green's *Leavenworth Case* (1878), the first detective novel written by a woman. Wharton's place in American letters has been appreciated – she has undergone both a feminist and a Hollywood renaissance – but her finest readers, her most gifted readers, continue to be her own stellar, if younger contemporaries: the consciously resistant Willa Cather and her most acute respondent, William Faulkner.

Through her fiction and her writing about fiction, Wharton entered the critical conversation in ways that changed the course of American literature by opening the door to the divergent voices that speak in the Faulkner of *As I Lay Dying*, the Toni Morrison of *Sula* (1973), the Ernest Gaines of *A Gathering of Old Men* (1983), and the Louise Erdrich of *Love Medicine* (1985, 1993). Clearly drawing on rich cultural inheritances, resoundingly influential streams of oral allusions, and literary legacies of experimental prose that include the work of Sherwood Anderson and Jean Toomer as well as Faulkner and the more immediate and thronging presence of Morrison herself, these current writers tend to acknowledge Faulkner, who – whether he is seen as a source of formal inspiration or as a semiotic provocateur – threatens to emerge in the role of a shared ancestor. Yet the Faulkner these writers have chosen to honor is the Faulkner who is Wharton's most direct literary descendant. This Faulkner, a figure who, like Wharton herself, was paradoxically more writer than man, answered Wharton's novels and literary critiques with a depth that continues to resonate in late twentieth- and early twenty-first-century American literature despite the fact that he and many others appear never to have uttered her name.

Whatever Wharton's reservations about the postwar literary generation, she paid younger writers the compliment of reading their work. Her essays and letters mention numerous modernists by name, revealing her to have been a serious if generally unsympathetic reader of, among others, Virginia Woolf, James Joyce, T. S. Eliot, and, not least, Faulkner, whose name she sometimes misspelled. Reading Faulkner's *Sanctuary* (1931), for instance, reawakened Wharton's interest in an idea for a long-planned (but never completed) essay "on the new school of fiction" she imagined titling "Wuthering Depths" (letter of June 8, 1931, quoted in Wharton 1996: 174). Only months before she died, Faulkner was again on her mind, "Palates accustomed to William Falkner [*sic*] no longer care for delicate fare" (letter of March 1, 1937, quoted in Benstock 1994: 389). Tellingly, a late letter to Bernard Berenson offers qualified praise for Faulkner, possibly for his treatment of the incest theme in *The Sound and the Fury*. About recent fiction by the controversial young Italian novelist Alberto Moravia, Wharton "remain[s] unconverted & incorrigible – because Faulkner & [Ferdinand] Céline did it *first*, & did it *nastier*." Parenthetically, she adds, she herself has "an incest donnée up [her] sleeve that wd make them all look like nursery-rhymes" (Aug. 14, 1935, in Wharton 1988: 589).

Ironically, at the height of her fame, when in 1921 she had just been awarded the Pulitzer Prize, Wharton wondered whether younger writers in the United States read her at all. In response to a "kind, ... generous & ... unexpected" letter from Sinclair Lewis, she confesses, "It is the first sign I have ever had – literally – that '*les jeunes*' at home had ever read a word of me. I had long since resigned myself to the idea that I was regarded by you all as the – say the Mrs. Humphry Ward of the Western Hemisphere" (6 Aug. 1921, in Wharton 1988: 445). A passage from a late notebook voices similar concerns: "When I get glimpses, in books & reviews, of the things people are going to assert about me after I am dead, I feel I must have the courage & perseverance, some day, to forestall them" (*Quaderno dello Studente*, quoted in Colquitt et al. 1999: 13).

Wharton's worries about her literary legacy proved prescient: until 1975, when Lewis's *Edith Wharton: A Biography* appeared, the most influential study of the novelist's life was Percy Lubbock's masterfully misogynistic *Portrait of Edith Wharton* (1947). Savaging her character and her career – and even her "yapping" Pekinese – Lubbock posits that Wharton's "little literary talent" paled in comparison to that of Henry James, whose "disciple" she became (Lubbock 1947: 26, 243, 146). As Lewis comments, Lubbock's portrait was "surreptitiously false in many places" (Lewis 1975: 516). Beginning with Lewis, a succession of biographers has in recent decades crafted other, more generously conceived (and more true) portraits of Wharton. They include Cynthia Griffin Wolff's *A Feast of Words: The Triumph of Edith Wharton* (1977),

---

Figure 27.1 Edith Wharton and the new woman author

Edith Wharton's lifetime (1862–1937) spanned a crucial period in the transformation of women's authorship in America. The domestic and sentimental novelists of the mid-century who preceded her were, with few exceptions, wives and mothers who did not consciously view themselves as professionals, despite the enormous popular success of their works. Her contemporaries – Jewett, Chopin, Freeman, Murfree, Woolson – were identified as regionalist authors; although they were often quite worldly and self-consciously professional, their works were not overly popular and they enjoyed only limited critical acclaim. Born into upper-crust New York society, Wharton fought against the social strictures that made authorship a demeaning occupation for a woman, just as she struggled with a new mass literary marketplace that made both her and her books into commodities that exposed her private world to public view.

Wharton's novels also crossed the admittedly permeable boundaries of historical and literary genres. On the one hand, she wrote realist novels of manners like *The House of Mirth*, *The Custom of the Country*, and *The Age of Innocence*. Such novels, despite the fact that they critiqued society's codes, particularly those of gender and marriage, earned her the reputation of a "genteel" writer in the mode of Henry James, with the implication that she was somewhat isolated from the lives of ordinary people and indifferent to the problems of the non-wealthy. But she also brought the world of naturalism into the drawing rooms and showed that high society could be as red in tooth and claw as the Yukon wilds of Jack London or the battlefields of Stephen Crane. In addition, she worked within the paradigm of regionalism, depicting not only the regions of town houses and country estates, but also the enclaves of the rural poor in the Berkshires. Lastly, she anticipated many of the defining elements of literary modernism. Like Howells, Twain, and her friend James, she was a major influence on a new generation of authors who would emerge in American fiction between the world wars. For many years not given her full due by academic critics, she is now viewed as one of the greatest novelists and storywriters of the twentieth century. (Photograph courtesy of The Lilly Library, Indiana University, Bloomington, Indiana.)

Gloria C. Erlich's *The Sexual Education of Edith Wharton* (1992), Susan Goodman's *Edith Wharton's Inner Circle* (1994), Eleanor Dwight's *Edith Wharton: An Extraordinary Life* (1994), Shari Benstock's *No Gifts from Chance: A Biography of Edith Wharton* (1994), and Alan Price's *The End of the Age of Innocence: Edith Wharton and the First World War* (1996). Taken together, these life studies offer compelling portraits of a complex artist in a manner that suggests the kaleidoscopic nature of the biographer's art. Read dialogically – Benstock with Dwight, Goodman with Price, Wolff with Erlich – these biographies (all by American scholars) make clear that even the subtlest shift of the biographer's hand can transfigure our vision of Wharton. That image will undoubtedly change again with the forthcoming biography by the noted British scholar Hermione Lee, whose work promises, for American audiences, an "outside" view of Wharton.

Formerly slighted as "our literary aristocrat" (Vernon L. Parrington) or as "Henry James's heiress" (Q. D. Leavis), Wharton is now judged a major force in American letters, as is reflected in the rapid rise of Wharton scholarship over the past thirty years. Invaluable resources for those seeking access to Wharton and her critics include Stephen Garrison's *Edith Wharton: A Descriptive Bibliography* (1990), Kristin O. Lauer and Margaret P. Murray's *Edith Wharton: An Annotated Secondary Bibliography* (1990), James W. Tuttleton, Kristin O. Lauer, and Margaret P. Murray's *Edith Wharton: The Contemporary Reviews* (1992), Frederick Wegener's *Edith Wharton: The Uncollected Critical Writings* (1996), Sarah Bird Wright's *Edith Wharton A to Z: The Essential Guide to the Life and Work* (1998), Helen Killoran's *The Critical Reception of Edith Wharton* (2001), and Carol J. Singley's *A Historical Guide to Edith Wharton* (2003). Indeed, to scan the critical canon is to realize that Wharton – from her juvenilia to the posthumous *Buccaneers* (1938) – has always attracted notice. Yet, as Killoran aptly observes, Wharton's "was, and is, a puzzling genius" (2001: 1).

Her name "long . . . public property," Wharton in some ways has come to resemble her own early heroine, Margaret Aubyn, "the famous novelist" from *The Touchstone* whose most private thoughts and feelings are exposed – "her whole self laid bare" – when, shortly after her death, the man who was "for years" Aubyn's sole "intimate friend" sells his most valuable possession: her letters. Importantly, when Stephen Glennard finally perceives what he has done ("It was myself I sold") he also experiences the stirrings of love:

> He knew, of course, that they [the letters] were wonderful; that, unlike the authors who give their essence to the public and kept only a dry rind for their friends, Mrs. Aubyn had stored of her rarest vintage for this hidden sacrament of tenderness. Sometimes, indeed, he had been oppressed, humiliated almost, by the multiplicity of her allusions, the wide scope of her interests, her persistence in forcing her superabundance of thought and emotion into the shallow receptacle of his sympathy. . . . He was almost frightened now at the wealth in his hands; the obligation of her love had never weighed on him like this gift of her imagination: it was as though he had accepted from her something to which even a reciprocal tenderness could not have justified his claim.

This passage brilliantly illuminates Wharton's own dilemma as a woman of genius and of passion, and anticipates as well the challenges her critics and biographers continue to face as they confront "the multiplicity of . . . allusions" and "the wide scope of . . . interests" that contribute to the wealth of Wharton's literary gift.

In the first half of the twentieth century, when women were the second sex and professors of literature were overwhelmingly male, Wharton's reputation declined even as a veritable who's who of American and British letters – including Carl Van Doren, Edmund Wilson, Q. D. Leavis, John Crowe Ransom, Diana Trilling, Lionel Trilling, Irving Howe, and Alfred Kazin – at times begrudgingly evaluated her work. Toward the end of the century, with the advent of feminist, gender, and cultural studies, a growing community of scholars, most of them women, has seen Wharton anew. Feminist luminaries such as Elaine Showalter, Susan Gubar, Sandra M. Gilbert, and Lillian S. Robinson have sensitively examined Wharton's lifelong study of the painful calculus of marriage and divorce, continuing a discussion that began as early as 1953, when in the first major book-length critical study of Wharton, Blake Nevius detected "a lurking feminism" in the fiction, a notion that is still open to debate (1953: 85). Among recent participants in this and other sophisticated arguments about Wharton's politics, sexual and otherwise, are Elizabeth Ammons, Dale Bauer, and Candace Waid. Wharton's relationship to myriad traditions – literary, artistic, linguistic, ethnographic, religious, philosophical, and scientific – has been thoughtfully documented by Nancy Bentley, Kathy A. Fedorko, Hildegard Hoeller, Helen Killoran, Elsa Nettels, Claire Preston, and Carol J. Singley. Additional clues concerning the mysterious alchemy between Wharton's prodigious reading and her creative process may be found in George Ramsden's meticulous catalogue of Wharton's extant library. (Half of her books were destroyed in the Second World War.) These and other touchstones from the first century of Wharton studies suggest that scholars have only barely begun to explore the secret garden of her art.

Selected Primary Texts by Edith Wharton

Verses. 1878.

The Decoration of Houses (with Ogden Codman, Jr.). 1897.

The Greater Inclination. 1899.

The Touchstone. 1900.

Crucial Instances. 1901.

The Valley of Decision. 1902.

Translation of *The Joy of Living (Es Lebe das Leben): A Play in Five Acts*, by Hermann Sudermann. 1903.

Sanctuary. 1903.

The Descent of Man and Other Stories. 1904.

Italian Villas and their Gardens. 1904.

Italian Backgrounds. 1905.

The House of Mirth. 1905.

Madame de Treymes. 1907.

The Fruit of the Tree. 1907.

The Hermit and the Wild Woman and Other Stories. 1908.

A Motor-Flight Through France. 1908.

Artemis to Actæon and Other Verse. 1909.

Tales of Men and Ghosts. 1910.

Ethan Frome. 1911.

The Reef. 1912.

The Custom of the Country. 1913.

Fighting France, from Dunkerque to Belfort. 1915.

The Book of the Homeless (Le livre des sans-foyer) (ed.). 1916.

Xingu and Other Stories. 1916.

Summer. 1917.

The Marne. 1918.

French Ways and Their Meaning. 1919.

In Morocco. 1920.

The Age of Innocence. 1920.

The Glimpses of the Moon. 1922.

A Son at the Front. 1923.

Old New York: False Dawn (The 'Forties), The Old Maid (The 'Fifties), The Spark (The 'Sixties), New Year's Day (The 'Seventies). 1924.

The Mother's Recompense. 1925.

The Writing of Fiction. 1925.

Here and Beyond. 1926.

Twelve Poems. 1926.

Twilight Sleep. 1927.

The Children. 1928.

Hudson River Bracketed. 1929.

Certain People. 1930.

The Gods Arrive. 1932.

Human Nature. 1933.

A Backward Glance. 1934.

The World Over. 1936.

Ghosts. 1937.

The Buccaneers. 1938.

LATER COLLECTIONS

Wharton, Edith (1969). *Eternal Passion in English Poetry* (comp., with Robert Norton, and collaboration of Gaillard Lapsley). Freeport, NY: Books for Libraries Press. (first publ. 1939.)

Wharton, Edith (1988). *The Letters of Edith Wharton*, ed. R. W. B. Lewis and Nancy Lewis. New York: Scribner.

Wharton, Edith (1990). *Edith Wharton: Novellas and Other Writings*, ed. Cynthia Griffin Wolff. New York: Library of America.

Wharton, Edith (1996). *Edith Wharton: The Uncollected Critical Writings*, ed. Frederick Wegener. Princeton: Princeton University Press.

REFERENCES AND FURTHER READING

Ammons, Elizabeth (1980). *Edith Wharton's Argument with America*. Athens, Ga.: University of Georgia Press.

Bauer, Dale (1994). *Edith Wharton's Brave New Politics*. Madison: University of Wisconsin Press.

Bell, Millicent, ed. (1995). *The Cambridge Companion to Edith Wharton*. Cambridge, UK: Cambridge University Press.

Benstock, Shari (1994). *No Gifts from Chance: A Biography of Edith Wharton*. New York: Scribner.

Bentley, Nancy (1995). *The Ethnography of Manners: Hawthorne, James, Wharton*. Cambridge, UK: Cambridge University Press.

Cather, Willa (1931). "My First Novels (There Were Two)." *Colophon*, pt. 6, n.p.

Colquitt, Clare; Goodman, Susan; and Waid, Candace, eds. (1999). *A Forward Glance: New Essays on Edith Wharton*. Newark: University of Delaware Press; London: Associated University Presses.

Dwight, Eleanor (1994). *Edith Wharton: An Extraordinary Life*. New York: Harry H. Abrams.

Erlich, Gloria C. (1992). *The Sexual Education of Edith Wharton*. Berkeley: University of California Press.

Fedorko, Kathy A. (1995). *Gender and the Gothic in the Fiction of Edith Wharton*. Tuscaloosa: University of Alabama Press.

Fryer, Judith (1986). *Felicitous Space: The Imaginative Structures of Edith Wharton and Willa Cather*. Chapel Hill, NC: University of North Carolina Press.

Garrison, Stephen (1990). *Edith Wharton: A Descriptive Bibliography*. Pittsburgh: University of Pittsburgh Press.

Gilbert, Sandra M. (1985). "Life's Empty Pack: Notes toward a Literary Daughteronomy." *Critical Inquiry* 11, 355–84.

Gilbert, Sandra M., and Gubar, Susan (1988). "Angel of Devastation: Edith Wharton on the

Arts of the Enslaved." In *No Man's Land: The Place of the Woman Writer in the Twentieth-Century*, vol. 2: *Sexchanges*, 123–68. New Haven: Yale University Press.

Goodman, Susan (1994). *Edith Wharton's Inner Circle*. Austin: University of Texas Press.

Greeson, Jennifer Rae (2003). "Wharton's Manuscript Outlines for *The Age of Innocence*." In Edith Wharton, *The Age of Innocence*, ed. Candace Waid, 413–21. New York: Norton.

Hoeller, Hildegard (2000). *Edith Wharton's Dialogue with Realism and Sentimental Fiction*. Gainesville, Fla.: University Press of Florida.

Howe, Irving, ed. (1962). *Edith Wharton: A Collection of Critical Essays*. Englewood Cliffs: Prentice-Hall. (Twentieth Century Views.)

Kazin, Alfred (1942). "Two Educations: Edith Wharton and Theodore Dreiser." In *On Native Grounds: An Interpretation of Modern American Prose Literature*, 73–90. New York: Harcourt. Excerpted in Howe (ed.), *Edith Wharton*, 89–94.

Killoran, Helen (1996). *Edith Wharton: Art and Allusion*. Tuscaloosa: University of Alabama Press.

Killoran, Helen (2001). *The Critical Reception of Edith Wharton*. Rochester: Camden.

Lauer, Kristin O., and Murray, Margaret P. (1990). *Edith Wharton: An Annotated Secondary Bibliography*. New York: Garland.

Leavis, Q. D. (1938). "Henry James's Heiress: The Importance of Edith Wharton." *Scrutiny* 7, 261–76. Repr. in Howe (ed.), *Edith Wharton*, 73–88.

Levenson, J. C., et al., eds. (1988). *The Letters of Henry Adams*, vol. 6: *1906–1918*. Cambridge, Mass.: Belknap/Harvard University Press.

Lewis, R. W. B. (1975). *Edith Wharton: A Biography*. New York: Harper.

Lubbock, Percy (1947). *Portrait of Edith Wharton*. New York: Appleton-Century.

Nettels, Elsa (1997). *Language and Gender in American Fiction: Howells, James, Wharton, and Cather*. Charlottesville: University Press of Virginia.

Nevius, Blake (1953). *Edith Wharton: A Study of her Fiction*. Berkeley: University of California Press.

Olin-Ammentorp, Julie (2004). *Edith Wharton's Writings from the Great War*. Gainesville: University Press of Florida.

Parrington, Vernon L. (1921). "Our Literary Aristocrat." Review of *The Age of Innocence*. *Pacific Review* 2, 157–60. Repr. in Howe (ed.), *Edith Wharton*, 151–4.

Preston, Claire (2000). *Edith Wharton's Social Register*. London: Macmillan; New York: St. Martin's.

Price, Alan (1996). *The End of the Age of Innocence: Edith Wharton and the First World War*. New York: St. Martin's.

Ramsden, George, comp. (1999). *Edith Wharton's Library: A Catalogue*. Settrington, UK: Stone Trough Books.

Ransom, John Crowe (1936). "Characters and Character: A Note on Fiction." *American Review* 6, 271–88.

Robinson, Lillian (1994). "The Traffic in Women: A Cultural Critique of *The House of Mirth*." In Edith Wharton, *The House of Mirth*, ed. Shari Benstock, 340–58. Boston: St. Martin's. (Case Studies in Contemporary Criticism.)

Showalter, Elaine (1985). "The Death of the Lady (Novelist): Wharton's *The House of Mirth*." *Representations* 9, 133–49.

Singley, Carol J. (1995). *Edith Wharton: Matters of Mind and Spirit*. Cambridge, UK: Cambridge University Press.

Singley, Carol J., ed. (2003). *A Historical Guide to Edith Wharton*. New York: Oxford University Press.

Trilling, Diana (1947). "*The House of Mirth* Revisited." *Harper's Bazaar* 81. Repr. in Howe (ed.), *Edith Wharton*, 103–18.

Trilling, Lionel (1956). "The Morality of Inertia." In Robert M. MacIver (ed.), *Great Moral Dilemmas in Literature, Past and Present*, 37–46. New York: Harper. Repr. in Howe (ed.), *Edith Wharton*, 137–46.

Tuttleton, James W.; Lauer, Kristin O.; and Murray, Margaret P., eds. (1992). *Edith Wharton: The Contemporary Reviews*. Cambridge, UK: Cambridge University Press.

Van Doren, Carl (1922). *Contemporary American Novelists, 1900–1920*. New York: Macmillan.

Van Doren, Carl (1940). *The American Novel, 1789–1939*. New York: Macmillan. (Rev. and enlarged edn. of *The American Novel*, 1921.)

Waid, Candace (1991). *Edith Wharton's Letters from the Underworld: Fictions of Women and Writing*. Chapel Hill: University of North Carolina Press.

Waid, Candace (2003). "The Business of Society: Contemporary Commentary on the New York Aristocracy." In Waid (ed.), *Age of Innocence*, 311–13.

Wharton, Edith (1975). "Beatrice Palmato." In R. W. B. Lewis, *Edith Wharton: A Biography*, 544–8. New York: Harper and Row.

Wharton, Edith (1981). *"The House of Mirth" : The Play of the Novel*, dramatized by Edith Wharton and Clyde Fitch, ed. Glenn Loney. London and Toronto: Associated University Presses.

Wharton, Edith (1990). "Life and I." In *Edith Wharton: Novellas and Other Writings*, ed. Cynthia Griffin Wolff, 1069–96. New York: Library of America.

Wharton, Edith (1992). *The Cruise of the Vanadis*. New York: Rizzoli.

Wharton, Edith (1993). *Fast and Loose and The Buccaneers*, ed. Viola Hopkins Winner. Charlottesville: University Press of Virginia.

Wharton, Edith (1994). "The Life Apart (*L'âme close*)." In Kenneth M. Price and Phyllis McBride, "'The Life Apart': Text and Contexts of Edith Wharton's Love Diary." *American Literature* 66, 663–88.

Wharton, Edith (1995). *Ethan Frome*, ed. Kristin O. Lauer and Cynthia Griffin Wolff. New York: Norton Critical Editions.

Wharton, Edith (1998). *A Backward Glance*, intr. Louis Auchincloss. New York: Simon & Schuster.

Wharton, Edith (2003a). *The Age of Innocence*, ed. Candace Waid. New York: Norton.

Wilson, Edmund (1947). "Justice to Edith Wharton." In *The Wound and the Bow: Seven Studies in Literature*, 195–213. New York: Oxford University Press. Repr. in Howe (ed.), *Edith Wharton*, 19–31.

Wolff, Cynthia Griffin (1995). *A Feast of Words: The Triumph of Edith Wharton*, rev. edn. Reading, Mass.: Addison-Wesley. (First publ. New York: Oxford University Press, 1977.)

Wright, Sarah Bird (1998). *Edith Wharton A to Z: The Essential Guide to the Life and Work*. New York: Facts On File.

28

Sensations of Style: The Literary Realism of Stephen Crane

William E. Cain

Stephen Crane (1871–1900) performed his literary work with great confidence. He wrote *The Red Badge of Courage* (1895) because he believed that he could do better than *La Débâcle* (1892), Émile Zola's book about two soldiers in the Franco-Prussian war, and he planned a novel titled *Peace and War* that would improve upon the job that Leo Tolstoy had done. Not in awe of any author, Crane said that *War and Peace* (1865–9) should have been slashed by two-thirds. As his first biographer Thomas Beer noted (1923), Crane "adored Tolstoy the superb and ruthless artist, but for Tolstoy the emotional pedagogue, the pilgrim of redemption, he had no use" (Beer 1923: 166).

In his life and writing, Crane was curious about and eager for extreme sensations. His stories, poems, and novels project cosmic speculations, but these should not be taken too seriously. Crane is not grappling with ideas about God and the universe, but, rather, representing them, expressing them, because he wants to know in the act of writing what they feel like. He enjoyed being provocative, making use of his peerless command of imagery and brash irony to gibe at the beliefs that overconfident (and hence deluded) persons had accepted.

Crane's work is "the expression in literary art of certain enormous repudiations," his friend H. G. Wells declared. Crane repudiates religion, family, and community and, more than that, offers no alternatives. As Alfred Kazin maintains in *On Native Grounds* (1942), "the surest thing one can say about Crane is that he cared not a jot which way the world went" (Kazin 1970: 68). Crane claimed he had been "a Socialist once for two weeks but when a couple of Socialists assured me I had no right to think differently from any other Socialist and then quarreled with each other about what Socialism meant, I ran away."

Crane regarded himself as superior to his Methodist relatives who led "nicely laundered lives." In a pocket notebook, he penned a quote he believed was from Emerson (no scholar has yet found the source): "Congratulate yourselves if you have done something strange and extravagant and broken the monotony of a decorous age."

Later, he reflected: "I used to like church and prayer meetings when I was a kid but that cooled off and when I was thirteen or about that, my brother Will told me not to believe in Hell after my uncle had been boring me about the lake of fire and the rest of the sideshows." On his deathbed he observed: "When you come to the hedge that we must all go over – it isn't bad. You feel sleepy and you don't care – just a little dreamy anxiety – which world you're really in – that's all."

An adventurer and thrill-seeker, Crane took pleasure in being where the action was, but not because of any position or cause he embraced. It was intense feeling he craved, an intensity that in his reading about major events and experiences he rarely found addressed to his satisfaction. About the accounts of the Civil War he sampled in the *Battles and Leaders* series (first published in *Century Illustrated Monthly Magazine* in the mid-1880s and later in a four-volume set, 1884–7), Crane said: "I wonder that *some* of these fellows don't tell how they *felt* in those scraps." "They spout eternally of what they *did*, but they are emotionless as rocks."

What would a young man, misled by his reading and by stories heard in town about the glories of war, feel as he approached the field of battle and faced the enemy for the first time? What would he feel, really feel, as he fled in terror and then returned to fight like a demon? These were the plotline questions to which Crane imagined the youthful Henry Fleming's responses; and he presented them in *The Red Badge of Courage*, the book with which any assessment of Crane must begin. He had material to work with and consult. He had heard stories told by Civil War vets; he read books, among them Tolstoy's *Sebastopol* (1855–6), and studied photographs. His brother Edmund was an expert on Civil War battles and tactics; and veterans of the 124th New York, some of whom Crane knew, provided him with information about the battle of Chancellorsville, Virginia, where the Confederate army had defeated a superior Union force in May 1863. But *The Red Badge of Courage* is not dependent on these sources. It is a feat of the imagination, a demonstration of literary prowess, a visionary book.

The Red Badge of Courage is an exhilarating reading experience in the mesmerizing potency of its language, the outlandish mockery of its tone, and the Salvador Dali- and René Magritte-like transformations of places and persons and things that Crane generates nonstop, as in this sequence of paragraphs depicting the terrified youth's flight:

> He slowly lifted his rifle and catching a glimpse of the thickspread field he blazed at a cantering cluster. He stopped then and began to peer as best as he could through the smoke. He caught changing views of the ground covered with men who were all running like pursued imps, and yelling.
>
> To the youth it was an onslaught of redoubtable dragons. He became like the man who lost his legs at the approach of the red and green monster. He waited in a sort of a horrified, listening attitude. He seemed to shut his eyes and wait to be gobbled.
>
> A man near him who up to this time had been working feverishly at his rifle suddenly stopped and ran with howls. A lad whose face had borne an expression of

exalted courage, the majesty of he who dares give his life, was, at an instant, smitten abject. He blanched like one who has come to the edge of a cliff at midnight and is suddenly made aware. There was a revelation. He, too, threw down his gun and fled. There was no shame in his face. He ran like a rabbit.

Others began to scamper away through the smoke. The youth turned his head, shaken from his trance by this movement as if the regiment was leaving him behind. He saw the few fleeting forms.

He yelled then with fright and swung about. For a moment, in the great clamor, he was like a proverbial chicken. He lost the direction of safety. Destruction threatened him from all points.

Directly he began to speed toward the rear in great leaps. His rifle and cap were gone. His unbuttoned coat bulged in the wind. The flap of his cartridge box bobbed wildly, and his canteen, by its slender cord, swung out behind. On his face was all the horror of those things which he imagined. (ch. 6)

Crane is also brilliant at more quietly grotesque effects, as in a later scene where Henry Fleming wanders through the woods:

At length he reached a place where the high, arching boughs made a chapel. He softly pushed the green doors aside and entered. Pine needles were a gentle brown carpet. There was a religious half-light.

Near the threshold he stopped, horror-stricken at the sight of a thing.

He was being looked at by a dead man who was seated with his back against a columnlike tree. The corpse was dressed in a uniform that once had been blue, but was now faded to a melancholy shade of green. The eyes, staring at the youth, had changed to the dull hue to be seen on the side of a dead fish. The mouth was open. Its red had changed to an appalling yellow. Over the gray skin of the face ran little ants. One was trundling some sort of bundle along the upper lip. (ch. 7)

As these passages show, Crane's central concern is the experience of war as a maximal situation confronted by a frightened consciousness. John Berryman, in his illuminating biography (1950; rev. 1962), thus is on the mark when he contends that in *The Red Badge of Courage* Crane indicates "no interest in the causes, meaning, or outcome" of the Civil War. Lincoln and Davis, Grant and Lee, slavery and abolition: the political leaders, generals, large-scale military strategies, and fiery passions that provoked and propelled the war do not matter to him. With captivating flamboyance and precision, Crane delineates the operations of his protagonist Henry Fleming's mind in crisis. Detached from his characters, scrutinizing them, but aware of how completely absorbing they are to themselves, Crane knows that it is not fear that troubles Henry Fleming, but the fear that others will see he is afraid. Running away isn't so bad. What's bad is that others might find out.

Crane chose the Civil War for his setting because many of his readers knew it first-hand and because many more were saturated in memoirs, illustrated books, battle records and reports, stories, and reunions related to it. Crane hence had something to capitalize upon, much he could take for granted, and even more to set himself against. *The Red Badge of Courage* struck Crane's contemporaries (including many Civil War veterans) as realistic, as believable and persuasive, even as it also seemed new to them, unlike anything about the war they had read.

In an effort to locate sources for this newness, modern scholars have linked Crane to a host of authors, philosophers, and social theorists, including Jacob Riis, William James, Darwin and Spencer, Zola and Tolstoy, Flaubert and Chekhov, Hamlin Garland and William Dean Howells, Henry James, Joseph Conrad, and even French impressionist (e.g. Claude Monet) and pointillist (e.g. Georges Seurat) painters. But these connections do not help much to explain how Crane's writing came to be the way it is in *The Red Badge of Courage* and in the other novels, stories, and poems. Berryman may offer the best image for understanding Crane, a writer "alone in a room with the English language, trying to get human feelings right."

Writing with both poise and bravado, Crane registers the dizzying turns and twists of a fearful, guilt-ridden, and (after Henry's heroics) contentedly relieved young man ("he was a man": ch. 24) who has in a frenzy of self-control mastered an experience that instant to instant threatened to overwhelm him. It is missing Crane's point to ask the question about this novel that critics so often debate: has Henry Fleming matured or is he self-deceived? Crane is exploring the coincidence of maturity and self-deception; he is working toward a conception of a character's psychology to which the customary distinctions and categories cannot do justice.

To put this another way: Crane is not offering a choice between free will and determinism, but, rather, showing that Henry Fleming needs both of these terms to understand and get through the crisis that assails him. He blames himself, others, the universe; he feels ashamed by his own actions, indicts others for what they have done to him, and lashes out at the forces that expose men so pitilessly to injustice and humiliation. Much of the weird, grim, ironic humor of *The Red Badge of Courage* comes from Henry's oscillations, as Crane pointedly sends him from one extreme of feeling to another and back again. But this is also where the novel's intellectual challenge and seriousness lie as well. For Crane, free will and determinism are names we give to a process that includes both at one and the same time. Singling out one or the other, as though it were primary and mattered more, is inevitable yet misleading, a sign of the limits of our common vocabulary for describing why persons act, and think and feel, as they do.

Crane was heartened by the acclaim he received for the true-to-life quality of *The Red Badge of Courage*. In a letter he said that the reviewers "all insist that I am a veteran of the civil war, whereas the fact is, as you know, I never smelled even the powder of a sham battle" (Crane 1988: vol. 1, 322). He had not been in battle, but he could render the experience of it with amazing clarity and conviction. From his boyhood, he had yearned to make his body "a testing ground for all the sensations of life," and he pushed and tested himself at every opportunity. Physically unimpressive at 5 feet 6 inches and 125 pounds, with blond hair and blue-gray eyes, he played baseball all-out, with "frantic glee," according to a teammate, and frantic, feverish behavior is repeatedly featured in Crane's descriptive language in *The Red Badge of Courage*. Crane relished football, too, and similarly applied its lessons to his book: "I have never been in a battle, of course, and I believe that I got my sense of the rage of conflict on the football field. The psychology is the same. The opposing team is an enemy tribe" (quoted in Stallman 1968: 181).

Crane was born in Newark, New Jersey, on November 1, 1871, the fourteenth and youngest child (nine survived) of the Reverend Jonathan Townley Crane (b. 1819) and Mary Helen Peck Crane (b. 1827). His mother was forty-five when Stephen was born; the four children born before him had all died in infancy. His father, a graduate of the College of New Jersey (now Princeton University), was the presiding elder of Methodist churches in the Newark district, and also an author committed to producing ten pages a day. In *An Essay on Dancing* (1848), *Popular Amusements* (1869), *Arts of Intoxication* (1870), and other books, he decried the use of alcohol and tobacco, card-playing, and other ungodly diversions, all of which his son Stephen would later embrace. One of the father's injunctions was: "a rigid iron rule for the guidance of all, young and old, learned and unlearned: TOTAL ABSTINENCE FROM NOVEL READING HENCEFORTH AND FOREVER" (quoted in Crane 1960: 5).

The elder Crane's way with words, as well as his religious view, shaped to an extent the writer that his son became. In, for example, one of his many essays on temptation and sin, Crane's father wrote: "The Scriptures tell us that Noah planted a vineyard and on one occasion drank of the wine until he was drunken. Very possibly the process of fermentation had not before been noticed, the results were not known, and the consequences in this case were wholly unexpected." Make the irony more glaring and heighten the detachment already in the tone, and one comes close to the feeling for life's peculiarities and humankind's follies that took hold of Stephen Crane.

Crane's family lived in Bloomington and Paterson, New Jersey, before settling in April 1878 in Port Jervis, in southeastern New York, where Crane's father was pastor of the Drew Methodist Church and where Crane began grammar school in September. Crane's father died in February 1880 of "paralysis of the heart," and three years later his wife and the younger children moved to the coastal resort town of Asbury Park (120 miles away from Port Jervis). Mrs. Crane, the daughter of a Methodist minister and the niece of a Methodist bishop, wrote essays for Methodist journals and New York and Philadelphia papers, gave lectures, and was a member of the Women's Christian Temperance Union. She kept the level of piety in the household high.

Crane attended Pennington Seminary, a coeducational Methodist boarding school in New Jersey where his father had served as principal in the 1850s. In January 1888, aged sixteen, he entered Claverack College and Hudson River Institute, a junior college and military school in Columbia County, New York. Fond of playing soldier and proud of ancestors who had participated in the American Revolution (one of them had commanded a New Jersey infantry regiment), Crane was happy at Claverack, saying that he had "a bully time" (quoted in Stallman 1968: 18).

During the fall 1890 semester Crane was a student at Lafayette College in Pennsylvania. He was asked to leave because of "scholastic delinquencies," having failed nearly all of his courses. He spent the spring 1891 semester at Syracuse University (which had been co-founded by his mother's uncle, Jesse Peck) in upstate New York, but was no more successful as a student there. A haphazard reader, Crane skimmed popular magazines and newspapers, perused novels on his own, including *Anna Karenina* and *War and Peace*, and thumbed through military histories. He asserted that "humanity was a more interesting study" than books and academic courses; his amusements were playing baseball, attending the theater, and keeping company with women. He told a friend "college life is a waste of time" and said he intended to become a newspaper reporter.

Crane had begun doing newspaper work as early as summer 1888, assisting his brother Townley, who headed a news agency in Asbury Park. In the fall of 1891 he did not return to Syracuse but chose instead to explore the slums, brothels, and saloons of the Bowery, on the lower east side of New York City. His mother was gravely ill (she died of cancer in December) and Crane was poor, intermittently writing for newspapers and living with friends in run-down, shabby New York apartments and off and on at a brother's house in New Jersey.

By early the following year, however, Crane had completed and revised the draft of *Maggie*, his first major work of fiction, the story of a mistreated but innocent girl and her harsh life in a New York City slum. The novel does not emerge from Crane's Bowery experiences but apparently preceded them. The scholar R. W. Stallman has concluded that Crane wrote the first draft of *Maggie* while at Syracuse: "here he read an English translation of Flaubert's *Madame Bovary* and then began writing his Bowery version of that novel, substituting for the as-yet-unexplored demi-world of the Bowery his knowledge of Syracuse's red-light district" (1968: 32). Crane's fiction about New York slum life took place before his forays into its depths. As Stallman explains, Crane "argued for personal experience as the basis of art, but he also argued for imaginative experience" (Crane 1952: xxxi). Going a step further, the critic Christopher Benfey has proposed with only slight exaggeration that *Maggie*, "well underway by the fall of 1891," was "less the result of Crane's experiments than their cause" (1992: 61).

Unable to find a commercial publisher, Crane published his novel privately, with the full title of *Maggie, A Girl of the Streets (A Story of New York)*, in March–April 1893. He borrowed $700 from his brother to meet the cost of printing, and the book appeared in yellow paper wrappers under the pseudonym Johnston Smith, with a modest print run of 1,100 copies.

Crane affirmed he had written with a purpose, noting in an inscription in gift copies that he sought in *Maggie* "to show that environment is a tremendous thing in the world and frequently shapes lives regardless. If one proves that theory, one makes room in Heaven for all sorts of souls (notably an occasional street girl) who are not confidently expected to be there by many excellent people." Though sometimes rebuking Crane's descriptions as overdone, as too brutal and sordid, reviewers commended *Maggie* for showing the deprivations, economic and emotional, of slum life. The novelist Hamlin Garland (whom Crane had heard lecture in August 1891) and W. D. Howells, Dean of American letters, especially admired it.

Maggie is partially the product of its era, as Crane's own reference to the impact of "environment" suggests. Zola's many novels, including *Thérèse Raquin* (1867), *L'Assomoir* (1877), and *Germinal* (1885) were well known and influential, and their renderings of fate, heredity, and environment were adapted and developed within an American context at the turn of the century by Frank Norris in *McTeague* (1899) and *The Octopus* (1901) and by Theodore Dreiser in *Sister Carrie* (1900) as well as by Crane some years earlier. But Crane chose to work on a smaller scale; he was more selective, without the huge obsessiveness about sociological detail that Zola, Norris, and Dreiser demonstrated. Nature is indifferent (or, it often seems, hostile) to human struggle; specific conditions of social life harass or block the achievement of virtue and indeed make typical kinds of moral judgment simplifying and inappropriate; persons act less by choices than by compulsions: in *Maggie*, Crane, akin to the major naturalists, expresses and explores these views. Norris perhaps was touching on this point when he stated in a review: "the author is writing, as it were, from the outside. There is a certain lack of sympathy apparent" (*The Wave*, July 4, 1896; quoted in Stallman 1968: 544). But Crane has a piercing clarity in his sentences that the other naturalists do not; though engaged with related themes, he differs from them in his conception and practice of literary language. His prose is taut and intense; the ironic pitch of the tone and startling phrases and images used in unexpected places for uncanny effects are more surreal than realistic; and yet it is absorbing and convincingly authentic for all its lurid qualities.

Crane exhibits his Bowery scenes and characters in forbidding yet flamboyant terms:

> Eventually they entered into a dark region where, from a careening building, a dozen gruesome doorways gave up loads of babies to the street and the gutter. (ch. 2)
>
> The wife put her immense hands on her hips and with a chieftain-like stride approached her husband. (ch. 2)

And he plays off his narrative voice – mocking, menacing, relentlessly ironic – against the fierce directness of the characters' words to one another:

> "You've been drinkin, Mary," he said. "You'd better let up on the bot', ol woman, or you'll get done."
>
> "You're a liar, I ain't had a drop," she roared in reply.
>
> They had a lurid altercation, in which they damned each other's souls with frequence. (ch. 2)

Crane's sentences carry condensed power, deliberately overbright and volcanic. A little like Emerson, he often appears at his most effective when taken by the sentence. Yet in *Maggie* many of his sequences of sentences effectively capture the eerie dissonances of scenes and situations:

Across from the bar a smaller counter held a collection of plates upon which swarmed frayed fragments of crackers, slices of boiled ham, disheveled bits of cheese, and pickles swimming in vinegar. An odor of grasping, begrimed hands and munching mouths pervaded. (ch. 11)

She went into the blackness of the final block. The shutters of the tall buildings were closed like grim lips. The structures seemed to have eyes that looked over her, beyond her, at other things. Afar off the lights of the avenues glittered as if from an impossible distance. Street car bells jingled with a sound of merriment. (ch. 17)

Crane offers no new message in *Maggie*; the degradation caused by coarsening, corrupting poverty had been presented before and would be again by many writers, social critics, and photographers. Nor was he advancing a case for reform. "You can't find preaching on any page of *Maggie*," he said. "An artist has no business to preach." What Crane offered (and took pleasure in) was an unprecedented style.

Crane was disappointed by the response to *Maggie*: "I remember how I looked forward to its publication, and pictured the sensation I thought it would make. It fell flat. Nobody seemed to notice it or care for it" (Crane 1988: vol. 1, 232). But, determined and in need of money, he was already planning a novel about the soldier Henry Fleming when the first book was published. He worked on it during the summer and fall, at his brother Edmund's home in Lake View, New Jersey, and in an old studio he shared with artist and illustrator friends in the former Art Students League building on East 23rd Street (Crane said that they lived on sardines, buns, and potato salad and took turns sleeping on the floor). His supporter Hamlin Garland said that Crane's "fingers were yellow with cigarette reek, and he looked like a man badly nourished" (Crane 1960: 301).

The Red Badge of Courage was first published in a much-shortened form (18,000 of the manuscript's 55,000 words) in the Philadelphia *Press* in December 1894, and, through syndication, in a number of other newspapers. From late January to mid-May 1895, Crane worked as a correspondent in the American West and in Mexico, but by early fall he had prepared a revised version of the manuscript, and it was published – Crane called it "a psychological portrayal of fear" – by D. Appleton and Company in October 1895. While not a moneymaker for Crane, it was a critical success, and he wrote five more Civil War stories between September 1895 and February 1896, including "The Veteran" and "An Episode of War." A new (and revised) edition of *Maggie* was published as well, and the twenty-three-year-old Crane, a celebrity author, now received dozens of invitations to write journalistic pieces and submit stories.

Crane was also a poet. In May 1895 his first book of verse was published – *The Black Riders and Other Lines* (1895): sixty-eight poems, all of them untitled, each placed high on the page and presented in capital letters. Terse, bold, and enigmatic, the poems show affinities with the work of Emily Dickinson (the first collections of whose poems appeared in 1890 and 1891) and the poetical sketches and songs of William Blake.

The best poem is the first:

> Black riders came from the sea.
> There was clang and clang of spear and shield,
> And clash and clash of hoof and heel,
> Wild shouts and the wave of hair
> In the rush upon the wind:
> Thus the ride of sin.

The majority of the poems, while stark and striking, are more awkward:

> Many red devils ran from my heart
> And out upon the page,
> They were so tiny
> The pen could mash them.
> And many struggled in the ink.
> It was strange
> To write in this red muck
> Of things from my heart.

In a letter of October 2, 1894, Howells told Crane: "These things are too orphic for me" (Crane 1960: 40). But the positive reactions to and sales of *The Red Badge of Courage* led to a wider audience for Crane's verse: "the poetry became of wider interest and was frequently reviewed in the context of the popularity of the novel" (Crane 1972: xxxiii).

From this point to his death in 1900, Crane wrote and published much, and frequently at top speed, in order to pay his debts. His story about a mother's fanatical devotion to her son, *George's Mother*, which he had begun in 1893 and completed in late 1894, appeared in early June 1896, and later in the same month an expurgated edition of *Maggie* was published. Hoping to capitalize still further on the success of *The Red Badge of Courage*, Crane assembled stories for a collection titled *The Little Regiment, and Other Episodes of the American Civil War*, published in December 1896.

In this same month Crane found the love of his life, Cora Howorth Taylor, the proprietor of the Hotel de Dream, a high-class bawdy house in Jacksonville, Florida, where Crane had stopped en route to cover the Cuban revolution. Cora was an avid reader and a world traveler; she was six years older than Crane, and had been married twice. Prior to meeting her, Crane had relationships, romances, and sexual flings with a number of women, including prostitutes (in summer 1896 he had lived in a brothel). He wrote erotic verse (which he destroyed) and, according to one report, had started a novel, *Flowers in Asphalt*, about a boy street-walker. Cora's spirit of revolt and unconventional behavior made her the right match for Crane, as is suggested by one of her diary entries: "Unenthusiastic natures, how much they miss! . . . I have lived five years in one all my life. I have never economized in sensation, emotion. I am a spendthrift in every way" (Gilkes 1960: 46). She also wrote: "One of the greatest pleasures of having been what is called bad is that one has so much to say to the good. Good people love hearing about sin . . . " (Gilkes 1960: 50).

While making the trip from Florida to Cuba on the steamer *Commodore*, which was illegally conveying arms to Cuban insurrectionists, Crane was shipwrecked on the morning of January 2, 1897. Fifteen miles from shore, he drifted for thirty hours with several other men in a ten-foot dinghy. Crane himself behaved bravely: "That man Crane is the spunkiest fellow out," the Captain remarked; and one of the crew added, "that newspaper feller was a nervy man. He didn't seem to know what fear was" (quoted in Stallman, 1968: 247, 248). Crane reported on this experience at sea in a newspaper account, "Stephen Crane's Own Story" (*New York Press*, January 7) and drew upon it for his story "The Open Boat," which in its narrative tone conveys the uncannily detached mood of panicky fatalism that he had perfected.

In spring 1897 Crane traveled with Cora to the Mediterranean to report on the war between Turkey and Greece. In June 1897 he returned to London, and the next month he and Cora (identifying themselves as Mr. and Mrs. Stephen Crane) rented a house in Oxted, Surrey, in southeast England. During the summer and fall he enjoyed friendships with Joseph Conrad, Edward Garnett, and Ford Madox Hueffer (Ford). He wrote "The Monster," "The Bride Comes to Yellow Sky," and "The Blue Hotel," three of his best stories. "I don't believe in inspiration," he observed. "I am one of those who believe that an enthusiasm of concentration in hard work is what a writer must depend on to bring him to the end he has in view" (quoted in Stallman 1968: 168).

A master of the short-story form, Crane had not only a powerful kind of concentration, but also a rare command of an unusual brooding tone. In his stories he satirizes humankind's overestimation of its powers, its inability to absorb the fact of its littleness in the midst of large, implacable nature. Yet even as he dramatizes the futility of human effort, Crane records the necessity and rightness of individual struggle, no matter how flailing and pathetic it might seem. Crane's own disciplined virtuosity, at his best, is a counter-statement against the implications of his own world-view.

By early 1898 Crane was on another newspaper assignment, traveling again to Cuba to cover the Spanish–American War and the exploits of Teddy Roosevelt and his volunteer cavalry regiment, the Rough Riders. Crane's journalistic pieces, twenty of which had appeared in the New York *World*, and twenty more in the New York *Journal*, were later included in *Wounds in the Rain: A Collection of Stories Relating to the Spanish–American War of 1898* (October 1900).

After nine months away from Cora, including three months in Havana, Crane made his way back to New York in November and then on December 31 sailed for England, where the two of them in February 1899 rented a dilapidated fourteenth-century manor, Brede Place, in Sussex. As Lilian Gilkes (1960) has stated, Crane was "in process of exchanging his early bohemianism for the new look of an English squire." There was no gas, electricity, or plumbing. Servants refused to spend the night there because of the legend that the house was haunted. Conrad, who esteemed Crane's writing and valued his friendship, judged the residence "uninhabitable" (Conrad 1923: 26).

Crane became friends with Henry James (who bicycled from seven miles away in Rye) and H. G. Wells, and proceeded busily with both his prose and poetry. He published two collections of stories, *The Open Boat and Other Tales of Adventure* (April 1898) and *The Monster and Other Stories* (December 1899), and in between a volume of verse, *War is Kind* (May 1899). Suffering from tuberculosis, Crane traveled to a sanitarium in Badenweiler, in the Black Forest of Germany. But the treatments were unsuccessful, and on June 5, 1900 he died. His body was returned to the United States and buried in the Crane family plot in Hillside, New Jersey.

Though his career was brief, Crane amassed an impressive body of work. In addition to the books already cited, he wrote two other novels, *The Third Violet* (1897) and *Active Service* (1899, about the Greco-Turkish War). Another collection, *Whilomville Stories*, was published two months after his death, and additional posthumous books followed: *Great Battles of the World* (1900); *Last Words* (1902, edited by Cora Taylor), which gathered early writings and new tales and sketches; *The O'Ruddy: A Romance* (1903, completed by the editor and journalist Robert Barr); and *Men, Women, and Boats* (1921), which brought together stories that had not been previously printed. *The Work of Stephen Crane*, a twelve-volume set edited by Wilson Follett, was published in 1925–7, and *The Collected Poems of Stephen Crane*, again edited by Follett, appeared in 1930.

There are abundant signs of the still greater author whom Crane might have become had he lived, above all in "The Monster," a long story of 21,000 words that took Crane two months to complete and that is the most complex and exploratory piece of fiction he wrote. "The Monster" tells of a black servant, Henry Johnson, who saves the son of a local doctor, Ned Trescott, from a house fire but whose face is horribly disfigured by burning acid and whose mind is deranged from the shock. Trescott is indebted to Johnson and provides for him, but, as the story unfolds, the doctor increasingly is ostracized by the townspeople who find Johnson's appearance repellent and frightening.

On one level, "The Monster" examines race relations and racism in America, suggesting that "the monster" is not the disfigured black man but the cruel community that shuns and torments him. Crane may have modeled Johnson on a black man, his face eaten away by cancer, who lived in Port Jervis, and in the background too is the lynching in the town of a black man (accused of rape) that occurred in June 1892. Henry Johnson performed a brave act; he is not a monster; but then again, "monster" is the identity that racial stereotypes of the era warned that each black man harbored just beneath the surface of his skin. Women and children recoil from Johnson, alarmed that he poses a mortal (that is, sexual) danger to them. At one point he is chased through the streets by an angry mob hurling rocks at him, a ghastly enactment of the racial violence commonplace in the South and to an extent in the North in the 1890s.

In "The Monster," Crane inquires into the racialized interconnectedness of black and white persons that Harriet Beecher Stowe had set forth in *Uncle Tom's Cabin* (1852), that Melville had weighed ominously in "Benito Cereno" (1855), that preoccupied Mark Twain in *Adventures of Huckleberry Finn* (1884) and *Pudd'nhead Wilson* (1894), and that Faulkner, Wright, Ellison, and Baldwin would grapple with in later decades. But the special power of "The Monster" lies in the innovative recasting of his style that Crane developed for it. As John Berryman pointed out, the story "initiates a revolution in Crane's aesthetic":

> Details of the exceptional, the colored, the fantastic, the cursory, will indeed be found; but on the whole he attacks his subject directly, and the change is great. Crane must have been thinking hard during the months preceding, agreeing with himself to give up half his tools and try something new. The story is ambitious in a new way: it studies not one individual or two, and a dog or a horse, but an entire community, Negroes and whites, doctors, a judge, a police chief, wives, boys, a barber, loungers, girls. (1962: 192)

Crane beautifully controls his fervent, phantasmagorical powers of literary imagination, as in the climactic scene, dreadful and opulent in its imagery, where Johnson, after desperately rescuing the boy, falls amid the flames and is scarred by the acid:

> Johnson halted for a moment on the threshold. He cried out again in the negro wail that had in it the sadness of the swamps. Then he rushed across the room. An orange-colored flame leaped like a panther at the lavender trousers. This animal bit deeply into Johnson. There was an explosion at one side, and suddenly before him there reared a delicate, trembling sapphire shape like a fairy lady. With a quiet smile she blocked his path and doomed him and Jimmie. Johnson shrieked, and then ducked in the manner of his race in fights. He aimed to pass under the left guard of the sapphire lady. But she was swifter than eagles, and her talons caught in him as he plunged past her. Bowing his head as if his neck had been struck, Johnson lurched forward, twisting this way and that way. He fell on his back. The still form in the blanket flung from his arms, rolled to the edge of the floor and beneath the window.
>
> Johnson had fallen with his head at the base of an old-fashioned desk. There was a row of jars upon the top of this desk. For the most part, they were silent amid this rioting, but there was one which seemed to hold a scintillant and writhing serpent.
>
> Suddenly the glass splintered, and a ruby-red snakelike thing poured its thick length out upon the top of the old desk. It coiled and hesitated, and then began to swim a languorous way down the mahogany slant. At the angle it waved its sizzling molten head to and fro over the closed eyes of the man beneath it. Then, in a moment, with mystic impulse, it moved again, and the red snake flowed directly down into Johnson's upturned face.
>
> Afterwards the trail of this creature seemed to reek, and amid flames and low explosions drops like red-hot jewels pattered softly down it at leisurely intervals. (section 7)

Trescott is right, or so it appears, to feel indebted to the black man who rescued his boy, but he soon faces the disturbing consequences of his gratitude. Trescott's son and young friends view Johnson as a freak; Trescott's patients scornfully abandon him; his friends and associates cast doubt on the wisdom of his loyalty to Johnson as the community fixates on the black "thing" as a threat to its safety; and, in the closing scene of the story, all the more devastating for its restraint, he must comfort his wife, whom the women of the town have ostracized:

> He pulled a chair close to hers. Later, as he cast his eye over the zone of light shed by the dull red panes, he saw that a low table had been drawn close to the stove, and that it was burdened with many small cups and plates of uncut tea-cake. He remembered that the day was Wednesday, and that his wife received on Wednesdays.
>
> "Who was here to-day, Gracie?" he asked.
>
> From his shoulder there came a mumble, "Mrs. Twelve."
>
> "Was she – um," he said. "Why – didn't Anna Hagenthorpe come over?"
>
> The mumble from his shoulder continued, "She wasn't well enough."
>
> Glancing down at the cups, Trescott mechanically counted them. There were fifteen of them. "There, there," he said. "Don't cry, Grace. Don't cry."
>
> The wind was whining round the house, and the snow beat aslant upon the windows. Sometimes the coal in the stove settled with a crumbling sound, and the four panes of mica flashed a sudden new crimson. As he sat holding her head on his shoulder, Trescott found himself occasionally trying to count the cups. There were fifteen of them. (section 24)

In the language of this scene, the critic Michael Fried hears "the intimation – it seems more than just a bare possibility – that Johnson will now have to be abandoned" (1987: 142). But the momentum of the story implies still more disquieting possibilities and questions. Johnson became a monster when the acid poured on his face. In another sense, however, he became a monster by failing to die when he saved the boy, as the initial reports stated and as the townspeople at first assumed; if he had not subverted their expectations, he would have been memorialized as a self-sacrificing brave man, even an angel of mercy, whatever (indeed, because of) his disfigurement. In view of the consequences for Johnson, Dr. Trescott, his wife, and so many others, including other blacks who also find him repulsive, it would have been better if Johnson had died, or else had not been prompted to rescue Trescott's son in the first place.

"The Monster" bears witness to Crane's complex moral intelligence and depth of reflection, dramatized through an authoritative form of verbal art that is piercingly direct when it needs to be and richly metaphorical when that is called for too. The author of a half-dozen of American literature's most significant works, Crane moved in "The Monster" to a new height of expertise and insight, and his early death, at age twenty-nine, was an immense loss for American literature. But his achievement was substantial – and unmistakably original. The controlled tensions of his language crucially influenced Cather and Hemingway, and his daring extravagances of imagery inspired Faulkner and Ellison, among others. Like the longer-lived Mark Twain, Crane matters both for the novels and stories that he wrote and for the literary work that his potent example did so much to make possible.

Selected Primary Texts by Stephen Crane

Maggie, A Girl of the Streets (A Story of New York). 1893.

The Black Riders and Other Lines. 1895.

The Red Badge of Courage; an Episode of the American Civil War. 1895.

The Little Regiment, and Other Episodes of the American Civil War. 1896.

The Third Violet. 1897.

The Open Boat and Other Tales of Adventure. 1898.

Active Service. 1899.

War Is Kind. 1899.

The Monster and Other Stories. 1899.

Bowery Tales. 1900.

Great Battles of the World. 1900.

Whilomville Stories. 1900.

Wounds in the Rain: A Collection of Stories Relating to the Spanish–American War of 1898. 1900.

Last Words. 1902.

The O'Ruddy: A Romance. 1903.

Men, Women, and Boats. 1921.

Later Collections

Crane, Stephen (1925–7). *The Work of Stephen Crane*, ed. Wilson Follett. 12 vols. New York: Knopf.

Crane, Stephen (1930). *Collected Poems*, ed. Wilson Follett. New York: Knopf.

Crane, Stephen (1952). *Stephen Crane: An Omnibus*, ed. R. W. Stallman. New York: Knopf.

Crane, Stephen (1960). *Letters*, ed. R. W. Stallman and Lillian Gilkes. New York: New York University Press.

Crane, Stephen (1963a). *Complete Short Stories and Sketches*, ed. Thomas A. Gullason. New York: Doubleday.

Crane, Stephen (1963b). *Uncollected Writings.* Upsala, Minn.: Upsala University Press.

Crane, Stephen (1964). *The War Dispatches*, ed. R. W. Stallman and E. R. Hagemann.

Crane, Stephen (1966). *The New York City Sketches of Stephen Crane, and Related Pieces*, ed. R. W. Stallman and E. R. Hagemann. New York: New York University Press.

Crane, Stephen (1967). *Complete Novels*, ed. Thomas A. Gullason. New York: Doubleday.

Crane, Stephen (1968). *Sullivan County Tales and Sketches*, ed. R. W. Stallman. Ames: Iowa State University Press.

Crane, Stephen (1969). *The Portable Stephen Crane*, ed. Joseph Katz. New York: Viking.

Crane, Stephen (1969–76). *Works*, ed. Fredson Bowers. 10 vols. Charlottesville: University of Virginia Press.

Crane, Stephen (1972). *Complete Poems*, ed. Joseph Katz. New York: Cooper Square.

Crane, Stephen (1984). *Prose and Poetry*, ed. J. C. Levenson. New York: Library of America.

Crane, Stephen (1988). *Correspondence*, ed. Stanley Wertheim and Paul Sorrentino. 2 vols. New York: Columbia University Press.

Crane, Stephen (2000). *The Red Badge of Courage; Maggie, a Girl of the Streets; and Other Selected Writings: Complete Texts with Introduction, Historical Contexts, Critical Essays*, ed. Phyllis Frus and Stanley Corkin. Boston: Houghton Mifflin.

References and Further Reading

Åhnebrink, Lars (1961). *The Beginnings of Naturalism in American Fiction: A Study of the Works of Hamlin Garland, Stephen Crane, and Frank Norris, with Special Reference to Some European Influences, 1891–1903.* New York: Russell & Russell.

Bassan, Maurice, ed. (1967). *Stephen Crane: A Collection of Critical Essays.* Englewood Cliffs, NJ: Prentice-Hall.

Beer, Thomas (1923). *Stephen Crane: A Study in American Letters.* New York: Knopf.

Benfey, Christopher (1992). *The Double Life of Stephen Crane*. New York: Knopf.

Berryman, John (1962). *Stephen Crane: A Critical Biography*, rev. edn. New York: Farrar, Straus, Giroux. (First publ. 1950.)

Brown, Bill (1996). *The Material Unconscious: American Amusement, Stephen Crane, and the Economies of Play*. Cambridge, Mass.: Harvard University Press.

Colvert, James B. (1984). *Stephen Crane*. San Diego: Harcourt Brace Jovanovich.

Conrad, Joseph (1923). "Introduction." In Thomas Beer, *Stephen Crane: A Study in American Letters*, 1–35. New York: Knopf.

Crane, Stephen (1979). *Maggie, a Girl of the Streets (A Story of New York): An Authoritative Text, Backgrounds and Sources, The Author and the Novel, Reviews and Criticism*, ed. Thomas A. Gullason. New York: Norton.

Crane, Stephen (1982). *The Red Badge of Courage; an Episode of the American Civil War, Newly Edited from Crane's Original Manuscript*, ed. Henry Binder. New York: Norton.

Crane, Stephen (1994). *The Red Badge of Courage: An Authoritative Text, Backgrounds and Sources, Criticism*, ed. Donald Pizer. New York: Norton.

Crane, Stephen (1999). *Maggie, a Girl of the Streets: A Story of New York*, ed. Kevin J. Hayes. Boston: Bedford/St. Martin's.

Davis, Linda H. (1998). *Badge of Courage: The Life of Stephen Crane*. Boston: Houghton Mifflin.

Dooley, Patrick Kiaran (1992). *Stephen Crane: An Annotated Bibliography of Secondary Scholarship*. New York: Hall.

Ellison, Ralph (1995). *Collected Essays*, ed. John F. Callahan. New York: Modern Library.

Fried, Michael (1987). *Realism, Writing, Disfiguration: On Thomas Eakins and Stephen Crane*. Chicago: University of Chicago Press.

Gandal, Keith (1997). *The Virtues of the Vicious: Jacob Riis, Stephen Crane, and the Spectacle of the Slum*. New York: Oxford University Press.

Gibson, Donald B. (1968). *The Fiction of Stephen Crane*. Carbondale: Southern Illinois University Press.

Gibson, Donald B. (1988). *The Red Badge of Courage: Redefining the Hero*. Boston: Twayne.

Gilkes, Lillian (1960). *Cora Crane: A Biography of Mrs. Stephen Crane*. Bloomington: Indiana University Press.

Gullason, Thomas A., ed. (1972). *Stephen Crane's Career: Perspectives and Evaluations*. New York: New York University Press.

Halliburton, David (1989). *The Color of the Sky: A Study of Stephen Crane*. New York: Cambridge University Press.

Hoffman, Daniel (1957). *The Poetry of Stephen Crane*. New York: Columbia University Press.

Katz, Joseph, ed. (1972). *Stephen Crane in Transition: Centenary Essays*. DeKalb: Northern Illinois University Press.

Kazin, Alfred (1970). *On Native Grounds: An Interpretation of American Prose Literature*. New York: Harcourt Brace Jovanovich. (First publ. 1942.)

Monteiro, George (2000). *Stephen Crane's Blue Badge of Courage*. Baton Rouge: Louisiana State University Press.

Nagel, James (1980). *Stephen Crane and Literary Impressionism*. University Park: Pennsylvania State University Press.

Pizer, Donald, ed. (1990). *Critical Essays on Stephen Crane's* The Red Badge of Courage. Boston: Hall.

Robertson, Michael (1997). *Stephen Crane, Journalism, and the Making of Modern American Literature*. New York: Columbia University Press.

Schaefer, Michael W. (1996). *A Reader's Guide to the Short Stories of Stephen Crane*. New York: Hall.

Solomon, Eric (1966). *Stephen Crane, from Parody to Realism*. Cambridge, Mass.: Harvard University Press.

Stallman, R. W. (1968). *Stephen Crane: A Biography*. New York: Braziller.

Stallman, R. W. (1972). *Stephen Crane: A Critical Bibliography*. Ames: Iowa State University Press.

Weatherford, Richard M. (1973). *Stephen Crane: The Critical Heritage*. Boston: Routledge & Kegan Paul.

Wertheim, Stanley (1997). *A Stephen Crane Encyclopedia*. Westport, Conn.: Greenwood.

Wertheim, Stanley, and Sorrentino, Paul (1994). *The Crane Log: A Documentary Life of Stephen Crane, 1871–1900*. New York: Hall.

Wolford, Chester L. (1983). *The Anger of Stephen Crane: Fiction and the Epic Tradition*. Lincoln: University of Nebraska Press.

Wolford, Chester L. (1989). *Stephen Crane: A Study of the Short Fiction*. Boston: Twayne.

29

Theodore Dreiser and the Force
of the Personal

Clare Virginia Eby

It seems fitting that Theodore Dreiser (1871–1945), like many American realists and naturalists, should have come to fiction by way of journalism. He proudly recorded a copyreader's assessment of some of his early news writing: "you have your faults, but you do know how to observe." In one of his autobiographies Dreiser reflects on his journalistic apprenticeship, tracing his young adulthood in Chicago, St. Louis, and other cities before settling in New York for several years, all before he would emerge as the controversial author of his first novel, *Sister Carrie* (1900). A characteristic passage from *Newspaper Days* (1922) encapsulates what would become Dreiser's signature orientation. Casting himself as an eyewitness, he observes the "degraded poor" of Chicago. "Always I was intensely curious," he writes, about "the why thereof. Why didn't society do better by them, why didn't they do better by themselves? Was government to blame? Or they? Or who? Always the miseries of the poor... fascinated me."

Several aspects of this passage make it characteristic of Dreiser, one being its subject matter. He is among the most important chroniclers of wealth and poverty in the United States, especially as financial position became newly visible in the booming urban centers. But in this passage the perspective of the observer is at least as pronounced as that of the observed, and it is the autobiographer's orientation toward his subject that marks the passage as truly Dreiserian. His speculation is abstract but hardly detached; the border between fascinated writer and those impoverished people who constitute his subject is permeable, as is the border between the poor and the principles that Dreiser feels they exemplify. Human specimens of abstract principles, laws, and forces always mesmerize Dreiser, prompting intense curiosity and equally intense speculation. Are individuals responsible for the positions they occupy, he repeatedly asks, or is society, biology, or some extrahuman force responsible? No reader of Dreiser's novels can avoid such questions, especially not in the face of ruminating narrators who routinely halt plots to pose them. In his concern with a panoply of forces – scientific, cosmic, psychological, cultural, and socioeconomic –

Dreiser shares the preoccupations of his generation. Yet as Ronald Martin puts it, of all the realists and naturalists Dreiser seems most "at home in the world of force" (1981: 217). Impersonal forces pervade his pages not simply because of the era's fascination with scientific and pseudoscientific systems but also because Dreiser, along with his characters, takes these forces so personally. This personal register of the impersonal, we might say, is his hallmark. It determines what he writes about: we can trace its imprint through Dreiser's recurring subjects, such as social class, consumer culture, and sexuality. The personal register also deeply influences core aspects of his aesthetic ideals, views on morality, and philosophical beliefs.

Social class is perhaps the most immediate and pervasive of all the impersonal forces that Dreiser knew intimately. Many years ago, F. O. Matthiessen observed that Dreiser was the first major American author from the wrong side of the tracks. Numerous authors whose ethnicity, race, or class made them appear marginal to earlier generations now justifiably claim readers' attention, but it remains true that poverty and social marginalization marked Dreiser's childhood and decisively influenced his outlook. In *Dawn* (1931), the autobiography covering his earliest years, he recalls being sent home one November from his Catholic school in Sullivan, Indiana, for not wearing any shoes. The incident "certainly did impress and even humiliate me," recalls Dreiser. No wonder that as a child he became "sharply aware of what it meant to have less as opposed to more." Consider Dreiser's wonder when he glimpsed a rich man's house in Terre Haute: "My face is pressed between the two iron pickets of the fence, to see. What could so great an animal be?" Young Dreiser's dreams of happiness, renown, comfort, and romance were entwined, as so often happens in America, with dreams of socio-economic advancement, yet he never forgot the poverty of his youth. Thus he can remark, practically in the same breath, that "I was . . . tremendously fascinated by the rise of the various captains of industry" and that "the underdog always interested me, – his needs, his woes, his simplicities."

Dreiser captures the range of social positions because, as he once put it, "life at close range . . . fascinated me." He excels at depicting the effect of class position on the individual psyche, on the singular personality: in other words, at depicting the personal. This preoccupation can be traced back to some of his earliest writings. In an 1897 column for *Ev'ry Month*, a music magazine he edited (in fact writing most of the contents himself), Dreiser reflects on the "wide gap between the very rich and the very poor." Again he approaches sociological speculation, wondering if this income gap might serve some social purpose: "It may be necessary that some should drudge and slave, and others walk in elegance." But Dreiser's perspective moves, as always, rapidly between the global and the local: he notes that the poor, the "drudges[,] are so numerous. . . . They have to struggle so hard for bread. They have to wear such wretched clothes. Their days are all toil, and their nights weariness." But what makes the position of the poor intolerable is not the work, the deprivation, the struggle, nor the exhaustion; rather, their lives are intolerable because "With all this they are cursed with minds and hearts." The poor laugh, they cry, "they work, work, work, until they are yellow and faded and limp – and they are humans."

This deceptively simple insight into the humanity of the poor is one of Dreiser's most important. Another, although a note he hits less frequently, is the humanity of the rich.

Differentiations of social class in America comprise one of Dreiser's most important subjects. Although his novels are remarkable for their treatment of middle-class striving, they portray nearly the full range of social classes. He has the working poor down cold, as illustrated in the early scenes of *Jennie Gerhardt* (1911), when the children pick up coal from railroad tracks to heat their house on Christmas Eve. In *An American Tragedy* (1925), Dreiser hauntingly captures social marginality in the Griffiths family of Kansas City, who humiliate their son Clyde by their streetcorner evangelism. Clyde knows that "Other boys did not do such things" as preach on the street, and the work seems "shabby and even degrading" to him. Dreiser captures also the smug superiority of the rich in the Kane family of *Jennie Gerhardt*, and again in the Lycurgus branch of the Griffiths family of *An American Tragedy*. In the latter novel, snobbish Samuel Griffiths instructs his family not to pay their cousin "any social attention," lest Clyde erroneously conclude he was on an "equal footing with any of us." Even blood relatives must never forget that they are, as haughty cousin Gilbert puts it, "employees first, last and all the time." Rationalizing inequity as a form of inspiration, the upper-crust Griffithses maintain that "there had to be higher and higher social orders to which the lower social classes could aspire." Yet when it comes to the figure at the top of the social heap, the robber baron millionaire, this figure has never been more sympathetically drawn than in Frank Cowperwood of *The Trilogy of Desire* (*The Financier* [1912]; *The Titan* [1914], and *The Stoic* [1947]). Dreiser invests the trilogy's hero with "fascinating individuality" and "immense creative force."

Dreiser excels at giving the abstraction of social class a human face because he understood that such concepts as *position* and *status* suggest a stability that individuals rarely experience. The lived experience of social class in the United States has less to do with fixed position than with continual movement – whether striving for a higher position, or struggling to maintain one that threatens to slip away. The two main characters in *Sister Carrie* demonstrate this principle in unforgettable detail. Carrie Meeber and George Hurstwood are both scarred by social marginality; although they experience it at different times in their lives and with different consequences, their wounds from it never heal. For Carrie, the degradation of working in a Chicago shoe factory and living with the Hansons becomes her overriding motivation, albeit a negative one: she doesn't know what she wants to become, but she knows that she isn't – won't be – can't be – a factory worker, nor like her sister Minnie. The Hansons expect Carrie to "submit ... to a solemn round of industry," but after one day of imbibing their dreary Protestant work ethic, Carrie feels suffocated. She likewise finds the monotonous strain of factory work first "distasteful," then "nauseating." The littered, smelly room where she works offends her, while her co-workers disgust her. The impact persists long after she has left the shop: "Toil, now that she was free of it, seemed even a more desolate thing than when she was part of it." To signify the imminent change (albeit in uncertain direction), Dreiser concludes the chapter about Carrie's first day in the factory by quietly noting that "her heart revolted." Many chapters later, he uses the same phrase when Carrie is on the brink of leaving Hurstwood, who sees nothing untoward in expecting her to scale down her wants; again Carrie's "heart revolted." Through fits and starts, she struggles, edging upward through the novel as she moves away from what she detests.

Hurstwood's experience of marginality is more devastating, and literally becomes lethal after he loses his comfortable position. The chapter in which Dreiser introduces Hurstwood carefully situates him: "a very acceptable individual of our great American upper class – the first grade below the luxuriously rich." This social position is all-important in Hurstwood's early and later sense of who he is: the manager in Chicago, the "ex-manager" in New York. As the figurehead of Chicago's swank bar, Fitzgerald and Moy's (Hannah and Hogg's in the Pennsylvania Edition), Hurstwood is alert to the nuances of social position. "He had a finely graduated scale of informality and friendship" which determines the tone and content of his conversation with each customer, giving to each, not according to his need but according to his social position. In all, Hurstwood appears "a very successful and well-known man about town," one who "looked the part" and who therefore strikes other strivers such as Charles Drouet as "someone worth knowing." But that is the Hurstwood of Chicago; he becomes "an inconspicuous drop in an ocean like New York." Simply put, after moving east, "Hurstwood was nothing."

The reasons for the withering of Hurstwood's success and vitality surely include his age, his unwitting theft from his employers, his impending divorce from a wife eager to destroy him; but Dreiser considers the most important an abstract social force, an "atmosphere." "The great create an atmosphere which reacts badly upon the small," the narrator explains, going on to remark how this social atmosphere *feels* – how it can literally hurt its unsuspecting victims. "Walk among the magnificent residences, the splendid equipages, the gilded shops, restaurants, resorts of all kinds . . . and you shall know of what is the atmosphere of the high and mighty," the narrator generalizes before swooping in to note its effect on Hurstwood: the "atmosphere of this realm work[s] its desperate results in the soul of man. It is like a chemical reagent." As social atmospheres can destroy, so can they create. When Carrie first encounters the "friendly environment" of the Chicago amateur theater, she glimpses what will become her way out, or rather up. Carrie's upward mobility and Hurstwood's downward plummet are aspects of the same story – the story of how social atmosphere and class position are everything, and how very intimate they can feel.

Class position is personal in another respect, for Americans tend to equate financial success with personal superiority (and likewise, poverty with moral failure). Dreiser captures the human toll of this equation in the shame that his poor characters feel. In the first chapter of *Jennie Gerhardt*, the title character is embarrassed to seek work cleaning the floors of the principal hotel in Columbus, Ohio, "not because it irritated her to work, but because she hated people to know." Jennie is an unusual character for Dreiser in that her social ambitions are so subdued. More typical is Clyde Griffiths of

An American Tragedy, through whose ascent Dreiser anatomizes America's core beliefs about social mobility. Foremost among these beliefs is the naïve assumption that a class system doesn't really operate in the United States, since anyone can supposedly achieve success and even fame. Dreiser's portrayal of this dream in *An American Tragedy* is at once deeply sympathetic and profoundly skeptical. The siren song of individual happiness achieved by social advancement rings in the ears of Clyde, as it does for most of Dreiser's characters. The siren appears to sing of individual accomplishment and personal achievement, beckoning a way to achieve one's inmost desires. The devastating irony is that Clyde's inmost desires, while felt as intensely personal, are constructed, even mass-produced, by vast social forces. In fact, as Dreiser proclaimed in a retrospective essay titled "I Find the Real American Tragedy," Clyde's problem is over-identification with American values. Dreiser affirmed that Clyde's desires reflected "not an *anti-social* dream as Americans should see it, but rather a *pro-social* dream. *He was really doing the kind of thing which Americans should and would have said was the wise and moral thing for him to do had he not committed a murder*" (Dreiser's emphasis). Clyde so successfully embodies the contradictions of the American class system that he goes from the society pages to death row, making readers wonder if it might not be the class structure that is criminal.

Dreiser shows the deep impress of social class on consciousness. All of his novels have strong autobiographical dimensions, but the work that most closely follows the trajectory of his own life is *The "Genius"* (1915). Here Dreiser traces Eugene Witla's ascent from a comfortable if dreary middle-class, Midwestern origin (the author giving his protagonist a higher initial social position than he himself occupied), through early achievement as a painter of urban scenes (bringing him aesthetic renown but not commercial success) to a neurasthenic breakdown, from which he emerges to build a career as a financially and professionally successful advertising director. During Witla's breakdown period (loosely modeled on Dreiser's own experience during the early 1900s), financial hardship compounds his psychological problems. Like Hurstwood before him, Witla learns from painful experience how difficult it is to get work, much more so when in poor health. Watching other men "wearily or hopelessly waiting" to be interviewed for jobs, Witla realizes, "It was like the grinding of the millstones, upper and nether. These [men] were the chaff. He was a part of the chaff at present, or in danger of becoming so. . . . He might go down, down, and there might never be an opportunity for him to rise any more." Such is the devastating experience of downward mobility, making the individual fear he is no more than the waste product of an industrial process. Paradoxically, Witla secures work for which he has no experience because although "As a laborer he was nothing: as an artist he could get a position as a laborer." He thus learns the critical lesson that being an artist grants him a type of celebrity independent of – and more marketable than – any artwork he produces.

The marketability of select identities in a consumer society is another of Dreiser's most salient themes, and his novels sensitively register how notions of identity change along with the development of mass markets. Nowhere is the personal response more memorable than in Dreiser's treatment of consumer desire. Carrie Meeber is an instructive guide here; fashionable clothes literally talk to her:

> '"My dear," said the lace collar she secured from Partridge's, "I fit you beautifully; don't give me up."'
> '"Ah, such little feet," said the leather of the soft new shoes; "how effectively I cover them."'

In a novel which has such barely articulate characters, the eloquence of consumer goods in *Sister Carrie* is all the more palpable. The showy Chicago department stores produce unquenchable longings: "Carrie passed along the busy aisles, much affected by the remarkable displays of trinkets, dress goods, stationery, and jewelry. Each separate counter was a showplace of dazzling interest and attraction. She could not help feeling the claim of each trinket and valuable upon her personally." Dreiser captures with astounding insight how institutions of mass production and distribution such as the department store instill desire by establishing a faux-personal relationship with the unsuspecting consumer. Through his attention to such intimate effects of life under consumer culture, Dreiser records another refrain of the siren's song.

Perhaps the best explanation for the symbiotic relationship between people and the objects they acquire comes in *The Financier*, the first volume of the aptly titled *Trilogy of Desire*, which traces the acquisitive career of the charismatic Frank Cowperwood (modeled on streetcar magnate Charles Tyson Yerkes). Cowperwood begins early in the trilogy to amass an art collection which he enshrines in his Philadelphia home, both for his own aesthetic pleasure and to conspicuously display his commercial success. Dreiser's narrator explains:

> The effect of a house of this character on its owner is unmistakable. We think we are individual, separate, above houses and material objects generally; but there is a subtle connection which makes them reflect us quite as much as we reflect them. They lend dignity, subtlety, force, each to the other, and what beauty, or lack of it, there is, is shot back and forth from one to the other as a shuttle in a loom, weaving, weaving. Cut the thread, separate a man from that which is rightfully his own, characteristic of him, and you have a peculiar figure, half success, half failure, much as a spider without its web.

The owner is not separate from, much less superior to, what he owns. Dreiser not only posits here an inviolable relationship between the financier and his acquisitions; he also indicates that to strip a man of his material goods is to reduce him to an incomplete self.

A lengthy narrative interpolation in *Jennie Gerhardt* enlarges upon this idea. Dreiser begins with the seemingly familiar notion that humanity's higher principles are being degraded by the culture's pervasive materialism: "We live in an age in which the impact of materialized forces is well-nigh irresistible; the spiritual nature is overwhelmed by the shock." But Dreiser's target here is not exactly materialism or consumerism; he takes aim at the whole technology of modern life:

> The tremendous and complicated development of our material civilization, the multiplicity and variety of our social forms, the depth, subtlety and sophistry of our mental cogitations, gathered, remultiplied, and phatasmagorically disseminated as they are by these other agencies – the railroad, the express and post-office, the telegraph, telephone, the newspaper and, in short, the whole art of printing and distributing – have so combined as to produce what may be termed a kaleidoscopic glitter, a dazzling and confusing showpiece which is much more apt to weary and undo than to enlighten and strengthen the observing mind.

His concern, again, is with the human consequences – the most intimate effects, those impressed on the individual consciousness – of technology. Telegraphs and railroads do not simply carry words, freight, and people; they "dazzl[e]" and "confus[e]" the observer. The narrator catalogues the psychological symptoms of technological change: "It produces a sort of intellectual fatigue by which we see the ranks of the victims of insomnia, melancholia and insanity recruited." Thus it is not simply that social marginality causes emotional wounds (pace Carrie and Hurstwood); the kaleidoscopic profusion of new technologies inflicts psychological pain as well.

Cowperwood is the one Dreiser character who rides the crest of rapid technological change. Indeed, his street-railway empire, begun in Philadelphia in *The Financier*, consolidated in Chicago in *The Titan*, and extended to the London underground system in *The Stoic*, depends upon pre-empting the commercial potential of technology. In *The Titan* Cowperwood realizes that adopting recent innovations in San Francisco public transportation (the cable cars) could solve the transportation problems plaguing Chicago's North and West Sides. He seizes upon this new system of traction, "together with the arrival of the arc light, the telephone, and other inventions," and introduces them in Chicago. In London, he again grasps the latest technologies, proposing to unify the subway system by "electrification, lighting, the new method of separate motor power for each car, air brakes, and automatic signals." Later in *The Stoic*, Cowperwood is "building the largest electrical power plant in the world." Although his mastery of technological change sets Cowperwood apart from Dreiser's less practical characters, the lesson remains the same: impose your will on external forces, or they will impose upon you. The same principle characterizes Cowperwood's relationship to the city – especially Chicago, a location of perennial importance in Dreiser. The narrator remarks toward the end of *The Titan* that "The great external element in Cowperwood's financial success . . . was the fact that Chicago was developing constantly," growing from "a soggy, messy plain strewn with shanties, ragged sidewalks, a higgledy-piggledy business heart" to "truly an astounding metropolis." The city's growth is Cowperwood's own; its force is his force.

Cowperwood, however, is the exception. The challenge to most of Dreiser's characters lies in negotiating a path through all the forces that impinge upon them personally. Little wonder that drift, chance, and randomness abound in his novels. Moreover, Dreiser's characters experience strong internal compulsions – biological and psychological drives, particularly for romantic fulfillment and sexual gratification. An additional force comes from cultural mores. These forces often pull an individual in different directions: whereas one may feel a strong biological and psychological pull toward sexual gratification, cultural forces urge restraint. Dreiser depicts this struggle between biological and cultural forces time and time again, perhaps most blatantly in the premarital sex play of Witla and his fiancée Angela Blue of *The "Genius."* The day after she nearly abandons herself to the sexual release she craves, Angela, though technically still a virgin, mourns for her lost chastity: "Oh Eugene, I don't understand myself now...I thought I was better than that." Witla's response, "We're none of us better than that," captures Dreiser's conviction that sexuality is among the strongest of internal compulsions acting on women as well as men. These are iconoclastic views for a Midwestern youth at the turn of the century. No wonder that Witla concludes, "His own moral laxity was a puzzle to him. . . . the subtlety of the universe was always with him . . . For a given order or society no doubt he was out of place."

Hurstwood, of course, learns a similar lesson about displacement when he moves to New York; but it would be inaccurate to assume that Dreiser's characters only want to find a comfortable social and material place. Most seek to discern nothing less than their places in the universe, though few apart from perhaps Witla (or Cowperwood, when he stares at the stars from the Philadelphia penitentiary in *The Financier*) would put it in those terms.

Dreiser models Witla's philosophical inquiry closely after his own. As Dreiser proclaimed that reading Herbert Spencer, the Social Darwinist philosopher who lionized Force with a capital F, "quite blew me to bits intellectually," so does Witla find reading Spencer "made him wonder what life really was. He had walked the streets for a long time after reading some of these things, speculating on the play of forces, the decay of matter," and other equally ponderous subjects. Part of the lesson Witla gleans is the arbitrary nature of social and moral codes and indeed, the impermanence of entire human societies: "Philosophies came and went, governments came and went, races arose and disappeared." Now the lesson hits Witla hard – and personally. The personal register becomes clearest in, of all places, a stroll through New York's Natural History Museum, where the iconoclastic artist peruses the skeletal remains of prehistoric animals and "marvelled at the forces which produced them, the indifference, apparently, with which they had been allowed to die." This lesson, which we might call Elementary Darwinism, does more than blow Witla to bits intellectually; it "almost broke his heart." His self-importance smashed, Witla "wandered about dazed, hurt, moody, like a lost child." Dinosaur bones shatter his emotional composure, reducing the proud artist to a little boy.

Other characters, especially Dreiser's men, experience a similar sense of existential anguish when confronting their insignificance in the cosmos. *Jennie Gerhardt*'s flawed hero Lester Kane articulates a despair that has been correctly identified as part of Dreiser's own. Lester's gloom arises from the recognition that "The individual doesn't count much," and that realization racks him. His tough guy posturings – "All of us are more or less pawns"; "life is more or less of a farce" – do not assuage the pain of his personal insignificance. The contrast between Lester's attitude and that of the magnanimous woman he casts aside (a philosophy which also represents a core aspect of Dreiser's thinking) is instructive. Although Jennie has been discarded by Lester, she "did not endeavor to explain or adjust the moral and ethical entanglements." Nor does she try "to put ocean into a tea-cup, or to tie up the shifting universe in a mess of strings called law." She lacks her lover's sophisticated tools for conceptualizing how life is organized – "History, physics, chemistry, botany, geology and sociology were not fixed departments in her brain as they were in Lester's." Jennie knows only that life is both very good and very bad: "She could not understand what it was all about, but still, . . . it was beautiful. One could live, somehow, under any circumstances." Her perspective, tolerant of mysteries without becoming cynical about them, articulates a heroic philosophy in the face of the incomprehensible. Lester sees the indifference of life's forces as a personal assault, a diminishment of his humanity; although he succeeds in worldly terms, he is personally beaten, crushed, coerced. Jennie does not take things so personally.

An entirely different sort of heroic philosophy in the face of impersonal forces distinguishes Frank Cowperwood. In the first chapter of *The Financier*, young Cowperwood begins pondering "how this thing he had come into – this life – was organized." Rejecting traditional explanations (he doesn't believe his mother's reiteration of the Adam and Eve story), Cowperwood discovers a workable philosophy while observing a lobster and a squid in an aquarium. The lobster, considering the other its "rightful prey," repeatedly "snapped off" bits of the squid. The incident "answered . . . that riddle" for Cowperwood, who concludes that the order of the universe is eat or be eaten, and resolves to secure a position on top of the food chain. The marine encounter "cleared things up considerably intellectually" for boy Cowperwood, remarks the narrator in what turns out to be quite an understatement. In fact, the financier extracts from the fishtank a streamlined, simplified philosophy. He believes in "strength and weakness," but "Right and wrong? He did not know about those." As he puts it, "I satisfy myself." Cowperwood is ruthless, his philosophy almost ridiculously simplistic (particularly when compared to the tolerance for mystery that characterizes Jennie Gerhardt's world-view). But the financier is charismatic and his philosophy extremely successful, and the reason lies in Cowperwood's complete and successful personalization of the lesson of the fishtank.

Dreiser himself spent much of his life trying to ascertain "how life is organized," a phrase he repeatedly invoked. "Naturally inclined to seek to solve the riddle of existence . . . always digging at the whyness of everything," he shares Lester's cynicism, Jennie's tolerance of mystery, and Witla's insistence on relativity, and he craved Cowperwood's certainty. The one thing he was reasonably sure of was that conventional morality was a sham.

Morality is one of the most pervasive forces that the Dreiserian character confronts, and seemingly one of the strongest. However, as Dreiser insists, morality is a man-made force, not divinely sanctioned, a premise instrumental in dismantling its power. "The world is dosed with too much religion," Dreiser skeptically begins the coda to *The Titan*, "and the professional moralist is at best a manufacturer of shoddy wares." As he remarks in an important essay, the dominant ethical point of view "does not accord with the facts of life as I have noted or experienced them" – and in Dreiser's work, the "I" consistently wins out over conventional morality. In his quarrel with established moral codes, Dreiser effects something of the revenge of the person against the arbitrary force. Consider, for instance, Carrie Meeber. On one hand, she clearly has internalized her culture's moral strictures, for after beginning her liaison with Drouet, "she looked into her mind, a mirror prepared of her own and the world's opinions, and saw a worse" version of herself. On the other hand, the narrator knows better: "Actions such as hers are measured by an arbitrary scale," he intones, a position that must have been more shocking to readers of tender moral sensibilities than the heroine's sexual decisions, or the author's refusing to punish her for them. The narrator insists that the collective wisdom of humanity produces but "an infantile perception of morals," which simultaneously excuses Carrie's inability to articulate a position beyond conventional morality while allowing Dreiser to present her life story as more true, more accurate, than any moral codes.

Dreiser in fact adopted this sort of personalized empiricism as the linchpin of his aesthetic. In a 1903 manifesto titled "True Art Speaks Plainly," he insists that "Truth is what is . . . To express what we see honestly and without subterfuge: this is morality as well as art." Besides affirming the moral obligation of the artist to deal honestly with unsavory subjects, Dreiser maintains that morality itself should be reconceptualized: instead of painting idealistic pictures of how humans should behave (but rarely do), simply render realistically what you see around you. Consequently, for Dreiser, "The sum and substance of literary as well as social morality may be expressed in three words – tell the truth." In the fiction, this position is most clearly realized in the descriptions of Eugene Witla's paintings: "Everything he touched seemed to have romance in beauty, and yet it was real and mostly grim and shabby." Each of his urban scenes "seemed to say: 'I'm dirty, I am commonplace, I am grim, I am shabby, but I am life!' And there was no apologizing for anything. . . . no glossing anything over. Bang! Smash! Crack came the facts one after another, with a bitter, brutal insistence on their so-ness." For Dreiser, the "so-ness" of facts is more authoritative than an entire museum of pretty pictures.

The most salient facts for Dreiser are always the human and personal ones. Notwithstanding the vast forces that impinge upon the individual, the human being emerges as a complex creature in Dreiser's novels – far more intricate than any of the prefabricated interpretations that betray human complexity. Take, for instance, his treatment of culpability in the ambiguous crimes of *Sister Carrie* and *An American Tragedy*. The narrator instructs the reader to withhold judgment on Hurstwood's theft of $10,000 from his Chicago employer's safe in *Sister Carrie*, for "Those who have never heard that solemn voice of the ghostly clock which ticks with awful distinctness, 'thou shalt,' 'thou shalt not,' 'thou shalt,' 'thou shalt not,' are in no position to judge." No reader could call Hurstwood's theft premeditated, and while we have the certainty of premeditation when it comes to evaluating Clyde's plot to murder Roberta in *An American Tragedy*, we also know that at the decisive moment, he loses his will, she falls into the water accidentally, and Clyde leaves her to drown. Exactly what Clyde is guilty of remains for most readers a tortured question, problematical in a way that highlights the inadequacy of the public version of events circulated by the media and legal system in Book 3. After reading *An American Tragedy*, the celebrated lawyer Clarence Darrow told Dreiser that it was in fact impossible to decide the question of Clyde's guilt (Elias 1970: 222). That verdict must have pleased the author, who maintained "there was an entire misunderstanding, or perhaps I had better say non-apprehension, of the conditions or circumstances surrounding the victims of that murder *before* the murder was committed" (Dreiser's emphasis). Dreiser's insistence on the intricacy of Clyde's crime is part of his broader affirmation of human complexity. As he once remarked, "The most futile thing in this world is any attempt . . . at exact definition of character."

Although Dreiser attacks the simplifications that pass as collective wisdom in numerous guises, the assault seems especially urgent when the subject is sexual morality, on which point he found Americans particularly prone to dishonesty, hypocrisy, and maliciousness. When it comes to those who invoke morality to condemn an individual who deviates from the reigning sexual code, Dreiser becomes outraged. His indignation is especially palpable in *Jennie Gerhardt*, where Lester's affluent family disapproves of Jennie's class position as much as they do of their affair. Money, morality, and sexuality are fused in the threat of Lester's father to disinherit him if he doesn't abandon Jennie: "How do you suppose I can seriously contemplate entrusting my share of my fortune to a man who has so little regard for what the world regards as right and proper?" Dreiser's outrage stems in part from the pitting of forces that he believed to be among the strongest and most legitimate influences on humans – for sexual gratification and companionship – against the man-made force of morality, and also from the fact that the latter is contaminated by monetary and status considerations. In short, according to Dreiser, "moral" positions concerning sexual behavior are generally immoral.

An American Tragedy shows the deep implication of money and status with sexual morality not only in the murder plot, but also and with especial clarity through the protagonists' unsuccessful attempt to procure an abortion. Roberta and Clyde fail to terminate her pregnancy not because abortion is a crime but rather because access to it is determined by one's class position. Dreiser first approaches this controversial point obliquely. Clyde knows that youths from the upper middle class who impregnate their girlfriends are able to procure abortions, but he lacks the intimacy necessary to approach them for the "helpful information" he needs. A doctor whom Roberta approaches provides merely platitudes – conveniently forgetting the "several cases in the past ten years where family and other neighborhood and religious consider-ations had made it [an abortion] seem quite advisable, [so] he had assisted in extricating from the consequences of their folly several young girls of good family who had fallen from grace and could not otherwise be rescued." Neither the evasive clichés in which Dreiser couches Dr. Glenn's rationalization, nor the doctor's hiding behind an image of himself as chivalrous rescuer of "girls of good family," can mask the moral bankruptcy of his willingness to help some women and not others. The tortured complexities of Clyde and Roberta's enactment of one of the oldest stories in the world – unwanted pregnancy leading to his entrapment and her desperation – are obliterated in the monotonous yet inevitable simplification into "sex crime." The real sex crime that Dreiser exposes in *An American Tragedy* is the national criminalization of sexuality in the first place – the fact that when Roberta feels the stirrings of desire for Clyde, she should feel "as guilty as though she had been caught red-handed in some dreadful crime."

Perhaps the ultimate lesson of *An American Tragedy* is that life is "one of those whirling tempests of fact and reality in which the ordinary charts and compasses of moral measurement were . . . of small use." The Dreiser character who best grasps that lesson is Frank Cowperwood, which largely accounts for the author's evident fascination with him. "How shall we explain these subtleties of temperament and desire?" inquires *The Financier*'s narrator in a classically Dreiserian query. "Is there no law outside of the subtle will and power of the individual to achieve?" Cowperwood thinks not. While "Dogma may bind some minds; fear, others," the financier knows that "Life cannot be put into any mold." Cowperwood captures what Eugene Witla intuits – that "life was somehow bigger and subtler and darker than any given theory." "How could the ordinary rules of life or the accustomed paths of men be expected to control" the mighty Frank Cowperwood? Dreiser asks rhetorically. Cowperwood expands upon the idea set forth in *Sister Carrie* about morality as an "arbitrary scale"; for the financier, "Morality varied . . . with conditions." He understands that life, not morality, is the ultimate force, and believes himself to embody that force. (Cowperwood, in fact, tries to continue embodying the life force after his death, as we learn in *The Stoic*, when he lays the plans to transform his Fifth Avenue mansion into a public museum and to build a hospital named after himself in the Bronx.) Cowperwood's positioning of himself as a force to be reckoned with marks this character as Dreiser's ultimate revenge of the personal.

There is a great deal of Dreiser's personality in all his major characters, and it is instructive that Cowperwood alone achieves such certainty. The more typical pattern is a ceaseless, even frenetic quest that lands characters in speculative quagmires. Sometimes the terminal point for a Dreiser character is a semblance of certainty, as appears to be the case finally for Clyde Griffiths. After his long odyssey through *An American Tragedy*, Clyde ends up embracing what he had spent years running from: Christianity. But how sincere is his conversion, under the guidance of Reverend McMillan, at the end of the novel? Even after Clyde issues his public statement affirming his acceptance of Jesus Christ, the man on death row remains "still dubious at moments. Was he truly saved?" The narrator's explanation of the protagonist's turn to faith is that "Clyde was now doing what every other human in related circumstances invariably does – seeking . . . some superhuman or supernatural personality or power." Clyde is looking for help, for comfort, for absolution, but even more, he is seeking "the personalization and humanization of forces." That quest aligns him with all of Dreiser's characters, and with the author himself. Part of Dreiser believed that we are all – to invoke his first chapter title for *Sister Carrie* – Waifs amid Forces. Yet another part of Dreiser believed that his own writing was a powerful force to be reckoned with, and literary history has justified his self-confidence. During the difficult period when he had to fight to have his first novel published, Dreiser insisted to the publisher who was trying to withdraw from his commitment to bring out *Sister Carrie* that "A great book will destroy conditions." It was at once a personal promise and also an impersonal one – a promise repeatedly fulfilled in the works of Theodore Dreiser.

SELECTED PRIMARY TEXTS BY THEODORE DREISER

Sister Carrie. 1900.
"True Art Speaks Plainly." 1903.
Jennie Gerhardt. 1911.
The Financier. 1912.
The Titan. 1914.
The "Genius." 1915.
Twelve Men. 1919.
Hey Rub-A-Dub-Dub: A Book of the Mystery and Wonder and Terror of Life. 1920.
Newspaper Days. 1922. (First publ. as *A Book About Myself*.)

An American Tragedy. 1925.
A Gallery of Women. 1929.
Dawn. 1931.
"I Find the Real American Tragedy." 1935.
The Bulwark. 1946.
The Stoic. 1947.
An Amateur Laborer. 1983.
American Diaries 1902–1926. 1983.
Theodore Dreiser's Ev'ry Month. 1996.

REFERENCES AND FURTHER READING

Bell, Michael Davitt (1993). *The Problem of American Realism: Studies in the Cultural History of a Literary Idea*. Chicago: University of Chicago Press.

Bowlby, Rachel (1985). *Just Looking: Consumer Culture in Dreiser, Gissing, and Zola*. New York: Metheun.

Cassuto, Leonard, and Eby, Clare, eds. (2004). *The Cambridge Companion to Theodore Dreiser*. Cambridge, UK: Cambridge University Press.

Eby, Clare Virginia (1988). *Dreiser and Veblen, Saboteurs of the Status Quo*. Columbia: University of Missouri Press.

Elias, Robert H. (1970). *Theodore Dreiser: Apostle of Nature*. Ithaca, NY: Cornell University Press. (First publ. 1949.)

Fisher, Philip (1985). *Hard Facts: Setting and Form in the American Novel*. New York: Oxford University Press.

Gerber, Philip L. (1992). *Theodore Dreiser*, rev. edn. New York: Twayne. (First publ. 1964.)

Gogol, Miriam, ed. (1995). *Theodore Dreiser: Beyond Naturalism*. New York: New York University Press.

Howard, June (1985). *Form and History in American Literary Naturalism*. Chapel Hill: University of North Carolina Press.

Hussman, Lawrence E., Jr. (1983). *Dreiser and his Fiction: A Twentieth-Century Quest*. Philadelphia: University of Pennsylvania Press.

Kaplan, Amy (1988). *The Social Construction of American Realism*. Chicago: University of Chicago Press.

Lehan, Richard (1969). *Theodore Dreiser: His World and his Novels*. Carbondale: Southern Illinois University Press.

Lingeman, Richard (1986). *Theodore Dreiser: At the Gates of the City, 1871–1907*. New York: Putnam.

Lingeman, Richard (1990). *Theodore Dreiser: An American Journey, 1908–1945*. New York: Putnam.

Martin, Ronald (1981). *American Literature and the Universe of Force*. Durham, NC: Duke University Press.

Matthiessen, F. O. (1951). *Theodore Dreiser*. New York: William Sloane.

Michaels, Walter Benn (1987). *The Gold Standard and the Logic of Naturalism: American Literature at the Turn of the Century*. Berkeley: University of California Press.

Mitchell, Lee Clark (1989). *Determined Fictions: American Literary Naturalism*. New York: Columbia University Press.

Moers, Ellen (1969). *Two Dreisers*. New York: Viking.

Orlov, Paul (1998). *An American Tragedy: The Perils of the Self Seeking "Success."* Lewisburg, Pa.: Bucknell University Press.

Pizer, Donald (1976). *The Novels of Theodore Dreiser: A Critical Study*. Minneapolis: University of Minnesota Press.

Pizer, Donald, ed. (1991). *New Essays on "Sister Carrie."* Cambridge, UK: Cambridge University Press.

Salzman, Jack (1972). *Theodore Dreiser: The Critical Reception*. New York: David Lewis.

Sundquist, Eric J., ed. (1982). *American Realism: New Essays*. Baltimore: Johns Hopkins University Press.

Swanberg, W. A. (1965). *Dreiser*. New York: Scribner.

Walcutt, Charles Child (1956). *American Literary Naturalism: A Divided Stream*. Minneapolis: University of Minnesota Press.

Warren, Robert Penn (1971). *Homage to Theodore Dreiser*. New York: Random House.

West, James L. W., III (1985). *A Sister Carrie Portfolio*. Charlottesville: University Press of Virginia.

West, James L. W., III, ed. (1995). *Dreiser's "Jennie Gerhardt": New Essays on the Restored Text*. Philadelphia: University of Pennsylvania Press.

Wilson, Christopher (1985). *The Labor of Words: Literary Professionalism in the Progressive Era*. Athens, Ga.: University of Georgia Press.

Zanine, Louis J. (1993). *Mechanism and Mysticism: The Influence of Science on the Thought and Work of Theodore Dreiser*. Philadelphia: University of Pennsylvania Press.

Index